The Sound Reinforcement Handbook

Second Edition

Written For Yamaha By
Gary Davis & Ralph Jones

Inside Design & Illustration by
Gary Davis & Associates
Cover Design by Lee Savoit

Published by

HAL•LEONARD™
CORPORATION
7777 W. BLUEMOUND RD. P.O. BOX 13819 MILWAUKEE, WI 53213

ISBN: 0-88188-900-8

First Edition	First Printing:	December, 1987
	Second Printing:	February, 1989
	Third Printing:	April, 1989
Second Edition	First Printing:	June, 1989
	Second Printing:	February, 1990

Printed in the U.S.A.

PREFACE

In 1974, the people at Yamaha asked me to write some spec sheets for a dozen or so new guitar amplifiers and small mixers. As soon as that job was done, they showed me a new product. It was a console, one intended to be a major departure – a leap into the heart of the professional sound reinforcement market – for a company then known primarily as a musical instrument manufacturer (or a motorcycle manufacturer, if you were not a musician). Yamaha said they wanted to firmly establish themselves as a leader, and they felt that a comprehensive instruction manual for the new console would help do the job. We had only a prototype board and some sketchy specs, but no detailed drawings or data, so I contacted engineer John Windt, and we measured the performance. Working with pencil and portable typewriter, I created the first draft of the PM-1000 Operating Manual.

The PM-1000 console did put Yamaha on the map, insofar as the professional sound reinforcement business is concerned. The manual was so popular that it had to be reprinted many times (far exceeding the number of consoles built). It became a standard text in several college courses due to its detailed discussions of the basics of sound reinforcement.

During the ensuing decade, Yamaha asked me to write manuals for a variety of amps, signal processors, mixers and so forth, and to maintain the same standard of excellence we began with the PM-1000 manual. Unfortunately, it is very expensive to produce and print 30 to 60 pages of instructions for every product, and it is difficult to justify – especially when only 8 to 16 pages contain the "hard core" operational data. For this reason, both Yamaha and I had pondered the concept of a generalized guide for sound reinforcement, apart from any individual operating manuals.

Finally, 10 years after the PM-1000 manual was published, Yamaha decided to move forward with this project. We anticipated a book of 96 to 160 pages in length, and expected it would take a year to complete. The first edition of *The Sound Reinforcement Handbook* was comprised of 384 pages, some 256 illustrations, and took three years to complete. The first printing of 10,000 copies sold out in a year, and while we were completing this second edition, another two runs totalling nearly 5,000 more copies had to be printed. Clearly, the book has been well received, and we're grateful.

The Sound Reinforcement Handbook is the largest project I have ever undertaken. It would not have been possible without the support and patience of the people at Yamaha Corporation of America, and at their parent company, Yamaha Corporation of Japan. All of us were able to endure the strain of gathering data, editing it, and producing this book for one reason: we had an important goal to achieve.

That goal was to create a useful reference for anyone who is interested in learning the basics of sound reinforcement. In this second edition, we have improved many of the illustrations, and added entirely new topics, corrected a number of minor errors and typos (perhaps created new ones). We have made the book much easier to use by completely reorganizing the chapters and creating an index.

We had originally planned the first edition for looseleaf binding, with the intent to publish updates periodically. The cost, however, would have been prohibitive, and so this soft cover format was adopted, with the prospect of a new edition when the need arises. We all hope you enjoy and learn from this one.

Gary D. Davis
Santa Monica, California
June, 1989

This handbook is dedicated to the sound reinforcement industry, and to all those people who have worked so hard to bring better sound and music to the world. We particularly wish to acknowledge the late Deane Jensen for his advancement of sound.

Acknowledgements

My associate Ralph Jones made a substantial contribution to the writing and illustrations that are in this handbook. Ralph's background with Meyer Sound Labs, and his formal music education, served to balance the knowledge I have gleaned from my involvement with many other sound equipment manufacturers, and my own physics background. Many thanks, Ralph. And thanks also to your wife, Claudette, who helped with some of the early deadlines.

As I mentioned in the Preface, the people at Yamaha Corporation of America and of Japan (formerly Nippon-Gakki in Japan) have supported this project — both financially and with considerable assistance in terms of suggested contents, proof reading, and helping to secure expert consulting assistance when that was required. They also deserve praise for giving me a free hand to write as much as was required, to include all we wished (including a number of competitors' names, when that information seemed important), and to not make this a sales presentation for any particular Yamaha equipment. Special thanks go to John Gatts and Bob Davis for overseeing the project at Yamaha, and to Craig Olsen for his help with the initial outline. Nancy Mastroianni, a skilled proof reader, was employed by Yamaha to highlight my inconsistent hyphenation, dangling participles, and other typographical errors. Soundman Steve Getson of Trenton, NJ, kindly identified many typos after the first printing. At our request, Brian Weiss of Word'sworth also did extensive proof reading. Mind you, we exercised our right of editorial license, so if some of the usage remains non-standard, it may not be Brian's or Nancy's fault.

Bob Davis, who collated all the comments and edits at Yamaha for both editions, was assisted by Yamaha District Manager Ray Bloom and by independent consultant Rolly Brook. Without this valuable input, I would still be choking on my left foot. Thanks, guys.

I made many phone calls to engineer John Windt, whose extensive knowledge of system grounding and system design added considerably to this book. Thanks also to the late Deane Jensen (of Jensen Transformers, Inc.), who provided very useful information on transformer and differential balancing, mic splitting, and other aspects of circuit design.

Lynn McCroskey and Alvis Wales of Sonics, Associates were very helpful with regard to interconnect of balanced and unbalanced circuitry, and they also made some useful suggestions regarding the relatively minor direct effects of wind on sound propagation.

Bill Swintek of Swintek Wireless Microphones gave us permission to use portions of data we wrote for him several years ago, and the people at HME submitted a major portion of the data dealing with wireless microphones and wireless intercom systems, which together make this portion of the book far more accurate and complete than it otherwise would have been.

Thanks to engineer Bob Ludwig for explaining the pros and cons of console placement. Thanks to Crown International Corporation for sending photos and information on their PZM microphones.

Composer/synthesist/consultant Christopher L. Stone of Dragonsense Studio was most helpful in guiding our MIDI and SMPTE discussions, and special thanks go to Jim Cooper of J.L. Cooper Electronics for proof reading the MIDI material and offering valuable corrections and suggestions.

I also wish to thank Carolyn and Don Davis, whose Syn-Aud-Con seminar and whose book, *Sound System Engineering,* have significantly augmented my understanding of sound and acoustics.

Last, but certainly not least, many thanks to Georgia Galey, my hard-working office manager who did so much to help bring this book from concept to reality: typing some data into the computer, proofing the typed and typeset copy, following up on phone calls, photocopying and the necessary go-fer jobs — in other words, filling in wherever and whenever she could. *GDD*

PS: The answer to the unasked question: No. Bob Davis, Don Davis and Gary Davis are not related to one another. They all just happen to share the same surname and work in the same general industry.

Sound Reinforcement Handbook
Table of Contents

Sound Reinforcement Handbook

Sound Reinforcement Handbook
List of Illustrations

SECTION 1.
WHAT IS A SOUND SYSTEM?

In today's technologically sophisticated world, audio systems of various types are a part of almost everyone's daily life. Nearly every home has a stereo or a simple radio. Most businesses use some type of intercom/paging system. Some auto sound systems are more sophisticated than many home stereos.

This handbook deals with a specific class of audio system which is properly referred to as a reinforcement system. For the purposes of this handbook, the term sound system is used exclusively to refer to reinforcement systems. Reinforcement systems of varying levels of sophistication are used routinely by amateurs and professionals for public address and music performance.

Sound reinforcement systems are not generally as simple as home stereos. Although they operate on the same principles, they require a higher level of understanding from their users.

This handbook is an introduction to those principles. Its purpose is to give you the understanding necessary to design and operate moderate-scale reinforcement systems. It can also serve as a reference when questions concerning such systems arise. Section 1 introduces the basic concept of the sound system.

1.1 THE AUDIO SIGNAL

1.1.1 Sound Waves

What we hear as sound is a class of physical kinetic energy called acoustical energy. Acoustical energy consists of fluctuating waves of pressure in a physical medium — usually air.

A single complete cycle of an acoustical pressure wave consists of one half-cycle of compression (higher pressure) of the air molecules, followed by one half-cycle of rarefaction (lower pressure) of the molecules. Sounds of higher amplitude (louder) compress and rarefy the air molecules to a greater extent than do lower amplitude (softer) sounds.

The rate of air pressure fluctuation is called the frequency of the wave. In order to be classified as sound, waves of pressure in air must fluctuate at a rate between 20 and 20,000 complete cycles per second (cps). Frequency corresponds to the musical attribute of pitch. Although pitch is a more complex attribute than frequency (it also involves amplitude), generally speaking the higher the frequency, the higher the perceived pitch of the sound. The unit Hertz (Hz) is now used to indicate frequency in cycles per second:

20 Hz = 20 cps

The amount of time required for one complete cycle of a sound wave is called the period of the wave. A wave's period is expressed in seconds per cycle, and is found by using the equation:

Period = 1 ÷ Frequency

Sound waves travel through air at the speed of 1130 ft/sec (344 m/sec)... at sea level on a standard temperature day (which is 59 degrees Farenheit or 15 degrees Celsius). The speed of sound is independent of frequency. The physical distance covered by one complete cycle of a given frequency sound as it passes through air is called the wavelength. Wavelength is expressed by the equation:

Wavelength = $\dfrac{\text{Speed of sound}}{\text{Frequency}}$

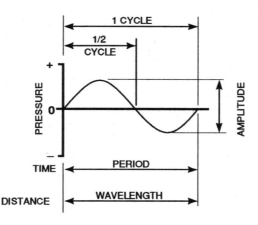

Figure 1-1. Representation of a
sound wave (one cycle
of a sine wave in air)

1.1.2 The Electrical Representation of Sound

An audio signal is an electrical representation of a sound, in the form of a fluctuating voltage or current. Within the limits of audio equipment, the signal voltage or current fluctuates at exactly the same rate as the acoustical energy that it represents, and the amplitudes of the acoustical sound wave and the electrical audio signal are scaled proportionately.

The amplitude, or strength, of an audio signal is called the signal level. Many different operating levels exist in audio systems. Level (acoustical or electrical) is specified in decibels. Section 4 describes the decibel in detail.

is expressed on the graph in relationship to a time reference called T_0. This happens to be the start time of the wave, although it could be designated at any time within the wave's period.

The time reference may also be another signal. If it is, the reference signal must resemble the signal whose phase is being measured: we can meaningfully compare only objects that are alike, or at least related. For example, Figure 1-3 shows an audio signal processor with one input (V_{IN}) and one output (V_{OUT}). The phase of the output signal is expressed in relation to the input signal.

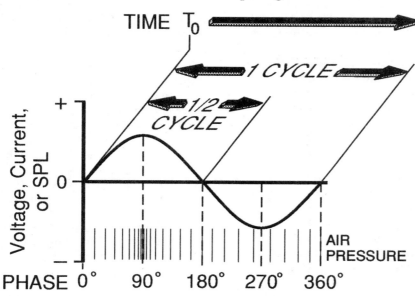

Figure 1-2. Representation of an audio signal (one cycle of a sine wave)

1.1.3 Phase

The time relationship of a sound wave (or an audio signal) to a known time reference is called the phase of the signal. Phase is expressed in degrees. One complete cycle of a sine wave equals 360 degrees.

The time reference may be an arbitrarily chosen, fixed instant in time. For example, Figure 1-2 shows a type of audio signal called a sine wave. A sine wave is a pure tone, a fundamental frequency with no harmonics (representing something like the sound of a flute). The phase of the sine wave

In Figure 1-3(b), the output is said to be in phase with the input (both sine waves cross zero at the same time, going in the same direction). In (c), the output is 90 degrees out of phase with the input (one sine wave crosses zero when the other is at maximum, both going in the same direction). In 1-3 (d), the output is 180 degrees out of phase with the input (both sine waves cross zero at the same time, but going in opposite directions). Note that these phase relationships may change at different frequencies, and often do with real-world audio circuits.

1.1.4 Adding Sine Waves

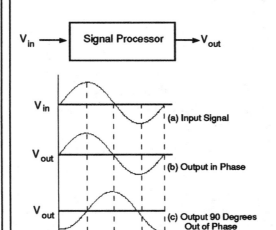

Figure 1-3. Phase relationships
between input and output signals

Phase is very important in sound systems. The main reason that phase must be controlled is that it affects how sounds add together.

When audio signals are mixed in a console, or when sound waves mix in the air, they add algebraically. Figure 1-4 shows the effect of phase on the addition of two sine waves of equal level and frequency, but at different phase relationships.

In Figure 1-4 (a), the sine waves are in phase; they add to form a sine wave of twice the level of either one. In (b), the sine waves are 90 degrees out of phase. They add to form a sine wave that is 1.414 times higher in level than either one. In (c), the sine waves are 180 degrees out of phase; they totally cancel one another.

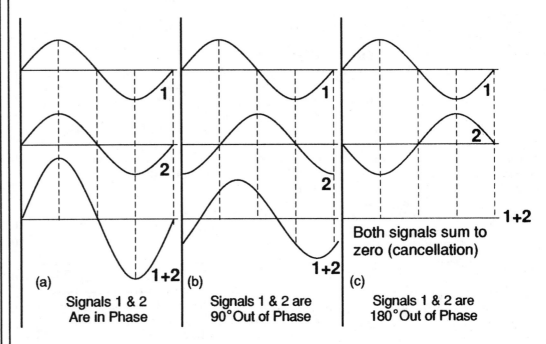

Figure 1-4. Phase affects the way two sine waves add together

1.2 The Basic Purpose of a Sound System

A sound system is a functional arrangement of electronic components that is designed to amplify (increase the strength of) sound. This may be done for any of several reasons. The three most common reasons are:

A) *To help people hear something better.* For example, one person speaking on a stage may not be heard well at the back of a large hall. A sound system may be used to make the sound more clearly audible. In this case, the intention is to make the voice at the back of the hall sound as loud as (not louder than) it is when heard up close.

B) *To make sound louder for artistic reasons.* A vocal group in a small club may be clearly audible but not necessarily very exciting. A sound system can give the group much greater musical impact by making it seem "larger than life."

C) *To enable people to hear sound in remote locations.* Seminars or meetings sometimes draw larger crowds than the meeting room will hold. A sound system can bring the speeches and discussion to a second room, so that the overflow crowd can hear them.

There are also sound systems which are designed to reproduce recorded or broadcast sound. In this case the general requirements may be similar to the live sound reinforcement system, except that a tape reproducer, compact disc player, phonograph, or radio tuner will be substituted for the microphone or electronic musical instrument, and there will be less concern about feedback.

1.3 A Conceptual Model of a Sound System

Sound systems amplify sound by converting it into electrical energy, increasing the power of the electrical energy by electronic means, and then converting the more powerful electrical energy back into sound.

In audio electronics, devices that convert energy from one form into another are called transducers. Devices that change one or more aspects of an audio signal are called signal processors. Using these terms, we can model a sound system in its simplest form, as illustrated below in Figure 1-5.

The input transducer (i.e., mic or pickup) converts sound into a fluctuating electrical current or voltage which is a precise representation of the sound. The fluctuating current or voltage is referred to as an audio signal.

The signal processing alters one or more characteristics of the audio signal. In the simplest case, it increases the power of the signal (a signal processor that does this is called an amplifier). In practical sound systems, this block of the diagram represents a multitude of devices — preamplifiers, mixers, effects units, power amplifiers, and so on.

The output transducer (i.e., the loudspeaker or headphones) converts the amplified or otherwise processed audio signal back into sound.

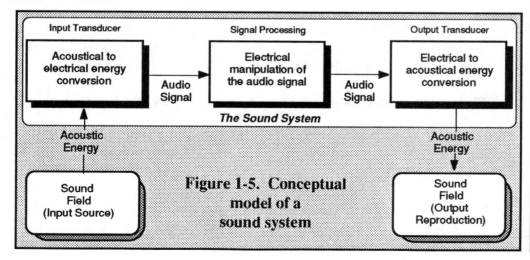

Figure 1-5. Conceptual model of a sound system

1.4 Input Transducers

In a sound system, input transducers convert sound into audio signals. The types of input transducers most commonly encountered in sound reinforcement systems are:

A) **Air Pressure or Velocity Microphones** — convert sound waves traveling in air into an audio signal traveling in the mic cable.

B) **Contact Pickups** — convert sound waves in a dense medium (wood, metal, skin) into an audio signal. Sometimes used on acoustic stringed instruments such as guitar, mandolin, violin, etc. Usually of the crystal type, occasionally capacitive.

C) **Magnetic Pickups** — convert fluctuating waves of induced magnetism into an audio signal. Found on electric stringed instruments.

D) **Tape Heads** — convert fluctuating magnetic fields (imprinted on magnetic recording tape) into an audio signal.

E) **Phonograph Pickups (cartridges)** — convert physical movement of a stylus ("needle") into an audio signal. In professional systems, the moving-magnet type cartridge is the most common.

F) **Laser Pickups** — convert imprinted patterns on a compact disc into a digital data stream that is then translated by a DAC (Digital-to-Analog Converter) into an analog audio signal.

G) **Optical Pickups** — convert variations in the density or transparent area of a photographic film into an audio signal. Used for most motion picture sound tracks.

Each type of input transducer has its own characteristics, which must be understood if the transducer is to be used properly. Section 10 of this handbook deals with microphones in detail.

1.5 Output Transducers

In a sound system, output transducers convert audio signals back into sound. The types of output transducers most commonly encountered in sound reinforcement systems are:

A) **Woofer loudspeakers** — designed specifically to reproduce low frequencies (usually below 500 Hz). Woofers sometimes are used to reproduce both low frequencies and some mid frequencies (normally not higher than 1.5 kHz). Typically, cone-type drivers are used as woofers, measuring from 8 to 18 inches in diameter.

B) **Midrange loudspeakers** — (formerly called "squawkers," though this is an archaic term from the hi-fi world) — designed specifically to reproduce mid frequencies (typically above 500 Hz). The highest frequency reproduced by a midrange unit is usually not higher than 6 kHz. If a cone-type driver is used as a midrange loudspeaker, its diameter typically ranges from 5 to 12 inches; if a compression driver is used, its diaphragm diameter may range from 2.5 inches to 4 inches (with a few special units up to about 9 inches in diameter).

C) **Tweeter loudspeakers** — designed to reproduce the highest frequencies (normally higher than 1.5 kHz, and usually above 6 kHz). If a cone-type driver is used, its diaphragm diameter usually ranges from 2 to 5 inches; compression driver diaphragms range from under 1.5 inches to about 4 inches.

D) **Full-range loudspeakers** — integrated systems incorporating woofer and tweeter (and, if used, midrange) drivers in a single enclosure. As the name implies, they are designed to reproduce the full audio range (more or less). In practical terms, their range rarely extends below about 60 Hz.

NOTE: *A full-range driver is a single loudspeaker which alone is designed to reproduce the full audio frequency range; this is not the same as a full range multi-driver system.*

E) **Subwoofer loudspeakers** — used to extend the low frequency range of full-range systems to include frequencies down to 20 or 30 Hz. Their range rarely extends above about 300 Hz. Cone-type drivers are used nearly exclusively, and typically measure from 15 to 24 inches in diameter, although a few special units are available with cone diameters approaching 5 feet.

F) **Supertweeter loudspeakers** — used to extend the range of full-range systems in the highest frequencies (usually above 10 kHz). Typically, these are either compression drivers or piezoelectric drivers in professional sound systems, although hi-fi type systems use some more esoteric technologies.

G) **Monitor loudspeakers** — full-range loudspeakers that are pointed at the performer on stage, rather than out into the audience. They are used to return a portion of the program to the performer, to help him or her stay in tune and in time, and are sometimes loosely referred to as "foldback." In recording studios, a studio monitor or control room monitor loudspeaker is a full range, high accuracy loudspeaker system designed to permit evaluation of the sound being recorded.

H) **Headphones** — full-range transducers designed to fit snugly on the ears. Some designs block out ambient (external) sound, while others do not. Headphones are sometimes used in sound systems as monitors for click-tracks, and may be used by engineers to check a live mix or a recording during a performance. Headphones also appear as components of intercom systems.

Each type of output transducer has its own characteristics, which must be understood if the transducer is to be used properly. Section 13 of this manual deals with output transducers in detail.

Figure 1-6 (next page) shows a simple practical sound system, such as might be used for a panel discussion in a lecture hall.

The system in Figure 1-6 is designed to amplify the voice of three panelists (or board members, etc). The system can be conceptually analyzed as having three sections: (a) the input transducers, (b) signal processing, and (c) the output transducers:

A) **Input Transducers** — Three microphones convert the sound they pick up from the panelists into audio signals that travel down the cables to the signal processing equipment.

B) **Signal Processing** — The three microphones are connected to individual inputs on the mixing console. The console serves the following functions:

1) **Preamplification** — The console's microphone input section amplifies the level of the audio signal from each microphone, bringing it up to line level.

2) **Equalization** — The console provides the means to adjust the tonal balance of each microphone individually. This allows the console oprator to achieve a more pleasing or more intelligible sound quality.

3) **Mixing** — The console adds the equalized signals of the microphones together to produce a single line-level output signal.

The output of the console is connected to a power amplifier. The power amplifier boosts the console's line level (0.1 to 100 milliwatts) output signal to a level suitable to drive the loudspeaker (0.5 to 500 watts).

C) **Output Transducer** — The loudspeaker converts the power amplifier output signal back into sound. The level of the sound is much higher than that of the three panelists speaking unaided.

There is another less obvious, but equally important aspect of the sound system: the environment. When the sound output of the loudspeaker propagates into the hall, it is altered by the acoustical characteristics of the space.

The room may have little effect on the clarity of the sound if, for example, the room is "dead" or nonreverberant. If the room is highly reverberant, and the sound system is not designed and installed to deal with the acoustics of the space, the effect on the sound may be so severe as to render the sound

system useless.

The environment is an integral part of the sound system, and its effects must be considered when the system is installed. Sections 5 and 6 of this manual deal in detail with the effects of the environment on sound systems.

Every sound system, no matter how large, is merely an extension of this basic model. The same principles that apply to this simple sound system also apply to large-scale concert reinforcement systems.

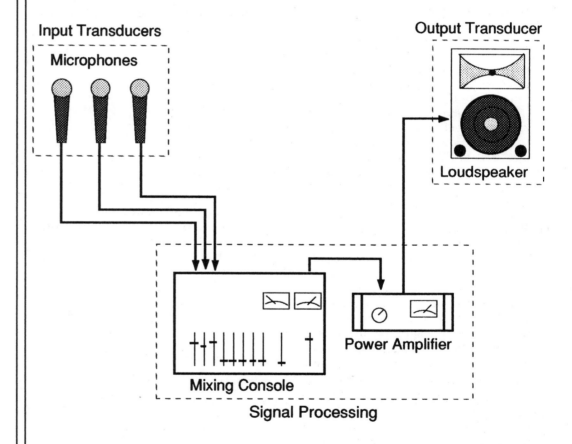

Figure 1-6. A simple sound system

SECTION 2.
FREQUENCY RESPONSE

2.1 A Definition

One of the most commonly-used terms in audio is *frequency response*. In Section 2, we define this term, examine how it applies to various types of audio equipment, and describe the relationship between frequency response and program material.

The frequency response of a device describes the relationship between the device's input and output with regard to signal frequency and amplitude. Another term for this is magnitude response. In its most common usage, the frequency response describes the usable range of signal frequencies which the device will pass from input to output.

Consider the system shown in Figure 2-1. An unknown signal processing element (or black box) is fed from a variable-frequency sine wave generator, and a device for indicating sine wave level in decibels is connected to its output.

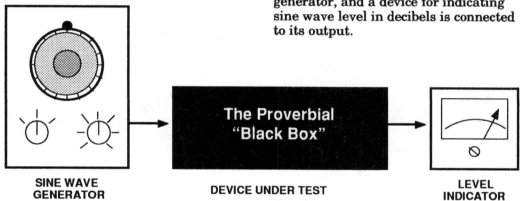

| SINE WAVE GENERATOR | DEVICE UNDER TEST | LEVEL INDICATOR |

Figure 2-1. Model for measuring frequency response

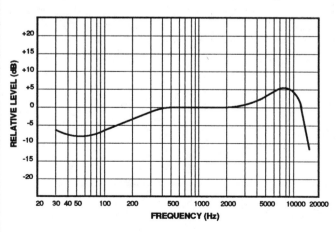

Figure 2-2. Plotted frequency response (relative level versus frequency) of "Black Box" in Figure 2-1

The ideal oscillator produces the same output level at all frequencies (in reality the linearity is not always perfect), so the input level to the black box is constant. As we sweep the oscillator frequency throughout the audio range, however, we may see that the output level of the black box, as registered by our meter, changes. If we make note of the level at each frequency on a graph, we can produce a chart like that shown in Figure 2-2. Here, the output level (vertical axis) is plotted against frequency (horizontal axis).

The graph of Figure 2-2 is called a frequency response plot. It shows us the range of frequencies that the black box will pass from input to output, and what fluctuations in output level (if any) occur within that range.

It is important to understand that the frequency response plot assumes a constant input level to the device under test. For precisely this reason, it gives us an indication of the fidelity with which the device transfers a signal from input to output. The less deviation there is in output level across the stated frequency band, the more faithfully the signal at the output will reflect the signal at the input.

NOTES:

1. If the input to a device under test is not constant in level at all frequencies, a correction may be made to the output plot (or the input level can be intentionally varied to make it constant). The resulting plot is said to be "normalized."

2. The term "frequency response" is used only to refer to signal processing devices and transducers — that is, any devices through which a signal passes. When referring to signal generating devices (oscillators, musical instruments, and so on), the proper term to use is "frequency range."

In its simplest form, a typical frequency response specification might read:

FREQUENCY RESPONSE:
30 Hz to 18 kHz, ± 3 dB

Note that the range (from 30 Hz to 18 kHz) is accompanied by the qualifier, "+ or − 3 dB." This is called the tolerance of the specification. The tolerance tells us the maximum deviation in output level that we can expect over the stated range if the input level remains the same at all frequencies.

Without a stated tolerance, the frequency response specification is useless, since we are left to guess the unit's effect on the signal. There might, in fact, be horrendous peaks and/or dips in the response — and these could alter the signal considerably. While a tolerance of ±3 dB is often assumed if not specified, such an assumption is at your own risk... there is usually a reason why such an important qualifier is omitted from a specification!

Figure 2-3 shows how such a specification is derived from the frequency response plot.

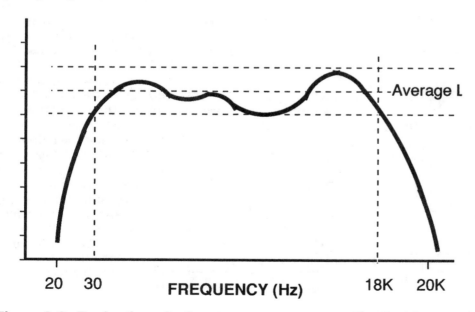

Figure 2-3. Derivation of a frequency response specification from a plot

Some audio devices exhibit extraordinarily flat frequency response, as shown in Figure 2-4. Such a response curve would be characteristic of a power amplifier or line amplifier, for example.

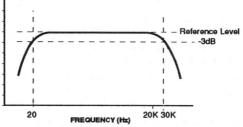

Figure 2-4. A plot of "flat" frequency response

In such cases, the frequency response limits are usually taken to be those points where the unit's output is 3 dB below the average (reference) level. The frequency response specification for the device plotted in Figure 2-4, then, would read:

FREQUENCY RESPONSE:
20 Hz to 30 kHz, +0, -3 dB.

If the frequency response of the device in question greatly exceeds the total range of human hearing (20 Hz to 20 kHz), the frequency response may be specified by simply stating the total response deviation within the audible range. The specification for the device whose response is shown in Figure 2–5, for example, might read:

FREQUENCY RESPONSE:
20 Hz to 20 kHz, +0, -1 dB.

Alternately, if one chooses the -3 dB points as the frequency limits, the specification would read:

FREQUENCY RESPONSE:
10 Hz to 40 kHz, +0, -3 dB.

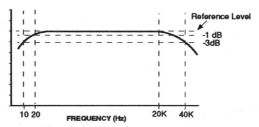

Figure 2-5. A "flat" frequency response plot of a device with1 very wide bandwidth

2.1.2 Octave Relationships And Measurements

Frequency response measurements and specifications are sometimes made on an octave or ⅓-octave basis. Such measurements are far lower in resolution than those described above. They are widely used with loudspeakers, however, because they provide good correlation with the characteristics of human hearing (and can be adjusted by corresponding one octave or ⅓-octave equalizers or filter sets).

The octave is a special musical interval between two tones, formed when the ratio between the frequencies of the tones is 2:1. The ear hears an equivalence between the tones when this is the case (for this reason, pitches at successive octaves in the musical scale are named with the same letter).

With regard to frequency, the octave interval is much wider at high frequencies than at low frequencies. For example, one octave above 40 Hz is 80 Hz (a 40 cycle wide interval), but an octave above 1,000 Hz is 2,000 Hz (a 1,000 cycle wide interval). Yet we hear both of these intervals as musically similar!

This is because the ear's response to frequency is logarithmic in character. (Logarithms are discussed in the Appendix of this handbook). Accordingly, audio response plots such as those shown earlier in this section employ a logarithmic scale to indicate frequency. On this type of scale, the divisions are packed closer and closer together as the frequency increases... up to a decade (10, 100, 1000, etc.), then the spacing interval repeats. Octave and ⅓-octave measurements are designed to divide the linear audio frequency scale, which we do not perceive to be linear, into perceptually equal increments. In frequency response measurements and specifications, then, the average level in each incremental division is given — normally in bar graph form, as shown in Figure 2-6 (next page).

Here, the center frequencies of the bands are spaced ⅓ octave apart. The specific frequencies given on the horizontal axis are standard center frequencies for ⅓-octave measurements: these same centers are also used for the filters in ⅓-octave graphic equalizers. The standard used is known as "ISO" (International Standards Organization), so you know if you have an equalizer with ISO standard octave or ⅓-octave spacing, it will coincide with the bands measured on an ISO standard Real Time Analyzer.

Instead of a sine wave, the excitation signal used for measurements like this is a special signal called pink noise. Pink noise is a randomly-generated signal that excites all the audio frequencies with equal energy per octave. It sounds very much like a rushing waterfall.

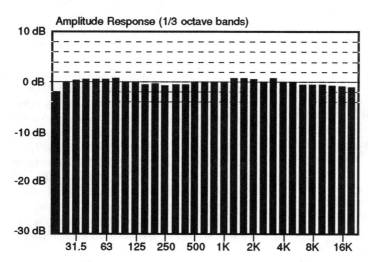

Figure 2-6. Frequency response measured In ⅓-octave bands

A practical audio system is a network of many different types of devices through which the signal must pass on its way to the listeners' ears. Each stage in the system will have specific frequency response characteristics, and will therefore modify the signal to some degree. The overall frequency response of the system is a function of the combined responses of all the various elements in the chain.

The audio elements that exhibit the flattest frequency response characteristics are electronic circuits and cables.

Since there are more frequencies packed into each upper octave than each lower octave, pink noise rolls off at higher frequencies. This means there is less energy at any single high frequency than at any single low frequency so that when all the noise in an octave is added up, it equals all the noise in any other octave. When pink noise is used as the excitation signal, the output of the device under test is filtered in octave or ⅓-octave bands, and the average energy in each band is measured separately.

It is important to note that measurements like this can conceal as much as they reveal. While they provide a good picture of the general characteristic of a device's frequency response, very narrow peaks or dips may be completely missed by the technique. In a reverberant space, the measurement may say more about the room than about the loudspeaker under test.

2.2.1 Electronic Circuits And Cables

Cables are electrically the simplest possible elements in the audio system, and this fact accounts for their generally good response. Cables may introduce response problems at the frequency extremes, however, and the extent of such problems is determined by the design of the cable, its length, and the type of circuitry to which it is connected.

The typical audio cable consists of one or two signal conductors surrounded by insulation and a shielding conductor, as shown in Figure 2-7.

The audio signal is carried in the central conductor(s). The shielding conductor is connected to the electrical ground point in the circuit, and serves to catch most induced static or radio interference signals, shunting them off to ground. (Hum, which is often caused by electromagnetic interference, is not generally attenuated by shields unless they are in the form of iron conduit; instead, twisting the dual conductors in a balanced circuit is the best means to reduce hum. This is due to a characteristic known as Common Mode Rejection, which is explained in Section 11.6.)

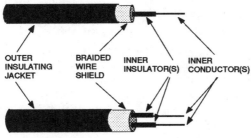

2-CONDUCTOR SHIELDED CABLE
(UNBALANCED LINE)

OUTER INSULATING JACKET | BRAIDED WIRE SHIELD | INNER INSULATOR(S) | INNER CONDUCTOR(S)

3-CONDUCTOR SHIELDED CABLE
(USUALLY BALANCED LINE)

Figure 2-7. Construction of typical audio cables

***NOTE:** The next paragraph may be a bit complex, but it does explain why cables can affect frequency response.*

Frequency response problems associated with cables are generally due to capacitance between the signal conductor(s) and shield in the cable, and capacitance between the conductors themselves. This capacitance, in conjunction with the resistance of the cable, can act like an R-C low pass filter, cutting off high frequencies and dulling the sound. The effect is proportional to the length of the cable, and is worse over very long cable runs, but is mostly dependent on the output impedance of the circuit that drives the cable. Special line driver amplifiers are used to send signals over long cables. Some cables also exhibit considerable inductance between conductors, and depending on the resistance (and impedance) of the circuit, the result can be an R-L high pass filter that cuts off low frequency response. This is why it is important to use the right type of cable for a given job.

Electronic circuits represent a highly developed and controlled technology. Unless they are specifically designed to alter the frequency spectrum (like tone controls, for example), circuits can be and generally are made very flat in frequency response.

Figure 2-8 shows a typical frequency response plot of a high quality audio power amplifier. Note that the response is absolutely flat throughout the audio range, falling off only at the frequency extremes.

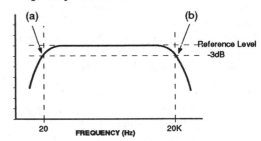

Figure 2-8. Frequency response of a typical audio power amplifier

The low-frequency rolloff indicated in Figure 2-8(a) is sometimes called a subsonic filter pole. Its effect is to reject ultra-low frequencies that could damage loudspeakers and/or modulate the audio to produce undesirable distortion.

The high-frequency rolloff (b) is sometimes called a TIM (transient intermodulation distortion) filter. This intentional limiting of high-frequency response serves to minimize TIM, and also helps to reject supersonic frequencies that can damage tweeters.

Similar characteristics can be expected of any professional audio signal processor. An exception is the digital delay or digital signal processor, both of which use very steep input and output low pass filters (so-called anti-aliasing and reconstruction filters) to avoid problems associated with the digital signal processing; in these devices, there will be a significant rolloff above the cutoff frequency of the device — as high as 150 dB per octave. Unless the design intentionally limits the response, however, analog audio signal processors should be flat throughout the audio range.

2.2.2 Microphones

Contemporary microphone technology is also highly developed, and it is possible to make microphones with very flat frequency response throughout the audio range. Because practical microphones are used in part for their musical or sonic characteristics, however, they may exhibit certain types of controlled deviations from flat response.

One such deviation is called a presence peak. This is a broad peak in response of 3 to 6 dB, centered in the region between about 2 kHz and 5 kHz. It has the effect of adding a bit of crispness to the spoken voice, and can increase the intelligibility of words.

Condenser type microphones often exhibit a peak in the neighborhood of 8 kHz to 10 kHz. This is generally due to diaphragm resonance, and can lend a slightly brittle or bright quality to the sound.

Ribbon type microphones sometimes exhibit both a presence peak and a slight low-frequency rise, usually around 200 Hz. This lends to them a warm sound quality, making them popular choices for both voice and certain instruments.

Generally speaking, the response of practical dynamic microphones used in sound work falls off rapidly in the octave above 10 kHz. Similarly, their low-frequency response may fall off gradually below about 100 Hz. Additionally, the angle of sound incidence upon the microphone may affect the frequency response so sounds coming in from the sides may sound different from those picked up on-axis; this is particularly evident with directional mics. A sound reinforcement mic that is popular for solo vocals or individual instruments may have a harsh response, with many resonances that actually brighten the apparent sound and help it to cut through a complex mix; these same characteristics may make such a mic unsuitable for pickup of multiple instruments or voices, and less-than-ideal for recording work. No one mic is ideal for every application.

The exact characteristic of any microphone is determined by a complex set of design factors, and one is well-advised both to check the data sheet and to try out the microphone. A new series of microphones introduced by Yamaha in 1986 utilizes unique

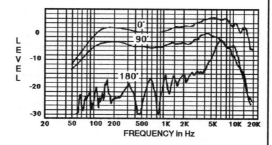

Figure 2-9. On and off axis frequency response of a typical cardioid (unidirectional) dynamic microphone

materials (beryllium laminated diaphragms) and innovative manufacturing techniques (screen-etched precision ports, for example) to achieve extended response and very smooth off-axis characteristics. In any case, some of the most important characteristics of a microphone may never be fully measured and documented. The selection of a microphone for a given application remains a highly subjective task, and the ear is the best guide.

2.2.3 Loudspeakers

Of all the elements in practical sound systems, loudspeakers are subject to the greatest variations in frequency response. It is not uncommon to find narrow peaks and dips of 10 dB or more in a loudspeaker's response. In fact, an overall response tolerance of ±4 dB, measured on a 1/3-octave basis, is considered very good.

This seemingly broad tolerance is considered good partly because loudspeaker transducers are asked to handle relatively large amounts of power and produce fairly high sound pressures, so their design must allow compromises for durability and efficiency. Practical loudspeakers also must use several transducers to reproduce the full audio range; the marrying of these transducers to form a single functional unit is a complex matter, and can drastically affect the system frequency response.

Sound reinforcement loudspeakers can be divided into two basic classes: full-range loudspeakers, and special units that cover limited ranges. The latter are used to augment the former, extending their response.

Generally, full-range reinforcement loudspeakers will have a frequency response extending from about 100 Hz to between 10 kHz and 15 kHz. In most applications, this response is sufficient. Some smaller loudspeakers, such as those used for paging, may have more limited response — but for voice, it is generally true that the loudspeaker response should extend from about 300 Hz to at least 3.5 kHz.

Of the special, limited-range units, the most common are subwoofers and tweeters. Subwoofers are loudspeakers designed to operate only below 300 Hz (typically below 100 Hz), and usually perform down to about 30 Hz. They are used to extend the bass response of systems. Tweeters usually work above 5 to 8 kHz, and are used to extend the system's high-frequency response.

Practical loudspeakers are directional — that is, they concentrate the sound that they radiate in a specific direction. As you move away from their primary axis, the sound not only drops in level, but the frequency response gets rougher.

For further information on the frequency response characteristics of loudspeakers, see Section 13, "Loudspeakers."

In order to relate the frequency response of a device or system to its sonic characteristics, we need to get a sense of the frequency ranges covered by typical program sources.

2.3 Voice and Instrument Ranges

2.3.1 The Speaking Voice

Compared with the full range of human hearing, the speaking voice covers a relatively narrow frequency band — roughly from 100 Hz to 6 kHz. Within that range, the power distribution of speech is heavily weighted in the frequencies below about 1 kHz, with some 80 percent of the energy concentrated in the range below 500 Hz.

While speech has very little high-frequency content, however, almost all of the energy of consonants occurs above 1 kHz. Therefore, loss of high frequencies can drastically affect speech intelligibility.

As a practical minimum, the bandwidth of a speech reproduction system must extend from 300 Hz to 3.5 kHz. This is the frequency response of a typical telephone receiver, and other types of utility communications devices exhibit similarly limited response. Generally, intelligibility may be improved by introducing a presence peak in the response of 3 to 6 dB in the region between 2 kHz and 5 kHz.

Sound reinforcement applications require somewhat higher fidelity than a telephone, however. For this reason, public address systems should be reasonably flat from 100 Hz to at least 8 kHz. A presence peak can improve intelligibility in such systems, too — but it can also increase the likelihood of feedback, so it must be approached with care.

2.3.2 The Singing Voice and Musical Instruments

Figure 2-10 (next page) is a very useful graph which describes the frequency ranges of musical instruments and trained singing voices.

Musical signals are much more difficult to characterize than speech. The frequency range and power spectrum of a particular musical signal depend in large part on stylistic matters — the instrumental complement, the arrangement, the style of production, and so on. Some styles of music, for example, depend heavily on energy between 20 Hz and 100 Hz to achieve their full intended impact, while those frequencies may be entirely absent in other styles.

The sound reinforcement professional therefore must learn to use his or her ears to carefully analyze musical material and correlate the sonic experience with system performance. The ability to do this comes only with long practice listening to a variety of equipment with different sound sources. In sound work it's very important to always listen carefully and examine what you hear, gradually building a mental catalog of experiences from which to draw.

2.3.3 Harmonics

Looking at Figure 2-10, we see that it seems to show the frequency range covered by musical instruments as limited to about 4 kHz. Yet we know that human hearing extends far beyond this limit, and that a sound system whose frequency response is

this limited will sound dull, lacking in highs. The apparent discrepancy is due to the fact that Figure 2-10 does not take harmonics into account.

Every musical sound that we hear is in fact a composite of sine waves at different frequencies and amplitudes. These sine waves combine to form the sound, and their frequency and amplitude relationships determine the quality, or timbre, of the sound. The ultimate waveform may be more of a triangle, squarewave or something not easily described in a word.

When a musical note with a complex waveform has a distinct pitch (as opposed to noise), that waveform can ultimately be created by combining a set of precisely related sine waves. These sine waves are called harmonics, and their frequencies are related in simple integer multiples. The sine wave frequency at the pitch that we hear as the note is the fundamental, and it is usually (though not always) the strongest (highest amplitude) of the set of sine waves which comprises the complex waveform.

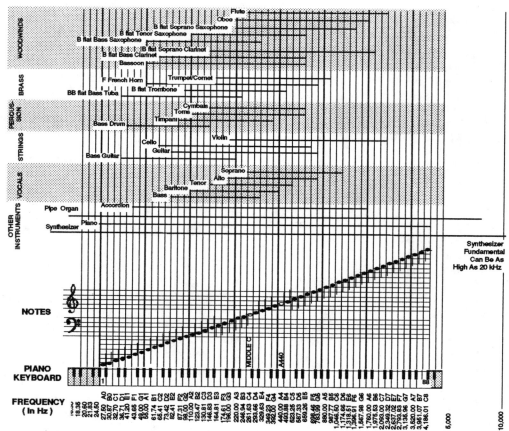

Figure 2-10. Frequency range of typical instruments and singing voices

2.4 Effect of Acoustical Factors

Above the fundamental there are additional sine wave components whose frequencies are multiples of the fundamental frequency. If the fundamental is at 500 Hz, for example, the harmonics will occur at 1 kHz, 1.5 kHz, 2 kHz, 2.5 kHz, and so on. Figure 2-11 is a graphical illustration of the harmonic spectrum of a musical sound.

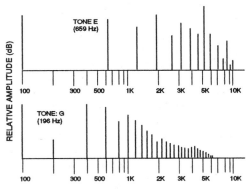

Figure 2-11. Harmonic content of open strings of the violin. The lower tones have more closely packed harmonics.

As the frequency multiplier increases, the amplitude (or strength) of the harmonic usually decreases so the upper harmonics are generally much lower in level than the fundamental. But this is not always the case. Sometimes, individual harmonics are louder than the fundamental. In such cases, the sound quality becomes more pinched or like that of a reed instrument (i.e., like an oboe, clarinet, and so forth).

If the sine wave components of a sound are not related in simple integer multiples, the sense of pitch is lost and the sound quality approaches noise. Drum sounds, for example, have very complex sets of components with non-integral frequency relationships.

Regardless of whether the sine wave components of sound occur at integral multiples, their precise amplitude relationships determine the sound quality. For this reason, flat frequency response is very important in a sound system. If the response is very rough, the quality of the sounds will be altered.

The frequency response of any sound system is affected by the environment in which it works.

Outdoors, the main factors affecting the system's response are wind, temperature, and air absorption. Wind tends to deflect sound very slightly as it travels, and gusty wind can appear to modulate the sound. Temperature gradients can also deflect sound, and to an even greater degree than wind gradients. Air absorption affects mainly high frequencies. As sound travels through air, the energy of the highs is lost more quickly than that of the lows. That is why sounds heard at a distance appear muffled. The degree to which the air absorbs high frequency energy is affected by the relative humidity.

Indoors, the predominant factors affecting a system's response are reflections from wall, ceiling and floor surfaces, and room resonances. Reflections not only cause reverberation effects, but also can cause cancellations at specific frequencies which show up as dips in the system response. Room resonances can cause dips or, more commonly, peaks in the response. All these effects will color the sound of the system.

The effect of environmental factors on sound systems is dealt with in detail in Section 5 ("Sound Outdoors") and Section 6 ("Sound Indoors").

SECTION 3.
THE DECIBEL, SOUND LEVEL, AND RELATED ITEMS

3.1 WHAT IS A DECIBEL?

Numerous attempts have been made to explain one of the most common, yet confusing terms in audio, the "dB." "dB" is an abbreviation for "decibel," and it need not be all that difficult to grasp, if properly presented. If you're one of the many people who is "a little fuzzy" about decibels, the following explanations should clear things up for you.

3.1.1 A Mathematical Definition of the dB

The dB always describes a ratio of two quantities... quantities that are most often related to power. The reason that the dB is used is that it is logarithmic*, and therefore smaller numbers can be used to express values that otherwise would require more digits. Also, since our ears' sensitivity is "logarithmic," dB values relate to how we hear better than do absolute numbers or simple ratios. Thus, the dB was intended to simplify things, not to complicate them.

The decibel is actual $\frac{1}{10}$ of a **Bel** (a unit named after Alexander Graham Bell, which is why the "B" of dB is upper case). What's a Bel?

A Bel is defined as the logarithm of an electrical, acoustic, or other *power ratio.* (We are describing the ratio of watts — this ratio does not refer to raising numbers to a power, although that, too, is part of log math.) To express the relationship of two power values, P_0 watts and P_1 watts, in Bels:

$$\text{Bel} = \log (P_1 \div P_0)$$

The decibel is more convenient to use in sound systems, primarily because the number scaling is more natural. Since a decibel (dB) is $\frac{1}{10}$ of a

Bel, it can be mathematically expressed by the equation:

$$dB = 10 \log (P_1 \div P_2)$$

To make it clear that the above is 10 times the log of P_1/P_2, we may sometimes add a dot (•) to indicate multiplication... i.e.:

$$dB = 10 \bullet \log (P_1 \div P_2)$$

(This is the same as the previous equation)

If you are not familiar with logs, it may not make much sense to you that the right half of the Bel equation is multiplied by 10 to get a value that's supposed to be $\frac{1}{10}$ of a Bel. This is correct, though.

It's not really important for you to grasp the logarithm concept just now... it's simply important that you realize that a logarithm describes the ratio of two powers, not the power value themselves. To demonstrate this, let's plug in some real values in the dB equation.

PROBLEM: What is the ratio, in dB, of 2 watts to 1 watt?

$$\begin{aligned} dB &= 10 \bullet \log (P_1 \div P_0) \\ &= 10 \bullet \log (2 \div 1) \\ &= 10 \bullet \log 2 \\ &= 10 \bullet .301 \\ &= 3.01 \\ &\approx 3 \end{aligned}$$

so the ratio of 2 watts to 1 watt is 3 dB.

NOTE: *If you don't have a calculator that gives log values, or a book with log tables, then you need to know that the logarithm of 2 is .301 in order to solve the above equation. A calculator that can perform log calculations helps a lot.*

* "Logarithmic" pertains to "logarithms," which are explained in the Appendix.

PROBLEM: What is the ratio, in dB, of 100 watts to 10 watts?

$$dB = 10 \cdot \log (P_1 \div P_0)$$
$$= 10 \cdot \log (100 \div 10)$$
$$= 10 \cdot \log 10$$
$$= 10 \cdot 1$$
$$= 10$$

so the ratio of 100 watts to 10 watts is 10 dB.

The two previous problems point out interesting aspects of using the dB to express power ratios:
A) whenever one power is twice another, it is 3 dB greater (or if it is half the power, it is 3 dB less),
B) whenever one power is ten times another, it is 10 dB greater (or if it is $1/10$ the power, it is 10 dB less).

One can begin to see the reason for using dB by expressing a few other power values. For instance, how much greater than 100 watts is 1,000 watts? That's a 10:1 ratio, so, again, it is 10 dB. What is the relationship of one milliwatt to $1/10$ watt? One milliwatt is $1/1000$ watt, and that's $1/100$ of $1/10$ watt, which means it is 10 dB below $1/10$ watt.

The dB can be used to express voltage ratios, as explained below. The decibel relationship of power ratios is *not* the same as that for voltage ratios.

Power is proportional to the square of the voltage. Without going into detail here, this means that where voltage is concerned, the dB relationships are doubled relative to power. That is...

$$dB_{volts} = 20 \log (E_1 \div E_0)$$

where E_0 and E_1 are the two voltage values. Consider what this means. While twice the power is a 3 dB increase, twice the voltage is a 6 dB increase. Similarly while 10 times the power is a 10 dB increase, 10 times the voltage is a 20 dB increase. The following equations should clarify this relationship:

What is the ratio of 100 watts to 10 watts, in dB?

$$dB_{watts} = 10 \cdot \log (P_1 \div P_0)$$
$$= 10 \cdot \log (100 \div 10)$$
$$= 10 \cdot \log 10$$
$$= 10 \cdot 1$$
$$= 10 \text{ dB}$$

What is the ratio of 100 volts to 10 volts, in dB?

$$dB_{volts} = 20 \cdot \log (E_1 \div E_0)$$
$$= 20 \cdot \log (100 \div 10)$$
$$= 20 \cdot \log 10$$
$$= 20 \text{ dB}$$

Now, why is 10 times the power a 10 dB increase, but 10 times the voltage a 20 dB increase? Let's calculate the actual power delivered into an 8 ohm load by the 10 volt and 100 volt outputs. The equation for power is:

$$P = E^2 \div R$$

That is, power in watts = voltage squared divided by the resistance in ohms. We see that power is proportional to voltage squared; double the voltage, you get four times the power. Armed with this knowledge, let's plug the two values for E (voltage) of 10 and 100 volts into the above equation:

$$P = 10^2 \div 8$$
$$= 100 \div 8$$
$$= 12.5 \text{ watts}$$

$$P = 100^2 \div 8$$
$$= 10,000 \div 8$$
$$= 1,250 \text{ watts}$$

As you can see, using ten times the voltage produces a power output that is 100 times as great. Now let's take the power ratio of the two output powers obtained using 10 and 100 volts (i.e., 12.5 watts and 1,250 watts)...

$$dB_{watts} = 10 \cdot \log (P_1 \div P_0)$$
$$= 10 \cdot \log (1250 \div 12.5)$$
$$= 10 \cdot \log (100)$$
$$= 10 \cdot 2$$
$$= 20 \text{ dB}$$

As you can see, while 100 volts is ten times 10 volts, when we refer back to the power values from which the dB is derived, we find this represents a 20 dB power ratio. This is why voltages have twice the multiplier before the log in the dB equation. The same holds true, by the way, for current relationships (i.e., dB in current uses the 20 log equation).

If we use a reference value of 1 watt for P_0, then the dB = 10 log $(P_1 \div P_0)$ equation yields the following relationships:

Power Value of P_1 (Watts)	Level in dB (Relative to 1 Watt P_0)
1	0
10	10
100	20
200	23
400	26
800	29
1,000	30
2,000	33
4,000	36
8,000	39
10,000	40
20,000	43
40,000	46
80,000	49
100,000	50

Table 3-1. Large power ratios (expressed in dB)

The value of using dB to express relative levels should be apparent here, since a mere 50 dB denotes a 100,000:1 ratio (one hundred thousand watts in this case). For finding smaller dB values (i.e., for power ratios between 1:1 and 10:1), the following chart may be helpful:

Power Value of P_1 (Watts)	Level in dB (relative to 1 watt P_0)
1.0	0
1.25	1
1.6	2
2.0	3
2.5	4
3.15	5
4.0	6
5.0	7
6.3	8
8.0	9
10.0	10

3.1.2 Relative Versus Absolute Levels

The key concept is that "dB," in itself, has no absolute value. However, when a standard reference value is used for "0 dB," then any number of dB above or below that implied or stated zero reference may be used to describe a specific quantity. We'll give several examples of "specifications" to illustrate this concept.

EXAMPLE A: "The console's maximum output level is +20 dB."

That statement is meaningless because the zero reference for "dB" is not specified. It's like telling a stranger "I can only do 20," without providing a clue as to what the 20 describes.

EXAMPLE B: "The console's maximum output level is 20 dB above 1 milliwatt."

Example B makes a specific claim. It actually tells us that the console is capable of delivering 100 milliwatts (0.1 watt) into some load. How do we know it can deliver 100 milliwatts? Of the 20 dB expressed, the first 10 dB represents a tenfold power increase (from 1 mW to 10 mW), and the next 10 dB another tenfold increase (from 10 mW to 100 mW). Of course, the above statement is awkward, so more "compact" ways of expressing the same idea have been developed, as explained in the next subsection.

Table 3-2. Small power ratios (expressed in dB)

3.2 Relating the Decibel to Electrical Signal Levels

3.2.1 dBm

The term **dBm** expresses an electrical power level, and is always referenced to 1 milliwatt. That is, 0 dBm = 1 milliwatt. dBm has no direct relationship to voltage or impedance.

The dBm was actually set forth as an industry standard in the *Proceedings of the Institute of Radio Engineers*, Volume 28, in January 1940, in an article by H.A. Chinn, D.K. Gannett and R.M. Moris titled "A New Standard Volume Indicator and Reference Level."

The typical circuit in which dBm was measured when the term was first devised was a 600 ohm telephone line. In the IRE article, the reference level was 0.001 watts, which is one milliwatt. It so happens that this amount of power is dissipated when a voltage of 0.775 V_{rms} is applied to a 600 ohm line.* For this reason, many people mistakenly believe that 0 dBm means "0.775 volts," but that is only the case in a 600 ohm circuit. 0 dBm does, however, always means one milliwatt.

EXAMPLE C: "The console's maximum output level is +20 dBm."

Example C tells us exactly the same thing as Example B, in Section 3.1.2, but in fewer words. Instead of stating "the maximum output level is 100 milliwatts," we say it is "+20 dBm."

EXAMPLE D: "The mixer's maximum output level is +20 dBm into 600 ohms."

Example D tells us that the output is virtually the same as that expressed in Examples B and C, but it gives us the additional information that the load is 600 ohms. This allows us to calculate that the maximum output voltage into that load is 7.75 volts rms, even though the output voltage is not given in the specification.

*The term "RMS" is an abbreviation for Root Mean Square, as explained in Section 3.4.

3.2.2 dBu

Most modern audio equipment (consoles, tape decks, signal processors, etc.) is sensitive to voltage levels. Power output isn't really a consideration, except in the case of power amplifiers driving loudspeakers, in which case "watts," rather than any "dB" quantity, is the most common term.

The term "dBm" expresses a power ratio so how does it relate to voltage? Not directly, although the voltage can be calculated if the impedance is known.* That complicates things, and, as we said earlier, the whole concept of the dB is to simplify the numbers involved. For that reason, another dB term was devised... **dBu**.

dBu is a more appropriate term for expressing output or input voltage. This brings up a major source of confusion with the **dB**... the dB is often used with different zero references; dBm implies one zero reference, and dBu implies another. We'll go on to explain these and show the relationship between several commonly used "dB" terms.

The voltage represented by **dBu** is equivalent to that represented by **dBm** if, and only if, the dBm figure is derived with a 600 ohm load. However, the dBu value is not dependent on the load: 0 dBu is always 0.775 volts.

The dBu was specified as a standard unit in order to avoid confusion with another voltage-related dB unit, the dBV, as explained in Section 3.2.5.

EXAMPLE E: "The console's maximum output level is +20 dBu into a 10k ohm or higher impedance load."

Example E tells us that the console's maximum output voltage is 7.75 volts, just as we calculated for Example D, but there is a significant difference. The output in Example D would drive 600 ohms, whereas Example E speci-

* In fact, about the only time that "dBm" is appropriate these days is when the equipment is driving very long cables, like those used in large sound reinforcement systems or multi-studio broadcast production complexes, where true 600 ohm balanced circuits are essential to reduce susceptibility to induced noise and high frequency losses.

3.2.3 dBV and dBv

fies a minimum load impedance of 10,000 ohms; if this console were connected to a 600 ohm termination, its output would probably drop in voltage, increase in distortion, and might burn out.

How can we make these assumptions? One learns to read between the lines. Example D refers the output level to power (dBm), so if a given power level is to be delivered, and the load impedance is higher, then a higher voltage would have to be delivered to equal that same power output. Conversely, Example E states a minimum specified load impedance, and connection to a lower impedance load would tend to draw more power from the output. Draining more power from an output circuit that is not capable of delivering the power (which we imply from the dBu/voltage specification and the minimum impedance) will result in reduced output voltage and possible distortion or component failure.

The dBu is a relatively recent voltage-referenced term. For many years, dBV denoted a voltage-reference, with 0 dBV = 1 volt rms. During that period, it became common practice to use a lower case "v," as adopted by the National Association of Broadcasters (NAB) and others, to denote the voltage value corresponding to the power indicated in dBm (that is, dBv was a voltage-related term with 0 dBv = 0.775 volts). "dBv" with the lower case "v" was convenient because the dB values would tend to be the same as though "dBm" were used *provided the "dBm" output was specified to drive 600 ohm loads*, making it easier to compare dBu specs with products specified in dBm. The convenience factor here only makes sense where a voltage sensitive (read "high impedance") input is involved, and can lead to serious errors elsewhere.

EXAMPLE F:
1) "The nominal output level is +4 dBv."
2) "The nominal output level is +4 dBV."

The above two statements, (1) and (2), appear to be identical, but upon closer scrutiny, you will notice the former uses a lower case "v" and the latter an upper case "V" after the "dB." This means that the first output

Level in dBu (or dBm across 600 ohms)

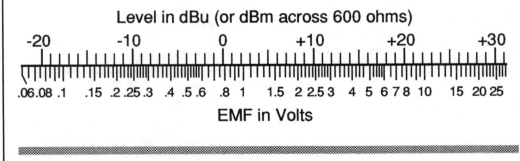

EMF in Volts

Level in dBu (or dBm across 600 ohms)

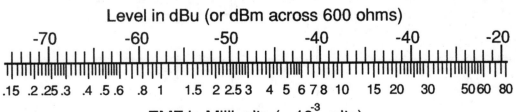

EMF in Millivolts (= 10^{-3} volts)

Figure 3-1. Nomograph relating level in dBu (or dBm across 600 ohms) to voltage

specified will deliver a nominal output of 1.23 volts rms, whereas the second mixer specified will deliver a nominal output level of 1.6 volts rms.

Unfortunately, people often did not distinguish clearly between "dBv" (a 0.775 volt zero reference — if one assumes a 600 ohm circuit) and "dBV" (a 1 volt zero reference without regard to circuit impedance). To avoid confusion, the capital "V" was then made the 1-volt zero reference standard by the International Electrotechnical Commission (IEC), while the NAB agreed to use a small "u" to denote the voltage value that might be obtained when the customary 600 ohm load is used to measure the dBm (although the load itself must be minimal). The "u" in "dBu" thus stands for "unloaded," a term engineers use to describe an output which works into no load (an open circuit) or an insignificant load (such as the typical high impedance inputs of modern audio equipment).

EXAMPLE G:
1) "The nominal output level is +4 dBv."
2) "The nominal output level is +4 dBu."

The two statements, (1) and (2), are identical, although the latter is the preferable usage today. Both indicate the nominal output level is 1.23 V rms.

To recap, the only difference between dBu (or dBv) and dBV is the actual voltage chosen as the reference for "0 dB." 0 dBV is 1 volt, whereas 0 dBu and 0 dBv are 0.775 volts.

NOTE: *If you are familiar with older Yamaha manuals, you will recognize the dBu as being the same unit Yamaha formerly described "dBv" (with a lower case "v") or just as "dB."*

3.2.4 Converting dBV to dBu (or to dBm across 600 ohms)

So long as you're dealing with voltage (not power), you can convert dBV to dBu (or dBm across 600 ohms) by adding 2.2 dB to whatever dBV value you have. To convert dBu (dBm) to dBV, it's just the other way around — you subtract 2.2 dB from the dBu value.

Table 3.3 (below) shows the relationship between common values of dBV and dBu, and the voltages they represent.

3.2.5 Relating dBV, dBu and dBm to Specifications

In many products, you may see phono jack inputs and outputs rated in dBV (1 volt reference) because that is the standard generally applied to such equipment, while the XLR connector output levels and some phone jack output levels are rated in dBm (1 milliwatt reference) or dBu (0.775 volt reference).

Typically, line level phono jack inputs and outputs are intended for use with high impedance equipment, which is basically sensitive to voltage rather than power, so their nominal levels may be specified as "-10 dBV."

Level in dBV (0 dBV = 1 V Without Reference to Impedance, Which is Usually High)	Voltage (RMS)	Level in dBu or dBm (0 dBu = 0.775V unterminated; 0 dBm = 0.775V across a 600 ohm load impedance)
+6.0	2.0	+8.2
+4.0	1.6	+6.2
+1.78	1.23	+4.0
0.0	1.00	2.2
-2.2	0.775	0.0
-6.0	0.5	-3.8
-8.2	0.388	-6.0
-10.0	0.316	-7.8
-12.0	0.250	-9.8
-12.2	0.245	-10.0
-20.0	0.100	-17.8

Table 3-3. Conversion factors for dBV and dBu

This standard is the one which has been used for many years in the consumer audio equipment business. Typical line level XLR connector inputs and outputs are intended for use with low or high impedance equipment. Since older low impedance equipment was sensitive to power, XLR connector nominal levels were often specified as "+4 dBm" or "+8 dBm," levels characteristic of sound reinforcement and recording, or of broadcast, respectively. (while dBu values would probably suffice today, old practices linger and the dBm is still used.) Phone jack inputs and outputs are usually specified at the higher levels and lower impedances characteristic of XLRs, though exceptions exist.

A low impedance line output generally may be connected to higher impedance inputs, without much change in level. Be aware that if a high impedance output is connected to a low impedance input, that output may be somewhat overloaded (which can increase the distortion and lower the signal level), and the frequency response may be adversely affected. In some cases, the equipment could be damaged, so check the specifications carefully.

3.2.6 dBW

We have explained that the dBm is a measure of electrical power, a ratio referenced to 1 milliwatt. dBm is handy when dealing with the miniscule power (in the millionths of a watt) output of microphones, and the modest levels in signal processors (in the milliwatts). One magazine wished to express larger power numbers without larger dB values... for example, the multi-hundred watt output of large power amplifiers. For this reason, that magazine established another dB power reference: dBW.

0 dBW is 1 watt. Therefore, a 100 watt power amplifier is a 20 dBW amplifier (10 log (100÷1) = 10 log (100) = 10 • 2 = 20 dB). A 1000 watt amplifier is a 30 dBW amplifier, and so forth. In fact, if we are referring to amplifier power, the dB values in Tables 3-1 and 3-2 can be considered "dBW" (decibels, referenced to 1 watt of electrical power).

3.3 Relating the Decibel to Acoustic Levels

The term "sound level" generally refers to the sound pressure level, although it may refer to sound power. While sound power is a rarely used term, be sure you make the distinction. The sound power is the total sound energy radiated by a louspeaker (or other device) in all directions. The sound pressure is the level measured per unit area at a particular location relative to the sound source.

3.3.1 dB SPL

The dB may be used to describe sound pressure levels. Another term for voltage is electromotive Fforce (EMF). The force of air pressing against the resistance of an eardrum is analogous to the force of a battery pushing electrons against the resistance in a circuit. Therefore, when a dB describes a sound pressure level ratio, the "20 log" equation is used:

$$dB_{SPL} = 20 \log (p_1/p_0)$$

where p_0 and p_1 are the sound pressures, in dynes per square centimeter or Newtons per square meter.

This equation tells us that if one SPL is twice another, it is 6 dB greater; if it is 10 times another, it is 20 dB greater, and so forth.

How do we perceive SPL? It turns out that a sound which is 3 dB higher in level than another is barely perceived to be louder; a sound which is 10 dB higher in level is perceived to be about twice as loud. (Loudness, by the way, is a subjective quantity, and is also greatly influenced by frequency and absolute sound level.)

Does SPL have an absolute reference value, and therefore do "SPLs" have quantifiable meaning? Yes, generally 0 dB SPL is defined as the threshold of hearing (of a young, undamaged ear) in the ear's most sensitive range, between 1 kHz and 4 kHz. It represents a pressure level of 0.0002 dynes/cm^2, which is the same as 0.000002 Newtons/m^2. Rather than merely relate various SPLs to various pressures, it is perhaps more meaningful to relate SPLs to common sources of

	dB
.45 ACP Colt Pistol (25 feet)	140
50 HP Siren (100 feet)	130
Threshold of Pain	
	120
Rock Music (10 feet)	110
Film Scoring (20 feet)	
	100
Loud Classical Music	
Heavy Street Traffic (5 feet)	90
Cabin of Jet Aircraft (Cruise Configuration)	80
	70
Average Conversation (3 feet)	60
	50
Average Suburban Home (night)	
Quiet Auditorium	40
Quiet Recording Studio	30
Quiet Whisper (5 feet)	
Extremely Quiet Recording Studio	20
Rustling Leaves	
Anechoic Chamber*	10
Threshold of Hearing	0
(Youths, 1 kHz to 4 kHz)	

Typical Recording Studio Control Room Monitors for:

NOTE: Sound may be audible below 0 dB SPL. This Value was based on limited research.

* Note that some anechoic chambers may be very noisy; the fact that a chamber does not reflect sound internally does not mean it effectively blocks external sounds from entering. Negative SPLs, while possible, are not given since, by definition, they are below the threshold of audibility.

Table 3-4. Typical sound pressure levels of various sources (at indicated distances to ear, where appropriate to specify)

sound, as is done in the following chart. Naturally, these figures are approximations.

3.3.2 dB PWL

Acoustic power is expressed in acoustic watts, and can be described with a dB term, **dB PWL**. This term shares the same "10 log" equation as other power ratios:

$$dB_{PWL} = 10 \log (P_1/P_0)$$

Acoustic power and dB PWL come into play when calculating the reverb time of an enclosed space, or the efficiency of a loudspeaker system, but they are seldom seen on specification sheets and seldom used by the average sound system operator. It is much more common to use dB SPL because the sound pressure is more directly related to perceived loudness (and is easily measured).

If, instead of electrical watts, we use acoustic watts in Tables 3-1 and 3-2, then those dB values can be considered "dB PWL" (decibels, sound power).

Incidentally, there is no set relationship between dB PW L and dBW; the former expresses acoustic power, and the latter electrical power. If a loudspeaker is fed 20 dBW, it might generate as little as 10 dB PWL. In English... feed 100 watts into a loudspeaker, it might generate as little as 10 watts acoustic power. This would indicate a conversion efficiency of 10 percent, which is *high* for a cone loudspeaker in a vented box!

3.4 What is RMS?

"RMS" is an abbreviation for Root Mean Square. This is a mathematical expression used in audio to describe the level of a signal. RMS is particularly useful in describing the energy of a complex waveform or a sine wave. It is not the peak level, nor the average, but rather it is obtained by squaring all the instantaneous voltages along a waveform, averaging the squared values, and taking the square root of that number. For a periodic signal, such as a sine wave, the peak value can be multiplied by a constant to derive the rms value of that wave. However, for an aperiodic signal such as speech or music, the rms value can only be measured using a specialized meter or detector circuit.

The rms value of a sine wave is 0.707 times the peak value of the wave, as indicated in Figure 3-2.

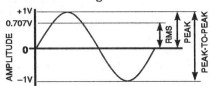

Figure 3-2. The rms value of a sine wave

You may recall that many power amplifier manufacturers used to boast their amps delivered "X watts rms Power," and that this was supposed to be much better than "X watts music power." In this context, the rms value of the audio signal was correlated to the equivalent power that would be dissipated by a DC signal. For example, consider an amplifier rated at 200 watts rms into 8 ohms. Such an amp should deliver 40 volts rms into an 8 ohm load. Remember that $E=\sqrt{PZ}$, or Voltage = Square Root of Power x Impedance ($E = \sqrt{200 \cdot 8 \text{ ohms}} = \sqrt{1600} = 40$ volts). If a 40 volt DC source were dissipated by an 8 ohm resistive load, it would produce the same amount of heat in that load as the 40 volt rms sine wave (or other audio signal).

Why is the rms value of a signal used? For one thing, the rms value correlates well with the real work being done by the amplifier. When so-called "program" or "music" power ratings are employed, the actual work being done is highly subjective — it depends largely on the nature of the program source. The rms value of any program will pretty much reflect the energy content of that source. There is just one minor problem: the term "rms power" is meaningless.

Why? Power is the product of voltage times current. Typically, in a power amp, one is measuring the rms value of the output voltage and multiplying it by the rms value of the output current. This *does not* result in the rms power because the voltage and current are not in phase, and hence the rms values do not multiply to form a mathematically valid value. The intent of an rms power rating is valid, but not the term itself. Manufacturers are still driving amplifiers with sine wave test signals and connecting the amp outputs to dummy loads. They obtain the rms value of the sine wave output voltage, and calculate a value for the power output based on that voltage and the load resistance or impedance. Those who wish to be technically correct list this rating as "continuous average sine wave power," rather than "rms power."

RMS values are not the exclusive domain of power amplifiers. In most (but not all) cases, when you see a voltage listed for input sensitivity on a preamplifier or line amp, it is the rms voltage. For example, you may recall that 0 dBm is 1 milliwatt which equals 0.775 volts rms across a 600 ohm circuit, and 0 dBV is 1 volt rms.

RMS values have another benefit in audio measurements. They are similar to, but not the same as, average values. The average value of a signal does not change much even when there are very high level transient peaks. Conversely, the peak level can vary wildly without a major effect on average level. When we wish to evaluate the loudness of a signal (the perceived level by a human listener), the rms value corresponds more closely with the sensitivity of our ears to audio energy. Hence, many compressors, noise reduction systems, and other signal processors employ rms detector circuitry. One notable exception is the broadcast limiter, where even momentary transient peaks can cause overmodulation and consequent signal splatter (spurious emissions), so peak detectors are often used in this application.

Three of the most often misused or carelessly used terms in audio are volume, level, and gain. It's important to have a clear understanding of these terms, and to agree on how they will be used.

VOLUME is defined as power level. In terms of audio equipment, then, if you turn up the volume, you are increasing the power. Unfortunately, the term is loosely used to describe sound intensity or the magnitude of an electrical signal. Of course, volume also refers to the cubic dimension of a space. Our favorite approach is to avoid the term altogether, since there are better terms that are far less ambiguous.

LEVEL is defined as the magnitude of a quantity in relation to an arbitrary reference value. Sound Pressure Level, for example, expresses level in dB relative to 0.0002 dynes per square centimeter. The audio level in a signal processor, for example, may be expressed in dBm, which is referenced to 1 milliwatt.

GAIN has several definitions. If not specified, it is usually assumed to be transmission gain, which is the power increase of a signal, usually expressed in dB. Sometimes, the increase in voltage is expressed as voltage gain, but one must be careful here because a voltage gain may represent a power loss... depending on the relative impedances involved. A common area where this very confusion reigns is with voltage and power levels between signal processors and loudspeakers.

EXAMPLE: The output voltage of a given signal processor is measured to be 0.775 volts rms. This signal is fed to a power amplifier, and then to a loudspeaker. The voltage applied to the louspeaker is 0.775 volts rms. What is the gain of the amplifier?

The answer... you don't have enough information to give an answer. On first glance, you might guess "0 dB" or no gain, since the voltage is the same at the amplifier's input and output. If you specified "0 dB voltage gain," you'd be safe, but that wouldn't really express anything of meaning. Instead,

you need to know the power dissipated at the input to the amplifier, and at the loudspeaker. To know this, you need to know the impedances.

EXAMPLE: An amplifier having 600 ohms actual input impedance is fed a 0.775 volt rms signal. It delivers 0.775 volts rms to an 8 ohm loudspeaker. What is the gain of the amplifier?

First, we calculate the input power:

$$
\begin{aligned}
P &= E^2 \div Z \\
&= 0.775^2 \div 600 \\
&= 0.600625 \div 600 \\
&= 0.001 \\
&= 1 \text{ milliwatt}
\end{aligned}
$$

You already knew this, because 0.775 volts across 600 ohms is 0 dBm, or 1 milliwatt.

Next, we calculate the power delivered to the loudspeaker load:

$$
\begin{aligned}
P &= E^2 \div Z \\
&= 0.775^2 \div 8 \\
&= 0.600625 \div 8 \\
&= 0.075 \text{ watts} \\
&= 75 \text{ milliwatts}
\end{aligned}
$$

Now, we calculate the ratio, in dB, of the output power to the input power:

$$
\begin{aligned}
dB_{power} &= 10 \log (P_1 \div P_o) \\
&= 10 \log (75 \div 1) \\
&= 10 \log 75 \\
&= 10 \cdot 1.875061263 \\
&\approx 19 \text{ dB}
\end{aligned}
$$

We now see that even though the input and output voltages are the same, the amplifier has a gain of 19 dB. In fact, since the reference value at the input is 0 dBm, the 75 mW output is, in fact, +19 dBm.

3.6 Loudness

The concepts of sound pressure level, the dB, and frequency response have been treated in previous sections. **Loudness** is related to these items.

Some people use the term "loudness" interchangeably with "SPL" or "volume." This is incorrect since "loudness" has a very distinct, and not so simple, meaning.

3.6.1 Equal Loudness Contours and Phons

One can use a sound level meter to measure the sound pressure in dB SPL. If a test signal with flat frequency response across the audio bandwidth (noise or sine wave), is fed through an amplifier with flat response, and to a theoretically ideal loudspeaker with perfectly flat response, to a listener outdoors, the result should be uniform sound pressure at all frequencies. A sound level meter set to flat response (linear scale, or, lacking that, a "C" weighted scale) would indicate the same number of dB SPL as the test signal is swept across the audio range (or as the meter's filter is swept across a broadband noise signal).

You can be certain, however, that the listener will not perceive this theoretically "flat" sound system to be so. Indeed, over the years it has been demonstrated that human hearing itself does not have flat frequency response. Two scientists, Fletcher and Munson,

described this phenomenon with a set of so-called equal loudness contours. Others obtained more accurate representations, such as the Robinson & Dodson curves shown in Figure 3-2. They show how much sound pressure a representative sample of people needs at various frequencies in order to feel that the sound is of the same intensity they hear at 1 kHz. In general, it takes more sound pressure at lower frequencies, and at very high frequencies, for us to believe a sound is equally loud as a sound at 1 kHz. The lower the absolute sound levels involved (the lower curves on the chart), the less sensitive we are to low frequencies.

Another term, the **phon**, was coined to specify loudness. As you can see in Figure 3-3, the numerical value of a phon is always identical to the sound pressure level in dB SPL at 1kHz. At other frequencies, the scales differ. Follow the top line, for example. At 1 kHz, it coincides with the horizontal line representing 120 dB SPL (scale on left side of chart). We call this the 120 phon contour. At about 3.5 k Hz, the 120 phon contour dips to about 105 dB SPL. At the two extremes of the line, 45 Hz and 9,500 Hz, it reaches 130 dB SPL. (There are a number of different families of equal loudness contours, measured under varying conditions; all look something like this one, however.)

What this tells us is that a loudspeaker must generate 130 dB SPL at 45 Hz or at 9.5 kHz in order for us to perceive the sound to be as loud as a 120 dB SPL sound at 1 kHz; our ears are less sensitive at the extremes. However, at 3.5 kHz, the same loudspeaker would have to generate only 105 dB SPL for us to perceive the sound as being as loud as a 1 kHz sound at 120 dB SPL; our ears are more sensitive.

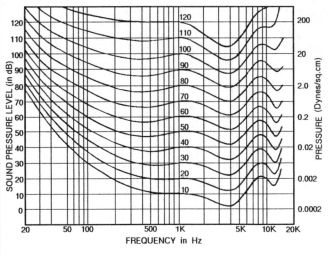

Figure 3-3. Equal loudness contours

3.6.2 What We Can Deduce From Equal Loudness Contours

If you examine the whole set of equal loudness contours, you'll see that peak hearing sensitivity comes between 3 and 4 kHz. It turns out that this is the frequency range where the outer ear's canal is resonant. If you realize how small the ear drum is, you can also see why it has difficulty responding to low frequency (long wavelength) sound, which is why the equal loudness contours sweep upward at lower frequencies. The mass of the eardrum and other constitutents of the ear limit high frequency response, which can be seen in the upward trend of the contours at higher frequencies, but here we see some anomalies — perhaps due to physiological limitations in the cochlea (the inner ear) as well as localized resonances. The fact that all the contours have slightly different curvatures simply tells us our hearing is not linear... that is, the sensitivity changes with absolute level.

The fact that the ear is not linear guided the makers of sound level meters to use a corrective filter — the inverse of the typical equal loudness contour — when measuring SPL. The filter has a so-called "A weighting" characteristic, as indicated in Figure 3–3. Notice that the "A curve" is down 30 dB at 50 Hz, and over 45 dB at 20 Hz relative to the 1 kHz reference, then rises a few dB at between 1.5 and 3 kHz, and falls below the 1 kHz sensi-tivity beyond 6 kHz. This is roughly the inverse of the 40 phon equal loudness curve illustrated in Figure 3–3.

Given the sensitivity characteristic of the ear, the "A weighted" curve is most suitable for low level sound measurement (see Figure 3-4). Remember that 40 dB SPL (at 1 kHz) is equivalent to the sound of a very quiet auditorium or of the average quiet residence. In the presence of loud sounds, such as rock concerts, the ear has a "flatter" sensitivity characteristic. This can be seen by comparing the 100 or 110 phon equal loudness curves (which are the typical loudness at such concerts) to the 40 phon curve. In order for the measured sound level to more closely correspond to the perceived sound level, one would want a flatter response from the SPL meter. This is the function of the B and C weighting scales. In apparent conflict with this common-sense approach, O.S.H.A. (Occupational Safety & Health Administration) and most government agencies that get involved with sound level monitoring continue to use the A scale for measuring loud noises. Since this causes them to obtain lower readings than they otherwise would, the inappropriate use of the A scale works in favor of those who don't want to be restricted.

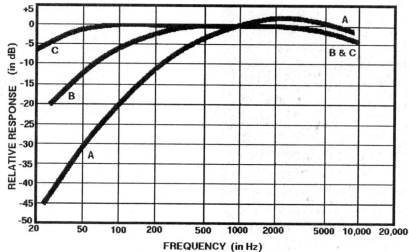

Figure 3-4. Filter curves for sound level meter weighting characteristics

You may see weighting expressed in many ways:

"dB (A)" means the same as "dB SPL, A weighted."

"dB (A wtd.)" means the same as above.

"dB SPL (A weighted)" ditto... same as above.

Incidentally, when the loudness exceeds 120 phons, most people become uncomfortable. The threshold of pain for most of us lies somewhere between 120 dB SPL and 130 dB SPL at 1 kHz.

Children and women tend to be more sensitive than adult men, as a group.

CAUTION: The levels which may cause permanent hearing damage vary with individuals, and with the length of exposure to the sound. Sometimes a "temporary threshold shift" will occur, reducing one's sensitivity to sound for anywhere from a few minutes to many hours, but without any long-term damage. Repeated exposure to a given level of sound, however, may produce permanent threshold shift (or other physiological damage) that would not be caused by an isolated exposure to that same level of sound. It is beyond the scope of this book to detail the "danger" levels, but anyone responsible for sound reinforcement should be cautious about delivering levels above 95 dB(C) SPL to an audience for any prolonged period. In addition, government regulation in some locations may stipulate the maximum peak and/or average sound levels.

3.6.3 Loudness Compensation

Many hi-fi preamplifiers and car stereo systems are equipped with loudness switches or controls. In essence, such features are designed for use at low SPL listening levels. The simple loudness switch will generally insert a fixed amount of bass boost at lower frequencies. More elaborate circuits will also add some high frequency boost, and the most elaborate circuits provide continuously variable controls that simultaneously lower the overall level while boosting lows and highs (actually, they probably just dip the midrange). You'll recognize this as the creation of a response characteristic akin to the inverse of the equal-loudness contours in Figure 3-2. This makes the music seem more natural at less than earsplitting levels.

Use of the loudness feature on such systems is probably *not* a good idea at high levels, unless you like exaggerated response. You can take a hint from this approach and use corrective equalization to boost low and high end response in any sound system when overall listening levels are low. If you're setting up a system for reinforcement of an all-acoustic instrument group in a small club, you may wish to set the sound level meter on the A scale (which will automatically give you the desired contour when you equalize for flat response on the weighted meter)... or even a little extra boost at the low and high ends. Just watch out for feedback, and remember to get rid of that EQ weighting if the next act is a high energy rock group.

4.1 DYNAMIC RANGE

4.1.1 Definition

The difference, in decibels, between the loudest and the quietest portion of a program is known as its *dynamic range*. Sometimes, the quietest portion of a program will be obscured by ambient noise. In this case, the dynamic range is the difference, in dB, between the loudest part of the program and the noise floor. In other words, dynamic range defines the maximum change in audible program levels.

Dynamic range also applies to sound systems. Every sound system has an inherent noise floor, which is the residual electronic noise in the system. The dynamic range of a sound system is equal to the difference between the peak output level of the system and the electro-acoustic noise floor.

4.1.2 Dynamic Range of a Typical Rock Concert

We'll describe a concert with about the widest dynamic range you're ever likely to encounter. The sound levels at the microphones (not in the audience) may range from 40 dB SPL (the audience, wind, and traffic noise at the mic during a very quiet, momentary pause) to 130 dB SPL (beyond the threshold of pain... but then, the performer is shouting into the mic, not into someone's ear). What is the dynamic range of this concert? It is obtained by subtracting the noise floor from the peak levels:

Dynamic Range...
= (Peak Level) − (Noise Floor)
= 130 dB SPL − 40 dB SPL
= 90 dB

The concert has a 90 dB dynamic range at the microphone.

NOTE: We specified the dynamic range in just plain "dB," not in "dB SPL." Remember, dB is a ratio, and in this case we are simply describing the relationship of 130 dB SPL to 40 dB SPL; the difference is 90 dB, but that has nothing at all to do with a sound level of 90 dB SPL referenced to 0.0002 dynes per cm². Dynamic range is nearly always specified in dB, and should never be expressed in dB SPL, dBm, dBu or any other specifically referenced dB value.

4.1.3 Electrical Dynamic Range of the Sound System

What is the dynamic range required of the sound system for such a concert? The electrical signal level in the sound system (given in dBu) is proportional to the original sound pressure level (in dB SPL) at the microphone. The actual electrical levels, of course, will depend on the sensitivity of the microphones, the gain in the preamplifiers, power amplifiers, and so forth, but these values, once established, remain fairly constant so we'll assume they are constant and look at the nominal level (that is, the level specified and designed for) in the electronics.

Thus, when the sound levels reach 130 dB SPL at the mic, the maximum line levels (at the mixing console's output) may reach +24 dBu (12.3 volts), and maximum output levels from each power amplifier may peak at 250 watts (of course, there may be dozens of such power amplifiers, each peaking at 250 watts, but let's keep things simple for now). Similarly, when the sound level falls to 40 dB SPL, the minimum line level falls to -66 dBu (388 microvolts) and power amplifier output level falls to 250 nanowatts (250 billionths of a watt).

When the acoustical program from the mic is converted to an electrical signal at the mixing console output, does it still have the same dynamic range?

Dynamic Range...
= (Peak Level) − (Noise Floor)
= +24 dBu− (-66 dBu)
= 90 dB

Yes, this program retains the same dynamic range at the mixing console output as at the mic, but how about at the power amplifier output? We didn't express any dB relationship for the 250 nanowatts or 250 watts, but it can be calculated with the formulas given in Part I, Section 3, as follows:

$$dB = 10 \log (P_1 \div P_0)$$
$$= 10 \log (250 \div 0.000000250)$$
$$= 10 \log (1{,}000{,}000{,}000)$$
$$= 10 \log (1 \times 10^9)$$
$$= 10 \cdot 9$$
$$= 90 \text{ dB}$$

This dB SPL to dBu or dBm or dBW correspondence is maintained throughout the sound system, from the original source at the microphone, through the electrical portion of the sound system, to the speaker system output. The important thing to understand is that a dB is a dB. If the sound level changes 90 dB, so does the electrical power. We realize this may seem odd, since we described two different equations for dB ($10 \log (P_1 \div P_0)$ and $20 \log (V_1 \div V_0)$) in Part I, Section 3... but the 10 log and 20 log figures drop out when the ratios themselves are described in dB. The difference in dB between two sound pressure levels will always correspond directly to the difference in dBm (power) or dBu (voltage) in the electrical circuit being excited by that sound... assuming linear amplification (i.e., no compression, EQ, limiting, or clipping).

A similar relationship exists for any type of sound reinforcement, recording studio, disco, or broadcast system.

We described the dynamic range of the program going into the microphone, and of the electrical signal through the console and power amps, but what of the sound coming out of the loudspeaker system? If you haven't already guessed, it also must have the same dynamic range. If the speakers aren't capable of this range, then they're probably going to either distort (or burn out) on the peaks, be incapable of responding to the lowest power levels, or experience some combination of these problems.

What are the actual sound levels that must be reproduced? That all depends on the distance between the loudspeakers and the audience, and how loud one wants the sound to be at the audience. Let's assume that we don't want to shatter eardrums... we don't want people in the audience to feel their ears are one inch from the lead vocalist's tongue during a maximum shout. The peak sound level we might accept as a reasonable facsimile of this excitement is 120 dB SPL. Without going through the math (we cover some of that in Part I, Section 5), take our word for it that these particular speakers must (cumulatively) generate 130 dB SPL in this particular environment. Well, we know if they generate 130 dB SPL on peaks, they're going to have to generate 40 dB SPL during the quietest passages, and will have a 90 dB dynamic range.

From this, we also know that if the sound reaching the audience during peaks was attenuated by air and distance by 10 dB from 130 dB SPL to 120 dB SPL, the 40 dB SPL generated by the speakers during quiet passages will also be attenuated. When the 40 dB drops to 30 dB, it will be below the ambient noise level in the audience. This means that the audience may not hear the very quietest parts of the show. This illustrates why some electronic manipulation of dynamic range is often called for. In this case, compression of the loudest peaks would allow the level to be turned up so the quiet passages are louder. Such processing is covered in Section 4.3.

4.2 HEADROOM

4.2.1 Definition

The *average electronic line level* in the concert sound system just described in Section 4.1 is +4 dBu (1.23 volts), corresponding to an average sound level of 110 dB SPL at the microphone. This average level is usually called the nominal program level. The difference between the nominal and the highest (peak) levels in a program is the headroom. Given the levels at the microphone, let's calculate the headroom required for the concert sound system previously described.

Headroom...
= (Peak Level) – (Nominal Level)
= 130 dB SPL – 110 dB SPL
= 20 dB

Once again, the headroom is always expressed in just plain dB since it merely describes a ratio, not an absolute level; 20 dB is the headroom, not 20 dB SPL. Similarly, the electrical headroom is 20 dB, as calculated here:

Headroom...
= (Peak Level) - (Nominal Level)
= +24 dBu – (+4 dBu)
= 20 dB

Again, 20 dB is the headroom, not 20 dBu. Provided the amplifier is operated just below its clipping level at maximum peaks of 250 watts, and at nominal levels of 2.5 watts, then it also operates with 20 dB of headroom. How do we know that? Calculate it, as explained in Section 3.

$$dB = 10 \log (P_1 \div P_0)$$
$$= 10 \log (250 \div 2.5 \text{ watts})$$
$$= 10 \log (100)$$
$$= 10 \bullet 2$$
$$= 20 \text{ dB}$$

Figure 4-1 illustrates headroom and dynamic range in a typical sound system, both in acoustical and electrical terms. The S/N Ratio shown in this illustration refers to *Signal-To-Noise Ratio*, which represents the difference between the nominal level and the noise floor. It is shown so you can see how this specification is related to dynamic range and headroom. There is, however, one tricky aspect to the relationship between S/N, headroom and dynamic range: you can't always add the S/N ratio to the headroom and come up with the dynamic range.

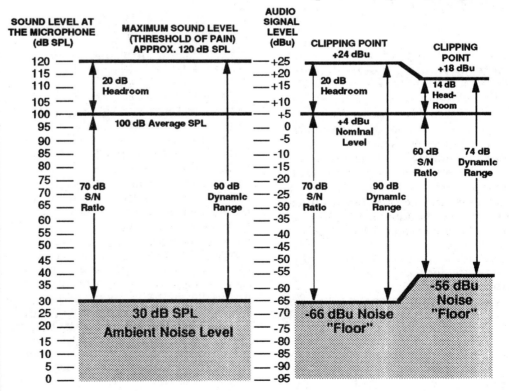

Figure 4-1. Dynamic range and headroom

The last statement seems to contradict our definitions – but not if you read between the lines. You see, *dynamic range* is the difference between the loudest and quietest portions of the *program signal*. The program may be a sine wave, voice, or some musically recognizable signal. Such program signals can often be audibly distinguished even when their level is several dB below the *noise floor* of the sound system! After all, noise is pretty much a random, wideband signal, whereas program is structured and, relatively speaking, a narrow band signal.

The *S/N Ratio*, on the other hand, begins at the noise floor and goes to some arbitrary nominal level. If this is added to the *headroom*, which goes from that nominal level to the maximum level, the number of dB can be less than the dynamic range... if one allows the possibility of a recognizable signal which is below the noise floor.

The problem is how to decide how many dB below the noise floor the program may be distinguishing. It depends a lot upon the specific program, the nature of the noise, and the listener. It's a safer bet, and eminently easier to measure, to go with our original assumption that the dynamic range begins at the noise floor... even if it is not technically accurate all the time, it's repeatable.

4.2.2 Why Headroom is Important

Headroom, as a specification, tells us something about the ability of the sound system to handle loud program peaks. Given two sound systems that both operate at the same nominal level, the system with the greater headroom will be able to handle louder peaks before distorting or destroying itself. Headroom requirements change with the nature of the program material and the purpose for which the sound system is operated.

A sound system intended for paging in a loud factory environment may need to have a very high nominal sound level (to overcome machinery noise), but it need not have more than a few dB of headroom... perhaps 6 dB at most. This is because all it is doing is reproducing speech, or warning sounds, and they can be controlled to remain within a very narrow sound level range. In fact, if the paging system operates at 110 dB SPL nominal level, 6 dB of headroom would yield peaks of 116 dB SPL. This is only a few dB below the threshold of pain. If the 20 dB of headroom found in the concert system previously described were applied here, peaks would reach 130 dB SPL, and the workers would probably file a class action lawsuit for hearing damage after the first few paging announcements.

On the other hand, a sound system intended to reinforce a symphony orchestra concert may need to have more than 20 dB of headroom. This is because the average level of the orchestra may be very low... say 90 dB, but on loud peaks a given tympani or plucked violin string, or some other instrument may indeed reach 120 dB SPL (if only momentarily). That represents 30 dB headroom. If the sound system is capable of only 20 dB of headroom, those brief peaks will be distorted. Perhaps this would be acceptable in a dense, loud rock concert, but a classically trained ear may recognize even this momentary distortion as sounding unnatural, and the sound system may well be rejected by the performers, conductor, and/or audience.

Does this mean that more power amplifiers and speakers are needed for a symphony concert than for a rock concert? Not at all. The same amount of equipment, or probably less, will suffice and can be set up to provide the extra 10 dB of headroom.

Remember, 10 dB is the equivalent of 10 times more power, so how can you get 10 dB more headroom from the same system? Well, if you read carefully, you'll see we described exactly the same peak SPL requirement... 120 dB in this case. We simply need more headroom. If we're not going to turn up the maximum level, we can reduce the nominal level... which is exactly what has been done. We went from 100 dB SPL to 90 dB SPL nominal, which gave us the extra 10 dB of headroom. Actually, we would undoubtedly have an extraordinarily good sound system with a peak capability of just 117 dB SPL for the orchestra (27 dB headroom), so we could get rid of half the power amps and speakers (3 dB is half the power).

4.3 MANIPULATING DYNAMIC RANGE IN A PRACTICAL SOUND SYSTEM

Seldom are the dynamic range and headroom exhibited by a program an exact match to the capability of a given sound system. Good sound system design should take into account the requirements of the typical program, but even here there are practical and financial constraints that sometimes call for compromise. How can such compromise be made? It happens all the time. If one plans for it, the sonic results will generally be much more acceptable.

4.3.1 Why Not Build a Sound System with Excess Dynamic Range?

A sound system's dynamic range can be increased by increasing the maximum sound level capability, or by making the environment quieter. Sometimes acoustic treatment can be applied, and this is a good approach in concert halls (not only to increase dynamic range, but to cut down on excess reverberation). At other times, particularly with portable sound systems, there is virtually no practical way to do much to the ambient noise levels. That leaves the "increase the sound level" option.

Increasing the maximum sound level capability of a sound system runs the costs of the system up very rapidly (exponentially, in fact). That's because every 3 dB increase in sound level requires exactly twice the capability in both power amplifiers and loudspeakers. One could keep the same amplifiers and obtain loudspeakers that are more sensitive... which is not a bad idea, but then it's a pretty good bet that sensitive loudspeakers are already in use. Besides, in many cases sensitive loudspeakers are larger and more costly, and there may not be physical space to mount (or travel with) such loudspeakers. It may be possible to use more highly directional loudspeakers (horns with a narrower dispersion angle, for example), which will focus

the available power into a smaller area, and therefore deliver higher SPL to that area. Otherwise, it's back to more or larger power amplifiers.

It is not at all impossible to spend thousands of dollars per dB SPL of extra capability in very large sound systems. For this reason it is often essential to find ways to reduce the dynamic range requirements. Except for small systems, where a 3 dB increase may mean one more amplifier and loudspeaker, it's generally too costly to build in more dynamic range than is absoutely necessary.

4.3.2 What Happens When the Sound System is Inadequate?

When the dynamic range of the program material exceeds the dynamic range capability of the sound system, some combination of the following will result:
a) Program peaks will be distorted due to clipping and/or loudspeaker break-up, and/or
b) Quiet passages will not be heard because they will be below the electrical and/or acoustic noise floor.

Let's explore how this might occur in the same theoretical concert sound setup we described in Section 4.1. As you may recall, in that situation the acoustic levels at the mic ranged from 40 dB SPL to 130 dB SPL, representing a dynamic range of 90 dB. The corresponding signal levels at the mixing console output ranged from −66 dBu (388 μV) to +24 dBu (12.3 V), again a 90 dB dynamic range. Finally, the power amplifier output went from a minimum of 0.25 μW to 250 W, also a 90 dB dynamic range.

EXAMPLE: Suppose that the sound system for the concert just described is carried by two semi-trailer trucks, and the one with the electronics become disabled on the highway. A local sound system (less loudspeakers) therefore has to be be rented at the last minute. The rental sound system is equipped with a noisier mic preamplifier circuit, and a less capable console output line amplifier than the equipment stuck on the highway. We are lucky enough to rent the same power amps, and we still have our own loudspeakers. So we measure the rented electronics and find they have an electronic noise floor of -56 dBu (1.23 millivolts), and a peak output level of +18 dBu (6.16 volts). What is the dynamic range of this newly assembled system?

To solve the problem:
1) The dynamic range is no better than the weakest link. In this case, we know the electronic circuitry is the weak link.

dynamic range...
= (Peak Level) - (Noise Floor)
= +18 dBu - (-56 dBu)
= 74 dB

The dynamic range of this system would only be 74 dB.
2) Since the band has not changed its act, we know the program still has an acoustic dynamic range of 90 dB, as shown in Figure 4-1. It is apparent that 16 dB of the program will be "lost" in the sound system (90 dB - 74 dB = 16 dB).

How is the 16 dB of program lost? There may be extreme clipping of program peaks, where the console output cannot rise high enough in level to follow the highest program levels. Quiet passages, corresponding to the lowest signal levels, may be buried in the noise. Typically, portions of that 16 dB difference in dynamic range between the sound system capability and the sound field at the microphone will be lost in both ways. This illustrates why, for high quality, high level sound reinforcement or music reproduction, it is necessary that the sound system be capable of low noise levels and high output capability.

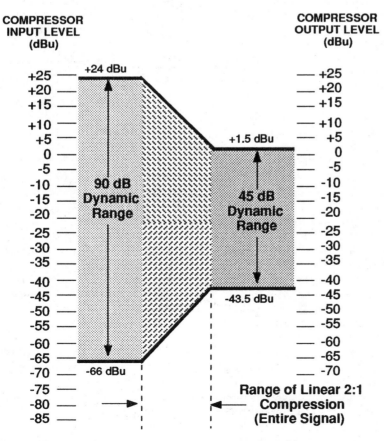

Figure 4-2. 2:1 Compression of a 90 dB program

4.3.3 How to Fit Wide Program Dynamics Into a Sound System with Limited Dynamic Range

So far, we have described linear electronics. That is, for every 2 dB change of input level, the output level also changes by 2 dB. This need not be the case however. Suppose for every 2 dB change of input level, the output would change only 1 dB. What would then happen to the dynamic range of the program? It would be cut in half. The 90 dB dynamic range would become 45 dB, as shown in Figure 4-2.

In fact, this is exactly what can be done with a simple signal processing device known as a *compressor*. By setting the compressor for a relatively gentle compression ratio of 2:1, every dB of input level change will result in half a dB of output level change. Such compression can generally be tolerated in all but the most critical musical reproduction, and, in fact, often much higher compression ratios are used.

In the example in Section 4.3.2, we need only to get the program dynamics from 90 dB down to 74 dB... only a 16 dB reduction in dynamic range. It is possible to set the compressor for a 1.21:1 compression ratio, which would squeeze 90 dB down to 74 dB as shown in Figure 4-3. (Some adjustment of actual levels may be required, also illustrated in Figure 4-3.) This is probably a much better idea than using 2:1 compression because it preserves as much of the impact and natural sound of the program as possible while still allowing it to fit within the constraints of the sound system.

It may be that we do not want any compression because, after all, it can have side effects, such as making quiet breath sounds louder, creating a pumping effect in some cases, and increasing the distortion of low frequency signals. Still, distorting on peaks is not acceptable either, so we may use another approach: apply compression only above a given

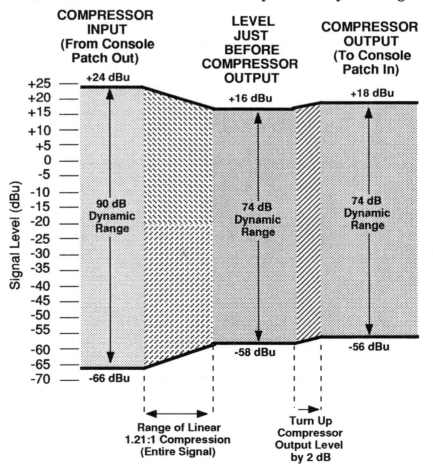

Figure 4-3. 1.21:1 Compression of a 90 dB program

threshold. Below a given signal level, no compression at all occurs. If the threshold level is chosen to approximate the nominal program level, this ensures that most of the program sounds completely natural. Above that threshold we use whatever amount of compression is necessary to prevent clipping. This is illustrated in Figure 4–3, where 1.43:1 compression is selected above a +4 dBu threshold. This approach squeezes the headroom requirement, but doesn't help with the quieter portions of the program, as can be seen from the fact that the dynamic range is reduced to only 84 dB; 10 dB of the program will still be lost in the noise. If the threshold were set lower, or the compression ratio to a higher value, then more dynamic range would be conserved, and the overall signal level at the compressor output could be increased to stay above the console's noise floor.

Some devices permit compression to be applied above a set threshold, and the compression ratio to be very high (anywhere from 8:1 to as high as 20:1 or even infinity:1). These devices are known as *limiters*, and the effect is known as *limiting*. The term is appropriate, since such a device limits the output level from rising any higher, with infinite compression, or very much higher, with 10:1 compression, regardless of further increases in input signal. For example, suppose the threshold is set at +15 dBu, and the compression ratio is 10:1. So long as the input to the compressor is below +15 dBu, the limiter's output level exactly matches its input. When the input rises above +15 dBu, the output changes very little. How little? Well, with a 10:1 ratio, 10 dB of input change will produce 1 dB of output change. That means a +25 dBu input signal will cause the limiter output to

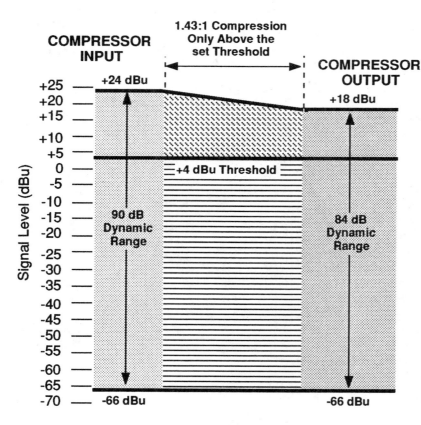

Figure 4-4. 1.43:1 Compression above a threshold

rise just 1 dB, to +16 dBu. Since few, if any, input sources will deliver as much as +25 dBu under any circumstances, the limiter essentially has restricted all input signals above +16 dBu so they cannot drive the output higher than +16 dBu.

Many devices can be set for compression or limiting, and hence are known as *compressor/limiters*.

We have made a broad assumption here that the compressor is inserted somewhere after the console's mic pre-amplifier and before the output stage, and that all the noise and headroom problems in the console occur after the compressor. This is, of course, not likely to be the case, since mic preamps often are a source of noise. Still, the summing amplifiers in consoles can be the bottleneck in terms of headroom, so using a compressor at the input stage can help. It is also very often the case that the console has plenty of headroom and dynamic range, and the real constraint to dynamic range is the power amplifier/loudspeaker system. In this case, compression at any point before the power amplifiers will help.

There is a special case where compression and its opposite, expansion, are used to overcome limited dynamic range in one portion of a sound system. That case occurs with an analog audio tape recorder, where the dynamic range often is limited by the noise floor and distortion levels of the tape oxide rather than the electronics. There is a common method used to avoid program losses due to tape saturation and hiss. Many professional and consumer tape machines are equipped with a noise reduction system, also known as a *compander* (as designed by firms like Dolby Laboratories, Inc. and dbx, Inc.).

A compander noise reduction system allows the original program dynamics to be maintained throughout the recording and playback process by compressing the program dynamic range before it goes onto the tape, and complementarily expanding the dynamic range as the program is retrieved from the tape. This type of system is illustrated in Figure 4-5 on the next page.

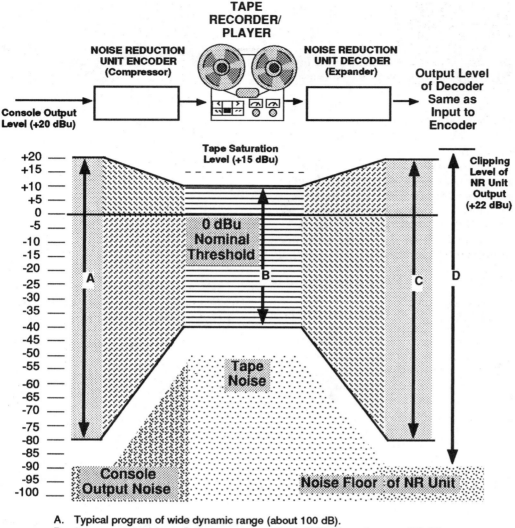

A. Typical program of wide dynamic range (about 100 dB).
B. 2:1 compressed (encoded) program occupies half the dynamic range (50 dB).
C. 1:2 expanded (decoded) program restores original dynamic range (100 dB)
   while keeping tape noise below the quietest program material.

**Figure 4-5. How a compander tape noise reduction system
overcomes dynamic range limitations**

4.3.4 How Much Headroom is Adequate?

Recall that headroom is the amount of level available above the average (nominal) signal for peaks in the program.

The choice of a headroom figure depends on the type of program material, the application, and the available budget for amplifiers. For a musical application where high fidelity is the ultimate consideration, 15 dB to 20 dB of headroom is desirable. For most sound reinforcement applications, especially with large numbers of amplifiers, where economics play an important role, a 10 dB headroom figure is usually adequate. In these applications, a compressor or limiter can help hold program peaks within the chosen headroom value, and thus avoid clipping problems. For the extreme situation (as in a factory) where background music and paging must be heard over high continuous noise levels, yet maximum levels must be restricted to avoid dangerously high sound pressure levels, a headroom figure of as low as 5 dB or 6 dB is not unusual. To achieve such a low headroom figure, an extreme amount of compression and/or limiting will be necessary, causing the sound to be somewhat unnatural, but allowing the message to cut through.

Section 5.
Sound Outdoors

Section 5 discusses the behavior of sound outdoors, and the effect of that behavior on sound systems.

Outdoor environments are essentially free of reflecting surfaces or obstructing objects, and the principles presented in this chapter therefore assume "free field" conditions. The behavior of sound indoors is presented in Section 6.

Doubling the radius (a–b) spreads the power over four times the surface area, so SPL falls off by the inverse square of the distance from the source.

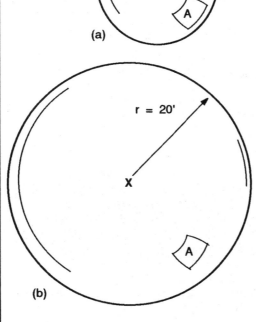

Figure 5-1. Acoustic power or sound pressure: the inverse square law

5.1 The Inverse Square Law

The inverse square law describes the relationship between sound pressure level and distance from the source. The law assumes:

a) A point source of sound (omni directional radiator)
b) Free field conditions (no reflective boundaries).

The inverse square law states that the intensity of the sound varies with the square of the distance. In other words:

for each doubling of the distance from the source, the measured sound pressure will drop by 6 dB.

For example, if a loudspeaker's continuous output measures 100 dB SPL at 10 feet, then at 20 feet the sound pressure level will be 94 dB (100 − 6 = 94).

A 6 dB difference in SPL corresponds to a sound pressure ratio of two to one. This is not a 2:1 loudness difference, however; a 10 dB difference represents about a 2:1 loudness change (see Section 3.3). Therefore, if you are twice as far from a point source as another observer, the sound will be a little more than half as loud for you as it is for that observer. Figure 5-1 illustrates the reason for this 6 dB decrease in SPL at twice the distance.

A point source of sound is located at X. In Figure 5-1(a), a sphere with a radius of 10 feet surrounds the point source. The sphere represents an even distribution of the acoustical energy of the source in a free field. In (b), our source is surrounded by a sphere with a radius of 20 feet (double the distance). The area of this sphere is four times that of the sphere in (a).

Consider a window of equal area in each sphere. Since the acoustical energy of the point source X is spread over four times as much area in (b) as it is in (a), one fourth as much acoustical energy will pass through the window in (b) as will pass through the window in (a).

A 4:1 acoustical power ratio expressed in decibels is 6 dB, corresponding to a 2:1 SPL ratio.

NOTE: *The sound **power** in dB does not change with distance because the power emitted by a source is a measure of the total energy (over time) emitted in all directions. A 100 watt light bulb's candlepower output (analogous to a speaker system's acoustic power output) remains the same, regardless of the distance from which one observes it, but the light intensity (analogous to SPL) does fall off with distance. The brightness of light falling on a given surface decreases as distance increases from the bulb, just as SPL falls off with distance.*

5.1.1 Inverse Square Law Calculations

Calculations based on the inverse square law are a routine part of sound reinforcement. To see how they may be used, consider the following examples.

EXAMPLE 1: A loudspeaker has a sensitivity rating of 102 dB SPL, 1 watt, 1 meter. How loud will the speaker be at 30 feet when driven by a noise signal at 1 watt continuous power? (Assume the loudspeaker is outdoors in a free field environment with no reverberant field.)

To solve the problem:
1) First convert from feet to meters, since that is the unit used in the sensitivity specification:

30 feet ÷ 3.28 feet/meter ≈ 9 meters

2) Calculate the inverse square loss, using the decibel equation for SPL:

$20 \cdot \log (9\text{meters}:1\text{meter}) = 20 \log (9)$
$20 \cdot \log (9) = 20 \cdot .9542425094$
$= 19 \text{ dB}$

3) Subtract the loss (19 dB) from the SPL at 1 meter (102 dB):

102 - 19 = 83 dB SPL

Answer:
The level at 30 feet will be 83 dB SPL.

EXAMPLE 2: You are asked to provide sound reinforcement for a parade grandstand. The depth of the audience seating area is 100 feet. You wish to place a full range loudspeaker with a sensitivity rating of 98 dB SPL (at 1 meter, 1 watt input) at the front of the seating area. The loudspeaker is stated to be capable of handling 100 watts continuous. What will the maximum SPL be at the back of the audience?

The steps to solving the problem are:

1) Calculate the ratio between 1 watt and 100 watts in dB, using the decibel equation for power:

$10 \log (100 \text{ watts} \div 1 \text{ watt}) = 10 \cdot \log (100)$
$= 10 \cdot 2$
$= 20 \text{ dB}$

2) Add this figure to the sensitivity of 98 dB (which is the SPL at 1 watt) to obtain the SPL at 100 watts (at a distance of 1 meter):

98 + 20 = 118 dB SPL

3) Calculate the inverse square loss, using the decibel equation for SPL:

100 feet ÷ 3.28 ≈ 30 meters

$20 \log (30 \text{ meters}) = 20 \cdot 1.477121255$
$= 29.542 \text{ dB}$

which we round off to 30 dB.

4) Subtract the loss from the SPL obtained in step (2):

118 - 30 = 88 dB SPL

If the system is driven to its maximum capabilities, the level at the back of the audience will be 88 dB SPL.

5.2 Effects of Environmental Factors

Sound propagated outdoors is subject to the influence of environmental factors that are not significantly present indoors. Such influences can cause the behavior of sound systems to deviate from that predicted by inverse square calculations.

The principal factors affecting sound outdoors are wind, temperature gradients, and humidity. The effects of these factors are most noticeable in large-scale outdoor events, such as sports events or rock concerts.

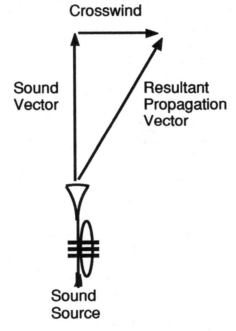

Figure 5-2. Sound and wind vectors (exaggerated)

5.2.1 Wind

Wind effects are divided into two classes — velocity effects and gradient effects.

The effect of wind velocity is illustrated in Figure 5-2 (below, left). A crosswind will add a velocity vector to a propagating sound wave and can shift the direction of propagation of the sound, making it appear to come from a different location.

Wind velocity gradient effects occur when one air layer is moving at a different speed than an adjacent layer; usually one layer is above the other. Such a gradient might be encountered when the audience area is shielded from the wind by a barrier, such as a stand of trees or a wall. The effect of velocity gradients on sound is shown in Figure 5-3 below.

Since wind velocity adds a vector to the propagating sound wave, refraction occurs when sound passes through a velocity gradient. Assuming horizontally stratified wind layers, when the sound is propagating against the wind, it is refracted upward. When it propagates with the wind, it is refracted downward. With vertical propagation, the sound will be refracted to the left or right.

This said, the actual effect of wind is minimal because (except in a hurricane) wind speed, relative to the speed of sound, is negligible. Drastically shifting wind, though, can destabilize a stereo image. Wind appears to have a greater effect because it often brings temperature gradients with it, as explained on the next page.

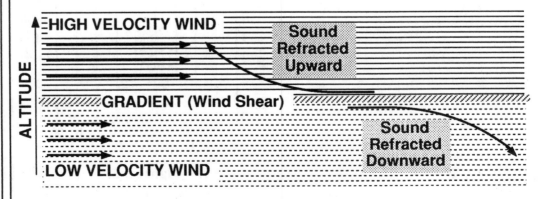

Figure 5-3. Effect of wind velocity gradient on sound propagation

5.2.2 Temperature Gradients

The speed of sound is also affected by temperature. Sound passes through hot air (because it is less dense) faster than it passes through colder air. For this reason, temperature gradients also cause refraction effects.

Figure 5-4 illustrates the effects of temperature gradients on sound outdoors. In (a), the upper air is warm while the lower air is cold. Such conditions may be found in the morning, when the ground is still cool from the previous night and the upper air is warmed by the sun. Under these conditions, sound tends to "bounce" between the gradient and the ground, forming regions of higher and lower sound intensity.

In Figure 5-4(b), the opposite case is shown. Such conditions may occur in the evening, when the ground is still warm. Sound in this case tends to refract upward.

5.2.3 Humidity

As sound propagates through air, the air absorbs energy from the sound wave, attenuating (weakening) it. The effect is significant only at frequencies above 2 kHz, and increases with frequency. This is the reason why, when we hear thunder in the distance, it is only a low rumble. The high frequency "crack" has been attenuated more rapidly than the low frequency portion of the noise.

The attenuation of sound in air is affected by the relative humidity. Dry air absorbs far more acoustical energy than does moist air. This is because moist air is *less dense* than dry air (water vapor weighs less than air).

Figure 5-5 shows the absorption of sound energy by the air, graphed in relation to relative humidity.

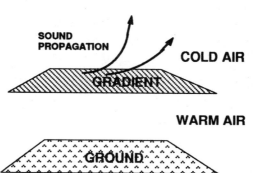
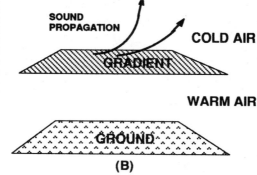

Figure 5-4. Effect of temperature gradients on sound propagation

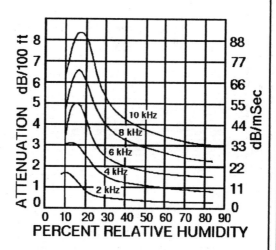

**Figure 5-5.
Absorption of sound in air
vs. relative humidity**

5.3 Feedback Control

Consider a basic sound system consisting of a single loudspeaker, a microphone, and an amplifier (Figure 5-6). A performer stands at the microphone, and a listener sits in the audience.

With the system powered up, by advancing the gain of the amplifier you will reach a point where the system starts to ring. This ringing is called feedback. The bold arrows in the figure indicate the feedback path. Some of the sound from the loudspeaker is picked up by the microphone and re-injected into the system, forming a continuous loop.

Feedback occurs when the gain in the loop reaches unity (gain of 0 dB). The feedback locks onto a frequency for which the loop path is non-inverting (in phase).

If we turn the gain down so that the feedback just stops (loop gain just under unity), the system's frequency response will still be erratic. This is because when the loop gain is near unity, the system still resonates at those frequencies for which the loop path is in phase.

As a rule of thumb, then, a sound system should be operated about 6 dB below the onset of feedback. This practice will allow a reasonable safety margin to control feedback, and assure that the sound quality will be reasonably natural (or at least that it won't be hollow or ringy due to feedback effects).

5.3.1 Maximum Gain (Available Gain Before Feedback)

We are now ready to introduce the important concept of maximum acoustic gain.

Referring to Figure 5-7, assume that both the loudspeaker and the microphone are omnidirectional. The microphone is one foot from the lecturer. The level of the lecturer's speaking voice, measured at the microphone, is 70 dB SPL. To simplify our calculations, we will assume that we are outdoors, so we need not factor reverberation into the equations.

With the system turned off, the level of speech that the listener hears can be found using a simple inverse square calculation from the ratio of D_0 to D_s.

$$70 \text{ dB} - [20 \log (D_0 \div D_s)]$$
$$= 70 - [20 \log (20 \div 1)]$$
$$= 70 - (20 \log 20)$$
$$= 70 - (20 \bullet 1.301)$$
$$= 70 - 26$$
$$= 44 \text{ dB}$$

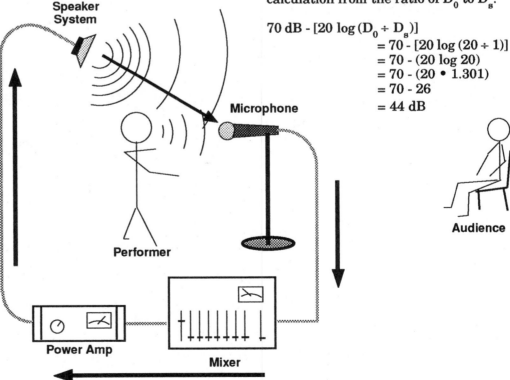

Speaker System

Microphone

Performer

Mixer

Power Amp

Audience

Figure 5-6. Typical acoustical and electrical feedback path

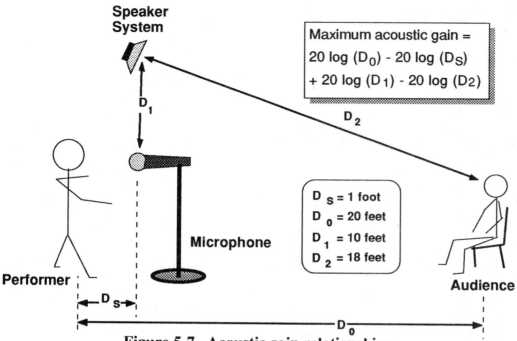

Speaker System

Maximum acoustic gain =
$20 \log (D_0) - 20 \log (D_S)$
$+ 20 \log (D_1) - 20 \log (D_2)$

D_1

D_2

Microphone

$D_S = 1$ foot
$D_0 = 20$ feet
$D_1 = 10$ feet
$D_2 = 18$ feet

Performer

D_S

Audience

D_0

Figure 5-7. Acoustic gain relationships

With the system off, the level that the listener hears is 44 dB SPL.

Now we turn the sound system on and bring up the amplifier gain. Feedback will occur at unity loop gain — that is, when the loudspeaker produces the same level at the microphone as does the lecturer's voice (70 dB SPL).

To find the level that the listener hears from the system, we apply an inverse square calculation to the ratio between D_1 (the distance between the loudspeaker and microphone) and D_2 (the distance between the loudspeaker and the listener).

$$70 \text{ dB} - [20 \log (D_2 \div D_1)]...$$
$$= 70 - [20 \log (18 \div 10)]$$
$$= 70 - (20 \bullet .2552725)$$
$$= 70 - 5$$
$$= 65 \text{ dB}$$

The acoustic gain of the system is the difference between the level that the listener hears with the system off, and that which he hears with it on. In this case, it is:

$$65 \text{ dB} - 44 \text{ dB} = 21 \text{ dB}$$

This figure is based on the feedback point. If we now allow a 6 dB margin below feedback, the practical maximum acoustic gain is reduced to 15 dB.

From this discussion, we can write a general equation for maximum acoustic gain:

Max gain...
$$= \text{ndB} - 20 \log (D_2 \div D_1) - \text{ndB} - 20 \log (D_0 \div D_s)$$

where ndB = the SPL of the lecturer's voice.

Simplifying, and adding a 6 dB margin, we get the standard equation:

Max gain...
$$= 20 \log (D_0) - 20 \log (D_s) + 20 \log (D_1) - 20 \log (D_2) - 6$$

or, Max gain...
$$= 20 \log(20) - 20 \log(1) + 20 \log(10) - 20 \log (18) - 6$$
$$= 26 - 0 + 20 - 25 - 6 = 15$$

Note that the factor ndB cancels out and the gain is independent of the level of the source. The equation also proves that we can increase the system gain by:

A) decreasing the distance between the source and the microphone (D_s), and/or...

B) increasing the distance between the loudspeaker and the microphone (D_1).

5.3.2 Using Directional Microphones and Loudspeakers

The calculations for acoustic gain presented in the previous subsection are based on the assumption that both the microphone and the loudspeaker are omnidirectional. In actual sound reinforcement work, however, omnidirectional elements are not often used, for reasons that will become clear as you read the following text.

Figure 5-8 (next two pages) presents a set of polar plots of (a) a typical cardioid microphone and (b) a typical reinforcement loudspeaker. Note that each has distinct directional characteristics. These characteristics can be used to increase the acoustic gain of a sound system.

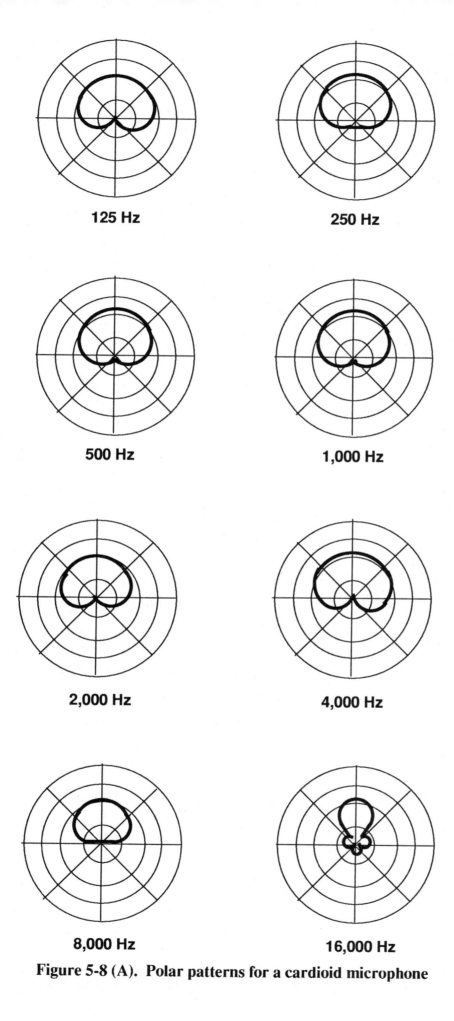

125 Hz

250 Hz

500 Hz

1,000 Hz

2,000 Hz

4,000 Hz

8,000 Hz

16,000 Hz

Figure 5-8 (A). Polar patterns for a cardioid microphone

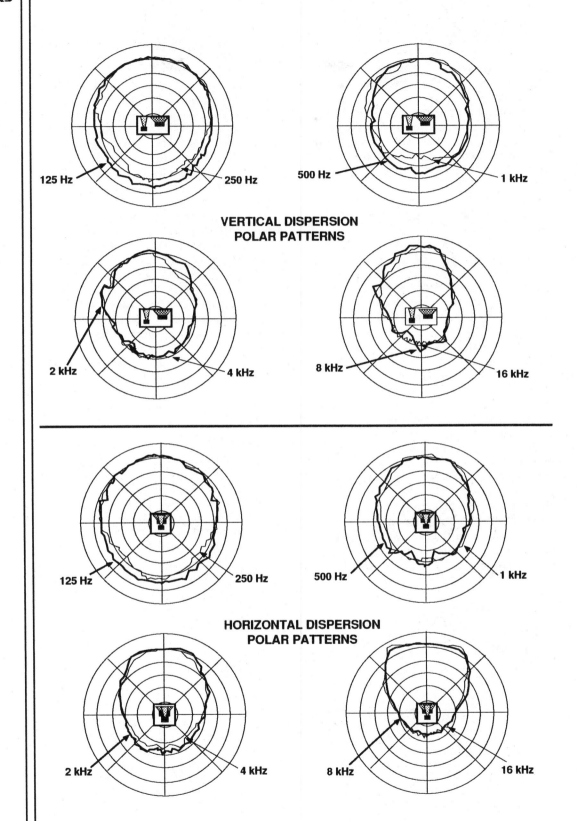

Figure 5-8 (B). Polar patterns for a sound reinforcement loudspeaker

Consider Figure 5-9, which presents a situation similar to that which we analyzed in Section 5.3.1.

Let's replace the omnidirectional loudspeaker with the directional one that is graphed in Figure 5-8. If we orient the loudspeaker such that the microphone lies on the -6 dB angle of the loudspeaker's polar response, then the sound arriving at the microphone from the loudspeaker will be 6 dB lower in level, compared with the omnidirectional loudspeaker. This 6 dB advantage adds directly to the sound system's maximum gain.

If we now replace the omnidirectional microphone with the cardioid whose polar response is shown in Figure 5-8, and orient the microphone so that the loudspeaker lies on its −6 dB angle, we obtain a similar advantage.

Theoretically, we've just added 12 dB to our sound system's maximum gain!

In practice, things are not quite that simple. At low frequencies, full-range loudspeaker systems become omnidirectional — no matter how directional they may be at mid and high frequencies. (The effect is examined in greater detail in Section 13.) Also, the directional characteristics of a cardioid microphone are not the same at all frequencies (See Section 10). In fact, *if the cardioid microphone does not have reasonably flat, smooth response, a smooth omnidirectional mic may provide the same practical maximum gain.*

You can test this effect by setting up a simple reinforcement system with a cardioid microphone and a full-range loudspeaker. If you place the microphone in front of the loudspeaker and slowly bring up the gain, the system will feed back at a high frequency. Place the microphone behind the loudspeaker and advance the gain, and it will feed back at a lower frequency.

In practice, then, directional elements will generally give you about a

6 dB gain advantage (twice as much gain). By examining the equation for maximum gain at the end of Section 5.3.1, you will see that decreasing Ds (distance between the source and the microphone) can dramatically affect the available system gain before feedback. Similarly, increasing D1 (distance between the microphone and the loudspeaker) also increases the available gain.

The best approach to feedback control, then, is:

A) Use directional elements (properly placed and aimed);

B) Keep the loudspeaker as far away from the microphone as practical (which is one reason why many loudspeaker systems are flown high above the stage); and

C) Keep the microphone close to the source (which is why many vocal performers seem to be swallowing their mics).

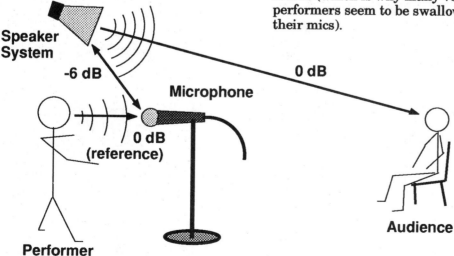

Figure 5-9. Using directional elements in a sound system can increase maximum available gain before feedback

SECTION 6.
Sound Indoors

6.1 BOUNDARIES

Section 6 discusses the behavior of sound indoors. The foundation for this discussion was laid in Section 5 ("Sound Outdoors").

In comparison with its behavior in free field, sound indoors exhibits quite complex behavior. Decades of acoustics research have been spent attempting to quantify the effects of a reverberant field. These efforts have yielded a body of equations that are used to describe how sound behaves in a given room.

We make no effort to present those calculations in detail here. Such effort would not serve our present purpose. Instead, this chapter presents the basic principles of indoor acoustics, using simple mathematics where necessary.

The walls, ceiling, and floor of a room are, to some extent, both flexible and porous to sound. Figure 6-1 shows what happens when a sound wave strikes such a boundary surface.

Part of the wave energy is reflected, as shown in Figure 6-1(a). The percentage of the energy that is reflected is related to the stiffness of the surface.

Wave energy that is not reflected enters the boundary. Part of this energy is absorbed (b) by the boundary material through conversion into heat. The remainder (c) is transmitted through the boundary. Both effects (a) and (b) are related to the flexibility and porosity of the boundary.

When sound strikes a smaller obstacle (not a wall or ceiling, but perhaps a podium or pulpit), it bends around that object. This is known as refraction, and is shown in Figure 6-2.

Refraction, reflection, transmission, and absorption are all dependent on the frequency of the sound wave and the angle at which it strikes the boundary. The percentages are not generally dependent on the intensity of the sound.

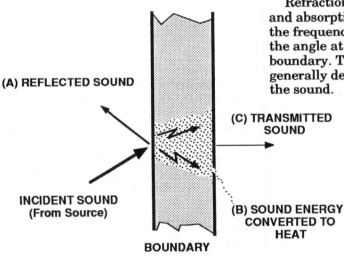

(A) REFLECTED SOUND

(C) TRANSMITTED SOUND

INCIDENT SOUND (From Source)

(B) SOUND ENERGY CONVERTED TO HEAT

BOUNDARY

Figure 6-1. Effect of boundary surfaces on sound transmission and reflection

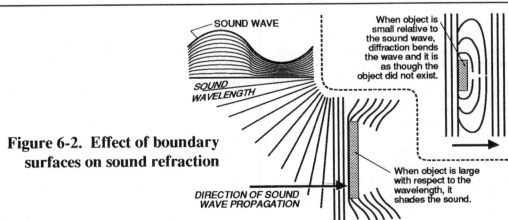

Figure 6-2. Effect of boundary surfaces on sound refraction

SOUND WAVE

SOUND WAVELENGTH

When object is small relative to the sound wave, diffraction bends the wave and it is as though the object did not exist.

DIRECTION OF SOUND WAVE PROPAGATION

When object is large with respect to the wavelength, it shades the sound.

6.1.1 The Absorption Coefficient

In architectural acoustics, a measure of the energy lost when a sound wave strikes a given material is specified by the absorption coefficient of the material. The concept of the absorption coefficient was developed by Dr. Wallace Sabine, who is regarded as the father of modern architectural acoustics.

Sabine defined an open window — which does not reflect any sound — as the perfect absorber, assigning it a coefficient of 1 (100%). Similarly, he gave the perfect reflective surface a coefficient of 0. The absorption coefficient of any material is thus a number between 0 and 1, which is readily converted into a percentage.

The relationship between the absorption coefficient of a boundary material and the intensity of the reflected sound wave is therefore a simple one. For example, consider that a given boundary material has an absorption coefficient of 0.15. To determine the effect of the boundary on a sound wave:

1) Convert the coefficient into a percentage

$$0.15 = 15\%$$

15% of the sound is absorbed by the material.

2) To get the amount reflected, subtract from 100%

$$100 - 15 = 85\%$$

85% of the sound is reflected.

3) Finally, the conversion to dB is a 10 log function

$$10 \log 0.85 = -0.7 \text{ dB}$$

The reflected sound pressure is 0.7 dB lower than the incident sound pressure.

This computation can be reduced to a single equation relating the reduction in sound level to the absorption coefficient:

$$ndB = 10 \log (1 \div (1 - a))$$

where 'ndB' = the reduction in sound level, and 'a' = the absorption coefficient.

Table 6-1 gives absorption coefficients for a number of different typical boundaries. The coefficients for each material are given at different frequencies, since the effect varies with frequency.

MATERIAL	Frequency (Hz)		
	125	1k	4k
Brick Wall (18" Thick, unpainted)	.02	.04	.07
Brick Wall (18" Thick, painted)	.01	.02	.02
Interior Plaster (On metal lath)	.02	.06	.03
Poured Concrete	.01	.02	.03
Pine Flooring	.09	.08	.10
Carpeting (With pad)	.10	.30	.70
Drapes (Cotton, 2x fullness)	.07	.80	.50
Drapes (Velour, 2x fullness)	.15	.75	.65
Acoustic Tile (5/8", #1 Mount*)	.15	.70	.65
Acoustic Tile (5/8", #2 Mount*)	.25	.70	.65
Acoustic Tile (5/8", #7 Mount*)	.50	.75	.65
Tectum Panels (1", #2 Mount*)	.08	.55	.65
Tectum Panels (1", #7 Mount*)	.35	.35	.65
Plywood Panel (1/8", 2" Air space)	.30	.10	.07
Plywood Cylinders (2 Layers, 1/8")	.35	.20	.18
Perforated Transite (w/Pad, #7 Mount*)	.90	.95	.45
Occupied Audience Seating Area	.50	.95	.85
Upholstered Theatre Seats (Hard Floor)	.45	.90	.70

* #1 Mount is cemented directly to plaster or concrete,
  #2 Mount is fastened to nominal 1" thick furring strips,
  #7 Mount is suspended ceiling w/ 16" air space above.

Table 6-1. Approximate absorption coefficients of common materials

Note that for mid and high frequencies an occupied audience area has an absorption coefficient very close to 1 (complete absorption). This is why the presence of an audience can have an enormous effect on the acoustics of a hall, and will provide a significant contrast with unupholstered seats on a hard floor. As we shall see in subsequent chapters, this fact is very important to the design of indoor sound systems.

6.2 Standing Waves

One significant effect of hard boundary surfaces is the formation of what are called standing waves.

Figure 6-3 shows what happens when a continuous sound, at one frequency, strikes a reflective boundary head-on. The reflected sound wave combines with subsequent incoming waves. Where the wave crests (maximum pressure) coincide, they combine and reinforce one another. The troughs (minimum pressure) also combine.

The result is a stationary pattern in the air, consisting of zones of low pressure (called nodes), alternating with zones of high pressure (called antinodes). The phenomenon is known as a standing wave.

Walking through such a standing wave zone, you can easily identify physical places where the sound is very loud, and others where the sound is very soft. Note that these alternate maximal and minmal air pressure zones are spaced at distances of ½ wavelength. Their position in space depends on the frequency of the sound.

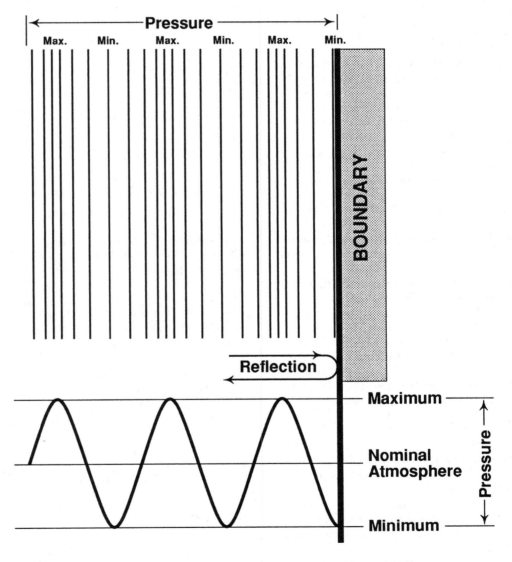

Figure 6-3. Formation of a standing wave by reflection at a boundary

6.2.1 Standing Waves in a Room

Now consider Figure 6-4, which shows two parallel walls. The walls are assumed to be highly reflective. In the center, we place a point source of sound.

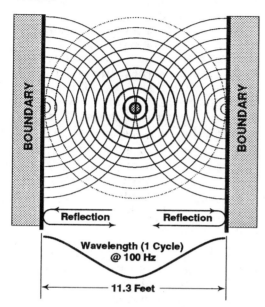

Figure 6-4. Formation of a standing wave in a room

Suppose our point source emits a brief tone. The sound waves travel out in all directions, with those propagated to the sides eventually reaching the walls. Some energy is absorbed by the walls; most is reflected back. Reflected waves from each wall travel to the other wall, reflecting again. The process continues until the energy of the sound is completely dissipated by absorption in the air and the walls.

In this situation, standing waves will be formed if — and only if — the wavelength of the sound "fits" the distance between the walls. Such standing waves are also called room resonances, natural frequencies, or modes.

For example, the wavelength of a 100 Hz tone is:

1130 ft/sec. ÷ 100 cycles/sec. = 11.3 ft./cycle

If the walls in Figure 6-4 are 11.3 feet apart, then successively reflected waves will reinforce each other, forming stationary nodal and antinodal points in the room. The same effect will occur at frequencies that are integral multiples of 100 (200 Hz, 300 Hz, etc.). This is illustrated in Figure 6-5.

Suppose that the area between the walls held an audience, and that the 100 Hz tone was a bass note in a musical passage. Those audience members seated at nodal points might have trouble hearing the note, while those seated at antinodes would hear it as unnaturally loud! Obviously, standing wave phenomena can drastically affect the quality of sound in a room.

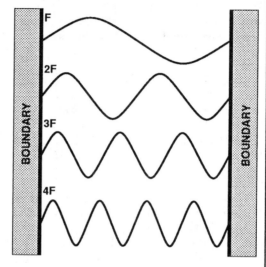

Figure 6-5. Room modes at harmonic frequencies

In rooms, the situation is much more complicated than what we have described here. There are three such simple resonance systems (one between each set of opposite walls, and one from floor to ceiling), and two more complicated ones (one involving all four walls, and one involving all six surfaces). Consequently, a given room will exhibit many such resonances at different frequencies.

Good acoustical design takes room resonances into account, and strives to minimize them through use of non-parallel walls and various types of absorptive treatments. One of the most effective and simple treatments is to hang drapes.

Notice in Figure 6-3 that the zone spaced ¼ wavelength from the reflecting surface is a node. In this zone, the pressure is minimum but the air particle velocity is maximum. Absorptive material hung at this point will have far greater effect on the standing wave than its absorption coefficient would indicate.

6.3 Reverberation

Another substantial and much discussed effect of boundary reflection is reverberation. Reverberation is modeled as described below.

Imagine a point source of sound at the center of an enclosed room. We turn on the source, and sound radiates outward in all directions, eventually striking the boundaries of the room. Some of its energy is absorbed, some is transmitted through the boundary, and most is reflected back into the room.

After a certain time, enough reflections have occurred that the space is essentially filled with a random field of sound waves. If the source remains on, the system reaches a state of equilibrium such that the energy being introduced by the source exactly equals the energy dissipated in boundary transmission and absorption.

Acousticians describe this equilibrium in statistical terms. Ignoring for the moment any standing-wave resonances or focused reflections, we can say that the sound pressure is the same at all points that are not too near the source.

Let's say that we now turn off the source. The remaining sound waves in the room continue to ricochet from boundary to boundary, losing energy with each reflection. At some point, all the remaining energy in the system dissipates, and the sound ceases.

This decaying of the sound is what we perceive as reverberation. The amount of time that it takes for the acoustical energy to drop by 60 dB is called the decay time, or reverberation time, abbreviated RT_{60}.

The length and spectral characteristic of the decay – together with any resonances – form the acoustic signature, or characteristic sound, of a room. These factors are obviously determined by the absorptive qualities of the room boundaries, and by the volume and shape of the room.

NOTE: There are several related equations, named after the people who developed them, for calculating the reverb time based on absorptivity of a given environment: Sabine, Norris-Eyring, and Hopkins-Stryker. The unit of absorption in Sabine's equation is the Sabin. It is beyond the scope of this book to go into details of these equations, which are shown below.

	MKS units: S = Surface area in m^2 V = Volume in m^3	English units: S = Surface area in ft^2 V = Volume in ft^3
Sabine Gives best correspondence with published absorption coefficients where $\bar{\alpha} < 0.2$.	$T = \dfrac{0.16V}{S\bar{\alpha}}$	$T = \dfrac{0.49V}{S\bar{\alpha}}$
Eyring Preferred formula for well-behaved rooms having $\bar{\alpha} \gtrsim 0.2$.	$T = \dfrac{0.16V}{-S \ln(1-\bar{\alpha})}$	$T = \dfrac{0.49V}{-S \ln(1-\bar{\alpha})}$
Fitzroy For rectangular rooms with poorly distributed absorption. α_x, α_y and α_z are average absorption coefficients of opposing pairs of surfaces with total areas of x, y and z.	$T = \dfrac{0.16V}{S^2}\left(\dfrac{x^2}{X\,\alpha_x} + \dfrac{y^2}{Y\,\alpha_y} + \dfrac{z^2}{Z\,\alpha_z}\right)$	$T = \dfrac{0.49V}{S^2}\left(\dfrac{x^2}{X\,\alpha_x} + \dfrac{y^2}{Y\,\alpha_y} + \dfrac{z^2}{Z\,\alpha_z}\right)$
	T = Decay time (in seconds) for 60 dB level reduction.	

Figure 6-6. Reverberation time equations

Relatively short to moderate reverberation with a smooth spectral characteristic is perceived as pleasant, natural, and musical. Excessive reverberation makes it difficult to understand speech, and can destroy the texture and impact of music. Most of us have strained to understand an announcement in a large, hard-surfaced gymnasium, arena or transportation terminal... not because it wasn't loud enough, but because there was too much reverberation. To be successful with indoor sound systems we must be careful in handling reverberation.

We have said that the reverberant field in a room is the same intensity everywhere in the space. What relevance does the inverse square law have indoors, then?

In order to answer the question, we must distinguish between the direct sound (the initial sound emitted by the source, before reflection), and the reverberant sound.

For the direct sound, the inverse square law is valid indoors just as it is outdoors. In terms of pure sound pressure once the reverberant field is activated, it adds a second pressure component.

Figure 6-7 shows an omnidirectional loudspeaker radiating sound in a reverberant field. The direct sound of the loudspeaker propagates into the space, diminishing in intensity according to the inverse square law. Initially,

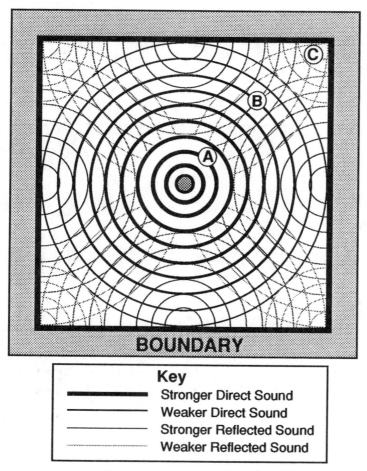

BOUNDARY

Key
—— Stronger Direct Sound
—— Weaker Direct Sound
—— Stronger Reflected Sound
······ Weaker Reflected Sound

Figure 6-7. Development of a reverberant field from a theoretical point source of sound in the center of an acoustic environment

there is primarily direct sound all over, as can be seen in Figure 6-7(a). At a certain distance from the loudspeaker, and after the sound has existed long enough to reverberate, the intensity of the direct sound equals that of the diffuse reverberant sound (b). Ultimately, at a sufficient distance from the loudspeaker, the reverberant sound is predominant and swamps out the direct sound (c).

The distance from the acoustic center of the source to the point at which the intensity of the direct sound equals that of the reverberant field is called the critical distance.

As we move further away, beyond the critical distance, into the region where the reverberant field predominates, the intensity of the sound levels off to a statistically constant value, assuming the sound source continues to excite the room at the same level.

It follows logically and intuitively that we can increase the critical distance by using a directional loudspeaker. If we concentrate the power of the system along a given axis which corresponds to an absorptive area (such as an audience), the direct sound

will predominate over a longer distance along that axis. This is not only because the sound energy is concentrated more in a forward direction, but also because there is less energy radiated and reflected toward the sides, and hence less energy to reflect from walls, ceiling, floor, etc. so that the reverberant field does not receive as much of the loudspeaker's energy. Since a directional loudspeaker's power decreases the farther we go off-axis, we must be aware that we will gain critical distance on-axis at the expense of the off-axis critical distance. Figure 6-8 illustrates this situation.

The real benefit of the horn is that it increases the direct level in a portion of the environment.

Since the direct sound follows the inverse square law, and we assume that the reverberant field's intensity is equal everywhere, it also follows that the ratio of direct-to-reverberant sound is an inverse square relationship. In other words, given that the ratio of direct to reverbant sound is 1:1 at the critical distance, then at twice the critical distance the direct sound will be 6 dB below the reverberant sound (half the level).

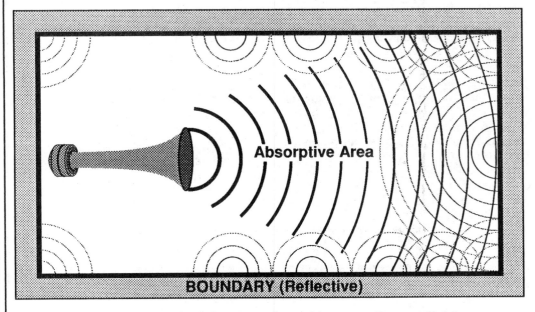

Absorptive Area

BOUNDARY (Reflective)

Figure 6-8. Directional radiator in a reverberant field

6.4.1 Implications For Sound Reinforcement

The preceding discussion reveals a fundamental reason why directional elements are the norm in sound reinforcement. Obviously, we don't want the direct sound of the system to be swamped by the reverberant sound. If we can increase a system's critical distance, then we have a better chance of maintaining clarity (or intelligibility) over greater distances.

A theoretical structure – buttressed by experimental evidence – has been constructed by acousticians, relating calculated critical distances and direct-to-reverberant ratios to intelligibility in speech reinforcement. This area is somewhat complex, and good modeling requires a solid mathematical background – and benefits from some help in the form of a well-programmed computer. For this reason, we will not go into detail in this basic handbook.

In any case, using such data, acousticians have developed methods for calculating the behavior of speech reinforcement systems in relation to hall acoustics. These methods are used routinely by consultants and contractors to design such systems.

Once we get into the field of music reinforcement, all bets are off, and such quantitative judgments are much more difficult to make. Here we enter a realm in which individual taste and subjective impressions reign.

Let us take it as given that we want the sound our system delivers to be as clear as possible, and that we wish to have as much control over the sound as we can. These two criteria imply that we wish to maximize the system's critical distance — that is, minimize the extent to which we excite the reverberant field — so that the audience hears mostly direct sound. The specific techniques for doing so are presented in Sections 17 and 18.

SECTION 7.
Block Diagrams

7.1 GENERAL DISCUSSION

Section 7 describes the function and symbolic conventions of block diagrams. We have shown a number of common variations of the symbols used to identify various electronic components and functions. Since manufacturers seem to invent their own symbols on a regular basis, some interpretation will undoubtedly be required in order to read any given block diagram. Still, the majority of symbols and signal flow indications are reasonably standardized so study of this material will be valuable in gaining an understanding of block diagrams.

In order to take full advantage of the properties of any piece of equipment, we must fully understand how that equipment works — both in and of itself, and also in relation to any components to which it is connected. One important tool for gaining that understanding is the block diagram.

A block diagram is a graphic description of the signal path through a device. The block diagram treats the device as a system constructed of individual functional entities that are connected in a specific way. It employs simplified notation, representing the various functions of the device as single blocks.

The purpose of this method of notation is to present the logical structure of the equipment in a simple, readily accessible form.

Most manufacturers of active signal processing equipment (consoles, delay lines, equalizers, and so on) provide block diagrams of their products. A block diagram may be found in the product data sheet (this is usually the case with complex equipment such as consoles), or it may be published in the instruction manual.

The block diagram is different, both in appearance and function, from another type of diagram called the schematic. Schematics present the component-level details of the actual circuitry of a device. Manufacturers may or may not publish schematic diagrams in instruction manuals (depending upon internal corporate policies and restrictions dictated by Underwriter's Laboratories where U.L. approvals are sought), but schematics are always included in the service manual.

The reason for this is that the information given in a schematic is necessary for servicing the unit, but not normally necessary for operating it. The method of organization and notation used in schematics is tailored to the needs of the service technician — needs which are different from those of the end user.

Schematic diagrams are sometimes organized according to component location on various circuit boards (to facilitate parts identification for servicing). This can make the actual signal flow difficult to follow. Block diagrams may be organized to show parts locations within modules, etc., but they are primarily organized to make it easy to see the signal flow. Schematics must show all connections, including power and grounding, whereas block diagrams often omit these connections to avoid visual clutter. Schematics must show all components in a circuit, whereas block diagrams show only the significant functional items, for example, an amplifier instead of a collection of transistors, diodes, capacitors, and resistors.

To the technically sophisticated user, block diagrams and schematics can be used as complementary tools. The block diagram serves as an invaluable aid in interpreting a schematic — since it presents the logical organization of the device — and aids in identifying the functions of various sections of the circuitry. Likewise, the schematic provides information that may be useful, for example, in unusual interfacing situations.

The needs of the end user are generally best served by the block diagram, rather than the schematic. After all, he or she needs first to know how the equipment works, and how it can be used — not how it is constructed at the component level.

Figure 7-1 shows the symbols that are commonly used in block diagrams. Some of these symbols also appear in schematics.

The following note applies to figure 7-1:

NOTE 1: This symbol is subject to the greatest variation in usage of any of the common block diagram symbols. The strict constructionist philosophy of block diagrams holds that this symbol is used to represent only simple amplifier functions (gain stages, drive amplifiers, active summing amplifiers, and so on). All other active (as distinguished from passive) functions are represented by a rectangle, appropriately labeled.

A looser attitude, which holds that the symbol should be used for all active functions (equalization stages, for example), is also common. In this case, the symbol is accompanied by a label defining its function.

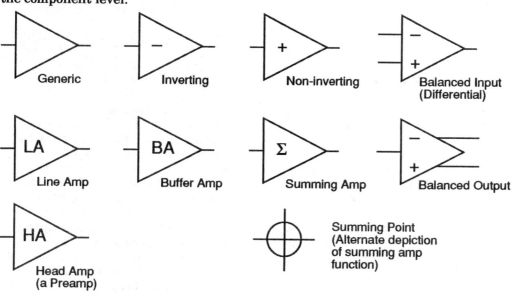

Figure 7-1. Block diagram symbols: amplifiers

7.2 Symbolic Conventions

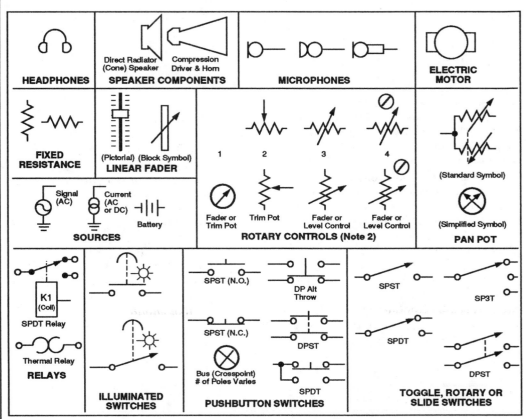

Figure 7-2. Block diagram symbols: miscellaneous components

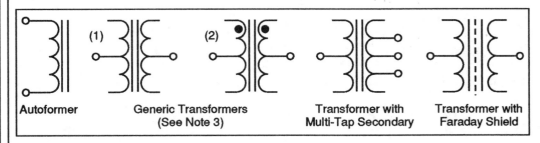

Figure 7-3. Block diagram symbols: transformers

NOTE 2: *On rare occasions, symbols (2) and (3) are reserved for internal trim controls that are not normally accessible to the user. In this case, symbol (4) may be used for a screwdriver-adjustable trim that is user-accessible. Symbols (2) & (3) also may be used to denote a linear fader.*

NOTE 3: *Symbol (1) indicates a transformer without indicating the polarity of connection. It is assumed to be connected in phase unless otherwise explicitly stated. The symbol (2) shows a common way of indicating transformer polarity. The dot corresponds to the + (in-phase) connection of the windings. If one dot is on top and the other below, the output is reversed in polarity.*

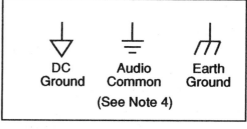

Figure 7-4. Block Diagram Symbols: Grounds

NOTE 4: Some manufacturers do not distinguish between circuit ground and earth (or chassis) ground in block diagrams. In such a case, one or another of these symbols might be used to indicate simply ground. This practice is confusing, at best.

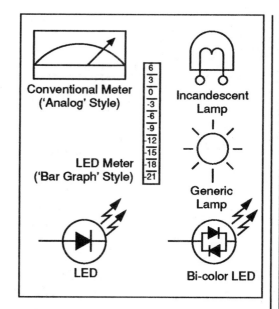

Figure 7-5. Block Diagram Symbols: Indicators

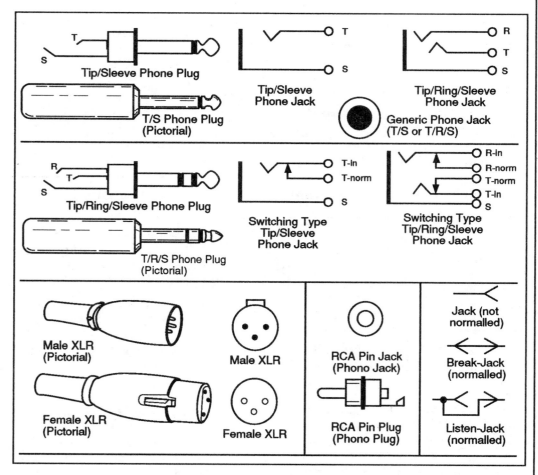

Figure 7-6. Block Diagram Symbols: Connectors

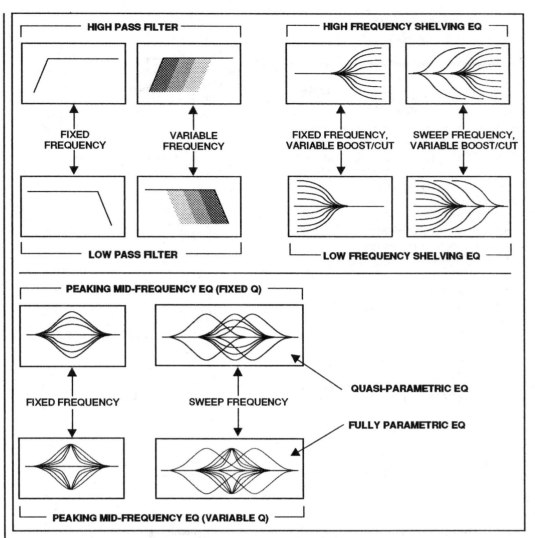

Figure 7-7. Block Diagram Symbols: Filters and Equalizers

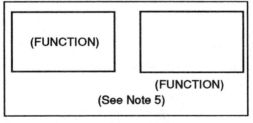

Figure 7-8. Block Diagram Symbols: Other Functions

In some block diagrams, you may see other symbols than those shown here. This may be because there is no convention for indicating what is shown in the diagram, or simply because the draftsman was feeling creative. Generally speaking, a responsible technical draftsman will label his drawings clearly, and provide a key to any nonstandard symbols.

NOTE 5: *A simple rule regarding symbols in block diagrams is, "When in doubt, draw a box and label it." This solution is becoming increasingly common, particularly in diagrams of digital signal processors. Some block diagrams consist of nothing but labeled boxes interconnected with lines. This purist approach has considerable merit in that it avoids any potential confusion arising from varying standards of symbol usage.*

7.3 Notational Conventions

Block diagrams are drawn to conform to the way Western languages are written: the signal flow is normally left-to- right and, as necessary, top-to-bottom. This practice is only violated in rare instances, and generally only for reasons of clarity, aesthetics, or economy of space.

Functional blocks, however they may be drawn, are connected with lines representing the signal path. Arrows may or may not be used to indicate the direction of signal flow; if the left-to-right rule is followed, they are not necessary.

Figure 7-9 presents some standard notational conventions.

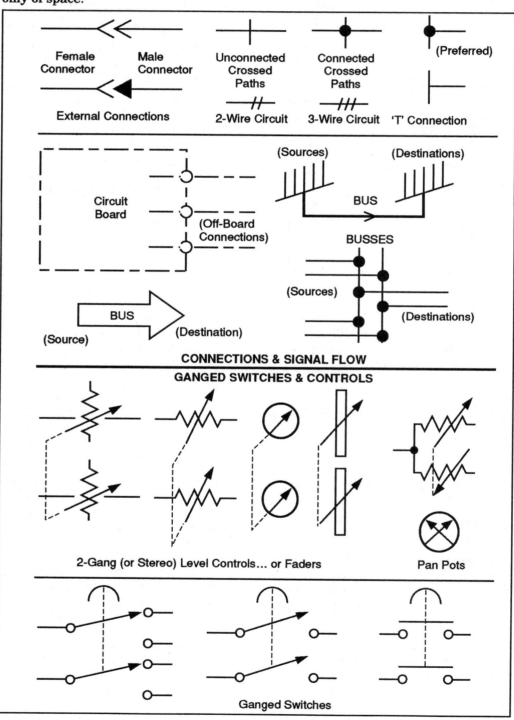

Figure 7-9. Block diagram notation

7.4 Analysis of Simple Block Diagrams

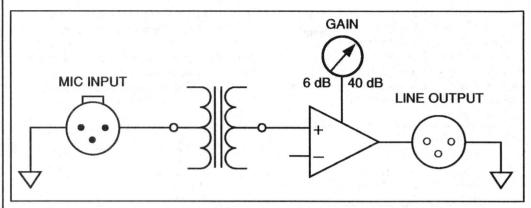

Figure 7-10. Microphone preamplifier block diagram

EXAMPLE 1. Figure 7-10 shows the block diagram of a microphone preamplifier. From it, we can deduce a number of things about the unit.

Beginning from the left (following the convention for signal flow), we see first that the unit has an XLR-type input connector. While not specifically labeled, we can assume pin 1 is the ground connection.

We can also assume pins 2 and 3 of the input connector are both signal pins, as they are connected to the primary winding of a transformer. The input is shown to be transformer-isolated.

The transformer secondary is connected to a differential input amplifier (as indicated by the '+' and '-' amplifier connections... single-ended amplifiers are normally shown with just a single line going in and a single line going out). A rotary gain control is shown, and from the way that it is drawn we surmise that it directly controls the gain of the amplifier (rather than being a level control that precedes or follows a fixed-gain amplifier). From the labeling beside the control, we see that the gain is variable from 6 dB to 40 dB.

The amplifier stage has a balanced output, and is not transformer-coupled, but rather drives the output connector directly.

This diagram gives us sufficient information to determine the input/output polarity of the preamp. Tracing from pin 2 of the input, we note that it is connected to the '+' side of the transformer primary. The '+' side of the

secondary is connected to the '+' input of the amplifier, and the '+' output of the amplifier we can assume is connected to pin 2 of the output connector (since this is the prevailing standard). Likewise, pin 3 follows the '-' connections from input to output.

For this preamplifier, therefore, pin 2 of the XLR-type connectors is the '+' or non-inverting pin.

***NOTE:** In most single-ended, inter-stage amplifiers, the signal source is actually connected to the '-' (inverting) input of the amplifier. This reverses the polarity of the signal, but allows gain and distortion controlling feedback to be more easily routed in the circuit. The reason the output is not reversed in polarity is that either (A) there are an even number of amplifier stages so the polarity reversals cancel out, or (B) the input or output terminals are internally reversed in polarity.*

EXAMPLE 2. Figure 7-11 (next page) shows a block diagram of a graphic equalizer.

This unit also uses XLR-type connectors, but the pins have not been labeled. Knowing the pin arrangement of such connectors, however, and knowing that pin 1 is always ground, we can deduce what the connections are.

Pins 2 and 3 are connected as the inputs to a differential amplifier, and no transformer is shown, so we know that this is an electronically balanced input. We do not know for certain that pin 2 is "high" and pin 3 is "low," but it

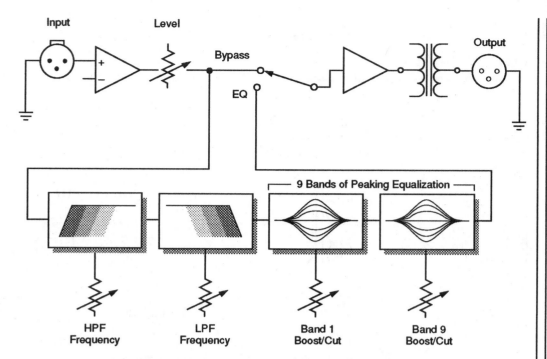

Figure 7-11. Graphic equalizer block diagram

appears so from the layout of the XLR. The input amplifier appears to have a fixed gain (although there is no indication of what that gain is), and is followed by a level control.

At this point, the signal path splits, and one branch goes to the output amplifier, while the other goes to a side chain of filter stages. These are obviously the equalization stages, and they are shown connected in series.

The first is a high-pass filter with a variable cutoff frequency. While its frequency range is not shown, it seems reasonable to conclude that this stage is a variable low-cut acting on the lowest frequencies. (This we can check by looking at the data sheet.)

The high-pass filter is followed by a variable-frequency low-pass filter. This is undoubtedly acting on the highest frequencies, functioning as a high-cut filter. Again, the data sheet should give us its frequency range.

The succeeding stages are the familiar bandpass stages of the graphic equalizer. Two are shown, with the dotted connecting line and accompanying bracket and label telling us that these are representative of nine stages, all presumably identical except for frequency range. Each is shown to have a single boost/cut control. While the block diagram does not indicate this, we might assume that the design uses sliders for these controls. This is another question that the data sheet should resolve.

The output of the last filter stage connects to the other pole of the switch that feeds the output amplifier. This is labeled "EQ/Bypass." We can see the logic of its operation. The wiper of the switch connects to the output amplifier. In the BYPASS position (wiper up), the output amplifier sees only the signal coming from the input. It is assumed that signals do not back up in the signal path, so nothing from the filter stages moves into the circuit immediately after the level control. With the EQ/BYPASS switch in the EQ position (wiper down), the output amplifier sees the input signal after it has passed through the filter and EQ stages.

The output amplifier is shown using the simple, general symbol for an amplifier stage. We make the assumption that it is non-inverting, since there is no indication to the contrary. (This may be checked in the data sheet or instruction manual to verify signal polarity.)

The output amplifier drives a transformer, which is connected across pins 2 and 3 of the output connector (again, an XLR type), indicating the output is balanced and transformer-coupled.

To trace polarity in this device, we might make certain assumptions:

1) The output amplifier is non-inverting;
2) The transformer is wired in phase (polarity is not indicated);

3) The EQ path is non-inverting.

Given these three assumptions, we could conclude that the unit is non-inverting and that pin 2 of the XLR-type connectors is the '+' pin.

Any of the three assumptions above could be wrong. The fact is that this block diagram gives little information regarding polarity. For instance, many output amplifiers are inverting (the polarity is reversed as signal passes through the amp)... and sometimes pin 3 is the + or high connection in an XLR. Making assumptions can be misleading, and we should consult the data sheet or manual in order to learn what the input/output polarity of this device really is.

EXAMPLE 3. Figure 7-12 shows the block diagram of a digital delay unit.

This is the most simplified (but not the most simple) diagram that we have dealt with. Neither the input nor output connector is shown, and some of the blocks represent fairly complex functions. This block diagram clearly concerns itself only with the logical structure of the device. Details such as connectors, input or output coupling, and input/output polarity and gain all must be obtained from the specifications section of the data sheet or instruction manual.

Nonetheless, we can learn a great deal about the device from the block diagram.

The input is buffered by an amplifier whose gain is determined by a control marked "Input

Level." The buffer is followed by a low-pass stage, whose function presumably is to reject hypersonic frequencies.

After the low-pass stage, the signal path splits. One branch bypasses the bulk of the circuitry, and is connected to a control labeled "Mix." The other end of this control connects to the output of the main signal processing chain, and the wiper of the control connects to the output block. We can deduce that the control is used to vary the mix between the dry (unprocessed) signal derived just after the input high pass filter and the wet (delayed) signal.

The other branch from the low-pass filter output connects to a switch that accepts a second input coming from farther down the line. The switch is labeled "Feedback In/Out." We see that the second input to the switch is a feedback path, and the switch allows us to select feedback if we want it.

The next block we encounter is a rectangle labeled "A/D." We know that this is a digital delay, so this must be the analog-to-digital converter. Hereafter, the audio signal is no longer analog, but instead is in the digital domain.

The output of the A/D converter (sometimes labeled "ADC") connects to a block labeled "Memory." This is where the actual delaying of the data occurs. (For a more detailed description of the theory of digital delays, see Section 14.) Two switches connect to the block at the top, and are labeled "Delay Time Select." From this, we

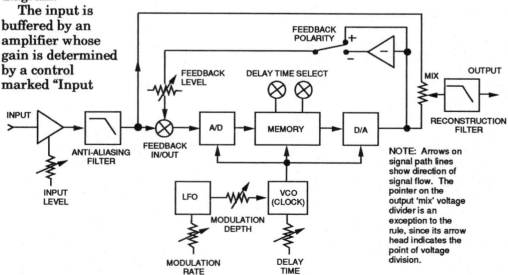

Figure 7-12. Digital delay block diagram

deduce that delay times are switched in ranges by two front panel switches.

The output of the "Memory" block connects to a block labeled "D/A." This is obviously the digital-to-analog converter (sometimes labeled "DAC") from here on, the signal is once again back in the analog domain.

At the output of the D/A converter, the signal path again splits. One branch connects to the "Mix" control, analyzed earlier. The wiper of the "Mix" control connects to another low-pass filter, whose function we assume to be to remove the memory section's digital clock frequency so that it does not appear at the output. At this point, we have completed the main signal paths, but some branches remain to be analyzed.

The second branch from the D/A output splits once again, with one sub-branch connected to an inverting amplifier that connects to a switch. The other sub-branch is a feed forward path around the inverter to the other pole of the switch. The switch is labeled "Feedback Polarity," and the two positions are labeled + and -. This is the feedback path that we're following, and the switch allows us to select between in-phase and out-of-phase (reversed polarity) feedback. The feedback is used to generate multiple echoes, reverberation effects, or flanging, depending on the delay time.

The wiper of the switch connects to a control labeled "Feedback Level," which connects back to the "Feedback In/Out" switch. We know we can control the amount of feedback, as well as defeating the feedback function if we so desire. We also know the signal flows right-to-left due to the arrow on the line exiting the "feedback level" control.

All that remains for us to analyze is a side chain at the bottom of the diagram. This side chain provides the clock signal for the digital processing section of the device. It is a control signal path, not an audio signal path.

The clock signal for all three digital blocks comes from a block labeled "VCO." The letters stand for voltage controlled oscillator. We know that the clock rate of this device, which controls the delay time, is voltage-controllable.

We also see that there is a panel control associated with the VCO,

labeled "Delay Time." Within ranges determined by the range switches, we have continuous control of the delay time.

Another signal path enters the VCO at the side. Tracing this path back, we see that it originates with a block labeled "LFO." The letters stand for low frequency oscillator. This designation is normally reserved for oscillators designed to work at sub-audio frequencies (from as low as .001 Hz up to 20 Hz... or as high as 100 Hz). This section is labeled "Modulation." The LFO therefore provides a modulating signal for the clock VCO, varying the basic clock rate in a periodic pattern (from experience, we assume the modulation wave to be a triangle waveform unless otherwise noted).

The LFO is connected to the clock VCO through a control labeled "Depth." This controls the amplitude of the modulating signal, and thus the extent to which it affects the clock rate. Finally, we see that the LFO frequency is varied with a panel control labeled "Modulation Rate."

7.5 SUMMATION

Techniques similar to those used in the previous examples can be used to analyze far more complicated block diagrams. The basic principles remain the same in all cases: read the signal flow left-to-right unless explicitly notated otherwise, and proceed logically through one path at a time.

Some detective work will occasionally be necessary to ferret out the meaning of a symbol or a notation method. This is the mark of a poorly-made block diagram. A little logical thought is almost always rewarded.

The technique of block diagrams is easily extended to the diagramming of whole sound systems. Doing so often reveals potential problem areas, and a good system diagram can be a handy aid in operating the system. Some examples of system block diagrams may be found in Sections 17 and 18, which describe "putting it all together" in terms of the electronics and the loudspeakers.

8.1 General Discussion

Specifications help us to understand how an item works, be it a microphone, mixing console, amplifier, loudspeaker, signal processor, or even a length of cable. Specifications provide insight into the quality of design and construction, and guide us as to the suitability of the item for a given purpose. In a legal sense, once a manufacturer specifies a piece of equipment to perform in a certain way, he is responsible to make sure it does, at least when first sold. And the sound contractor may be held liable if specified system performance criteria are not met. It is important to understand the meaning of specifications.

8.1.1 Why Specs Are Not Always What They Seem

Unfortunately, specifications are all too often unclear themselves. We suspect that if the design engineers were responsible for publishing all specifications and sales information, without regard to product sales, specs would be a lot easier to comprehend, but the reality is that every manufacturer wants his product to appear as good as possible. For this reason, specs are often listed in such a way as to emphasize the strong points and overlook the weaker points of a product.

If specifications are honestly measured, you may think, and if the product legally is supposed to meet those specs, then can they really be twisted to favor a product? Yes, because there are many ways to measure a specification, and many ways to present it, all of which may be accurate but not necessarily useful at best, and misleading at worst. Mind you, this is not always intentional... some people in engineering, sales, and marketing really don't understand subtle aspects of product

design, performance, and specification. We recall one prominent ad where the console's output level was specified as "±24 dBm." Giving the manufacturer the benefit of the doubt, we assume the ad agency slipped – or maybe there really was a switch to toggle the console's maximum output level between 252 milliwatts (+24 dBm) and about 4 microwatts (-24 dBm). We hope you will take it upon yourself to learn enough to avoid such pitfalls.

8.1.2 Examples of Specs That Should Be Doubted

The following specifications describe an imaginary piece of signal processing equipment. They have been stated so as to appear useful, yet every single one is either misleading or completely meaningless. Can you tell why?

Seems like this is a reasonably well made item, whatever it does. Fairly low distortion, typical professional

Frequency Response:	
	30 Hz to 20 kHz
Harmonic Distortion:	
	Less than 1%
Intermodulation Distortion:	
	Less than 1%
Output Noise:	
	Better than –90 dB
Input Impedance:	
	600 ohms
Input Sensitivity:	
	0 dBV
Maximum Output Level:	
	+24 dBm
Output Impedance:	
	10k ohms
Crosstalk:	
	Under 60 dB
Dimensions:	
	19" W x 3-1/2" H x 8" D
Weight:	
	10 pounds

Figure 8-1. An inadequate signal processor specification

levels, low noise, standard rack mount size. Nothing very special here... or is there? The balance of Section 8 will explain why a little healthy skepticism is in order.

8.1.3 What to Look For

In general, a specification should provide sufficient information to enable any competent technician, using standard test equipment, to measure the equipment itself to verify the specification. If an elaborate test load was connected to the amplifier in order to obtain a specification, that load should also be explained in the spec. If the amplifier was measured at -10 degrees Fahrenheit, then that, too should be stated (after all, it might do wonders for the power rating to operate the amplifier in a freezer). For input noise specs, it makes a difference whether an input is shorted or connected to a specific impedance. For output level specs, the load is significant. The bandwidth is significant for impedance, noise and level specs. You get the idea... a very simple spec may be easier to read, but it is also easier to fudge.

Section 2 goes into a fair amount of detail with regard to the proper means of measuring and evaluating the frequency response of various equipment, and the power bandwidth of amplifiers. Here we will quickly review the difference between power bandwidth, frequency response, and frequency range, and then cite a few pitfalls in their measurement and specification.

8.2.1 Distinguishing Frequency Response, Frequency Range, and Power Bandwidth

The term frequency response is a description of the ability of a device to accurately reproduce, at its output, the signals which appear at its input. With microphones, this describes the relationship between the acoustic pressure at the diaphragm and the electrical signal at the mic connector (i.e.,dB SPL to dBV, dBu or dBm). With preamplifiers, mixers, and power amps, frequency response describes the power or voltage waveform's amplitude relationship between input and output connectors, and so forth. There are at least two important aspects to such a specification:

A) The extremes beyond which response falls off unacceptably or becomes too erratic to be considered useful; and

B) The degree of deviation (tolerance) within those extremes.

There are instances where specifying a frequency response makes little or no sense.

If a device is intended to alter the spectral balance of a sound, then specifying its frequency response, per se, may be useless. For example, what is the frequency response of an electronic music synthesizer? We could examine the keyboard and look up the fundamental frequencies corresponding to the notes... but then, there are harmonics and variable frequency oscillators and so forth, so how can we really know? Well, we could simply measure the maximum and minimum frequencies that could possibly be produced at the most extreme settings of the instrument for every note on the keyboard. The real issue here is that this is generating original sound, not reproducing anything, so the whole concept of frequency response goes out the window. The term frequency range is appropriate. If we do, in fact, measure the highest and lowest frequencies that might be generated, we can then specify these as follows:

Synthesizer Frequency Range:
    16 Hz to 22 kHz

In the special case of power amplifiers, frequency response may be extremely flat, with wide bandwidth, at low power levels, but may be substantially degraded at higher power levels. In fact, this is usually the case. Therefore, the frequency response of an amplifier is generally measured at 1 watt output (or some other low level). In order to see what the amplifier does at higher power, the power bandwidth is described; this specification tells the number of Hz between the points where the output power drops by 3 dB (half the power) relative to the midband (typically 1 kHz) when the amplifier is developing its maximum rated power. The following examples might be given for a properly specified, real world amplifier.

Frequency Response:
    10 Hz to 50 kHz, +0 dB, -1 dB (at 1 watt output into 8 ohms)

Power Bandwidth:
    25 Hz to 28 kHz (@ 250 watts into 8 ohms, ≤ 0.1% THD, both channels driven)

Observe that the power bandwidth is considerably less than the frequency response bandwidth. Also note that no tolerance is required on the power bandwidth spec because by definition the spec merely tells us where the power drops 3 dB relative to the midband power of 250 watts (i.e., to 125 watts). Figure 8-2 illustrates the actual response curves for these specifications.

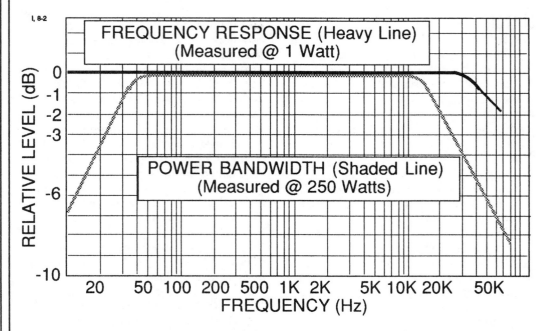

Figure 8-2. Frequency Rresponse and power bandwidth curves are not identical

8.2.2 Graphic Versus Printed Specs

As you can see from the preceding examples, specifications may be presented graphically, as well as in typed form. In fact, most frequency response specs are first plotted on a graph, and then the written specs are generated from the graph. Wherever possible, it is better to see the graph, since this provides far more information about what is happening between, and even beyond, the extreme ends of the stated frequency response and power bandwidth.

Looking at Figure 8-2, for example, notice that the low end frequency response doesn't actually fall off one bit at 10 Hz, although from the printed spec, you might have guessed it was down 1 dB. True, the high end response does drop by 1 dB at 50 kHz. Why was this amp not specified to below 10 Hz? Well, for one thing, it's not a DC-coupled amplifier, so it's not supposed to go down to DC (which is the same as 0 Hz AC). Since 10 Hz is well below the audio range, there simply was no point in specifying it to, say, 8 Hz (which may be where it was down 1 dB). Besides, the graph paper used did not go below 10 Hz, so response any lower would have been difficult to document. In this case, the printed spec did not hide anything, and in fact was apparently more conservative than the actual performance.

Even with graphic plots of frequency response or power bandwidth, it is important to know such things as the load impedance and operating level.

Quiz:

Now, do you know why the frequency response spec in Figure 8-1 is meaningless? If you said, "no tolerance (no + or - so many dB) was stated," you're correct. If you said, "no power level is given," you would also be correct, assuming this was a power amp. In the absence of a stated output level, 1 watt is generally assumed for measuring power amplifier frequency response.

8.2.3 What is a Good Frequency Response Spec?

With any spec, good must be judged in the context of the application, the balance of the system's performance, and cost versus benefits. If this sounds like hedging, it is. There is no one answer.

Certainly, the flatter and wider a frequency response spec, the more accurately a system reproduces sounds. But, it is pointless to have amplifiers and loudspeakers that are flat to below 30 Hz when there is no program material present below 40 Hz (which is generally the case in a sound reinforcement system). In fact, it is often desirable to restrict low frequency response to block mic rumble and wind noise, and to protect woofer cones in the event a mic is dropped.

If the sound system is to be used for paging, then the low frequency response need not go much below 200 Hz. Similarly, it is pointless to have power amplifiers and loudspeakers that are capable of flat response to 18 kHz in such a system. The human speaking voice simply doesn't generate frequencies that high, so all the system would do is to reproduce hiss and noise above 5 kHz or so. In this kind of application, a frequency response spec of "150 Hz to 10 kHz, ± 6 dB" would be considered excellent... and actually preferable to the proverbial "20 Hz to 20 kHz" idealized spec.

In fact, let's examine that "20 Hz to 20 kHz" syndrome. For many of us, those numbers have been ingrained as the gospel of required response in a decent sound system. Where do they come from? Well, a long time ago research demonstrated that young ears can detect sounds as low as 20 Hz and as high as 20 kHz, and not much beyond that. Below 20 Hz, we begin to feel the sound instead of hearing it. In fact, there is almost no musical signal below 30 Hz except for the lowest organ notes on large pipe organs, the thump of a very large drum, or an occasional synthesizer tuned down an octave below the keyboard. While a few very sensitive adult ears can hear a few thousand cycles above 20 kHz (characteristically recording engineers or musicians playing non amplified instruments), most adult humans in today's civilized, western cultures cannot hear much above 16 kHz — at best. And the only natural sounds that

8.3 Noise

go up that high are the very highest harmonics of high pitched musical notes. Given this information, a system exhibiting "flat" response from 25 Hz to 18 kHz would give most listeners a breathtaking, very pleasing experience. Even a 35 Hz to 16 kHz system would sound very good to most people.

If we examine recorded or broadcast music, there are other considerations. In records, high pass filters often restrict the lowest recorded frequencies to 40 Hz or 50 Hz (occasionally there is some program with frequencies below 50 Hz, but records almost never go below 20 Hz). In compact discs or digital tapes, the highest frequencies may "hit a brick wall" due to very steep filters at 17 kHz to 20 kHz. The best FM radio broadcasts seldom have any energy below 30 Hz (because the source material has no frequencies that low), and since the stereo pilot tone is at 19 kHz, their high frequency response is restricted to something below 18 kHz... often as low as 15 kHz. In any case, flat response beyond these limits is, in itself, no virtue. The only real justification for extended frequency response is that it suggests flatter phase response within the desired audio passband, and that flat phase response (if it exists) may improve the sound quality of the system.

This last point raises another issue. Specs are often interrelated. If one spec is terrible, then something else is probably suffering, too, whether apparent or not from the other specs listed.

One definition of noise is akin to the definition of a weed. What's a weed? It's the flower you didn't plant and don't want to grow. What's noise? It's the sound you didn't intentionally create, and don't want to hear.

While this definition is hardly technical, it does get the point across. Noise is important to quantify (and generally to minimize) in electronic circuits because it can mask portions of the program, thus reducing available dynamic range. High noise levels are very annoying and fatiguing to the listener, and actually color the sound. Noise also wastes amplifier power, increases effective distortion, and hastens loudspeaker failure by generating unnecessary heat.

On the other hand, some types of noise are very useful as test signals for calibration of electronic equipment, frequency response alignment of speaker systems, or music synthesis.

8.3.1 What is Noise?

When the old man walks in on his teenagers, who are listening to the latest new-wave rock group at unnaturally high levels of distortion, and says "What's that noise you're listening to?" he's not discussing the kind of noise we're concerned with just now. We're more interested in the scientific aspects of noise.

There are many kinds of signals that qualify as noise, and these are given convenient names like white noise, pink noise, hum, buzz, static, popcorn noise, and so forth. Of these, only the first two types (white and pink) are intentionally created — for use as test signals (in this case, the noise is more like the flowers). The other types of noise are unwanted, of no practical value (the weeds).

White and pink noise are both comprised of a random signal, with all audio frequencies present, over time, and at various signal levels. Such noise is generated by the random thermal motion of electrons, and is therefore called random noise. When this thermal noise is amplified, we perceive it as hiss.

8.3.2 White Noise

Assuming one is listening to relatively good headphones or loudspeakers, the noise that one hears when a high quality amplifier's gain (or level, or volume) control is turned all the way up, with no input signal present, is known as white noise. White noise is unfiltered, unaltered thermal noise.

When the energy content of a white noise signal is averaged (integrated over time), it will be found to contain equal energy per Hz. What does this mean?

If one measures a 100 Hz wide window between 100 Hz and 200 Hz, and then again between 1,500 Hz and 1,600 Hz, or 10,000 Hz and 10,100 Hz, the amount of energy will be exactly the same in each case. Plotting the power of white noise, with respect to frequency, will result in a 3 dB per octave buildup in level as the frequency rises, as shown in Figure 8-3. Why is this so? When we say the energy rises 3 dB per octave, we have to consider what an octave is. It is a doubling of the frequency. From 20 Hz to 40 Hz is one octave. From 100 Hz to 200 Hz is one octave. From 4,000 Hz to 8,000 Hz is one octave. Notice that as the frequency rises, there are more actual Hz in each octave: 20 Hz in the octave between 20 Hz and 40 Hz, compared to 4,000 Hz in the octave between 4,000 Hz and 8,000 Hz. We

have stated that white noise has equal energy per Hz. That means that if there are more Hz in a given octave, there will be more energy in that octave. That's why white noise shows a 3 dB per octave increase.

There are noise generators that produce white noise. Lacking one, you can get a pretty good facsimile of it by adjusting an FM radio so it is not tuned to any station, and turning off its muting circuit. The resulting hiss is basically white noise.

White noise is used to calibrate electronic equipment. It provides a signal with which to measure levels, and it drives the circuitry at all frequencies simultaneously. It is almost never used for testing loudspeakers, as explained in the following text.

8.3.3 Pink Noise

Pink noise is white noise that has been modified with a pinking filter (really). Such a filter is nothing more than a 3 dB per octave roll-off that commences at a sub-audio frequency and continues to reduce the level as the frequency goes higher and higher. In essence, it nullifies the 3 dB per octave rise in energy of the white noise signal to create noise which has equal energy per octave.

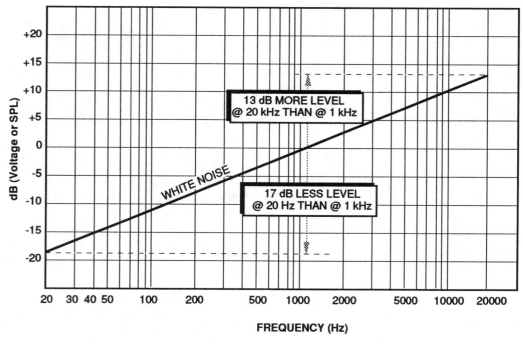

Figure 8-3. White noise energy vs. frequency

Since pink noise has equal energy per octave, it is more useful as a loudspeaker test and calibration signal. For one thing, it makes it easier to get a flat plot on a ⅓-octave real time analyzer, since the level will be uniform with respect to the octave scaling. But, there is a more important reason to use pink noise.

Musical programs typically have much more energy at low frequencies than at higher frequencies. The very highest octave in a sound system is driven primarily by harmonics of musical notes, and most of these are at a considerably reduced level relative to the fundamental. Were white noise to be used as the test signal, it would be delivering far more energy to the high frequency drivers than to the midrange or low frequency drivers. This would be a very unrealistic test, and would tend to burn up a lot of tweeters without making the woofers work very hard at all. Pink noise is balanced to more closely simulate the kind of signals the sound system will actually be required to reproduce.

This section of the manual is about specifications, which means it's also about testing. If you read a loudspeaker power specification, and it states that noise was used as a sound source, that noise has probably been shaped— that is, it has been filtered in some way.

Pink noise itself is a shaped signal, shaped by the pinking filter. True pink noise (or white noise) will have unrestricted bandwidth, and it really doesn't make sense to feed a given driver frequencies that are beyond its intended range of operation... that only causes excess heat (at higher frequencies) and excess diaphragm excursion (at lower frequencies).

To create an appropriate signal, the noise is subjected to further bandpass filtering. If a woofer is being tested for power handling or sensitivity, and is intended for use in the 40 Hz to 500 Hz range, then the noise source should be shaped with a 40 Hz high pass and a 500 Hz low pass filter. It is important to note not only the frequencies, but also the slope rates of such filters (as explained in Section 8.9) since this all affects the specified performance.

Some manufacturers use specially created filters to shape the noise, often with reasonable justification. It is important, when comparing specs, to examine the filters that were used on

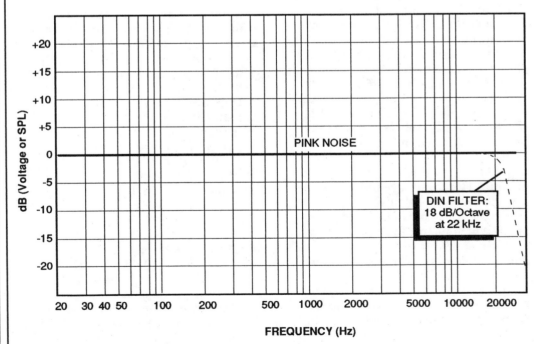

Figure 8-4. Pink noise energy vs. frequency

the noise. (Unfortunately, some manufacturers measure woofer sensitivity in the 1 kHz to 2 kHz range, which makes the numbers look better, but is worthless since the units are beamy at those frequencies and are used at much lower frequencies.)

8.3.5 EIN: A Measure of Mic Preamplifier Noise

Using noise as a test signal is one thing. Finding it at the output of a mixing console, a signal processor or a power amplifier that is supposed to be *quiet* is quite another matter.

In circuits that have microphone inputs, one common specification is the Equivalent Input Noise, abbreviated EIN. This is a measure of how quiet the mic preamp really is... except it's measured at the device's output, typically at the output of a mixing console. To determine the EIN, one actually measures the noise at the output, then subtracts the amount of amplifier gain. The math is usually a bit more complex than simply measuring so many dBm at the output and then subtracting so many dB for the gain. Typically, the measurement is done with a resistor connected across the input (usually 150 ohms) to represent the microphone and to keep out spurious signals. Calculations must account for the actual impedance of the input termination, as well as the temperature (remember, noise is thermally generated, so heat will affect it). The bandwidth of the circuit is also important, since the wider the bandwidth, the more overall noise energy will be present (as shown in Figures 8–3 and 8–4).

What is a good EIN spec for a mic preamp? Here were are in luck. There is a theoretically calculable minimum noise (the thermal noise of the resistor) below which no mic preamp will ever go. Given a 20 Hz to 20 kHz bandwidth and a 150 ohm input resistor, at 59°F, that resistor's theoretical minimum is –131.9 dBm. Notice that EIN should always be specified in dBm, since it represents the noise power.

If you see an EIN specified with the input shorted, beware... such a specification makes no sense. For one thing, what good is a mic preamp if its input has a dead short circuit across it? Wire, which has very little resistance, will generate much less thermal noise than a 150 ohm resistor, so the EIN will probably look a lot better than it should. The chances are such a spec was either measured by someone who didn't know any better (not a good omen in terms of the circuit design), or by someone who felt the EIN spec was necessary for shopping comparisons, but who also felt it necessary to improve the numbers that describe a noisy input.

NOTE: Some differential amplifiers are specified with regard to "equivalent input wideband noise voltage." In this measurement, the input of the amp is shorted, and the output voltage is then divided by the DC gain of the amplifier. This type of measurement is not particularly applicable to audio equipment.

8.3.6 Specifying Output Noise

Output noise is a useful specification for any electronic device. It accounts for all the sources of noise within the device: preamplifiers, filters, summing amplifiers, buffer amplifiers, solid state switches, power supply leakage, and so forth. Particularly in mixing consoles, it is one of the most easily manipulated specifications... because so many things affect the output noise.

Here are four typical output noise specifications:
a) **Output Noise:**
   Better than 90 dB below maximum output.
b) **Hum and Noise:**
   Less than -70 dBm.
c) **Hum and Noise:**
   Less than -85 dBm (20 Hz to 20 kHz).
d) **Hum and Noise:**
   Less than -70 dBm (20 Hz to 20 kHz, one input level and one master level control at nominal position, all other level controls at minimum, input pad bypassed, 600 ohm input and output terminations).

Did you guess that these four specifications are all describing the same mixing console? They are, but why do they differ so much? The answer lies (pun intended) in the level of detail provided.

In (a), only output noise is cited, and we don't know if power supply hum was a component of that noise. A skeptical reader might assume there was considerable hum, and that a notch filter was used to remove that hum so the noise figure would look better. This might hold up in court, but it is not exactly ethical (if intentional), and it certainly doesn't tell us much about real-world performance. So let's assume that it really is a hum and noise spec. If so, why is the figure 90 dB? Well, it's spec'd at 90 dB (or more) below the maximum output level. If the maximum output level is +24 dBm, this spec could be interpreted to be "Better than -66 dBm," which is really not as good as spec (b).

We really don't like spec (b) either, because it lacks essential information... like the bandwidth of the noise. If a 100 Hz to 10 kHz shaping filter were used ahead of the noise meter, a lot of hum and/or high frequency hiss present in the actual output would go unrevealed by this specification. Once again, let's assume the manufacturer is not hiding something, and a reasonable bandwidth of 20 Hz to 20 kHz were used. There's still some important information missing, as illustrated by specs (c) and (d).

Remember, these specs all describe the same console. Why, then, does spec (c) claim to be 15 dB quieter than spec (b)? Here the bandwidth is given, and it is reasonably wide. Was it that spec (b) had a miniscule bandwidth? Not likely. No, a look at spec (d) suggests the answer. It has to do with where the console's level controls are set. You know that when you turn up the level, the noise generally increases... and usually the more channels you add to a mix, the more noise. Well, in spec (c), all the level controls were set at minimum, so the output was very quiet... but what good is a console with all the level controls shut down? In spec (d) we see one input and one master circuit contributing to the output noise, and we get a reasonable indication of true performance. We also

are told that the input and output are terminated by (connected to) 600 ohms. We already know the termination can have a significant effect on the noise level from the EIN discussion.

Incidentally, the mere specification of a 20 Hz to 20 kHz noise bandwidth does not tell us how such a bandwidth was obtained. If very gradual filters are used, significant noise can be present above 20 kHz. For example, a 6 dB per octave roll-off would mean that at 40 kHz, a white noise source would have been attenuated only about 3dB, since it rises at 3 dB per octave. Clearly, either a much steeper filter, or one that begins at a lower frequency, is called for.

Around 1974, Yamaha engineers and technicians began measuring noise with a special filter because, at the time, there was no standard noise filter for testing mixing consoles and other electronics. By selecting a -6 dB per octave low pass filter with its knee (−3 dB point) at 12.47 kHz, they obtained the equivalent high frequency noise energy to an infinite dB per octave "brick wall" filter set at 20 kHz. The resulting noise measurement was intended to give more meaningful results relative to the range of human hearing.

Now a European DIN (Deutsche Industrie Normen) standard specifies a noise filter for such measurements. It basically is down 3 dB at 22 kHz, and rolls off at 12 dB per octave above that. This type of filter admits about 2 dB more noise than the previously described Yamaha filter, but it is now being built into many audio test sets.

Other manufacturers, mindful of the reduced sensitivity of the ear to high and low frequencies, have instead used an "A" weighting filter when measuring noise (the filter is described in Section 3.6). This filter yields "human" results, and, like the DIN filter, is also widely available for purchase. Remember that "A" weighting yields better looking noise specs than a simple 20 kHz low pass filter because large portions of the low and high ends of the audible spectrum are rolled off.

Quiz:

Why is the output noise spec in Figure 8-1 less than useless? Well, it tells us even less than example spec (a) above. We don't know the bandwidth, the level control settings, or the termination. Beyond that, the output level of -90 dB is not referenced to anything... not to 1 milliwatt (as it would be if stated in dBm), nor to maximum output level (which would enable the output noise level to be ascertained).

8.3.7 Other Types of Noise

You may recall we briefly cited hum, buzz, static, and popcorn noise at the beginning of this section. These are all types of noise, and are seldom specified. Hum is generally the result of leakage of AC power line energy into the audio circuit. It can be caused by a poorly isolated power transformer, a power supply problem, or indirectly by electromagnetic coupling of AC magnetic fields into cables or other components. It can be caused by excess harmonic distortion on the AC line itself. While AC power lines are normally 60 Hz in the U.S.A. (or 50 Hz in some other parts of the world), hum is comprised primarily of sine wave components at 120 Hz, 180 Hz, and other harmonics of 60 Hz (or 100 Hz, 150 Hz, etc. for 50 Hz power lines).

Buzz is similar to hum, but contains harmonically related noise energy across the audio spectrum, including high frequency energy. It is often caused by SCR dimmers (silicon controlled rectifiers) that "chop" the 60 Hz AC power line sine wave. The resulting steep waveform is the cause of harmonic distortion that readily couples into nearby audio circuitry (especially if the shielding and/or grounding in the system is not correct). An analyzer screen photo of SCR induced buzz is shown in Figure 8-5.

Static can be caused by distant lightning, by intermittent sparking of power lines, generators or electric motors, or by radio frequency energy that enters the sound equipment and is rectified. The latter is also known as RFI, which is an abbreviation for radio frequency interference.

Proper grounding and shielding, both within a given piece of equipment, and for the overall sound system, go a long way toward minimizing problems with hum, buzz, and static.

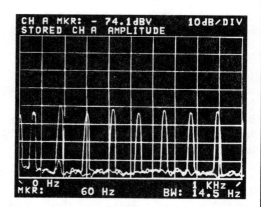

Figure 8-5. Frequency spectrum of noise induced by an SCR dimmer on a 60 Hz AC power line

Popcorn noise is not obtained by placing a mic near a heated pan of popping corn, although it sounds similar. It is a sporadic, crackling sound that can be caused by internal breakdown within transistors, or by dirty patch-points or other connections. It should never be present in properly designed sound equipment that uses high quality components and is in good operating condition.

8.4 Harmonic Distortion

Distortion is any unwanted change that occurs in an audio signal. There are many types of distortion. Distortion can alter the amplitude, alter the phase, or create spurious frequencies that were not present in the input signal. Harmonic distortion is one form of the latter type of distortion.

Harmonic distortion colors the sound, making it unnatural. When it occurs in the signal processing or amplification circuitry, it gives the impression the loudspeakers are breaking up because harmonic distortion is also created when loudspeakers are overdriven. Perhaps most dangerously, harmonic distortion can actually promote premature loudspeaker failure, as explained in Sections 12 and 13.

As with noise, there are times when distortion is a desired result, mainly in guitar amplifier/speaker systems, where the coloration caused by the distortion becomes part of the sound the musician seeks to create. A special type of signal processor, an exciter, also uses high frequency distortion components to brighten the sound. These are the exceptions to the rule and we can pretty much assume that distortion is generally something to be avoided.

8.4.1 What is Harmonic Distortion?

Harmonic distortion is comprised of one or more signal components that are whole number multiples of the input frequency. For example, if a pure 100 Hz sine wave is applied to the input of a circuit, and the output contains not only 100 Hz, but also 200 Hz, 300 Hz, 400 Hz and 500 Hz signals, the output can be said to contain 2nd, 3rd, 4th and 5th harmonics. These harmonics are distortion, since they were not part of the input signal.

NOTE: The human ear tends to find odd-order harmonics (i.e., 3rd, 5th, 7th, etc.) more objectionable than even-order harmonics (i.e., 2nd, 4th, 6th). Higher order harmonics (i.e., 6th or 7th) will tend to be more objectionable than lower order harmonics (2nd or 3rd).

In describing distortion, we describe the relative level of the harmonic components, compared to the primary input signal component, at the output of the device being tested. The distortion components can either be specified in level (i.e., so many dB below the signal), or in percent (i.e., so many percent of the signal). Harmonic distortion can be specified for individual harmonics, or as a composite value representing all the harmonics. The latter is more common, and is called Total Harmonic Distortion (THD).

Harmonic distortion can be caused by the clipping of a waveform (when an

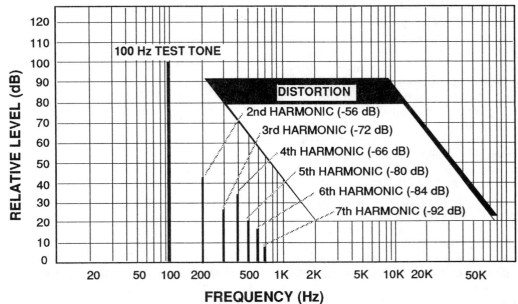

Figure 8-6. Graphic representation of harmonic distortion

amplifier is driven to a point where the output cannot produce adequate voltage to trace the input waveform). It can be caused by other circuit faults or design errors. In loudspeakers, it can be caused by resonances, voice coil rubbing or striking against the magnetic structure, or diaphragm break-up. It is beyond the scope of this handbook to explore the origins of harmonic distortion in any greater detail.

8.4.2 Measuring Harmonic Distortion

One method of measuring harmonic distortion is to inject a single frequency, sine wave test signal at the input of the device under test, and to then use a deep, very narrow band rejection filter to eliminate that same test signal at the device's output. Typically, such a filter would cut the test signal by at least 80 dB. One then takes a simple voltage measurement of everything that's left at the output and calls that the total harmonic distortion. The problem with this measurement is that it also measures any noise present at the output. This is why manufacturers sometimes print a spec like this:

Total Distortion & Noise:
Less than 1% at +4 dBm.

If this spec is accompanied by a very low output noise specification, you can assume that most of the 1% is, in fact, distortion... if the noise is high, then perhaps a lot of the measured distortion is actually noise voltage. It is not necessary to be a detective if the equipment is measured using a wave analyzer.

By using a wave analyzer, which precisely indicates signals present in bands as narrow as $1/10$ octave... or a spectrum analyzer that provides a detailed graphic view of the entire output waveform, with respect to frequency and amplitude, individual harmonic frequencies can be identified and measured. Using such equipment, individual harmonics may be specified. For example, it is not uncommon to see the following specification:

Harmonic Distortion:
2nd Harmonic, -60 dB,
3rd Harmonic, −75 dB, relative to maximum rated output at 1 kHz.

We know such a spec has been measured with an analyzer, rather than a notch filter. It is less susceptible to inaccuracies due to noise, unless there is a very high noise level. With an analyzer, we generally view the noise voltage. Therefore, if we want to convert a dB distortion spec into a percent spec, we use the following formula:

$$\%\text{Distortion}_{(V \text{ or } SPL)} = 100 \bullet 10^{\pm dB/20}$$

PROBLEM: What is the percent 2nd harmonic distortion of an output whose 2nd harmonic is 60 dB below the +4 dBu signal?

$$
\begin{aligned}
\%\text{ Distortion} &= 100 \bullet 10^{-60/20} \\
&= 100 \bullet 10^{-3} \\
&= 100 \bullet .001 \\
&= 0.1\% \ 2^{nd}
\end{aligned}
$$
Harmonic Distortion

This equation can be used for individual harmonics, or for total harmonic distortion. If we are looking at dB in relation to output power, then the equation is modified to reflect the 10 log relationship, as follows:

$$\%\text{Distortion}_{(Power)} = 100 \bullet 10^{\pm dB/10}$$

PROBLEM: What is the percent 2nd HD of an output rated as follows:

Second Harmonic Distortion:
30 dB below maximum rated output of 100 watts.

$$
\begin{aligned}
\%\text{HD}_{pwr} &= 100 \bullet 10^{-30/10} \\
&= 100 \bullet 10^{-3} \\
&= 100 \bullet .001 \\
&= 0.1\%
\end{aligned}
$$
2nd Harmonic Distortion

Notice that the -60 dB distortion number in the first problem dB, was referenced to voltage (as indicated by the dBu spec). In the second problem, the -30 dB distortion number was referenced to power. Note that both values represent a distortion of 0.1%. This is why percentages are most often used in describing distortion — they avoid confusion.

The same formulas apply to 3rd harmonic, 4th harmonic or total harmonic distortion. Figure 8-7 provides a handy graphic reference based on these formulas, so you don't have to do the math if the values can be found on the chart.

If you want to go in the opposite direction, that is, to find the ratio in dB represented by a percent distortion, use the following formulas:

For power ratios:
$$dB = 10 \log (\% \div 100)$$

For voltage ratios (or SPL ratios):
$$dB = 20 \log (\% \div 100)$$

If you have separate specs for 2nd harmonic, 3rd harmonic, and so forth, you cannot simply add the figures to obtain the THD. Instead, you need to add the dB value of each harmonic using the following formula (then you can find the % THD using one of the previously stated voltage/SPL referenced formulas):

$$\text{Total dB} = 10 \log (10^{dB1/10} + 10^{dB2/10} \ldots + 10^{dBn/10})$$

PROBLEM: What is the % THD for a circuit whose 2nd harmonic distortion is –40 dB, third harmonic is –65 dB, fourth harmonic is –50 dB, fifth harmonic is –70 dB, and all subsequent harmonics are negligible (below –80 dB) relative to 252 mW (+24 dBm) output?

$$\text{Total dB} = 10 \log (10^{-40/10} + 10^{-65/10} + 10^{-50/10} + 10^{-70/10})$$

$$\text{Total dB} = 10 \log (10^{-4} + 10^{-6.5} + 10^{-5} + 10^{-7})$$

$$= 10 \log (.0001 + .0000003162 + .00001 + .0000001)$$

$$= 10 \log (.0001104162)$$

$$= 10 (-3.956967203)$$

$$= -39.6 \text{ dB (approx)}$$

As you can see, the total distortion, in dB is not much greater than the second harmonic (0.4 dB). The higher order harmonics are so much lower in level that they are almost negligible in this case. Now let's convert the number of dB to a percentage.

$$\%THD = 100 \cdot 10^{-39.6/10}$$

$$= 100 \cdot 10^{-3.96}$$

$$= 100 \cdot 0.0001096$$

$$= .001\%$$

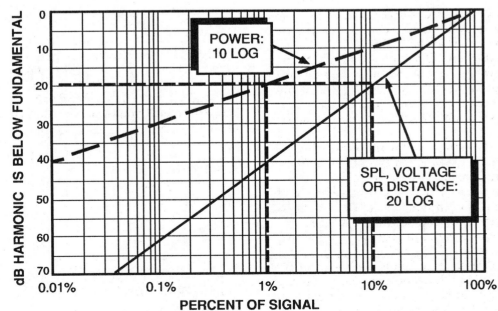

POWER: 10 LOG

SPL, VOLTAGE OR DISTANCE: 20 LOG

dB HARMONIC IS BELOW FUNDAMENTAL

PERCENT OF SIGNAL

Figure 8-7. Relationship of dB to percent of signal

8.4.3 Factors Affecting Harmonic Distortion Specifications

None of the distortion specs presented so far in this section have been thorough. There are many things we would like to know about a harmonic distortion spec in order to determine whether it represents an appropriate measurement of a real world operating condition, and to be able to duplicate the measurement ourselves. It would be wise to ask the following questions:

a) At what operating level, or levels, was the measurement made?
b) At what frequency, or over what frequency range, was the measurement made?
c) What input termination and output load were used?
c) Was noise part of the measurement, or was this a pure distortion test?

The distortion in almost all circuits will rise dramatically and suddenly as the maximum output voltage or power is reached. This is the result of clipping. The distortion will usually be rated at some level below this rise. It is important to note that the percent distortion may also rise at very low output levels. In this case, it is usually a matter of running into the residual noise of the test equipment, or the equipment under test. That is, the harmonic components can only be so many dB below the signal when the signal is very close to the noise floor. A special case exists with digital audio

equipment, where the actual distortion components may remain at a fairly constant level regardless of the output power. In this case, the percent distortion will decrease as the output power is increased.

Distortion will sometimes be higher at low frequencies in transformer-coupled equipment, particularly at higher levels, due to transformer core saturation. In most audio circuits, distortion generally rises at higher frequencies. This is why many manufacturers provide actual distortion graphs, illustrating the %THD versus frequency and level, as shown in Figure 8-8. Such graphs are useful, and are often derived at 100 Hz, 1 kHz, and 10 kHz, which are representative of the audio spectrum.

It is not unusual to see the midband (1 kHz) distortion be lower than the low and high frequency distortion. Our ears, being most sensitive at mid frequencies, will tend to hear this as being most natural, anyway. We are also very tolerant of low frequency distortion. Sometimes it is even perceived as sounding good.

You may notice that the highest end of the audio spectrum is not represented in Figure 8-8. Why not show a 20 kHz plot? Well, what would be the 2nd harmonic of 20 kHz? Right, 40 kHz... well above the audio spectrum... and the other harmonics would be higher than that. The 2nd harmonic

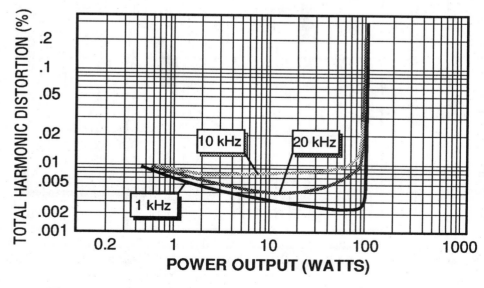

Figure 8-8. THD Plot for a typical power amplifier output

of 10 kHz, however, is 20 kHz. These higher frequencies can affect audible frequencies (via intermodulation products), but given a limited amount of space, a 10 kHz spec is probably more useful. Time for a quiz.

Quiz:
Why was the harmonic distortion spec in Figure 8-1 worthless? (To save you the trouble of page flipping, it was: Harmonic Distortion: Less than 1%.)

Of course you know the answer: no level was specified, nor was a frequency (or frequency range), or a load... we don't really know if it's THD or one or more specific harmonics (we'd assume THD).

8.5 Intermodulation Distortion

Intermodulation distortion (abbreviated IM or IMD) occurs when at least two input signal frequencies interact to form new, non-harmonically related, output frequencies. Percent for percent, intermodulation distortion is usually more objectionable to the ear than harmonic distortion.

8.5.1 Measuring IM Distortion

There are a number of commonly used tests for IM. All involve the use of two sine wave tones, usually at different relative levels. The Society of Motion Picture and Television Engineers (SMPTE) has been concerned with IM for a long time... ever since the advent of film soundtracks. They devised one test for IM which is perhaps the most widely used today. You will often see this specified as: INTERMODULATION DISTORTION (SMPTE method).

SMPTE distortion tests utilize 60 Hz and 7 kHz tones in a 4:1 ratio—the 60 Hz tone is 12 dB higher in level than the 7 kHz tone (2:1 is a 6 dB voltage ratio, so 4:1 is a 12 dB ratio). Sharp notch filters then eliminate the 60 Hz and 7 kHz components from the output, and everything that's left is assumed to be intermodulation distortion. As with THD, this technique can result in noise being factored into the IM spec, so it is preferable to use a wave analyzer.

One important item. The SMPTE IM test must be based on peak voltage measurement, whereas most other noise and distortion tests are based on rms measurement. Since the 7 kHz rides atop the 60 Hz waveform, it is important to use an oscilloscope when adjusting the output level (the test signal looks like a fuzzy 60 Hz waveform). Because the level is turned down to account for the peak voltage, a correction factor of about 1.5 dB is used before calculating the actual percent distortion.

Other tests for IM utilize different frequencies and different ratios (for example, 14 kHz and 15 kHz, 1:1). The most common test, by far, is the SMPTE test.

8.5.2 Sources of IM Distortion

Amplifiers are the major source of IM distortion in electronic circuits. Well-behaved amplifiers tend not to generate much IM. In loudspeakers, IM can be caused by Doppler effect. The diaphragm of a driver may be moving back and forth at a lower frequency, and the higher frequency waveform then rides on that moving diaphragm, causing the frequency of the higher frequency wave to shift up as the diaphragm moves closer to the listener, and to shift down as the diaphragm moves away. This is the same effect that causes the pitch of a train whistle or truck horn to rise as the train or truck approaches the listener, and fall as it passes and moves away.

8.5.3 How Much Distortion is Tolerable?

As we stated, IM distortion tends to be more objectionable than harmonic distortion, so it stands to reason that the IM spec should be at least as low, if not lower than the THD spec. This is generally the case with well designed equipment. When we ask, "How much IM is tolerable?", we might just as well ask "How much distortion of any kind is tolerable?"

The answer is not simple. It depends on the maximum sound pressure levels to be generated, the dynamic range of the sound system, and the nature of the program. If the distortion components are sufficiently low in level that they will be low enough to be buried below the ambient noise of the environment by at least 10 dB SPL, then the distortion will probably be inaudible. To calculate the actual values, you'll have to take the percent distortion at maximum output level, convert that to dB, and subtract that number of dB from the maximum sound level. Then see if the result is below the measured or specified noise floor of the system. You'll probably find that anything below 1% will be fine for all but the most critical sound systems.

One cannot simply look at the distortion of a loudspeaker, at say 5%, and assume that it is so high that it will mask any distortion from the electronics. Most of the loudspeaker's

distortion may be second harmonic, and may not be very objectionable. On the other hand, if the 1% distortion in the amplifier is mostly intermodulation, or odd-order harmonic distortion, these components may well be heard through the loudspeaker. This illustrates why it is important to keep distortion low throughout the signal chain.

8.5.4 Transient Intermodulation Distortion

Transient Intermodulation Distortion, or TIM, is a special case of IM. It occurs only momentarily during brief "transients" — high level, sharply sloped peaks in the program. TIM is generally the result of improper amplifier design, and amplifiers using a lot of negative feedback to improve stability are most susceptible to TIM. It is difficult to measure this spec, and there is as yet no consensus on the proper method of measurement, so few manufacturers will list it on a spec sheet. It's an audible aberration that is best avoided.

Quiz:

Why was the intermodulation distortion spec in Figure 8-1 worthless? (To save you the trouble of page flipping, it was: Intermodulation Distortion: Less than 1%.)

The answer is similar to the previous quiz. No level was specified, nor were the test signal frequencies and ratio, nor was the load.

8.6 Input and Output Impedances

Impedance is defined as the total opposition to the flow of alternating current (read that "audio signal") in an electrical circuit, and is measured in ohms. So much for definitions. But what does impedance mean to the operator of a sound system?

The impedance of an output – of something that supplies audio power – is a measure of how easily the power will flow from that output. This impedance is known as source impedance because it is the impedance of the source of signals.

The impedance of an input – of something to which a signal is applied – is a measure of how much power that input will tend to draw (from a given output voltage). This impedance is known as the load impedance because it is the impedance that determines how loaded down the output will be. The load impedance is also known as the termination or terminating impedance.

In most modern, line level audio circuits, it is considered beneficial for the output's source impedance to be as low as practical, and the input's load impedance to be as high as practical within limits, as is explained later in this section. Refer to Figure 8-10 to see how the input load impedance of one device (Z_{IN}) terminates the output source impedance (Z_{OUT}) of the device feeding it.

A circuit where the input termination impedance is a minimum of some 10 times the source impedance of the output driving that input is said to be a bridging input, and the output is said to be bridged.

In some modern equipment, and in most older equipment, it was desirable for the input's terminating impedance to be roughly the same as the output's source impedance. Such circuits are said to be matched.

It is important for you to know whether the output of a particular piece of equipment is supposed to be matched or bridged, or whether that doesn't matter. When there is an impedance mismatch (which means the source and load are not right for one another, whether matched or bridged), the results can range from improper frequency response to excess distortion to incorrect operating levels to circuit failure. In terms of specifications, it is important to know what impedances were used when measuring the specs in order for the specs to be reproducible.

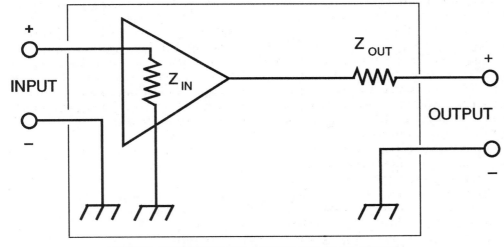

SIGNAL PROCESSOR, MIXER OR AMPLIFIER

Figure 8-9. Block diagram showing input termination resistance (Z_{IN}) and output source impedance (Z_{OUT})

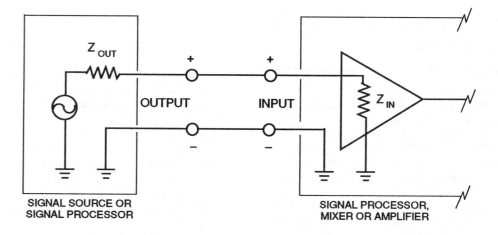

Figure 8-10. Block diagram illustrates how load impedance of an input terminates source impedance of a preceding output

8.6.1 Confusion About Input And Output Impedances

The specification of input and output impedance would seem to be straightforward, based on the information we have presented so far. Unfortunately, in an attempt to help the user of equipment, many manufacturers have contributed to significant confusion.

8.6.1.1 Output Impedance

EXAMPLE: What is the source impedance of the output in this specification?

Output Impedance:
600 ohms

If you guessed 600 ohms, you may be right. On the other hand, you may be dead wrong! Sometimes, instead of specifying the actual source impedance of an output, a manufacturer will specify the impedance of the load into which the output is designed to operate. In the above example, it is entirely possible that 600 ohms was not the source impedance, but rather the intended minimum load impedance. How would you know? You wouldn't unless you studied the circuit schematic or called the manufacturer and spoke with an engineer who knew the product. For this reason, a much better, less ambiguous specification for that input would be:

Output Source Impedance:
100 ohms
Minimum Load Impedance:
600 ohms

Sometimes the minimum recommended load impedance is not the same as the minimum acceptable load impedance, and neither may be the same as the output's source impedance. In this case, a clear, unambiguous specification might look like this:

Output Source Impedance:
200 ohms
Minimum Load Impedance:
600 ohms. Recommended Load Impedance: 2k ohms or higher

Quiz:
What was the actual output source impedance of the device specified in Figure 8-1? You will recall the spec read "Output Impedance: 10k ohms."

Did you answer 10,000 ohms? You're probably incorrect, but we really don't know from that spec.

Why do we think 10,000 ohms is probably the the intended load, rather than the actual source impedance? Experience tells us that the output source impedance of line level, professional sound equipment that is intended to drive low actual load impedances tends to fall in the 50 ohm to 600 ohm range, while the source impedance of outputs that are intended to drive 10k ohm actual load impedances tends to fall in the 600 ohm to 2000 ohm range. The spec of 10,000 ohms therefore appears to be a suggested load impedance to bridge the output (although it is possible that it's an actual output source impedance). That's why the spec in Figure 8-1 is not very useful.

8.6.1.2 Input Impedance

Just as output impedance specs can be ambiguous, so, too can input impedance specs. Sometimes the manufacturer will list the actual terminating impedance of the input, whereas sometimes the intended source impedance of the circuit driving the input will be listed. Ideally, both should be plainly spelled out.

Quiz:
What was the actual input termination impedance of the device specified in Figure 8-1? You will recall the spec read, "Input Impedance: 600 ohms."

Well, it might be 600 ohms. Or it might be 5,000 or 10,000 ohms and intended to bridge a 600 ohm output. Once again, you simply don't have enough information to know, for sure, anything about the input impedance. If we had to guess (and sometimes we do), we'd guess this is a bridging input, and that its terminating impedance is high. Why? The "Input Sensitivity" spec in Figure 8-1 is rated in dBV, which is a voltage-referenced spec. If the input actually had a 600 ohm input impedance, its sensitivity would probably be spec'd in dBm, which is a very convenient figure to use with an actual 600 ohm impedance. The fact that "dBV" was used suggests an input which is more voltage than power sensitive, which suggests high impedance. Hence our educated guess.

What is an unambiguous way to specify input impedance? Here are a few examples:

A BRIDGING INPUT —

Input Load Impedance:
(or, Input Termination Impedance:)
   5,000 ohms
Intended For Sources Of:
   600 ohms

Another way to specify this
   BRIDGING INPUT —

Input Impedance:
   5,000 ohms (for use with 600 ohm
   or lower source impedances)

A MATCHING INPUT —

Input Load Impedance:
   600 ohms, matching

Another way to specify this Matching Input:

Input Impedance:
   600 ohms
Intended For Source Impedance of:
   600 ohms

A MICROPHONE INPUT
(Neither Matching nor Bridging) —

Microphone Input Impedance:
   1,400 ohms (for use with 50 to
   200 ohm mics).

8.6.2 The Implications of Impedance Mismatches

When we speak of a mismatch, we simply mean that the input source impedance is not appropriate for the output of the device that is connected to the input (or vice-versa, depending on your point of view). A mismatch does not imply a matching or a bridging circuit, per se, just an incorrect one for the particular equipment involved.

To understand what happens with mismatched impedances, it may be useful to review how output source impedance is determined. Refer to Figure 8-11. When the source imped-ance of an output (Z_{OUT}) is measured, the voltage across the output is first measured with an open circuit, or very high resistance load. The resistance of the load (Z_L) is then reduced (usually with an impedance bridge or a box that allows switching in resistors of lower and lower value). Gradually, as the load increases (resistance decreases), it pulls down the output voltage. At the point where the open circuit voltage (V_O) drops to half its initial value (–6 dB with respect to voltage), the load is disconnected, and its resistance is checked. This resistance is assumed to be equal to the actual source imped-ance of the output because half the output voltage (and half the power) is being dissipated by the load.

What happens when an output is connected to too low an actual load impedance? What would happen, for example, if you connected the 600 ohm output of a mixing console to an 8 ohm loudpeaker?

While a few console and preamp outputs are capable of operating into very low impedances (8 ohms) — primarily for driving headphones — typical line levels (measured in milli-watts or dBm) cannot drive speakers to usable levels. Not only is the power insufficient for more than *whisper* levels, the console circuits are designed to operate into loads of 600 ohms to 50,000 ohms. They simply cannot deliver even their few milliwatts of rated power to a typical 8 ohm speaker without being overloaded. Let's see what would happen.

PROBLEM: *How serious an overload would an 8 ohm load present to a 600 ohm, +24 dBm output?* First, we must calculate (or look up in Table 8-1 (in the following sub-section) the power represented by +24 dBm.

$$
\begin{aligned}
\text{Power} &= 0.001 \bullet 10^{dBm/10} \\
&= 0.001 \bullet 10^{24/10} \\
&= 0.001 \bullet 10^{2.4} \\
&= 0.001 \bullet 251 \\
&= 0.251 \text{ watts} \\
&\approx \tfrac{1}{4} \text{ watt}
\end{aligned}
$$

The maximum specified output power, therefore is 250 milliwatts. How much power would be drawn by an 8 ohm load? In order to know this, we need to know the voltage represented by the +24 dBm output. Fortunately,

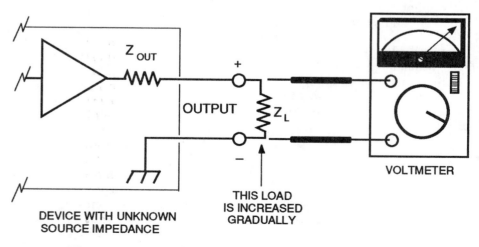

DEVICE WITH UNKNOWN
SOURCE IMPEDANCE

Z_{OUT}

OUTPUT

$+$

Z_L

$-$

THIS LOAD
IS INCREASED
GRADUALLY

VOLTMETER

Figure 8-11. Measuring output source impedance

we know the specified load impedance (600 ohms), so the voltage would be:

$$\text{Voltage} = \sqrt{W \cdot Z}$$
$$= \sqrt{.251 \cdot 600}$$
$$= \sqrt{150.6}$$
$$= 12.27 \text{ volts}$$

Given that the output delivers 12.27 volts into 600 ohms, how many watts would 8 ohms try to draw?

$$\text{Power} = E^2 \div Z$$
$$= 12.27^2 \div 8$$
$$= 150.6 \div 8$$
$$= 18.8 \text{ watts}$$

Clearly, an output that is designed to deliver a maximum power of $\frac{1}{4}$ watt will not be able to deliver 18.8 watts into an 8 ohm load, or any other load. Such an output would be severely overloaded, and would poop out before driving the loudspeaker.

It may be that 12.27 volts is sufficient, because we may only need 18 watts to drive the speaker. However, in order to deliver that voltage into 8 ohms, a power amplifier must be used. The line amp in the console can't supply the needed current.

We went into considerable detail in the previous example to illustrate why an impedance mismatch can cause a serious problem. Some impedance mismatches are less severe, but can still cause problems.

Consider the case of the typical low impedance dynamic microphone, as used in professional sound reinforcement. The microphone may have an actual output source impedance of 50 to 200 ohms. It is typically designed to operate into a mic preamp with 1000 to 1500 ohms input termination impednce. (This is basically a bridging input, since it is roughly ten times the output impedance of the mic.) If the mic is connected to an actual 200 ohm input impedance (as a less knowledgeable circuit designer might inadvertently build for a 200 ohm mic), the output voltage of the mic will drop 6 dB. The signal-to-noise performance will therefore be degraded. Since the inductance of the mic element (or transformer secondary) and the input impedance form a tuned circuit, the

frequency response of the mic will also be degraded, causing a rise in low end response. Conversely, if the mic is connected to a capacitively coupled input (common with condenser mics) the frequency response may fall at the low end.

NOTE: *In cases where an input has too low an impedance so that it could overload the source device, it is possible to use resistors to build out the input to avoid overloading it. There will be some loss of level, however. Moreover, this requires a separate device (a special pad or a special cable, which can complicate an installation and, in the case of portable systems, can create a potential problem if the build-out resistors are inadvertently omitted or are installed in the wrong circuit.*

It is thus important to ensure that the impedance specifications are complete, and that you understand what they mean, in order to get the most from the sound system. It is certainly essential to know the source and load impedances if one is to obtain accurate values (or at least match manufacturer's specified values) when measuring the input and output levels, noise and frequency response of sound equipment.

8.6.3 Impedance and Frequency

Impedance is not a fixed parameter in a circuit. By its very nature, it varies with frequency. When we accept an impedance specification that ignores the frequency, we are ignoring an important factor. Loudspeakers, in particular, undergo drastic changes in impedance in the vicinity of their resonant frequency, often with a 4:1 difference (12 dB) in impedance between the peak and the minimum or nominal impedance. Amplifiers and other signal processors may be somewhat better, but the impedance will still change at different frequencies. For this reason, you will sometimes see an impedance specification that cites frequency, like this:

Input Load Impedance:
    15k ohms minimum (below 5 kHz),
    10k ohms minimum (5 to 20 kHz).

Power amplifiers often indicate a frequency range for their output source impedance, but they do it indirectly in the damping factor specification. The higher the damping factor, the more control the amplifier can ostensibly exert over the loudspeaker diaphragm. Damping factor is simply the output load impedance (say 8 ohms for a loudspeaker) divided by the amplifier's actual output source impedance (say 0.02 ohms). In this example, the damping factor is 400. The output source impedance typically rises at higher frequencies, which means the damping factor goes down. For this reason, you may see a specification like this:

Damping Factor: (8 ohm load)
    400 minimum below 250 Hz;
    50 minimum below 10 kHz.

What does the above tell us? It tells that the amp's output impedance is no more than 0.02 ohms (but may be less) below 250 Hz. It also tells us the output impedance rises (probably gradually) above 250 Hz to a maximum of 0.16 ohms at 10 kHz. We surmise this because it is typical for source impedance to rise with frequency, and the 8 ohm load divided by the damping factor of 50 equals 0.16 ohms. You see, sometimes you can read between the lines in a spec.*

---

* If you really want to read between the lines, you'll realize that the actual <u>load</u> impedance of the loudspeaker system probably rises as it approaches 10 kHz. Therefore the actual, not calculated, damping factor may not be degraded to the extent suggested by the above specification. A 16 ohm load divided by the same 0.16 ohm amplifier source impedance represents a damping factor of 100, not 50.

8.7 Standard Operating Levels

There are many ways to specify input and output levels in sound equipment. Complicating the matter, there is no single standard operating level at which all equipment operates. This section of the handbook explores typical operating levels, and how they are specified. Prior to reading this material, the reader is encouraged to review Section 3, which discusses the decibel in detail.

When we speak of level, if it is not explicit, we are usually describing the voltage or sound pressure (a 20 log function). However, levels often pertain to power (a 10 log function). We'll try to be concise here, but the term *level* remains ambiguous in common usage.

8.7.1 General Classification of Levels

There are a number of different standard operating levels in audio circuitry. It is often awkward to refer to a specific level (i.e., +4 dBu) when one merely wishes to describe a general sensitivity range. For this reason, most audio engineers think of operating levels in three general categories:

A. Mic Level or Low Level
This range extends from no signal up to about -20 dBu (77.5 mV), or −20 dBm (77.5 mV across 600 ohms = 10 millionths of a watt). It includes the outputs of microphones, guitar pickups, phono cartridges, and tape heads, prior to any form of amplification (i.e., before any mic, phono, or tape preamps). While some mics can put out more level in the presence of very loud sounds, and a hard-picked guitar can go 20 dB above this level (to 0 dBu or higher), this remains the nominal, or average range.

B. Line Level or Medium Level
This range extends from -20 dBu or −20 dBm to +30 dBu (24.5 V) or +30 dBm (24.5 V across 600 ohms = 1 watt). It includes electronic keyboard (synthesizer) outputs, preamp and console outputs, and most of the inputs and outputs of typical signal processing equipment such as limiters, compres-

sors, signal delays, reverbs, tape decks, and equalizers. In other words, it covers the output levels of nearly all equipment except power amplifiers. Nominal line level (the average level) of a great deal of equipment will be −10 dBu/dBm (245 millivolts), +4 dBu/dBm (1.23 V) or +8 dBu/dBm (1.95 V).

C. Speaker Level and High Level

This covers all levels at or above +30 dBu (24.5V)... or +30 dBm (24.5 V across 600 ohms = 1 watt). These levels include power amplifier speaker outputs, AC power lines, and DC control cables carrying more than 24 volts.

8.7.2 Expressing the Wide Power Range of a Sound System

We have described the general classifications of audio levels (with respect to voltage). Let's review this in terms of the signal power at various points in a sound reinforcement system.

The lowest power levels in a typical sound system are present at the output of microphones or phono cartridges. Normal speech at about one meter from the average dynamic microphone produces a power output from the microphone of about one trillionth of a watt. Phono cartridges playing an average program selection produce as much as a thousand times this output — averaging a few billionths of a watt. These signals are very weak, and engineers know that they cannot be run around a chassis or down a long cable without extreme susceptibility to noise and frequency response errors. That is why microphone and phono preamps are used to boost these very low signal levels to an intermediate range called line level. Line levels are between 10 millionths of a watt and 250 thousandths of a watt (¼ watt). These levels are related to the "dBm" unit of measurement as illustrated in the following chart.

-20 dBm	= 10 microwatts	= 0.00001 watts
0 dBm	= 1 milliwatt	= 0.001 watts
+4 dBm	= 2.5 milliwatts	= 0.0025 watts
+24 dBm	= 250 milliwatts	= 0.250 watts
+30 dBm	= 1000 milliwatts	= 1.0 watts
+40 dBm	=	= 10.0 watts
+50 dBm	=	= 100.0 watts

Table 8-1. dBm related to power levels in circuits

The output power delivered by individual amplifiers in a typical sound system ranges from a low of about 50 watts (to power one or two high frequency compression drivers) to as much as 1,000 watts or more (to drive multiple low-frequency enclosures). Rather than express these power outputs in dBm, the watt is generally used. Sometimes, however, the power is rated in dBW, where 0 dBW = 1 watt (refer to Table 8-2).

Power Output (in watts)	Power Output (in dBW)
0.1	-10.0
1.0	0.0
10.0	+10.0
20.0	+13.0
30.0	+14.7
40.0	+16.0
50.0	+17.0
60.0	+17.8
70.0	+18.5
80.0	+19.0
90.0	+19.5
100.0	+20.0
200.0	+23.0
250.0	+24.0
400.0	+26.0
500.0	+27.0
800.0	+29.0
1,000.0	+30.0
2,000.0	+33.0
4,000.0	+36.0
8,000.0	+39.0
10,000.0	+40.0
100,000.0	+50.0 dBW
100,000.0	+80.0 dBm

Table 8-2. Power output in watts and dBW

When you examine Tables 8– often used for specification. It is easier to write "–20 dBm" than to write "0.00001 watts," and it is easier to write "+4 dBW" than "10,000 watts." Of course, these tables also illustrate why it is important to make sure you know the correct reference value for the particular dB scale being used in a spec. For example, what is the power output represented by +30 dB?

If you answered "I can't tell," you're right. An output of +30 dBm is 1 watt, whereas +30 dBW is 1000 watts! This sizeable difference is because the dBm is referenced to 1 milliwatt, and the dBW to 1 watt.

8.7.3 How Impedance Relates to Level Specifications

As you know from Section 3, the power dissipated by a given output voltage will vary with the impedance into which the output operates. Remember the formula for power is:

$$P = E^2 \div Z$$

where, in this case, P is the output power in watts, E is the output voltage, and Z is the load impedance.

What happens when the load impedance is altered? Assuming a constant output voltage (a good assumption for most of today's transitorized preamps and power amps), if the impedance is lowered (fewer ohms), the output power demands are increased, and vice versa.

8.7.3.1 Power vs Impedance

We can assume a device will deliver its rated output power (in dBm, dBW or watts) to a load equal to the device's specified output load impedance. In the absence of a specified load impedance, we would want to avoid operating into a load less than the device's actual output source impedance (i.e., *never operate an amp into a load anywhere near its actual output source impedance*). Given the above formula, we see that when this output is operated into

a higher load impedance, fewer actual watts (or milliwatts) are drawn from the device's output. What this really means is that the output level (in dBm, dBW or watts) will be less than the specified value at the specified load impedance. You can often see this with a power amplifier's output specification, where it may be rated at 200 watts into 4 ohms, but just 100 watts into 8 ohms... because it simply cannot deliver any more than 28.3 volts rms across the output terminals, even if the load is reduced from 4 to 8 ohms. (Right, a higher impedance is less of a load.)

8.7.3.2 Overloading an Output

While in theory the 4 ohm power rating of an amplifier should be twice the 8 ohm power rating, in reality many amplifiers cannot deliver double the power into half the impedance. If you see a specification like this, it tells you something about the amplifier design:

Power Output:
100 watts into 8 ohms
175 watts into 4 ohms

The fact that the 4 ohm rating is 175 watts instead of 200 watts suggests a thermal or power supply limitation. The circuitry simply overheats, or the power supply cannot deliver enough current to satisfy the greater load at 4 ohms. In this case, one could simply turn down the input attenuator on the amplifier to ensure that the maximum power restriction is not exceeded (or else the amplifier's protection circuitry or fuse may do the job more dramatically).

Sometimes the amplifier may be electronically and physically capable of operating into a lower impedance than is specified, but it may simply become very warm (or hot) when doing so. Underwriter's Laboratories (UL) in the USA, or the Canadian Standards Approval (CSA) criteria will not allow an amplifier to be specified to operate into loads which, in their opinion, cause the amplifier to get too warm. They are not concerned with audio performance, but strictly with fire hazards. Even if the amp sounds OK when operating into too great a load, this practice increases the potential for damage, fire hazard, or tripping AC breakers in the power distribution system.

A common problem with high power amplifiers only shows up when multiple amps are used. When banks of these amps are installed in large sound systems, they draw so much power on loud peaks that the AC main's voltage sags, causing interaction with the consoles and other low level signal processing equipment through the power supplies, and a terrible low frequency feedback/distortion loop. On many occasions, this equipment can trip the main AC service breakers. Particularly when driving woofers, the AC power source must be stiff. Most manufacturers incorporate current-limiting circuitry in their amplifiers, or install appropriately rated circuit breakers, to avoid such disasters.

In the case of a preamplifier, mixing console, or other line level audio signal processor, reducing the load impedance will also cause the output to try to deliver more power to the load. When overloaded, such outputs will often exhibit increased distortion, which may be followed by circuit component failure as the load is increased.

For the reasons just listed, it is not reasonable to fudge an output power specification by testing the output with a low load impedance. It should be tested with a realistic load.

8.7.3.3 How The Load Affects Output Voltage

The very nature of the source impedance test procedure, as outlined in Section 8.6, tells us that with lower load impedances, the amp runs out of power (it is limited in its ability to deliver more current to the load). This does not mean that the voltage will rise with higher load impedances. Generally it will not. Therefore, when a piece of equipment is specified to operate at some maximum voltage level, say +24 dBu (12.3 volts rms), it can be expected to deliver that level to any impedance that is equal to or greater than the minimum specified load impedance.

Note that this behavior, with respect to a constant (or nearly so) output voltage level above the minimum load impedance is not the same as the output power level, which will fall linearly with a rising load impedance.

This suggests why the line output of most modern sound equipment is specified in dBu or dBV rather than dBm: the number of dBu or dBV won't change as the output is connected to various loads, whereas the number of dBm will.

8.7.4 What Happens When Hi-Fi and Pro Equipment Mix?

This brief topic belongs as much to Section 8.6 as to 8.7 because it deals with impedance and level mismatches. While some professional sound equipment finds its way into home hi-fi systems, and some consumer hi-fi equipment finds its way into professional sound systems, there are often significant differences in operating levels and impedances that make this a risky proposition.

8.7.4.1 Hi-Fi Output to Pro Equipment Input

A piece of consumer sound equipment may operate at considerably lower nominal (average) line levels than +4 dBu. This is typically around −16 dBu (123 mV) to -10 dBu (245 mV) into 10,000 ohm or higher impedance loads. Peak output levels in such equipment may not go above +4 dBu (1.23 V). The output current available here would be inadequate to drive a 600-ohm terminated circuit, and even if the professional equipment has a higher impedance input, the output voltage of the hi-fi equipment may still be inadequate. The typical result is too-low levels into the professional equipment, and too-high distortion in the overloaded hi-fi output. This can damage loudspeakers (due to the high frequency energy content of the clipped waveform), and it can damage the hi-fi equipment (due to overloading of its output circuitry). There are exceptions, but this points out one of the reasons why it's important to read and understand the input and output level and impedance specifications when using consumer sound equipment in a professional application.

8.7.4.2 Pro Equipment Output to Hi-Fi Input

If a nominal +4 dBu (or +4 dBm) output from a mixing console or professional sound system signal processor (such as a graphic EQ) is connected to a typical hi-fi preamplifier's auxiliary or line input, the chances are excellent that the input will be overdriven. Because the input is expecting to see a nominal -10 dBu to -16 dBu signal, it is going to be driven with 14 to 20 dB too much signal. Sometimes the hi-fi unit's volume control can be adjusted to take care of the excess level, but in some equipment the signal will drive a preamp into clipping* before it ever reaches a volume control. This is generally the case at the preamp out-to-main amp in input, which comes after the volume control in an integrated hi-fi amplifier. If the professional equipment's output level is reduced, signal-to-noise ratio may suffer. The impedance mismatch, going in this direction, is not likely to cause any problems for the circuitry itself, but it can cause frequency response errors.

---

* *Clipping* is a condition that occurs when the amplifier (or other circuit) is either overloaded or is being driven beyond the output capability of the circuitry. The waveform cannot be accurately traced because the available voltage (or current) is not adequate, and consequently a portion of the waveform is *clipped* flat. This causes harmonic distortion, and is generally heard as a defect in the sound.

Signal leakage from one circuit to another, or between cables, is always present to some extent in any sound system. Leakage can occur between channels of a mixing console, a stereo signal processor, or an amplifier. It can also occur between the input and output of a single channel.

Generally, this leakage, or crosstalk as it is called, is held to acceptably low levels. When it is not, it disrupts performances or degrades the overall sound. Severe output-to-input crosstalk can cause feedback or very high frequency oscillation (too high in frequency to be audible) that increases distortion and can even burn out circuits if not detected and eliminated. Inter-channel crosstalk in a stereo system reduces separation. Inter-channel crosstalk in a multi-channel mixing console makes it sound like channels that are turned off are still on, causes cancellation of signals that otherwise would not be mixed together, and allows leakage of test signals or other off-line signals into the main program channel. Crosstalk through switches and controls can keep circuits from really shutting off when you want them out of the mix. There is no good reason to welcome crosstalk.

Some manufacturers specify the opposite of crosstalk in stereo sound equipment: separation. We prefer this term when applied to transducers, such as phonograph cartridges. In such devices, the electromechanical ability of the cartridge to differentiate the horizontal and vertical components of a record groove into left and right channel signals can properly be called separation. The cartridge is separating the signal components. The degree to which it is not successful (the remaining bleed of left into right and vice-versa) is crosstalk.

Crosstalk, like all other audio parameters, can be specified in many ways. It is seldom adequately described.

8.8.1 What Causes Crosstalk?

Crosstalk can be caused by inductive or capacitive coupling between separate circuits, and can be aggravated by poor circuit design, by poor physical component layout within equipment, and by improper cabling techniques. When audio flows through wires, it creates changing magnetic fields, which cut across nearby conductors, inducing voltages in them. The induced voltage is crosstalk. If two transformers are near one another, and their magnetic fields interact, the crosstalk between the two can be very high. When wires or circuit components carry signal voltages, and are near other wires or signal components, the two can behave as plates of a capacitor (albeit with very low capacitance due to small surface area and large distance). This causes the voltage to capacitively couple between circuits.

8.8.2 Crosstalk in Cables

When two cables, particularly long cables as from a stage to a mixing console in the back of the house, are bundled in close proximity, there is a lot of area exposed whereby capacitive and/or inductive coupling of signals can occur. So-called snakes or multi-core cables are the most susceptible to such coupling. So long as the cables in a single bundle are confined to microphone-level signals, the crosstalk will generally remain at acceptably low levels. However, if just one cable is carrying a high level signal, such as the output from a synthesizer or a hot electric guitar, or a line-level signal going the other way— from the console to an on-stage power amp, then the crosstalk from the higher-level cable can induce unacceptably high voltages in the mic-level cables. Remember that the mic-level cables will be amplified, and all that gain will also amplify the crosstalk components. The crosstalk specifications obtained for a given piece of equipment can be rapidly eroded if the hookup between components is not done with care.

The best way to avoid cable crosstalk is to use separate, not multi-core, cable, and to bundle it loosely, not tightly. If line-level cables must run to the same place as mic-level cables,

separate them by the greatest distance practical, and where they cross, have them cross as close to a right angle as possible.

These same techniques apply to signals routed within mixing consoles, which is one reason why some consoles exhibit better crosstalk performance than others.

8.8.3 Specification of Crosstalk

Inter-channel crosstalk is generally measured by applying a test signal (typically a sine wave) to one channel, and no signal to the other channel(s), and then measuring the output signal appearing in the other channel(s). The value is given in dB below the signal at the driven output. Thus, if an output is driven to 0 dBu, and the signal measured at an adjacent, undriven channel's output is -60 dBu, the crosstalk would be specified as:

Crosstalk (Adjacent Channels):
    -60 dB

Unfortunately, the situation is seldom that simple. Crosstalk values will change with frequency. If the crosstalk is caused by inductive coupling, it will be greater at low frequencies. If caused by capacitive coupling, it will be greater at high frequencies. The frequency at which the crosstalk is measured is thus important. Some manufacturers will provide this information, as follows:

Crosstalk (Adjacent Channels):
    Equal to or better than -60 dB below 1 kHz; -50 dB at 10 kHz

An even more useful crosstalk specification is provided by graphing the crosstalk between channels, as shown in Figure 8-12 (next page).

Notice in Figure 8-12 that when channel 1 is driven, the crosstalk into channel 3 is greater at frequencies between 10 kHz and 20 kHz than the crosstalk into channel 1 when channel 3 is driven. This is not at all unusual, but it would not be revealed by a simple printed specification. The knowledge of this type of information might, for example, allow someone to decide to run the SMPTE time code signal through channel 3 (since it exhibits less high frequency crosstalk). The printed spec for the crosstalk illustrated in Figure 8-12 might read like this:

Crosstalk (Between CH 1 & CH 3):
Better than -60 dB below 10 kHz; better than -55 dB at 20 kHz

Some confusion occurs with crosstalk specs due to the differences in the way some people choose to express the same thing. For example, the above spec could be written:

Crosstalk (Between CH 1 & CH 3):
Better than 60 dB below 10 kHz; better than 55 dB at 20 kHz

— same idea, without the minus signs. Or, it might be written:

Crosstalk (Between CH 1 & CH 3):
At least 60 dB below 10 kHz; at least 55 dB at 20 kHz

— again, same idea, with "at least" instead of "better than." Or it might be written:

Crosstalk (Between CH 1 & CH 3):
Below 60 dB at 100 Hz, 1kHz and 10 kHz; below 55 dB at 20 kHz

In this last example, we substitute three discrete frequencies (100 Hz, 1 kHz and 10 kHz) instead of the otherwise implied "at any frequency below 10 kHz." We don't like this specification because it leaves us wondering if there may not be some glitch with a lot of crosstalk at 275 Hz and 3.6 kHz, although the other methods, including the graph, show this is not the case here. The other thing we don't like about this last example is the use of the phrase "below 60 dB" since it is somewhat ambiguous. Does it mean "less than 60 dB" as in "worse than 60 dB" as in "maybe 55 dB below the driven channel", or does it mean what the graph tells us is the case?

Input-to-output crosstalk is specified in a similar manner, although it's trickier to measure. Still, such a spec should contain the number of dB crosstalk, and the applicable frequencies.

As with other specs, it's probably a good idea to know how the inputs and outputs are terminated. It is also a

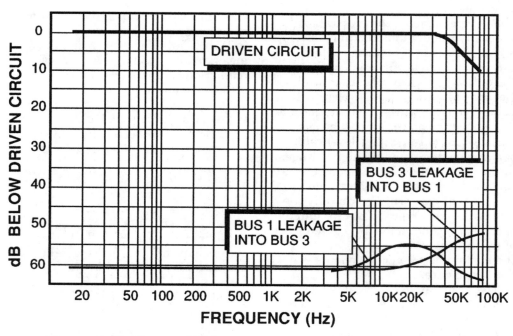

Figure 8-12. Crosstalk between two busses in a mixing console

good idea, especially in complex systems, to know how various pan pots and gain controls are set, since this can definitely affect crosstalk.

Crosstalk always is present in controls, switches, faders, etc. The issues is not whether it exists, but how low it is. Crosstalk can be measured across almost any circuit paths, and it will always have some impact on performance — it is not unlike distortion, even at low levels, so it is to be avoided.

While there are dozens of circuits across which one can measure the crosstalk, we can't suggest you demand this information in a spec because at present few manufacturers provide it. To be fair, it does take up a lot of space to list all these data, and some responsible manufacturers instead choose to simplify the presentation of the most critical information so it is more readily digestible. There is always a trade-off between readability and completely descriptive specifications.

Quiz:
In Figure 8-1, why was the crosstalk spec meaningless? You will recall it stated, "Crosstalk: Under 60 dB."

We don't know if the measurement is for adjacent channels (usually a worst case spec) or between more widely spaced channels. We don't know what frequency range is described by the spec (it could be that there is very low crosstalk below 500 Hz, but that it rises subtantially above that). In fact, we don't know whether "under 60 dB" means there is less than 60 dB of separation between circuits (i.e., the crosstalk may be down only 50 dB from the driven channel), or if it means there is less than 60 dB leakage. We assume the latter.

8.9 Filter Slope Rates and Turnover Frequencies

There are many types of filters: high pass (low cut), low pass (high cut), bandpass, notch, and so forth. They are generally specified as to the slope rate at which they attenuate signal below or above a specified turnover frequency.

The turnover frequency (or knee) of a filter is the frequency at which the level has dropped 3 dB relative to the level in the filter's pass band. The slope rate, expressed in dB per octave, is the rate at which the level drops beyond the turnover frequency.

Filters tend to have one of several standard slope rates: 6 dB, 12 dB, 18 dB, or 24 dB per octave. In digital audio equipment, where brick wall filters are required to prevent aliasing distortion, special filters with higher sloper rates of 48 dB per octave to as much as 150 dB per octave may be found.

The reason filters are specified in multiples of 6 dB per octave is that one filter pole — one section of a filter circuit — produces that much attenuation per octave. The more sections, or poles, the more dB per octave. For this reason, some filters are specified not in dB per octave attenuation, but by the number of poles in the circuit, as follows:

High Pass Filter:
18 dB per octave below 80 Hz

or,

High Pass Filter:
80 Hz, 3 pole

Refering to Figure 8-13 (next page), we see that this filter actually begins to attenuate frequencies above 100 Hz. The attenuation there is very slight, and reaches -3 dB at 80 Hz, which is the specified turnover point. Between 80 Hz and 40 Hz (1 octave), the level drops 18 dB. Note that the level at 40 Hz is 21 dB below the passband level. By the time the frequency reaches 20 Hz, the filter is down another 18 dB to -39 dB. Realizing that -40 dB is $1/100$ the voltage, or $1/10,000$ the power, we see that this filter is very effective in removing any 20 Hz or subsonic components from the signal. Even at 40 Hz, the power is less than $^1/_{100}$ that in the passband, which gets rid of a lot of rumble, wind noise, and vocal pops.

Square waves are sometimes used as test signals. There may be good reasons to do this, but often the results are misinterpreted. The primary value in using a square wave, rather than a sine wave, is that it is comprised of many frequencies at once, covering virtually the entire frequency spectrum. A square wave is thus a very wideband signal, and observing it on an oscilloscope can immediately tell us much about the high and low frequency response of a circuit, as well as any resonances in the circuit that may be excited by transients (as represented by the steep leading edge of the square wave).

Isn't the square wave the same as noise, which is a wideband signal with all frequencies? No, there is a big difference. In a square wave, not all frequencies are present, just a lot of them, and they are harmonically related. Moreover, they share a specific level relationship. When all these sine wave frequencies are added together, in the correct phase and level relationship, they form the square wave. In fact, this is the key to why square wave testing is so useful. A phase shift or an anomaly in frequency response will cause some of the sine wave compo-

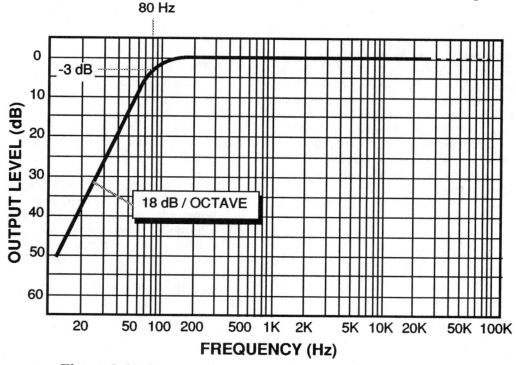

Figure 8-13. Frequency response of an 80 Hz, 3-pole filter

nents of the square wave to add in such a way that the wave is no longer square.

The very steep leading and trailing edges on each sine wave also provide an opportunity to evaluate the rise time capability (and slew rate) of a circuit.

Incidentally, even a theoretically perfect square wave need not be square. It should be symmetrical, but the height of the wave is merely a function of its level, and of the gain or loss of the test equipment. So long as the wave is comprised of right angles and straight lines, it can be considered "square."

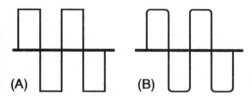

Figure 8-14. A theoretically perfect square wave (A) and a good square wave from a function generator (B)

We will not go into great detail about evaluation of square wave oscilloscope photos. It is simply beyond the scope of this handbook. We do show a few illustrations of typical square waves and suggest what they tell us about the circuits that produced them.

8.10.1 Oscilloscopes

Dual trace oscilloscopes allow one signal to be shown on the top part of the display, and another on the bottom. The typical application is to show an input test signal on the top, and the signal output of the device being tested on the bottom (or vice-versa). This allows rapid comparison of changes in the waveform caused by the circuit under test.

When oscilloscopes display square waves, they very often fail to display (or the display is very faint) the rising leading edge and falling trailing edge of the wave. Instead, you may see only a series of dashed lines representing the flat top and bottom of the square,

as shown in Figure 8-15. This display is perfectly normal, and does not indicate any problem in the circuitry or the scope.

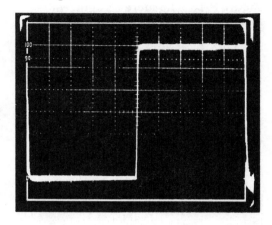

Figure 8-15. An oscilloscope display of a near-perfect square wave

The horizontal scale on the scope represents time, and one division (one box) can be set to be 50 microseconds, or 100 microseconds, or 1 millisecond, or whatever scale the scope allows. By observing the period for one wave, one can calculate the frequency. The ability to shift the time base is of importance to us because it serves to magnify the square wave for closer scrutiny. The same signal that looked very square in Figure 8-15 shows a finite rise time in Figure 8-16, where the horizontal time base scale has been stretched out.

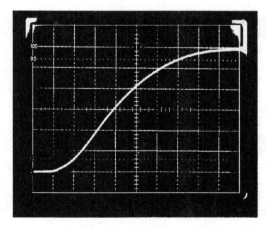

Figure 8-16. "Magnification" of the square wave in Figure 8-15, with expanded time base

Note that the time it takes for the signal to rise from 10% to 90% of its maximum value is defined as the square wave's rise time, as shown in Figure 8-16. The more recognizeable display of this same square wave in Figure 8-15 is such that a rise time would be very difficult to measure.

Viewed left-to-right, when the flat top of a square wave tilts down to the right, or the bottom tilts up, this suggests a deficiency in low frequency response. Actually, unless the circuit is capable of passing DC, all square waves will exhibit some of this tilt, as shown in Figure 8-17.

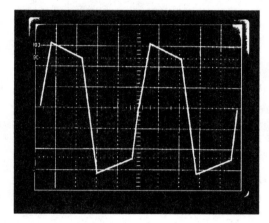

Figure 8-17. Square wave oscilloscope photo of a circuit with 6 dB per octave roll-off below 1 kHz

The opposite tilt to that shown in Figure 8-17, with an upward tilt from left to right, would suggest a roll-off of high frequencies.

When the beginning part of the flat top or bottom of the square wave shows ripples, it indicates the circuit is ringing, or is resonant and is being excited by the steep transient of the leading edge. The more ripples, and/or the larger their amplitude, the worse the problem. This indicates the circuit may not be properly terminated, or that the design itself is deficient. See Figure 8-18.

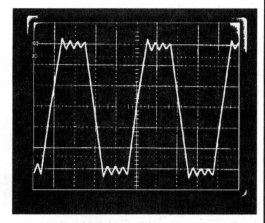

Figure 8-18. Square wave oscilloscope photo of a circuit which is improperly terminated and is ringing

Sine waves can be helpful as test signals, too. The upper and lower portions of a square wave should be symmetrical. If they are not, as shown in Figure 8-19, then it is likely that there is a problem with the circuit under test; it may have a transistor improperly biased, or one half of a bipolar power supply may be lower in voltage than the other, etc.

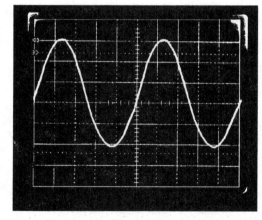

Figure 8-19. Sine wave oscilloscope photo of a bipolar amplifier with imbalanced power supplies

There are more things that can be gleaned from scope photos of square waves, but the preceding should give you an idea of the major items.

8.10.2 What Not To Expect With Square Waves

First of all, a square wave is not a natural, musical signal. It can be created by a synthesizer, but basically it's artificial. Music and voice consist of complex waves. There is no valid reason for any sound system or audio amplifier to have to pass square waves perfectly. In fact, without DC response, it's impossible... and audio does not go down to DC. A loudspeaker (or at least a single driver) cannot possibly produce a square wave because once it produces peak sound pressure when the diaphragm moves forward or backward, there is no way to sustain that pressure during the "flat" part of the waveform. Still, as illustrated previously, square waves can be useful as diagnostic tools. The important concept here is that circuits which don't reproduce accurate square waves can still sound very good.

If crosstalk tests are made using square waves, you can expect worse measurements because of the greater high frequency content; the ideal square wave is full of harmonics, whereas a pure sine wave has none.

8.11 Miscellany

We neglected to quiz you on the last two specifications on the chart in Figure 8-1. While the *Dimensions* and *Weight* would seem to be straightforward, here, too, there are catches. Below those two specs are repeated:

Dimensions:
 19" W x 3-½" H x 8" D

Weight:
 10 pounds

Given that the width of the unit is 19 inches, we would suspect it is intended for standard rack mounting. Given that its height is 3-½ inches, a whole number multiple of the standard 1-¾ inch high single rack space, we can be almost sure this is a rack-mountable device. We would then want to know how much of its depth lies behind the front panel, and how much of it is comprised of knobs and handles. The problem here is that we have only a single depth spec. We would prefer to see this:

Dimensions:
 19" W x 3-½" H x 8" overall depth; depth behind front panel, 7-¼".

The weight is not specified to be net (the weight of the equipment) or gross (the shipping weight, including packing materials). It would be nice to see both, or at least to know which this is.

In terms of metric conversions for weight and dimensions, here's all you need to know:

1 inch	= 2.54 cm	= 25.4 mm
1 meter	= 39.37 inches	= 3.28 feet
1 foot	= 30.5 cm	= .305 meter
1 cm	= 0.394 inch	
1 pound	= 0.455 kg	
1 kg	= 2.2 pounds	
1 oz	= 0.284 kg	= 28.4 grams

SECTION 9.
WHY EARS DON'T ALWAYS CORRELATE WITH SPECS

This section of the manual examines a few of the many reasons why it is seldom possible to know what something will sound like merely by reading its specifications, no matter how much you know about specifications. The two opposite, extreme points of view are:

a) "If it sounds good, the heck with the specs," or

b) "If the specs are good, then it must sound good."

Ideally, equipment ought to sound good and exhibit good specs. In reality, this is not always the case. We believe that specifications are important, and should be considered in any decision to buy, rent, use, or recommend sound equipment. But the equipment must sound good when properly installed in an appropriate sound system so one must not disregard the "golden ears" approach, either.

Note that in this context, when we use the term *ears* or *by ear* we understand that this includes our brain for processing and evaluating the raw data from the ears.

9.1 DIFFERENT POINTS OF VIEW

Any performance specification, whether written or graphic, is merely a representation of some physical behavior. It is not the behavior itself.

When evaluating how a sound system may actually sound, those who would rely entirely upon measurements and specifications are making judgements based on a representation. One may indeed learn a lot about the performance of a system from carefully reviewing the specs... especially with the insight gained from studying Section 8 of this handbook. The final criterion, however, is "Does it sound good?" or, in more practical terms, "Does it sound good enough for the intended application?" Ultimately, if the experience is listening, then listening should be the preferred, first-hand means to evaluate the sound.

9.1.1 Calibrated Mics vs Ears

When acoustic measurements are made of a sound system, a calibrated microphone is typically utilized. This is nothing more than a conventionally manufactured mic that is made to very strict tolerances, and then calibrated to a standard so any frequency response deviations can be compensated by the associated test equipment.

Our ears work differently. First, we normally work with two at all times. They are non-linear with respect to amplitude (reference the Fletcher-Munson equal loudness contours). They do, however, measure time of arrival of reflected sounds, and thereby provide phase information to our brains instead of the amplitude variation logged by the calibrated mic (which will result from phase additions and cancellations between reflected and direct (or multiple reflected) sound waves arriving at a single mic diaphragm.

Then, too, the microphone is connected to test equipment, and that equipment generally will examine only one or two parameters of the sound at a time: for example, distortion or amplitude response or phase response. Our ears listen to and evaluate all these factors at once, which can make a major difference.

9.1.2 Average Ears vs. "Golden Ears"

Just as the average man on the street could not be expected to walk into an athletic stadium and instantly become a referee qualified to make critical calls for a professional sports contest, neither can the average person be expected to make critical aural evaluations of a professional sound system. Most mixing engineers, as well as many musicians and producers, spend a lot of years fine-tuning their perceptions of sound. If you're not among these people, you may find this hard to believe, but many audio professionals really do hear things that the average person does not hear. Their eardrums may not vibrate any differently than the next person's, but they have acquired a heightened nerve-brain sensitivity and a greater ability to carefully interpret those physical vibrations. As a result, they often demand sonic improvements for defects that the average person may not perceive at all, or may discount as being unimportant. These audio professionals, along with many amateur audiophiles, should be treated with respect because they generally do have the so-called "golden ears" that have led to many of the refinements and improvements in sound equipment. From our experience, we'd give the golden ear the benefit of the doubt. If a qualified person claims to hear something significant in a sound system, and you don't hear it and can't seem to measure it, then you're probably not performing the appropriate tests.

There are, of course, wide areas of disagreement as to what sounds good and what sounds better. If someone just loves heavy bass, a flat amplitude response sound system will seem *thin*

and lacking *guts* to that person. That's why it is important to find outfirst what people want, and to have them demonstrate what they do and do not like, in order to interpret their criticisms or requests for a given system or piece of sound equipment.

9.2 Test Equipment Measurements vs. Listening Tests

It is never really possible to listen to a single component. There is always some kind of signal generator or signal source, some sort of amplifier, possibly a mixer or signal processor, and an output transducer (loudspeaker or headphone). In order to hear any one of these components, you will always be hearing the result as colored by the other components, as well as by the acoustic environment. On the other hand, you can test a given component by feeding a calibrated test signal to the input, and measuring the output directly, with no other equipment and few environmental factors to color the measurements.

9.2.1 Test Signals vs. Program Material

Consistent with this approach, many professionals will calibrate loudspeakers using single-frequency test tones or band-limited noise. Tones or noise are useful for balancing the output levels, and for adjusting equalization, but they are not representative of actual program material.

As an example, let's consider a stereo pair of full range loudspeakers,

each channel driven by one channel of a power amplifier. The amplifier, in turn, is preceeded by a pair of $\frac{1}{3}$-octave graphic equalizers. (Refer to Figure 9–1). Due to minor manufacturing variations in the loudspeakers, and a stage layout that is not entirely symmetrical (few are once equipment and props are in place), the listener perceives some difference between the left and right channels during the sound check. While repositioning the loudspeakers might improve the balance, this is not practical because they are hanging above the stage in semi-permanent fixtures. Therefore, the sound engineer (or contractor, or producer... whomever is responsible) reasons, the graphic EQ should be adjusted to obtain a better balance between the two loudspeakers.

The engineer wants as close a match as possible over a broad range of frequencies, so he drives each channel of the EQ/amp/speaker system with the same pink noise source (one at a time), measures the results on a real-time audio spectrum analyzer, and moves graphic EQ filter sliders up and down to get the best possible match between the two channels. This is a simplification, of course, but let's assume that the procedure works to the extent that the spectra for the two loudspeaker channels are within a dB of one another using the pink noise. Now what does it sound like?

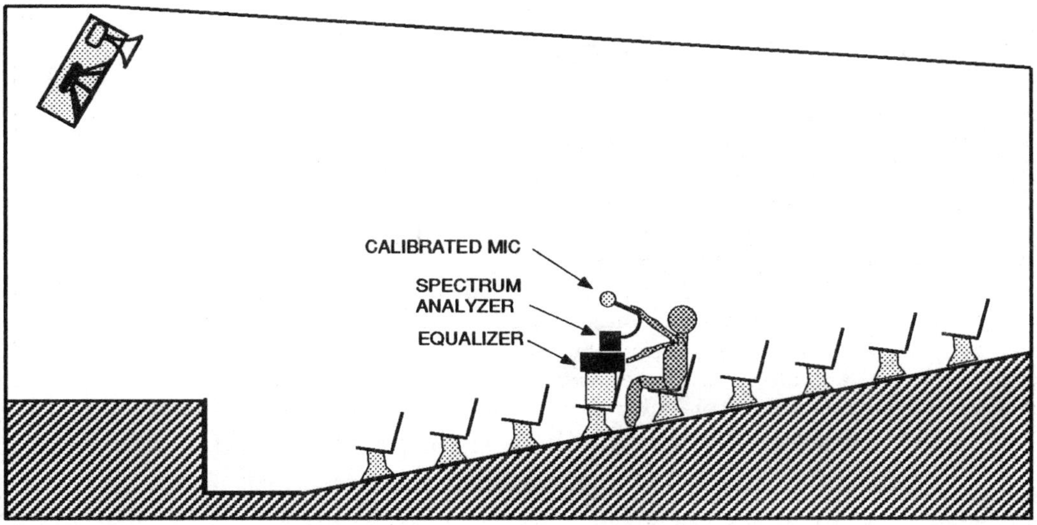

CALIBRATED MIC
SPECTRUM ANALYZER
EQUALIZER

Figure 9-1. Simplified illustration of loudspeaker system being fine-tuned to the environment

Running typical stereo program material through the system provides inconclusive results... the image may be wandering somewhat, and certain transients sound different in the two channels. Feeding the identical (mono) program to both channels yields even less pleasing results, with an obvious imbalance in sound quality between the two loudspeakers. What has occurred?

The carefully measured results using expensive test equipment, which indicated virtually identical output from each channel, are not verified by the listening tests.

There are probably several reasons why this hypothetical example often occurs in reality. For one thing, the spectrum analyzer was measuring only the amplitude of the signals, one channel at a time, not the phase shift within a channel or delay between the two. When program material is piped into the system, and the human ears are employed as the *analyzer*, then the other factors are measured. Equalization not only adjusts the amplitude in a given band (which is all the analyzer was evaluating), it also creates phase shift, and possibly other changes as

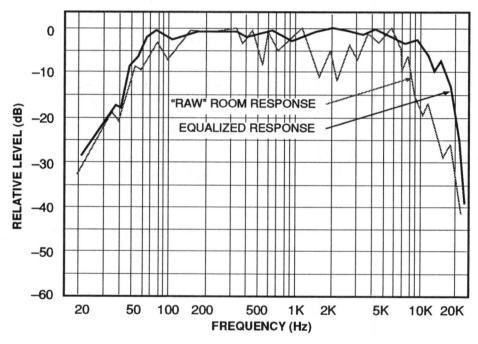

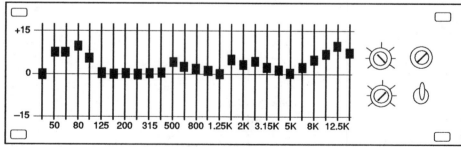

1/3 OCTAVE GRAPHIC EQUALIZER

Figure 9-2. Comparison of uncorrected and corrected spectrum analysis for a sound system, along with graphic EQ settings needed to achieve the corrections.

NOTE: *Phase shift, background noise, and changes in distortion and group delay are not directly indicated by the spectrum analyzer. Therefore, EQ corrections will not always produce the expected change in the curve.*

well, including various forms of distortion, and group delay (which may change the directional characteristics of the system, hence the reverberant field and certain comb filter effects due to interaction of direct and reflected sound waves). Since the EQ settings are not identical in each channel, the perceived sound quality changes, even though the amplitude response may be made nearly identical.

This illustrates one reason why instrumentation and ears don't always correspond. There is yet another factor involved, as detailed in Section 9.2.2.

9.2.2 Location and Number of Test Microphones

Normally, human hearing utilizes a pair of *mics* that we call ears, and their physical location in space is constantly changing to some extent (unless one's head is in a dental examination chair,

well braced against motion). The two ears receive slightly different versions of whatever sound source is exciting the environment... versions that differ in time of arrival and frequency balance. When sounds reflect from room boundaries, they often reach the two ears a split second apart, with the head shadowing (partially blocking and reducing the amplitude of) the higher frequencies at the ear opposite the sound source or the reflecting surface.

Reflections cancel or reinforce one another at different points in space, and at different frequencies at the same point. At the highest frequencies, the increased or decreased acoustic levels change as one moves just a few tenths of an inch. However, with the slight rocking and twisting motion of the head, one's ears and brain are able to construct an average of the sound field in the vicinity of the listener, and the result is what we perceive to be the sound of the system and the environment.

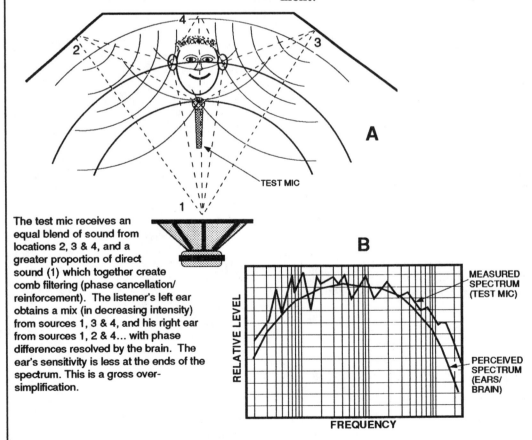

The test mic receives an equal blend of sound from locations 2, 3 & 4, and a greater proportion of direct sound (1) which together create comb filtering (phase cancellation/reinforcement). The listener's left ear obtains a mix (in decreasing intensity) from sources 1, 3 & 4, and his right ear from sources 1, 2 & 4... with phase differences resolved by the brain. The ear's sensitivity is less at the ends of the spectrum. This is a gross over-simplification.

Figure 9-3. Sound field comparison:
(A) Sound field at human ears and at a test mic
(B) Representative frequency response at the mic or ears

When a calibrated microphone hears sound for a spectrum analyzer, it *hears* it at only a single point. That point does not vary, assuming a fixed mic. Reflections that reinforce or cancel at a given frequency will tend to do so in a fixed, unvarying relationship, so that one can often observe deep notches and peaks (comb filtering) in the measured frequency response of the sound system. If you were to move the mic just a few inches to one side, the entire spectrum would probably change. Moving a few feet would, once again, cause major changes in the measured response. Therefore, it is misleading to make EQ or other adjustments merely by measuring the results at one point.

In fact, at least one test equipment manufacturer has offered a multiplexing system that averages three mics together to display a closer facsimile of the average sound field. However, it is important to note that the brain independently processes two different acoustic measurements, whereas mixing mic inputs together electrically will cause signal cancellation and reinforcement that do not yield the same kind of results as independent processing. For this reason, some analyzer manufacturers provide memories so that the response can be measured in several locations, and then the measured graphs can be overlaid on the analyzer display for human visual interpretation. This is an improvement, but it's not the same thing as our constantly shifting ears.

We often think of dynamic range in terms of the difference between the maximum level the sound system is capable of producing, and the background noise of the environment. Indeed, this is what we hear at concerts, speeches or shows. But test equipment also has a dynamic range, and often that range is considerably less than the dynamic range of the sound system. Until recently, for example, most spectrum analyzers could display only 30 dB on screen. Now better units generally display a 60 dB range, and some can do better. A good sound system, though, may be capable of 80 dB or, in some cases, 100 dB of useable dynamic range, and our ears have a range of some 120 dB or better. It's obvious that the spectrum analyzer cannot measure things that we may be hearing. Of course the analyzer may have attenuation pads or range switches so that it can ultimately measure all the sound, but it can't do it simultaneously the way our ears do.

Spectrum analyzers are not alone in this regard. Most audio test equipment — even the voltmeter — is limited in the scope of values it can measure without range switching. If an IM distortion product is 65 dB below the fundamental frequencies, it may not show up on the test equipment,but it may be very audible to the casual listener. This is yet another factor to consider when pondering why we may hear things that differ from what we measure.

9.3 Static vs Dynamic Tests

As we've hinted earlier, sometimes the ears don't match the tests simply because the right tests are not made. This is particularly evident when one considers the nature of static test signals (i.e., a sine wave tone or a steady noise signal) versus the typical program material (sharp attacks, wide dynamic changes, and sudden jumps in frequency).

Many tests are now made using tone bursts, which come closer to a program signal in this regard, but few printed specifications indicate the results of such tests.

When a circuit, or even a transformer or transducer, is subjected to a tone burst (or a loud percussive note), the component can ring. That is, the voltage in the circuit can overshoot the intended value, then resonate up and down until it settles. (Some circuits don't settle down, but instead go into oscillation; they are said to be unstable.) The same circuit may not exhibit any such behavior if the input signal is gradually increased in level, or is a steady state signal.

Ringing is often caused by improper loading, not only in terms of the load impedance itself, but in terms of how much capacitive or inductive reactance is part of that impedance. A power amplifier, for example, may perform flawlessly when bench tested with an 8 ohm, non-inductive resistor. Even the most stringent tone bursts may cause no aberrations. Connect that same amplifier to an 8 ohm electrostatic loudspeaker, which is mostly capacitive reactance, and it may sound awful. It may ring to the point of incipient oscillation, and its protection circuitry may trip so often as to chatter. The ringing may occur because a resonant circuit has been created. The protection problems may occur because reactive loads can force the output stage of the amplifier to dissipate up to twice the power of an equivalent (in ohms) purely resistive load.

The difference between static and dynamic testing is recognized in at least one specification, Transient Intermodulation Distortion (or TIM). In the early 1970s this measurement was first proposed as a way to quantify the audible distortion that occurred with

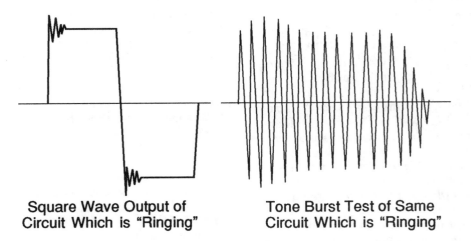

Square Wave Output of Circuit Which is "Ringing"

Tone Burst Test of Same Circuit Which is "Ringing"

Figure 9-4. A Square wave which shows "ringing" and a tone burst test of that same circuit

We can hear ringing as a form of distortion. Ideally there should be no overshoot or ringing in the circuitry of sound reinforcement or recording equipment. Equipment that is not tested with pulse or burst signals may look great on paper, but may perform disappointingly due to this type of circuit problem.

certain transient signals, even though the steady-state I.M. measurement would not indicate a serious distortion problem. It is interesting to note that this specification was long considered somewhat controversial, and not easily measured.

9.4 Masking Effects And Equipment Interaction

It is easy to make assumptions about specifications that do not reflect actual, perceived sound. Let's take a specific example: harmonic distortion. If a loudspeaker is rated at 1% T.H.D., and a power amplifier at 0.1% T.H.D., would you expect to hear the amplifier's distortion through the loudspeaker? Most people would answer, "no." In fact, many loudspeakers have measurable distortion of greater than 1%, and if one were to perform an A-B comparison to different power amps each having 0.1% T.H.D. ratings through such a speaker, the differences in sound quality would very possibly be audible. Why?

Well, the very term T.H.D. implies a sum—a total of various distortion components. As discussed earlier, the ear finds some harmonics more objectionable than others. Specifically, odd-order harmonics (3rd, 5th, 7th, etc.) are more harsh, and even-order harmonics (2nd, 4th, 6th, etc.) are more musical to the average listener. Also, higher order harmonics (6th, 7th, 8th, 9th, etc.) are more noticeable and objectionable than lower order harmonics (2nd, 3rd, 4th).

If the loudspeaker with 1% T.H.D. generates mostly 2nd and 4th harmonics, and the power amplifier with 0.1% T.H.D. happens to generate an inordinate amount of 5th and 7th harmonics, it may well be that the predominant audible problem is caused by the power amp. In this case, the much higher *total* percentage distortion in the loudspeaker does not mask the high order odd harmonics generated by the amp.

Granted, this is an extreme example, but it makes our point. Don't assume that a high noise level or distortion level in one piece of equipment makes it impossible to hear lesser noise or distortion in other components. A digital delay line's quantizing noise, for example, may be audible even though it is several dB below the noise floor of the analog equalizer to which it is connected. The organized digital hash can be recognized through the random analog hiss, even sometimes when it is below the room's noise level. (In fact, digital noise can be a real problem.) Similarly, some program signals can be heard below the noise floor, which is why the effective dynamic range may not exactly match the mathematical sum of the measured signal-to-noise ratio plus headroom.

Then, too, there are other psychoacoustic factors that may affect our perception of measurable performance defects. For example, tape recordings and certain synthesizers will exhibit a type of noise known as modulation noise. This consists of noise sidebands that accompany a given note. Fortunately, the ear tends not to hear sidebands within an octave or so on either side of the actual note, a so-called masking effect, and residual wideband noise tends to obscure the relatively low modulation noise energy beyond that 2-octave wide masking window. An exception can occur with a recording of a strong, low frequency note on a very quiet recorder. Say the note is at 82 Hz. It will have modulation noise sidebands at lower and higher frequencies. The lower frequency sidebands tend not to be audible because the ear is even less sensitive at the lowest frequencies, and because they are within the masking window. The higher frequency sidebands, however, occur in a frequency range where the ear is more sensitive, and may not be entirely masked by the note. What may be heard, then, is an increase in hiss when the note is played. If you listen to certain tape recordings, particularly of classical piano or guitar on an analog recorder in which noise reduction is used, you may be aware of this modulation noise. In most cases the residual background noise of the tape, along with the inherent masking of nearby frequencies by the very program signal that causes the modulation noise (or by other notes) will make the modulation noise inaudible. What can be measured may not be heard.

SECTION 10.
MICROPHONES

10.1 Methods of Transduction

Microphone is a generic term that is used to refer to any element which transforms acoustic energy (sound) into electrical energy (the audio signal). A microphone is therefore one type from a larger class of elements called transducers — devices which translate energy of one form into energy of another form.

The fidelity with which a microphone generates an electrical representation of a sound depends, in part, on the method by which it performs the energy conversion. Historically, a number of different methods have been developed for varying purposes, and today a wide variety of microphone types may be found in everyday use.

10.1.1 Dynamic

By far the most common type of microphone in contemporary sound work is the dynamic. The dynamic microphone is like a miniature loudspeaker — in fact, some dynamic elements serve dual functions as both loudspeaker and microphone (for example, in intercoms).

Figure 10-1 illustrates the basic construction of a dynamic microphone.

A flexibly-mounted diaphragm, Figure 10-1 (a), is coupled to a coil of fine wire (b). The coil is mounted in the air gap of a magnet (c) such that it is free to move back and forth within the gap.

When sound strikes the diaphragm, the diaphragm surface vibrates in response. The motion of the diaphragm couples directly to the coil, which moves back and forth in the field of the magnet. As the coil cuts through the lines of magnetic force in the gap, a small electrical current is induced in the wire. The magnitude and direction of that current is directly related to the motion of the coil, and the current thus is an electrical representation of the incident sound wave.

Dynamic microphones are highly dependable, rugged and reliable. For this reason, they are extremely common in stage use, where physical strength is very important. They are also reasonably insensitive to environmental factors, and thus find extensive use in outdoor paging applications. Finally, because moving-coil technology is fairly refined and is capable of very good sonic characteristics, dynamic microphones also are widely used in recording studios.

10.1.2 Condenser

Next to the dynamic, the most common microphone type is the condenser. Figure 10-2 illustrates the construction of a condenser element.

A gold-coated plastic diaphragm, Figure 10-2 (a), is mounted above a conductive back plate (b), which is often made of gold-plated ceramic. The diaphragm and back plate, separated by a small volume of air (c), form an electrical component called a capacitor (or condenser).

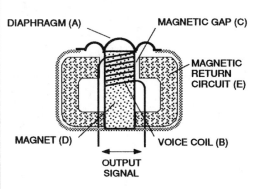

DIAPHRAGM (A)   MAGNETIC GAP (C)

MAGNETIC RETURN CIRCUIT (E)

MAGNET (D)   VOICE COIL (B)

OUTPUT SIGNAL

Figure 10-1. Construction of a dynamic microphone

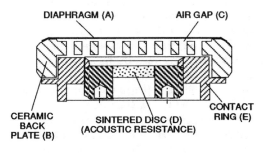

DIAPHRAGM (A)   AIR GAP (C)

CERAMIC BACK PLATE (B)   SINTERED DISC (D) (ACOUSTIC RESISTANCE)   CONTACT RING (E)

Figure 10-2. Construction of a condenser microphone

A polarizing voltage of between 9 and 48 volts is applied to the diaphragm by an external power supply, charging it with a fixed, static voltage. When the diaphragm vibrates in response to a sound, it moves closer to and farther from the back plate. As it does so, the electrical charge that it induces in the back plate changes proportionally. The fluctuating voltage on the back plate is therefore an electrical representation of the diaphragm motion.

Condenser microphone elements produce a signal voltage with almost no power. Thus they present a very high impedance. For these reasons, all condenser microphones incorporate an amplifier, which drives the microphone line. Its function is both to boost the signal level and to isolate the element from the lower impedance of the input to which the microphone is connected. Early condenser microphones employed tube amplifiers and thus were physically quite large. Modern condensers use transistor amplifiers, and can be made very small.

Because the diaphragm of a condenser is not loaded down with the mass of a coil, it can respond very quickly and accurately to an incident sound. Condensers therefore generally have excellent sonic characteristics, and are widely used in recording. Being somewhat more sensitive to physical shocks and environmental factors (humidity), however, classic condensers are less often used in sound reinforcement.

10.1.3 Electret Condenser

The electret is a special class of condenser microphone. Electrets incorporate diaphragms made of a unique plastic material that retains a static charge indefinitely. The manufacturer charges the diaphragm when the element is made (usually by irradiating it with an electron beam), and no external polarizing voltage is required.

Electrets still require a built-in amplifier, however, and this is normally a transistor unit. The amplifier often is powered with a battery — between 1.5 and 9 volts — housed in the microphone case. (In some designs, the amplifier and battery are housed in a small case that is connected to the element by a cable. Increasingly, phantom power is being used instead of a built-in battery on electret condenser models.) The purpose of the amplifier here is primarily to buffer the high impedance condenser capsule output from the relatively lower impedance of the mic input.

Electrets are increasingly common in both recording and reinforcement. Because they may be made very small, electrets make possible some unique close-miking techniques. The technology is also relatively inexpensive, so electret elements are often used in consumer products. Electrets can be of high quality, and some very fine electret microphones are available for professional recording and laboratory applications.

10.1.4 Ribbon

Ribbon microphones employ a transduction method that is similar to that of dynamics. Figure 10-3 illustrates the construction of a typical ribbon element.

A very light, thin, corrugated metal ribbon, Figure 10-3 (a), is stretched within the air gap of a powerful magnet (b). The ribbon is clamped at the ends, but is free to move throughout its length.

When sound strikes the ribbon, the ribbon vibrates in response. As is the case with the dynamic coil element, the moving ribbon cuts the magnetic lines of force in the air gap, and a voltage is thereby induced in the ribbon. The

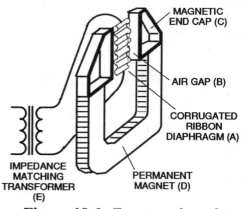

Figure 10-3. Construction of a ribbon microphone

voltage is very small and the ribbon impedance very low, so all ribbon microphones incorporate a built-in transformer. The transformer serves the dual functions of boosting the signal voltage and isolating the ribbon impedance from the load presented by the input to which the microphone is connected.

Early ribbon microphones were extremely fragile. The ribbon could be damaged simply by blowing or coughing into the microphone! Not many microphone manufacturers now make ribbon units, but those that are available are much more rugged than older units. All but a few modern ribbon mics remain more fragile than dynamic or condenser units, so they are used primarily in recording (a couple of notable exceptions are used for reinforcment).

Ribbon microphones usually have excellent sonic characteristics, with great warmth and gentle high-frequency response. They also have excellent transient response and very low self-noise. For these reasons, some ribbon mics are prized as vocal microphones, and are also very effective with acoustic instruments.

10.1.5 Carbon

The carbon type is among the earliest microphone elements ever developed. Figure 10-4 illustrates the construction of a typical carbon element.

A small cup, Figure 10-4 (a), is packed with pulverized carbon and enclosed at one end by a brass disk called a button (b), which is coupled to a circular metal diaphragm (c). The button and a back plate at the rear of the cylinder form the connection terminals. A battery (d) provides an activating voltage across the carbon.

When sound strikes the diaphragm, the carbon granules in the button vibrate, becoming alternately more and less dense as the diaphragm moves. The electrical resistance of the carbon thereby fluctuates, and converts the battery voltage into a corresponding fluctuating current that is an electrical representation of the sound. The current is stepped up by a transformer (e), which also serves to isolate the low

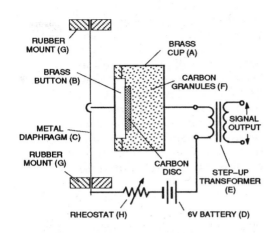

Figure 10-4. Construction of a carbon microphone

impedance of the element from that of the input to which it is connected, and to block the battery DC from the input.

Carbon microphones are not known for excellent sonic characteristics, but they are quite inexpensive, and rugged. For this reason, they are still widely used in utility sound applications. (The standard telephone mic element has long been a carbon type, although dynamic mics are used in many newer phones.) Carbon microphones can lose some efficiency and become noisy if the granules in the button become compacted, but simply tapping the element against a hard surface usually cures the problem.

Another very early microphone type is the piezoelectric. Figure 10-5 illustrates the principle of piezoelectric microphones.

A flexible diaphragm, Figure 10-5 (a) is coupled to a crystal element (b) by a drive pin (c). The crystal element is of a material that exhibits the piezoelectric (*pressure-electric*) effect. When it is physically deformed by pressure or torsion, the crystal generates an electrical voltage (potential) across its faces.

When sound strikes the diaphragm it vibrates, and the crystal is thereby deformed slightly. The crystal generates a voltage in response to this bending, and this varying voltage is an electrical representation of the sound.

Piezoelectric microphones (sometimes called *crystal* or *ceramic* types), like carbon types, are not generally known for their sound quality, but are quite inexpensive. Properly implemented, a crystal element can perform very well, and the principle is often used for contact-type pickups.

Piezo elements are high-impedance devices, and they produce substantial output levels. They can be damaged irreparably by physical abuse, and are susceptible to both heat and humidity.

In addition to the method of

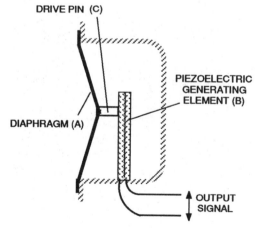

Figure 10-5. Construction of a piezoelectric microphone

transduction and pickup pattern, microphones are further classified according to their functional design. Many different microphone designs are available, and each is optimized for a specific range of applications.

10.2.1 Hand-Held

By far the most prominent microphone design is the hand-held type. Figure 10-6 shows a few typical hand-held microphones.

As the name implies, this micro-

Figure 10-6. A few typical hand-held microphones

phone is designed so that it may be held in hand by a lecturer or singer. Of course, such microphones also are very often mounted on a stand using a threaded mounting clip.

The most common pattern in hand-held microphones is the cardioid, although other patterns are available. Whatever the pickup pattern or type of capsule (sound generating element), if it's in a hand-held mic, it must be well isolated from physical vibration to prevent handling noise, and the capsule must be protected from being dropped. Rubber shock mounts and protective screens are standard features of most hand-held mics.

10.2.2 Stand-Mounting

10.2.3 Lavalier

Some microphones are designed specifically for stand (or boom) mounting only; Figure 10-7 shows examples of such microphones.

Lavalier microphones are very small elements that are designed to pin directly to clothing or to be hung on a lanyard around the neck. Figure 10-8 (next page) shows a typical lavalier microphone.

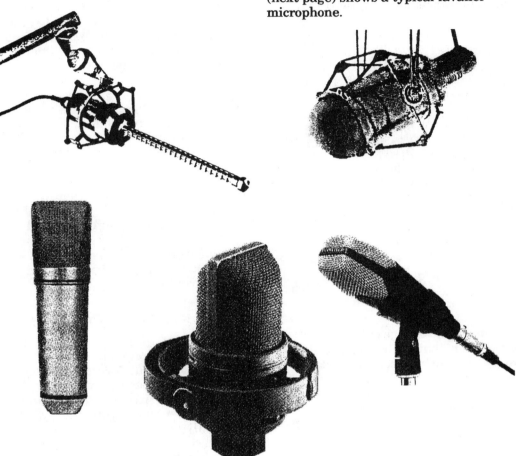

Figure 10-7. Stand mount microphones

Microphones like this are most commonly made for recording. Typically, older tube-type condensers were made for stand-mounting only, being too large for convenient hand-held use. Even the most modern mics, however, may be designed for stand mount in the studio because more elaborate external shock and vibration isolation is then possible. Video and motion picture production mics, mounted on booms, are often elaborately shock mounted to keep vibration out of the mic. Smaller, very unobtrusive modern stand-mounting microphones are usually electret types, and are designed specifically for reinforcement and broadcasting applications where appearance is a primary consideration.

It used to be that lavaliers were nearly always dynamics, since they were much less costly to build in the required small package. Modern lavalier microphones are almost always electret condenser types, since electret elements now can be made very small in size, offering excellent top-end response and sensitivity for a reasonable cost. The most common pattern for lavaliers is omnidirectional, although recently some cardioid and hypercardioid types have been introduced. The omni pattern has several advantages in this application. It does not emphasize the already resonant chest cavity because it does not have proximity effect, and it can be clipped in different orientations without its sound quality changing. This is crucial if the sound is to remain consistent.

Lavalier microphones are widely used in television broadcasting, since they can be made very unobtrusive. For the same reason, they are also often used in theatre (coupled with a wireless transmission system).

Figure 10-8. A typical lavalier microphone

A major advantage of lavalier elements is that, since they are affixed to the speaker's person, the distance between source and microphone is constant and sound quality therefore is more consistent. Lavaliers must be mounted with care to avoid extraneous noise from clothing.

10.2.4 Contact Pickup

Contact pickups are microphone elements that are designed to detect sound waves in a solid medium, rather than in air. Figure 10-9 shows one type of contact pickup.

Contact pickups are most commonly piezoelectric devices, although the dynamic principle has been used for this application, also. A recent type of contact transducer that has garnered considerable interest in sound reinforcement circles uses the condenser principle, and comes in the form of a flexible strip.

Contact pickups are used almost exclusively for instruments (the exception is throat microphones, which are sometimes used in communications), and their placement is extremely critical. The complex resonant characteris-

tics of instrument bodies result in radically different sound qualities in different locations, and considerable experimentation is necessary to achieve satisfactory results. The means by which they are affixed to the instrument can affect the sound quality and the instrument. A sticky wax is often used, since it can be removed without damaging the instrument.

Figure 10-9. A typical contact microphone

Because contact pickups rarely yield a true sound quality, they are not often used in recording, except for special effects. In reinforcement, however, they offer exceptional resistance to feedback, but they can be very susceptible to handling noise.

10.2.5 Pressure Response

The so-called pressure response microphone is a fairly recent development, and is subject to patent and trademark restrictions. The commercial implementation of the principle is commonly called the PZM™, and is manufactured under a licensing agreement by Crown International of Elkhart, Indiana. Figure 10-10 shows one of the Crown PZM™ units.

The microphone element is placed extremely close to and facing a flat plate. In theory, the microphone samples pressure variations in the tiny air gap between the element and the plate, rather than responding to air velocity.

Figure 10-10. A Crown Pressure Zone Microphone (Courtesy of Crown International Corp.)

10.2.7 Parabolic

The parabolic microphone is actually a conventional mic element coupled with a reflector that concentrates sound on the element. Figure 1-12 (a) shows the principle of operation, and Figure 10-12 (b) a polar pattern for this type of mic.

The parabolic reflector is a cup-shaped surface whose cross section is a curve that is called a parabola. Mathematically, the parabola is built around a focal point and a plane surface. Acoustically, the parabolic reflector concentrates all sound that arrives along the primary axis to a point located at the mathematical focus. It is thus highly directional, and serves to increase the sensitivity of the mic element dramatically.

Parabolic microphones are used widely in nature recording. Since their low-frequency response is directly related to their size, practical hand-held units are limited to frequencies above about 1 kHz and thus are most useful for bird and insect songs. For years they have been seen on the sidelines at football games so broadcast audiences can listen to on-field sounds, such as bodies colliding on a football field. Parabolic microphones are never used in reinforcement.

Originally developed for recording and implemented using condenser instrumentation elements, the pressure zone principle offers certain benefits. Among these are good imaging qualities and, if the element is mounted on a floor or wall, freedom from path-length cancellations. Low-frequency response of the pressure-zone microphone is directly related to the size of the boundary plate. The larger the plate, the better the pickup of lows.

Pressure-zone microphones are sometimes used in sound reinforcement, but since they are inherently omnidirectional, they offer little help with feedback. Recently, directional units have been developed to deal with this problem, and are finding some application in conferencing situations as well as instrument amplification.

10.2.6 Shotgun

The shotgun microphone is a highly directional unit. Figure 1-11 shows a typical shotgun microphone.

Shotgun microphones are most often used in broadcasting, and they are particularly popular in film work, where isolating actors' dialog from ambient noise is a constant concern. They are also sometimes employed creatively for special effects in the studio. Shotgun mics are also used for long distance pickup in some sports events. Successful use of shotgun microphones in reinforcement is rare.

Figure 10-11. A typical shotgun microphone

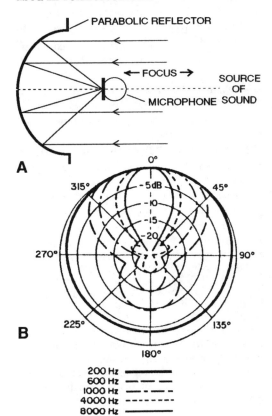

Figure 10-12. A Parabolic mic:
(a) Principle of operation
(b) Polar response

10.2.8 Multi-Element Arrays

A few special microphones have been constructed using two or more transducer elements. Such units normally require auxilliary networks to control the combining of signals from the elements.

One such unit is called a two-way cardioid microphone. This device uses two elements — one for high frequencies and another for lows — much like a two-way loudspeaker. A crossover network combines the signals from the two elements, crossing over at about 500 Hz. Advantages of the technique are wide and flat frequency response both on and off axis, and absence of proximity effect (see Sections 10.3.2 and 10.3.3).*

Another multi-element system is the stereo recording microphone, which incorporates two identical elements in a single body. Several manufacturers produce such units, usually employing condenser elements. Some advantages in recording are relative freedom from phase discrepancies between channels, ease of use, and unobtrusive appearance (which is of particular benefit in live recording).

An unusual application of multi-element technology is the Calrec Soundfield™ microphone, designed by Calrec of England for stereo recording. Four condenser elements are mounted in a tetrahedral arrangement and connected with a special active combining network. The unit produces a set of signals which, when recorded on a multitrack recorder, can be reprocessed in the studio to steer the stereo image as desired. Both imaging and sound quality are said to be excellent, and the unit is finding increasing use in professional recording.

---

* Originally, all cardioid mics were dual-element mics, though the two elements were used to achieve directionality... a large, expensive method to build a mic. Other cardioid mics used complex plumbing (ducts and ports) to achieve directionality with a single element, though these were very large and expensive, too. In 1940, the first single-element self-patterning cardioid mic was developed, ultimately leading to smaller cardioid mics.

10.2.9 Noise-Cancelling Microphones

Noise-cancelling (or differential) microphones employ either two mic capsules wired in reverse polarity, or a single diaphragm that is open on both sides to sound pickup. Such mics tend to discriminate for close on-axis sound sources, which produce higher pressure on one side of the diaphragm (or one one of the capsules) than on the other. More distant and off-axis sounds tend to produce equal pressures on both sides of the single diaphragm (or on both capsules) and thus are cancelled.

Differential microphones are used for speech communication only, and are most beneficial in noisy environments like factories or airplane cockpits. (If you are using one, be sure you're speaking directly into it at a distance of less than 2 inches — or it will treat your voice, however loud, like noise and reject it.)

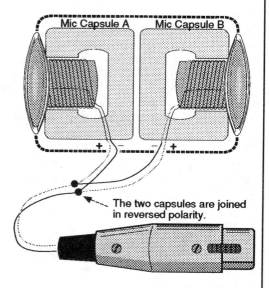

Figure 10-13. Cross-sectional view of a dual-element differential microphone.

10.3 Acoustical And Electrical Characteristics

The acoustical and electrical characteristics of a microphone together determine both the quality of its performance and its suitability for a particular application or system. No single factor predominates; all work together, and it is important to understand the range of qualities that may be expected in typical professional and semi-professional equipment. After all, even a mediocre system has a better chance of performing well if the sound source is clean, and even the best sound system can't make a poor quality mic sound good.

10.3.1 Pickup Patterns

Microphones are classified not only by the method of transduction but also by their pickup pattern. The pickup pattern is the way in which the element responds to sounds coming in from different directions, and there are several different standard patterns. (This is akin to the polar response of a loudspeaker... in reverse.)

10.3.1.1 Omnidirectional

Omnidirectional elements, as their name implies, pick up sound more-or-less equally from all directions. Figure 10-15 (next page) shows a set of polar response patterns for a typical omni microphone.

One might think that omnidirectional microphones are never used in sound reinforcement, since they offer no protection from feedback. This is generally the case, but not entirely so. There is a myth that cardioids are better, but omnis have better low frequency response, and less susceptibility to breath noise and wind noise. Because omnidirectional mics tend to have much smoother frequency response than directional mics, there are fewer peaks to trigger feedback, so sometimes a good omni is as useful (or more so) as a mediocre directional mic. Lavalier mics (mics worn on a lanyard around the neck, or clipped to a shirt) are often omnis. Omni mics are quite

useful in recording, and virtually every studio owns at least a few of them.

10.3.1.2 Cardioid

The cardioid is unreservedly the most popular of all microphone pickup patterns. Figure 10-14 shows a typical cardioid polar response pattern.

Note that the pattern is heart-shaped — hence the name "cardioid." As Figure 10-14 clearly shows, the cardioid microphone is most sensitive to sounds coming in on the primary axis, and rejects sounds from the sides and rear of the microphone.

The directional qualities of the cardioid make it a natural choice for sound reinforcement, since they help in reducing feedback and increasing system gain (see Section 5.3, "Feedback Control"). This effect is overrated, and omnidirectional mics are often a better choice for close work than is a cardioid. Cardioids tend to have more coloration when sound does not arrive on axis because their directional qualities vary with frequency.

Cardioids are quite common in recording, since they can be used to diminish unwanted sounds arriving from off-axis. Their frequency response is usually rougher than that of an omni and they are somewhat more sensitive to wind noise and breath popping.

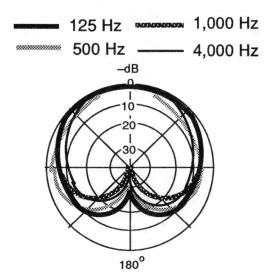

Figure 10-14. Polar pattern of a cardioid microphone

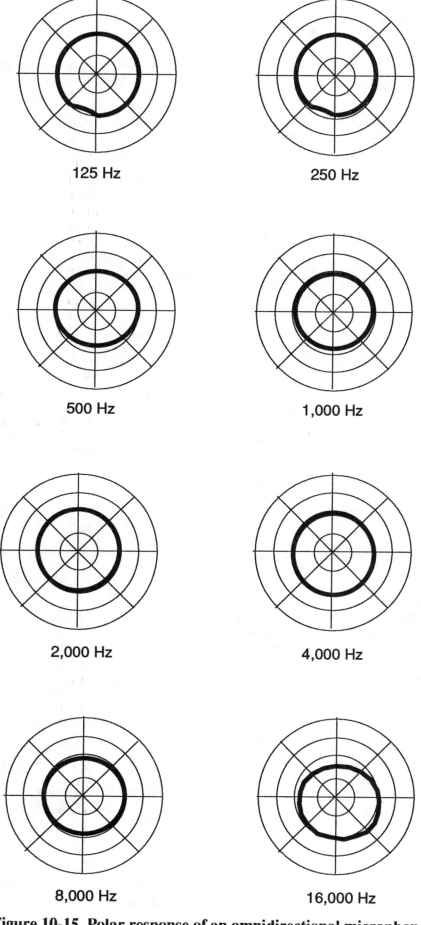

125 Hz

250 Hz

500 Hz

1,000 Hz

2,000 Hz

4,000 Hz

8,000 Hz

16,000 Hz

Figure 10-15. Polar response of an omnidirectional microphone

10.3.1.3 Bidirectional or Figure-8

A somewhat more unusual but very useful pickup pattern is the so-called figure-8 or bidirectional. Figure 10-16 shows a typical polar response plot of a bidirectional element.

The derivation of the name for this pattern is obvious from Figure 10-16. Bidirectional elements are most sensitive to sounds coming in from the front or rear of the microphone, and reject sounds from the sides.

Figure-8 microphones are very useful in circumstances where pickup of two separate voices is desired — for example, in an interview situation or a barbershop quartet (where opposing singers can see each other and be picked up, but the audience is off axis and is not picked up). In recording and reinforcement, the figure-8 may be used to pick up two adjacent instruments when separate control is not desired. For example, it may be placed between two tom-toms in a drum set.

10.3.1.4 Supercardioid

The supercardioid is a highly directional microphone element. Figure 10–17 shows a polar response plot of a typical supercardioid microphone.

Note that, in contrast to the cardioid, the supercardioid does exhibit more of a rear pickup lobe, though small. It thus supplies far less rejection of sounds coming in directly from the rear than does the cardioid. The forward pickup lobe is far more concentrated and the supercardioid offers superior rejection of sounds coming in from the sides.

Supercardioids are used in special situations where greater side rejection is desired, but some rear pickup may be tolerated. Because of the concentrated forward lobe, they also may "reach" farther than a typical cardioid, and are sometimes used for pickup of distant sources.

Incidentally, the supercardioid is similar to, but not identical to another very directional microphone, the hypercardioid.

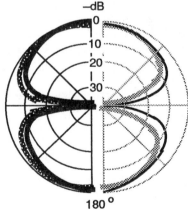

Figure 10-16. Polar pattern of a figure 8 microphone

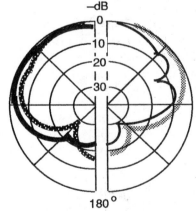

Figure 10-17. Polar pattern of a supercardioid microphone

The frequency response of a microphone is a measure of the consistency with which it translates a given sound pressure level into a given audio signal level at different frequencies.

We could say that an ideal microphone would translate a given pressure level to the same signal level no matter what the frequency (within the limits of the audio band, or 20 Hz to 20 kHz). Such a microphone would be said to have flat frequency response.

While some recording microphones and many instrumentation microphones closely approach this ideal, most of the units used in professional sound work deviate from flat response — sometimes quite significantly. But frequency response variations are not necessarily bad. They are often introduced intentionally in order to produce specific performance advantages in practical applications. If you know the response of a particular microphone, you may be able to use that response to compensate for deficiencies in the quality of a sound source.

At the low end, it is not uncommon for a microphone's response to fall off below about 100 Hz, particularly in the case of vocal microphones. Since the human voice is generally incapable of producing energy that low in frequency, the effect of this limitation is to discriminate for voice frequencies, and simultaneously help to eliminate extraneous noise. For instrument amplification and recording, response to 50 Hz or below is preferred.

Many microphones exhibit a response peak in the upper frequencies. This is called a presence peak, and again is characteristic of vocal microphones. A presence peak can help to increase the intelligibility of words, so it may be a desirable characteristic. But it can also increase the possibility of feedback in sound reinforcement and is generally to be avoided in mics used for recording.

It is most important, in the case of directional microphones, that the frequency response remain reasonably flat off-axis, although the sensitivity drops. Otherwise there will be a change in tonality if the person or instrument being picked up by the mic shifts off axis. Hand-held mics are most susceptible, since a slight change in the angle on which they are held

will change the tonal color unless the mic has uniform frequency response off axis. Even if a mic remains in a stand, the response should be uniform off axis, or any reverberant energy will have a distorted tonal color.

Uniform frequency response off axis is characteristic of good quality mics, and is one performance aspect to look for in selecting a microphone. It is probably more important than the absolute sensitivity or the actual response on axis. Remember, if the frequency response gets rough off-axis, then the quality of a voice will change as the performer moves around in front of the mic. This is hardly desirable!

Frequency response variations are a major factor governing a microphone's characteristic sound. It is important that the sound of a mic be matched to the application and the sound source, and this is best done by ear. You can get a clue from the spec sheet. For instance, a rising response with a peak in the 5 to 8 kHz range indicates the mic is probably optimized for lead vocals, some solo instruments, and for ordinary speech reinforcement. A mic with extended low frequency response and not particularly extended high frequency response would be useful for drums or other low frequency instruments. A mic with very flat response may be useful in recording, as well as in reinforcement. Since transient quality, coloration, and other factors affecting sound quality are difficult to measure with any single specification, it is difficult to provide useful guidelines for selection of a mic simply by reading the spec sheet. When in doubt, listen.

10.3.3 Proximity Effect

Proximity effect is an increase in low-frequency response when a microphone is very close to the sound source, and is an inherent characteristic of directional microphones (omnis do not exhibit the effect). Figure 10-18 illustrates proximity effect.

Proximity effect increases dramatically when the microphone is less than 2 feet away from the source, and can produce 16 dB or more of bass boost. (Actually, the overall sound level increases due to the closer proximity of the sound source to the mic, but higher frequencies are cancelled more than lower ones by the mic at this distance, so there is the equivalent of bass boost.) This can sometimes cause preamplifier overload, resulting in gross distortion. Announcers and vocalists often use proximity effect to add fullness to the sound of the voice and an experienced performer incorporates it as part of his or her mic technique. Public speakers, by contrast, are often naive about the effect, and it often destroys intelligibility in public address applications (a low cut filter is usually an effective cure in this case).

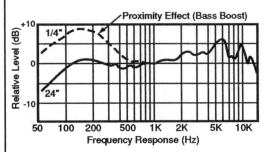

Figure 10-18. Proximity Effect

10.3.4 Transient Response

Transient response is a measure of a microphone's ability to render very sharp, fast musical attacks and signal peaks. The main limitation on transient response is diaphragm mass, so condensers and ribbon mics generally exhibit better transient response than even the best dynamics. Figure 10-19 shows a transient response comparison between a typical dynamic (top trace) and a condenser (bottom trace).

Transient response is not very important in vocal reproduction, but it attains great importance with percussive sources such as drums, piano and plucked string instruments. The transient nature of such sources is an integral part of their musical personality, so the ability to render transients accurately is highly desirable when working with them — either in reinforcement or recording. A ribbon or condenser is the best choice here.

Generally speaking, the smaller a microphone, the better its transient response will be. This is because a smaller diaphragm has less mass and thus responds more quickly. The trend in recent years has been toward smaller microphones — this is due in part to the development of better electret elements — so transient response has been getting better. As a rule, you can expect modern electret units to have excellent transient characteristics.

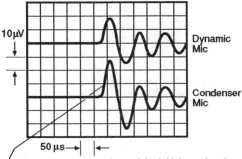

Note the steep wavefront of the initial transient is much more accurately traced by the condenser mic. The rest of the test signal is lower in frequency and amplitude, and is reproduced about the same by either mic.

Figure 10-19. Comparison of transient response in typical condenser and dynamic microphones

10.3.5 Output Level or Sensitivity

Since the transduction element invariably is very small, microphones generate small signal levels when compared with line-level devices such as mixing consoles or tape machines. For this reason, a microphone requires a preamplifier to bring its output signal up to line level (see Section 11). This function is normally included in the mixing console or recorder to which the microphone is connected. (The impedance converter contained in condenser-type mics should not be confused with a preamplifier. Condenser mics still require a preamplifier to be consistent with line level.)

Microphone output level is always specified with reference to a specific input sound pressure level, usually at 1000 Hz. The specification is thus an indicator of the sensitivity of the unit. A more sensitive microphone will produce more output level at a given SPL.

Two reference SPL levels are commonly used for microphone ouput level specifications. These are 74 dB SPL (which is the level of an average speaking voice at a distance of 3 feet) and 94 dB SPL (corresponding to a relatively loud speaking voice at 1 foot). These levels may also be expressed as:

74 dB SPL = 1 microbar or 1 dyne/cm^2

94 dB SPL = 10 microbar or 10 dyne/cm^2

Microbars and dynes-per-square-centimeter are both units of pressure.

The microphone output signal level is given in dB, with either of two different references: dBV (dB re 1 volt) and dBm (dB re 1 milliwatt). The first is a voltage reference and the second is a power reference, so the two units are not directly comparable without knowing the specific load impedance (see Sections 13 and 14).

A typical microphone sensitivity specification, then, might read:

SENSITIVITY:
-74 dBm re 1mW/microbar

Translated, this means that the microphone will deliver a signal at 1 microbar whose power is 74 dB below one milliwatt. To determine the signal voltage that this power level corresponds to, we need to know the load impedance.

A more useful form of sensitivity specification is:

SENSITIVITY:
Output level of -47 dBV at 94 dB SPL

This specification needs no translation, and allows direct and simple calculation of the output signal voltage at various sound pressure levels.

10.3.6 Overload

Distortion in a sound system is often blamed on microphone overload. In fact, it is rarely the mic that is overloading, but usually the preamplifier stage to which it is connected. A good quality professional microphone should be able to withstand sound pressure levels of 140 dB SPL or more without overloading. This is 10 dB beyond the threshold of pain!

The overload point of a microphone can be very important in some reinforcement applications, however. While the peak level seen by a mic from a rock vocalist who swallows the microphone may be 130 dB SPL or a bit more, the peak levels encountered when close-miking drums can easily be 140 dB SPL. For such applications, then, we should look for a unit with an overload point approaching 150 dB SPL. With condenser mics, the overload point will be reduced if a lower battery (or phantom power) voltage is applied. If your battery-powered mic becomes distorted for no apparent reason, replace the battery. If a phantom powered mic develops distortion at high sound levels (high, but still within the realm the mic should be able to handle), you can try using a higher phantom voltage supply, if permitted by the mic manufacturer.

It is important to relate the overload point of a microphone to its sensitivity. Consider, for example, a mic with a sensitivity rating of -47 dBV at 94 dB SPL. If we use this mic in close proximity to a drum, it may see peak levels of 140 dB SPL. The output level then would be:

$$-47 + (140 - 94) = -1 \text{ dBV}$$

or very close to 1 volt! This will certainly overload the mixer's preamplifier stage unless a pad is used to drop the signal level. (Most quality mixers will provide such a pad, either switch-activated or in the form of a continuous rotary control.)

10.3.7 Impedance

The source impedance of a microphone is the equivalent total AC resistance to current flow that would be seen looking into the microphone's output (see Section 8). Source impedance determines the size of the load that the microphone can comfortably drive. Ideally, a microphone should be connected to a load whose input impedance is roughly ten times the mic's source, or output, impedance.

Microphones are usually divided into two basic classes: high impedance and low impedance. Most professional microphones are low impedance devices, meaning that their source impedance is below 150 ohms (so they should be terminated by a 1,000 to 1,500 ohm input). Piezoelectric contact pickups, guitar pickups and inexpensive microphones are usually high impedance, meaning that their source impedance is 25 kohms or greater (they benefit from 50 kohm to 250 kohm actual load impedances).

Low impedance microphones are preferred in sound reinforcement and recording since, properly connected, they are far less susceptible to extraneous noise pickup in the cable (they are sensing more current than voltage, so noise must have more energy to get into the circuit). Such devices usually require a transformer, when they are connected to a high impedance input, to preserve their noise immunity. More important, low impedance mics can drive cables hundreds of feet long, whereas high impedance mics are limited to about 20 foot long cables.

High impedance microphones and pickups require a transformer or buffer amplifier when they are used with low-impedance inputs and/or long mic cables. In this case, the transformer converts the devices' high impedance to a low impedance suitable for driving the connection. High impedance mics and pickups usually produce a larger

output signal voltage, which may be why they are often used in inexpensive equipment. Another reason is that without the cost of the transformer or buffer amplifier, or the 3-pin XLR type connector, such mics are usually less expensive to manufacture than a low impedance mic.

Microphone impedance bears no consistent relationship to price and quality. It is a design factor that is weighed like any other in optimizing a mic for a given application. The important point is simply that we must know the source impedance of the microphone, and provide the appropriate circuit or matching transformer to mate it with the input to which it will be connected.

10.3.8 Balanced and Unbalanced Connections

An unbalanced connection is a two-wire system. One wire carries the audio signal, and the other (called the shield) is connected to ground, or the electrical reference point. Another term for unbalanced circuits is single-ended, although we don't feel the term is particularly precise since it is also used to describe the operation of certain noise reduction systems.

A balanced connection is a three-wire system. Two separate wires carry the signal — one inverted in polarity with respect to the other — and the third is the shield, which again is connected to ground.

Balanced connections are almost always used for low impedance microphones. The balanced system is more immune to noise, and is by far the preferred method in professional audio. The most common balanced connector is the three-pin XLR-type, which is chosen for several reasons. It has 3 conductors, it is shielded, it locks in place, and the ground pin makes contact first to bleed static from the cable and avoid pops.

Unbalanced connections are used for high-impedance microphones and pickups, and sometimes for low impedance mics in consumer equipment. The unbalanced system is susceptible to noise pickup, and is generally not preferred in professional work. The most common unbalanced microphone connector is the ¼-inch phone connector.

Particularly for microphones, balanced connections should be used wherever possible. Sometimes this will require the addition of an external transformer at the mixer input, but the advantages in noise immunity and reliability more than justify the added expense.

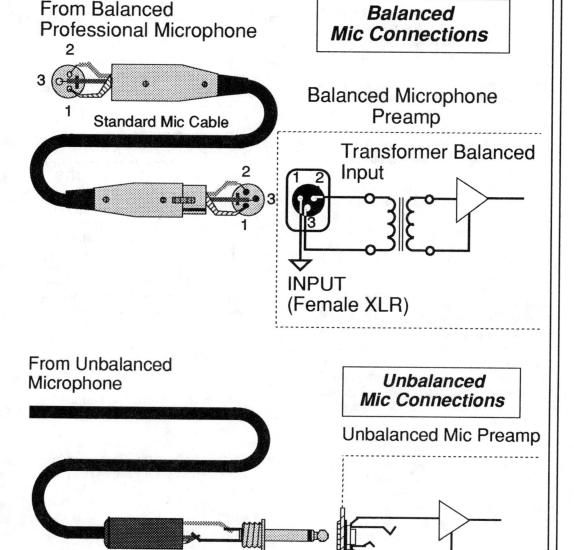

From Balanced
Professional Microphone

2
3
1
Standard Mic Cable

2
3
1

**Balanced
Mic Connections**

Balanced Microphone
Preamp

Transformer Balanced
Input

1   2
3

INPUT
(Female XLR)

From Unbalanced
Microphone

**Unbalanced
Mic Connections**

Unbalanced Mic Preamp

INPUT
(Female 1/4"
Tip/Sleeve Phone Jack)

Figure 10-20. Balanced and unbalanced microphone connections

10.4 Application Information

10.4.1 Windscreens and Pop Filters

Every microphone is, to some extent, susceptible to extraneous noise from breath pops or, outdoors, from wind. In severe cases, these noises can destroy intelligibility or damage particularly sensitive loudspeakers. For the most part, the effect of air noise is more pronounced with directional microphones, such as those used in both recording and reinforcement.

Every microphone manufacturer provides some sort of windscreen, which is basically an air velocity filter that protects the diaphragm element from air noise. The most common modern type is made of highly porous acoustical foam. Typical foam and metal mesh covered foam windscreens are shown in Figure 10-21.

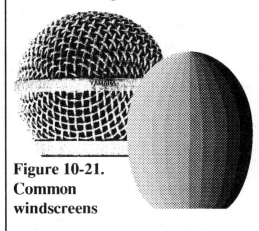

Figure 10-21. Common windscreens

The foam is essentially transparent to sound pressure waves, but acts like a kind of labyrinth for high velocity wind or breath gusts. The air gusts lose their energy as they travel through the channels in the foam, so that they dissipate before reaching the diaphragm.

In recording studios, breath pops are occasionally a problem while recording vocalists. A simple pop filter consisting of nylon mesh stretched on a small hoop can help. The hoop is mounted directly to the microphone, about 3 to 6 inches away from the microphone body. The vocalist sings at the microphone through the nylon mesh, which stops the gusts produced by explosive consonants such as p's and t's.

In an emergency, a makeshift windscreen can be made from a white athletic sock slipped over the microphone. While this is hardly the most attractive solution from a visual standpoint, it can save the day in outdoor paging applications. Then, too, you might just try switching from a cardioid to an omnidirectional mic, which may sufficiently reduce wind noise or vocal pops to eliminate the need for any sort of wind sock or filter.

10.4.2 Shock Mounts

Stand mounted microphones are sometimes subject to physical vibrations coupled from the stand to the mic housing through the mounting clip. To diminish this source of extraneous noise, some microphone manufacturers provide shock absorbing mounts. One typical such mount is shown in Figure 10-22.

Here, the mic is suspended within a frame by a kind of cat's cradle of elastic bands, which effectively absorbs noises from jarring of the stand.

In an emergency, a makeshift shock mount may be improvised with a piece of acoustical foam or kitchen sponge and some duct tape. Wrap the foam or sponge around the mic housing and secure it with a bit of tape, then fix the mic to the stand with more tape. Again, this may look a bit scruffy, but it can greatly improve shock isolation.

Figure 10-22. A typical shock-mounted microphone on a stand

10.4.3 Phantom Power

Condenser microphones require a polarizing voltage and power for their built-in amplifiers. Sometimes provision is made to supply this voltage directly through the microphone cable. The procedure is called phantom powering, and the most common phantom supply voltage available in mixing consoles is 48 VDC, although 24 V supplies are widely used. Most phantom powered mics can operate on a wide range of supply voltages from as little as 1.5 or 9 volts up to 50 volts.

In a phantom power system, the polarizing supply voltage is placed on both of the signal lines in a balanced connection, with the same polarity on each line. Dynamic microphones connected in a balanced system with a phantom power input are then protected from damage, theoretically, since the system results in a net zero DC potential across the coil. A dynamic mic connected unbalanced to a phantom power input may be destroyed, however!

It is therefore very important to be aware of whether a mixing console input is wired for phantom power. Most such inputs provide a switch to disable the phantom power when it is not needed. Always be sure that this switch is set to *off* when dynamics, or electret condensers with internal batteries, are connected to the input.

Figure 10-23 illustrates how phantom power is delivered to the impedance converter in a mic along the same conductors that carry audio from the mic to the console preamplifier.

10.4.4 Effect of the Number of Open Microphones (NOM)

As we learned in Sections 5 and 6, a primary concern in sound reinforcement is maximizing a system's acoustic gain. To do so, we must:

a) keep the distance between the mic and loudspeaker as large as is practical;
b) keep the distance between the mic and the source as small as is practical; and
c) use directional mics and loudspeakers, placed so that their interaction is minimized.

All the calculations in our discussion of system gain and feedback control assume a single mic. It is intuitively obvious that as we add mics to a system, the potential acoustic gain must decrease and feedback potential rise. In actual fact, every time you double the number of open mics (mics that are turned on or whose level is brought up on the mixing console), the system gain must be reduced by 3 dB to avoid feedback.

In operating a sound system, then, we need to be aware that it is best at any given time to turn on only those mics that are required. So long as a given microphone is not used at any time, it should be muted, or its fader on the mixer should be brought down. There is something to be said for using the least number of mics that you can get away with. It's fine to try to duplicate studio quality in stage work, but using six or eight mics on the drum set might be self-defeating.

All of this means more work and a greater demand for creativity from the sound engineer, but it can result in higher system gain, better sound quality, and less potential for feedback.

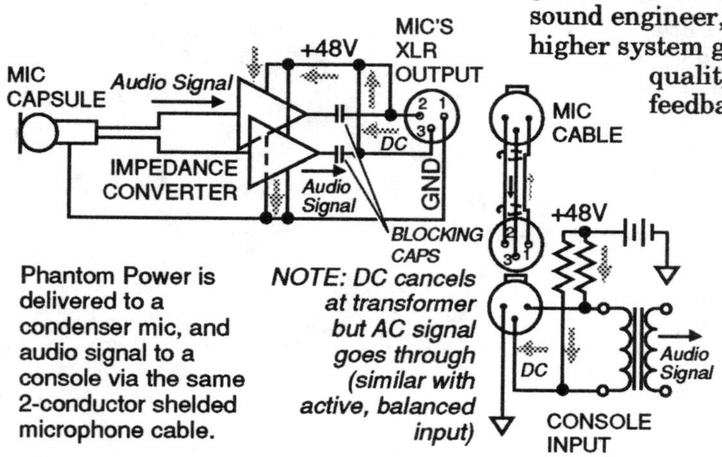

Phantom Power is delivered to a condenser mic, and audio signal to a console via the same 2-conductor shelded microphone cable.

NOTE: DC cancels at transformer but AC signal goes through (similar with active, balanced input)

Figure 10-23. How phantom power and audio share the same cable.

10.4.5 Gain and Microphone Placement

System gain can also be enhanced by good mic placement techniques. In general terms, the closer that we can mic sound sources in a reinforcement system, the less electrical gain we will need. This means both cleaner sound and less potential for feedback.

It can also mean greater potential for overloading the preamplifier input (see Section 1.3.5, "Overload"). In close-miking situations, if gross distortion is encountered, it is most likely to be due to the preamp — not the mic — and it may be necessary to use a pad at the preamp input. The mics used should have high SPL capability so that mic overload is avoided.

Public speakers can present problems if they are unused to working with a microphone. A lecturer who wanders around in front of the mic will produce a widely varying signal level, particularly if the mic is a cardioid. The best solution with such a source is to use a lavalier. The sound quality and level will be much more consistent, making the engineer's job much easier, and the result better.

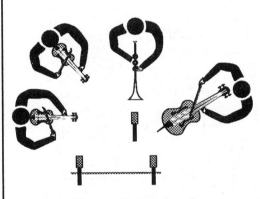

Figure 10-24. Spaced pair stereo placement, with a separate soloist mic

10.4.6 Stereo Recording

Ironically, one of the subjects most open to debate in professional sound is simple, two-microphone stereo recording. A number of different techniques have been proposed and used — each requiring particular pickup patterns and placements — with varying degrees of success. Since sound is a highly subjective matter, of course, each method has its avid proponents.

A full discussion of all the various methods of stereo recording is beyond the scope of this handbook, and we will confine our discussion to the three most common techniques: the spaced pair, X-Y, and M-S methods.

The spaced pair is an extremely simple and successful technique. Two microphones are used, and these are placed on stands spaced 6 to 8 feet apart and 6 feet or so above the ground. Either omnidirectional or cardioid units may be used. Omnis can offer slightly better quality, but less rejection of audience noise and reverberation. A third mic may be used to feature a soloist, if desired. Figure 10–24 illustrates the technique.

While the spaced pair can yield acceptable results, it is susceptible to delay problems (or localization problems) associated with the different path lengths from sources to the two microphones. In an attempt to improve stereo imaging, some recordists use a technique called X-Y.

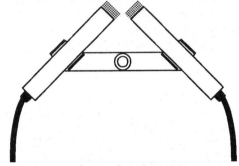

Figure 10-25. Stereo microphones in an X–Y configuration

The technique requires two cardioid units, preferrably with matched characteristcs. The two are mounted on the same stand with a special mounting bar and angled at about 45 to 60 degrees, with the diaphragms as close together as possible. Stereo imaging may be compromised (there is disagreement here), but is generally quite good when heard with headphones and acceptable over loudspeakers. Figure 10-25 illustrates the technique.

A third technique that is often used for recording for broadcast is the M-S method (an abbreviation for Mid-Side Stereophony). M-S recording requires one cardioid and one figure-8 element, placed on the same stand with their patterns oriented as shown in Figure 10-26.

Stereo information is extracted from the mic signals by a matrix which produces a sum channel (the two added together) and a difference channel (the figure-8 signal subtracted from the cardioid signal). The technique is valued for broadcast because it retains mono compatibility. The sum of the two signals cancels the figure-8 signal, leaving only the cardioid signal.

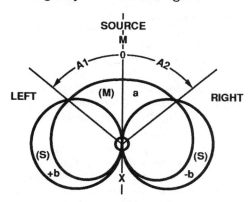

Figure 10-26. Sensitivity patterns of cardioid & figure-8 mics in an M–S stereo configuration

Some information in the wireless intercom and wireless mic sections of the handbook was originally written by Gary Davis and Associates in cooperation with Bill Swintek of Swintek Enterprises, Inc., of Sunnyvale, CA (a wireless microphone and intercom system manufacturer) for a 1983 magazine article. That copy has been edited and expanded here, and is used with the permission of Swintek Enterprises. The majority of the wireless mic and intercom information here was provided by HME Electronics, Inc. of San Diego, CA, also a manufacturer of wireless mic and intercom equipment. We are appreciative of the assistance provided by both of these companies.

10.5.1 What is a Wireless Intercom?

A wireless intercom is a system with which two or more people can communicate from reasonable distances apart. Its equipment is miniaturized, and is not connected by wires or cables, thus providing maximum mobility to its users.

There are two basic types of professional, wireless intercom systems. One type is operated with a console base station and one or more wireless, remote units. The other type is operated with a battery powered, wireless transceiver and one or more wireless, remote units. The remote units consist of small belt pack transceivers, and headsets with attached microphones. The base station operator can communicate with all crew or team members using the belt packs, simultaneously.

10.5.2 Who Uses Wireless Intercoms?

Wireless intercom systems have become a necessary part of many communication networks in recent years. The flexibility provided through their use is indispensable in many production, training, security and industrial applications. Rapid growth in the videotape production industry has created a need for wireless intercoms to be used as extensions of wired systems already in place. They are invaluable as communication aids between directors, stage managers and camera, lighting and sound crews in theater and film productions. In sports events, wireless intercoms are not only used by coaches, spotters and players, but also by sportscasters and news production crews. In activities such as stunt filming, circus acts and gymnastics, in which cues and timing are crucial to safety and successful performance, the wireless intercom has become a critical asset. The applications of wireless intercom systems are limited only by the imagination of their users.

10.5.3 What Is The Background of Wireless Intercoms?

Early intercom systems generally consisted of fixed units, which were wired in place. Any mobility depended on the length of cable connecting their headsets to base stations. As the users moved around, the cables had to be dragged with them and lifted over obstacles. Outside interference noise was also a problem.

Walkie talkies were the earliest form of wireless intercoms used. They were heavy and cumbersome and had to be connected to large batteries from which they obtained their power. Their reception was easily distorted and noisy. Wireless communication has come a long way since the walkie talkie.

Technological advances since the late 1960s have tremendously affected both the size and performance of wireless intercoms. The development of semiconductor technology improved their dynamic range and audio quality significantly.

Technology in the early 1970s introduced the integrated circuit compandor, which was incorporated into wireless intercoms to reduce noise. Later, the application of diversity reception minimized the problem of dropouts (transmission losses), greatly improving system reliability. The Federal Communications Commission

(FCC) allocation of specified frequency bands for wireless intercoms has eliminated radio interference from other services.

Today's wireless intercoms perform as well as conventional, wired intercoms. In the 1980s they are being manufactured with improved dynamic range and smaller transponders, a result of better compandor integrated circuitry and advanced circuit design techniques. A variety of wireless intercom equipment is presently available in various configurations.

10.5.4 Types of Wireless Intercoms

There are three basic types of wireless intercom systems: simplex, half duplex and full duplex. A simplex system permits one-way communication only, such as ordinary radio broadcasting in which the listener can hear the announcer but cannot respond. A half duplex system operates like a walkie talkie, allowing the users to communicate one at a time, only while pressing a button. A full duplex system, however, provides continuous two-way communication without pressing a button. This is the most desirable type of system, since it provides complete hands-free mobility to the user with the advantages of normal uninterrupted conversation. Brief descriptions of each type of system are given below.

• **Simplex**
Since only one-way communication is possible in a simplex system, it is useful only in dispersing information

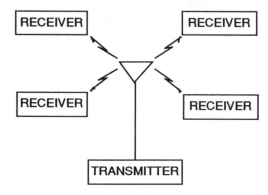

Figure 10-27. Simplex wireless intercom system

when no reply is necessary. Paging systems at airports or in department stores and hospitals are simplex systems. Because of its simple circuitry, this is the least expensive type of intercom system. (Refer to Figure 10-27.)

• **Half-duplex**
Because of its affordable price range and the fact that it provides two-way communication capabilities, this is the most popular type of wireless communication system. (Refer to Figure 10-28.) Half-duplex systems consist of one unit which serves as the base station and several remote units. The base station may either be a console which plugs into an AC outlet or is powered by a 12 volt battery, or it may be a mobile belt-pack unit with a miniaturized transceiver. The base station operator, usually a director or crew supervisor, can communicate freely with all crew members, transmitting and receiving simultaneously. His instructions can be heard by all crew members at once. Thus, priority messages from the director reach all crew members without delay. The base station also simultaneously rebroadcasts all incoming messages. Each crew member's communication with the base station can thereby be heard by all fellow crew members. Although crew members cannot communicate directly with each other, they can communicate via their supervisor or director. Crew members can hear incoming messages at all times. In order to transmit from a remote unit, crew member must press a button on their belt packs. Only one member is able to transmit at a time. The half duplex is cost effective and efficient for most operations.

• **Full-duplex**
This is the ideal form of wireless intercom system since it provides the only truly hands-free operation. With a full duplex intercom, uninterrrupted communication is possible, as in a normal telephone conversation. The major difference in this system and the half duplex is that a full duplex intercom is capable of continuous transmission in both directions. It is not necessary to press a button to transmit. (See Figure 10-29.) The discrete full-duplex system, operates with only two units: a base station and one remote unit. Transmitting and receiving by these units is done on two different frequencies. A message is transmitted on one frequency by one of the units and received on that same frequency by the other and visa versa. If a larger communication network is required with more than two wireless belt packs, the system becomes complex. In order to accomplish this, a base station that will transmit to all the wireless belt packs on a single frequency is needed. At the same time, separate receivers for each wireless belt pac are necessary at the base station. The base station then functions as a repeater, receiving messages from each remote unit and retransmitting them back to all the remote receivers at once on a single frequency. The complexity of this extended full duplex system increases its cost significantly and is therefore not cost effective for all operations. Currently available systems permit use of four to six full duplex, wireless remote belt pack units in this fashion, providing full hands-free communication to all users at once.

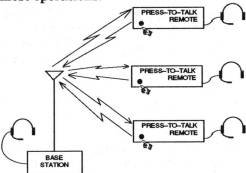

Figure 10-28. Half-duplex wireless intercom system

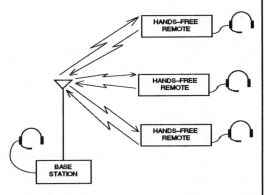

Figure 10-29. Full-duplex wireless intercom system

• **Integrated Systems**

There are as many varied configuration requirements for wireless intercom systems as there are users. Systems may be integrated in almost any imaginable combination. One user may need to link a PA system (simplex) to a full duplex system. Another user may want to hook up several half duplex wireless belt pack units to an existing cabled intercom system. A typical remote belt pack transceiver has provisions for either half duplex (push-to-talk) operation or may be switched to full duplex, which provides continuous hands-free transmission and reception. With nine volt alkaline batteries, the belt packs may operate continuously for eight to ten hours. More than four wireless belt packs may easily be accomodated by adding base station for additional channels, or by letting several belt packs use the same transmit frequency. In this case, push-to-talk is mandatory because only one signal can be transmitted without interference at a given time. Wired stations, generally used at fixed positions for cameras and lights, are the most cost effective. But the director or crew supervisor may prefer wireless stations for mobility. Wireless systems are also needed for positions that are not practical to wire. Whatever its application, the wireless intercom provides greater mobility than its cabled counterpart.

Audio bandwidth is not a critical factor with wireless intercom systems. Some frequency bands are more subject to interference from adjacent frequencies than other. For example, the 400 to 470 MHz, ultra-high-frequency band, of which wireless intercoms and microphones utilize the 450 to 451 and 455 to 456 MHz frequencies, is also used by police, fire and public health service radios. Any time nearby frequencies such as these are in intermittent use, there is a risk of random interference that was not detected during equipment setup.

The most practical and commonly used frequency band for wireless intercom systems in the U.S.A. is the VHF band, from 26 to 27, 35 to 43 and 154 to 174 MHz. Different manufacturers use different frequencies, and their systems are necessarily preset to those given frequencies. The buyer must be aware of these factors in choosing the most appropriate system in order to avoid interference from local broadcast. Interference from harmonics of scheduled broadcast must also be considered. That is, if an FM radio program is being broadcast at 88 MHz, it will also appear at 176 MHz, and other multiples of the primary broadcast frequency.

Some manufacturers utilize a "split-band" system. In this type of system, the base station may transmit on the VHF high band, while the remote units transmit at VHF low band. In split-band operation, coordination with the FCC is important to be sure that both frequencies are in compliance with the same section under FCC regulations.

To operate a wireless intercom legally in the United States, a Federal Communication Commission station license is required. The type of license depends on the use to which your intercom will be put. Local FCC offices or the equipment manufacturer should

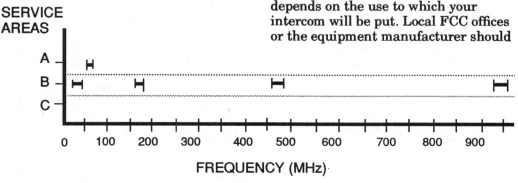

Figure 10-30. Wireless intercom frequency bands

be contacted for further information. Figure 10-30 indicates the radio frequency allocations for wireless intercoms in the United States. In other countries different frequency allocations as well as operating regulations may apply. Local authorities should be consulted prior to system selection or operation.

10.5.6 Improved Range and Noise Reduction

There are now numerous systems designed for improved audio range and noise reduction. Wireless intercom systems do not need to have high level dynamic range since they are used primarily for speaking and do not have to produce a natural or enhanced musical quality. However, it has been demonstrated that the natural voice quality of today's systems is less fatiguing over a long period of time than the highly compressed audio sound of a few years ago. This is a benefit of the improved range and signal-to-noise ratio of state-of-the-art wireless intercom technology.

Prior to the late 1970s, most wireless intercoms could not efficiently reduce unwanted noise. Today, many systems include compander circuitry, the most advanced noise reduction technology. In a compander circuit, a full-range compressor is built into the intercom transmitter and an audio expander into the receiver. When the signal is compressed, the audio level remains well above the residual noise floor. When it is expanded again, the noise is reduced and the signal is much cleaner and relatively noise-free. Low level hiss and static are virtually eliminated. Companding the audio signal also provides improved dynamic range over a straight transmission. In some cases the wireless intercom may actually be quieter than its cabled counterpart.

10.5.7 Evaluating and Selecting a System

There are a number of criteria that must be considered in evaluating and selecting a wireless intercom system suitable for professional use. Ideally such a system must work perfectly and reliably in a variety of tough environments with good intelligibility and must be useable near strong RF fields, lighting dimmers and other sources of electromagnetic interference.

• **Operating Frequency**
If a wireless intercom is going to be used effectively at frequencies adjacent to other strong signals which might interfere with the clarity of its

reception, the extra expense of a more complex receiver will be necessary. Thus the operating frequency of a wireless intercom system is a factor to be considered in selecting your equipment.

• **Diplexer**

Wireless intercom and microphone systems normally operate on like frequency bands, thereby often benefitting by combining systems, enabling a director or crew supervisor to have closed and open communication. Up to 24 discrete VHF high-band microphones and intercoms can be operated in the space of a single TV channel. However, such complex systems often experience desensing, the muting of a receiver because another mic or intercom is transmitting in close proximity, thus limiting its effective range. Some systems have antenna diplexers and may therefore be immune to the desensing problem.

• **Side Tone**

An important feature to look for in an intercom is side tone which confirms that communication is actually taking place. Side tone simply means that the user hears his voice as he talks, but only after it has been retransmitted to him. Non-duplex systems cannot offer side tone or have local side tone in which the voice is fed directly into the earpiece through a preamp and thus does not confirm two-way communication.

• **Headsets**

Some wireless intercoms are built entirely into headsets. While these units are very compact, they are often heavy and uncomfortable as well as poor in serviceability and sound quality. In other intercoms the transceiver is packaged separately and is designed to work with a variety of headsets. This will usually be most cost effective for the buyer who already has headsets. To assure compatibility, investigation should be made regarding which kind of headsets are best suited to the particular transceiver under consideration.

• **Batteries**

The type of batteries used in a wireless intercom must also be considered. A rechargeable system can be economical over a long period of time. On the other hand, fresh throw-away batteries before each show provide confidence that a wireless intercom will last to the end of the show. The system should be capable of operating at least 4 to 6 hours on one set of batteries. Rechargeable nickel-cadmium batteries are more economical in the long run, but they are also more difficult to maintain. If not deep-cycled (fully discharged and recharged), they will not yield nearly as long an operating life between charges as a set of fresh, non-rechargeable alkaline batteries.

• **Future Needs**

One of the most important considerations to be made in wireless intercom selection is future needs. A system should be compatible with other types of systems and equipment to allow the greatest possible adaptability to future needs. Perhaps one system may be somewhat more expensive than another, but it may be much more economical in the long run in maximizing future operational capabilities.

10.5.8 Conclusions

Today's wireless intercoms are a great improvement over the cabled systems of just a few years ago. The mobility they provide is an invaluable asset to nearly any industry. Their versatility, through integration with existing cabled intercom systems, as well as with wireless or cabled microphone systems, is another advantage. Their audio bandwidth and signal clarity far exceeds the requirements of most users. They excel in sound quality, and in their ability to solve many types of production communication problems.

10.5.9 Glossary of Wireless Intercom Terms

Bandwidth — The range of frequencies within which performance falls, with respect to some characteristic – usually the -3 dB points.

Belt pack — Communication equipment worn on a belt. In a wireless intercom system, the belt pack (or belt-pac) usually includes a transmitter, a receiver and a headset with built-in microphone.

Compander — A combination of a compressor at one point in a communication path for reducing the amplitude range of signals, followed by an expander at another point for a complementary increase in the amplitude range.

Compressor — A signal processor that, for a given input amplitude range, produces a smaller output amplitude range.

Diplexer — An electronic apparatus which allows a single antenna to connect to a transmitter and receiver simultaneously.

Diversity Reception — Where a signal is obtained by combination or selection or both, of two or more sources of received-signal energy that carry the same modulation or intelligence, but that may differ in strength or signal-to-noise ratio at any given instant minimizes the effects of fading.

Dynamic Range — The difference, in decibels, between the overload (or maximum) level and the minimum useable signal level in a system.

Expander — A signal processor that, for a given amplitude range of input voltages, produces a larger range of output voltages.

Frequency Band — A continuous range of frequencies extending between given low and high frequency limits.

Integrated Circuit — A combination of electronic circuits, each of which has an independent function, but are linked together as an interdependent network; usually packaged in a single, small chip or semiconductor-based microcircuit.

Preamplifier — An amplifier which boosts a low-level signal, providing enough level for the signal to be further processed.

Repeater — An electronic device which receives a signal and then transmits the same signal on a different frequency.

RF Field — An energy field (a definable area) where radio frequency signals are prevalent.

Semiconductor — An electronic conductor, with resistivity in the range between metals and insulators, in which the electric charge-carrier concentration increases with increasing temperature (over some temperature range).

Signal-to-Noise Ratio — The ratio of the level of the signal to that of the noise level (usually expressed in dB).

Split Band — A communication system in which signals are transmitted in opposite directions on different frequency bands.

State-of-the-Art — The most modern technology available to solve a problem in a unique way for the first time.

Transceiver — The combination of radio transmitting and receiving equipment in a common housing, usually for portable or mobile use, and employing common circuit components for both transmitting and receiving.

Transponder — A receiver-transmitter combination that receives a signal and retransmits it at a different carrier frequency.

10.6 Wireless Microphone Systems

10.6.1 What is a Wireless Mic?

A wireless microphone system is a small scale version of a typical commercial FM broadcasting system. In a commercial broadcasting system, a radio announcer speaks into a microphone that is connected to a high-power transmitter in a fixed location. The transmitted voice is picked up by an FM receiver and heard through a speaker or headset.

In a wireless microphone system, the components are miniaturized but the same principles apply. The transmitter is small enough to fit into the microphone handle or into a small pocket sized case. Since the microphone and transmitter are battery powered, the user is free to move around while speaking or singing into the mic. The transmitted voice is picked up by a receiver that is wired to a speaker.

Two types of microphones are available with wireless mic systems: the handheld mic, with a transmitter in its handle; and the lavalier mic, which is small enough to be concealed as a lapel pin or hung around the neck. Lavalier mics are wired to miniature body-pack transmitters, which fit into a pocket or clip onto a belt.

10.6.2 Who Uses Wireless Mics?

Wireless microphones are widely used today in television and videotape production. They eliminate the need for stage personnel to feed cables around cameras, props, etc. For location film production, as well as ENG (Electronic News Gathering) and EFP (Electronic Field Production), wireless mics make it possible to obtain usable first take sound tracks in situations that previously required post-production dialogue looping. The cost saving can be significant.

Handheld mics are used by performers on camera where they provide the freedom needed to move around the stage and gesture spontaneously. They are used by speakers and entertainers who need to pass the mic from one person to another. In concerts, handheld wireless mics permit vocalists to walk and dance around the stage and even into the audience without restriction and with no chance of shock in the event of rain.

Lavalier mics are used in game shows, soap operas and dance routines. They eliminate the need for boom mics and help to alleviate visual clutter. Lavalier mics are used by MCs, panelists, lecturers, clergy, stage actors, and dancers because they can be concealed easily and provide hands-free mobility. Some lavalier transmitter models have high impedance line inputs that accept cords to create wireless electric guitars.

10.6.3 What is the Background of Wireless Mics?

Technological advances since the late 1960s have tremendously affected both the size and performance of wireless mics. Until that time wireless mics were large and used miniature vacuum tubes, offering limited dynamic range and poor audio quality. The development of semiconductor technology in the late 1960s reduced these problems significantly.

Technology in the early 1970s introduced the integrated circuit compandor which was incorporated into wireless mics to reduce noise. At about the same time, the FCC authorized the use of frequencies in TV channels 7-13 for wireless mics. Thus the wireless microphone's most serious problem, radio interference from other services, was virtually eliminated. Later, the application of diversity reception minimized the problem of dropouts (transmission losses due to cancellation of radio waves), greatly improving system reliability.

Today's wireless mics perform as well as conventional wired mics. In the 1980s, wireless mics are being manufactured with improved dynamic range and smaller transmitters, a result of better compandor integrated circuitry and advanced circuit design techniques. A variety of standard microphones with different sound characteristics is available.

10.6.4. Radio Frequencies Used

There are no international standards for wireless mic radio frequency allocations. Performance is not controlled for transmitter power limits, frequency stability, or RF bandwidth occupancy. Wireless mics could therefore, theoretically, operate at any frequency. Certain frequency bands, are more commonly used. (Refer to Figure 10-31.)

taneously without RF intermodulation products causing interference.

• Wireless mics are permitted to operate in the commercial FM broadcasting band, providing their power is not greater than 50 μV/M radiation at 15 meters. With this power restriction, it is not practical to use this band for professional applications in which

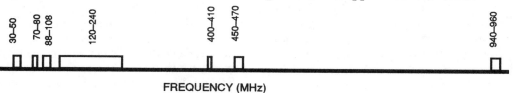

FREQUENCY (MHz)

Figure 10-31. Commonly used international frequency bands

In the United States, the FCC regulates the operation of wireless mics at specified frequency bands. Frequency bands typically used are shown in Figure 10-32. The applicable Federal Communications Commission regulations are as follows:

reliable transmission performance is expected.

• Wireless mics may operated on a shared basis with business radio service. Continuous radio transmission is authorized if the transmitter power is limited to 120 mW. The business radio service frequencies for wireless

SERVICE AREAS

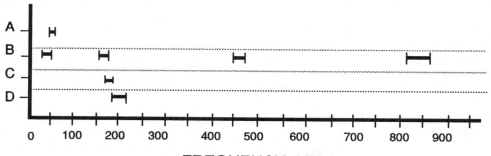

FREQUENCY (MHz)

Figure 10-32. Wireless microphone frequency bands used in the United States

• Low power communication devices may operate in the 49.81 MHz to 49.90 MHz band (Figure 10-32 (a)). Power is limited to 10,000 μV/M radiation at a 3 meter distance (approximately 1 to 5 mW) and with a 5 kHz audio frequency limit. This segment of the RF spectrum is susceptible to man-made noise generated by auto ignition, flourescent lights, dimmers, etc. The restriction imposed by the FCC on low-power equipment aggravates the problem of signal-to-noise ratio in this band. Because these frequencies are evenly spaced (15 kHz apart), only three wireless mics can operate simul-

mics are: 30.76 MHz to 43 MHz, VHF low-band; 150 MHz to 173.4 MHz, VHF high-band: 457MHz to 470 MHz, UHF low-band; and 806 MHz to 866 MHz, UHF high-band (Figure 10-32 (b)). At 150 MHz and higher, man-made noise decreases significantly. With the higher power and larger transmission bandwidth allowed by the FCC, along with many more available frequencies and the shorter antenna requirement, operation in the VHF high-band and higher is desirable. The major disadvantage is interference from other business radio services. An operating station license is required and the transmitter must be type accepted under FCC regulations. Contact your local FCC office for aForm 25 if you want to obtain a license. Anyone can operate a wireless mic system at these frequencies. Specific frequencies designated in this part of the regulation for wireless mics are known as "B frequencies." The bands are from 169.445 MHz to 170.245 MHz, from 171.045 MHz to 171.845 MHz , from 169.505 MHz to 170.305 MHz and from 171.105 MHz to 171.905 MHz (Figure 10-32 (c)). "B" frequency transmissions must not exceed a bandwidth of 54 kHz and output power of 50 mW.

• For broadcasting, video production, and filmmaking applications, wireless mics may operate in the 174 MHz to 216 MHz range (TV channels 7 thru 13), on a non-interference basis. (Figure 10-32(d)). This means that for a given location, wireless mics may operate on unused TV channels. Transmitter power is limited to 50 mW. An operating station license is required for broadcasters and filmmakers and the transmitter used must be type accepted under FCC regulations. This VHF high-band offers the best operating area for wireless mics. It is free of citizens band (CB) and business radio interference, and any commercial broadcast stations that might cause interference operate on a schedule, and thus can be avoided easily.

10.6.5 Technical Problems

• **Transmission Loss**
There is a calculated transmission loss between transmitter and receiver through use of an isotropic antenna. Less transmitter power is required for an equivalent signal strength at the receiver as frequency is lowered. One problem with wireless microphones is the difficulty in designing antennas that are small but efficient in the VHF low-band area. However, for the VHF high-band, small and efficient antennas are practical.
Interference from other radio services is the major problem at both VHF and UHF. The only clear channels available are the unused TV

channels in a given location and the "B" channels. For touring groups the TV channels become a problem, as a clear TV channel in one city may not be clear in another. Therefore, the "B" channels are recommeded for this purpose.

• **Dropout**
Loss of reception at the receiver of a wireless mic due to radio wave cancellation called multipath reflections is usually referred to as dropout. This problem has several possible sources. Dropout characteristics are different between VHF and UHF frequency bands. The dropout zones are much shorter at UHF where rapid flutter is often heard.
Loss of reception may also be caused by a transmitter being too far from the receiver. This may be corrected by relocating either the transmitter and receiver antennas closer to each other.
The power of a signal received by an antenna is a critical factor in causing dropout. When examining practical solutions and limitations in alleviating dropout, it is important to consider that not all of the power transmitted will reach the receiver. A wireless mic transmitter radiates power in many directions simultaneously, depending on the specific mechanical configuration of the antenna system. This makes the transmission vulnerable to many types of interference.
System performance is degraded by path losses due to interfering objects between the transmitter and receiver, such as other equipment or people, as well as by the position of the transmitter antenna and interfering signals due to multipath reflections.
Several paths can occur when the environment in which the wireless microphone is operating contains objects such as cameras, lighting equipment, or stage props made of metal or other materials that reflect radio signals. Due to phase differential of the arriving signal, the resultant signal can be enhanced or totally cancelled, creating multipath dropouts. These path losses affect the total power received at the antenna. Multipath cancellation is the most common cause of dropout.

- **Use a High Gain Receiving Antenna at the Mix Positon**

High gain antennas can improve the S/N ratio, and may thus reduce fades and dropouts if they are due to weak signals. Signal cancellations will not be aided. High gain receiving antennas are generally also a bad idea because: (a) the transmitter is constantly moving around with the performer so the antenna would have to be continuously re-aimed, and (b) much of the received radio signal is actually caught on the bounce from walls, props, etc., so even if one stood offstage and aimed a beam antenna at the performer, it could be aiming at the wrong target.

- **Place the Receiving Antenna(s) and Receiver(s) Near the Mic(s) and Run Audio Signals Back to the Mix Positon**

With wireless mics, an alternative is to place the receiving antenna(s) on or above the stage, run a moderate length antenna cable to a nearby wireless mic receiver, and then run as long a standard audio cable as necessary between the receiver's audio output and the mixing console's input. Most receivers provide line level outputs that are ideal in this situation. This keeps the mic transmitting antenna(s) and the receiving antenna(s) reasonably close, which optimizes the RF S/N ratio.

- **Diversity Reception**

In some wireless microphone installations, it may be impossible to locate a single antenna to eliminate multipath dropout or signal fading. The technique that has been adapted for wireless microphones to minimize multipath dropouts is called diversity reception. This is the application of two or more receiving antennas to receive signals that have been diverted into more than one path (multipath). The idea, in general, is that if the signal is weak at one antenna, it will probably be stronger at the other, at any given instant. Diversity reception enhances the performance of a wireless mic system. It is usually effective, although nothing will guarantee a total absence of dead spots. There are a number of different ways to accomplish diversity reception, and each manufacturer of wireless microphones tends to favor

one approach or another. The conditions required to achieve this reception are:

- a single transmitter source
- uncorrelated, statistically independent signals
- multiple receiving antenna systems

The success of any diversity reception system depends on the degree to which the independently received signals are uncorrelated. If a diversity reception system cannot produce uncorrelated, statistically independent signals, then diversity reception does not exist. A diagram of a basic diversity reception system is shown in Figure 10-33.

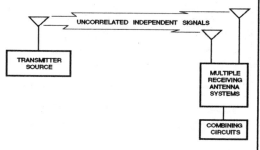

Figure 10-33. Diversity reception system

Implementation of a diversity reception system can be accomplished in several ways, but all system implementations have the need to combine the received, independent signals in some method. The major drawback with any multiple reception diversity system is cost. Combining techniques are chosen based on cost and the degree of improvement required. The less predictable or less closely related the signals, the more significant the benefits of the diversity system.

There are various techniques of diversity reception based on the exact method for processing and extracting the transmitted signals. Space diversity is the technique most commonly used for wireless mics. Space diversity can be implemented in many different ways, but the three basic requirements of diversity reception mentioned earlier must be satisfied. Two or more receiving antennas are required and must be at least one half wavelength apart (typically 3 feet). The amount of separation determines the degree of the uncorrelated signals. Polarization diversity is a method of space diversity in which the antennas on the receiving system are placed at angles to each other in order to capture the uncorrelated, independent signal. Each antenna provides an independent path that is selected or combined to produce the desired signal improvement. These selecting and combining methods of processing the independent signals are shown in Table 10-1.

COMBINING METHOD	TECHNIQUE
Selection (Also referred to as 'switching' or 'optimal switching'	Switches to optimum input
Maximal ratio (also referred to as 'variable gain')	Adds signals with variable gain amplifiers
Equal gain (also referred to as 'linear adder')	Adds signals linearly

Table 10-1. Combining methods for diversity reception

In space diversity the incoming signal with the best signal-to-noise ratio is selected from the two or more antennas used. This signal selection, illustrated in Figure 10-34, can be accomplished either prior to or after audio detection.

Another method of signal improvement is that of combining the incoming independent signals. The two methods of doing this are called maximal ratio combining and equal gain combining. The techniques for maximal ratio and equal gain combining are illustrated in Figure 10-35. In maximal ratio combining, independent signals are combined in order to derive the maximum signal voltage/noise power ratios from each of them. A modification of this approach is equal gain combining in which all incoming signals are set to an average constant value. A comparison of the signal selection and combining methods is shown in Figure 10-36 and Table 10-2.

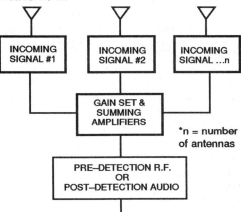

Figure 10-35. Maximal ratio combining and equal gain combining

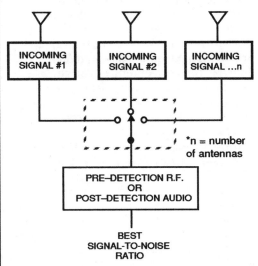

Figure 10-34. Space diversity signal selection

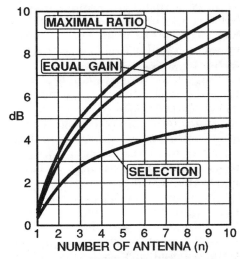

Figure 10-36. Comparison of signal selection and combining methods

Clearly, the maximal ratio combining method offers the best possibility for improvement over a non-diversity system, although it is the most difficult to implement. Wireless mics typically use selection or equal gain combining diversity. The choice is based on greatest reduction of the probability of dropouts. Any of the selection/combining techniques can be implemented in the pre-detection or post-detection stage of the receiver.

mic's receiver. The net result is flat audio response through the transmitter/receiver chain, but any hiss that enters the system as a result of the radio transmission is also cut by the de-emphasis.

Audio companders are available with variable gain amplifiers, which respond to changing input levels. Without a compandor, a wireless mic would be more subject to noise from its transmission medium and would be

Method	Advantages	Disadvantages
Selection	No no-phasing required	Switching transients
Maximal ratio combining	Best improvement in S/N ratio	Cost and complexity
Equal gain combining	Improvement in S/N ratio, Low cost	Co-phasing for optimum performance

Table 10-2. Comparison of space diversity
signal reception methods

• **Companders**

The compander was originally used to reduce static and increase the dynamic range on telephone lines. A compander is a two part system consisting of a compressor, which reduces the audio range by providing more gain to weak signals and an expander, which restores the signal to its original dynamic range ratio. The degree to which the audio energy is compressed (and subsequently expanded) is referred to as compression ratio. Typically, a wireless microphone uses a ratio of 2:1. This compression keeps loud sounds from overmodulating the transmitter and keeps quiet sounds above the hiss and static. Expansion restores the loud sounds after reception and further reduces any low-level hiss or static.

Almost all FM wireless mic systems use some form of pre-emphasis and de-emphasis to reduce hiss or high-frequency noise. Basically, the high frequencies are boosted (pre-emphasized) at the mic's transmitter and, conversely, cut (de-emphasized) at the

unacceptable for most professional applications. Compander systems are subject to phenomena known as breathing or pumping. This soft hissing is most noticeable during low input levels. Pre-emphasis networks (similar to those used in FM) are used to further improve the transmitted signal. Although the audio compander is required for professional applications, an alternate system, called a limiter, is also available. The limiter can only prevent peak levels from becoming distorted. Hence the dynamic range, without distortion, is increased at the input by up to 40 dB, but the output remains constant with no improvement in dynamic range.

10.6.7 Multiple Microphone Systems

A wireless microphone requires system design and analysis consistent with the channels and particular design being used. When using multiple wireless mics, the following interference sources must be considered:

- transmitter spurious emissions
- transmitter and receiver intermodulation
- Splatter

Spurious signals are generated within the transmitter due to mixing products created in multiplying the crystal oscillator to the carrier frequency. These mixing products, if they fall within the bandwidth of the receiver, will be heard as squeals or chirping sounds. The spurious outputs of the transmitter are discrete spectral signals (*splatter*), and typically cannot be removed easily once a transmitter is designed.

Transmitter intermodulation (IM) occurs when a carrier frequency from another source is coupled into the output stage of a transmitter and becomes a second signal source. The transmitted IM products will overwhelm the receiver and will be recognized as acceptable signals, thus creating the chirping and squeals and overall sensitivity degradation.

10.6.8 Compatibility of Wireless Mic Systems

Wireless mics from one manufacturer will not usually be compatible with equipment from another manufacturer (in fact, sometimes different lines made by the same manufacturer may not be compatible). This is because of the different frequencies and different noise reduction circuits used by the various manufacturers, which can result in signal distortion. To assure compatibility, check with your factory representative before adding other manufacturers' equipment to your existing wireless microphone system. What follow are descriptions of a few areas that breed incompatibility:

- **FM deviation**
  Deviation (the amount the carrier frequency changes for a given amount of audio input) may vary with different manufacturers' equipment. NFM (narrow band FM) transmitters will not yield good results with wideband FM receivers, and a wideband transmitter will sound even worse with an NFM receiver. The deviation set by one maker of wireless mics simply may not be appropriate for that set by another maker.

- **Companding**
  There are no legal or even industry-wide standards regarding the use of companding. Some manufacturers use none, some use it only on certain models, and others offer it on their entire line. Expanding an uncompressed signal, or vice-versa, will create horrible sounding audio. But just because both mic transmitter and receiver use companding, there is no guarantee of success. If one manufacturer relies on 1.5:1 compression and 1:1.5 expansion, while another sets his equipment for 2:1 compression and 1:2 expansion, then using one system's mic with the other system's receiver will result in dynamic errors. Incorrect decoding of the companded signal can cause surging (with too much expansion) or too little dynamic range (with too little expansion). Beyond that, the method of level detection (peak, average or rms) may vary, so even with the same compression/expansion ratios, the equipment may still be incompatible.

  NOTE: An ordinary audio tape noise reduction system is not suitable for wireless mic signal processing because the noise spectrum of tape and that of FM radio broadcast differ, and hence different pre-emphasis curves are required for optimum results. So if you have a compander-type mic and an ordinary receiver, your dbx or Dolby tape decoder will not help you out, even though the noise avoidance principle may be about the same.

- **Pre- and De-Emphasis**
  A similar problem exists with pre-emphasis and de-emphasis. Everyone uses different turnover frequencies, and different amounts of boost and complementary cut. Intermix one type

of mic transmitter with another type of receiver, and the frequency response of the overall wireless mic system may be seriously degraded.

10.6.9 Antenna Cables

Antenna cables for wireless microphone systems should always be coaxial type as these are not prone to interference. Proper connectors should also be used. Use of improper connectors or cable can cause signal loss and performance degradation.

Be aware that not all coaxial cable is the same. Polyfoam cable (foam center dielectric) has lower losses and holds up better in portable use than standard cable. Moreover, there are genuine differences in the shielding on some brands of cable.

In cable runs of over 100 feet, it is generally advantageous to install an RF preamplifier. Placing the preamp at or near the antenna raises the signal well above the noise, improving the signal-to-noise ratio before cable attenuation takes its toll. The preamp, if adjustable, should be set for only enough gain to compensate for cable losses. Excess gain can overload the receiver, defeat squelch circuits, or increase intermodulation distortion.

Table 10-3 (next page) shows the two types of cable most commonly used in wireless microphone systems and indicates whether or not preamps are necessary at various cable lengths.

10.6.10 Evaluating Wireless Microphone Systems

There are a number of criteria that must be considered in selecting a wireless microphone system suitable for professional use. It must be reliable in a variety of tough environments with good intelligibility and must be usable near strong RF fields, light dimmers and other sources of electromagnetic interference. This relates directly to the type of modulation (standard or narrow-band FM), the operating frequency (HF, VHF, or UHF), the receiver selectivity, and so forth. Ideally the system should be capable of operating at least 4 to 6

hours on one set of batteries. Rechargeable nickel-cadmium batteries, as described in Section 10.5.7, offer a trade off of long-term economy against the need for increased maintenance.

Published specifications are of little use in evaluating wireless microphone performance. Depending on the manufacturer, specifications may be exaggerated or have qualified conditions that may not be applicable in actual use. Because RF power output is limited by the FCC, most systems operating in the same band are comparable in transmission distance, but other parameters more critical to performance and reliability should be carefully examined. The following considerations should be evaluated prior to selection of a wireless microphone system:

- **Construction**
  For reliable operation, the equipment should meet accepted design standards, such as spacing between lines on the printed circuit boards, stress reliefs on wire bends, clearance between components, and manufacturing tolerance. In evaluating assembly techniques, one should consider soldering (avoid solder bridges, splashes, cold joints) and the overall workmanship (there should be no flux on printed circuit boards). The battery compartment should be readily accessible and mechanically durable.

- **Comparison**
  The following comparison tests can be made by getting a wired mic which uses the same element as your wireless mic and feeding both outputs into a mixer or an A-B switch.
  Frequency response: Both mics should sound identical; one should be no more *brilliant* than the other.
  Gain: Output levels should be nearly identical.
  Phase: With both mics placed near each other, a properly phased wireless mic will not show any cancellation vs. the wired version.
  Dynamic range: Shout into the mic. Listen for distortion at high levels. Note any pumping action or other compandor characteristics.
  Noise floor: With gain level on the mixer set about equal, listen for overall noise floor differences.

- **Radio Frequency**

Set the receiver squelch for normal quieting. Remove the transmitter antenna, if possible, to induce dropout. Listen for squelch action when dropout occurs. A good design will minimize the annoying sound of dropout.

Ultimately, if a handheld wireless mic is being used for TV production, or a concert that is being videotaped, or with live projection TV effects, the mic's looks can be as important as its performance, especially when the audio can be dubbed in post production. Remember that the performer cares a lot about visual æsthetics.

Today better professional wireless microphone equipment is as good as, or superior to many of the tape machines or sound systems to which the mics are connected. A wireless mic can never be better than, only as good as, a wired version of the same type. Because wireless mics are sophisticated radio systems as well as audio systems, care must be taken in setup, and a thorough understanding of the system's parameters is advisable. Wireless systems offer many practical advantages to the user.

COAXIAL CABLE LENGTH (FEET)	TYPICAL RG-58/U (dB loss @ 150 MHz)*	RF PREAMP NEEDED?	POLYFOAM RG-8/U (dB loss @ 150 MHz)*	RF PREAMP NEEDED?
50	3.0	No	1.0	No
75	4.5	Optional	1.5	No
100	6.0	Yes	2.0	No
125	7.5	Yes	2.5	No
150	9.0	Yes	3.0	Optional
175	10.5	Yes	3.5	Yes
200	12.0	Yes	4.0	Yes
250	13.5	Yes	5.0	Yes
300	15.0	Yes	6.0	Yes
400	16.5	Yes	8.0	

Table 10-3. Cable/preamp recommendations for wireless mic systems

(*There is a wide variation between similar cables, depending on how they are manufactured. Also, loss is logarithmically less at lower frequencies)

Compander — A combination of a compressor at one point in a communication path for reducing the amplitude range of signals, followed by an expander at another point for a complementary increase in the amplitude range.

Compressor — A signal processor that for a given input amplitude range produces a smaller output range.

Cordless Mic — An older term for wireless mic.

Dead Spot — Those locations completely within the coverage area where the signal strength is below the level needed for reliable communication.

De-emphasis — The use of an amplitude-frequency characteristic complementary to that used for pre-emphasis earlier in the system. (See pre-emphasis)

Diversity Reception — (Defined in Section 10.5.9.)

Dynamic Range — The difference, in decibels, between the overload (or maximuim) level and the minimum acceptable signal level in a system or signal processor.

Expander — A signal processor that for a given amplitude range of input voltages produces a larger range of output voltages.

Intermodulation — The modulation of the components of a complex wave by each other, as a result of which waves are produced that have frequencies equal to the sums and differences of integral multiples of the frequency components of the original complex wave.

Isotropic Radiator — A hypothetical antenna having equal radiation intensity in all directions.

Limiter — A signal processor in which some characteristic of the output is automatically prevented from exceeding a predetermined value.

Multipath Transmission — The propagation phenomenon that results in signals reaching the radio receiving antenna by two or more paths.

Polarization Diversity Reception — That form of diversity reception that utilizes separate vertically and horizontally polarized receiving antennas.

Pre-emphasis — A process in a system designed to emphasize the magnitude of some frequency components with respect to the magnitude of others, to reduce adverse effects, such as noise, in subsequent parts of the system. A specific type of equalization.

Space Diversity Reception — That form of diversity reception that utilizes receiving antennas placed in different locations.

Squelch Circuit — A circuit for preventing a radio receiver from producing audio-frequency output in the absence of a signal having predetermined characteristics.

SECTION 11.
PREAMPLIfiERS, SMAll MIXERS
& MIXING CONSOLES

11.1 GENERAL Discussion

The terms *mixer*, *mixing console*, *console*, *board*, and *desk* are often used interchangeably. All are used for combining and re-routing audio signals from a set of inputs to a set of outputs, usually with some added signal processing, and level adjustment. What, then, is the distinction?

Console is, in fact, an abbreviation for mixing console. Mixer, in our opinion, generally refers to a small unit, either rack mountable or with fewer than 10 to 12 input channels. The larger units, then, are the consoles. (We won't argue with anyone who wants to call something with 16 inputs a mixer, but we find the distinction useful.)

Board is a less formal word sometimes used to describe a mixing console. Finally, desk is the popular British term for this same equipment.

A preamplifier is a circuit (or a device which contains a circuit) that boosts a weaker audio signal to a level suitable for further mixing and signal processing. Almost all mixers and consoles that have microphone or phono inputs include preamplifiers. Some stand-alone preamplifiers include rudimentary mixing controls, which somewhat blurs the distinction with small mixers.

Now that we understand the terms (we do, don't we?), let's examine some of the designs, features and performance criteria that pertain to the actual equipment.

(Refer to Figure 11-1 on the following two pages for diagrams of typical mixer and console configurations).

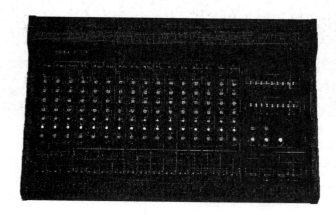

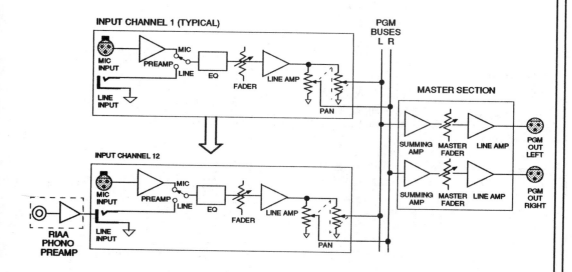

Figure 11-1. The relationship between a preamp, a mixer and a console:

(A) A small 12-input channel x stereo output mixer with an external RIAA preamp for a phonograph

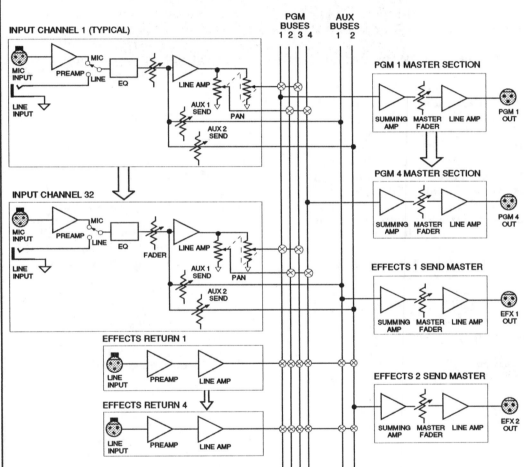

Figure 11-1. The relationship between a preamp, a mixer and a console:
(B) A large 24-input channel x 4 output console with
2 effects send and return circuits

11.2.1 What Are They, and What Do They Do?

Preamplifiers are used to boost the weak -70 dBu to -50 dBu nominal output levels of microphones (mic preamps) or phonograph cartridges (phono preamps) to levels from −20 dBu to +4 dBu. In terms of voltage, the boost is from levels measured in micro-volts (millionths of a volt) to between $1/10$ volt and 2 volts. The power involved is boosted from tenths of a microwatt (tenths of a millionth of a watt) to between $1/100,000$ watt and $2/1,000$ watt.

The preamplifier is the first active stage, the first electronic circuit that processes the microphone (or phono) signal connected to a mixer or console. Preamplifiers are also used to boost certain guitar pickups, although here they often act more as an impedance converter (boosting the power so the guitar pickup is not overloaded by the console's or power amp's input impedance) than as a voltage booster, since guitar pickups can generate voltages that are equal to the line-level voltage of the typical mixer.

> **NOTE:** *The input channel of a mixer or other audio device may be casually referred to as a preamp, but in fact a preamp is merely a portion of an input channel. It is a circuit that is required to complete any channel with a mic or phono input, but a channel contains more than a preamp.*

Preamplifier design is very important since this is the circuit with the most gain, and hence the greatest chance to amplify its own distortion and noise. Together, the actual impedance of the source that is connected to a preamp's input, and the actual impedance of the load into which the preamp's output is terminated both have a major impact on the performance of the preamp. A good preamp must be designed for minimum noise and distortion when used with specified signal source and termination impedances. This is one reason why a preamp that is optimized for an electric guitar (which has a very high source impedance of tens to hundreds of thousands of ohms) will not do a good job with a typical professional microphone (which has a source impedance of 50 to 200 ohms).

Preamplifiers generally are designed to operate within a certain gain range. When you operate the trim control on a console's input channel, you generally are adjusting the gain of the pre-amplifier. If operated at unity gain (no amplification), many preamplifiers will become unstable and may exhibit increased distortion or a tendency to oscillate. Therefore, design engineers will generally provide attenuation pads before and/or after the preamplifier. This enables the signal to be knocked down so that the preamp can always be operated with some gain. Another approach is to bypass the preamplifier when the input signal is of sufficiently high level, which is why line inputs are provided. The line input generally comes after the preamplifier.

Of course, if you have another line input source and only mic input channels are available, you can always knock down the line signal to mic level by using a 20 to 50 dB attenuation pad, or you can be lucky and find an insert or patch jack in the mic input circuit after the mic preamp, and connect the line input signal there.

If a mixer or console is designed with line inputs only, a microphone cannot be plugged in directly. There will not be enough gain and the impedance will probably be incorrect, too. However, an external microphone preamplifier can be used to boost the mic output prior to connection to the line input. Some mic preamps are battery powered, and are housed in a small mini-box or even in a compact, in-line package with male and female XLRs. Carrying a spare in-line mic preamp (or two) can be a good idea if one is concerned about running short of mic inputs, since it allows instant conversion of a spare line input (such as an effects return) to accept a mic. With battery powered preamps one always runs the risk that the battery will give up before the show is over, so use a fresh battery.

11.2.2 Impedance Converters

Condenser microphones sometimes confuse people because they often have a form of preamplifier built in. In fact, the preamp in the typical condenser microphone is designed primarily as an impedance converter, giving the mic an effective output impedance of 50 to 200 ohms instead of the condenser element's very high output impedance. This makes it possible for the mic to drive long lines with lower susceptibility to hum, noise, and high frequency loss, and it also makes the mic compatible with the microphone inputs of most mixers and consoles. The impedance converter circuit in the mic (or in an associated in-line package) can provide a few dB of boost so that the average condenser mic is somewhat hotter than the average dynamic mic — but still not hot enough to drive a line input directly. It may be necessary to turn down the trim control, or add some attenuation ahead of the mic preamp in the console's microphone input. (This same discussion applies to certain electric guitars that have built-in preamps, although they may actually provide enough level to drive a line input directly.)

11.2.3 Phono Preamps

The phonograph preamp is a special type of preamplifier. The basic amplification, per se, is nothing special. However, the phono preamp includes a specific equalization characteristic known as R.I.A.A. EQ (Recording Industry Association of America). Due to the limitations of vinyl and record cutting heads, many years ago the R.I.A.A. standardized on a curve that provides about 15 dB of cut at 20 Hz and 20 dB of boost at 20 kHz (relative to flat response at 1 kHz) when the records are made. Then, upon playback, the reciprocal EQ curve is applied in the preamp. Reducing the low frequencies applied to the record reduces the width of the grooves, allowing more time to fit on a side, and also reduces the tendency to skip. Boosting the highs keeps them above the inherent hiss caused by imperfections in the vinyl material, and allows the reciprocal high cut upon playback to also cut any induced hiss. Because this special EQ is required, a standard mic input will not do a satisfactory job for phono playback. Similarly, a phono preamp will severely color the sound from a microphone.

The special class of phono cartridge known as moving coil cartridges output considerably less voltage than the typical dynamic, moving magnet, electret, or even a low cost crystal or ceramic phono cartridge. The moving coil cartridge will require either a specialized voltage step-up transformer, or a special moving coil preamp. Such preamps, again, are specialized and should not be used for mic signals. They may include R.I.A.A. EQ, or may be designed as a pre-preamp, for use ahead of a standard R.I.A.A. phono preamp.

Several companies make small, rack mountable mixers that are one or two rack spaces high (1-¾"or 3-½" x 19"). Some accept mics, some line inputs, others a combination. Sometimes limited channel equalization is provided (perhaps a bass and treble control), occasionally multi-band EQ is provided, but often no EQ is available. Sometimes there will be an auxiliary bus for effects or monitoring, but not always. These tend to be very basic units. In simple applications, such as providing a few inputs for mixing a cabaret performance, a hotel meeting room or a small conference, such mixers may be all that is required. These compact mixers also have a place in large, sophisticated sound systems. They can be used in a modular fashion, mixing additional mic or line inputs together for a submixed feed to the main console, which expands the overall system capability. They can also serve as a discrete, if somewhat limited, fall back system in the event of catastrophic failure of the main mixing console. We know of at least one major rock concert that was completed only because the sound company carried a pair of 6-input mic mixers to augment the main console, which didn't make it through the show.

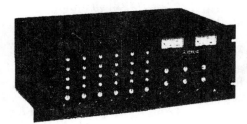

Figure 11-2. A rack mount mic or line mixer

Sometimes the rack mount mixer can be used to enhance the capability of the main mixing console. For example, if an additional mix of the inputs is needed for a remote feed or a monitor feed, and no more busses are available in the console, the input channels' direct out or insert out jacks can be patched into an external mixer (or daisy chained to several), which are then used to create the additional mix(es).

Small mixers are very popular in broadcast applications, especially remotes. Here, the basic rack mount design may be augmented by a variety of specialized features, including an output level meter, phantom power, a built-in battery and/or DC input for operating the unit, and perhaps even a special output for connection to a telephone line.

Some small mixers may be designed for stand-alone use, not necessarily for rack mounting. These units generally have from 6 to 12 input channels, and are designed primarily for use in small clubs, in schools, for meetings, multi-image, or A-V (Audio-Visual) presentations, for occasional recording, and so forth. This type of mixer may look very much like a scaled down console, and may include many of the same features such as input pads, straight-line faders, multi-band EQ, auxiliary/effects busses, a wrist bolster (arm rest), patch points, and so forth. Some of these smaller mixers actually have features that are nearly identical to certain larger consoles, and therefore make an ideal choice for an occasional expander to the larger mixing system.

Figure 11-3. A typical small, stand-alone mixer

The more complex a mixer (or console), and the greater the number of channels, the more critical the performance of a given circuit. With only a few mics, if each mic input is a bit noisy (or a bit distorted), the overall effect may not be too bad. Multiply that noise or distortion by 20 or 40 inputs, and the problem cannot be tolerated. In evaluating the performance specifications of the small mixer, the ultimate application must be considered. If the mixer is to stand alone in a small sound reinforcement system, less stringent standards may be just fine. If the mixer is to contribute to a large sound system (as a submixer), or is to be part of a recording system where the sound goes through the equipment multiple times, then higher standards are beneficial. Similarly, a small mixer used strictly for paging and background music need not have anywhere near the performance quality of a similar unit used for foreground music. It is important, therefore, not to equate size with quality, but instead to evaluate each separately.

11.4 Consoles

11.4.1 What is a Console?

A mixing console is a complex audio system. Not only does it preamplify and assign input signals to different outputs, it also allows for a variety of different mixes and special signal routing and processing. The basic path of the signal is as follows: mic or line input to mixing bus to master level control to output. There are generally a number of inputs, of course, with each input being assignable to the busses. Sometimes assignment is via on/off (assigned/not assigned) switches, and sometimes it is via level controls, whereby some portion of the signal is assigned to a given bus.

The console will generally provide equalization, and possibly high pass filters, for each input channel, and sometimes for the output mixes. Other components or functions may be included in the console such as compressors, test oscillators, talkback circuits, and muting logic. Patching facilities are usually part of the console, too, allowing signals to be rerouted so that the signal path inside the console is altered, or so that external equipment can be properly integrated with the mixing system. In short, the console is the heart of the sound system.

11.4.2 How Mixes Differ: Pre & Post Fader Considerations

Different mixes are used for different purposes. The main (or primary) output mix in a sound reinforcement console is used to drive the main amplifier/loudspeaker system. There may be one or more auxiliary mixes used for driving effects, such as reverb or echo, which, in turn, are mixed back into the main mix. One may want more of some input channels and less of others to contribute to a given effects mix, which is why proportional assignment controls are provided for assignment to the effects bus.

The overall output level applied to any assigned main mixing bus(es) from each input channel is generally adjusted by means of a fader. The main or primary bus is nearly always post-fader. These days, most faders are linear (straight line) controls, rather than rotary controls. However, smaller mixers, and some larger broadcast consoles, still use rotary faders because they occupy less panel space than linear types, which is sometimes essential in crowded control rooms or remote trucks. On the other hand, some old timers just prefer rotary faders because they grew up with them.

The signal applied to the auxiliary or effects mixing bus(ses) may be derived before (pre) or after (post) the channel's fader. This pre or post fader signal still must go through the auxiliary or effects send level control before it is applied to the aux or efx bus. When an auxiliary or effects mix is derived pre fader, fader adjustments made to alter the primary mix will not affect that auxiliary mix. Only the send level control adjusts this mix. Post fader auxiliary or effects sends are still subject to the send level control, but they also track fader changes.

Post fader sends are often used for feeding echo or reverb devices because one generally wants the echo sound to fade out when the channel is faded out of the mix. Sometimes, for special effects, one may prefer a pre fader echo send; when the channel is faded, its echo component lingers until the echo send control is turned down, giving the appearance of a sound moving off into the distance.

Auxiliary mixes for stage monitoring or sub-mixes for remote use are generally derived pre fader. In this way, channel fader adjustments that are intended to fine tune the main house mix will not distract performers on stage or cause inappropriate imbalances in broadcast or recording feeds. It is important to remember that performers on stage use their monitor mixes to judge their own playing or vocal dynamics, and the balance between band members. If these balances are arbitrarily changed during a performance because the mixing engineer is attempting to alter the house mix and the monitor feeds happen to be derived post fader, the entire performance will be adversely affected. On

the other hand, there may be exceptions, particularly in small clubs where the stage monitor speakers spill into the audience to a large extent, where compromises must be accepted, and the stage monitor mix is best done post fader.

11.4.3 Panning, Summing, and Master Faders

When a pair of busses is used to carry a stereo signal, it is generally necessary to be able to assign a given input to either or both of these busses in an adjustable proportion. The relative signal level on the left and right busses of the stereo pair will determine the perceived stereo position of the sound image. It is possible to use a pair of individual send level controls to assign different amounts of signal to the two busses, but such an arrangement is, at best, inconvenient. Instead, so called pan pots are more commonly employed. Their function is depicted in Figure 11-4 on the next page.

A pan pot (short for panoramic potentiometer) is nothing more than a pair of specially tapered pots (level controls) wired back-to-back so that as the level going out of one pot increases, the level going out of the other decreases. In sound system applications, it is desirable to taper the resistance elements in the two sections of the pan pot so that when the pot is centered, the output level from each section is 3 dB less than it would be if the pot were turned all the way up for the individual section (all the way to one side). The total POWER then coming out of the loudspeaker system will be the same with the pot centered as with the pot to one side or the other (two amplifiers each producing 3 dB less than full power equal the same as one amplifier producing full power). It turns out that the resistance curve necessary to maintain uniform output in the system follows the geometric sine and cosine functions. Pan pots that do not adhere to these functions should be avoided. A pair of pots, for example, that maintain full output at both sides until centered, then begin attenuating one side when moved past center, will produce a 3 dB level build-up at the center. Such pots are really intended for use as a balance control (altering the stereo balance of an overall program, as in a car stereo system).

NOTE: It is possible to establish a stereo image by means other than simple manipulation of relative level. In fact, humans perceive stereo position by evaluating not only the relative level of a given sound reaching both ears (which is what pan pots alter), but also by evaluating the relative phase and group delay of the sound. Some forms of stereo encoding, binaural recording, and holographic or spatial sound processors utilize phase differences to achieve stereo imaging. Relative levels determine stereo image in 99.9% of commercially available mixers and consoles.

We know signals are routed to a given mixing bus either by pan pots, or by assign switches, or both, but how are they actually applied to the busses and the console outputs? In the most common circuit arrangement, after each channel's assign switch, pan pot or send pot, the signal goes through a summing resistor and is then applied to a common wire (the bus wire). The signals applied to that bus are then fed to a summing amplifier or a combining amplifier which makes up for signal loss through the send controls and summing resistors. Following that, the signal goes through a master fader or master send level control, then to an output booster amplifier, and to the console output.

The summing resistors after each circuit prevent unwanted interaction between circuits; that is, they create a one way street so the audio flows in the desired direction. It is possible to apply too much signal to a given bus, causing the summing amplifier to be overdriven. When the summing amplifier clips, pulling down the master fader may reduce the level, but that comes *after* the summing amp, so the distortion remains. As more channels are added to a given mix, or as the level on the channels is increased, one must guard against bus summing amp overdrive. If distortion is heard when the one more channel is added, the chances are that the master fader won't help. Instead, pull down all the input channel faders (or auxiliary mix send level controls) for those channels contributing to the offending mix. This reduces the level on the bus, as shown in Figure 11-5 on the following pages. Then, if more output level is required, raise the master fader.

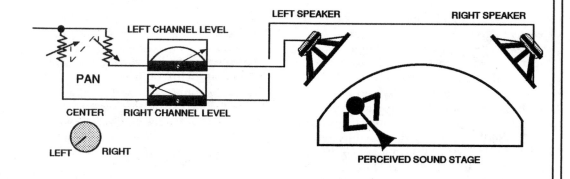

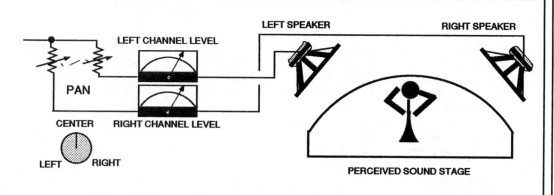

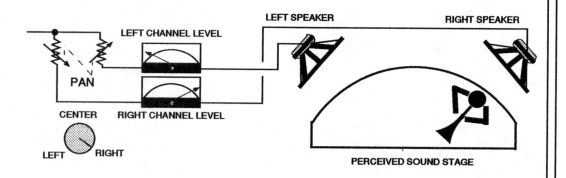

Figure 11-4. How pan pots work

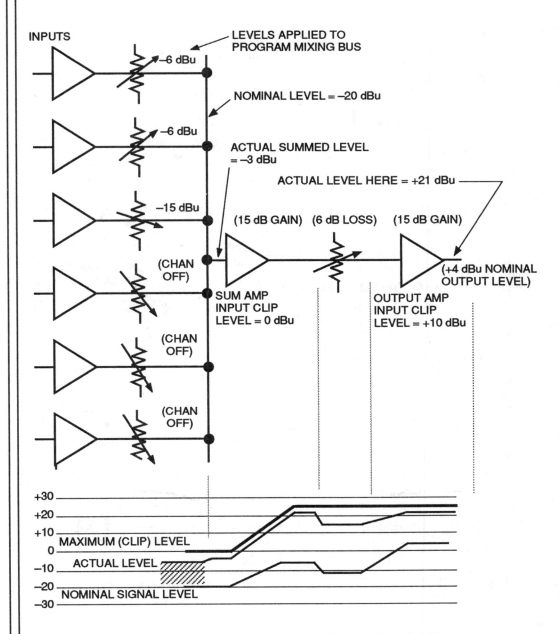

INPUTS

LEVELS APPLIED TO
PROGRAM MIXING BUS

−6 dBu

NOMINAL LEVEL = −20 dBu

−6 dBu

ACTUAL SUMMED LEVEL
= −3 dBu

ACTUAL LEVEL HERE = +21 dBu

−15 dBu

(15 dB GAIN)   (6 dB LOSS)   (15 dB GAIN)

(CHAN
OFF)

SUM AMP
INPUT CLIP
LEVEL = 0 dBu

(+4 dBu NOMINAL
OUTPUT LEVEL)

(CHAN
OFF)

OUTPUT AMP
INPUT CLIP
LEVEL = +10 dBu

(CHAN
OFF)

+30
+20
+10
0
MAXIMUM (CLIP) LEVEL
−10
ACTUAL LEVEL
−20
NOMINAL SIGNAL LEVEL
−30

**Figure 11-5. How summing amplifiers are overdriven,
and how to correct the problem:**

A) Several input channels apply signal at higher-than-nominal level to the
program mixing bus. The level applied to the summing amp remains below
its clip level, however.

Illustration continued on next page

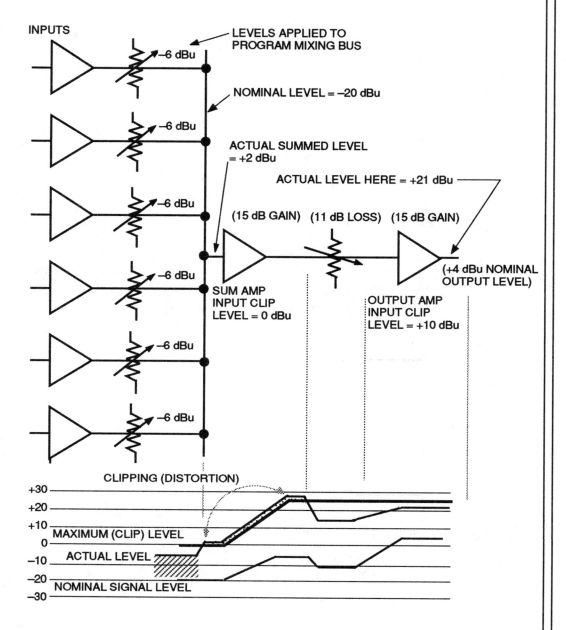

Figure 11-5. How summing amplifiers are overdriven, and how to correct the problem:

B) Additional inputs raise the level on the program bus sufficiently high to drive the summing amp into clipping. Turning down the bus master control keeps the output level the same as in (A), but cannot eliminate the distortion from the clipped summing amp.

Illustration continued on next page

...*Figure 11-5, Continued*

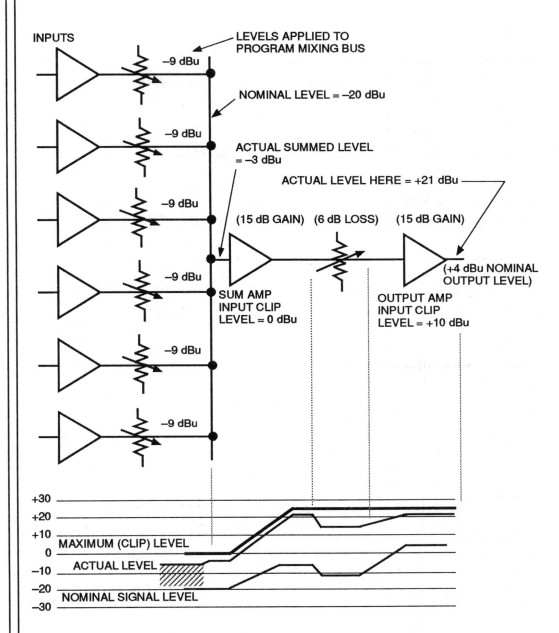

Figure 11-5. How summing amplifiers are overdriven, and how to correct the problem:

C) Turning down all inputs several dB avoids clipping, and master control can be left at original setting.

11.5 Understanding Console Specifications

A detailed discussion about general specifications can be found in Section 8. This discussion pertains to those specifications of special importance to mixers and consoles.

11.5.1 How Many Inputs, Mixes, and Outputs?

The description of a console usually includes some reference to the number of input channels and the number of primary (main mixing bus) outputs. If a console is said to be a 24 x 8 system, it is implied that there are 24 input channels and 8 primary mixing busses.

Sometimes there are sub-mixes within a console. For example, it may be possible to further mix the 8 busses in the previous example to derive a stereo mix. Such a console would be described as a 24 x 8 x 2 console.

This shorthand for describing a console's mixing capability breaks down when one tries to describe more complex systems. For example, suppose the above console also has a mix matrix with 8 outputs, and 11 sources can be mixed into each of those 8 outputs. The matrix is an 11 x 8 matrix. But is the console a 24 x 8 x 8 x 2 or a 24 x 8 x 11 x 2 or a 24 x 8 x 11 x 8 x 2? The shorthand becomes a liability. It's probably best to describe the console as a 24 x 8 x 2 with an 11 x 8 matrix. Similar wording would describe a recording console with a separate monitor mixing section, i.e., a 48 x 24 x 2 console with a 24 x 2 monitor section (48 inputs, 24 primary busses, and a stereo bus plus a 24 input by stereo output monitor). Refer to Figure 11-6 on the next page.

The number of auxiliary mixing busses is seldom included in this numerical shorthand. Neither are the total number of input and output connectors. These items are simply listed in the general specifications.

11.5.2 Signal-To-Noise Ratio

There is no single S/N ratio specification that can adequately describe a mixing console. One must specify a given signal path through the console, as well as the gain and attenuation controls affecting that signal path, in order to adequately specify any S/N ratio in a console. One may be interested, for example, in the S/N ratio from mic input to main output, with the channel fader and master fader at nominal position, with the input trim set for a nominal -60 dB input signal, and with no pad. This will provide some idea of the S/N ratio for one channel, but what happens when several channels add together? It may be desirable to specify S/N ratio with several or all input channels contributing to the mix, in which case (for real world results) the channel faders may have to be pulled down a few dB from nominal. One may get a very different S/N ratio in this case. Then, too, the S/N ratio obtained when a line input signal is applied to the input channel may be significantly different than that obtained from the mic input; if it is much better, we may suspect a noisy mic preamp. Once again, the S/N ratio at an auxiliary mix output, or from an effects return to a main output, is something to examine.

If a console's output noise is specified with all faders down, this gives some idea of the quietest one can make the system, but it provides little information about how the system will perform. If at least one input and one output are not up then the noise figures are useless. Moreover, mixing and equalization controls should be in positions that are normally used. It would be cheating to turn down the channels' high frequency EQ when measuring the S/N from input to output, since any hiss in the input preamp would be attenuated by the EQ, giving a false impression of actual performance.

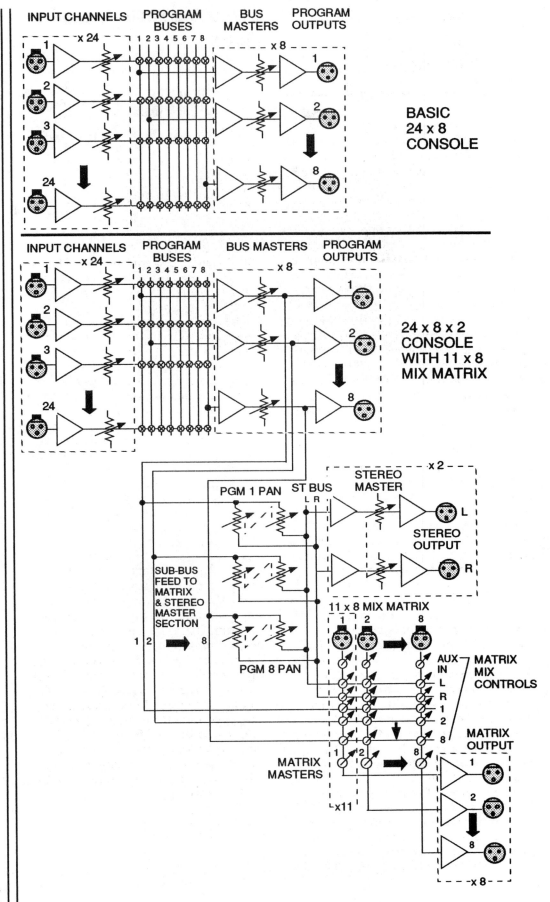

**Figure 11-6. Simplified block diagrams of
different mixer configurations**

Most of us would assume that the controls are flat and appropriate, but it is better to specify everything in detail than to assume. We once measured a console (the manufacturer shall go unnamed) where the high frequencies rolled off (like a treble tone control being turned down) when the master output fader was raised. The result was very nice looking S/N figures, and a very dull sounding mix. This same console, however, was specified to have very flat frequency response. They didn't tell anyone that it was measured with the master faders nearly all the way down, in a position that would never be used for any practical work. To be fair, most manufacturers are not hiding something by not specifying every last control setting. There are so many controls on a console that the ideal spec would occupy many pages.

There are many stages or circuit elements in a mixer or mixing console where the signal level can be altered: input attenuators, preamps and trim controls, channel faders and send controls, summing amps, master faders, booster amps, and output amps. The overall voltage gain (the increase in dBu level) from input to output, then, is dependent on a combination of many settings. With a low-level mic input some consoles run out of gain before the output level is adequate to drive the rest of the sound system. With loud concerts or hand-held vocal mics, almost any console will have adequate gain. With a distant mic (hung overhead or a mic mouse at the foot of a theatrical stage), particularly a low-sensitivity mic, and a relatively quiet sound source (a person speaking in normal voice), the console may not have sufficient gain. How much gain is enough?

In most cases, 60 to 70 dB of gain is sufficient. This will establish a +4 dBu nominal output level with a -56 dBu to -66 dBu mic input signal. In the low level situations described above, a console with as much as 80 to 90 dB of voltage gain may be desirable. Why don't all consoles offer 80 dB to 90 dB of gain? There is a trade off. With added gain comes added noise. Therefore, some consoles are equipped with a gain switch in the output stage, providing the extra gain when necessary, and avoiding the extra noise when the gain is not needed.

It is important to note that the maximum voltage gain specified, and the maximum gain you can actually use in a live mixing situation, may not be the same. Some consoles are specified with a high gain value, but the nature of the console's circuitry is such that the circuits generate excess noise or, in some cases, excess distortion due to headroom limitations in the circuit where the gain is increased.

2.5.4 Headroom

Headroom, as we defined it previously, is the difference (in dB) between the maximum level a circuit can handle and the nominal level in that circuit. In a console, the actual headroom available will vary at different points. An input circuit may have 25 dB of headroom (at a certain combination of attenuator, preamp gain trim, and channel fader settings), and an output circuit may have 20 dB of headroom (for example, +24 dBm maximum output capability with +4 dBm nominal level). If a single headroom specification were given for this console, we would assume it to be 20 dB because this is the lower figure. The actual value could be even less. For example, if the internal gain structure of the console were not well thought out, it would be possible for a given mixing bus to have less than 20 dB of headroom. In this case, even though the input and output have 20 dB headroom, the console would be restricted by the bus capability.

So that you can determine the headroom throughout a console, some manufacturers (notably Yamaha) include a gain structure diagram with the specifications. This diagram, an example of which is shown in Figure 11-7, illustrates the nominal

level and the maximum level before clipping at every key point along the signal path from input to output. By measuring the vertical distance between the upper clip line and the nominal level line, you can determine the headroom at any stage.

We don't mean to imply that a console must have at least 20 dB of headroom. The requirement depends on the intended application and the desired quality level. Simple mixers, for example, which are intended primarily for voice sound reinforcement or background music, need no more than 10 to 15 dB of headroom. A console with +4 dBm nominal and +18 dBm maximum output level can have no more than 14 dB of headroom, and such systems are not uncommon. For high quality musical sound reinforcement, particularly with many channels, or for recording work, we feel that 20 dB should be a minimum headroom requirement. This means that program peaks that are 20 dB above the nominal level (and some percussive instruments peak higher than that above the average level) will not be distorted. It also allows for some margin of error in the console setup and operation, as explained in Section 11.7.

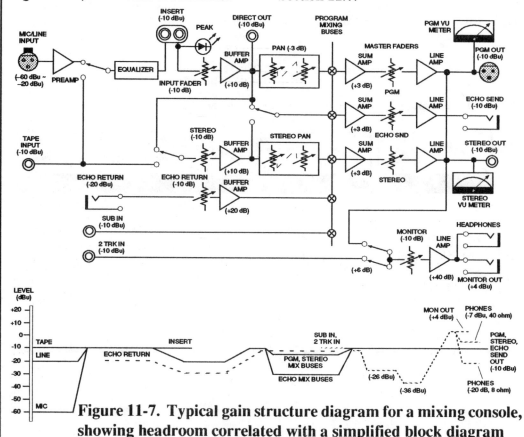

Figure 11-7. Typical gain structure diagram for a mixing console, showing headroom correlated with a simplified block diagram

11.5.5 Indicators

Almost all consoles, and a large number of mixers, have some form of level meters or indicators. They may be VU meters or LED bar graphs, or some other readout. It is important to learn not only the type of readout, but how it is calibrated; i.e., what does "0" on the meter represent?

A "VU" (volume unit) meter is a specific type of meter, with carefully defined response characteristics. It is designed to provide a reasonable way to estimate the loudness of a signal. The indication is something like the average signal level, but it is not precisely an average or RMS measurement. Not all meters that appear to have VU scales are actually VU meters. It is important to learn whether the meter has true VU ballistics, which means that the needle movement follows a predictable pattern with which most mixing engineers are familiar so that levels can be accurately judged, or whether it has some other characteristic. Peak meters (or PPM's – Peak Programme Meters – as the British call them) will jump around more, and will read higher than VU meters. They are most useful for avoiding overmodulation in broadcasting, saturation of tape, and mechanical

destruction of drivers due to over-excursion.

Peak, VU and average meters should indicate the same level on a continuous sine wave test signal. However, there is often a 10 to 25 dB difference between the instantaneous peak signal level and the level indicated by a VU or an average signal level meter.

Sometimes a VU type meter will include a peak LED which turns on when the instantaneous signal level reaches some preset threshold, thus providing a warning of clipping or overmodulation even if the VU pointer is moving in a safe zone. (See Figure 11-8 on the previous page.)

The difference between the average level (or VU level) and the clip point *may* be detected on a meter that has an integral Peak LED, but such displays are not particularly informative. Recently, one manufacturer has devised a special loudness meter that simultaneously displays the peak and average levels at all times, using a meter-like scale comprised of green, yellow and red LEDs. This meter gives a continuous indication of the headroom and of the program dynamics. Refer to Section 16.7 for additional details.

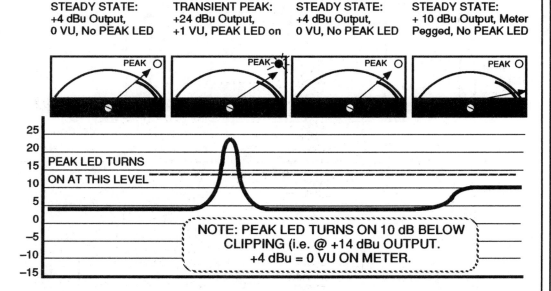

STEADY STATE:
+4 dBu Output,
0 VU, No PEAK LED

TRANSIENT PEAK:
+24 dBu Output,
+1 VU, PEAK LED on

STEADY STATE:
+4 dBu Output,
0 VU, No PEAK LED

STEADY STATE:
+ 10 dBu Output, Meter
Pegged, No PEAK LED

PEAK LED TURNS
ON AT THIS LEVEL

NOTE: PEAK LED TURNS ON 10 dB BELOW
CLIPPING (i.e. @ +14 dBu OUTPUT.
+4 dBu = 0 VU ON METER.

Figure 11-8. How a typical VU meter with peak indicator responds to a test signal

11.6 TRANSFORMER ISOLATED VS. ELECTRONICALLY BALANCED INPUTS & OUTPUTS

As you probably know, balanced wiring helps eliminate some types of externally generated noise. The two wires of the balanced cable carry the same signal, but each wire is opposite in signal polarity to the other. In a balanced input, both of the signal-carrying wires have the same potential difference with respect to ground (they are balanced with respect to ground), and the input is designed to recognize only the difference in voltage between the two wires, hence the term *balanced differential input*. Should any electrostatic interference or noise cut across a balanced cable, the noise voltage will appear equally — with the same polarity — on both signal-carrying wires. The noise is therefore cancelled or rejected by the input circuit. (This is why the term common mode rejection applies; signals in common to the two center wires are rejected.)

A floating input or output is similar to a balanced circuit, except there is NO reference to ground. True floating circuits can be created with transformers, but never with single-IC differential amplifiers. It takes two ICs, or the equivalent in discrete circuitry, to make a true floating input circuit. The use of a transformer, however, does not automatically mean the circuit is floating. If the transformer has a grounded center tap, then the circuit is balanced with respect to ground. In fact, if there is capacitive leakage (which there usually is), there is likely to be some degree of imbalance with respect to ground in the transformer. In most cases there is no practical difference in operation between balanced and floating circuits. Incidentally, the slang term for a circuit with a transformer input or output is a circuit with *iron* (ostensibly because these transformers have iron or some related magnetic alloy in their cores).

So much for terminology. Now, why does some equipment utilize amplifiers, and other transformers, to implement a balanced circuit?

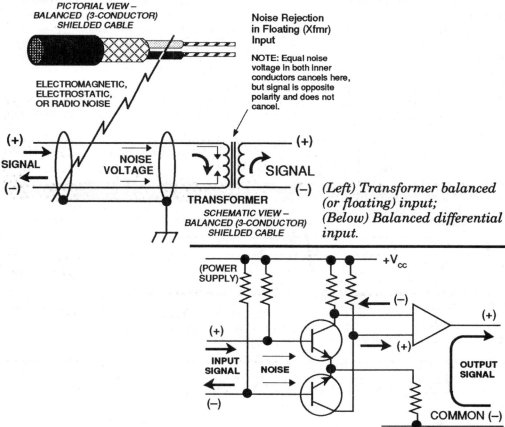

PICTORIAL VIEW –
BALANCED (3-CONDUCTOR)
SHIELDED CABLE

ELECTROMAGNETIC,
ELECTROSTATIC,
OR RADIO NOISE

Noise Rejection
in Floating (Xfmr)
Input

NOTE: Equal noise voltage in both inner conductors cancels here, but signal is opposite polarity and does not cancel.

(+)
SIGNAL
(−)

NOISE
VOLTAGE

SIGNAL
(+)
(−)

TRANSFORMER

SCHEMATIC VIEW –
BALANCED (3-CONDUCTOR)
SHIELDED CABLE

(Left) Transformer balanced (or floating) input; (Below) Balanced differential input.

(POWER SUPPLY)
+V_cc

(+)
INPUT SIGNAL
(−)

NOISE

(−)
(+)

OUTPUT SIGNAL

COMMON (−)

Figure 11-9. Noise rejection in a balanced line

11.6.1 Transformers vs. Differential Amps: Price Concerns

There are two means to achieving a balanced input: with a transformer or with a differentially balanced amplifier (an electronically balanced input). Each approach has its potential benefits and potential disadvantages. There is no best way to balance an input or output. It really depends on the goals, the specific circuit design and components used, and the environment in which the equipment is used.

There is a popular misconception that balanced, differential amplifier input circuits have a more transparent sound than most transformer inputs. There is a technical reason why some transformer inputs sound less transparent, but the truth is that a high quality transformer input can sound as good as a high quality differential amp, and much better than an average differential amp input. The real issue is cost. A good transformer costs more than a good differential amp, and much more than an average differential amp. How much more? In 1989 U.S. dollars, differential amps cost as little as $2 for a barely acceptable unit, perhaps $10 for a good one, and up to $40 or so for a very good one. A poor quality input transformer costs $5, a good one $40, and the best quality transformers $60 to $90 a piece. (These are the raw component prices, not the cost of the components after wiring into the circuit plus adding manufacturing and sales markups). People often form their opinions regarding which sounds better based on listening comparisons with poor quality transformers and relatively high quality differential amps.

It is relatively easy to make a mediocre transformer, and easy to work it into a circuit; it is a passive circuit element, and thus requires fewer wires or connections. The problem with such transformers is that they have limited bandwidth, attenuating the high frequencies and saturating (distorting) at low frequencies. It is expensive to make a transformer that can handle high levels at low frequencies, since such transformers have larger cores (often made with more exotic alloys), and hence larger windings. The larger transformer takes up more space in the equipment, and adds to the weight as well (particularly when multiplied by many channels in a mixing console).

11.6.2 Discrete vs. IC Differential Amps

The differential input amplifier has risen in popularity, particularly with the wide availability of low cost amps packaged as single, integrated circuit chips that are easily inserted in circuit boards. Some people prefer a differential input amplifier to be an IC, others prefer a hybrid (a package containing an IC and discrete circuitry), and still others prefer a component amplifier (made from individual transistors and other components). The IC or hybrid circuit would seem to have the advantage of uniform temperature for all components, which would seem to be important because unequal drift in component values in the differential amp can unbalance the ostensibly balanced circuit. But the most critical components are external to the IC or hybrid, so there is no inherent thermal stability advantage to the IC.

The most critical components in the differential amplifier are those components controlling the gain of each half of the amp. The amplifier usually has high open loop gain, which is controlled by selecting and matching capacitors and resistors in the feedback loop (which are external to IC diff amps). The match should be better than 0.05%— perhaps a close as 0.01%—so that the best common mode rejection ratio can be realized. (A 0.1% tolerance yields no better than 60 dB common mode rejection ratio (CMRR), whereas a 0.01% tolerance can yield 80 dB CMRR!). Hence the need for stability and precision.

Indeed, aside from the IC not having any inherent thermal advantage, there are portions of a circuit which, ideally, should NOT be thermally coupled to other portions of a circuit. In this regard the discrete component amplifier enables the designer to better control thermal coupling (or the lack thereof). On the other hand, the IC amplifier has the advantage of more closely matched circuit values than a discrete component amplifier, which can yield better performance if the circuit is, in fact, optimized (which it may or may not be). It is not possible to make any blanket statements as to which type of differential amp, IC or discrete component, is best. It is really a matter of very specific design, quality, and construction considerations.

11.6.3 The Case for the Transformer

The differential amplifier, however it is made, offers the advantage of not being subject to core saturation with high level, low frequency signals. An inexpensive differential amp may sound better with a drum than does a medium quality transformer costing several times as much as the diff amp. On the other hand, not all differential amps are well designed, and some may not do a very good job of balancing an input. A good quality transformer can sound better than a differential amplifier because the capacitor(s) in the diff amp will do more to degrade the sound than the well designed transformer.

There are a number of reasons why input transformers are sometimes preferred. In the case of certain audio equipment that has an unbalanced input, a transformer can be added (externally or internally) to convert the unbalanced input to a balanced input. Beyond that, there are cases where a transformer is desirable even if the input is electronically balanced. For example, where there is a significant amount of electrostatically or electromagnetically induced noise, particularly high frequency, high energy noise (the spikes from silicon controlled rectifier (SCR) dimmers, for example), the common mode voltage (CMV) of an electronically balanced differential amplifier input may be insufficient. What occurs is this: the diff amp's specified common mode rejection ratio (CMRR), which may be excellent, suddenly goes to zero when the noise voltage rises above a certain value. That value (CMV) is generally about that of the power supply rails: typically 15 to 20 volts at best. Thus, an induced noise spike of 25 to 75 volts (not uncommon near SCR dimmers) will go right through the differential amplifier. The CMV of a transformer is dependent only on the insulation breakdown voltage of the windings, and is typically more than 100 volts. For this reason, in the presence of high noise voltages, input transformers are essential.

One of the major benefits of the transformer is in the area of grounding isolation when multiple input circuits are tied to a given microphone or instrument. In this splitter application, the transformer should have separate Faraday shields for each winding. The Faraday (electrostatic) shields are then each tied to the chassis ground of the respective equipment to which the winding is connected. This provides a continuous drain for electrostatic noise voltages without necessarily connecting the various chassis together. Thus, ground loop induced noise can be avoided. A casual examination of theory suggests that such measures may be unnecessary; just hook up the splitter transformer, tie the cable shield grounds to the various chassis, but cut the grounds at the transformer end, and everything will be shielded without ground loops. This approach tends to fall apart at high frequencies where non-uniform capacitive coupling occurs between the transformer windings and the shield. The use of separate Faraday shields should yield balanced capacitance to each shield from its associated winding. Then, even if you break the ground between the two chassis (to eliminate ground loops and low frequency hum), the windings remain more or less grounded at high frequencies due to the transformer winding's capacitive coupling to its electrostatic shield, which continues to reduce buzz and hiss despite the lifted ground. (We do not recommend lifting grounds, but if it is done, the cut shields should still be passed to ground via small capacitors.)

11.6.4 Transformers and AC Safety

There is never complete ground isolation with an electronically balanced input. Yet the mere use of an input transformer does not guarantee the ultimate in safety, either. Consider what happens when a performer is touching a mic and also touches an electrically hot item such as a guitar which is electrically live due to a fault in the guitar amp. If the mic is grounded, current will flow. **The performer can be subjected to very high currents, and to severe AC shock.** Even if the mic is transformer coupled, its case may be grounded, via the cable shield, to the chassis of the mixer, providing a low-resistance return path for the AC current. **The only real protection in such cases is to use AC power isolation transformers for the guitar or instrument amplifier(s).**

How do shock hazards like this occur? Problems can arise when the guitar amplifier chassis is connected to the AC neutral instead of ground (either by poor design, a loose wire, or a capacitive filter that breaks down). In such cases, there is no certainty of hazard because the AC neutral leg is not normally more than a few volts above ground potential. But if the AC distribution system is imperfect or the AC plug is inserted backwards (i.e., high and neutral are reversed), then the chassis of the guitar amp will be connected to the hot leg of the AC circuit. If the mic case or other equipment is grounded, and the performer touches both, *ZAP!* Using an isolation transformer on the AC feed to the guitar amp, while admittedly costly, will avoid such AC shock hazards. When an AC power transformer is used in this way, primarily for ground isolation, it is said to be an isolation transformer.

11.6.5 More on Transformers

If an audio input transformer is used to prevent a low impedance input from loading down a high impedance output, it is known as a bridging transformer (not to be confused with the bridged connections of a stereo power amp output in mono mode).

Many consoles today are provided with electronically balanced, differential amplifier inputs because these are more cost effective than high quality transformers, they weigh less, and in many situations they perform very adequately.

In the occasional situations where absolute isolation of the grounds between the console and the other equipment must be obtained, or where high common mode voltages are present, there is no viable substitute for a transformer. Sometimes the manufacturer will make provisions for installation of optional input transformers, or you can add them just ahead of the differential amplifier input. On the other hand, if a circuit is being designed from scratch to utilize a transformer, there is no reason to utilize a differential amplifier, since that merely places more components and more potential signal degradation in the signal path.

The balanced output carries similar, but not identical considerations with respect to the differential amplifier versus transformer issue. Input transformers often can be made smaller because they handle lower signal levels. If incorporated in the console, inexpensive resistive padding can be switched in ahead of the transformer to avoid saturation with higher level signals. The output transformer, on the other hand, will nearly always have to handle high level signals and cannot be padded. Therefore, output transformers can add significantly more to the weight. Output transformers tend to be a bit less costly to manufacture because of less complex shielding requirements, so their larger size may not add as much to the cost as would an input transformer that can handle high line levels. An electronically balanced output can drive a balanced cable, and feed a transformer-balanced input, thus achieving a measure of ground isolation and improved common mode rejection without the cost of dual transformers in the circuit. For complex fixed or portable installations (such as very large sound reinforcement systems or broadcast studio complexes) the absolute grounding isolation and higher CMV of transformers makes it advisable to use them on outputs and inputs.

> There are other ways to achieve isolation. The most common means is with a wireless radio mic. One can place an inductive loop around a stage, drive it with a large power amplifier, and pick up the magnetically radiated signal with smaller coils, as is done in some one-way stage communication systems. One can digitize the audio signal and transmit it by means of modulated light in fiber optics, but this is much more expensive than using a transformer, with no great performance advantage. One can use the audio signal to modulate a light, and pick up the light with an LDR (light dependent resistor), thus achieving isolation at the expense of increased noise and distortion. Some systems, such as those for hearing impaired theatre goers, even do this over 10 to 100 foot distances using infrared LEDs for transmitters and infrared photo sensors for receivers. The guitarist who places a microphone in front of the guitar amp's speaker, rather than plugging a line output from the guitar amp into the console, has achieved electric isolation between the guitar and console by means of an acoustic link.

One final comment: if you add a transformer to an input or output circuit, make sure the transformer's characteristics are correctly matched to the circuit. The source impedance and load termination impedance connected to a transformer have a major impact on the resulting performance. Incorrect impedances can cause ringing (by creating a resonant circuit), or degraded frequency and phase response. The transformer should be capable of handling the levels and frequency range involved. In many cases, even though the transformer has a 1:1 turns ratio, it should not be reversed in the circuit. There may be a difference in the performance when primary and secondary connections are swapped. It is best to speak with a knowledgeable applications engineer if you are planning to use any add-on transformer, unless the model is specifically recommended by the equipment manufacturer.

Avoid testing a transformer with a continuity checker or ohm meter. The DC current flowing through it can, in some cases, magnetize the core and create a permanent increase in the distortion level of the transformer. This is more of a problem with low cost, steel core transformers than with better nickel alloy core models. Still, if you want to check a transformer, it is safer to do it with an audio frequency test signal.

11.7 Gain Staging And Gain Structure

This section not only explains some of the basics of gain structure, it also discusses how to make adjustments of the mixing console to ensure optimum gain structure.

11.7.1 Why Does Gain Have To Be Manuipulated: A Review of Sound Levels Fed to the Console

An instrument amplifier, home hi-fi, or power amp usually has only one master volume control. That's easy to deal with, but when you are faced with that sea of controls called the modern mixing console, you may find anywhere from three to ten rotary controls or linear faders that all affect the same output! You can make a substantial improvement in the signal-to-noise ratio of your mixing system if you get the louder you need from exactly the right control. What's the right control? Well, the answer isn't simple, but if you understand the console's *gain structure*, you'll be able to figure out which controls are better for certain adjustments.

The actual electrical levels entering a console vary tremendously, depending on the sound level of the source, how far away it is from the microphone, how sensitive the mic is, or — if the source is a direct-wired electronic instrument — on the nominal output level of the instrument. Consider two extremes of acoustic level: the distantly-miked flute versus the mic inside a kick drum. What kind of electrical levels are involved? That depends on the microphone. Using standard, dynamic sound reinforcement mics, signal levels ranging from 0.00001 volts (caused by 40 dB SPL from the flute reaching the mic capsule) to as much as 10 volts (caused by 170 dB SPL peak pressures from the bass drum reaching the mic capsule — a high, but not impossible value) will appear at the input of the first amplifier in the mixing console. How much dynamic range is this? Since twice as loud to the human ear is 10 dB, you have the human require-

ment of 13 "twice as louds" (otherwise stated as 130 dB) as the range of input levels (170 dB SPL minus 40 dB SPL = 130 dB dynamic range). This considerable dynamic range is not the whole range of human hearing; the sensitivity of the ear goes down quite a bit lower.

In the real world, we would not normally listen with our heads inside bass drums, but we may well place a microphone there, one inch from the beater. And that can generate levels equal to a rifle shot at two feet!

To complicate matters further for the electronic engineer, electronic noise can offset the required dynamic range. If one is to prevent a console from adding noticeable noise to the mix, the noise level of the electronics must be lower than the lowest energy level that will be applied to the mixer in the presence of the quietest sounds. As a rule of thumb, the noise floor of the electronics should be at least 40 dB below the electrical level generated by the quietest sounds (or lower, if we can manage it). To view this figure in perspective, it's half the loudness four times. This noise is caused by random molecular motion due to heat, so-called Johnson noise in semiconductor junctions, and other arcane scientific phenomena. If the noise is 40 dB lower than the minimum music level, you'll have an acceptably quiet mix. In order to do that, you'll be adding the 130 dB of desired dynamics for the music on top of the 40 dB margin for noise protection, and the result is a 170 dB range. That's the four half as louds for noise free mixes and the 13 twice as louds for dynamic range for a total of 17 doublings in volume (each of which is 10 dB).

In other words, you have to add the program dynamics on top of a cushion that is above the equipment's inherent noise floor.

If we just line up those signal voltage numbers that our standard microphones generate, one on top of the other, you can see the size of the problem:

10.00000

...and then,

.00001

This range of 1,000,000:1 is considerable, and in practical terms it is not possible to handle it without an adjustment of the actual amount of amplification in the mic preamp. Ten volts coming out of a microphone, in itself, is not an unmanageable level. (Yes, you can get ten volts out of a dynamic mic; just stick it in the kick drum one inch from the beater location, and really play HARD!) The problem is designing a circuit that will handle ten volts today on the rock concert, and still have enough range to deal with the flute in the classical ensemble tomorrow.

Better mixing consoles have input circuitry designed to deal with these extremely high and low mic output voltages. The circuits still have extra capability for headroom (in case the sound gets louder) and the noise level (on better consoles) is so low as to ensure a quiet mix. In order to handle these levels, you must make some adjustments on the mixing console.

11.7.2 Gain Control at the Microphone Input

We'll start with the rule and then give you some explanation. When you are beginning your sound check, use as much amplification from this stage as you can! Most mixers have a knob called TRIM, GAIN, INPUT LEVEL, PAD, or INPUT ATTENUATION; some have a switchable PAD or AT-TENUATOR in addition to a continuously variable GAIN or TRIM control. We'll use the term GAIN to refer to the general function. Regardless of the label, such knobs all do about the same thing, though they may work a bit differently. For example, turning up the gain may be the same as reducing the pad. Be sure you know which way to turn the knob to make the level higher. If you can turn up this knob first so that there is maximum gain (minimum attenuation) before adjusting any of the other controls on your console, the mix will be quieter. The more gain you get from the mic preamp, the less you will need to add from the other amps in your console.

Of course if the incoming microphone signal is already high in level,

you need not turn up the GAIN all the way. Since you have more signal prior to preamplifcation, you need less amplification overall from your console, and the output noise should go down.

Here's a suggested method for arriving at the correct setting.

STEP 1

To set the GAIN, first turn it down all the way. On most consoles, this means full counterclockwise rotation. Make sure that any PAD or ATTENU-ATOR switch is NOT engaged. (In this formal approach, setting the PAD comes last.)

STEP 2

Set the channel's slide fader almost all the way to the top of its travel. Some consoles have a heavier line, arrow or some other mark on the slider scale that can be used as a normal or nominal setting for this procedure.

STEP 3

Set the submaster faders (if any) and the master faders to this same almost to the top position, or to the manufacturer's mark.

STEP 4

Now, turn up the GAIN as high as necessary until the VU meters indicate the desired level (typically peaking around zero, or two-thirds of full scale). This formal procedure ensures that you have, in fact, taken as much power from the microphone as possible before using amplification from another part of the console.

11.7.3 Input Attenuation or Padding

Suppose, as you went through the preceding steps, the sound you heard was distorted, and setting the GAIN lower didn't help. When you tried lowering the master, or you turned down the power amp sensitivity, the sound got quieter, but remained fuzzy. What can be done?

What's probably happening is that the level from the mic is simply too high to begin with (if there is an input transformer, the transformer core may be saturated before the sound ever gets to the GAIN control). Use the PAD, or MIC ATTENUATOR. Most Yamaha consoles include a pad (or multiple pad values) as part of the input module preamp circuitry, but with some other brands you may have to purchase or build an external pad for use between the mic cable and the console input. You switch in the PAD last, when you know that the electronic adjustments alone will not lower the signal from the microphone to a value that the preamp or input transformer will handle.

Why adjust the PAD last? Because a PAD is not going to help your signal-to-noise ratio. It discards signal coming in on the mic cable BEFORE it enters the preamplifier. One of the most common errors leading to poor signal-to-noise performance is keeping the PAD or MIC ATT engaged. That means that additional amplification must be used to make up for the discarded signal, and with amplification comes more noise.

11.7.4 Eliminating Other Causes of Signal-Level (and Gain) Related Distortion

Misunderstanding the basic setup of the microphone preamplifier is probably the primary cause of poor console performance, but there are a couple of other ways to improperly adjust and lose the quality that your console is capable of delivering.

11.7.4.1 Summing Amp Overdrive

On an 8 input channel or smaller mixer, it is difficult to overload the summing amplifier, but not impossible. It would happen this way:

You set all the mic preamp GAIN controls a bit too high, and all the input faders very close to the top of their travel. To get the output level down to a point where it doesn't overdrive the power amp input, you find that you have to set the submasters or master faders almost all the way down. The meters are reading the correct level, but the sound is slightly crunchy.

What's wrong? The first amp in the submaster or master module is getting too much signal.

In some larger consoles, a separate BUS TRIM is provided so you won't have to reset everything while the show is in progress. If you don't have such a control, the setting procedure for the mic preamps that we described in Section 11.7.2 should keep you out of trouble because it guides you to begin with the submasters and masters up.

11.7.4.2 Power Amp Overdrive

If the power amplifier is now clipping because it is overdriven, cut back on the input sensitivity of the power amp (i.e., turn down the amp's input level control). In addition to improving the signal-to-noise ratio, this readjustment will also give you more useable travel on your console's submasters and/or master faders.

What do you do if your power amp doesn't have an input control pot? Lower the level of everything on the console —INPUT GAIN, SUBMASTERS, and MASTERS—until you have a suitable output level. To retain adequate fader control travel on the submasters and masters, turn down the input GAIN as much as practical before resorting to pads or running all the input faders down too far. In short, don't take all the level reduction you need just from the masters. Spread it out.

11.8 Interface With Sub-Mixers

Larger mixing consoles, and sometimes smaller mixers, often have sub input, link or expander connections. Such connections generally apply line level signals directly to the main program mixing busses, and sometimes are also provided for auxiliary busses (echo/effects, cue, etc.). They are intended to permit another mixer or mixing console to be electronically joined so that both units' inputs can be combined onto the same busses, and controlled with one set of master faders. For convenient reference, the main mixing console may be called the master, and the sub-mixer the slave in such setups.

The concept of sub-mixing is not new, and it continues to offer benefits in a number of situations. No matter how large and complex a mixing console, it seems that there are times when just a few more inputs would be helpful for a particular job, and this is where the sub-mixer (or subsidiary mixing console) is ideal. For example, it may not be economical, or the physical space may not be available, to install a larger console to handle the occasional need for a few additional input channels. Sometimes the sub-mixer can be used to mix a separate stage act, or to mix only the electronic keyboards, which provides local control for the person concerned with that group of inputs. Then these pre-mixed inputs are fed to the main mixing console for distribution to the sound system amps and loudspeakers. It may be that a rental sound company wishes to keep maximum flexibility in their inventory, and would prefer to stock two 16-channel consoles, which can go out on separate jobs sometimes, and be linked to create one 32-channel console on occasion, rather than carry a single 32-channel console that can only be used for one job at a time.

The sub-mixer inputs on a console are generally specified to accept one of a few standard line levels, typically −20 dBu (78 mV), -10 dBV (316 mV), or +4 dBu (1.23 V) nominal. In most cases there are no input level controls on the sub-inputs, so those levels must be controlled by the master faders on the sub-mixer. So long as the impedances and levels are in the right range,

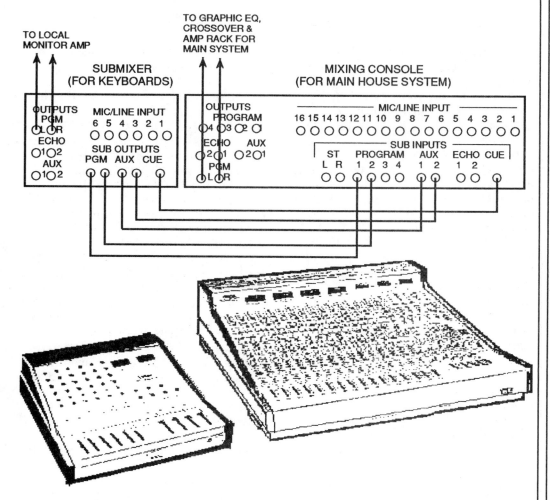

Figure 11-10. Block diagram of a sub-mixer connected to a main mixing console

without overloading the output of the sub-mixer or overdriving the input of the main console, almost any mixers and consoles can be linked in this way. These days, almost nobody sells something called a sub-mixer or an expander; you just use whatever unit you like. It may be a good idea to use a unit with similar signal quality (comparable specs), and possibly even made by the same company so the control layout is similar (which avoids confusion). You can even connect two identical, large mixing consoles with one designated as a sub-mixer. Be aware that a few mixers or consoles, generally older models, utilize a special multipin connector that is designated for a particular matching sub-mixer. In these cases, the sub-mixer may not include its own power supply, and the multipin connector on the main mixer or console will therefore feed DC power to the sub-

mixer. It may still be possible to use another brand or model sub-mixer with such a console, but a special adaptor cable would be required. If a console has no sub-mixer inputs, it can still accommodate a sub-mixer. You simply use one of the main console's input channels per sub-mixed bus, with the channel set up for line-level sources, or use a spare effects return or aux input on the main console to accommodate a sub-mix.

Remember that any time you add inputs to a mix, you add noise, so don't expect the system to be as quiet with the sub-mixer in the circuit. Be sure the polarity of the signals is correct. Even if you wire cables correctly, sometimes one mixer will invert the input signal whereas the other will not, so it may be a good idea to open two mics, side-by-side, one feeding the sub-mixer and one the main console, make a mono mix of the two mics on one bus in the main console, and flip the phase or reverse the polarity of one mic to see whether the sound increases or drops in level. If it increases, you may have to invert all the inputs on the sub-mixer, or use a polarity reversing adaptor in the link to the main console.

Sometimes a sub-mixer (i.e., any console) will have outputs that precede the master faders. Such outputs can be used to drive the main mixing console, thus allowing the sub-mixer's master faders to be manipulated for local use (i.e., for keyboard monitor speakers on stage) while the pre-fader outputs feed a consistent mix to the main console. In this case, it is a good idea to bring the sub-mixer outputs into inputs on the main mixing console that have level controls (i.e., input channels or aux returns) so that the sub-mixed signal can be balanced with the main mix.

It is best to connect a sub-mixer to the same leg or even the same outlet box of the AC power distribution system as the main mixing console. This will minimize differences in ground potential between the two units, and thus minimize chances for ground loop induced hum. While some would disconnect the sub-mixer's third prong if it has a grounded AC plug, and instead run a heavy ground wire from the sub-mixer chassis to the main console chassis, we do not recommend such a practice. Instead, it may be necessary to utilize transformer-isolated floating (and balanced) lines between the units. Be sure to perform a sound check with ALL stage equipment, including lights, turned on so that any potential hum or interference can be identified and minimized before the performance.

When using a sub-mixer, set up its gain structure as though it were the main mixing console, as explained in Section 11.7. Then adjust its master faders to produce the appropriate nominal output level so that, with the main console's master faders at their correct nominal position, the overall sound balance of the mix is correct. If the output of the sub-mixer is too high in level and requires that its master faders be operated way down near the lowest setting, then an external attenuation pad of an appropriate value should be inserted at the sub-input to the main console, and the sub-mixer's master faders returned to a more normal operating position. This will minimize noise and distortion.

Incidentally, there are situations where the main mixing console itself becomes a sub-mixer. For example, if there is a remote recording or broadcast truck covering a live event, some of the main sound reinforcement console's outputs may be fed to the truck's console. If there is a separate stage monitor mixing console which does not have a sufficient number of input channels, a sub-mix of several mics (say the entire drum mix) may be fed from the main console to the monitor console. The same considerations regarding correct level/impedance matching, gain structure, and grounding isolation apply here, too.

Stage monitoring systems are one of the important keys to a successful show. Sound reinforcement practice has evolved to the point where even small music clubs usually have some type of monitoring system, and large-scale concert monitor systems can be very elaborate. Despite their widespread use monitor systems are the subject of a lot of misunderstanding — particularly among musicians, who are the very ones to benefit most from a good monitor system.

11.9.1 What is a Stage Monitor System?

The stage monitor system is a specialized sound reinforcement system that operates independently of the house sound system. Like the house system, it consists of a console, equalizers (and, occasionally, other signal processors), power amplifiers and loudspeakers. Since the monitor system is used to help the musicians onstage hear their performance, the loudspeakers are pointed toward the stage rather than into the house.

The primary difference is that the monitor console has many separate output channels, each driving a separate amplifier and loudspeaker chain with a different mix, whereas house sound systems are monophonic or stereophonic (even if they do use a split stack up front and a few surround or fill speakers, many systems are mono).

Each monitor output mix is assigned to one or a few of the performers, and the mix that each hears is tailored to his or her particular needs. In order to stay on key and on cue, for example, the lead vocalist needs mostly to hear the background vocalists, along with perhaps a bit of the keyboard and guitar. Similarly, the bass player needs to hear the kick drum, and the drummer needs to hear the bass. The guitar player needs to hear both, while the keyboardist might need to hear the lead vocal and the guitar.

For this reason, monitor mixing consoles usually have eight or more output busses, and are designed for flexibility in assigning the inputs

proportionally to any combination of the outputs.

Monitor loudspeakers also are designed differently from house reinforcement speakers. Their frequency response is usually tailored more for voice reproduction, and their dispersion is often more focused to help control the sound onstage.

11.9.2 How is a Monitor System Set Up?

Figure 11-11 shows the signal flow of a typical stage monitor system. Each signal from the stage is routed to a splitter — usually a specialized transformer — which provides two separate, electrically isolated feeds (see Section 11.10). Another term for a splitter is a stage box. One feed from the stage box goes to the house console via the snake, which is a single multicore audio cable containing a number of individually shielded pairs of center conductors. The other feed is sent to the monitor console.

Each output of the monitor console feeds a separate equalizer (usually a graphic type, though parametrics are sometimes used) whose primary purpose is reducing peaks to control resonances and thus increase the available gain before feedback. The equalizers, in turn, feed power amplifiers that drive the monitor loudspeakers.

A cue bus output from the console feeds a separate monitor loudspeaker located right next to the console. The monitor engineer uses this output to check the separate mixes individually so that he can catch problems and fix them quickly. The graphic or parametric equalizers that are added to process the various output mixes are sometimes connected after the console output, but it is preferable to locate them in the console's master insert in/out loop. In this way, when the monitor engineer selects a given mix to feed the cue bus, the equalization is also audible.

Finally, there often are two side fill loudspeakers located at either side of the stage and fed from another mix.

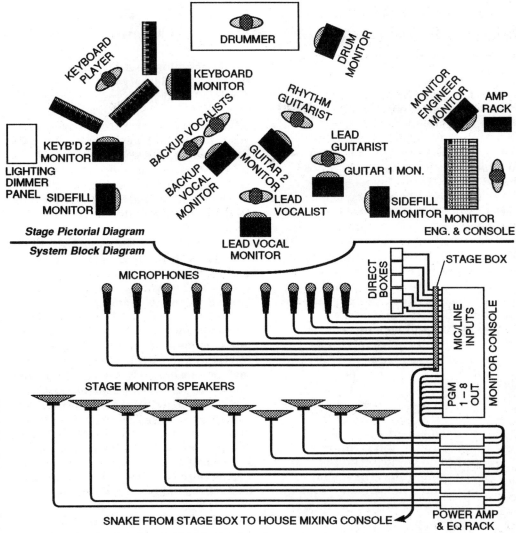

KEYBOARD PLAYER

DRUMMER

DRUM MONITOR

KEYBOARD MONITOR

RHYTHM GUITARIST

MONITOR ENGINEER MONITOR

AMP RACK

BACKUP VOCALISTS

LEAD GUITARIST

KEYB'D 2 MONITOR

LIGHTING DIMMER PANEL

BACKUP VOCAL MONITOR

GUITAR 2 MONITOR

GUITAR 1 MON.

SIDEFILL MONITOR

LEAD VOCALIST

SIDEFILL MONITOR

MONITOR ENG. & CONSOLE

Stage Pictorial Diagram

System Block Diagram

LEAD VOCAL MONITOR

STAGE BOX

DIRECT BOXES

MICROPHONES

MIC/LINE INPUTS

MONITOR CONSOLE

STAGE MONITOR SPEAKERS

PGM 1–8 OUT

SNAKE FROM STAGE BOX TO HOUSE MIXING CONSOLE

POWER AMP & EQ RACK

Figure 11-11. Block diagram of a typical stage monitor system

11.9.3 Why a Monitor Console is Preferable to a Mix From the Main House Console

In the early days of sound reinforcement — even in large concerts — the monitor mix was done from the main console out in the audience. As studio recording techniques became more sophisticated, musicians became increasingly discriminating about their onstage monitors because they became accustomed to playing along with selected tracks over headphones. Eventually, their desires simply exceeded both the capacities of house consoles and the ability of house soundmen to handle a large number of separate mixes. In order to satisfy the growing need for more sophisticated monitoring, concert engineers began using separate, onstage consoles for the monitors.

The out-front soundman was never in a very good position to mix monitors, anyway. Being located out in the house, he can't hear what it sounds like onstage. The musicians have to communicate with him using hand signals — and this can be quite confusing, especially in the middle of a show. Most important, the house engineer's primary responsibility is to manage the house mix. Once the show starts, he's got his hands full, and has very little time to worry about the monitors. This is why monitor mixing has become a separate job in sound reinforcement.

11.9.4 The Importance of a High Quality Monitor Mix

There are many reasons why a high quality monitor system is very important to the professional musician. Perhaps the most obvious one is that if the band members can't hear themselves clearly, they're going to have trouble staying in tune and in time — in which case, the potential for good sound quality in the house really doesn't matter! Especially when performers use pre-recorded tracks or sequencers (an increasingly common practice), they can get lost very quickly if they can't hear clearly... and a tape or sequencer can't make adjustments the way live players can. A good monitor system, then, can improve the musicians' performance.

The quality of the monitors also affects the quality of sound in the house. Regardless of how carefully the dispersion of the monitors is controlled, some of their sound inevitably spills out into the house, where the audience hears it directly. The sound of the monitors also gets into the onstage microphones and, if the monitor system is producing distortion, it will degrade the sound that the audience hears through the house sound system. Finally, the audio quality of a monitor system affects its susceptibility to feedback. Since feedback often starts on resonant spikes in the monitor loudspeakers, monitors with flatter (more accurate) frequency response will be less prone to feed back. It is a serious error to cut corners on a monitor system because you think it will not affect what the audience hears. It definitely will have an effect.

11.9.5 Other Benefits of a Separate Monitor Console

The monitor console can serve double or triple duty in a band's setup. Contemporary music relies increasingly on multiple-keyboard systems (often with MIDI-controlled synthesizer slaves) and electronic drums. As a consequence, there is a heightened need for onstage mixing consoles to provide submixes of the electronic instruments for the house console, and to the onstage monitor system.

A full monitor console can provide these submixes at the same time that it handles the monitor mixing. Figure 11-12 (next page) shows an example of such a setup using a 24-input x 4 aux bus x 8-main bus monitor console.

Input channels 1-11 are used as a submixer for a number of keyboard and guitar signals. Channels 14-18 handle the vocal mics, while 19-23 handle instrument mics. Channels 12 and 13 are the inputs from an effects processor, which is fed from the console's Aux output and is used to add some reverb, phasing or other effects to those monitor mixes that need it. Channel 24 is a spare input.

Aux outputs 1 and 2 supply stereo keyboard submixes for the house console and the keyboard player's amplifier/speaker system, while program outputs 1-8 handle the individual performers' monitor mixes. A built-in or separate intercom system is provided to talk with the soundman at the main house console.

The setup in Figure 11-12 offers a touring band numerous advantages. They have control over their own monitor mixes. They have two-way communications with their house sound engineer, allowing them even more control over their sound. And by combining the keyboard-submixing chore with monitor mixing, they save on the amount of equipment that they have to carry from one venue to the next — while substantially improving the quality of their sound.

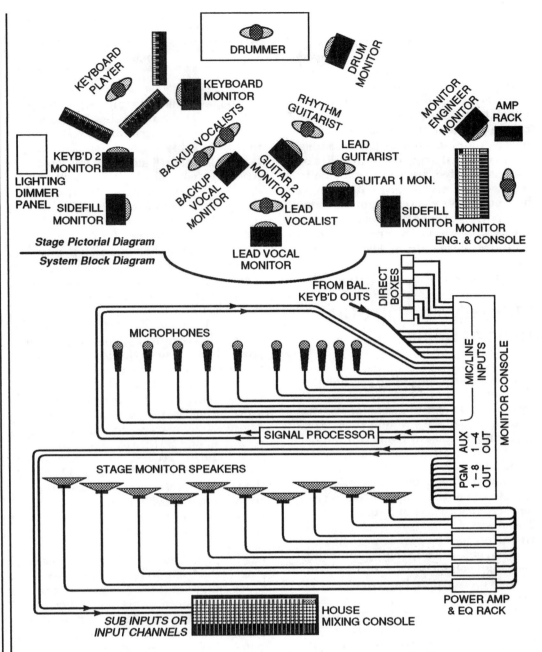

KEYBOARD
PLAYER

DRUMMER

DRUM
MONITOR

KEYBOARD
MONITOR

RHYTHM
GUITARIST

MONITOR
ENGINEER
MONITOR

AMP
RACK

KEYB'D 2
MONITOR

BACKUP VOCALISTS

LEAD
GUITARIST

LIGHTING
DIMMER
PANEL

SIDEFILL
MONITOR

BACKUP
VOCAL
MONITOR

GUITAR 2
MONITOR

GUITAR 1 MON.

LEAD
MONITOR

SIDEFILL
MONITOR

MONITOR
ENG. & CONSOLE

LEAD
VOCALIST

Stage Pictorial Diagram

System Block Diagram

LEAD VOCAL
MONITOR

FROM BAL.
KEYB'D OUTS

DIRECT
BOXES

MICROPHONES

MIC/LINE
INPUTS

MONITOR CONSOLE

SIGNAL PROCESSOR

AUX
1–4
OUT

PGM
1–8
OUT

STAGE MONITOR SPEAKERS

POWER AMP
& EQ RACK

*SUB INPUTS OR
INPUT CHANNELS*

HOUSE
MIXING CONSOLE

**Figure 11-12. A monitor mixing system which also
furnishes a submixed feed to the main house system**

11.9.6 Polarity (Phase) Reversal as a Tool to Fight Feedback

It is a common practice to ring out the monitor system before the performance. Ringing out is a method of tuning the equalization of each monitor channel to suppress resonances in the stage/monitor speaker system. The actual point at which feedback begins will change when performers are on stage, as mics are actually in use, and even with small changes in temperature and humidity (which can drastically affect the stage acoustics).

While graphic or parametric equalization is of great value in reducing feedback, so is the simple technique of reversing the polarity of a particular monitor console output. Unlike a main house mixing console, where various busses may be combined, or where the sound image from multiple speaker channels relies upon a specific phase (polarity) relationship between the channels, monitor mixes are each unique and are not intended to blend or overlap much. The absolute polarity of a sound has a lot to do with the point at which feedback occurs, and flipping that polarity can provide increased gain before feedback. Therefore, it is desirable to have polarity (or phase) reversal switches on each monitor console output. If these are not provided, then polarity reversing adaptors can be plugged into the output channels as required. It is still a good idea to have polarity reversing switches on each input, too, since multiple mic inputs are often blended onto a single bus, and these electrical signals (when they carry portions of the same sound source) must have the proper phase relationship in order to add constructively.

11.9.7 Eliminating SCR Dimmer Noise

SCR (silicon controlled rectifier) dimmers are widely employed in modern stage lighting control systems. Unlike the old wire wound rheostats, which might generate a local hum field due to strong 60 Hz electromagnetic radiation, SCR dimmers generate a widespread buzz due to the sharp wavefronts of the chopped AC waveform created by the dimming action. These waveforms can travel along AC wiring as high frequency parasitics, and can get into mic cables, inducing very high voltage spikes at the mixing console inputs. (See Figure 8-5 in Section 8.3.7.)

The resulting buzz can get into the mic inputs of the console, even if the console has high quality circuitry, when the inputs are electronically balanced. This type of interference is greatest when the monitor console or stage mic wiring run in close proximity to the SCR dimmer equipment, and where high power lighting is involved. As detailed in Section 11.7 and 11.10, there are situations where input transformers can provide increased CMRR (common mode rejection ratio) due to their higher CMV (common mode voltage) compared with electronically balanced differential inputs. If the monitor console does not have transformer-balanced (or floating) inputs, and SCR dimmer noise is a problem, it may be necessary to add transformers at the mic (or stage mic splitter box) *and* right at the console inputs.

The term mic splitting has nothing to do with the damage that can occur when a careless performer swings the mic by its cable, or intentionally slams it into the stage floor for visual impact. Actually, mic splitting refers to the division of the audio signal output from the mic to feed two or more different inputs. Typically, a mic signal will be split to simultaneously feed both a monitor mixing console and a main house mixing console (a 1:2 split), or it may feed these and also a remote broadcast or recording truck's console (a 1:3 split).

Splitting a signal is not that difficult. Theoretically, you can simply parallel-wire two or three connectors to the end of a cable and plug in. Sometimes a simple 1:2 Y connection can be used successfully. The trick is to avoid overloading the mic, which would degrade frequency response, transient response, and S/N ratio, and to avoid hum-inducing ground loops. There is also a danger, in hard wired splits of the type just described, that a short circuit in a mic cable to one console could kill the feed to all the other input(s) derived from that same mic, or that an electrical fault at a remote location could endanger a performer on stage. One solution is to double mic everything, but this approach is very costly, and doesn't work when it comes to the output of a guitar or synthesizer. For this reason, a transformer (sometimes with multiple secondary windings) can be used to achieve isolated splits from a single mic (or line level source).

To avoid ground loops in a Y connected split, why not cut the shield of the cable at the mic? This is possible, and actually works just fine in some installations, but it has drawbacks. For one thing, if the microphone is a phantom powered condenser mic, the shield connection is essential or there will be no return for the DC power that operates the amplifier/impedance converter within the mic case. Don't cut the shield, and you risk a ground loop. What can be done?

Again, the solution is to use a splitter transformer.

11.10.1 The Splitter Transformer

The main purpose of a splitter transformer is to isolate the shield grounds between two portions of a sound system. By using the setup illustrated, the stage mic (or keyboard mixer, guitar, etc.) is connected directly to the monitor console input. At the same time, the signal from the mic goes through a transformer. The transformer illustrated has two completely separate Faraday shields (electrostatic shields), one for the primary and one for the secondary. The primary shield is tied back to the monitor console, while the secondary shield is tied to the cable shield that goes to the main house console. In this way ground loop hum protection, and phantom power continuity are maintained for the stage mic (or instrument), while full shielding is also established between the split point and the main house console.

The particular transformer shown here is a Jensen model JE-MB-C, selected due to its very low distortion, low phase shift, wide bandwidth, and isolated shields. Information on this transformer, and on other similar transformers that provide additional splits (for feeding remote recording equipment, etc.) is available directly from Jensen Transformers, Inc., North Hollywood, CA.

You will notice that the circuit shown has a ground lift switch. When the switch is closed, the shields of the cable to the house console and the cable to the monitor console are electrically connected. This may be a good way to begin, but then, if hum and noise are detected, the ground can be lifted by opening the switch. You may find that you'll have to lift all but one of the grounds (on the several cables between the consoles) or every single ground. The situation will differ for each setup, sometimes for each venue given the same sound system.

Typically, stage boxes are constructed that each house from 8 to 24 transformers, and the associated connectors, switches, etc. There may be large, locking, multi-pin connectors that allow stage boxes to be joined to multicore cables, with the possibility of

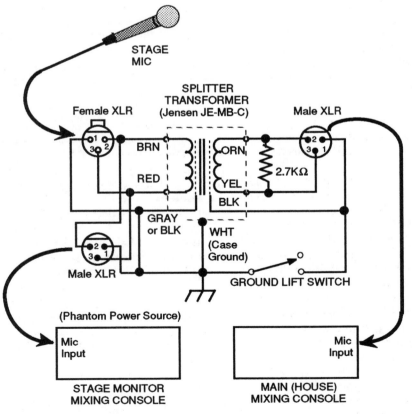

Figure 11-13. An isolated mic split feed that allows phantom powering of the mic

using different stage boxes or extending cables without the need to rewire the entire audio distribution system. This is a more convenient way to deal with the situation than constructing an individual splitter box for each channel. One transformer per channel is required. Why are these transformers not built into the console itself? They are not always necessary. (Avoid the trap of thinking that if you always have all the ground lift switches closed, you don't really need the transformers; remember, each ground on a given multway split should be tied to a separate Faraday shield in the transformer). Since transformers are very expensive, there is no use paying for them unless they're needed. Besides, building an input/splitter transformer into the monitor console would not necessarily provide grounding isolation for the cable to the house console (or to any other remote location).

There may be a few, rare instances when even the use of splitter transformers and proper grounding techniques may not be adequate to prevent noise from getting into the mixing system. This can occur in a very high noise environment, as when the monitor console and/or stage cables are located very near a high-power SCR dimmer lighting panel. Normally, the common mode rejection ratio or CMRR of the electronically balanced monitor console inputs is more than adquate to eliminate such noise when it cuts into the balanced cable from the microphone. But when the noise energy radiated by a nearby source is very strong, the common mode voltage (CMV) of the electronically balanced input may be exceeded. In this case, the CMRR goes to zero, and the only solutions would be either to (1) move the cables and/or console away from the noise source, or (2) provide additional noise protection. This topic is covered in greater detail in Section 11.6. Understand that the following remedies pertain to only the most severe, high-noise environments, and should not be necessary for most sound system installations.

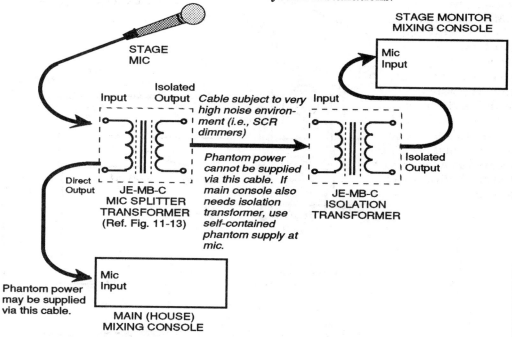

Figure 11-14. Use of additional transformers for isolation of electronically balanced inputs in the presence of extreme noise (SCR dimmers, forexample)

11.10.3 Splitting a Mic Without a Transformer

The first line of attack against severe noise is to use a very high density shielded cable, such as star quad type cable, which has four inner conductors in a double twisted configuration for extra noise cancellation. It is really double-balanced cable. (Star Quad type cable is available from Canare Cable, Inc., North Hollywood, CA.) Whether in single cables or snakes, this type of cable can make a significant difference in the noise immunity under most conditions.

If the special cable alone is not adequate, then it may be necessary to install additional transformers right at the inputs to the monitor console (if the console does not have transformer-isolated inputs) and, if the house console is not transformer isolated, possibly at the inputs to that console, too (Figure 11-14). These transformers should have the shortest possible cable to the console (6 inches to a foot or two) so that minimal noise exposure exists. The same Jensen JE-MB-C transformer (or equivalent) is suitable here. The advantage of using the extra transformer, even though the input is already electronically balanced, is that the transformer provides up to 200 volts peak common mode voltage, with an 85 dB CMRR at 1 kHz — a higher CMRR and much higher CMV (to fight the high peak noise voltages) than is possible with the electronically balanced input alone. This is a costly solution, and should be treated as a last resort in the most critical situations.

As described earlier, there are instances when microphones can be split to feed two consoles simply by using a Y adaptor. This technique is most successfully applied when the two consoles are similar in design, and when both are operated from the same AC system. It is not a good idea to use parallel hard wired splitting when feeding a remote recording or broadcast facility. When a mic is split without a transformer, there is no good way to avoid ground loops, except perhaps to cut the shield at the XLR connector of one console or the other. In this way, the chassis ground from the other console provide a drain for all currents induced in the shields of the cables from the mic to both consoles.

When a phantom powered mic is to be used, we recommend powering it from the monitor console on stage, if that console has the capability, since the DC power for the mic will travel through a shorter length of cable and will therefore be subject to less voltage drop (see Figure 11-15 on the previous page). This means that the shield must be connected at the monitor console in order to complete the phantom power circuit. If a shield has to be cut to avoid a ground loop, cut it at the house console input connector.

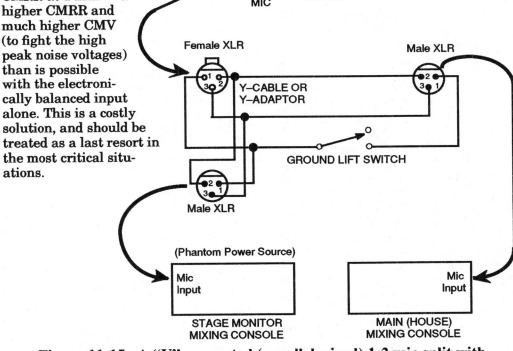

Figure 11-15. A "Y" connected (parallel wired) 1:2 mic split with hard wiring instead of a transformer

11.11. Reducing Feedback In The Stage Monitor System

Anyone who has dealt with stage monitor systems will tell you that it's a constant battle to obtain adequate volume levels for the performers without causing howling, ringing or other effects that all amount to electro-acoustic feedback. When you place a microphone near a loudspeaker which, ultimately, is fed by that mic, you're going to get feedback as soon as the speaker output reaches a critical sound pressure level at the mic.

In many cases, feedback can be controlled or eliminated by using signal delay in the amplifier / loudspeaker system. This is because the feedback can be caused by (a) notched response in the speaker system and/or (b) improper dispersion control in the speaker system, both of which are often traceable to time offset of the drivers at the crossover frequency or between identical drivers connected to different length horns. These time offsets create comb filters and distort the ideal polar response of the loudspeaker system; eliminating them can help tame feedback. It may require a digital signal delay with precision down to as little as 10 to 50 microseconds (translating to $^1/_8$ to $^5/_8$ inches offset of the acoustic center of the driver) in order to make effective corrections in this domain. Such time-based or position-based corrections should be made before any graphic or parametric EQ is applied for feedback control. Of course, the implementation of these very precise delay corrections is complex and costly. Instead, longer delays of 20 to 30 milliseconds will often satisfy the musicians (especially vocalists) with less overall level because the performers can hear themselves better. Then there is less of a feedback problem, too, because less gain is required.

11.11.1 Directional Microphones

The name of the game is increasing the available gain before feedback occurs. The first line of attack is to use cardioid microphones, and to make sure the back of these mics is directed at the nearest monitors. This seems obvious to anyone who has done any stage work, but there are some tricks. For example, the directionality of the mic typically depends on vents toward the rear of the mic head, or possibly in the mic handle. If the vents are covered, the directional characteristics go away and the feedback protection is lost. The same problem occurs if the mic head is swallowed — literally placed inside the mouth, or with a cupped hand over it. For this reason, performers should be instructed (with tact) about how not to hold the mic.

11.11.2 Polarity (Phase) Reversal

Given that a directional mic is used, what else can be done? Sometimes feedback can be eliminated by simply reversing the phase of the signal at either the mic or at the monitor speaker. We use the expression *reverse the phase,* but we really mean reverse the polarity by exchanging the two signal conductors in the audio line. Reversing the polarity can reduce feedback because, instead of having the direct and reinforced sound waveforms adding together and thereby exceeding the threshold of feedback, they subtract from one another.

Polarity reversal can be accomplished by exchanging the two wires that connect to the loudspeaker, by exchanging the two signal wires in the balanced audio line (using a phase-reversal adaptor), or by using a switch provided for this purpose in the mixing console. It's better to try this first at the monitor speaker because if you flip the polarity of the mic, it may alter the stereo image (if it's a stereo mix), render any recordings uncuttable (if a record is to be made), and make it impossible to get a proper mono blend with other mics (for house feed or broadcast). For the same reason that the polarity reversal reduces feedback (i.e., signal cancellation), out-of-phase inputs cannot be properly mixed to mono; the signal simply disappears! In record cutting, any out-of-phase information in the left and right channels causes vertical movement of the cutting stylus. Even if the cutter head manages to cut a groove with this vertical anti-phase information, the playback stylus can skip out of the groove, making the record unplayable. One way to check inputs for mono compatibility is to press the input cue or preview switches (if available on the console) for suspect channels and listen to the result in the headphones or via a speaker connected to the console's cue or monitor output. If the signals all remain clearly audible, the phase relationship is OK, but if a portion of the sound goes away, then one input is out-of-phase with respect to the other.

11.11.3 Ringing Out a Monitor System

Polarity (phase) reversal can allow somewhat more gain before feedback, but sooner or later most engineers realize that equalization is required to get the most gain before feedback.

The most common method of eliminating feedback in a stage monitor system is to ring out the monitor system before the performance. Ringing out is a method of tuning the equalization of each monitor channel to suppress resonances in the stage/monitor speaker system.

Why is it called ringing out? Any sound system will begin to howl at the frequency where the loop between mic and speaker is loudest. This loudest point can be caused by a peak in the speaker's response, a peak in the mic's response, by channel EQ boost in the console, by resonances and reflections in the acoustic environment or, most likely, by a combination of these factors. Just before a system takes off and howls you can usually hear a ringing sound, a slight resonance when almost any sound is amplified. By looking for, and tuning out, these incipient feedback points, one rings out the system.

Why do resonances occur? There are many reasons, including loudspeaker

response, acoustic reflection and/or absorption characteristics of the environment, and the mics themselves. Certainly, all directional mics exhibit different directional characteristics at different frequencies, so a mic that offers great back rejection (15 dB) at 2 kHz, may offer almost no protection at 200 Hz (3 dB); one might expect that some bass roll-off would aid in reducing the feedback from such a mic.

Where should the EQ be introduced? Well, one does not necessarily want to introduce EQ in the individual channels because the EQ needed to reduce feedback at one mic might not be right for the other mics. That EQ may also sound wrong to other performers when they hear the same mic on their monitors. It is possible to use some channel EQ to reduce feedback but it is generally better to apply equalization at the input to the power amp which drives the particular monitor speaker. Instead of connecting the equalizer after the monitor console's master output, it may be better to connect it in the master insert in/out patch point (if one is provided) so the engineer can hear the effect of the EQ while monitoring via the console's master cue/monitor facilities. Graphic EQ is most commonly used for ringing out monitor systems, and typically one-third octave resolution is preferred to one octave resolution. This offers a major benefit over channel EQ. Specifically, $1/3$–octave graphic equalization enables you to lower the level of a relatively narrow band of frequencies without affecting nearby frequencies. Resonances, reflections, and hence feedback all tend to occur in very narrow frequency bands, so the graphic EQ is able to do the job with minimal ducking of adjacent program frequencies which are not causing any problems.

Sometimes $1/6$- or $1/12$-octave graphic EQ is used because it further narrows any corrections. The typical feedback situation involves such a narrow band of frequencies that a notch filter of only 10 Hz bandwidth may be ideal for removing the feedback without removing adjacent program material. This high resolution means trickier setup, more tendency to drift out of adjustment as the stage temperature and humidity change (which changes the acoustics), and higher equipment costs. (For those who are very technically inclined, consider that feedback is a wavelength-related phenomenon, not a frequency domain phenomenon, so tuning a frequency-calibrated equalizer, no matter how stable, may not keep the feedback from drifting back in as the wavelengths change due to atmospheric conditions.)

Here's how to ring out the system. Set up the stage exactly as it will be used, with all mics in place and all controls set. If you can do this at a sound check, with performers standing at the mics, so much the better. (You might offer ear plugs because they are going to hear some howling.) Go through one monitor output at a time. Gradually turn up the volume until a slight ringing begins while a given mic is being talked (that is, while someone is speaking into the mic). Turn the level up slightly higher until a howl just begins. Then, using your golden ears or, preferably, a spectrum analyzer, identify the frequency at which this howling occurs. Locate the corresponding frequency band on the graphic equalizer, and pull that band down about 3 dB. Then bring up the monitor output level some more, while the same person is talking, until ringing/howling again commences. If it's at the same frequency, pull down the slider another few dB; if it's a different frequency, pull down that slider 3 dB. Eventually, you'll reach a point where many frequencies all start to howl at once, or where you've already adjusted most of the frequencies that begin to howl as you further raise the gain. That's when you can stop the EQ adjustments. You've gotten all the gain there is. Then go on to the next monitor speaker, perhaps with another mic if that is the primary mic feeding this new speaker. When you're done, you may find you've obtained from 3 to 15 dB more usable gain out of the monitor system.

One further note about feedback reduction. Use the console's built-in high pass filters whenever possible. If the console has a 60 to 100 Hz low cut (high pass) filter, preferably at 12 dB to 18 dB per octave, it will cut out a lot of noise (wind, vocal pops, mic stand rumble), and thus clean up the sound to reduce muddiness. What's more, low frequency resonances in the stage itself can be excited by the instruments and monitor speakers and then travel through the floor or the air and get into the mics. These resonances will be much less likely to create feedback if they are reduced by using the 80 Hz (or thereabouts) filters. The only outputs where you may not want to use the filter are those for the drummer and perhaps a keyboard player who wants to hear low synthesizer notes. For everyone else, it is better to insert the filter, and then remove it if someone complains (which is highly unlikely). If there are no suitable filters in the console, it may be possible to find one built into the graphic equalizer or even the power amp, or to add an in-line filter between the monitor console output and the stage power amps.

The best results are obtained if the procedure is followed each night — even if you're playing the same stage. This is because even small changes in temperature, humidity, and stage layout can drastically affect the stage acoustics.

It is essential to control the system gain so that it never gets to the point where feedback is a problem. Ringing out the monitors will help with this, but it is usually wise to allow about 10 dB of headroom in the system when establishing your initial settings during the sound check. The energy of live performance is very different from that of the sound check, and the stage level can rise rapidly if the performance is successful and the crowd is responding. Leaving a safe gain margin allows the flexibility to open up the monitors as the performance rises in intensity, without running into feedback or instability.

11.11.4 Aiming Monitor Loudspeakers

In placing and aiming a stage monitor, there are two basic criteria. First, since the function of the loudspeaker is to allow the performer to hear himself or herself, it must be aimed so that the performer stands or sits within the primary dispersion pattern of the system. Since onstage ambient levels can be fairly high, it is also important to place the monitor close to the performer.

Loudspeaker dispersion is most critical in the high frequencies, which affect voice intelligibility. The manufacturer's data sheet can provide valuable information about the dispersion characteristics of the monitor, and you should consult it in planning placements. This rough placement can then be fine-tuned (aimed) by ear, using recorded music.

As important as it is to get the sound where you want it, it is just as important to keep the sound from getting where you don't want it — and one such place is the performer's microphone. For this reason, monitors are usually placed in the maximum rejection area of the polar pattern for the vocal or instrument mic. Since that mic is almost always a cardioid, the maximum rejection area will be to the rear of the microphone, so the monitor should be placed such that the microphone stand is between the performer and the speaker, with the mic aimed so that its rear points at the loudspeaker.

In situations where the lead vocalist moves in a wide area onstage, some engineers use two monitors to cover the full stage. The most common practice has been to place the two monitors apart from one another and aimed so that their patterns intersect at center stage. This type of placement can be a mistake. The interaction of the two loudspeakers causes comb filtering, resulting in uneven frequency response and a much higher potential for feedback.

When using two stage monitors, the best approach is to place them close together with their rear corners touching, and splay them to cover the stage area. This technique results in much smoother coverage of the stage, and greatly reduces the possibility of feedback induced by comb filter peaks.

11.12 Equipment Placement

We discussed monitor loudspeaker placement in the preceeding paragraphs, but what about placement of the other key elements the monitor and house mixing consoles? Because the person operating the console has control of the sound quality and balance, it is important for the console to be physically located where the sound that operator hears is an appropriate reference.

We have already described some of the reasons why it is important to place the monitor console near the performers, preferably at the side of the stage (ease of hand signals to the operator for mixing requests, reference to the on stage sound field, and so forth). But exactly where at stageside should the console be located?

11.12.1 Additional Monitor Console Placement Factors

The monitor console will be on one side or the other of the stage. Sometimes the actual layout of performers, props and equipment will dictate which side of the stage is best for the monitor console. If there is no strong need to place it on one side or another, then it should probably be placed on the side opposite that where the stage lighting equipment (dimmers, power transformers, etc) are located. If there are no concerns with stage lighting equipment, then the monitor console should be on the side of the stage nearest the house console, which will tend to minimize the length of cable runs. It is also best if the monitor console is located very close to the power amplifier and related sound equipment racks on stage. Sometimes another helper is not there for backup, and the close placement means that if the monitor console operator must make adjustments or fix problems in the amps (even if they're the amps for the main house loudspeakers), it can be done without leaving the vicinity of the monitor console.

11.12.2 Main House Mixing Console Placement

One of the most important factors in obtaining a good sounding mix for the audience is the location of the house mixing console. What the audience hears is a direct result of the mixing balance, overall level, and equalization adjustments that the operator makes. And those adjustments are, in turn, based entirely on what that console operator hears. Place the console in an inappropriate location, and the sound may be OK for people at that location, but perhaps for nobody else.

The ideal location, then, is that location at which the sound is most representative of the sound heard by the greatest number of people in the audience. One might assume this to be about half the distance from the main house loudspeakers to the back of the audience, and on the central axis from the stage, but this is not generally the best position.

Many sound engineers prefer to do their mixing dead center in front of one of the main house speaker stacks (and typically there are two, although they carry the same mono mix). This gives the engineer a good on-axis reference where frequency response is most uniform, and avoids excess influence from spill of onstage sound. In fact, a location which is centered mid way between two speaker stacks is least desirable because of phase cancellations (and comb filtering) of sound from the two stacks. If one wishes to be near the middle of the audience (from left to right), then at least make sure the position is somewhat off center to reduce the phase problems.

A general rule of thumb with regard to the distance from the main house loudspeakers is this: measure the distance between the two main stacks (we're assuming there are two), and do

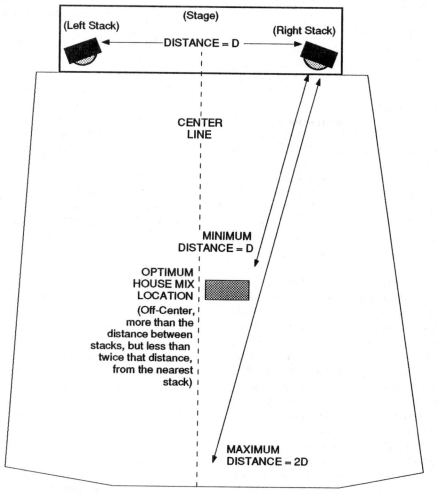

Figure 11-16. A suggested location for the mixing console in a concert hall

not locate the house console any closer than this distance from the nearest stack. Also, do not locate the console any further than twice that inter-stack distance. These relationships are shown in Figure 11-16. This rule does not always apply. In a larger venue, say a sports arena, the distance between stacks may be 50 feet. According to the formula, one would not want to be more than 100 feet from the stage stacks. However, the back of the audience may be 400 feet away, so the 100 foot limitation would place the console too close.

There is another problem — formulas or not — in being too far from the main loudspeakers (the above arena could present a problem here). At a distance, the time it takes for the sound to reach the console becomes significant, and the operator can miss cues. Instead of coming in on the quarter or half note cue, he may be a few full notes late. It is best to keep the console within 100 feet of the main loudspeakers, which keeps the time delay under 100 milliseconds. In smaller venues, even 100 feet may be too far back if it places the mixing console under a balcony or near a wall. A balcony or other overhang will change the acoustics (usually build up the bass and alter the reverberant field) such that the operator hears something that most of the audience does not.

If the house console is located too near the stage, there are other potential problems. Being close to the stage causes the operator to mix down too much in level, and the people near the back will be shouting for more volume. Also, spill from the monitor loudspeakers can influence the perceived mixing requirements for the house, and most of the audience may not be hearing that spill. Another factor — even if one decides that this near-stage position is a good idea acoustically — is that the best seats in the house, and certainly those that produce the most revenue, tend to be up front, and the show promoters are always reluctant to give up those revenue producers. In fact, it may take some convincing to get the needed seats removed mid-audience where the console belongs, but it's worth fighting for because the show quality depends on it.

12.1. GENERAL DISCUSSION

The audio power amplifier is a signal processing component whose function is – as its name implies – to increase the power of an audio signal. In sound systems, the power amplifier is always the final active component in the signal chain, located just before the loudspeakers.

Power amplifiers designed for professional use are generally simple in appearance compared to many hi-fi amplifiers. Aside from a line-level input and a high-level output for connection to the loudspeakers, they may have a power switch, sensitivity (volume) controls and, occasionally, meters. Many professional amplifiers omit one or more of even these bare amenities.

In small portable sound systems, the power amplifier may be built into the mixer, as a convenience. Such integrated devices are called powered mixers.

12.2 OHM'S LAW & RELATED EQUATIONS

Full comprehension of the function and application of power amplifiers requires an understanding of electrical power and its relationship to voltage, to resistance or impedance, and to current. These relationships are stated by Ohm's Law – one of the most important fundamental equations in electrical physics (and, hence, in audio).

12.2.1 Voltage, Resistance and Current

Consider the circuit of Figure 12-1. A DC voltage E from source S (a battery) is applied across a load resistance R. The completion of the circuit allows the flow of a current "I," represented by an arrow in the diagram. Current flows as a stream of electrons from the point of highest voltage (or potential) – the - terminal of the battery – to the point of lowest potential, which is the + terminal.

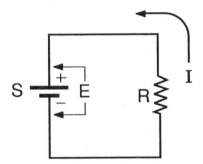

Figure 12-1. A simple DC circuit

The relationships among voltage, resistance and current in the circuit of Figure 12-1 are defined by Ohm's Law as follows:

$$I = E \div R$$

where:
I = current in amperes
E = electrical potential in volts
R = resistance in ohms

Suppose that we know the voltage to be 1 volt DC and the resistance to be 100 ohms. Using Ohm's Law, we can easily calculate the current through the load:

$$I = 1 \text{ volt} \div 100 \text{ ohms}$$
$$= .01 \text{ ampere}$$
$$= 10 \text{ milliamps}$$

By simple algebraic transpositions, we can restate the law to solve for any of the three quantities when the other two are known:

$$\boxed{I = E \div R} \quad \boxed{R = E \div I} \quad \boxed{E = I \bullet R}$$

In AC circuits, the complex quantity of impedance substitutes for resistance. Impedance is defined as the total opposition to flow of alternating current, including both DC resistance and the frequency-dependent opposition component, which is called reactance. The symbol for impedance is "Z," and, like resistance, the unit of impedance also is the ohm. Thus, in AC circuits:

$$\boxed{I = E \div Z} \quad \boxed{Z = E \div I} \quad \boxed{E = I \bullet Z}$$

where:
I = AC current in amperes
E = AC electrical potential in volts
Z = Impedance in ohms

For example, in Figure 12-2 an AC voltage E_{RMS} from source S is applied across load impedance Z. Current I flows through the load. Note that the direction of current flow alternates with the voltage: this is an alternating current (AC) circuit. Suppose that we know E to be 1 volt RMS, and Z to be 100 ohms. As above, we can easily find

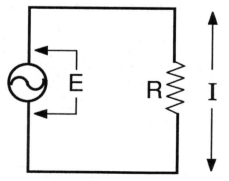

Figure 12-2. A simple AC circuit

I by Ohm's Law:
$$I \text{ (RMS)} = 1 \text{ volt RMS} \div 100 \text{ ohms}$$
$$= .01 \text{ amperes}$$
$$= 10 \text{ milliamps}$$

Note that in AC circuits impedance includes a frequency-dependent term called reactance. The value of a given load impedance in audio circuits generally changes with frequency. If the signal voltage remains constant, then the current through the load will be different at different frequencies. As indicated by Ohm's Law, the current will be inversely proportional to the impedance. As the impedance drops, the current will rise (and vice versa).

12.2.2 Electrical Power

Electrical power is the energy used to do the work when an electrical current is made to flow through a load resistance or impedance. The equation for power, though not part of Ohm's Law, is related, and is defined as follows:

$$\boxed{P = E \bullet I}$$

where:
P = power in watts
E = electrical potential in volts
I = current in amperes

By referring to the equations giving the relationships among voltage, resistance (or impedance) and current, we can rewrite the power equation, incorporating the resistance (or impedance) component:

$$\boxed{\begin{array}{l} P = E^2 \div R \text{ (or Z)} \\ P = I^2 \bullet R \text{ (or Z)} \end{array}}$$

Consider again the circuits of Figures 12-1 and 12-2. Knowing the voltage and resistance (or impedance), we can now calculate the power dissipated in each case.

In Figure 12-1, the voltage was 1 volt DC and the resistance was 100 ohms. To find the power:

$$P = E^2 \div R$$
$$= (1 \text{ volt})^2 \div 100 \text{ ohms}$$
$$= .01 \text{ watts}$$
$$= 10 \text{ milliwatts}$$

Since we chose the same voltage and impedance values in Figure 12-2, this calculation also describes that circuit. Since the circuit of Figure 12-2 is an AC circuit and the voltage is given as 1 volt RMS, we call the P term the average power. (The misnomer RMS power is sometimes used, indicating that the power was calculated from the RMS voltage or from the RMS current. Since voltage and current are out-of-phase in an AC circuit, simple multiplication of RMS voltage times RMS current does not yield RMS power.)

Figure 12-3 is a reference chart giving all the equations deriving from Ohm's Law. The parameters E, I, R (or Z) and P (or W) are shown in the central area, each occupying one of the four quadrants of the pie. To solve for a given parameter, find that parameter at the center of the chart and choose the equation in its quadrant that defines the quantity in terms that you have measured or know.

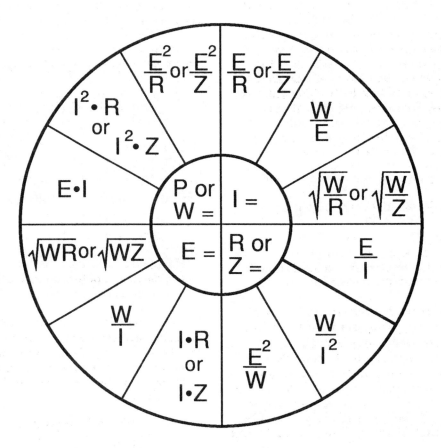

Figure 12-3. Ohm's Law Nomograph for AC or DC

Where:

I = AC current in amperes
E = AC electrical potential in volts
Z = Impedance in ohms
R = Resistance in ohms
P = Power in watts
W = Power in watts

NOTE: Equations referring to power and impedance are describing a Power Factor (PF), rather than pure DC power. This quantity accounts for the reactance of the load and the AC signal.

For example, suppose that we wish to know the power in the circuit of Figure 12-4 (next page). We know that the load resistance is 50 ohms, and we have measured the current through that resistance to be 20 milliamps.

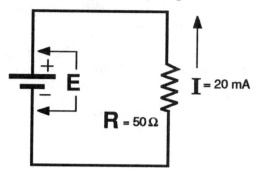

Figure 12-4. Sample Circuit for Power Calculation

From the chart of Figure 12-3, we look at the P (power) quadrant and find an equation that utilizes the I (current) and R (resistance) which we already know. The appropriate equation is:

$$P = I^2 \cdot R$$

Plugging in our measured values:

$$P = (.02 \text{ amperes})^2 \cdot 50 \text{ ohms}$$
$$= .0004 \cdot 50$$
$$= .02 \text{ watts} = 20 \text{ milliwatts}$$

Calculations based on Ohm's Law are extremely common in sound work. The chart of Figure 12-3 will serve as a useful reminder for all variations of the basic equation, and should be kept at hand as a reference.

12.2.4 Electrical Power and Amplifier Gain

We have said that the function of an audio power amplifier is to increase the power of an audio signal. What, precisely, does this mean?

Figure 12-5 shows a symbolic representation of a typical audio connection between a signal source, power amplifier, and loudspeaker. A signal source develops a signal voltage E_1 across the amplifier input impedance Z_1.

Let us presume that:

$$E_1 = 1 \text{ volt RMS}$$

$$Z_1 = 10 \text{ kohms (10,000 ohms)}$$

The signal power of the line-level connection, then, is given by the equation:

$$P = E_1^2 \div Z$$
$$= (1 \text{ volt})^2 \div 10,000 \text{ ohms}$$
$$= .0001 \text{ watts}$$

Expressed in dBm, the line-level signal power is:

$$\text{ndBm} = 10 \log (P_1 \div 1 \text{ milliwatt})$$
$$= 10 \log (10^{-4} \div 10^{-3})$$
$$= -10 \text{ dBm}$$

Now, let us consider that the voltage gain of the power amplifier is unity and the loudspeaker impedance is 8 ohms – that is:

$$E_1 = E_2$$

$$Z_2 = 8 \text{ ohms}$$

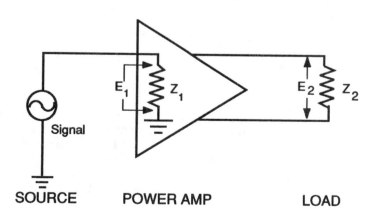

Figure 12-5. Typical Audio Circuit: A Signal Source, a Power Amplifier and a Load

The signal power transferred to the loudspeaker load is:

$$P = E_2^2 \div Z$$
$$= (1 \text{ volt})^2 \div 8 \text{ ohms}$$
$$= 0.125 \text{ watts}$$

Expressed in dBm, the loudspeaker-level signal power is:

$$ndBm = 10 \log (.125 \text{ watts} \div 10^{-3} \text{ watts})$$
$$= 20.9 \text{ dBm}$$

We can see that, while the voltage gain of the amplifier is unity, its power gain is considerably greater than unity. In dB, the power gain of this amplifier is:

$$A_v = (P_{out} \text{ in dB}) - (P_{in} \text{ in dB})$$
$$= 21 \text{ dBm} - (-10 \text{ dBm})$$
$$= 31 \text{ dB}$$

The power amplifier has effectively increased the audio signal power by 31 dB (a factor of about 1260:1).

NOTE: In this discussion, when we speak of amplifier gain, it is necessary to specify whether we are talking about voltage or power. By extension, when we use quantities expressed in dBm, it is extremely important to remember that dBm is a unit of power (decibels referred to 1 milliwatt), not of voltage.

12.3 Power Ratings of Amplifiers

The power rating of an amplifier states the power that the unit will deliver to a specified load — at a specified distortion level, and over a specified frequency range. For example, the power specification for a typical professional amplifier might read:

Power Output Level
Continuous average sine wave power at less than 0.05% THD, 20 Hz to 20 kHz:

Stereo, 8 ohms,
both channels driven...240 W/ch

Stereo, 4 ohms,
both channels driven...400 W/ch

Note that, since a 4 ohm figure is given, we can assume that the unit will safely handle loads as low as 4 ohms. We see, however, that the 4 ohm power figure is somewhat less than twice the 8 ohm figure. This is typical, and indicates protective current limiting, probably due to power supply limitations or component heating restrictions.

Output power specifications must be read carefully to avoid misinterpretation. For example, some manufacturers may provide less complete statements of output power than that given above. If the distortion value, bandwidth and load impedance are not given, the true performance of the amplifier cannot be adequately predicted.

Manufacturers may occasionally specify peak power in addition to average power. This often indicates that the power supply of the amplifier is operating near its limits, and sags under heavy continuous current demand — even though it may be capable of higher current for very brief periods. While such an amplifier may be suitable for home hi-fi use, where the unit's maximum output is rarely (if ever) needed, it won't serve well in a professional application.

12.3.1 FTC Preconditioning

A number of years ago, in response to wildly different means of rating power in consumer electronic equipment, the Federal Trade Commission defined a standard for rating consumer power amplifiers. Such power ratings are specified to be derived from tests made after a specific preconditioning cycle. The purpose of the preconditioning is to assure that the unit will perform reliably when it is heated to the highest temperature that it can be expected to reach in normal use.

FTC preconditioning involves operating the amplifier at one third the rated power, using a 1 kHz sine wave signal, into a resistance equivalent to the rated load impedance, for one hour. (In typical class B amplifier circuits, one-third power operation produces maximum heating of the output transistors.)

While professional amplifiers legally are not required to meet FTC preconditioning, an amplifier that is designed for professional service is likely to encounter worst case temperature conditions relatively frequently. A professional power amplifier should reasonably be expected not only to meet but to exceed the FTC preconditioning standard.

If an amplifier has been tested by its manufacturer according to FTC standards, the specifications normally will show this to be the case. For example, the power rating may be termed "FTC Power Rating." Alternately, the manufacturer may choose to mention FTC preconditioning in a footnote or elsewhere in the data sheet — either by name, or by a description of the procedure.

12.3.2 Power Bandwidth

The power bandwidth of an amplifier is a measure of its ability to produce high output power over a wide frequency range. As such, the power bandwidth specification complements the standard power specification described above, and can tell us more about the unit's performance.

Power bandwidth is a frequency-related specification, defined as the frequency range lying between those points at which the amplifier will produce at least half its rated power before clipping. It is sometimes specified as a numerical bandwidth (i.e., so many kilohertz) or may be given in the form of a graph, as in Figure 12-6.

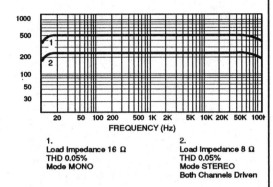

1.
Load Impedance 16 Ω
THD 0.05%
Mode MONO

2.
Load Impedance 8 Ω
THD 0.05%
Mode STEREO
Both Channels Driven

Figure 12-6. Power bandwidth of a power amplifier

Note that while this figure resembles a frequency response curve, it does not, in fact, represent the frequency response of the amplifier. What it shows is the maximum power output plotted against frequency. There is no assumption that the input drive level is the same across the band.

Power bandwidth can affect frequency response. If an amplifier's power bandwidth is limited — as is the case with most older, transformer-output designs — the amplifier's response may collapse at the frequency extremes when it is driven to maximum power, even though the amplifier might exhibit very wide frequency response at low power levels. In fact, a power amplifier's frequency response is generally measured at 1 watt output level, so power bandwidth problems do not affect the specification (even if they do affect actual performance).

The power bandwidth of modern OTL (output transformerless) transistor amplifiers is generally excellent, resembling that shown in Figure 12-6. Such amplifiers exhibit consistent frequency response at both low and high levels, and consequently reproduce program material at high power with far greater fidelity than older, transformer-coupled designs.

12.3.3 Slew Rate and Output Power

Slew rate is a measure of the ability of an amplifier to respond to very fast changes in signal voltage.

Assume an instantaneous step change in signal voltage at the input of the amplifier, as shown in Figure 12–7(a). The amplifier attempts to replicate that input step change at its output as exactly as possible, except perhaps at a higher voltage. Due to the inherent speed limitations of practical analog circuitry, the amplifier's output voltage change will occur somewhat more slowly than the input step, appearing as the steep ramp shown in Figure 12-7(b).

The slope of the ramping output voltage is called the slew rate of the amplifier. We specify slew rate in volts per microsecond (1 microsecond = $\frac{1}{1,000,000}$th of a second).

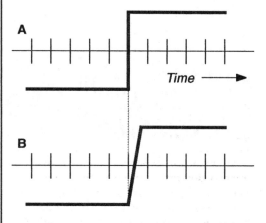

Figure 12-7. Slewing of a step

An amplifier's slew rate can affect its ability to render musical transients and complex waveforms with accuracy at high power levels. Note that this can be an important specification because sharply rising musical transients usually occur on peaks, where the power demand is greatest.

Figure 12-8 illustrates the importance of high slew rate in rendering step changes at high power levels. In (a), we see the instantaneous step change at the input of the amplifier. In (b), the amplifier reproduces that step change at low output level. We see that this is a fairly close approximation of the input step.

In (c) the same unit is asked to reproduce the same step change at a high output level. We see that the slew

rate of the unit has produced significant distortion of the signal (the input step, scaled in size, is superimposed over the output step as a dotted line for comparison). We can conclude that the higher the amplifier power, the higher the slew rate must be. After all, at any given frequency (a given number of cycles per second), a higher voltage (higher power) output will have to slew more volts per second (and more volts per microsecond).

As a rule of thumb, low-power amplifiers (up to 100 watts continuous per channel) should have a slew rate of at least 10 volts per microsecond. High-power amplifiers (over 200 watts) should have a slew rate of at least 30 volts per microsecond. The higher the slew rate, the better, up to a point. Too high a slew rate in a power amplifier may be associated with too wide a

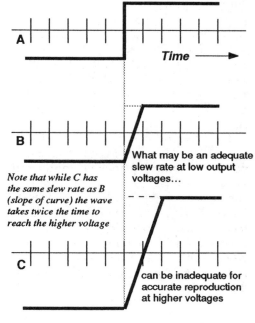

Note that while C has the same slew rate as B (slope of curve) the wave takes twice the time to reach the higher voltage

What may be an adequate slew rate at low output voltages…

can be inadequate for accurate reproduction at higher voltages

Figure 12-8. Slew rate requirements are greater for higher power amplifiers

bandwidth, which can allow the amplifier to pass radio frequency (RF) signals that serve only to increase distortion, waste power, and overheat drivers. Too high a slew rate may also suggest susceptibility to distortion or current limiting when subjected to the resulting back-EMF from a real world loudspeaker load.

3.3.4 Bridged Operation

The power specification of a professional amplifier will often include mention of mono operation, as follows:

Power Output Level
Continuous average sine wave power at less than 0.05% THD, 20 Hz to 20 kHz:

Stereo, 8 ohms,
both channels driven ....240 W/ch

Stereo, 4 ohms,
both channels driven ....400 W/ch

Mono, 8 ohms ....800 Watts

The mono specification above refers to the power capability of the amplifier in bridged operation. Bridging is usually selected by a rear-panel switch labeled Mono/Stereo or bridge/Normal, and requires special output connections.

When a power amplifier is bridged, both amplifier channels are fed the same signal (usually from the left input), but the signal polarity of one channel – usually the right channel – is reversed relative to the other channel. Both halves of the stereo amplifier then process the same signal, and the load is connected so as to draw power from both channels. The amplifier effectively becomes a single channel unit, even though both channels are used — hence the term mono. The output signals of a bridged amplifier when fed with a sine wave input are shown in Figure 12-9.

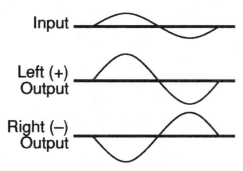

Figure 12-9. Bridged mono operation: sgnal polarity (phase) relationships

A bridged amplifier is connected to the load as shown in Figure 12-10. Note that the load is connected across the two hot output terminals. The left channel output is normally the positive connection, and the right is the negative. The load is thus driven in a push-pull mode, and the RMS voltage across it, for a given input signal level, is effectively double what it would be if the load were connected across one channel only.

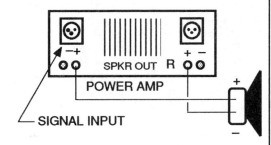

Figure 12-10. Power amp bridged output connection

CAUTION: See text for detailed description of bridging!

Note that the specification above gives mono output power for 8 ohms only. This is because the minimum allowable load impedance in bridged mode is typically double the minimum impedance for a single channel: 8 ohms in bridge = 4 ohms/channel in stereo. Because the output voltage is doubled, the power delivered into a given load impedance is quadrupled (power is proportional to the square of the voltage). While the amplifier can deliver the voltage, its power supply, heat sinks, fuses and output transistors typically cannot sustain the current that would be drawn if this amplifier were asked to drive a 4 ohm loudspeaker in bridged mode. Such a load would probably cause the amplifier distortion to rise significantly, the amp could current limit early, and it might well fail or destroy the loudspeaker. Thus the theoretical 4X power increase due to doubled voltage becomes a practical 2X power increase due to the doubled minimum impedance restriction in bridged mode.

Bridging must NEVER be confused with mono operation as it is commonly known in hi-fi equipment. In hi-fi, mono means that both amplifier channels reproduce the same signal, in phase (same polarity), and each channel output is connected to a different speaker. If two speakers are connected as a stereo pair to the outputs of a bridged amplifier, they will reproduce the same signal, but out of phase with one another. This can have disastrous consequences in sound reinforcement. If bridged connections are made to an amplifier with a hi-fi type mono mode (i.e., same polarity), the voltages applied to the + and - loudspeaker terminals will ride up and down together, meaning there is no electrical potential across the speaker (except for nonlinearities between the channels). Little, if any, sound will be produced, and damage to the amplifier may also occur.

NOTE: The term bridged, in this context, refers to the speaker load being connected across two channels' outputs, per Figure 12-10. Sometimes, in the context of low level audio signals (i.e., preamplifier outputs), the term bridged has another meaning; it may mean that the impedance of the load is at least 10 times the impedance of the signal source (as contrasted with matched where the impedance of the source and load are roughly the same. For example, a synthesizer with 2.5 kohm actual output impedance will be bridged by the 25 kohm actual input impedance of a particular mixer; this bridging has no relationship to the bridging of a power amp output being discussed in this section of the handbook.

12.3.5 The Effect of Clipping

When a power amplifier is asked to produce levels that exceed its design limits, clipping occurs. Clipping is illustrated in Figure 12-11.

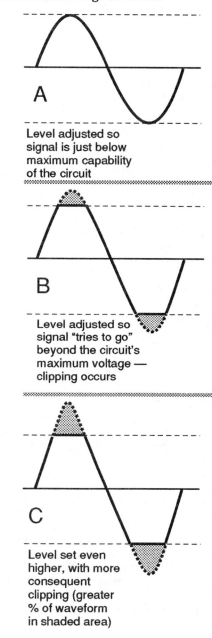

A

Level adjusted so signal is just below maximum capability of the circuit

B

Level adjusted so signal "tries to go" beyond the circuit's maximum voltage — clipping occurs

C

Level set even higher, with more consequent clipping (greater % of waveform in shaded area)

Figure 12-11. Clipping of a sine wave

In Figure 12-11(a), we see the amplifier output just before clipping, and this sine wave is an exact replica of the sine wave input to the amp. In (b), we have raised the input signal level slightly, and we see the onset of clipping. Note that those portions of the wave that lie beyond the output voltage capability of the amplifier are truncated. The amplifier cannot produce a higher output signal voltage, so it simply maintains its maximum output voltage until the input signal voltage drops to a level that it can accurately reproduce. As a consequence, the wave is flattened on the top and bottom.

If we further increase the input signal level, the peak-to-peak level of the output will not increase, but the slope of the rising and falling portions of the wave will become steeper, as shown in (c).

Clipping has two basic effects. Obviously, it greatly increases the distortion. This results in the generation of high frequency components that lend a very harsh quality to the sound, and may endanger high frequency drivers — particularly in passive crossover systems. More important, clipping dramatically increases the average power applied to the load, which can overheat voice coils on any drivers.

The waveform of Figure 12-11(a) is a sine wave, whose heating power is proportional to its RMS voltage. A severely clipped sine wave such as that shown in (c) resembles a square wave whose peak-to-peak amplitude is the same as that of the wave in (a). The heating power of this wave is proportional to its peak value, which is 1.414 times the RMS value of the sinewave shown in (a). This has the same effect as a 3 dB increase in voltage, or double the power!

Whenever an amplifier is driven into hard clipping — as will often occur on musical peaks in professional applications — the power applied to the load is thus double the maximum undistorted continuous power of the amplifier. For example, when a 200 watt amplifier (8 ohm rating) is driven into clipping on peaks while driving an 8 ohm loudspeaker, the peak power seen by that loudspeaker is 400 watts.

12.4 The Relationship Between Amplifier Power And SPL

The factor that relates amplifier power to sound pressure level for a given loudspeaker is the loudspeaker's sensitivity rating. Unless otherwise noted, sensitivity is generally specified in dB SPL at 1 watt at 1 meter, on axis (directly in front of the loudspeaker). For the purposes of sound system calculations, it may be regarded as the sound pressure level that would be measured at a distance of 1 meter from the loudspeaker when it is driven by a 1 watt signal (usually pink noise).

Consider a loudspeaker with a sensitivity rating of 93 dB SPL (1 W, 1m), and a rated maximum power handling capacity of 100 watts continuous, 400 watts peak. In order to find the maximum continuous and peak SPL capabilities of this loudspeaker, we need to find the increase, in decibels, between the 100 and 400 watt maximum power levels and the 1 watt at which sensitivity is specified. Remember, decibels express a ratio. Once the decibel ratios of 100 and 400 watts to 1 watt are calculated, they can simply be added to the SPL sensitivity figure to obtain the maximum SPL values.

Thus, to find the maximum continuous SPL:

$$\begin{aligned} ndB &= 10 \bullet \log (P_1 \div P_2) \\ &= 10 \bullet \log [(100 \text{ watts}) \div (1 \text{ watt})] \\ &= 10 \bullet \log 100 \\ &= 10 \bullet 2 \\ &= 20 \text{ dB} \end{aligned}$$

The 100 watt continuous power is 20 dB above the 1 watt power used to measure sensitivity. Since the loudspeaker delivers 93 dB SPL sensitivity (1W/1M), its maximum continuous SPL at 1 meter is...

$$\begin{aligned} SPL_{(continuous)} &= 93 \text{ dB} + 20 \text{ dB} \\ &= 113 \text{ dB SPL} \end{aligned}$$

Similarly, to find the maximum peak SPL:

$$ndB = 10 \cdot \log [(400 \text{ watts}) \div (1 \text{ watt})]$$
$$= 10 \cdot \log 400$$
$$= 10 \cdot 2.6$$
$$= 26 \text{ dB}$$

The 400 watt peak power is 26 dB above the 1 watt sensitivity, which provides a maximum peak SPL of...

$$SPL_{(peak)} = 93 \text{ dB} + 26 \text{ dB}$$
$$= 119 \text{ dB SPL}$$

If one of two loudspeakers is 3 dB more sensitive than the other, the less sensitive loudspeaker will require twice as much amplifier power to generate the same SPL as the more sensitive loudspeaker.

Suppose that we decide to drive the loudspeaker described above with a power amplifier rated at 50 watts continuous. What can we expect the maximum continuous and peak SPL to be?

If we assume that we will use the full continuous power of the amplifier, then the continuous SPL can be found as above:

$$ndB = 10 \log [(50 \text{ watts}) \div (1 \text{ watt})]$$
$$= 17 \text{ dB}$$

Having calculated that 50 watts is 17 dB above 1 watt, we again add that increase in dB to the sensitivity...

$$SPL_{(continuous)} = 93 \text{ dB} + 17 \text{ dB}$$
$$= 110 \text{ dB SPL}$$

To find the peak SPL, let us assume that the amplifier may clip on peaks. You will recall that clipping tends to square the waveform, delivering twice the power to the load, so the power then would seem to be 100 watts (2 x 50 watts).

$$ndB = 10 \log [(100 \text{ watts}) \div (1 \text{ watt})]$$
$$= 20 \text{ dB}$$

$$SPL_{(peak)} = 93 \text{ dB} + 20 \text{ dB}$$
$$= 113 \text{ dB SPL}$$

In practice, the amplifier will not be run at its full continuous power, since this would not allow any headroom at all for peaks. Besides, a loudspeaker cannot reproduce a square wave (clipped waveform). Thus, while the peak SPL probably will remain the same, the continuous SPL may be 6 dB or more below that which we have calculated, depending upon how much headroom is allowed. In low level applications, this may be fine. That judgment must be made based upon the demands of the application.

12.5 Matching Power Amplifiers To Loudspeakers

When choosing an amplifier for a loudspeaker system, we must consider a number of factors.

Unless the system will be used only at low levels, it is important that the amplifier's power rating not be too low. Otherwise, we won't be able to utilize the full SPL potential of the loudspeaker. An amplifier with inadequate power capability can, in fact, damage loudspeakers by stressing them more than a larger amp (the smaller amp will be driven into clipping, which produces a dense harmonic structure and artificially steep waveforms; this can overheat high frequency driver voice coils by feeding them more power than the program would otherwise have provided.) On the other hand, it is unwise — especially in professional applications — to choose an amplifier that is significantly more powerful than the loudspeaker can handle because it becomes too easy to destroy the loudspeaker thermally (with excess power) or mechanically (with excess excursion).

The amplifier must also be able to handle the load that the loudspeakers present. In order to avoid excessively loading the amplifier when multiple loudspeakers are connected to a single output, we need to know the impedance of each individual loudspeaker and we must calculate the net load impedance.

12.5.1 Interpreting Loudspeaker Power Ratings

A typical loudspeaker power rating might read as follows:

Power Handling
Continuous .... 120 watts
Program .... 240 watts
Peak .... 480 watts

What size power amplifier should be chosen to work with this loudspeaker? In order to answer the question, we need to know precisely what each of these ratings means.

Continuous power handling refers to the level of long term average power that the loudspeaker will handle. It is usually measured using a sine wave or weighted noise input. Properly used, the continuous power rating is a worst case specification, and represents maximum heating of the component voice coils.

Program power handling is measured using a test signal that approximates a real world program signal. Actual program signals have less long term heating effect for a given power level.

Peak power handling refers to the maximum instantaneous, short term power that the loudspeaker will handle. In this usage, short term refers to time intervals under a second (generally, no more than 1/10 second).

The structure of this power handling specification is designed to correspond to the nature of the program material:

The *continuous power* level corresponds to the long term average heating power of typical program material.

The *program power* level corresponds to maximum average levels of program material as they would be measured over medium term averaging periods (say, up to a minute).

The *peak power* level corresponds to peak levels in the program, which invariably last less than a second.

Some would say that this loudspeaker should be used with an amplifier rated at 480 watts per channel into 8 ohms. The philosophy behind this choice originates in hi-fi — the idea being that use of a high power amplifier allows undistorted (unclipped) reproduction of musical peaks.

At home listening levels, this may be fine. But in a professional application, the continuous SPL demand on the loudspeaker will be significantly greater. In fact, this 480 watt amplifier may be running no more than 6 dB below clipping (120 watts) on a long-term average basis. The amplifier could certainly clip on musical peaks—and the loudspeaker would then be asked to handle 960 watts!

The proper choice for this loudspeaker is an amplifier rated in the neighborhood of 220 watts per channel. This allows the full undistorted power of the amplifier for loud musical passages, while making certain that the peak power applied to the loudspeaker does not exceed its power handling capabilities. Similar reasoning can be applied to other loudspeaker specifications.

If a loudspeaker specification does not include a program power rating, but only gives continuous and peak, then the choice must be made by interpolation from those ratings.

For example, consider a loudspeaker rated to handle 200 watts continuous and 400 watts peak. Clearly, we must choose a 200 watt power amplifier, in order not to exceed the peak power rating. On the other hand, a loudspeaker rated to handle 100 watts continuous and 400 watts peak can be driven by a 200 watt amplifier as well, since we can reasonably assume that the system will be run with at least a 6 dB margin between the long term average level and the short term peak level.

If power handling, and the method used to determine this specification, is not clearly indicated, the loudspeaker should be considered unsuitable for professional applications.

12.5.2 Impedance Calculations

The impedance of a loudspeaker is the total opposition to AC current flow that it presents to the output of the power amplifier.

The amount of power extracted from the amplifier by the loudspeaker is inversely proportional to its impedance. The lower the impedance, the more power the loudspeaker will dissipate for a given signal voltage (assuming that the amplifier has that power to give). For this reason, amplifier power ratings are usually given at two or more load impedances, and the 4 ohm power is usually close to twice the 8 ohm power.

The load impedance seen by an amplifier must always be greater than zero. If it were equal to zero, the amplifier output would be shorted and the current demand would be infinite (since I=E÷Z, as Z approaches zero, I approaches infinite current).

Practically speaking, the load impedance on an amplifier should never be less than 4 ohms. While some amplifiers are rated for 2 ohm operation, it is not advisable to load an amplifier this heavily in professional use. Not only will the amplifier be stressed, but the loudspeaker cable will have to be exceptionally large in size, particularly over long runs, since any resistance in the cable will constitute a larger percentage of the load impedance, and will therefore waste a larger percentage of the amplifier's power.

Loudspeaker specifications will always include a figure called nominal impedance, given in ohms. Some may also give an impedance curve such as is shown in Figure12-12. Here, the impedance of the loudspeaker is plotted against frequency.

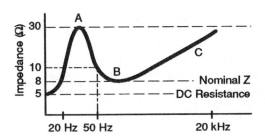

Figure 12-12. Typical Loudspeaker Impedance Curve

Note that the impedance is not at all constant with frequency. In fact, it varies quite widely. The impedance rise in the low end (a) is due to the natural resonance of the low frequency driver. The shape of this rise is affected by cabinet loading.

Following the rise is a trough (b), then a long rise (c). The nominal impedance is normally specified to be the minimum impedance at the trough (b). Standard values of loudspeaker impedance are 4, 8, and 16 ohms.

Connecting a single loudspeaker to an amplifier output is a simple affair. What happens, though, when we wish to drive two or more loudspeakers from that output? How will this affect the net impedance seen by the amplifier?

There are two basic ways to connect multiple loudspeakers to a single output: in series, and in parallel. These are shown in Figure 12-13.

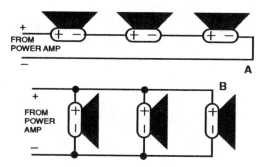

Figure 12-13. Series (A), and parallel (B) connection of loudspeakers

When loudspeakers are connected in series, as shown in (a), current from the amplifier passes serially through the loads, and the net impedance is the algebraic sum of the individual impedances. If we connect three loudspeakers — with impedances of 8, 8, and 4 ohms respectively — in series across an output, the net impedance will be:

$$Z_{net} = Z_1 + Z_2 + Z_3$$
$$= 8 + 8 + 4$$
$$= 20 \text{ ohms}$$

When loudspeakers are connected in parallel, as shown in (b), the net impedance is a bit more complicated to

calculate. It is described by the equation:

$$Z_{net} = \cfrac{1}{\cfrac{1}{Z_1} + \cfrac{1}{Z_2} + \dots \cfrac{1}{Z_n}}$$

Where n = the total number of parallel elements.

Luckily, in the special case in which we connect two loads of equal impedance in parallel, the complexity of the calculation is reduced. The net impedance is half the impedance of either one. If we connect two 8 ohm loudspeakers in parallel, the net impedance is 4 ohms. Where the impedances are unequal, or more than two loads are paralleled, then the equation above must be used to calculate the net impedance.

> **HINT:** *If more than two loudspeakers are connected in parallel, so long as all are the same impedance, then the net impedance of the load is equal to the impedance of one loudspeaker divided by the number of loudspeakers. For example, with three 8-ohm loudspeakers in parallel, the impedance is 8÷3, or 2.667 ohms.*

What are the relative advantages and disadvantages of parallel and series connection?

Series connection results in a higher impedance. If our loads are very low impedance, then the net impedance can be made greater by connecting them in series. On the other hand, if one of the loads fails and becomes an open circuit — which is the most common way that loudspeakers fail — then the entire connection is broken, and all the loudspeakers will cease to function. There also tends to be more interaction between functioning loudspeakers in series, which can increase distortion. Finally damping factor for any one loudspeaker is significantly degraded in series connections, which may have an adverse effect on low frequency reproduction.

By contrast, parallel connection inevitably results in a lower impedance. We are thus limited in how many loudspeakers we can connect in parallel before the impedance drops below the minimum that the amplifier will handle. If one loudspeaker fails, though, the others will keep working, and damping factor is not seriously degraded.

Parallel connection is thus by far the most reliable, and is for this reason the most common method of wiring professional speaker systems.

Finally, both series and parallel connection can be combined, as shown in Figure 12-14. This is called series /parallel connection.

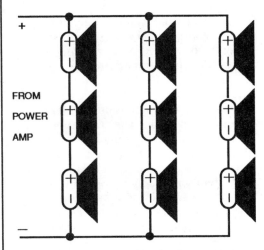

Figure 12-14. Series/parallel connection of loudspeakers

The net impedance of such a load must be calculated by first calculating the impedance of each branch of series-connected loudspeakers, and then calculating the net impedance value of these parallel-connected branches.

By employing series/parallel connection, a large number of loudspeakers can be connected to a single amplifier output, with the total amplifier power being shared among them. This method is only used in certain special circumstances in sound contracting, and is seldom used in sound reinforcement for several reasons.

First, it allows for only a small proportion of the total amplifier power for each loudspeaker. Second, it places a large part of the overall sound system at the mercy of a single amplifier; should that one amp fail, you can kiss the sound goodbye. Last, the connection is inherently complicated, which makes it both difficult to duplicate in portable applications and a real bother to troubleshoot.

In conclusion, sound reinforcement professionals generally rely on parallel connection of loudspeakers. In the case of low frequency drivers, two drivers per amplifier channel is the norm. In high frequency drivers, as many as four may be paralleled across a single output (if each is 16 ohms, which is a common impedance for compression drivers). In all cases, the net impedance is held to 4 ohms or higher.

NOTE: Be sure to use the actual impedance of the loudspeakers when calculating the impedance of multi-speaker (especially parallel) loads. At least one popular series of 16 ohm compression drivers is known to have an actual impedance of about 12 ohms in the frequency range of operation. This means that 4 in parallel would measure 3 ohms, not 4 ohms, which could overload a power amp rated at 4ohms minimum.

12.5.3 Constant-Voltage Distribution Systems

A method for connecting a large number of loudspeakers to a single amplifier output that is more reliable, and thus more widely used, than series/parallel connection is so-called constant voltage (CV) distribution. While CV systems are almost never used in live performance sound reinforcement, they are quite common in distributed paging and foreground/background music systems.

The constant voltage system relies on an amplifier whose output voltage is constant over a very wide range of load impedances (down to a practical minimum, usually 4 ohms). In the days of transformer coupled tube amplifiers, an output voltage that was independent of load was a rarity, and special design techniques had to be employed to implement CV systems. Modern professional transistor amplifiers generally deliver a load independent output voltage.

As shown in Figure 12-15 (next page), the CV system employs transformers wired in parallel across the signal distribution line. The transformers present a relatively high impedance to the line, and are provided with taps to vary the voltage delivered to each loudspeaker.

Because the amplifier's output voltage remains constant (more or less) as the load impedance changes, loudspeakers in different zones may be connected or disconnected at will, without appreciably changing the level at other locations. Moreover, since taps can be adjusted at each loudspeaker, the sound levels can be locally tailored to the environment without the use of unreliable, expensive and power-wasting pads and without having to use individual power amps for different areas. And since there is higher voltage and lower current, resistive loss in the cables are reduced, so smaller gauge wiring is sufficient over long distances, reducing overall system costs.

CV systems are not often used in reinforcement for several reasons. First, the power available to each loudspeaker is limited – not only because the total amplifier power is divided among many units, but also because a transformer capable of high power would be very large and costly. Second, the operation of a large number of loudspeakers again depends on the reliability of a single amplifier. Finally, CV transformers (particularly inexpensive ones) exhibit a widely varying impedance that can approach zero at low audio frequencies. The ability of a CV system to handle low frequencies is thus quite limited except with the most costly transformers. In fact, if the signal is not band limited, low frequencies may cause the amplifier to fail because it will be trying to drive what is essentially a short circuit.

Where the program bandwidth is limited, and SPL demands are low, CV systems offer a cost-effective solution to the problem of sound distribution. For this reason, they are commonly employed in paging and background systems such as one might find in hotels, department stores, sports stadiums, and airports.

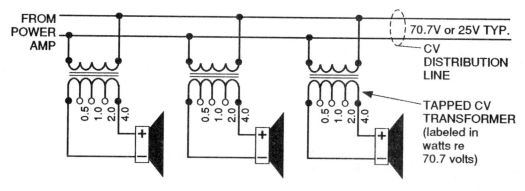

Figure 12-15. Constant Voltage Distributed Loudspeaker System

SECTION 13.
Loudspeakers

13.1 INTRODUCTION

Section 13 covers the broad subject of loudspeakers — as they are used in sound systems. Included in this discussion are: principles of acoustic transduction, types of loudspeakers and enclosures, loudspeaker specifications, acoustic performance, crossovers, distortion sources, and typical failure modes.

Loudspeaker is a generic term used to describe a wide variety of transducers that convert electrical energy into acoustical energy, or sound. The term also is commonly used to refer to systems of two or more transducers in a single enclosure, with or without a crossover.

For the sake of clarity, we will use the term driver to refer to individual transducers, and loudspeaker to refer to systems. A system of one or more drivers implemented as a free standing functional component — that is, mounted in an enclosure with or without crossover, or fitted with a horn, or otherwise completed for a specific function.

Applications of loudspeakers are discussed in Sections 17 and 18.

In a sound reinforcement system, loudspeakers play an important role as the final link between the sound source and the audience. Surprisingly, they are also the least understood components of that equipment chain.

To some people, loudspeakers are seen alternately as extraordinarily fragile and temperamental devices, or as powerful, magical things capable of acoustical miracles. Many sound reinforcement professionals, for example, accept it as inevitable that half of the drivers in their system will burn out every night there is a show. Other professionals have been known to claim obviously outrageous efficiency ratings or acoustical power figures for their systems.

Such attitudes can only thrive in a climate of ignorance. If the people setting up and operating a system are provided with the right information, loudspeakers can serve as simple and useful tools for attaining good sound — whatever one defines that to be.

This chapter is designed to provide that right information. The information presented here is largely practical rather than theoretical, and is intended to give you a working understanding of loudspeakers as they are used in sound reinforcement.

13.2 Common Methods Of Acoustic Transduction

Loudspeakers convert electrical energy into acoustical energy. There are a number of possible ways to effect this conversion, and some fairly esoteric methods have been employed — both in scientific applications and, occasionally, in hi-fi systems. Among the more esoteric transducers are venturi-modulated air streams and electro-magnetically modulated gas plasma systems. In the down-to-earth world of sound reinforcement, two methods overwhelmingly prevail— the electro-magnetically modulated diaphragm and the piezoelectrically modulated diaphragm. Of the two, the former is by far the most common.

13.2.1 Electromagnetic Transduction

The vast majority of loudspeakers — both high and low frequency — are built around electromagnetic linear motors. As such, loudspeakers are close relatives of other simple electric motors, solenoids, and so on. Figure 13-1 shows how such motors work.

If a direct current is now passed through the coil, the flow of electrons in the wire creates a *second magnetic field*, as shown in Figure 13-1 (d) around the coil. The polarity (north - south) of this field is dependent on the direction of current flow through the wire.

The electromagnetic field interacts with that of the permanent magnet. Assuming that the permanent magnet's position is fixed, the force resulting from the interaction of the two fields causes the coil to move.

If the flow of current in the coil is now reversed, then the polarity of the electromagnetic field is also reversed. This reverses the direction of the force acting on the coil, causing it to move in the opposite direction.

If the direction of the current is repeatedly reversed, the coil will move back and forth within the field of the magnet. The motion of the coil will be a physical representation of the alternations of the current.

This is the general principle by which electromagnetic motors work. Figure 13-2 shows the components of the type of electromagnetic motor that is found in most drivers.

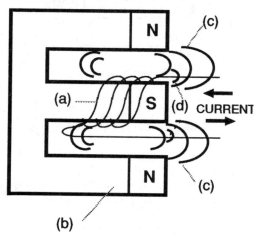

Figure 13-1. Operation of a linear electromagnetic motor

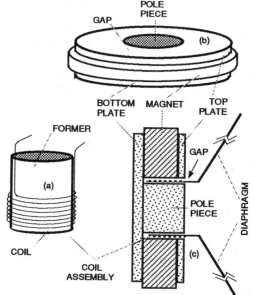

Figure 13-2. Components of a linear electromagnetic motor (In a typical driver)

A coil of wire, Figure 13-1 (a), is surrounded by a *permanent magnet* (b). The permanent magnet sets up stationary lines of *magnetic force* (c).

A typical coil assembly *(voice coil)* is shown in Figure13-2 (a). The coil wire may have a round or square cross section. The cylinder on which the coil is wound is called the *former*. The former may be made of specially-treated paper, or of a synthetic material.

A typical *magnet assembly* is shown in Figure 13-2 (b). The donut shaped permanent magnet is fitted top and bottom with plates made of a magnetic material (generally iron). Inserted in the center of the donut is a cylindrical slug of magnetic metal called the pole piece.

The cross section view, Figure 13–2 (c) reveals the positioning of the coil and pole piece.

Note that the top and bottom plates, along with the pole piece, carry and contain the magnetic field. The only air space that the field passes through lies between the top plate and the pole piece (there is a very slight amount of flux leakage beyond this area). This space between the top plate and the pole piece is called the *gap*. The effect of this design is to concentrate the magnetic field in the gap — where the coil is — and minimize leakage of the field into the surrounding air at any other point. The path of the flux field is called the *magnetic circuit*.

As shown in Figure 13-2, the coil is suspended in the gap, concentric with the pole piece. Alternating current from the power amplifier passes through the coil, causing it to move back and forth in the gap. The coil is attached to a suitable diaphragm, which couples its mechanical motion to the air.

13.2.2 Piezoelectric Transduction

The other transduction method that is used occasionally in sound reinforcement drivers is based on the piezoelectric effect.

Discovered in the late 19th century by Pierre and Jacques Curie, the piezoelectric (pressure electricity) effect is a property of certain crystalline materials. When such a crystal is mechanically deformed, electricity is generated. On the other hand, if an electric potential is applied across the crystal, it changes dimensions, expanding or contracting in the axis of electrical polarization.

The piezoelectric elements used in audio transducers are generally of the type known as bimorphs. Bimorphs are elements built in two layers of piezoelectric material, and are also called benders. Figure 13-3 shows the type of deformation that bimorphs undergo when a voltage is applied across them.

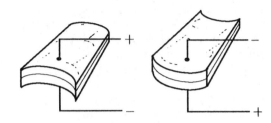

Figure 13-3. Bimorphs as used in piezoelectric drivers

Figure 13-4 shows the construction of a typical piezoelectric driver element. The drive voltage for the bender comes from the power amplifier. The bender, in turn, is joined to a diaphragm.

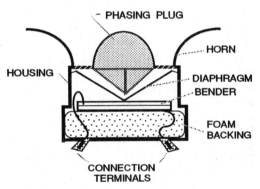

Figure 13-4. Cross-section of piezoelectric driver

Piezoelectric benders are capable of only limited excursion, and their response falls off drastically in the mid and low audio frequencies. At high frequencies, they offer fairly high efficiency with very low distortion. They are therefore used only for high-frequency drivers (usually acting above 5 kHz or so).

Efficient reproduction of low frequencies requires that a large volume of air be moved. This, in turn, requires one or both of the following:

1) Long diaphragm excursion

2) Large diaphragm area

You will recall from the previous section that piezoelectric benders have limited excursion capability and are not particularly efficient at low frequencies. In sound reinforcement, low frequency drivers are invariably electromagnetic linear motors with cone diaphragms. When flush mounted on the front of an enclosure (i.e., without a horn), this type of driver is also known as a direct radiator. Figure 13-5 shows a typical cone low frequency driver in cross section.

The motor, Figure 13-5 (a), is constructed as detailed previously in Section 13.2.1. The coil (b) is coupled to a cone shaped *diaphragm* (c).

The driver's diaphragm/coil assembly is attached to the *frame* (d) – also called a basket – at two points. The *spider* (e) accomplishes two tasks: it anchors the apex of the cone, and it centers the coil in the gap. The *surround* (f) anchors the base of the cone to the frame. Together, these elements are referred to as the suspension.

The gap is protected from foreign particles by a domed piece (g) mounted at the center of the cone. This is referred to as the *dome* or *dust cap*.

Flexible, multistrand wires (h) run from the connection terminals to the coil. These wires are called the *coil leads*, *tinsel leads*, or simply *leads*.

As shown in the accompanying front view, the perimeter of the frame is drilled at regular intervals for mounting. The most common number of mounting holes is six.

The driver size is specified in terms of cone diameter, measured at the base (widest diameter) of the cone. Standard sizes for low frequency drivers in sound reinforcement are 12, 15, and 18 inches

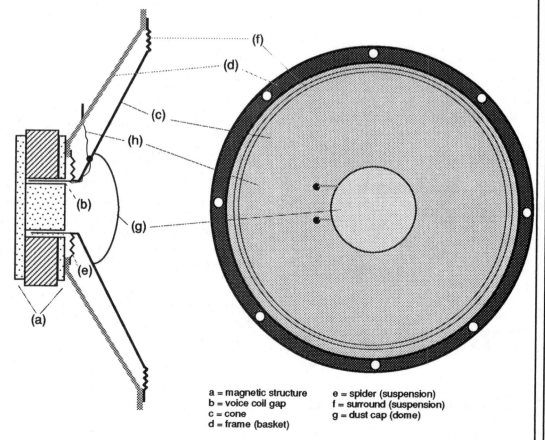

a = magnetic structure
b = voice coil gap
c = cone
d = frame (basket)

e = spider (suspension)
f = surround (suspension)
g = dust cap (dome)

Figure 13-5. Cross-section of a cone-type driver

(whose metric equivalents are 30.5, 38 and 45.7 cm). Because different manufacturers use different sized frames and measure cones differently, not all 12 inch drivers, for example, will be the same actual diameter.

The polarity of the connection terminals may be specified in any one of a number of ways. The most common method is color coding; the + terminal is red, and the − terminal is black. Other methods simply identify the + terminal, either with a colored mark, or by labeling it with a plus sign.

The common definition of driver polarity, illustrated inFigure13-6, is:

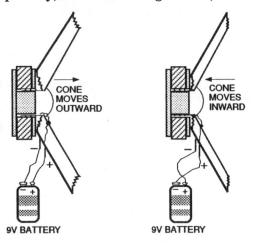

Figure 13-6. Testing driver polarity with a battery

A positive bias across the terminals causes the cone to move forward.

NOTE: *At least one popular speaker manufacturer has used the opposite of this polarity standard in a few loudspeakers. Then, too, when some speakers are reconed, their magnetic structures may be recharged with opposite polarity, thus changing the effective polarity of the electrical connections. To be sure, always check a loudspeaker by applying a low DC voltage to the terminals and observing diaphragm motion. With concentric cone / compression driver 2-way units, each section of the transducer should be checked individually.*

13.3.1 Directional Characteristics of Cone Drivers

The directional characteristics of a cone driver are dependent on the relationship between the size of the cone and the wavelength of the sound that the driver is reproducing. Figure 13-7 shows polar plots for a typical cone driver at various ratios between cone diameter and wavelength.

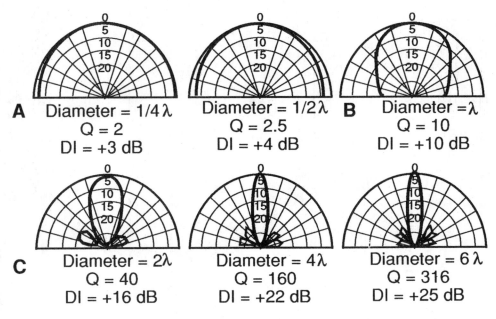

Figure 13-7. How the directional characteristics of a driver vary with wavelength

At low frequencies, where the wavelength is long compared to the size of the cone, the driver is omnidirectional, as indicated in Figure 13-7(a).

As the frequency rises, the wavelength gets shorter, and the directional pattern of the cone very gradually narrows. When the wavelength is equal to the cone diameter, the directional pattern is as shown in Figure 13-7(b). Note that the cone is now fairly directional: 45 degrees off axis, the level is approximately 6 dB lower than it is directly on axis.

At higher frequencies, the cone's directional pattern narrows very sharply. In Figure 13-7(c), the wavelength is half the diameter of the driver diaphragm; note that the driver is now highly directional. The beamwidth will continue to narrow as the frequency rises.

Cone type low frequency drivers are nearly always mounted in enclosures. The reason for this practice is illustrated in Figure 13-8, which shows a cone driver reproducing a low frequency sine wave in free space.

In the first half cycle of the sine wave, the cone moves forward, as shown in Figure 13-8(a). A compression front is generated at the front of the diaphragm, with a corresponding rarefaction at the rear.

The compressed air flows to the low-pressure zone at the back of the driver, in an attempt to equalize the air pressure. On the second half-cycle (b), the reverse occurs.

The result is that most of the sound wave is cancelled and very little acoustic energy is generated, even though the excursion of the cone may be very long.

This cancellation effect only occurs at low frequencies. At higher frequen-

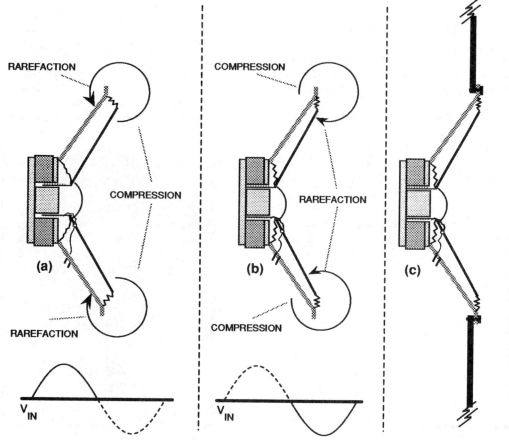

Figure 13-8. Reproduction of Low Frequencies by an Unbaffled Cone Driver Can Result in Acoustic Cancellation

This cancellation effect only occurs at low frequencies. At higher frequencies, the diaphragm moves very quickly, and the wavelengths are short compared with the distance to be traveled around the driver. There is not enough time for the air to travel the distance around the diaphragm, and little or no cancellation occurs.

By mounting the driver in a baffle, as illustrated in Figure 13-8 (c), we can increase the distance from one side of the driver to the other and thus minimize the cancellation. The larger the baffle, the longer the wavelength must be for cancellation to occur. Make it large enough, and the cancellation is entirely eliminated.

In practical loudspeakers, the baffle's function is assumed by the enclosure. The most common low-frequency enclosures used in sound reinforcement are the vented and the horn loaded enclosure.

13.4.1 Vented Enclosures

Vented enclosures are generally used for direct radiator, low frequency systems. A direct radiator system is one in which the driver diaphragm is coupled directly to the air (i.e., it is mounted on the surface of the enclo-

sure, without a horn in front or behind the driver).

Figure 13-9 shows both a cross-section and a front view of a typical vented enclosure.

Note that the enclosure features an opening, Figure 13-9 (a), in its front surface. The opening is called a port or vent. The internal volume of the enclosure and the port form what is called a Helmholtz resonator.

A bottle is another form of Helmholtz resonator. We know that if we blow across the neck of a bottle, we can produce a tone. The frequency (or pitch) of the tone is the resonant frequency of the resonator. Vented enclosures are designed to have a specific resonant frequency.

In a vented enclosure, the back wave from the driver is used to reinforce the front wave at the resonant frequency, as indicated by the arrows in the diagram. The resonant system of the enclosure and port shifts the phase of the back wave by 180 degrees, so that it is in phase with the front wave.

The area of the port and the size of the enclosure may be adjusted to tune the system. Tuning determines the frequency at which the system resonates; this is the frequency range where back-wave reinforcement occurs.

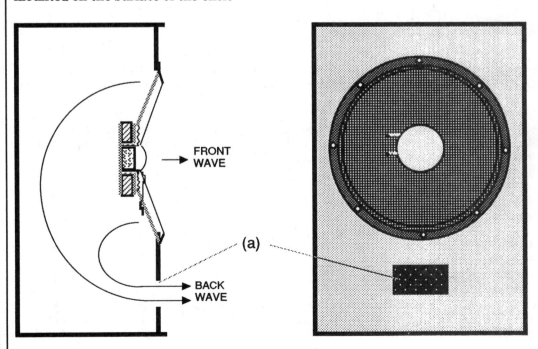

FRONT WAVE

BACK WAVE

(a)

Figure 13-9. A vented, direct-radiator low frequency enclosure

We generally choose the tuning of the enclosure in order to reinforce the very low frequency response of the driver, so as to get reasonably flat, low frequency response.

The interior of vented enclosures is always lined with absorbent material, usually fiberglass batting. The batting absorbs higher frequencies that otherwise could cause cancellations when bouncing around within the enclosure.

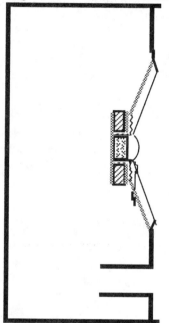

Figure 13-10. A ducted port low frequency enclosure

A variation of the vented enclosure uses what is called a *ducted port*, shown in cross-section in Figure 13-10.

Ducting adds another factor to the tuning of the enclosure system, in effect lowering the resonant frequency for a given size enclosure and port area. Ducting is normally used to extend the low frequency response of smaller enclosures.

In essence, the port (ducted or not) in a vented system acts as an acoustic equalizer which peaks the low frequency output so that the level does not fall off as the frequency is reduced... up to a point. The tradeoff in such systems is that below the frequency to which the port is tuned, the sound output level drops off much more rapidly than in a sealed or infinite baffle enclosure.

13.4.2 Low Frequency Horns

The other prevalent low-frequency enclosure type is the horn loaded enclosure. Low frequency horns can be very efficient, and are quite popular in sound reinforcement.

Horns also offer better directivity control than direct radiator enclosures. The directional characteristics of a low frequency horn are determined by the horn rather than by the driver size, and horns with large mouths retain directivity in the low frequencies. Since horn enclosures are more directional than direct radiator types, they are particularly useful in situations where long throws are required.

The most common flare used in horns is exponential. Figure 13-11 shows the shape of a classic, straight *exponential horn*.

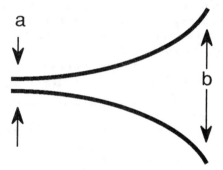

Figure 13-11. Cross-section of a straight exponential horn

Horns act as impedance-matching devices. The acoustical impedance at the throat of the horn, Figure 13-11 (a), is high and loads the driver diaphragm so that less excursion is needed to produce high sound pressures. The horn couples this high throat impedance to the low impedance that the mouth (b) sees from the surrounding free air.

The flare rate from the throat to the mouth, and the physical size of the horn, determine the cutoff frequency, which is the lowest frequency at which the horn is effective in controlling the driver diaphragm. Below the cutoff frequency, the driver diaphragm is no longer loaded by the throat impedance. (This is why horn loaded systems should not be fed frequencies below their cutoffs. The diaphragm will flop in an uncontrolled manner, causing distortion and a strong likelihood of premature self destruction.)

The diameter of the horn mouth (or equivalent diameter for a rectangular mouthed horn) should be at least one-quarter the wavelength of the cutoff frequency. For this reason, low frequency horns must, in theory, be very large if their response is to extend to the lowest end of the audio range.

When horns are arrayed together, their mouth areas couple acoustically to form the equivalent of a single large mouth. This effect permits us to design individual low-frequency horn enclosures of practical dimensions, then group the enclosures together as a block to extend the system's low frequency response.

A horn shaped like that in Figure 13-11, if it were to be effective at a low frequency, would be unwieldy. For this reason, practical low frequency horn enclosures are often of the *folded horn* type. As the name implies, folded horn enclosures are constructed by folding the horn back on itself to reduce its physical size.

One type of folded horn enclosure that is often used in sound reinforcement is the so-called *W-bin*, illustrated in cross-section in Figure 13-12.

As shown in Figure 13-12, the horn is folded in a W shape within a roughly rectangular enclosure. Another type of folded horn is shown in Figure 13-13.

The type of enclosure illustrated in Figure 13-13 is sometimes referred to as a *scoop*. It is an approximation of a curled horn.

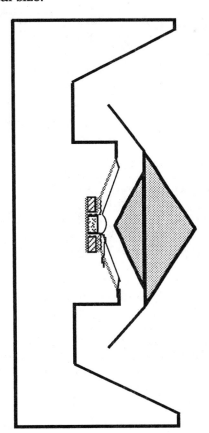

Figure 13-12. Cross-section of a folded, low frequency horn (a W-bin)

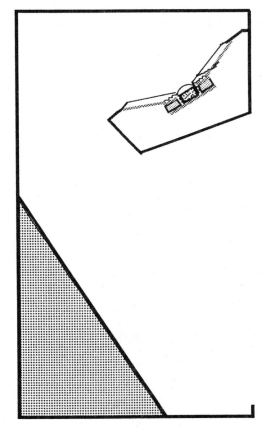

Figure 13-13. Cross-section of a folded, low frequency horn (a scoop)

13.5 High Frequency Drivers

In sound reinforcement, practical high frequency loudspeakers are most often horn-loaded. The drivers used at high frequencies are designed specifically to drive the high acoustical impedance found at the horn throat, and are thus called *compression drivers*. Figure 13-14 is a cross section of a typical compression driver.

erly designed phasing plug minimizes phase cancellations that would otherwise occur before the sound exits the driver.

The phasing plug feeds into an exponential *throat*, Figure 13-14 (e), covered at its opening with a *protective screen* (f) that prevents foreign objects from entering the driver.

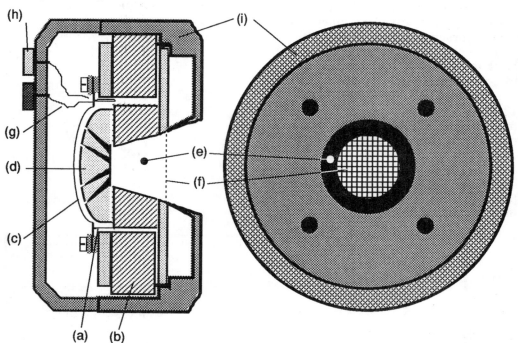

Figure 13-14. Cross-section of a typical compression driver

We see that the transduction component is the familiar electromagnetic linear motor of Section 13.2.1. The *coil*, Figure 13-14 (a), sits in the gap of a *permanent magnet* (b).

The *diaphragm* (c) is domed, rather than being a cone. The physical dimensions of the driver leave little room for excursion, but not much is needed. High frequency reproduction requires less excursion than low frequencies, and the high throat impedance of the horn also reduces the diaphragm excursion requirements.

At high frequencies, the wavelength of the sound is small compared with the diameter of the diaphragm. For this reason, the slotted structure (d) — called the *phasing plug* — is used to alter the diaphragm-to-horn path length of waves emanating from different areas of the diaphragm so that their phase is coherent. A prop-

Flexible wires (g) lead from the diaphragm assembly terminals to the outside *connection terminals* (h), located on the *dust cap* (i). Polarity labeling conventions are the same as for low-frequency drivers (see Section 13.3) — generally red for + and black for –.

The common definition of driver polarity is:

A positive bias across the terminals causes the diaphragm to move toward the front of the driver.

The accompanying front view in Figure 13-14 reveals the threaded holes in the front plate that are used to attach the driver to the horn. The most common number of mounting holes is four.

Supertweeters may also be used in sound reinforcement loudspeakers.

13.6 HiqH FREQUENCY HORNS

They may be of either the electromagnetic type described above, or the piezoelectric type. In either case, they are invariably horn loaded, and the horn is generally an integral part of the driver construction.

Figure 13-15 shows the construction of a typical piezoelectric supertweeter. A description of piezoelectric transduction is given a few pages back in Section 13.2.

Supertweeters such as that shown in this figure are used to reproduce frequencies above about 5 kHz.

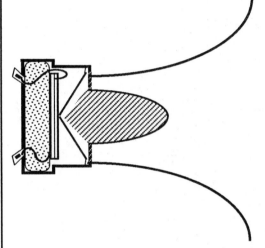

Figure 13-15. Cross-section of a piezoelectric supertweeter

High frequency horn design is a fairly refined art. Many types of high frequency horns are used in sound reinforcement. Because size is not a limiting factor, and because high frequencies do not bend around corners as readily, high frequency horns are not folded (although a few do have 90 degree bends in them).

The most important attribute that we desire in a high frequency horn for sound reinforcement is a controlled dispersion pattern. The horn should distribute high frequencies over a defined angle both in the horizontal and vertical axes. To the extent that it is possible acoustically, the angle of dispersion should be consistent over the full frequency range of interest — usually, up to about 16 kHz. That way the sound quality off axis will be close to that on axis.

The horizontal and vertical dispersion angles of a typical reinforcement high frequency horn will usually differ from one another, and with good reason. We usually need a fairly wide horizontal angle in order to cover a typical audience area. A similarly wide vertical angle would waste acoustic energy by directing it to areas where we don't need or want it — into free space or onto ceilings, for example.

The loudspeaker industry seems to have settled upon horizontal angles in the neighborhood of 80 to 90 degrees, and vertical angles on the order of 30 to 40 degrees. Narrower dispersion angles are also available in some horns. Horns with narrow dispersion concentrate sound in a smaller area, and are used for long throw applications.

The flare rate of contemporary high frequency horns varies from exponential to more complex functions related to an exponential rate. Compound flare rates may, in fact, be used— that is, the flare rate may change in different regions of the horn.

Some common types of simple, high frequency horns are: exponential, radial, and constant directivity.

Exponential horns employ exponential flare rates, often with different rates for the horizontal and vertical expansions, and sometimes with compound rates.

Radial horns are formed by defining a flare in two dimensions, then rotating that shape through a given arc around a central origin. The rotating shape defines the surface of the horn. Refer to Figure 13-16

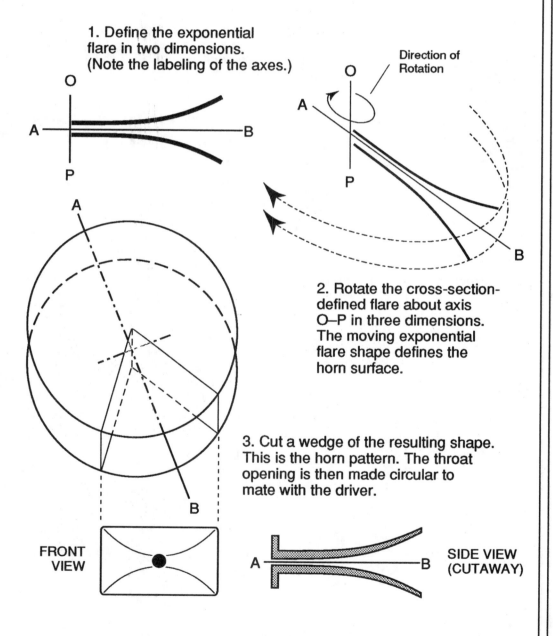

1. Define the exponential flare in two dimensions. (Note the labeling of the axes.)

Direction of Rotation

2. Rotate the cross-section-defined flare about axis O–P in three dimensions. The moving exponential flare shape defines the horn surface.

3. Cut a wedge of the resulting shape. This is the horn pattern. The throat opening is then made circular to mate with the driver.

FRONT VIEW

SIDE VIEW (CUTAWAY)

Figure 13-16. The design of an exponential radial horn

Constant directivity (CD) horns employ compound flare rates, with different rates in the horizontal and vertical axes. Refer to Figure 13-17. Because their directional characteristics are very consistent over a wide frequency range, constant directivity horns are becoming increasingly popular in sound reinforcement. The advantage is that once coverage is computed at a given frequency, the same coverage applies at all frequencies within the range where the horn exhibits constant coverage. This simplifies system design and often improves intelligibility.

The design of constant directivity horns requires the throat to narrow before flaring out to the mouth, which means they are subject to increased distortion caused by air turbulence

that occurs in the throat at high sound pressure levels. One of the tricky aspects of their design is to minimize this turbulence-induced distortion.

Some traditional (non CD) horn designs incorporate acoustic lenses to improve their high frequency dispersion characteristics. Lenses may be made of louvers (similar to Venetian blinds), or of layers of perforated metal.

Such lenses have both good and bad points. They can be effective in producing a controlled pattern, and will not normally introduce significant sound level losses. On the other hand, they can produce resonances at the lower frequencies of the horn's response, coloring the sound. In general, a well designed horn will not require a lens to produce adequate dispersion.

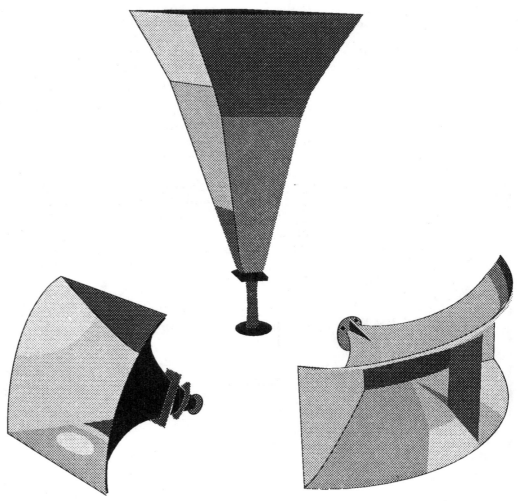

Figure 13-17. A variety of constant directivity horns

We have discussed low frequency and high frequency drivers and enclosures, each of which is designed only to reproduce a specific, limited frequency range. To reproduce the entire audio range, such drivers and enclosures are combined into multi-way systems.

Generally low and high frequency devices cannot be connected directly together to be driven by a single power amplifier's output. For one thing, the ragged acoustic outputs of the low and high drivers outside their respective frequency ranges may not add together properly. This would result in poor frequency response. Low frequencies, moreover, can actually damage high-frequency drivers (see Section 13.11, "Typical Failure Modes.")

For these reasons, it is necessary to somehow divide the full-range audio signal into its low and high frequency components, directing each only to the appropriate driver(s). This is the function of the crossover. Other terms for crossover are *frequency dividing network* or *crossover network*, all of which mean the same thing.

Figure 13-18 (a) shows a two-way loudspeaker system consisting of a direct radiator (a vented enclosure with a cone type low frequency driver) and a horn loaded high frequency driver. An idealized version of the crossover characteristic typically used for such a system is shown in (b).

Above a certain frequency, the input to the low frequency driver gradually falls off. The input to the high frequency driver also falls off below a certain frequency. The point along the frequency axis of the graph where the two curves meet is called the crossover point.

We can see that the crossover point is, for each driver, 3 dB down in relation to the flat portion of each frequency band. Three dB is one half the power output; in this crossover region the acoustic outputs of the two drivers add together to fill the 3 dB hole.

Similar principles apply in three-way systems. Figure 13-19 (next page) shows an idealized crossover characteristic for a such a system.

The rate at which the level to each driver falls off beyond the crossover point varies in different designs, and is called the *slope* of the crossover. Typical crossover slopes are 6, 12, 18 and 24 dB per octave The filters that create these slopes are known, respectively, as first, second, third or fourth order filters (each order represents another 6 dB per octave, and another circuit section in the filter network).

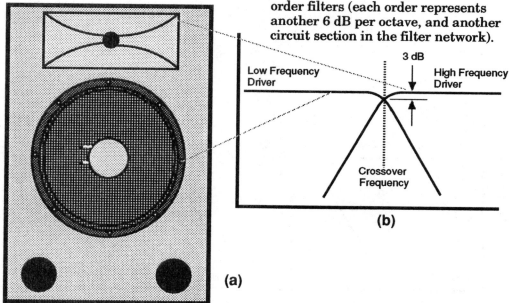

(a)

(b)

Figure 13-18. A typical 2-way loudspeaker system and its idealized crossover response characteristics

13.7.2 Passive, High Level Crossovers

A 6 dB/octave slope generally allows for too much overlap between the drivers. It may be OK for a crossover between two cone type drivers (though such gradual rates do exacerbate time alignment problems), but it does not adequately protect the high frequency compression driver from damaging low frequencies. The most commonly used crossover slopes in high level professional sound systems are 12 dB per octave and 18 dB per octave.

Two generic types of crossover are in common use in sound reinforcement: high level passive networks, and low level active networks.

Passive, high level crossovers are simple networks that are designed to pass high signal levels. They are inserted between the power amplifier output and the drivers. Passive crossovers are most often enclosed in the loudspeaker cabinet, as shown in Figure 13-20, although some are mounted externally.

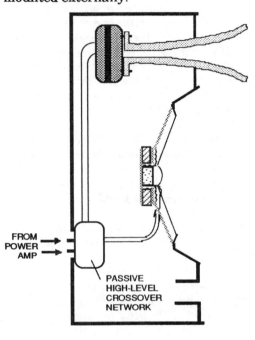

FROM
POWER
AMP

PASSIVE
HIGH-LEVEL
CROSSOVER
NETWORK

Figure 13-20. Typical location of a passive, high-level crossover network inside a loudspeaker enclosure

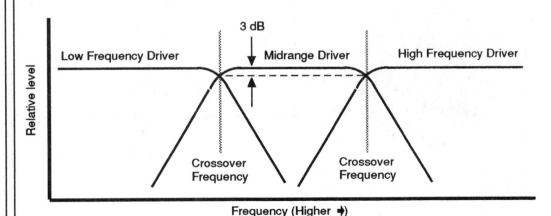

Figure 13-19. Idealized crossover response characteristics for a 3-way loudspeaker system

NOTE: Some passive crossovers are made to go between the signal source and the power amplifier. These are passive, low level crossovers. Since their function is almost identical to that of the active, low level crossover, and since they are not very common these days, we will not offer a separate discussion of this type of crossover. The only difference between the active and passive low level crossover is that the active unit also includes built-in line amplifiers to make up for loss in the filter networks. Refer to Section 13.7.3, "Active, Low Level Crossovers."

Passive crossover networks are composed of fundamental electronic components — capacitors, inductors and, occasionally, resistors. The design of such networks is a complicated affair, well beyond the scope of this handbook. We can, however, describe some of the general requirements for passive crossovers.

Since they are connected after the power amplifier output, the components in passive crossovers must be capable of withstanding high voltages. For example, a power amplifier rated at 250 watts continuous into 8 ohms is capable of producing 45 volts rms, or 127 volts peak-to-peak. Voltage is of particular concern in selecting capacitors, which are rated for specific maximum voltages. For a given capacitance value, as the voltage rating increases, so will the physical size (and price) of the capacitor.

Insertion loss, which is the loss associated with introducing the network between the amplifier and the driver, is another design concern. Passive crossovers should have minimal insertion loss. A crossover with an insertion loss of only 1 dB, when connected at the output of a 100-watt amplifier, will reduce the effective maximum power that the driver sees to 79 watts.

To minimize the insertion loss, inductor coils in crossover networks must be wound using large gauge wire. Crossover coils in large, high power sound reinforcement speaker systems are always air core types, since iron cores introduce distortion through core saturation.

Passive networks are sensitive to both source (driving) impedance and load impedance. Since contemporary power amplifiers exhibit near zero output impedance, source impedance is generally not a problem, except with very long cable runs. Load impedance is always a factor, and passive crossovers must be designed to work with the loads presented by the respective drivers. If a driver of the wrong impedance for a crossover is used, the actual crossover frequency will shift, and the results will vary from poor system frequency response to a high potential for blown high frequency drivers.

13.7.3 Active, Low Level Crossovers

Active crossover networks are designed to be inserted in the signal chain before the power amplifier. They thus work at far lower signal levels (milliwatts) than do passive, high level crossovers (hundreds of watts). Since active crossovers divide up the total frequency range before the power amplifier, separate amplifier channels are required for each driver or set of drivers, as shown in Figure 13-21. Another term for this type of unit is an *electronic crossover*.

A two way loudspeaker with an active crossover and two power amplifiers (or two halves of a stereo amplifier) each handling a different frequency band, is called a *biamplified* system. Similarly, a three way loudspeaker with active crossovers and three sections of power amplifier is a *triamplified* system.

NOTE: *Some systems combine active, low level crossovers with passive, high-level crossovers. For example, a three way loudspeaker system may utilize an active crossover to split the lowest from the mid and high frequencies, feeding each band to a separate power amplifier. The high frequency amplifier's output is then fed to a passive crossover, whose output goes to the mid and high frequency drivers. Such a system is biamplified, but is a three way system. Similarly, there are four way triamplified systems. This illustrates that bi- and tri- refer to the number of amplifier sections handling different frequency bands, not to the number of sections in the loudspeaker system.*

In spite of the fact that they can increase the total cost of a smaller system, active crossovers are widely used in professional sound because they offer significant advantages in system performance, as detailed in the following text. They can actually save

money in larger (multi-speaker system) installations.

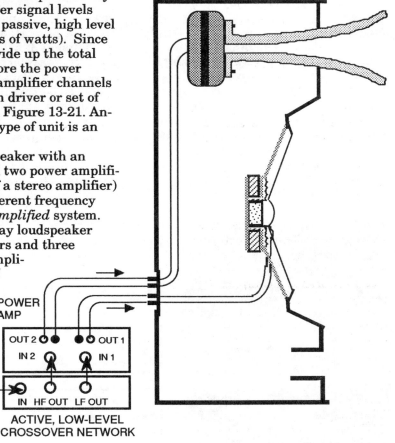

Figure 13-21. Typical location of an active (electronic) crossover network, just ahead of the power amplifiers

13.7.3.1 Headroom

Program material (music or speech) is made up of many different fundamental frequencies and their harmonics. Most music, especially popular music, is bass heavy; there is much more energy at low frequencies than at high frequencies. When both high and low frequency material are present in a program, such as a flute and a bass guitar, the high energy bass frequencies can use up most of the power in the power amplifier, leaving none for the high frequencies. The result can be severe clipping (distortion) of high frequency material. With an active, low level crossover, the high frequency material can be routed to its own power amplifier, avoiding the clipping problem. This results in an effective increase in headroom that is greater than would be obtained by simply using a single, equivalent, larger power amplifier.

Figure 13-22 (a) shows a low frequency waveform from a power amplifier output. The peak-to-peak voltage of the waveform is 121 volts, corresponding to 43 volts RMS. If this voltage were applied to an 8 ohm loudspeaker load, the power level would be about 230 watts (the formula is P=E²÷Z, so power is equal to (43 volts x 43 volts) ÷ 8 ohms = 1849÷8 = 231.1 watts).

of either signal by itself. For an amplifier to produce this voltage into an 8 ohm load, it would have to produce 54V RMS, and must have 365 watts power output capacity (remember that power is proportional to the square of the voltage). If a 230 watt amplifier is used, the waveform will be clipped.

If the same two waveforms were produced by two amplifiers, corresponding to the two graphs of Figure 13-22 (a) and (b), the total amplifier power capacity needed would be 246 watts (the sum of the two power values, 230 + 16), not 366 watts. Thus, using the two amplifiers to reproduce the low and high frequencies in a

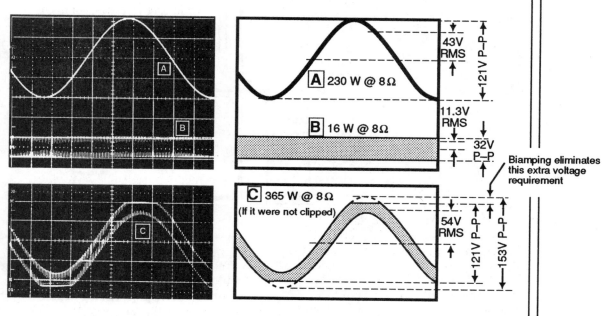

Figure 13-22. Oscilloscope photos and accompanying drawings illustrate the headroom advantage of a biamplified system

Figure 13-22 (b) shows a high frequency waveform from a power amplifier output. The peak-to-peak voltage is 32V and RMS voltage is 11.3V — less than shown in (a), and correspond to a 16 watt output into an 8 ohm load. The levels of these high and low frequency waveforms are typical of musical content.

Figure 13-22 (c) shows the effect of adding the signals of 13-22 (a) and (b), corresponding to a low frequency note and a high frequency note being played at the same time. Note that the total peak-to-peak voltage, which would be 153 volts if it were not clipped, is greater than the peak-to-peak voltage

biamplified arrangement reduces the total power amplifier capacity needed for clean reproduction.

NOTE: *The above discussion is somewhat oversimplified, since it assumes that the low and high frequency waveforms have a phase relationship that does add constructively at peaks. In typical program material, this happens sometimes, but not always. Still, the benefit of biamplification in reducing total required power capacity is valid in real world applications.*

13.7.3.2 Efficiency

A traditional, high level passive crossover is made up of capacitors, inductors and resistors. The resistors in the crossover use up some power... so do any losses in the capacitors and inductors. Biamplifying the system with an active, low level crossover removes these losses, thus improving the sound system's efficiency (i.e., more sound level for a given amount of power amplifier output).

13.7.3.3 Damping

The damping factor of a power amplifier is equal to the load impedance (the impedance of the loudspeaker system connected to it) divided by the amplifier's actual output impedance. An amplifier with a high damping factor can exert greater control over the motions of a loudspeaker diaphragm than an amplifier with a low damping factor, so high damping may improve sound quality. (This effect is disputed by a few engineers, though most accept its validity.) Connecting a passive crossover between the power amplifier and the loudspeaker system effectively increases the output impedance of the amplifier (as seen by the loudspeaker system), which degrades the damping factor. Using an active, low level crossover in a bi or tri amplified system instead of a high level crossover removes the passive components in the amplifier-to-loudspeaker path, and thus allows the true value of the amplifier's damping factor to be realized.

13.7.3.4 Distortion

An active, low level crossover avoids any possible non-linearities that might be caused by a passive, high level crossover. This is only one source of distortion avoided by the active crossover. As previously explained, the active crossover reduces the chance of clipping by adding headroom, so distortion in the amplifier is avoided.

If clipping does occur, amplifier-caused harmonic distortion may be less audible in the biamplified or triamplified system. For example, if the power amplifier in a conventional two-way

system (with high level passive crossover) clips during a very powerful, low frequency note, unwanted harmonics are generated. The conventional system will pass the harmonics through the passive crossover to the tweeter or high frequency compression driver, which will reproduce them audibly. In a biamplified system using the same loudspeaker components, there is no passive crossover after the power amplifiers. Even if the note does cause amplifier clipping (which is less likely), the clipped, low frequency note and its harmonics will go from the low frequency amplifier directly to the woofer (low frequency driver). Since the woofer is less sensitive to high frequencies than the tweeter (or midrange), the high frequency harmonics are attenuated by virtue of the woofer's inherent limitations. This serves to decrease audible distortion.

13.7.3.5 Biamp or Triamp vs. Conventional System

Bi- or triamplified systems offer a number of performance advantages, such as increased headroom. Audio program material is made up of many different frequencies and harmonics. In musical material, most of the energy is in the low frequencies, with very little in the highs. When both high and low frequencies are present in a signal, the stronger low frequencies can use up amplifier power, leaving little or no reserve for the highs so they are more apt to cause the power amplifier to clip. In a bi- or triamped system, a smaller amp can handle high frequencies, LF amp clipping is less of a factor, and less overall amplifier capacity is needed due to the efficiency improvement in the absence of the passive crossover(s).

Smaller bi- or triamped systems are more expensive than conventional system using high-level passive crossovers. Large bi- or triamplified systems require only one crossover network for multiple amplifiers and loudspeakers, whereas conventional systems have a high-level crossver for each loudspeaker – a more costly alternative. Also, a large bi- or triamped system's power capacity can be less than a conventional system, which is why the former is often more cost effective.

By using an appropriate crossover (as discussed in Section 13.7.1) to combine two or more drivers that reproduce different frequency bands, loudspeaker systems can be created that cover most of the audio frequency range. Such systems are referred to as full range loudspeakers.

NOTE: *A full range driver is a single loudspeaker that is intended to reproduce most of the audio frequency range. One example is the typical 6" x 9" oval car stereo loudspeaker. Such units cannot do a very good job at the extremes of the audio spectrum, nor can they generate the very high sound levels required of a full range sound reinforcement system. The full-range loudspeakers we discuss here are not single driver units, but rather are systems comprised of two or more individual loudspeakers (or drivers) that each reproduce a portion of the audio spectrum.*

In sound reinforcement, full range loudspeakers are usually two way or three way systems. They may employ passive crossovers, active crossovers, or a combination of the two. Systems comprised entirely of horn loaded loudspeakers or compression drivers are fairly common because of their high efficiency, although some professionals prefer the sound of direct radiator loudspeaker systems. Especially in smaller systems, the most common approach employs a combination of direct radiator low frequency drivers and horn loaded high frequency drivers.

Two basic approaches have been taken to the packaging of full range systems. These are illustrated in Figure 13-23.

One approach, Figure 13-23 (a), employs separate enclosures for each individual frequency range, these being stacked in various combinations to form the system. This philosophy was common in older sound systems, and is still used in many systems today.

Advantages that are claimed for separate enclosures include ease of handling and improved control over the

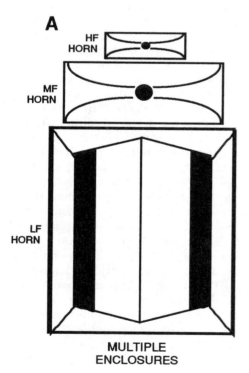

MULTIPLE
ENCLOSURES

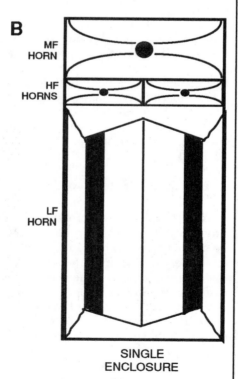

SINGLE
ENCLOSURE

Figure 13-23. Two of the many ways to package a 3-way loudspeaker system

13.8.1 Effect of Boundary Conditions

When a full range loudspeaker is used in an environment with boundary surfaces, its placement affects its perceived frequency response. When such effects are properly understood, they can be used as another trick for producing the desired sound quality.

Consider Figure 13-24. In (a), we see an omnidirectional radiator (a theoretical, idealized loudspeaker) in free field. We measure its sound pressure output at a distance d, and set this to be our reference pressure level, or 0 dB SPL.

If we now place a large reflective boundary (i.e., a wall, ceiling or floor) next to the omnidirectional loudspeaker, Figure 13-24(b), the sound that is radiated toward the boundary is reflected. We see that, as a result, the sound pressure at distance D increases by as much as 3 dB. The source is radiating its power into half as much space, and so this is called *half space loading*.

In Figure 13-24(c), the loudspeaker is placed at the junction of two perpendicular boundaries. Now its power is radiated into one quarter the space; this is called *quarter space loading*.

system. Many reinforcement professionals have come to feel that these advantages are outweighed by a number of disadvantages, such as the increased complexity of hookup (and thus greater potential for mistakes), lack of control over the phase alignment of the system, and the general physical instability of stacks (a pile of separate boxes can tumble down).

The most common contemporary approach, Figure 13-23(b), is the single full range enclosure. This approach is particularly convenient in the case of systems that use a passive crossover, since there is no necessity to daisy chain multiple connections from one cabinet to another. If an active crossover is used, a single multipin connector and multiconductor speaker cable can be used to simplify connections.

The setup and testing of full range systems is covered in Section 17 and Section 18.

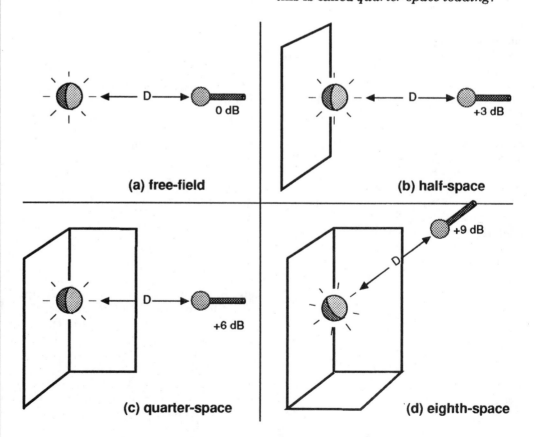

(a) free-field

(b) half-space

(c) quarter-space

(d) eighth-space

Figure 13-24. How SPL Increases Due To Boundary Effects

Note that the SPL has increased by 6 dB relative to the full space, omnidirectional situation in (a).

Finally, in Figure 13-24 (d) we place the source in a three sided corner. This reduces the space to one eighth of the free field, and is called *eighth space loading*. As before, the SPL increases by another 3 dB, to 9 dB more than (a).

Loading affects the output of practical full range systems, as well as this theoretical system, but the effect is not the same at all frequencies.

Note that our example assumes a theoretically omnidirectional radiator. Practical loudspeakers are omnidirectional only at low frequencies (where the wavelength is large compared with the size of the unit). At high frequencies practical loudspeakers have controlled directional characteristics, and radiate sound in one direction (presumably, away from the wall).

For this reason, if we place a full-range loudspeaker at a wall-ceiling junction or in a corner, the low frequencies will be boosted while the highs remain essentially unchanged (they are aimed away from the walls anyway, and so there is little or no reflected energy to reinforce the direct-radiated energy in front of the loudspeaker). If the loudspeaker is deficient in bass, or if we want a bass-heavy sound, the boost provided by the corner placement would be welcome. Otherwise, the system may require equalization to reduce bass output. Again, this can be a benefit. If we know that large amounts of low-frequency energy will be demanded from the system, we can use half-space or quarter-space placement to boost the lows acoustically, then use equalization to cut the lows back down electronically, thus increasing the system headroom (by decreasing power demands on the amplifier and loudspeaker system).

13.9 Loudspeaker Specifications

The specifications of a driver or loudspeaker system should give us all the basic information we need to use it in an application. The main attributes that are normally given in loudspeaker specifications are frequency response, power handling, sensitivity, impedance, and directional characteristics.

13.9.1 Frequency Response

Frequency response is a comparison, by frequency, of the on-axis sound pressure output level of a loudspeaker to its input power level. A typical full range loudspeaker frequency response specification might read:

Frequency Response:
30 Hz – 15,000 Hz, ±3 dB

The specification tells us the range of frequencies that the loudspeaker is designed to accurately reproduce (30 Hz to 15 kHz). It may be able to operate somewhat beyond this range if corrective equalization is applied, but the basic flat response region is defined by this specification.

The figure ±3 dB (or + or –3 dB) is called the tolerance of the specification. It tells us that within the stated frequency range, if we compare the output sound level to the input power level at any frequency, the ratio between the two will fall within a 6 dB window (+3 dB - (-3 dB) = 6 dB).

Frequency response can also be presented as a graph, as shown on the next page in Figure 13-25.

The horizontal axis is frequency, on a logarithmic scale. The vertical axis is sound pressure level, on a linear scale. The graph assumes an input signal to the loudspeaker that is equal at all frequencies. Note that this loudspeaker would barely satisfy the specification given on the previous page (30 Hz – 15 kHz, ±3 dB).

Frequency response deviations such as those shown in Figure 13-25 are considered normal for average, practical loudspeakers. Since they are complex transducing systems, loudspeakers' behavior in response to an excitation signal is subject to a number

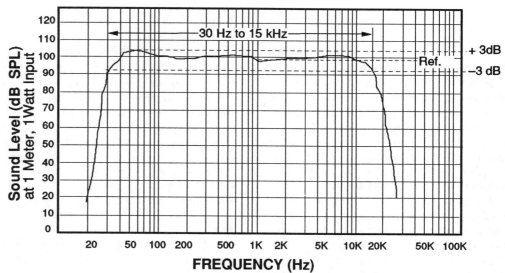

Figure 13-25. Graphic specification of loudspeaker frequency response

of interacting factors. As a result, loudspeaker frequency curves typically will be far rougher than frequency response curves for microphones or active signal processors. If you see a perfectly smooth response curve, it is probably not an accurate one. Sometimes the measuring technician will increase the damping or turn up the chart paper speed when plotting a response curve, which has the effect of mechanically eliminating some of the peaks and dips, but does not accurately reflect what the loudspeaker is doing.

At least one manufacturer provides curves that are composites of one-third octave band noise. The speaker output level is averaged within each band, and plotted as a short, straight, horizontal line. Such curves will never show small dips and peaks in the response, only larger trends. On the other hand, smaller peaks and dips are not generally significant, so the averaged noise band graphs are probably a reasonable specification. (The only problem with averaged noise graphs is that if there is a sharp peak in a live sound system that can trigger feedback, it will not be apparent. One would want to know about such peaks in order to tune a notch filter to reduce the peaks and thereby increase the usable gain of the sound system.)

We can see why graphs such as the one in Figure 13-25 are preferred to simple statements like "30 Hz – 15 kHz, ±3 dB." The graph gives a lot more information. From it, we can see where peaks and dips in the response occur, and how wide they are.

The frequency response of a loudspeaker has a great effect on how the loudspeaker sounds. The flatter the curve, the more accurately the loudspeaker reproduces sound.

Peaks and dips in the response color the sound. A peak in the high end will make the system sound brighter. A peak in the low end will make it seem bass heavy. A broad dip in the midrange will tend to lessen the strength of voice signals, making them less intelligible. Very narrow dips usually have a minimal effect on the sound, particularly on speech, although they can swallow a particular note without affecting adjacent notes on the musical scale.

13.9.2 Power Handling

The power handling specification indicates the amount of amplifier power that the loudspeaker can handle without damage. The specification has no relationship to either frequency response or distortion. Power handling may be specified in a number of ways.

Continuous power (sometimes incorrectly termed rms power) refers to the average power dissipated in the loudspeaker, often by a continuous sine wave signal. This is a worst case specification, representing a condition that results in maximum heating of the voice coil. A loudspeaker rarely encounters such a signal in practical use, unless there is a malfunction in the system or a synthesizer player has a finger resting on one key.

Program (or continuous program) power ratings are based on the power of a complex waveform that simulates actual program material. This power rating will always be higher than the continuous or rms power rating. Unfortunately, there is no standardized program for this rating, so different manufacturers' program ratings cannot be directly compared.

Peak power ratings refer to the maximum instantaneous (very short term) power that the speaker can handle. The peak power handling of a loudspeaker is limited by its maximum excursion, rather than by heating. The peak power rating will always be higher than either the continuous or the program rating.

EIA power handling refers to the use of a clipped, shaped noise signal that closely simulates the conditions of a music signal. The signal is specified in a standard promulgated by the Electronic Industries Association (EIA). It provides both an average level that tests the thermal capacity of the system, and peaks up to 6 dB above the average level to test the excursion capability of the system.

The EIA rating always represents the average level of the signal — not the peak level. Since the peaks may be 6 dB higher, an EIA rating of 50 watts, for example, corresponds to a peak rating of 200 watts. Similarly, an EIA rating of 150 watts corresponds to a peak rating of 600 watts.

Power ratings are one means to match the driver or loudspeaker with an appropriately rated power amplifier. The match is important. An amplifier with too little power will not allow the full capacity of the loudspeaker to be realized. If the underpowered amplifier is pushed too hard, driven into clipping to obtain the desired volume level, it will produce harmonics that can more readily destroy the loudspeaker due to voice coil overheating than a more powerful amplifier that is not clipping. On the other hand, too powerful an amplifier may destroy the loudspeaker due to overexcursion and/or overheating. The procedure for matching a power amplifier to a loudspeaker is further described in Section 12.5.

The sensitivity of a loudspeaker may be specified in several ways: dB SPL at one meter in front of the loudspeaker, with a one watt input signal is the most common rating. Other ratings may be derived using one watt at four feet, or one milliwatt at 30 feet. Assuming the most common case (one watt, one meter), there are still some differences between different manufacturers' specifications. The measurement microphone should be placed directly in front of the driver in a single driver loudspeaker, or in front of a point half way between the two drivers in a two way loudspeaker. Three way or more speaker systems do present a problem in terms of where the measurement mic is located because at 1 meter (39.37 inches), there can be significant SPL differences off axis from some drivers. Then, too, how is the one watt of input power measured? The input voltage is usually measured, squared, and divided by the loudspeaker impedance. What impedance is used? Typically, the nominal rated impedance will be used, but since the actual impedance of a loudspeaker varies with frequency, it is possible that the actual impedance at the tested frequency (or frequencies) is lower, which would then draw more power than the assumed 1 watt, which would artificially boost the sensitivity rating. For this reason, if one wants truly accurate sensitivity specifications, it is important to specify the test signal (usually a sine wave, which may be swept over a given frequency range, but sometimes a band-limited noise signal), and the means by which the input power was determined. It is desirable to specify either the actual input voltage or the assumed impedance for the input power calculation.

*NOTE: Sensitivity is often confused with efficiency. Sensitivity is the sound level produced by a given input power at a specified distance **directly in front** of the loudspeaker. Efficiency is the percentage of total acoustic power output radiated in all directions (distance doesn't matter) relative to a given input power. If two speakers have identical sensitivity, the one with wider dispersion is the more* *efficient. Given two loudspeakers with similar directional characteristics, we can get an idea of their relative efficiency by examining their sensitivity specifications.*

An increase of 3 dB in sensitivity creates an increase in sound pressure level in front of the loudspeaker that is the same as doubling the amplifier power. In other words, given two speakers, one 3 dB more sensitive than the other, if the more sensitive one were operated at 50 watts continuous, the less sensitive loudspeaker would have to be driven at 100 watts continuous to achieve the same sound pressure level on axis.

If the less sensitive loudspeaker in the previous example happens to have a wider dispersion angle, it is possible that it actually delivers the same or even more total acoustic power to the environment than the more sensitive speaker.

Typical calculations using sensitivity ratings may be found in Section 5, "Sound Outdoors."

Impedance is defined as the total opposition to the flow of alternating current in an electrical circuit. In loudspeaker specifications, the term *nominal impedance* is usually used. This reflects the fact that the actual impedance of a loudspeaker varies considerably with frequency. The nominal impedance of a loudspeaker is usually taken to be the minimum impedance that it presents to the power amplifier (above resonance). Figure 13-26 shows a typical impedance curve for a loudspeaker with a rated nominal impedance of 8 ohms.

The nominal impedance is directly related to the amount of power that a loudspeaker can extract from the amplifier. For example, if a power amplifier is rated at 100 watts into 8 ohms, an 8 ohm loudspeaker can extract 100 watts from that amplifier. A 16 ohm loudspeaker, can only extract only about 50 watts from the amplifier.

One would assume from this line of reasoning that a 4 ohm loudspeaker could extract 200 watts from the same amplifier. This may not be the case because, when driving a 4 ohm load, the power amplifier may current limit before that power output is reached. (Sometimes the relationship between impedance and clipping power is not mathematically precise in a power amplifier due to thermal or power supply limitations. The relationship between a power amplifier and its load impedance is discussed in Section 12.)

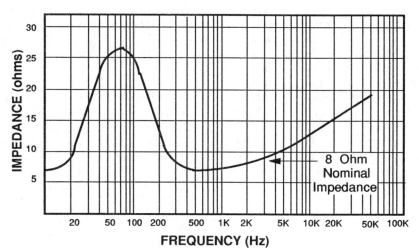

Figure 13-26. Graphic specification of loudspeaker impedance

13.9.5 Directional Characteristics

The directional characteristics of a loudspeaker may be specified in a number of ways. The most common method is to specify horizontal and vertical dispersion separately in degrees. These figures normally represent the angle that is bounded by the points where the sound pressure level is 6 dB lower than the on axis level. In this case, two facts are important to remember:

1) In the absence of any specified frequency range, the quoted figures represent an average that applies only to the mid and high frequencies, since the speaker becomes omnidirectional at low frequencies.

2) The quoted figures represent the total dispersion in the given axis — that is, a specification of 30 degrees vertical dispersion probably means +15 degrees and -15 degrees around the axis (the 0 degree line).

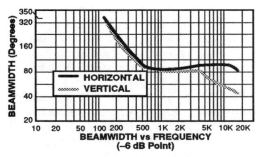

Figure 13-27. Beamwidth plot of a loudspeaker

Another method of presenting directional information is the beamwidth plot. A typical beamwidth plot is shown in Figure 13-27.

Note that this is really a slightly more detailed version of our first specification. The angular beamwidth between the -6 dB points is plotted here against frequency.

Still another method of presenting directional characteristics is to give a family of frequency response curves, as shown in Figure 13-28.

As in the case of the polar plot, curves such as these give us an idea of the frequency response on and off axis. In fact, this plot gives more information about sound quality along different, specific axes, though it gives less detailed information about dispersion at all angles. For sound reinforcement work, plots such as this are very useful.

Some loudspeaker specifications also include values for *directivity factor* and *directivity index*. These figures apply to families of calculations that are beyond the scope of this manual. They are generally used by acousticians and consultants in specifying speech reinforcement systems, and are less applicable to music reinforcement systems.

One more method of specifying the directional characteristics of a loudspeaker is the polar plot. Figure 13-29 (next page) shows typical horizontal and vertical polar plots for the same full-range loudspeaker depicted in Figure 13-27.

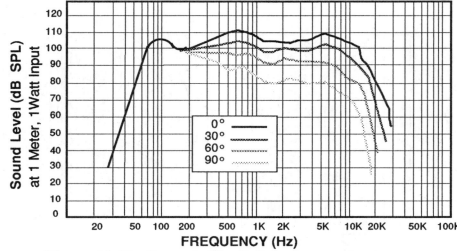

Figure 13-28. On and off-axis frequency response curves of a typical full-range loudspeaker system

Note that the loudspeaker's directional characteristics are shown in a number of different frequency ranges. From this information, we can deduce how the sound will change as we move off axis.

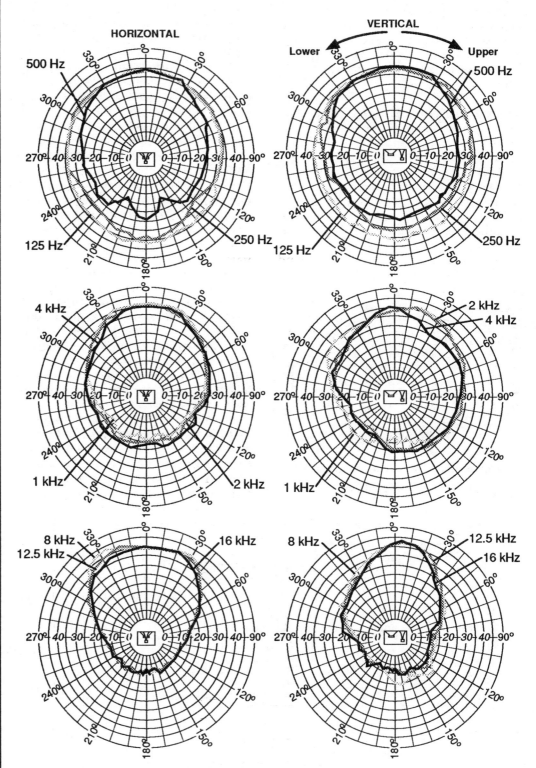

Figure 13-29. Polar plots illustrating the horizontal and vertical dispersion of a full-range loudspeaker system

There are many potential sources of distortion in drivers and loudspeaker systems. Some are inherent in the design of the driver, or in its enclosure or horn. Others are, to an extent, under the control of the system designer and operator. We will deal only with the latter case here.

13.10.1 Over Excursion

When the power amplifier – or another signal processing element in the chain – is asked to deliver an output signal level that exceeds its capabilities, clipping occurs.

Over excursion is the driver's equivalent of amplifier clipping. When a driver is asked to produce a higher sound pressure level than it is capable of delivering at a given frequency, over excursion occurs. On peaks, the diaphragm may slam against the driver frame, causing a burst of uncorrelated high frequency energy. In extreme cases, the coil will jump out of the gap, which can tear the suspension or may jam the voice coil out of the gap, quickly destroying the driver.

Over excursion produces gross distortion. It is an indication that the loudspeaker system cannot handle the power required by the application. The usual solution is to add more loudspeakers, thereby increasing the acoustic power generating capacity of the system so that adequate sound levels can be generated without overdriving the loudspeakers.

13.10.2 Intermodulation Distortion

Music signals are quite complex, and reinforcement of music demands that a loudspeaker faithfully reproduce many frequencies at once. Under some conditions, interaction can occur in the loudspeaker between two or more frequencies in a program, producing extra frequencies that were not present in the original signal. This is called intermodulation (IM), and the extra frequencies that are produced are a form of distortion.

One form of intermodulation distortion (IMD) was described in Section 13.7.3 (amplifier clipping of high frequency components in the presence of a strong low frequency tone). As we observed, this form of IM distortion occurs primarily in systems that employ passive crossovers.

Intermodulation distortion also occurs when a driver is pushed to the limits of its excursion by a very strong signal at one frequency while other, less strong frequencies are also present. As the driver reaches its mechanical limits, it strains against its suspension. This causes a soft clipping of the wave that it is attempting to reproduce. Any other frequencies that are present in the signal become modulated by the strong tone, generating IM distortion products.

A similar effect occurs when a driver is pushed hard enough that its voice coil leaves the magnetic gap of the motor assembly. The force of the permanent magnet is intentionally concentrated in the gap. If the voice coil moves beyond the gap, that force is no longer present, and the coil's motion

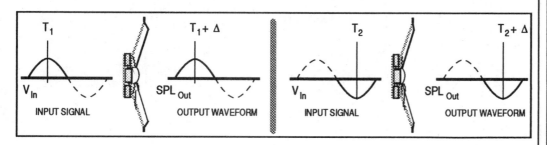

Figure 13-30. Pushing (and pulling) a driver "to the limits" with too much power can introduce distortion.

will no longer increase with increased current. The result is a form of clipping of the wave and, again, IM distortion products are generated. For this reason, low frequency drivers that are designed for long excursion generally employ over wound coils, so that a portion of the coil remains in the gap at all times.

A more subtle form of IM distortion may occur when a cone driver is used to reproduce a wide range of frequencies. The low frequencies cause the cone to travel fairly far in both directions at high speeds, while at the same time it is reproducing higher frequencies. Just as the pitch of a moving car's horn seems higher when it is moving toward us and lower as it moves away, so the motion of the cone that is caused by low frequencies will modulate the frequency of higher components, generating IM products. The effect is called *Doppler distortion*.

In horn loudspeakers, intermodulation distortion can result from nonlinear compression of the air in the throat of the horn. The effect is directly related to several factors: a higher compression ratio, a lower frequency, a higher sound pressure level, or a smaller horn throat diameter will serve to increase the distortion. For this reason, low and mid frequency horns are generally designed with relatively low compression ratios. This source of IM distortion is of particular concern in high frequency horn and driver design, since the need for greater efficiency at high frequencies usually results in the use of higher compression ratios.

13.10.3 Mechanical Defects

Simple mechanical problems in loudspeaker cabinets or drivers can also cause distortion. Most of these are easily remedied once they are identified.

Particularly in low frequency loudspeakers, vibration of the enclosure's walls can result in distortion. For this reason, low frequency enclosures usually require fairly thick, dense materials and extensive bracing. Cabinet resonance not only distorts the sound but also causes a loss of efficiency, since energy that could be projected by the system is instead dissipated in the enclosure walls.

A related source of distortion is poorly designed or loosely mounted cabinet hardware. Rattling handles, loose screws, undamped metal horns or lenses and the like will all generate spurious noises. Hardware must be carefully chosen, securely mounted and, if necessary, coated with a damping compound.

Low frequency enclosures must also be made with airtight seams, even if they are ported. The reason is that very high air pressures build up in the cabinet, even at moderate sound pressure levels. Air will be forced through every small opening, causing whistling or rushing sounds, and the distortion contribution of such sounds can be surprisingly high. Connector plates, handles and drivers all must be gasketed to seal any air leaks, and cabinet joints must be clean and tight.

Both high and low frequency drivers are very susceptible to foreign particles. Perhaps most dangerous are particles of iron or steel, since these will be attracted into the gap of the magnetic assembly and held there by the magnetic field. As the coil moves in and out, it will scrape against any particles in the gap, causing rubbing noises that will couple to the diaphragm very effectively. The result can be very nasty sounding. Missing dust caps must always be immediately replaced, and any repairs to loudspeakers should be made in a clean, dust-free environment.

Mechanical defects in the drivers themselves may also cause distortion. One of the most common such defects is coil rubbing. The voice coil, while moving in and out in the gap, comes in contact with the side walls of the gap.

Coil rubbing causes fairly high distortion, even if the coil is only slightly touching. The effect is caused either by a problem with the suspension such that the coil is not centered in the gap, or by a coil that is out of round. In either case, repair or replacement of the driver is indicated.

Finally, small mechanical defects in the driver – such as a poorly glued part of the suspension, flapping coil lead-in wires, or small deformations of the diaphragm (particularly in high frequency drivers) – may cause smaller amounts of distortion. Discovering these problems can sometimes require extensive troubleshooting. Everything counts, and any source of distortion is best tracked down and fixed. The result will be far better sound quality under all circumstances.

13.11 Typical Failure Modes

When a loudspeaker component fails, it is obviously important to identify and, if possible, correct the cause of the failure. In some cases, a fair amount of detective work will be required.

Failures in loudspeaker drivers are most often traceable to one of two sources: manufacturing defects or improper operation. Drivers may also fail due to problems in external signal processing components of the sound system. These problems are more difficult to trace, particularly if they occur only intermittently. Cooperation of the end user may be required to identify and correct the fault.

The starting point for identifying the cause of a loudspeaker failure is the failed component itself. By examining the symptoms and physical evidence, it is often possible to determine and correct the cause of the failure.

13.11.1 Manufacturing Defects

Manufacturers of professional audio equipment are sensitive to the fact that their customers' livelihoods depends in part on their products' quality and

Defect	Test	Result
Insufficient gluing of suspension components	Sine wave sweep	Buzzing sounds; Separation of (surround and spider) cone or diaphragm
Incomplete bonding of the voice coil to the diaphragm	Sine wave sweep	Buzzing sounds; Coil rubbing Separation of the coil from the diaphragm
Cold solder joints at coil lead-in wires	DC resistance of voice coil connection	Coil resistance greater than rated impedance of driver, or infinite
Faulty welds at the voice coil terminations on the coil former	DC resistance of voice coil connection	Coil resistance infinite or intermittent; sound ceases or is full of static
Poorly assembled driver frame or casing	Visual check Sine wave sweep	Cracks or breaks; loose parts Buzzing sounds; Coil rubbing

Table 13-1. Diagnosis of loudspeaker manufacturing defects

13.11.2 Improper Operation

consistency. For this reason, every major pro audio manufacturer employs some measure of quality control as an integral part of the manufacturing process.

Loudspeaker drivers, which are made and sold in quantity, are sometimes subjected only to spot checking, and the occasional defect may escape the manufacturer's attention and not show up until the driver is in the hands of the end user.

Manufacturing defects in drivers are usually mechanical in nature. Some common examples, and the symptoms that they may generate, are shown in Table 13-1.

The proper handling of manufacturing defects involves knowledge of, and respect for, the service and warranty policies of the manufacturer in question. When manufacturing problems are suspected, consult the supplier's published warranty policy, and communicate with their service or warranty return offices. Responsible manufacturers will welcome identification of such problems, since the information can aid the manufacturers in refining their procedures. Most important, follow the manufacturers' repair or return policies to preserve the rights of the end user.

Particularly with less sophisticated installations or less knowledgeable operators, improper connection or operation accounts for the great majority of component failures. Such failures take many forms, but they are usually catastrophic and readily identified.

Most failures resulting from improper operation can be identified through visual inspection of the failed component. In many cases, it will be necessary to disassemble or destroy the component in order to make a complete inspection. This will likely void any warranty that may apply, and this issue should be decided before undertaking inspection. Of course, if the failure was caused by improper operation, it will undoubtedly not be covered by the product warranty anyway! Still, it's beneficial to establish what caused a failure so that future failures can be prevented. In any case, if the failure might be covered by a warranty, consult the manufacturer before tearing the component to pieces.

Tables 13-2 (below) and 13-3 (next page) present common operation-induced failures in low frequency and high frequency drivers, respectively.

Symptom	Probable Cause
Voice coil looks charred	Excessive continuous amplifier power
Fused or blackened coil lead-in wires	Excessive continuous amplifier power
Voice coil out of gap	Excessive peak amplifier power
Torn suspension	Excessive peak amplifier power; possible out-of-phase connection, if used in a cluster
Coil rubbing	Improper mounting of driver resulting in deformation of frame; excessive continuous amplifier power resulting in separation of coil from former; dropping of cabinet or driver or severe vibration in shipping resulting in deformation of frame; Shifted pole piece.
Burned cone	Grossly excessive continuous amplifier power
Torn or punctured cone	Excessive peak amplifier power; careless transportation; Vandalism
Broken basket or misaligned magnet assembly	Dropping of cabinet or driver

Table 13-2. Diagnosis of low frequency driver failures resulting from improper use

Symptom	Probable Cause
Voice coil looks charred	Excessive continuous amplifier power; amplifier failure (DC at amp output)
Fused or blackened coil lead-in wires	Excessive continuous amplifier power
Diaphragm out of gap or smashed against the pole piece	Excessive peak amplifier power; connection to low frequency amplifier in biamplified system
Diaphragm cracked or pulverized	Excessive continuous amplifier power (often frequency related); excessive peak amplifier power; connection to low frequency amplifier in biamplified system
Diaphragm dimpled or torn	Mishandling of tools during attempted repair or disassembly
Coil rubbing	Dropping of cabinet or driver; improper replacement of diaphragm assembly; excessive continuous amplifier power resulting in separation of coil from former
Mechanical misalignment of magnet assembly or pole piece	Dropping of cabinet or driver

Table 13-3. Diagnosis of high frequency driver failures resulting fromimproper use

13.11.3 Failures Due To Other Components In The Signal Chain

The action of an amplifier or signal processor can result in a condition that destroys one or more loudspeaker components. Such problems may not be readily identifiable except by careful testing of the entire sound system. The physical condition of the failed driver(s) can provide clues that may help to identify the problem's source.

One common source of driver failure is a DC voltage at the output of a power amplifier. Such a condition usually affects only low frequency drivers, since high frequency drivers are usually capacitively coupled.

If the DC offset is significant, and of the wrong polarity, it will cause the coil to jump the gap and burn, resembling a failure caused by excessive peak amplifier power. If the polarity of the offset pulls the cone inward, the cone will usually be frozen in that position by the burned coil.

Less significant offsets may simply hold the cone continuously off center. In this case, the suspension components will eventually retain the off center position, and the cone will appear pushed in or out even when the driver is disconnected. The driver may not fail entirely, but it will usually generate a fair amount of distortion. (Similar distortion can occur when a loose suspended cone type speaker is hung vertically, allowing gravity to create a mechanical DC offset.)

If DC at the amplifier output is suspected, and the amplifier is AC coupled (does not pass DC), then the amplifier is failing or has failed. If the amplifier is DC coupled, the offset may be coming from a previous stage. In this case, the amplifier and the component feeding it must be tested separately.

High frequency oscillations in the signal chain may also destroy loudspeaker components — usually the high frequency driver(s), since the low frequency drivers are protected by the crossover filters. In biamplified systems, amplifier oscillation can cook low-frequency drivers just as readily.

Since they often occur at hypersonic frequencies, high frequency oscillations may not be noticed. In fact, they can cause coil burning when the system is first turned on, with no audio input

and no audible sound output from the loudspeakers!

Oscillations in a sound system may be difficult to track down. If they are suspected as a cause of driver failure, careful signal tracing with a wide band oscilloscope, beginning at the amplifier output and working backward, is usually required. There is a less scientific, but often effective and inexpensive, means to trace RF oscillation. Sometimes a portable AM radio receiver can be held near system cables and used to detect RF oscillations (which may either be heard as a noise while listening to a station, or as hash while tuned between stations).

Finally, turn-on or turn-off transients can destroy low and highfrequency drivers alike. Such transients occur when an electronic component produces a spike at its output when it is powered up or down. For this reason, the general rule to adopt is this:

Turn the amplifiers OFF first, and ON last.

This way, any power on/off transients generated by signal processors in the system never find their way to the loudspeakers.

SECTION 14.
SIGNAL PROCESSING EQUIPMENT

A *signal processor* is a device (or circuit) which alters the audio signal in some non-linear fashion. By that definition, a simple fader, level control or amplifier IS NOT a signal processor. An equalizer, filter, compressor, phaser, delay line, or other sound altering device IS a signal processor. In this section of the handbook we go into some detail on a variety of common signal processing devices, providing some historical perspective, how it works information, and limited notes regarding applications and use. The one product category we have omitted here is the crossover network (or frequency dividing network), which is covered in detail in Section13.7 (most people would not consider a crossover network to be a signal processor, although it certainly does alter the signal).

We discuss most signal processors as though they are discrete, self contained devices that are used outboard from the mixing console. In fact, many mixing consoles or even smaller mixers have some signal processors built-in: various types of input equalizers, graphic equalizers for outputs, echo or reverb, and sometimes compressor/limiter circuitry.

Another common term for a *signal processsor* is an *effects unit* or *effects device*, sometimes abbreviated EFX. Many signal processors are used primarily for special effects, such as the flangers and distortion generators (fuzz boxes) used by electric guitarists. Other signal processors are used to subtly shape the overall sound balance (equalizers), to control the perceived spaciousness of the sound or add perspective (reverb and delay) or to level the wide volume variations in a program (compressors) in such a way that no special effect is perceived. These same devices, when used with more extreme settings, will produce special effects. We prefer the term signal processor because it covers the device in all cases, whether used for mild enhancement or extreme special effects.

14.1.1 General Discussion

In the early days of the telephone industry, when long cables were used to transmit voice, a lot of signal loss (attenuation) occurred. Amplification could be used to make up for that loss, but it turned out that the loss was frequency dependent, with some frequencies suffering greater attenuation than others. Special circuitry was developed to differentially boost the frequencies that suffered the greater attenuation. Since these circuits made all frequencies more equal in level, the circuits were called *equalizers*. Originally the term *equalization* referred only to circuits that boosted certain areas of the audio frequency spectrum.

You may recognize that a circuit which acts on a certain portion of the frequency spectrum is a *filter*. Filters generally cut certain frequencies. If you cut most frequencies and allow certain frequencies to pass without being cut (a *band pass filter*), the net result is similar to having boosted those frequencies that pass through unaltered, especially when amplification (gain) is added to make up for the attenuated frequencies. Filters can thus be used, in a sense, to produce boost. Filters that act to cut frequen-

cies were eventually combined in a single unit with equalization circuits that act to boost certain frequencies, creating the reciprocal boost/cut devices that are widely used today.

While it is historically and technically accurate to use the term *equalization* only when referring to boost, common usage today applies the term to boost and cut circuits. You will also see the term *filter set* in some contexts, such as $^1\!/_3$ *octave filter set* where the term equalizer might or might not be equivalent (some filter sets provide cut only, and hence are really not equalizers at all). We are not too concerned with precise terminology, but we did think you should know why some people draw careful distinctions in this area.

14.1.2 Common Tone Controls

The typical *tone control* on a hi-fi amplifier or car stereo is a form of equalizer. It generally operates in just two *bands* low frequency (or bass) and high frequency (or treble). Figure 14-1 illustrates the appearance of standard bass and treble tone controls, along with a graph of the frequencies that might be affected as the controls are adjusted.

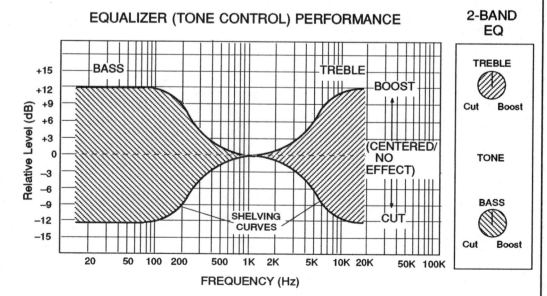

Figure 14-1. Typical bass and treble tone controls and how they alter frequency response

When you turn up the *bass* tone control, you increase the level of lower frequency sounds (boost them) relative to the rest of the program. This results in a richer or fuller sound or, in the extreme, in a boomy sound. Conversely, when you turn down the *bass* tone control, you decrease the level of these same frequencies (cut them), resulting in a thinner or tinny sound.

The graph in Figure 14-1 depicts one particular type of equalization known as a *shelving* characteristic or shelving curve. Let's examine the shelving type EQ created by the bass control. The graph indicates that the boost or cut gradually builds below the 1000 Hz hinge point. With the control set at one extreme or the other, the circuit produces 10 dB of boost or cut at 100 Hz, with less and less effect above that frequency. Below 100 Hz the amount of boost or cut remains constant, as shown by the response plot that has ceased to slope and is again level. This new boosted or cut level portion of the curve looks like a shelf, hence the term shelving.

The *treble* tone control operates like a mirror image of the *bass* control, boosting or cutting frequencies above the 1000 Hz hinge point, but providing no more than the maximum set boost or cut above 10 kHz (in the shelving region). The hinge point of such tone controls varies, and may not be the same for bass and treble circuits. The bass control might hinge at 500 Hz, and the treble control at 1.5 kHz, causing no change whatsoever between 500 Hz and 1,500 Hz when either control is adjusted. Also, the point where maximum EQ occurs may vary in the real world, with bass controls reaching maximum between 50 Hz and 150 Hz, and treble controls between 5 kHz and 12 kHz.

Figure 14-2 illustrates the effect of tone control settings of less than maximum boost or cut. As you can see, the shelving characteristic remains flat, and the hinge point remains the same, but the amount of boost or cut under the curve changes.

If one were to classify this particular set of tone controls as an equalizer (which it is), it would be be specified as a two-band, fixed frequency range equalizer having a shelving characteristic, and up to 10 dB of boost or cut at 100 Hz and 10 kHz.

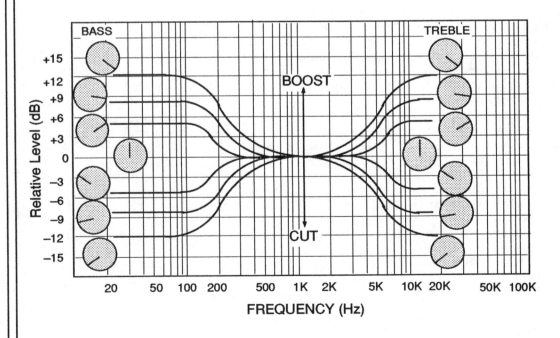

Figure 14-2. A typical family of bass and treble tone control curves, with control settings indicated

14.1.3. Multi-Band Conventional Equalizers

Each input channel on a typical mixer or mixing console may have a two band equalizer, similar to the hi-fi tone controls described in Section14.1.2, but it is more likely to have a somewhat more elaborate equalizer that affords separate, simultaneous control of at least three frequency bands. In the case of a three band equalizer, the middle frequency band (midrange) will always exhibit what is known as a *peaking* characteristic, as illustrated in Figure 14-3.

our ears are most sensitive (500 Hz to 4 kHz). Unfortunately, the selection of just a few EQ frequencies that are supposed to be good for everything seldom produces exactly the sound that someone wants for a very specific mixing job. For this reason, some manufacturers provide a way to alter the actual center frequencies of peaking EQ (or the knee frequencies of shelving EQ). Such a scheme, with a simple choice of two frequencies in each of four bands, is shown in

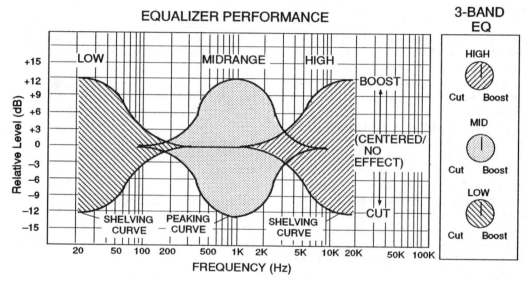

Figure 14-3. Typical 3-band equalizer characteristic

Another term for peaking is peak/ dip, which reflects the fact that the peak amount of equalization can be an increase in level due to boost (a peak in the frequency response curve) or a decrease in level due to cut (a dip in the response curve). All peaking equalizers have some center frequency at which maximum peak or dip occurs, and below or above which there is less and less effect until, at some distance from the center frequency (along the frequency axis) there is no effect. Contrast this with the shelving EQ, above (or below) whose effective frequency the amount of boost or cut remains constant.

Many mixing console channel equalizers provide two or more mid-band peaking equalization controls between a pair of shelving high and low frequency equalization controls, thus affording a greater degree of control of those frequencies where most of the music energy exists and where

Figure 14-4. Observe that the low and high bands have shelving type curves (still, with switchable frequencies) while the low mid and high mid bands have peaking type EQ.

There is a tendency to refer to a 3 band equalizer (per Figure 14-3) as a 3 knob EQ or a 4 band equalizer (per Figure 14-4) as a 4 knob EQ. The problem here is that there may be more than 4 knobs in a 4 band equalizer. The frequency selection switches may have control knobs, which would make this 4 band EQ an 8 knob EQ. We prefer citing the number of frequency bands that may be simultaneously controlled, not the number of knobs available to do that job. (Advanced, remotely controlled equalizers actually permit control of many bands, with respect to frequency, boost cut, and other parameters, using just two knobs and a few switches, which means your terminology must be precise.)

Where permitted by cost considerations and available panel space, it is generally desirable to be able to simultaneously control more frequency bands. This means that different aspects of the sound can be manipulated. Suppose an electric guitar is the input to a given mixing channel. With a 2 band EQ (tone controls), all one can do with the boost is lift the bass for a richer sound, which unfortunately also adds a boomy quality to certain bass notes... or lift the treble for more brightness, which, unfortunately also emphasizes the sound of fingers sliding on the strings. Processing this same guitar with a 4 band EQ is an entirely different story. Now the low frequency shelving EQ control can be rolled off to cut unwanted boominess, while a lower mid peaking EQ can apply some boost at around 200 Hz for a thick sound, the upper mid peaking EQ can apply some boost at 2.5 kHz to increase the punch, while the high frequency shelving EQ can roll off frequencies above 8 kHz to reduce extraneous noise. These selected EQ frequencies, the choice of how much boost or cut to apply, and whether the curve is peaking or shelving will depend on many factors: individual taste, the instrument or mic used, the acoustics of the environment, the sound system quality, the availability of specific EQ options, and more.

Some mixing consoles have been built with a choice of 20 or more discrete EQ frequencies, in 4 or 5 bands, on the input channel equalizers. Even this may not be adequate for pinpointing the desired sound, which is why other types of equalizers were developed, as explained in following paragraphs.

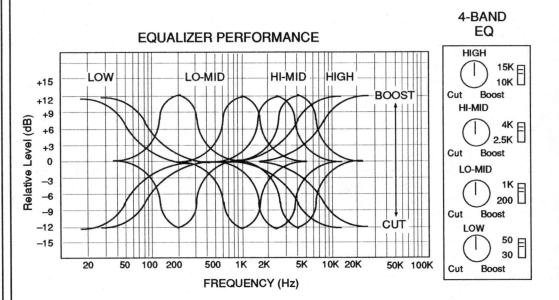

Figure 14-4. A 4-band equalizer with two switch-selectable frequencies per band

14.1.4 Sweep Type Equalizers

For years it was recognized that if one could sweep the center or knee frequency of an equalizer, this would provide much more precise control of the sound. The technique was very costly due to the nature of the electronic circuitry in early equalizers. The coils (inductors) were either fixed in value or very difficult to alter. Newer circuits utilize relatively less costly integrated circuit operational amplifiers, plus relatively inexpensive capacitors and resistors, to emulate the function of the inductor, with the added advantage of easily changed circuit values. This has made it practical to build stable, cost effective equalizers with sweepable frequency controls. The *sweep type equalizer* is much like the multi frequency conventional EQ discussed in Section 14.1.3, except that instead of switching the center or knee frequency, one can continuously adjust it. One such sweepable equalizer is illustrated in Figure 14-5.

The equalizer in Figure 14-5 has 4 knobs to cover 3 bands. In this case, the high and low bands are shelving type EQ, and the associated frequency knobs adjust the knee of the shelving curve, whereas the mid band is a peaking type EQ so its frequency knob adjusts the center frequency of the peak/dip effect. Some such EQs have sweepable center bands and fixed frequency high/low bands.

14.1.5 Parametric Equalizers

In all the equalizers discussed thus far in Section 14.1, the steepness of the EQ curve has been fixed. At a given value of boost or cut, the bandwidth of the peaking curve (the amount of the audio spectrum affected) has been set by the manufacturer and is not adjustable. Sometimes one wishes to have a very broad EQ curve, with a gentle onset and a very gradual buildup to maximum peak or cut (or to the shelving value) with respect to frequency. For example, to bring out a bit of presence in the overall mix of several vocalists, a broad peak at around 6 to 8 kHz may be called for. On the other hand, a certain note or a noise can be either accented or diminished in strength with minimal effect on adjacent frequencies. This aspect of the equalizer – the broadness or sharpness of the curve – is described by a specification called Q. The higher the Q, the sharper the curve.

A few equalizers are provided with switchable Q, but the majority of equalizers that provide any control of Q offer continuously variable Q between a broad and a narrow characteristic (typically Q of 0.5 through Q of 3 to 5). A very narrow notch filter, with only a few Hz bandwidth, may have a considerably higher Q. Such filters are not normally found on a mixing console channel equalizer, but are restricted to specialized uses, such as notching out harmonics of motion picture camera

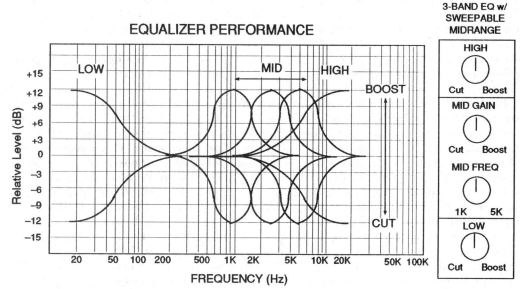

Figure 14-5. A 3-band equalizer with the middle band having a sweepable center frequency

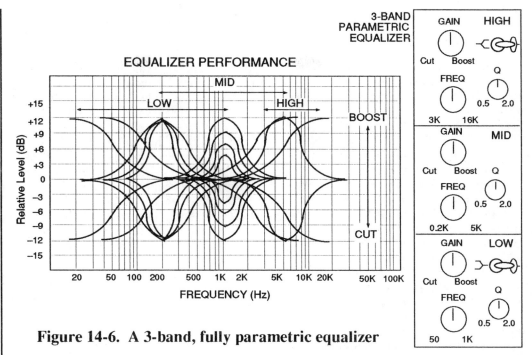

Figure 14-6. A 3-band, fully parametric equalizer

noise, or reducing the strong 120 Hz second harmonic of 60 Hz power line hum. Equalizers that provide both sweepable center frequencies and adjustable Q, as well as boost/cut controls, are known as *parametric equalizers* (because they allow you to adjust all the parameters of the equalization). A parametric equalizer is illustrated in Figure 14-6.

Usually there are several filters in a parametric EQ, and some outboard parametrics (packaged for use externally rather than built into a console) are set up for stereo operation so that adjusting one control affects two channels (which is desirable for keeping a stereo image in proper perspective). Each filter section in the parametric equalizer can either cut or boost frequencies within its band, and the range of center frequencies available from adjacent filters usually overlaps.

Some so called parametric equalizers do not have adjustable Q, and are really sweep type equalizers. Some offer parametric EQ in one or more bands (i.e., just the midrange band), but switchable or fixed frequency EQ in the other bands. These are not fully parametric as is the one illustrated in Figure 14-6. In reality, just about any conceivable combination of fixed frequency or sweep type or parametric EQ, with shelving and/or peaking curves has appeared at one time or another, so be sure to closely examine any equipment to determine how it actually works.

One of the alleged advantages of the parametric type EQ is that it enables the frequency needing help to be precisely selected, and the Q to be adjusted, so that a minimal amount of boost or cut can be applied, with correspondingly fewer ill effects on adjacent frequencies where the correction is not needed. By adjusting a filter for wide band rejection characteristics (low Q), it can perform room equalization in a similar manner to a graphic equalizer, or it can act as a variable frequency cut or boost tone control. In a narrow band reject mode (high Q), a parametric equalizer can be used for feedback control, or (as previously explained) to notch out hum frequencies without subtracting much of the adjacent program material.

Since all EQ causes phase shift, boost can reduce headroom and cut can eliminate desired portions of the program. The ability to use only the minimum amount of equalization required is thus a genuine advantage. Some people dislike parametric EQ because there are so many parameters that MUST be adjusted, and because it is difficult to make note of specific settings so they can later be duplicated in other mixing situations. If inexperienced operators will be using a mixing console, with minimal time to become familiar, it may be better to have simpler EQ. But a good parametric EQ in the hands of an experienced professional is quite a tool.

The debate over which type of EQ is best is complicated by the actual sound quality of some equalizer circuitry. For A higher quality fixed-frequency equalizer may sound much better, even if the correction cannot be as precise, than a mediocre quality parametric EQ. High quality equalizers exhibit less distortion and/or noise than lower quality units, and may give longer service without maintenance where better quality controls are employed. Some units exhibit somewhat lower phase shift, though this is more a function of the amount of boost or cut selected. As with all sound equipment (indeed, any technical equipment), the way a feature is provided is as important as the feature itself.

When applying parametric EQ to the program as a whole, rather than one channel, you should remember that excessive boost may reduce system headroom, create clipping and make extreme power demands on amplifiers and loudspeakers. In addition, a parametric equalizer may ring considerably at high Q (narrow) boost settings. Ringing is a problem caused when a filter begins to act like an oscillator. (Ringing is the tendency of a filter to resonate at its natural fre-quency when excited by a sine wave pulse at that frequency.) Ringing is present to some extent in all equalizers, but is usually masked by the reverberance in a sound system. High Q filters, though, can generate excessive ringing or resonance. Such ringing may be useful as an effect on a particular input source, but is generally not desirable when it affects the overall sound system. Used carefully, a parametric equalizer can be an extremely useful tool for sound reinforcement or for recording.

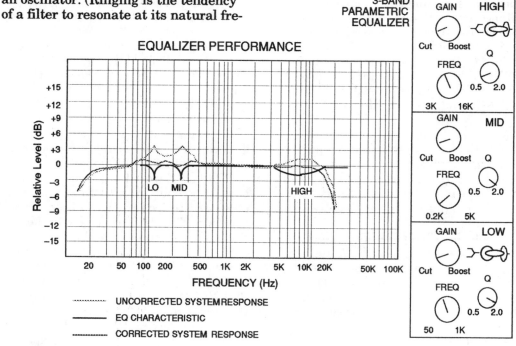

Figure 14-7. Correcting special problems with a parametric EQ

14.1.6 Graphic Equalizers

A *graphic equalizer* is a multi-frequency, band reject filter, or a band-pass/reject filter. Unlike typical three or four band input channel equalizers, a graphic equalizer can simultaneously operate on eight or more frequency bands, typically chosen to have one octave or one-third octave band centers. Most graphic equalizers use I.S.O. standardized band center frequencies. (I.S.O. is an abbreviation for the International Standards Organization.) Less common, but sometimes found are graphic equalizers with two-third octave, one-eighth octave, one-sixth octave and, on rare occasion, one-twelfth octave band centers.

The units are called graphic because most have linear slide controls. When they are set they create a visual image that resembles the overall frequency response curve of the EQ (NOT the response of the sound system!). Some graphic equalizers use rotary controls to accomplish the same thing (though they don't graph the EQ curve). A graphic equalizer may provide attenuation only (band reject), or, more commonly, attenuation and boost (band pass/band reject).

One octave, two-thirds octave and one-half octave graphic equalizers are considered to be broadband devices, useful for general corrections or alterations in the frequency response of a system. One third, one-sixth and one-twelfth octave equalizers may be considered narrowband devices although technically they are still broadband. Truly narrowband filters have a

bandwidth on the order of 4 to 10 Hz rather than one-twelfth of an octave. Why are we concerned about relatively broad or narrow band filters in the equalizers? It turns out that things like AC hum or motor generated noise occur in very narrow bands, and many room resonances are very narrow. Correcting them with broader filters means that some non-problem frequencies will be affected, which can have unwanted audible side effects. Consider that the one octave from 10 kHz to 20 kHz has a 10,000 Hz bandwidth and that the most narrowband graphic EQ on the market, with a one-twelfth octave filter, could affect a band as wide as 833 Hz in this region of the spectrum. It's true that in the octave from 20 Hz to 40 Hz, which is 20 Hz wide, that a one-twelfth octave filter could be less than 2 Hz wide. This shows us that a filter based on some fraction of an octave spacing covers more actual Hz (more bandwidth) as the frequency increases, and that when a pinpoint correction is needed, the more narrow the filter spacing, the better.

There are a number of reasons why few graphic equalizers are one-sixth or one-twelfth octave devices, however. For one thing, what can be covered in 27 to 31 one-third octave bands requires about 60 one-sixth octave bands or over 100 one-twelfth octave bands. That becomes a very expensive device, a very large device, and one which is very, very time consuming to use when tuning a room. Greater phase shift

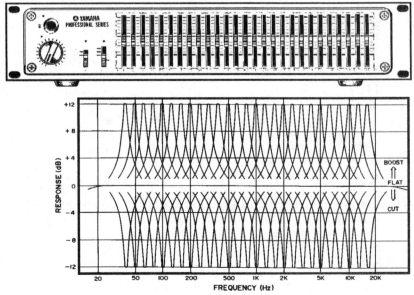

Figure 14-8. A one-third octave graphic equalizer

occurs with narrow filters, which can create unpleasant swishing sounds as program frequencies sweep through the equalized band. Beyond that, the frequencies requiring corrections may drift somewhat if the anomalies are dependent on room acoustics. In that case, the anomalies are more wavelength-related than frequency related so temperature, for example, can have a significant impact on the frequency at which resonant modes occur. (The less dense the air, the slower sound travels, hence a given wavelength will correspond to a different frequency.) With the more narrow band filters, the entire tuning process may have to be repeated when drift occurs, which may be impossible during a show. Here the broader filters are less critical, and may provide more stable sound system characteristics. Technology and the marketplace have, so far, determined that one octave graphic equalizers are useful for general tonal corrections, and one-third octave graphic equalizers are sufficient for most room tuning and feedback avoidance.

Graphic equalization reduces the effect of resonant peaks and dips in loudspeaker response and, to a lesser degree, in the acoustic environment, reducing the tendency for acoustic feedback to occur. As the overall gain (volume) of the sound system is turned up, feedback will first occur at that frequency (or frequencies) where the system has a peak. It typically begins as a slight ringing, and then becomes a loud howl. By using a graphic equalizer to attenuate the first peak, the overall system gain can be increased until the next (formerly lower) peak begins to feed back. That peak is then attenuated using another graphic EQ band, and the system gain can be further increased. When the peaks have all been leveled to the extent possible with the EQ, the overall system gain may increase from 6 dB to 10 dB above above the initial gain before feedback commences.

Another use of graphic equalization is to contour the frequency response of the mixing console's output to obtain the most pleasing sound quality or improved intelligibility. Flat response is seldom desired, and almost never realized in sound reinforcement applications. Audio may be reasonably flat over the middle of the audio spectrum, but the bottom end is sometimes boosted for effect or rolled off for power

handling and reverberant considerations, while the top end is usually rolled off somewhat due to typical listening preferences (although it may be boosted to overcome the differential attenuation of high frequencies by air over longer distances). Sometimes the middle portion of the spectrum (1 kHz to 5 kHz) must be boosted to improve the recognition of vocal consonants and sibilants, particularly when these sounds are masked by other sounds in nearby frequency bands.

The graphic equalizer is a very useful tool, but it cannot substitute for good acoustics or for well designed amplifier/loudspeaker systems. Excessive boost, especially at lower frequencies, drains much of the available amplifier power, over stresses the drivers in the loudspeaker system, and reduces overall system headroom. Excessive cut takes out noticeable portions of the program along with a desired response peak or noise component.

The signal driving each loudspeaker (each main cluster or each monitor mix) usually requires its own channel of graphic equalization, which is installed just after the mixing console output (or in the patch in/out loop of the output circuit), before any electronic crossover or the power amplifier. Stage monitor feeds, for example, may require very different equalization than house feeds. In recording and broadcast applications, the graphic equalization applied to the recording is usually for tonal considerations, and to avoid exceeding the frequency response limits of the medium. The studio monitors or audience foldback system might require graphic equalization to suit very different ends.

Some graphic equalizer circuitry is such that when boost is applied to two adjacent bands, there remains a large dip between the two band centers. If a frequency must be equalized between the two band centers, excess correction will be required at the band centers. Other equalizers maintain a smoother transition to adjacent bands, which means that less overall boost (or cut) for each band center control is required to grab frequencies in between. This latter performance is more desirable, and such equalizers are classified as having *combining* type filters. Non combining type multiband equalizers (or filter sets) are primarily intended for measurement purposes, not for program correction (see Figure 14-10).

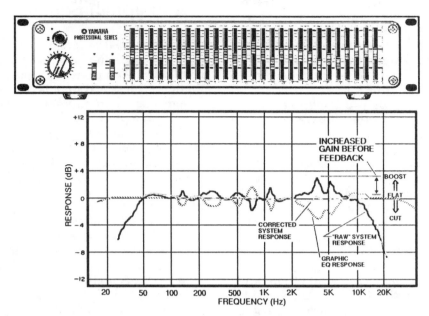

Figure 14-9. Reducing feedback and smoothing the overall system response with a graphic equalizer

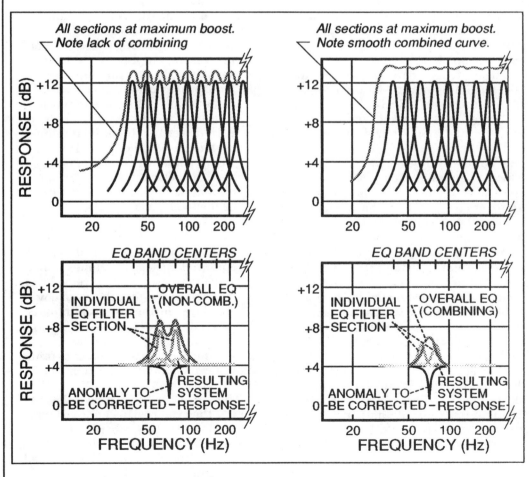

Figure 14-10. The difference between non combining and combining type filters in a graphic equalizer

14.1.7 Paragraphic Equalizers

A *paragraphic equalizer* is NOT a literary tool. It is a graphic equalizer with sweepable center frequencies instead of having the band centers fixed at I.S.O. or other predetermined frequencies. It may or may not have adjustable Q. As you can guess, the term is a contraction of parametric and graphic.

Such devices are generally used for tuning out feedback or other system anomalies. They can function exactly like a standard graphic equalizer, but with the added advantage of being able to sweep the filter center frequency to the exact point where the feedback node occurs, thus allowing a minimum of cut to be applied. Because the circuitry is more costly, and there are more knobs than on a standard graphic EQ, the paragraphic typically is not offered in one-third octave configurations. However, a one octave paragraphic still may have 8 to 10 filter sections, and *if* the sweep frequency range offers adequate overlap between sections, then it may be possible to get as much increase in effective system gain as with a conventional one-third octave graphic.

The difficulty with the paragraphic is determining how to obtain a smooth system response. This is aided considerably by using an audio spectrum analyzer and a pink noise source. Unlike the graphic equalizer, where it may be relatively easy to make an educated guess at the most appropriate EQ boost/cut slider, and then operate it to correct the problem, the paragraphic EQ offers no clear choice. Should one use this slider, or the one just above or below it? How much boost or cut should be used when searching for the optimum center frequency? These questions should be addressed in the owner's manual for the particular equalizer, since their answer depends on the available overlap in bands (if any), and the Q of the filters, whether fixed or adjustable. Once again, while the paragraphic EQ may offer more potential control, it also forces the operator to exercise considerably more judgment and skill in order to take advantage of that potential.

14.1.8 Tuning a Sound System with Graphic (or Paragraphic) Equalization

It is essential to recognize that equalization is the *LAST* step that should be taken in tuning a sound system. Unless a system is correctly designed and carefully set up, the equalization may not accomplish much, and may actually degrade the sound. Here are some of the things that should be checked prior to equalizing a system:

a) Check the overall performance (frequency response, noise and distortion characteristics) of each individual piece of equipment in the sound system, and of the system as a whole. A malfunctioning loudspeaker, for example, renders the equalization processess useless. Hum or high frequency oscillation can also skew your results.

b) Check to ensure the polarity is consistent from all input sources (microphones, direct instrument pickups, tape machines, etc.) through the mixing console, signal processors, amplifiers and loudspeakers. Be sure all amplifier/loudspeaker channels have the same polarity (they are in phase). This does not necessarily apply to each driver in a bi- or triamplified system, bi- or triamplified system, where polarity reversal may be specified. Consult the operation manual for the electronic crossover or the loudspeaker system.

c) Be sure to check the system with typical program signals at normal operating levels. Test tones or noise at reduced levels (or extreme levels) may not highlight otherwise obvious flaws during your preliminary listening evaluation.

An additional discussion of system tuning can be found in Section 17 of this handbook.

There are two basic approaches to tuning the system. One approach is to ring out the system, whereby feedback is induced and the equalization is then applied to knock down individual feedback frequencies (nodes). This procedure is described in Section 11.13. Another approach is to measure the

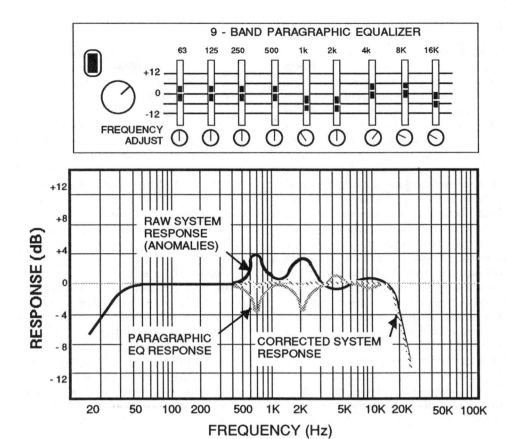

Figure 14-11. Reducing feedback and smoothing the overall system response with a paragraphic equalizer

frequency response and adjust the equalization to obtain the desired room curve. Sometimes this latter process is done with one octave graphic EQ, and then further refined by ringing out with one- third octave or parametric EQ.

When measuring the response of a system, use a suitable real time audio spectrum analyzer. If you're using one-third octave equalization, then the analyzer should be capable of at least one- third octave resolution. Portable devices with LED or LCD displays may be the most convenient, but remember that a unit with hard copy capability (a chart recorder or computer with printer) may be helpful in documenting your work, especially in fixed installations. Alternate means of measuring the system response, such as Time Delay Spectrometry (TDS), with its derivative, Time-Energy-Frequency (TEF) measurement system are available from certain vendors.

When you measure the system response, do it from a typical listening position. Then measure it again, perhaps three or four times, from different listening positions. Examine these data. If there are large discrep-

ancies in overall level or response, it may be necessary to first re-aim or relocate certain loudspeakers, or to change the power applied to certain of them. If the curves are similar, then average the results (some equipment will do this automatically). This gives you a representative measurement. Apply corrective equalization to lift the dips and/or knock down the peaks in the measured response. Measure the system response again (at several locations), and make further corrections. Three or four iterations may be necessary. You may be using a noise source or test tones for these measurements, so be sure to LISTEN to program material through the sound system before you complete your tuning. If something sounds bad, it may be necessary to strike a compromise between the EQ settings that yield a good looking curve and the settings that sound best to the trained ear. Finally, be sure to measure and document not only the system response, but also the EQ settings that produced it (in case someone rearranges the controls when you're not around).

14.1.9 High Pass And Low Pass Filters

A *high pass filter* (also known as a *low cut filter*) allows all frequencies above its cutoff point to pass through from filter input to filter output without attenuation, whereas frequencies below the cutoff are attenuated. The cutoff point is defined as that frequency where the signal has dropped 3 dB relative to the flat or bandpass region. Below the cutoff point, the filter will exhibit increasingly more attenuation (in dB) as the frequency goes lower and lower. The rate at which this attenuation occurs is defined in dB per octave. Standard high pass filters are available in 6 dB/octave increments, since each 6 dB represents one filter pole (one filter circuit element). Thus, 6 dB, 12 dB, 18 dB and 24 dB per octave HP filters are common.

High pass filters are ideal for rolling off (attenuating) the signal in an area where noise, distortion or other unwanted material is present. For example, the very low frequency rumble of footsteps and sympathetic vibrations that ripple along a stage floor can get into microphones via mic stands, then travel through the mixing console, into the power amps, and to the loudspeakers. These rumble components, which range from 5 Hz to 30 Hz or so, will not be reproduced by the majority of sound systems, but will use up an inordinate amount of amplifier power, thus reducing the power available to handle the desired program signal (with less headroom and more tendency for the amplifiers to clip and distort on program peaks). Low frequency rumble

and noise also can cause the low frequency loudspeaker diaphragms to move through excessive excursions, especially below the cutoff frequency of a horn loaded system, which can drastically increase distortion and may destroy the driver suspension. Even if the mic is hand held or has a very good shock mount, the wind or a vocalist's breath can induce low frequency noise in the 40 Hz to 70 Hz region where little to no usable program energy exists (for a vocal mic).

For these reasons, in almost any sound reinforcement system it is desirable to install a high pass filter with a cutoff frequency no lower than 20 Hz (a so-called sub-sonic filter). The optimum slope of such a filter is 18 dB per octave. Twelve dB per octave is OK, and 24 dB is probably more than you need (besides, higher slope rates cause more phase shift inside the pass band, which can produce unwanted audible artifacts).

The fact is that most sound systems reproduce very little below 40 Hz, so a high pass filter with a 40 Hz cutoff may have no direct effect on the program when inserted, other than protecting the drivers and reducing distortion. Such filters are often provided as standard equipment on the electronic crossover network or on a graphic or parametric equalizer, and are even provided on a few power amplifiers. The HP filter may have a fixed cutoff frequency, a few switch-selectable cutoff points, or a continuously adjustable cutoff frequency. If

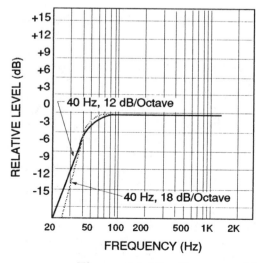
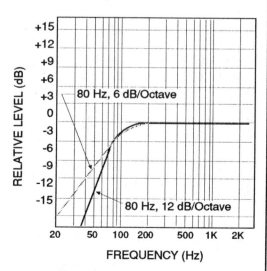

Figure 14-12. Common high pass filter characteristics

provided on your crossover, graphic equalizer, or power amp, we strongly recommend you use the HP filter. If you have more than one available in the signal path between the mixing console output and the amp input, use as many filters as necessary to obtain the desired 18 dB/octave slope rate. This might be a single 18 dB/octave filter, or a 6 dB filter in the graphic EQ plus a 12 dB filter in the crossover network. If the filters are provided in the power amps, use them (even if the system is biamped and the amp is for the high frequency drivers). The filters in the amps will also protect against any low frequency transients or distortion generated by the signal processors.

If no filter is available in the path from the console to the amplifiers, consider purchasing a separate high pass filter (cutoff somewhere between 20 Hz and 40 Hz) and inserting it in the signal path ahead of the power amplifier(s). An added benefit of such filters is loudspeaker protection. If a performer drops a microphone, the ensuing low frequency thud will be far less likely to propel all the woofer diaphragms into the audience.

To eliminate breath and wind noises in vocal or certain instrumental mics, and to reduce hum or sound leakage from nearby low frequency instruments, cutoffs above 40 Hz are best. However, one would not want to use an 80 Hz or 100 Hz HP filter to process the entire program. Such filters are often included in the input channel circuitry of the mixing console, and

should be used any time you do not hear a loss of desired program frequencies when you switch the filter into the circuit.

A *low pass filter* (also known as a *high cut filter*) is something like a high pass filter, only it attenuates frequencies above a certain cutoff point. Low pass filters are less common, but still widely found in sound systems. They can be used to roll off unnecessary portions of the frequency spectrum that are above the highest program frequencies, and which contain primarily hiss and noise. In some cases the loudspeaker or transmission system may have limited high frequency response, and if program frequencies above that limit are applied the result will be distortion. Instead of creating distortion with higher frequencies that will not be accurately reproduced it may be better to throw away such frequencies with a low pass filter. If you ever have to send a program through a limited bandwidth telephone line, for example, it is an excellent idea to low pass filter the program so it does not exceed the specified upper response limit of the phone line (or so it doesn't exceed it by much). Low pass filters will usually have 6 dB or 12 dB per octave slope rates, and may have cutoff points anywhere from 3 kHz (for a voice grade phone line) to 8 kHz (for an older motion picture theatre) to 15 kHz (for typical good quality sound reinforcement) to 18 kHz (for FM radio broadcast) to 20 kHz (for very high quality sound reinforcement).

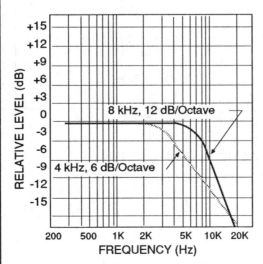
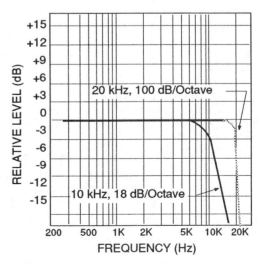

Figure 14-13. Common low pass filter characteristics

A special class of low pass filters, with very high slope rates (48 dB per octave to over 100 dB per octave), are used in digital signal processing and digital audio recording equipment. These filters are designed to be virtual brick walls that prevent frequencies above a given cutoff from reaching the digital circuitry. They prevent a very annoying audible problem known as aliasing, and are therefore known as *anti aliasing filters*. These filters are built into the digital equipment, so you need not be concerned with them (except that some such filters have more effect on the audible portion of the program than others, which is due to the rather severe phase shift and ringing associated with the high slope rate of certain designs).

A handful of special low pass filters have been offered for the express purpose of noise reduction. These filters not only have an adjustable cutoff point, but that cutoff is designed to slide up and down automatically in response to program material. When the program falls below a certain threshold (at a given frequency), the low pass cutoff point slides down in frequency. This has the effect of cutting off the hiss and noise components where there is no program present, and thus reducing the overall noise. These so-called *horizontal filters* can be tricky to set up, and can be audible in many cases, but they do offer a means to achieve single ended noise reduction (that is, noise reduction where the program signal was not treated with prior encoding).

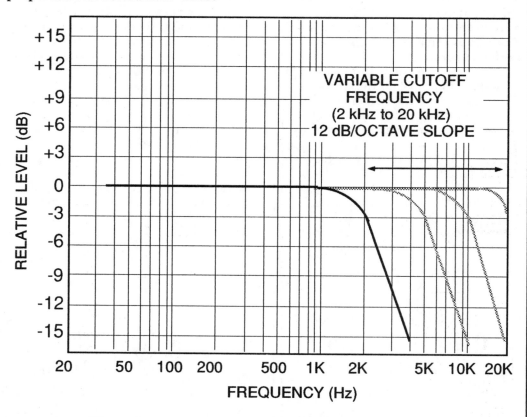

Figure 14-14. A horizontal (sliding) low pass filter functions as a single-ended noise reduction system

14.2 REVERBERATION AND DELAY

Reverberation consists of multiple, blended sound images (not individually discernable echoes) caused by reflection from walls, floor, ceiling and other surfaces which do not absorb all the sound. Reverberation occurs naturally in most indoor environments, and is more prominent with hard surfaced environments. Reverberation can also be created artificially by a number of means. Natural reverberation (from an *echo chamber*) and artificial reverberation (from an electronic or electroacoustic reverberator) can be used as an effect for live sound reinforcement, broadcast or recording. In this section of the handbook, we describe some of the many ways in which the effect can be created, and discuss its use. Refer also to Section 6, especially Section 6.3, which discusses reverberation in indoor environments.

Reverberation is often confused with *delay* (or *echo*), especially since some modern signal processors provide both.

Delay refers to one or more distinct sound images (*echoes*). In fact, true reverberation normally begins with a few relatively closely spaced echoes known as early reflections. These are caused by the initial bounce back of sound from nearby surfaces. As the sound continues to bounce around, the increasing number of reflections blend, creating the more homogeneous sound field we call reverberation. Figure 14–15 illustrates the natural occurence of reverberation, including early reflections.

The environment in Figure 14–15 is a small room, which means that the reflections occur within a short period of time. In larger volume environments, early reflections will be spread out over a longer period of time. Note that the vertical lines on the instrument's display each indicate a complete frequency spectrum (like looking at a frequency response plot on edge). The height of the vertical lines shows the amplitude. The horizontal spacing between vertical lines is a time scale.

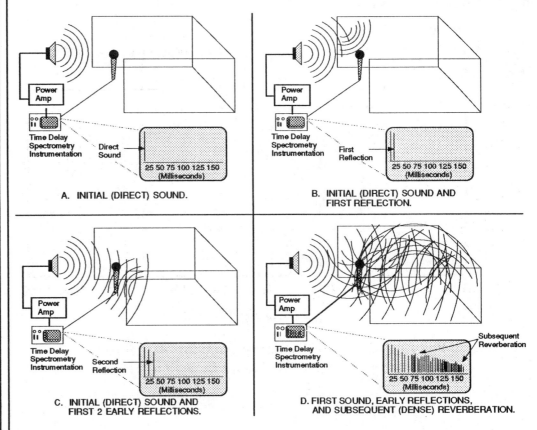

A. INITIAL (DIRECT) SOUND.

B. INITIAL (DIRECT) SOUND AND FIRST REFLECTION.

C. INITIAL (DIRECT) SOUND AND FIRST 2 EARLY REFLECTIONS.

D. FIRST SOUND, EARLY REFLECTIONS, AND SUBSEQUENT (DENSE) REVERBERATION.

Figure 14-15. Propagation of an impulse sound in the environment shows natural occurence of early reflections and subsequent reverberation.

You can see the sound decaying in level, with reflection density increasing (closer spacing) as time passes. By measuring the time it takes for the reverberant sound to decay 60 dB from the instant the original sound occurs, the RT_{60} of the environment is obtained.

In a large, outdoor space such as a canyon, there may be only one or a few reflections from distant surfaces, with a relatively large time span between them (more than 30 to 35 milliseconds). In this case there is no opportunity for a reverberant field to develop (the attenuation of air kills the sound before many reflections can develop), so what is heard is an echo.

In theory, if the echoes occurred closer together (in time), they would be equivalent to the early reflections of a reverberant field. We begin to see, then, that there is really a close relationship between echo and reverberation. Those electronic devices that create echo (delay lines) and those that create reverberation share many, many similarities, which is why some such units are capable of producing both effects.

The use of signal delay, though, is not restricted to the creation of echo effects. In many distributed

sound systems it is necessary to delay the signal fed to mid and rear loudspeaker clusters so that it reaches the listener just after the sound arriving from the stage. This requires a single, high quality delayed sound image (per speaker location). In such cases, the delay must be adjusted to allow for the time it takes for the sound to travel from the main (front) loudspeaker cluster to the delayed cluster, with perhaps as much as an extra 10 milliseconds added to ensure the sound is perceived as coming from the front. The calculations involved are discussed in Section 18.7. The acoustical implications are discussed in Section 6.3.

The following sub sections discuss some of the methods by which these effects are created, along with a few hints for obtaining the best results. One hint we feel applies to all such effects is this:

Any effect normally will constitute only a small proportion of the final program. If you don't like what you're hearing, and you've got the mixing console's reverb return level set equal to or higher than the program level, pulling down the effect level may improve the sound considerably.

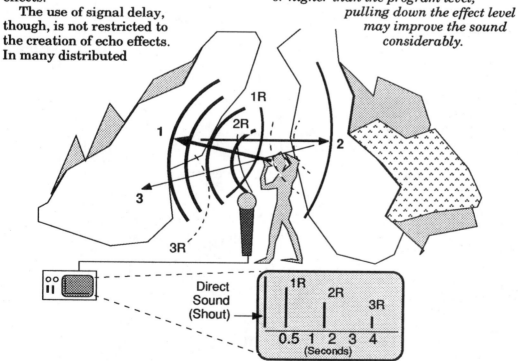

The first, second and third "contacts" of sound on the canyon walls are indicated by the numbered arrows. The subsequent reflections, as they reach the listner's ear (and the measurement mic), are numbered 1R, 2R and 3R. The third reflection is so weak as to barely be audible. These reflections are, in fact, echoes.

Figure 14-16. The natural occurence of echoes

14.2.1 Reverb Chambers

A *reverb chamber* is a room with a very live sound quality (reflective surfaces) that is equipped with one or two microphones (two for stereo reverb) and one or several loudspeakers. The echo send from the mixing console is fed to an amp and the speakers, and the preamplified mic signals are brought back to the mixing console's echo return (or the mics are connected directly to spare input channels). The sound from the speakers bounces around the walls, floor and ceiling, creating natural reverberation that is captured by the mic. A good chamber has none of the artificial sound some electronic effects units are said to exhibit, but it certainly can be subject to noise (mechanical vibration – or electronic from the amps), or to distortion (from the loudspeakers and mic). In fact, the chamber must be heavily isolated from leakage of external sounds (some studios used to use a hallway as their chamber, and more than one such recording has been interrupted by a door slamming or other more clandestine sounds).

Reverb chambers were the original means by which reverb was added to recordings or radio broadcasts. They still exist in a few locations; but a chamber is expensive to build, especially with today's high priced urban real estate. Unless the room is built to exactly the right dimensions, and finished with just the right materials, it won't function very well, and it's difficult to significantly change the sound once the room is built. If you want more than one reverb effect, or have more than one project in the works simultaneously, you may need several rooms (some older studios had three rooms dedicated to reverb, a very costly proposition). It's also impossible to take the chamber with you when you move. Chambers obviously have no application in portable sound reinforcement. For these reasons, the live chamber has largely been replaced by all electronic or electromechanical devices.

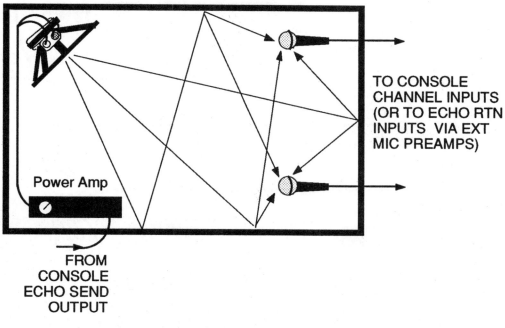

ROOM WITH HARD-SURFACED WALLS
(AN ACOUSTICALLY LIVE ROOM)

TO CONSOLE
CHANNEL INPUTS
(OR TO ECHO RTN
INPUTS VIA EXT
MIC PREAMPS)

Power Amp

FROM
CONSOLE
ECHO SEND
OUTPUT

Figure 14-17. General design of an actual reverb chamber

14.2.2 Duct Type Reverbs

Someone figured out that by attaching a small loudspeaker to one end of a common garden hose, and shoving a microphone in the other end of the hose, a reverb effect (with some echo) could be obtained. This rather straightforward technology found its way into commercial designs, some of which used sections of sewer pipe with larger loudspeakers and mics— same idea, though. An early unit of this genre, which may still be found in some studios, was the *Cooper Time Cube*. The cube system included a rack-mountable chassis with the driving electronics and mic preamp, along with a box that contained the tubing. There were frequency response limitations to such systems, as well as limited dynamic range, and a somewhat honky characteristic. It was also difficult to get more than one type of reverb sound from such a device. Still, they did work, and they were relatively compact and portable. (See Figure 14–18).

14.2.3 Spring Type Reverbs

The concept of a reverb is based on obtaining reflections of the sound. Early on, someone figured out that the sound could be converted to a mechanical wave that would accomplish the same thing. This was first accomplished by attaching a suitable transducer (a piezoelectric crystal or a loudspeaker-like voice coil) to a metal coil (a spring). The effects send signal from the mixing console drives the transducer, which twists the spring, and the sound then travels up and down the spring, a tortional wave reflecting off each anchored end. Another transducer attached to the other end of the spring converts these mechanical reflections back into an electrical signal, which is fed to the mixing console's effects return input (see Figure 14-19, next page).

It became apparent that a single spring had a very distinct, sometimes annoying sound quality, so a number of multiple spring designs were created. Some of these used three and four springs in parallel, each with a somewhat different wire gauge or diameter

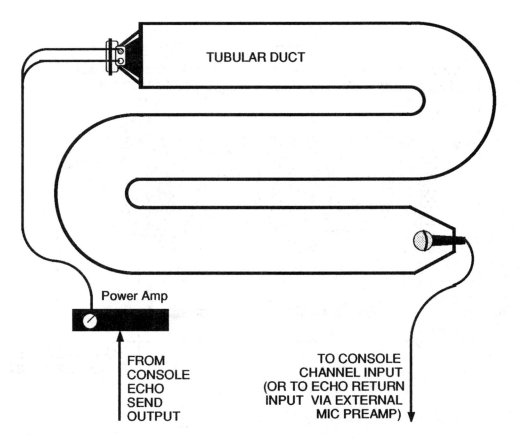

TUBULAR DUCT

Power Amp

FROM CONSOLE ECHO SEND OUTPUT

TO CONSOLE CHANNEL INPUT (OR TO ECHO RETURN INPUT VIA EXTERNAL MIC PREAMP)

Figure 14-18. General design of a duct type reverb

or tension so as to obtain a richer reverb texture (more random reflections). Some designs use fewer springs, but change each individual spring's characteristics over its length (by altering its coil diameter or the thickness of the wire in the coil).

Some spring type reverbs have mechanical adjustments that alter the damping on the spring, while others have a sliding damper which changes the spring length. Both of which are designed to alter the reverb decay time.

Springs, which may be from 8 to 12 inches or more in length, can be permanently stretched (or tangled) if they bounce around too much in shipping. For this reason, some spring type reverbs are equipped with a spring lock, a mechanical catch that traps the spring and prevents excess motion. These locks should always be released before using the reverb.

One of the more objectionable characteristics of the typical spring reverb is the tendency for it to produce a sproing – a metallic glitch – when a sharp edged transient waveform is

applied. In order to prevent this problem some spring reverbs include rise time limiting or a simple compressor/limiter circuit. If you are using a spring and run into this problem, try turning down the drive level or insert a compressor in the signal path just ahead of the reverb input.

Spring type reverbs can sound reasonably good, and are available at prices ranging from very inexpensive to somewhat costly, depending on the design. These units are most widely used for the reverb effect built into many guitar amplifiers. Springs, however, are generally deficient in transient and high frequency response, and most are not of sufficient quality for top notch recording or reinforcement work. They are also subject to mechanical feedback (the sound field can excite the springs directly), so they should not be placed too close to a loudspeaker or on a stage which is shaking with dancers, etc. Better quality units tend to have better mechanical isolation from external vibration.

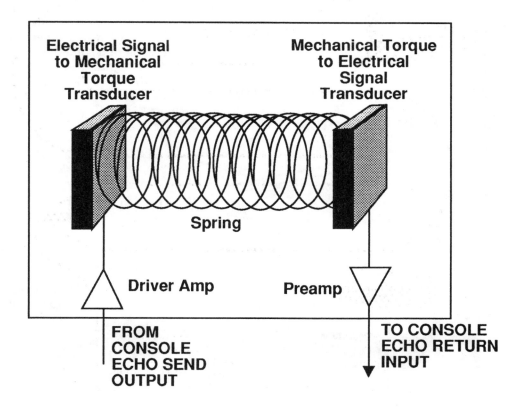

Figure 14-19. General design of a spring type reverb

14.2.4 Plate-Type Reverbs

The plate type reverb utilizes the same principle as the spring, but instead of a spring, a metal plate is suspended (with tension) in a frame. The metal plate is driven by one or more voice coil like transducers, which are fed an amplified signal from the mixing console's effects send output. The vibrations produced by the transducer(s) are reflected back and forth in the plate, bouncing at the plate edges. Contact mics or similar transducers convert the vibrations back into electrical signals for feed to the effects return circuit. See Figure 14-20 (next page).

The reverb quality can be altered by changing the tension on the plate suspension, and by moving a damper onto the plate surface. Major changes are possible if different sized plates are used, if the plates are made of different materials, or if transducer types and locations are changed.

Typical plates measure as much as 3 feet by 5 feet or more, and with the associated frame the weight can be several hundred pounds. Such units are widely used in recording or broadcast studios, but are impractical for travel. At least one manufacturer has developed a compact, more or less portable plate based on miniaturization (with a gold foil plate); the cost is high, but the convenience is there.

Plates, too, have their own reverb characteristic. They tend to do a better job with transients and high frequencies than do springs, and they are somewhat more immune to external vibration, although banging on the frame will certainly produce an audible result. Plate reverbs are usually more costly than spring reverbs.

14.2.5 Digital Reverberation

The reverb described thus far has used mechanical means to generate the sound reflections. In the mid 1970s, the first high quality digital reverberators were introduced. They had limited features compared to today's models, and cost upwards of $10,000.

Modern computer technology has made it cost effective to design a completely electronic reverb (see Figure 14–21, next page). In the digital reverb, incoming audio signal is converted to numerical representations of that signal by ADCs (Analog-to-Digital Converters). The numbers represent the voltage and polarity of the signal, and the speed at which the numbers change provide frequency information. Signal level is generally metered, adjusted, and sometimes limited while the signal is still analog (before the ADC). Once the signal is digitized, it is stored in RAM (random access memory). It is then read by the

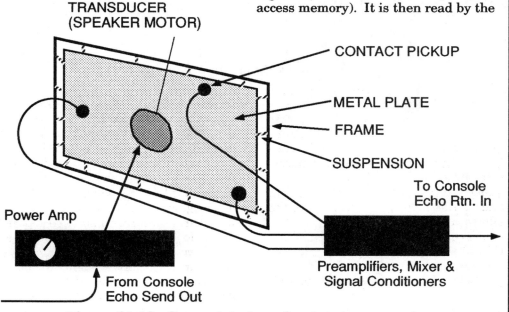

DRIVEN VOICE COIL TYPE TRANSDUCER (SPEAKER MOTOR)

CONTACT PICKUP

METAL PLATE

FRAME

SUSPENSION

To Console Echo Rtn. In

Power Amp

Preamplifiers, Mixer & Signal Conditioners

From Console Echo Send Out

Figure 14-20. General design of a plate type reverb

computer circuitry, and processed according to complex algorithms (an algorithm is simply a block diagram for a series of operations). These algorithms may alter the level of the signal while re-reading it out of memory at precise intervals. The frequency response of the signal may be altered on subsequent reads, and, depending on the sophistication of the device, the delay time (the time before the signal is read) may be different for different portions of the signal band. This frequency-dependent reverb time is something that occurs in natural reverberation, too. The digital circuitry may re-combine various versions of the signal, store that composite sound image, then process it. This process is continuous, since incoming sound must also be incorporated, even as earlier sounds are decaying. In short, there's a lot of mathematical manipulation going on inside the digital reverb.

numbers) must be increased, which means more numbers are required to store the signal for a given length of time. While memory costs and CPU (central processing unit — the brain) costs have come down recently, it still costs more to obtain a wider bandwidth in a digital reverb. With the proper design, 20 kHz bandwidth is relatively easy to achieve. On the other hand, it is seldom needed because, in the real world reverberation usually has significant roll-off at higher frequencies due to the selective attenuation of air at these frequencies. A reverb with 12 kHz to 15 kHz bandwidth may sound perfectly natural, especially when the effect is blended in with the direct, full bandwidth program.

Nearly every digital audio processor uses something known as an anti-aliasing filter. These are low pass filters comprised of multiple poles, with very sharp slope rates of from

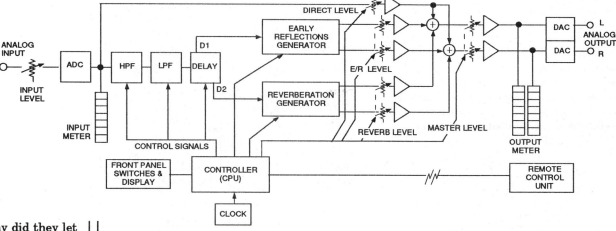

Figure 14-21. Block diagram of a digital reverb

"Why did they let the drawing flow into the margin?"

"So it would be large enough to read the type."

"Oh. I see."

YAMAHA
Sound Reinforcement
Handbook
Page 265

The digital representation of the sound is processed by a DAC (Digital-to-Analog Converter), where it again becomes an analog audio signal. The DAC output goes through a low pass filter (to smooth out any high frequency ripple in the converted signal), and then to a booster amp to drive the effects return input.

There are trade offs involved. Digital processing can use up a lot of computer memory. The wider the signal bandwidth, the more memory is used. That's because the *sampling rate* (the rate at which the ADC measures the incoming signal and converts it to

48 dB to 100 dB per octave, or even more. They are used to create a *brick wall* above which no signal frequencies can get into the digital processing circuitry. If these filters were not used, frequencies higher than one half the ADC sampling frequency would cause aliasing, which is a non-linear, very unnatural sounding distortion whereby distortion signals are created at lower and lower frequencies as the input signal frequency rises higher and higher above the so called Nyquist frequency (half the sampling rate).

Digital audio circuitry can represent the audio signal with different numbers of bits. The more bits, the higher the resolution of the number that represents the waveform, and the higher the cost (more bits take up more memory and require more number crunching by the computer). The most common values in professional audio are 14 bit and 16 bit digital words, although a few units use 18 to 24 bit resolution internally, then fold back to 16 bits for D–A conversion. With a given bandwidth, the more bits, the greater the potential dynamic range and the lower the distortion at low signal levels. This last statement must be qualified because certain error correction schemes and certain processing techniques can improve on 14 bit resolution or degrade 16 bit resolution to the point where there may be little practical difference between two given systems. There is no substitute for listening tests using actual program signals.

One area where digital reverbs (and other digital audio equipment) often run into problems is in the ADCs and DACs. There are many ways to convert signals, and doing it with the greatest accuracy, least noise, and least distortion will usually cost more. Another area where some units differ from others is in the type and quality of the anti-aliasing filters. Some filters have a significant and undesirable phase shift and level altering effect on the portion of the signal that is supposed to be unaltered. Other filters may not be steep enough, so high level, high frequency sounds may cause aliasing distortion. One method of reducing phase shift on the output side of a digital reverb (or other digital audio equipment) is to use a technique known as *oversampling*. In this case, the digital-to-analog converter operates at a higher frequency than the actual clock; typically two to four times the sampling rate. (There are still only a given number of samples, but each one is examined multiple times by the converter.) The resulting output reconstruction filter can thus be designed at two to four times the sampling frequency, and possibly with a gentler slope rate, which keeps most of the filter induced phase shift out of the audio passband.

One of the best aspects of the digital reverb is that its characteristics can be altered significantly by simply changing the internal algorithm (selecting a new program, in essence). A number of different programs typically are resident in read only memory (ROM), and some reverbs allow the operator to alter the programs to custom tailor the reverb characteristics. All programs operate in different ways, and one of the things that differentiates one model of reverb from the next is just how well one likes a particular program. For example, the number of early reflections, and their relative level and polarity, can have a lot to do with the realism and overall sound quality. Some units provide only one or a few reflections, others may provide from 6 to 40 early reflections with precise control over each. With more possible settings comes a greater responsibility to set the system up properly, which is why preset effects remain popular. There is a degree of magic in making a good sounding reverb.

Some digital reverbs not only enable the user to alter the program, but also enable those altered (or edited) programs to be stored in memory for future use. Many models also allow for remote control, whereby different programs can be selected, or the effect can be turned on and off, via time code controllers that are based on the Musical Instrument Digital Interface (MIDI), a standard time code specified by the Society of Motion Picture and Television Engineers (SMPTE), or a variety of dedicated remote controllers. Because the technology is much the same, some digital reverbs also offer the user other special effects (phasing, flanging, chorus, echo, gating, and so forth).

When working with digital reverbs, it is important to pay close attention to gain structure. Apply a signal to the device at the correct nominal level, not so high as to overdrive the ADC and not so low as to flirt with the effect's noise floor.

14.2.6 Tape Delay

Prior to the early 1970s, the only practical means of delaying an audio signal was to use recording tape. Primarily used in recording or broad-

14.2.7 Digital Delay

cast studios, tape delay was achieved by placing a tape recorder in monitor off the tape mode, feeding the signal to be delayed to the record head, then taking the delayed signal from the playback head. Since the playback head is located a finite distance after the record head, the signal delay time was then a function of the actual record-to-play head spacing and of how fast the tape was moving. This technique worked reasonably well, though it was limited with respect to the available range of delay and to the length of time it could be used before the reel of tape was exhausted. A variation on this theme was the Echoplex, an effects device that used a continuous loop of tape (whose running speed could be adjusted), one record head, and multiple playback heads (which could be adjusted in spacing). The Echoplex was certainly more portable than a studio tape deck, less costly, and produced the multiple echoes which performers wanted in the studio or on stage. The heads had to be cleaned and degaussed often, tape tended to wear out, and overall maintenance requirements were heavy.

Tape delay techniques were not well suited to driving remote speaker systems. Sound quality was poorer than the direct sound, suffering from tape hiss, wow, distortion, and frequency/phase response errors. The delay really could not be set to brief intervals. Also, instability caused the image to wander).

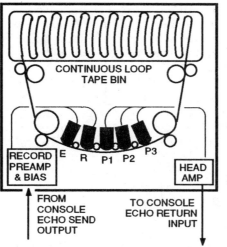

Figure 14-22. A tape delay unit
(E=erase head, R=record head,
P1-P3= playback heads)

Advances in digital technology in the early 1970s made it feasible to design a practical digital device to delay an audio signal. This device came to be known as a *digital delay line* (or DDL), probably in honor of the first signal delay. That first delay was conceived about a half century ago, before the advent of tape recording, and was used for a live radio broadcast. The audio was sent hundreds of miles down telephone lines to another city, then returned via phone lines. The time it took for the signal to propagate along those hundreds of miles of wire constituted the delay time. Digital technology now made this long line delay possible without the long line. Paradoxically, digital delays are now used to sync audio (by delaying it) with the video picture on transmissions where the video must travel thousands of extra miles to and from an orbiting satellite, yet the audio gets there faster by telephone or direct (earthbound) microwave relay.

The early digital delays cost well over \$1,000, and could provide from $1/10$ to $1/2$ second of delay to a single output. Longer delays or more output taps (at different delay times) cost even more. The bandwidth of these devices was often limited to 10 or 15 kHz, primarily due to the then very high cost of the digital memory. Nonetheless, the sound quality was generally better than taped delays, the delay time was crystal oscillator controlled (for stability and repeatability), and there was no regular maintenance required. These units were used primarily for delay of sound to remoted speakers (mid and rear of the house) in large sound reinforcement systems.

As technology marched on, bandwidths increased, the cost came down, and the digital delay line found new uses. Units that offer continuously adjustable delay times, reasonably wide bandwidths, and a variety of special effects capability are now available for a few hundred dollars (more on this shortly). A thousand dollars or less will buy 20 kHz bandwidth units with multiple outputs, and some of the more sophisticated delay lines that sell for \$2,000 to \$3,000 have as many as 8 individually adjustable outputs with delay times up to several seconds.

How does a digital delay line work? The input signal (analog audio) is sampled thousands of times per second and converted to a string of numbers that represent the ever changing voltage value of the signal. The numbers are digital audio, and they are created by an ADC (analog-to-digital converter). The exact rate at which the input signal is sampled determines the highest frequency which can be processed. The sampling rate must be a little bit more than twice the highest audio frequency. The numbers that represent the audio are then stored in RAM (random access memory) registers. A clock (crystal oscillator) generates strobe or sync signals that cause the memory in each register to shift to the next register in sequence. At some point, the memory is read by a DAC and the stored numbers are converted back to a continuously changing voltage—the analog audio signal output. The signal delay involved is dependent on two things: (1) the number of memory registers available, and (2) the speed of the shift clock. In some units the selection of longer delay times is available only at reduced bandwidth. This is because a fixed amount of memory is available, and the memory can be used either to store the greater number of samples required to represent higher frequencies, or to delay a smaller number of samples for a longer time.

Many digital delay systems include a variety of special effects capabilities. By varying the internal clock frequency, the speed at which the signal is read out can be changed, causing a shift in pitch. Often a low frequency oscillator (LFO) circuit is provided to modulate the clock, which produces a vibrato-like regular shift in pitch. Usually the LFO frequency (the speed) and the amount of modulation (the depth) are variable, and sometimes the LFO waveform is adjustable as well. Some units can be set to loop the sound, where the input is turned on for a set period of time and the resulting sound samples are continuously recirculated in the delay memory. The output samples this continuously recirculating sound without destroying it, and the result is an endless repeat. Footswitch and MIDI control of these parameters makes them useful as live performance tools for the musician or vocalist. Other effects include chorusing and flanging, in which very short delays, that vary somewhat in time are mixed in with the direct signal to get comb filter effects. These effects are discussed in greater detail in Section 14.4.

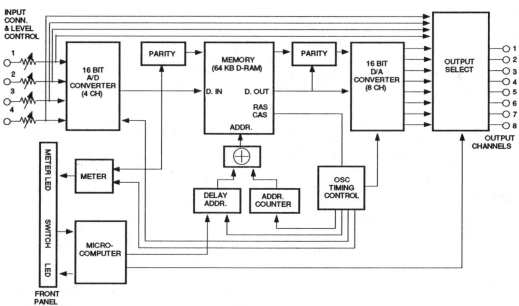

Figure 14-23. Block diagram of a 4-input x 8-output digital delay line

14.2.8 Analog Delay

An *analog delay* is an effects device that is similar to a digital delay in that it is an all-electronic device that temporarily stores the audio signal to create a time delay. The analog delay differs in the manner by which the audio signal is stored. Both units sample the input signal, chopping the waveform into thousands of equally timed segments per second. While the digital delay device converts each sample to a number, the analog delay unit converts each sample to an average voltage value. Instead of using an ADC, numerical (digital) memory registers, and a DAC, the analog delay line uses a sample and hold circuit to convert the continuous input signal to a string of voltage values, plus a large number of capacitive storage devices known as bucket brigade devices (BBDs). The reason they are called bucket brigade is that the voltage stored in one capacitive memory register (bucket) is poured into the next register (bucket) in sequence. The sampled voltage eventually reaches the output. The voltage is transferred from one register to another by a strobe signal, much like the digital delay's technology, and many of the same special effects are available in the typical analog delay line. The analog delay line is usually limited to a narrower bandwidth than the digital delay, and is generally somewhat noisier than the digital delay, although individual models must be compared. Analog delays became popular in the late 1970s because they were less expensive to produce than digital delays. They were, and still are, primarily intended for use as musical special effects devices more than for architectural sound delay.

Some musicians claim that the analog delay has a *warmer* or *fatter* sound than the digital delay. There are differences in the processing. We suspect that the differences today are as much a function of the specific design of the analog or digital delay as of the basic technologies themselves. In any case, as the cost of digital components has come down, and expertise in their application to audio has increased, digital delays have pushed the analog delay to a small corner of the market.

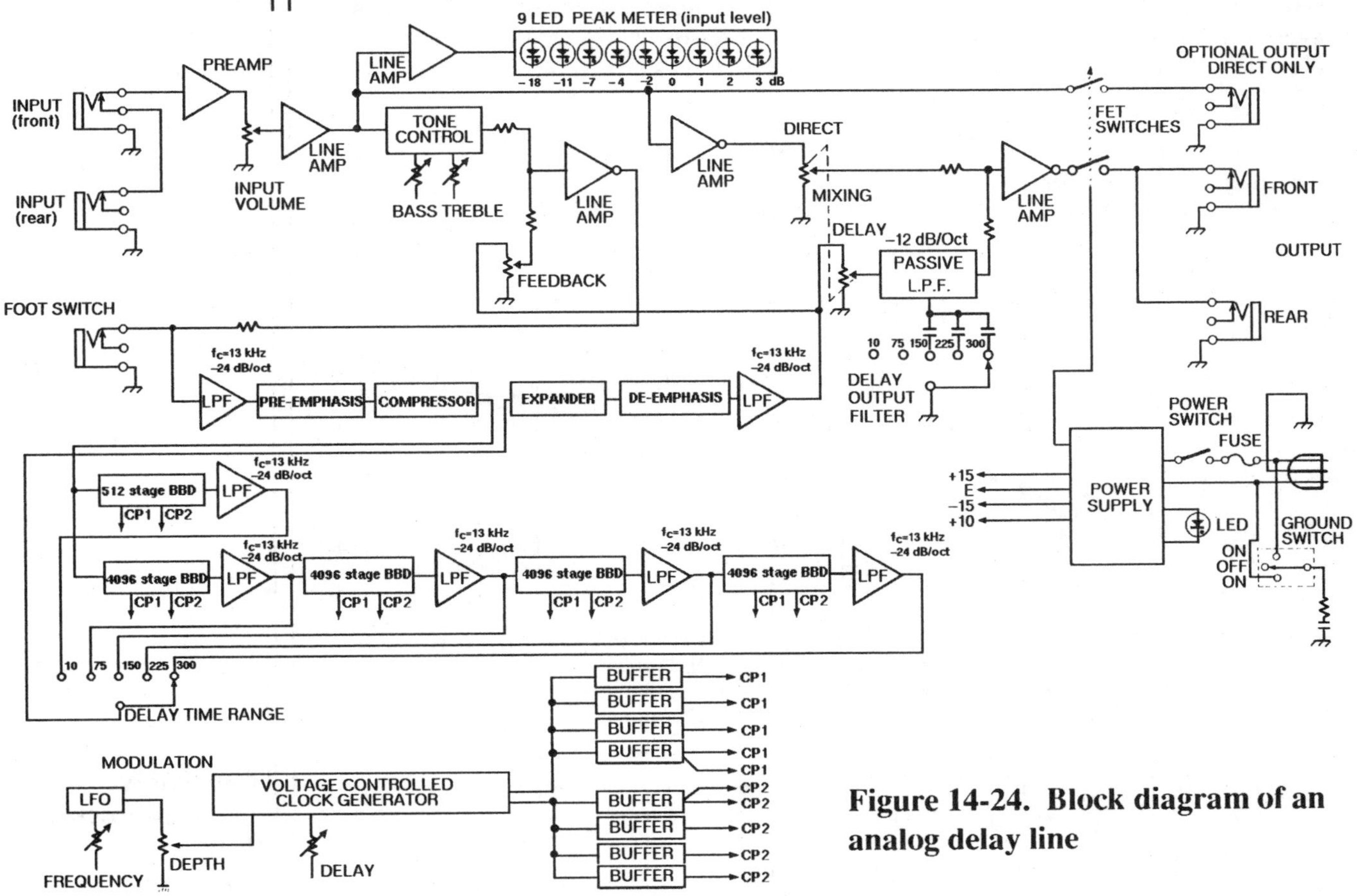

Figure 14-24. Block diagram of an analog delay line

14.3.1 General Discussion

Compressors and *limiters* are signal processors that reduce the dynamic range of the signal. The limiter is designed to prevent signals from exceeding a given (usually adjustable) threshold level. Sometimes the limiter is a brick wall, preventing any further rise in input level from resulting in any rise in output level above the set threshold. Sometimes the effect is to allow only a small (non-linear) rise in output level for further increases in input level above the set threshold. This action, because it eliminates the peaks in signal level in a program, is known as leveling, and some limiters are also known as audio leveling amplifiers.

The ratio of the change in output level (in dB) to the change in input level is known as the *compression ratio*. Most limiters will have a compression ratio of from 8:1 to 20:1 or even higher. If a unit is set to 8:1 compression then an increase in input level of 8 dB (assuming the input is above the set threshold value) will

result in a 1 dB increase in the output level. A few units offer infinite compression, where no amount of increase in input level (above threshold) will cause an increase in output level. Because the transfer characteristic (the slope of the plot of change in output to input level) changes at the threshold, the threshold is also known as the *rotation point*.

Limiters are generally used to process only the program peaks, which is why they are also known as *peak limiters*. In broadcast, such units prevent overmodulation of the transmitted signal. In sound reinforcement, they can be used to protect loudspeakers from mechanical destruction in the event of a dropped microphone (by limiting the peak level that will be fed to the amps and speakers). In record cutting, they prevent excess cutting stylus excursion, which would otherwise cause kissing of adjacent grooves and subsequent skipping when the pressed record is played back.

If the threshold is reduced so that most or all of the program is subject to compression, then the device functions as a compressor. Compressors generally use lower compression ratios than limiters. Typically 1.5:1 to 4:1. Com-

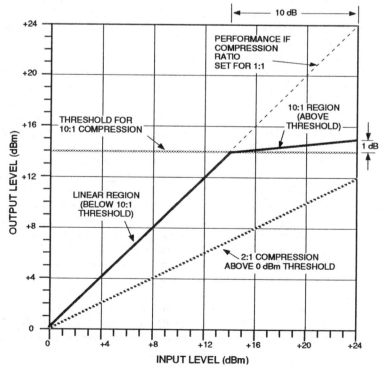

Figure 14-25. Compression and limiting characteristics

pression has a number of uses. In tape recording, broadcast, or sound reinforcement, compression is sometimes used to squeeze the dynamic range of a program to suit the storage or reproduction medium. If the noise floor to saturation point of the tape represents a 50 dB dynamic range, and the live program has a 100 dB dynamic range (noise floor to peak level), then 2:1 compression enables that program to fit on the tape. In any situation where the ambient noise level is high, yet the maximum sound level that can be reproduced is limited (i.e., industrial or commercial paging systems), compression can be used to squeeze the program into a very small dynamic range, and that range can be reproduced just below the maximum output capability of the sound system. Take the paging system in a stadium, for example. Let's say the ambient noise level during an event regularly exceeds 95 dB SPL (during cheers, applause, etc.) yet the maximum sound level the reinforcement system can deliver to the middle of the audience is 110 dB SPL (15 dB of effective dynamic range). The trained announcer's speaking voice may have a dynamic range of 30 dB (untrained voices vary more). By applying 2:1 compression to the voice, the entire program is squeezed down to 15 dB, which is then capable of being reproduced by the sound system at levels the audience can hear. (This is a somewhat oversimplified explanation, since coherent program such as voice can often be discerned below the level of random noise.)

Because the circuitry is almost identical, the real distinction between a compressor and a limiter is how the device is used. Many such devices are designed to perform both functions. They have a wide range of adjustable threshold and compression ratio values (and sometimes attack/ decay characteristics), and are therefore known as *compressor/limiters*. (Additional discussion of the need for such devices may be found in Section 4.3.)

14.3.2 How Compressor/ Limiters Work

There is generally a voltage controlled amplifier (VCA) whose gain can be varied by an applied voltage. A detector (or side chain) circuit is provided that contains the threshold and any attack/decay time adjustments, and that samples the input signal to create a control signal. The control signal is then applied to the VCA. There are typically input and output level controls as well, and there may be a meter circuit that can be switched to indicate the input level, output level and/or the amount of gain reduction at any instant.

One of the major factors that distinguishes one compressor/limiter from another is the method by which it detects the input signal level. Some units, particularly limiters for broadcast or record cutting, operate based on the instantaneous peak input signal level. Other units operate based on the average signal level. Still others detect the root mean square (rms) signal level. What is the difference? Peak level detection, particularly with a high compression ratio, can be used to absolutely prevent any output signal from exceeding a set value for even a fraction of a second. It will also duck the output level in the presence of a momentary peak, which in some cases is more of a problem than preventing the peak from reaching the output. Averaging and rms detection may allow a fraction of a cycle to several cycles of higher level audio to get through before the compression clamps down the level. This will result in a more natural sound, particularly when the threshold is set to apply moderate compression to a large percentage (or all) of the program.

Averaging the signal level is done by a relatively simple circuit. However, the numeric average of the signal voltage does not happen to correspond as closely to the way our ears perceive relative loudness as does rms detection. rms detection is trickier to achieve. With a pure sine wave signal, the rms value of the signal is 1.414 times the peak level, but with a complex audio signal the RMS value is not as easily derived. Fortunately, there are some clever engineers around who realized that light output of a lamp or an LED excited by an AC signal corresponds to the rms value of that signal. A light source (an LED) that is excited by the sampled input signal may be used to excite a light dependent resistor (LDR), which modulates the control voltage for the VCA. There are other, even more complex rms detectors in use which do not rely on LED/LDR technology.

The speed at which the gain is reduced in response to an increase in input signal level is defined either as the *attack time* (in milliseconds) or the *attack rate* (in dB per second). The term depends on the nature of the circuitry and how the manufacturer treats this parameter. The speed at which the gain is restored to the original value after the input stimulus is removed is known as the *release time* or *release rate*.

The detector, or side chain, circuit on some compressor/limiters is brought to a pair of input/output connectors. This permits signal processors to be used in the side chain. If you want more compression in response to high frequency signals, you insert an equalizer in the chain with the high frequencies boosted. This setup is often used for de-essing, whereby vocal sibilance is removed by differential compression. If low frequency EQ cut is used, the compressor allows drum

sounds to get through more or less unaltered, yet may clamp down on a relatively less powerful (but more threatening to tweeters) high synthesizer note. If a brief signal delay is inserted in the main signal path, and the side chain input is fed from a point ahead of the delay, a zero attack time can be achieved or even an unusual precompression effect where the compression is heard before the signal that causes it (this resembles the sound of a tape recording played backwards).

14.3.3 Setup Adjustments

There is no one attack or release value that is optimum for all situations. Too rapid an attack causes unnatural program level fluctuations, and considerable distortion of low frequency signals as the compressor tries to ride the waveform. Too slow an attack allows the output to exceed whatever level has been chosen as the desired maximum before the compressor/limiter acts. Too fast a release results in pumping or breathing as the gain changes rapidly, and too slow a release causes quieter portions of the program to be lost while the gain is

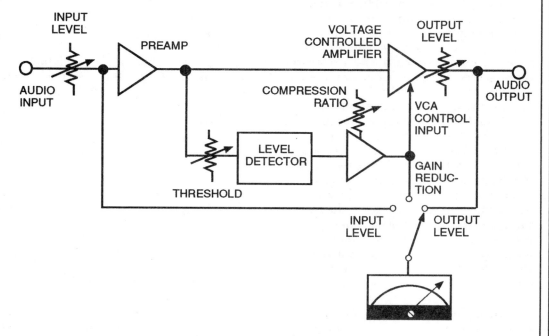

Figure 14-26. Block diagram of a compressor/limiter

still reduced in response to the no longer loud input stimulus. Manufacturers either provide for attack/release time values that automatically change in response to the input signal, or for manually adjustable attack and release times (or rates). While some people insist on manual adjustments, misadjustment causes major problems in the sound. Some models have both automatic and manual modes. If you decide to manually adjust these parameters, follow the suggestions provided by the manufacturer of the device. In the absence of that, here are a few hints:

With a given input signal, adjust the input level control (if any) so the input is well above the noise floor, but does not clip the input stage. Then set the threshold to whatever rotation point, and set the compression to whatever ratio, may be appropriate for the situation. For speaker protection, as an example, the threshold should be set to a point that prevents the power amplifiers from delivering whatever power level is established as the mechanical limit for the speakers. Suppose a loudspeaker is rated at 100 watts continuous and 200 watts peak, and the power amplifier is rated at 200 watts output to that speaker's rated load impedance (given a +4 dBu input). Let's also suppose that the power amp's input attenuator is turned down 10 dB. (For simplicity, we'll assume that the compressor's input and output level controls are adjusted for unity gain through the device when there is no compression.) In this case, a +14 dBu signal applied to the amp causes it to deliver 200 watts to the speakers. The threshold and compression ratio of the compressor/limiter must therefore be set to avoid exceeding +14 dBu. If you want to preserve as much as possible of the natural program dynamics, set the threshold to +10 dBu. Our criteria require that any input signal, no matter how loud, not cause the output to increase more than 4 dB beyond that value. We assume that due to the capabilities of the equipment feeding the compressor/limiter, no input signal will exceed +26 dBu. We subtract +10 from +26 and see that a 16 dB dynamic range must be compressed to 4 dB, and simple math shows us that a 4:1 compression ratio do the job. Had we

set the threshold at +13 dBu, we would have had to restrict the remaining 13 dB of possible input signal increase to a mere 1 dB of output signal increase (a 13:1 compression ratio). This would be OK, but very high compression ratios sound less natural since the effect comes in all at once. This is OK if you plan to watch the input levels carefully to avoid the above-threshold region and the limiting is really just brick wall protection.

With typical program material applied, listen to the output (and evaluate it with a meter or oscilloscope) as you adjust the attack. If you're using the system for limiting to protect loudspeakers, prevent overcutting, etc, use the fastest time or rate you can without audible distortion. If you're using the system for compression (to level vocals or to increase the sustain of an electric guitar), use the slowest attack you can, consistent with reasonable output level control. By providing greater apparent dynamic range, this avoids ruining the punch.

Set the decay time slow enough that you don't hear excessive pumping or breathing, yet fast enough that the program is not ducked unnecessarily after a loud passage.

14.4.1 General

A *noise gate* is a signal processor that turns off or significantly attenuates the audio signal passing through it when the signal level falls below a user adjustable threshold, as illustrated by Figure14-27 on the next page. The idea is that the desired program will pass through unaltered, but low-level hiss and noise (or leakage from other sound sources) will not be heard when the primary program is not present (presumably when the level is below the set threshold).

Those noise gates that literally shut off the signal flow when the program is below the threshold level will tend to have an audible effect as they cut in and out. The sudden change in background noise level may be disturbing. This is why some noise gates are designed to merely reduce the signal level by a finite amount (to lower the gain) when the level falls below the threshold. The effect is to reduce noise, but not to have a drastic, sudden change. To further avoid the audible modulation of background noise, these units may have automatic or adjustable time constants where after the level drops below the threshold, it takes so many milliseconds for the gain to be reduced.

The circuit that reduces the gain is an *expander*, although it is not known as such in this case. What is happening is that the noise floor of the program is being reduced, and hence the dynamic range of the program is being expanded.

When the expansion circuit works only below a set threshold, we call the device a noise gate. There are also signal processors that expand the entire program. In this case, the threshold is set to be any convenient zero point, typically at the nominal program level. Any signals falling below that threshold are expanded downward in level so they become even quieter than they already are, and signals above the threshold are expanded upward in level. The net result is a program with greater dynamic range. In this case, the device is called an expander. (See Figure 14-28 on the next page).

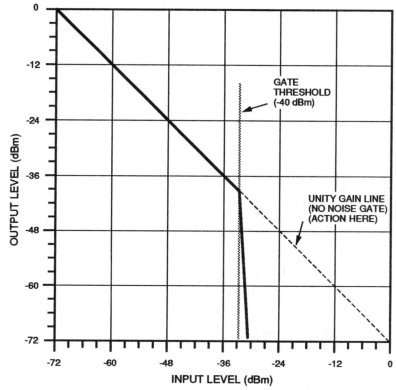

Figure 14-27. The action of a noise gate

14.4.2 Noise Gate Applications

Noise gates are useful for automatically muting temporarily unused mics in a recording or sound reinforcement system. The number of open mics reduces the available gain before feedback in a reinforcement system, and generally adds to the background noise in a recording. Particularly in complex, multichannel setups, the use of a noise gate can improve the sound without increasing the workload for the mixing engineer. Using a noise gate on the overall mixed program is of little value. It is difficult to find truly silent passages in a mixed program, so the gate might be cutting out quieter portions of desired audio signal. In order to be effective, with minimum audible side effects, each subgroup, or perhaps nearly each input to the mixing console, should be processed by its own noise gate. A noise gate is useful, too, in reducing the effects of crosstalk onto other circuits within a console. One noise gate per channel is very costly, and there are some input sources that just don't need a gate (i.e., a quiet, direct-input digital electronic keyboard), so these factors must be evaluated in setting up a system.

Noise gates can do more than simply quieting a noisy guitar, keyboard or vocal mic input when the instrument or singer is momentarily silent. They can actually tighten up a performance. Take the drummer as an example. It may be that the snare overshoots or resonates a bit too much, or that it is simply played a bit off-time with respect to the kick drum. In this case, the kick drum can be used to synchronize the snare. See Figure 14-29 (next page).

Nearly all units have a separate trigger or gate input, which is normally wired (internally) to derive signal from the main audio input to the gate unless a switch (or switched jack) causes the trigger signal to be derived externally. With the kick drum connected to the trigger input of the snare drum's noise gate, the downward expansion threshold is no longer triggered by the audio signal flowing through the gate's main program path, but by the kick drum. The trigger signal can be tapped from a direct output on the console's kick drum input strip. When the kick drum is played, its level opens up the noise gate on the channel that processes the snare, and when the kick sound abates,

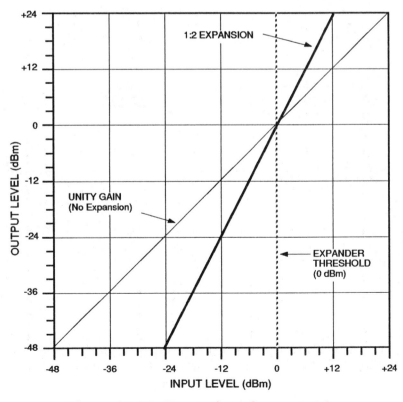

Figure 14-28. The action of an expander

14.4.3 Expander Applications

the snare input is shut off automatically so that the snare is forced into synchronization with the kick. The hold time (the period during which the noise gate remains open after the trigger signal drops below threshold) can be adjusted for as much snare overhang as desired.

Expanders are a component in most tape noise reduction systems. They do the decoding of the encoded (compressed) audio tape, simultaneously restoring the original dynamic range of the program and pushing down any added tape hiss or noise below the inherent program noise floor.

Expanders are also available as separately packaged signal processors. Consider the playback of an ordinary tape recording or record, or reception of a radio broadcast, any of which may have been compressed somewhat for better storage or transmission. This compression reduces the dynamic range, which takes out some of the

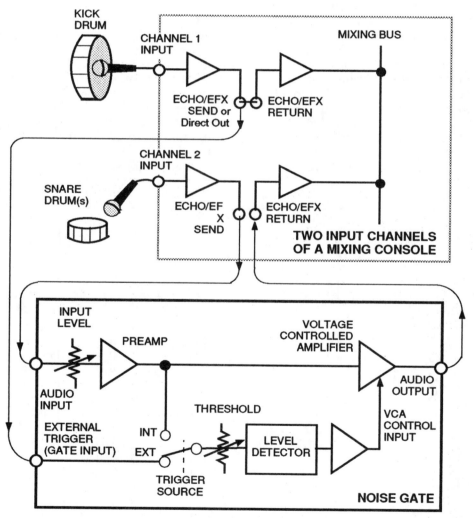

Note: Most of the time the internal trigger mode is set, and individual noise gates are used on each drum mic in order to suppress leakage from adjacent drums, and get a tighter drum mix. This setup is a specific case chosen to illustrate why and how external triggering may be used.

Figure 14-29. Using a noise gate to tighten a snare drum

punch in the program and makes the program less exciting — less natural sounding. In this case the expander restores some of the lost dynamic range. Unless severe compression was used, expansion ratios should be restricted to no higher than 1:1.4 if a natural sound is to be preserved. The problem with using too much expansion is that unless it is the exact inverse of the compression applied to the program it will cause unnatural surges in level. Expansion works best with a program that already has a reasonably wide dynamic range. If you take a severely compressed radio broadcast, for instance, with 6 dB dynamic range (yes, they do exist), even a high 1:2 expansion ratio will still give you a mere 6 dB increase (to 12 dB dynamic range... not very impressive). Process a modest 50 dB dynamic range program with 1:1.4 expansion, and the resulting 20 dB increase (to 70 dB dynamic range) may exceed the capability of many sound systems!

Expansion can restore (or create) the missing punch of a complete program mix or an individual signal in that mix. Depending on where the threshold is set, and how the unit is adjusted, the expander can also serve as a sort of single ended noise reduction process to quiet down a recording, broadcast or instrument signal that has too much hiss. Expansion can also be used to reduce residual crosstalk from adjacent tracks on a tape, channels on a mixer, or acoustic leakage of a nearby sound into a given mic.

Be sure to use an *expander* for these functions. Don't use the decoding circuit of a tape noise reduction system. Noise reduction decoders typically use some sort of frequency weighting, which produces erratic and unnatural expansion of a program that has not been processed with complementary, frequency weighted compression.

14.5 FLANGERS AND PHASERS

14.5.1 Flanging

Originally, *flanging* was achieved using reel-to-reel tape recorders. Two tape recorders would record and play back the same program, in synchronization. By alternately slowing down one machine, then the other, different phase cancellations occurred. The slowing down was achieved by using hand pressure against the flanges of the tape supply reels, hence the term *reel flanging*, or simply flanging.

The result of this alternate slowing down of one machine, then the other, with both outputs electrically mixed, was a series of changing interactions between the two outputs. There would be reinforcement (addition) and then cancellation (subtraction), which gave the effect of a sweeping comb filter. The sound can be described as swishing or tunneling.

Using a pair of hand tended tape machines is hardly convenient, nor does it produce easily repeatable effects. For this reason, electronic circuitry was devised to automatically create the same kind of effect. If a given signal is delayed, then mixed back with the original signal, the result is cancellation at a frequency whose period is twice the delay time. This cancellation also occurs at odd harmonics of the signal frequency. The depth of cancellation (or reinforcement) depends on the level balance between the direct and delayed sound. An equal balance produces maximum effect. A sweeping flange is created by continuously varying the time delay, typically with a low frequency oscillator (LFO) to modulate the delay clock. This causes the nulls (notches in response) to sweep across the program bandwidth, alternately boosting and cutting different frequencies in relationship to one another.

If the polarity of one signal (delayed or direct) is inverted with respect to the other, the result is called a negative flange. If the unit provides for some feedback of output to input, then a more exaggerated effect will occur.

If you haven't already guessed, flanging relies upon delay, and that means it is often available in effects-oriented digital (or analog) delay lines, as well as in some digital reverbs. Some *flangers* are specially packaged for guitar use. The entire effects device sits on the floor, has an on-off footswitch, perhaps has a foot operated pedal for player controlled sweeping instead of LFO generated sweeping, and has input and output connections optimized for guitar use.

The highest quality flanging can only be achieved with two channels of delay. This is because complete cancellation is not possible when the delayed and direct signal are always offset in time. With two delayed signals, there is no direct signal, but both channels are always delayed by a basic value (whatever that might be), and then the two channels sweep up and down in delay time opposite to each other, with the two delayed outputs being mixed to produce the effect. This affords an opportunity for greater depth of effect. It is also a much more costly way to go, so this approach is seldom implemented. (Incidentally, you won't hear a good flange unless the two signals are mixed together electrically. Using a stereo speaker system with each channel fed by a different delayed signal will not yield a flange.)

14.5.2 Phasing

Flanging and phasing have a somewhat similar sound, but are achieved in a very different way. A *phaser* or *phase shifter* is a device that contains one (or more) deep, high Q filters. (High Q means the filter has a very narrow bandwidth). A signal is split, with some of it going to the filter circuit, and some bypassing the filter. A lot of phase shift is created at frequencies on either side of the filter notch. By sweeping that notch up and down the frequency spectrum, and mixing the resulting signal back with the direct signal, a series of ever-changing phase cancellations results.

Changing the relative balance of direct and filtered sound also changes the nature of the effect. In some cases it is possible to reverse the polarity of one of the two component signals to

produce additional, unusual effects.

Phasing is popular for guitars, keyboards and vocals.

Because this effect relies upon a swept filter, rather than a swept delay, true phasing is seldom included in a digital delay or reverb system.

14.5.3 What To Look For

With any special effects processors, but particularly with flangers and phasers, it is important to obtain the right unit for the job. Devices meant for direct connection to a guitar may be too noisy, and may operate at the wrong levels for insertion in the signal processing send/receive loops of a mixing console. Conversely, a device is made for use with a mixing console may overload an electric guitar pickup, impairing the frequency response and degrading signal-to-noise ratios. Also, it may not have adequate gain, further increasing the noise.

Some of the differences between units relate to the available control of the effect — how deep it can be, how wide it can sweep, whether there are manual and automatic settings, remote control capability etc. These differences can be explored by looking at the front and rear panels. Some of the more important differences relate to the actual performance, which can only be determined with listening tests using program material that is the same or very close to that with which the device will be used. Sometimes it seems that an effect which sounds good with a guitar sounds awful with a piano, or what sounds good with a voice is inaudible with a guitar, and so forth. You may be able to make a correction with the available controls, but sometimes a given unit simply works better than another for a particular application.

14.6 EXCITERS

In 1975, a company called Aphex introduced the first *Aural Exciter*. This unit changed the signal in such a way that, when part of the Exciter-processed signal was mixed back in with the direct program, the apparent punch and intelligibility of the program was enhanced. This was achieved without changing the program frequency balance or gain appreciably. The exciter became popular for increasing apparent loudness of the overall program or of individual parts, especially in record cutting (where the benefit of more apparent level could be enjoyed without reducing the available recording time), in live sound reinforcement (where feedback and headroom were not sacrificed, as they would be with simple graphic or parametric EQ boost) or in broadcast (where greater penetration can be obtained without overmodulation).

While early units were only available for rent, later versions were sold, and later the circuit was implemented on integrated circuit chips and built in to other manufacturers' equipment (today the circuit is being used in special commercial intercom and telephone equipment). Other companies have emulated the function of Aphex's invention, although they use somewhat different approaches to the actual signal processing.

The Aphex Exciter works by splitting the input signal. Part of it goes directly to the output, and the other part goes through a high pass filter network and a harmonic generator, after which that processed signal is mixed back in with the direct signal at the output. This processing generates frequency dependent and amplitude dependent harmonics. Newer circuitry has increased the sensitivity to amplitude changes so that the system steepens a wavefront for a sharper apparent attack. This is done primarily with even harmonics so that the positive-going peak is accentuated. Interestingly, the psychoacoustic effect is much greater than any single specification, measured with conventional instrumentation, would indicate.

The key to proper use of any exciter is to use it in moderation. Only a small percentage of processed signal should be mixed back into the direct program feed.

A number of other companies have introduced processors that are supposed to perform similar signal manipulation, although Aphex claims to own the term "Aural Exciter", and reserves the rights to their specific process.

SECTION 15.
CABLING

15.1 THE IMPORTANCE OF GOOD CABLES

A given cable probably costs less than any other component in a sound system (unless it is a multi channel snake, which is pretty costly). Still, there may be hundreds of cables in a single system, so the cost can add up to a sizable figure. Hum, crackles, lost signal due to open circuits, or failed outputs due to shorted circuits can all be caused by a cable. If you think about it, regardless of how high the quality of your mics, mixing console, amplifiers and loudspeakers may be, the entire system can be degraded or silenced by a bad cable. You should never try to save money by cutting corners with cable. A system's worth of good cable is expensive.

High price alone does not guarantee a good product. There are major differences between similar looking cables. All wire is not the same, nor are all look alike connectors made the same way. Even if the overall diameter, wire gauge, and general construction are similar, two cables may have significantly different electrical and physical properties such as resistance, capacitance between conductors, inductance between conductors, overall flexibility, shielding density, durability, ability to withstand crushing or sharp bends, tensile strength, jacket friction (or lack thereof for use in conduits), and so forth. Almost all audio cables in a sound reinforcement system should utilize stranded conductors, yet many same-gauge wires use a different number of strands. More strands usually yield better flexibility and less chance of metal fatigue failure or failure after an inadvertent nick in the cable. Even the wire itself makes a difference. Pure copper is an excellent conductor, but lacks tensile strength. Copper/bronze inner conductors are strong yet adequately flexible. Aluminum is strong and lightweight, but has too much resistance for practical use in audio circuits.

Connectors may be well made, with low contact resistance (and low tendency to develop resistance over time), or perhaps not. They may be well secured to the cable, with thoroughly soldered shields and inner conductors and good strain relief, or they may be carelessly put together.

There is also the question of which type of cable to use: single or dual conductor shielded type? Cable with braided, wrapped or foil shields – or cable with no shield at all? Separate, loosely bundled cables for each channel, or a multicore snake with many channels sharing the same outer jacket?

The following paragraphs shed some light on the function and construction of various cables and connectors.

15.2 Types Of Cables, Their Construction, And Use

15.2.1 Electrostatic and Electromagnetic Shielding

Shielding for mic and line level cables is essential in most applications. Mic and line signals are relatively low in level, and will be amplified. Any noise entering the cable will be amplified along with the desired signal. The purpose of shielding is to exclude *electrostatic* fields— to intercept these spurious charges and drain them to ground so they do not get into the inner, signal carrying conductor(s) of the cable. In the case of an unbalanced cable with a single center conductor,

BALANCED SHIELDED CABLE
(3-conductor)

Electrostatic Noise

Electrostatic noise is blocked from reaching the inner conductor(s) by the shield, and instead flows around the shield and through the drain wire to the chassis.

CHASSIS

the shield also acts as a return path for the signal.

Higher frequency noise, including the very steep wavefronts generated by sparking, has shorter wavelengths and is therefore more of a problem for loosely braided or wrapped cable shields. (The shorter the wavelength, the easier it is for the noise to penetrate even minute spaces in the shielding.) The best shielding you can use in fixed (permanent) installations or within a rack or piece of equipment is a foil shield. Metal foil provides nearly 100% shielding effectiveness (known as shielding density), but such cables (i.e., Belden 8451 or Canare L–2B2AT) are not particularly strong or flexible, and the shielding will deteriorate if they are flexed very much. This is why cable with braided or wrapped wire shielding is more commonly used for mic and instrument

The noise current flows along the chassis, through the ground wire of the AC cord, and ultimately is shunted to earth.

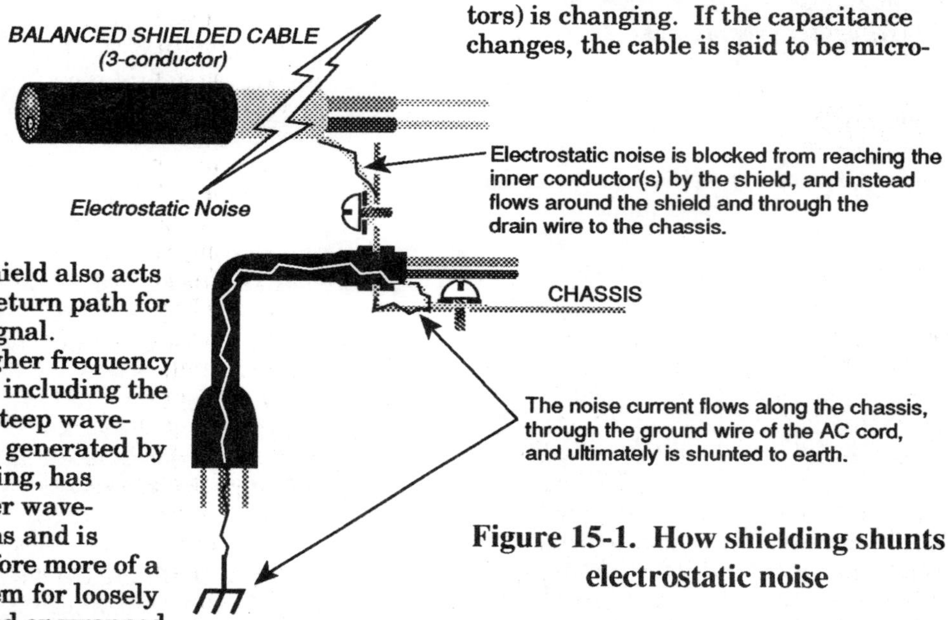

Figure 15-1. How shielding shunts electrostatic noise

connections to the sound system. Cables with wrapped (or swerved) shields may offer greater flexibility than similar braided shield cables, but the wrap will tend to open up with flexing, which not only degrades shielding density, but can also cause microphonic noise, as described below. Electrostatic charges may be caused by sparks at the armatures of motors or generators, by gas discharge lighting (neon or fluorescent), and other sources. These charges can capacitively couple into a cable. If the inter-conductor capacitance changes within a section of the cable itself, noise will also be induced. When you flex a cable and you hear it, there are two possible causes: either some wire strands are broken and are intermittently touching, or the capacitance between inner conductors (or shield and inner conductors) is changing. If the capacitance changes, the cable is said to be micro-

phonic. This is a major problem with phantom power in mic cables, although it can happen in any cable, and you definitely don't want this internally generated noise to occur in any sound system. The best way to avoid electrostatic noise and microphonic noise is to use cables with stable dielectric (insulating) material that won't let the center conductors migrate relative to the shield, and with a tightly braided shield that is well-trapped by the outer jacket so the shield itself does not open up as the cable is flexed. A rubber outer jacket is often favored for mic and instrument cables because it has a good feel and is flexible over a wide temperature range, but good quality vinyl has become popular, too. Vinyl pulls through a conduit better than rubber. In fact, there are special plenum cables that don't necessarily need conduit. These are jacketed with tough, slippery fluoropolymer resin compounds such as Pennwalt KYNAR®, Allied HALAR®, or DuPont TEFLON®, which can withstand temperatures of 125, 150, and 200 degrees centigrade, respectively. Jackets optimized for plenum or conduit installation tend to have inadequate flexibility for most other uses.

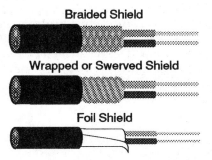

Braided Shield

Wrapped or Swerved Shield

Foil Shield

Figure 15-2. Different types of cable shielding

We stated that cable shielding is primarily for electrostatic noise, and this is true. But there is another type of noise. *Electromagnetic* noise may be generated by the coils in electric motors, ballast in fluorescent lighting, the coils in large rheostat type lighting dimmers, or the chopping of AC current by silicon controlled rectifier (SCR) dimmers. Such noise enters cable by means of inductive coupling. Normal cable shielding does not exclude electromagnetic fields (unless the shield is heavy iron or steel conduit). Magnetic fields are cancelled only by a balanced line, with twisted center conductors, and by sheer physical distance from the source.

Ground Loops are also a contributing factor in cable noise, but in this case the noise is being induced by currents flowing through the shield, and it matters not how dense the shield is or how tightly the center conductors are twisted. Only proper grounding will cure the problem.

15.2.2 Cable Self-Capacitance

While shielding is beneficial to the extent it excludes electrostatic noise, it can have a negative impact on a cable. It increases the overall distributed capacitance between signal-carrying conductors. Because a cable has finite resistance as well, the combination of capacitance plus resistance constitute a low pass filter. For a given wire gauge, the longer the cable and/or the greater the capacitance per foot, the lower the cutoff frequency of the filter. In practical terms, if you're using more than 100 feet of mic cable, you need to use cable with the lowest practical capacitance per foot. Be aware that on dual conductor shielded cables, there are two capacitance specs to examine: capacitance between center conductors, and capacitance between a center conductor and the shield. Cables with larger diameters inside the shield (we don't care about jacket thickness) tend to have lower capacitance due to greater spacing between conductors. There are, however, major variations in similar looking cables due to the tightness of the twist between center conductors, the dielectric constant* of the insulation, and other factors. You can go through complex calculations to figure out what effect a given cable might have on the high end frequency response of the system, but the bottom line is that the wrong cable may indeed affect the transient or overall high frequency response of the system. Output source impedance and input termination impedance must be considered when figuring out the actual high frequency losses. With older equipment, changing from a low impedance (600 ohm) termination to a high impedance (15 kohm) termination could cut in half the filter cutoff frequency, resulting in considerably more signal loss. Today, this is not as likely to occur. The equation for filter cutoff frequency is as follows:

$$f_o = \frac{1}{(2\pi RC)}$$

where f_o is the -3 dB point of the filter, π is 3.1416, R is the resistance of the

---

* *Dielectric constant* describes the electrical insulating properties of a material (whether cable insulation or ordinary air).

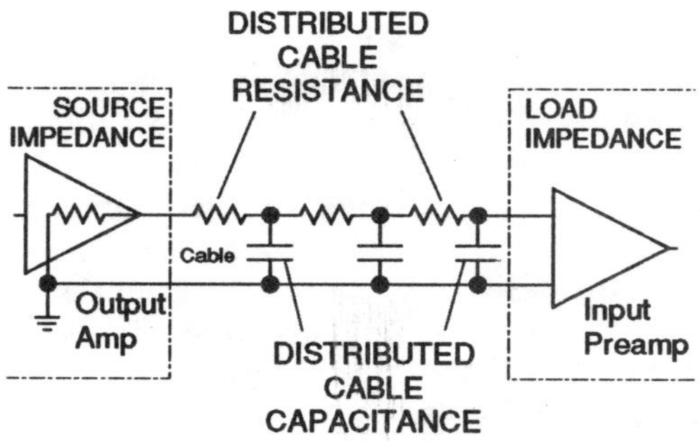

Figure 15-3. Cable resistance & capacitance create a low pass filter.

cable (in Ohms) and C is the capacitance of the cable (in Farads).

As you can see, higher capacitance or resistance causes the cutoff frequency of this 6 dB per octave low pass filter to slide lower and lower.

Cables used within equipment are generally shorter, and may have smaller diameters. The small diameter allows the cable to bend around short radii inside a chassis. Wire gauge of Nº 24 and Nº 26 American wire gauge (AWG) are OK in these applications because over these relatively short distances, overall resistance remains low. The larger insulation diameters required to reduce the capacitance per foot of cable are also less of a factor when relatively few feet of cable are involved. When such cables are misused to cover long cable runs, their extra capacitance and higher resistance will cause very noticeable degradation of system performance.

Single conductor shielded cables are intended for use in unbalanced circuits They will unbalance balanced circuits. Dual conductor shielded cables are primarily used for balanced circuits, although they may be used to good advantage where a balanced output is driving an unbalanced input. With unbalanced outputs driving unbalanced inputs, avoid using dual-conductor shielded cables because they can exhibit twice the specified capacitance in such a hookup, and this may cause a significant loss of high frequency and transient information. There are a few cables that utilize four center conductors, connected in pairs, to perform essentially the same function as a dual-conductor cable, but with greater immunity to electromagnetic noise. The principle of noise rejection by balanced circuits is covered in Section 11.6 of this handbook.

Some single conductor shielded cables appear to be similar to the coaxial cable used for TV and radio signals (i.e., RG-58, or RG-59), but there is a major difference. Coaxial cable for RF use generally has solid center conductors (or only a few strands of heavier wire), and the cable capacitance differs significantly from that of audio cable. The coax also tends to be less flexible. In other words, don't use RF cable for audio signals.

In dual-conductor cables, the inner pair of conductors is usually color coded either black and red or black and white. If black and red, by convention, the red wire should be the hot or high side of the pair. If black and white, the situation is not always clear. Many people prefer to make the white the hot side, but in AC wiring the black is hot, so you may find the black side of the audio cable wired this way, too. It really makes no difference at all, so long as the cable is wired with consistent polarity between the connectors at both ends. (Refer to Figures 15-4 (a) and 15-4 (b) for specific wiring details with various cable and connector types with different combinations of balanced and unbalanced terminations.)

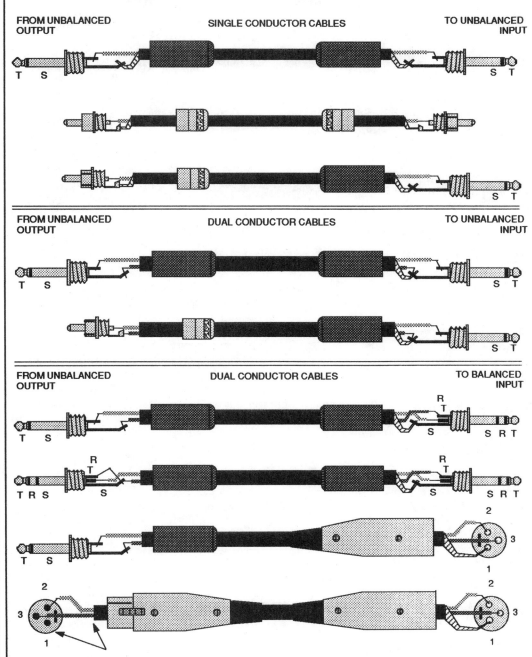

FROM UNBALANCED OUTPUT SINGLE CONDUCTOR CABLES TO UNBALANCED INPUT

FROM UNBALANCED OUTPUT DUAL CONDUCTOR CABLES TO UNBALANCED INPUT

FROM UNBALANCED OUTPUT DUAL CONDUCTOR CABLES TO BALANCED INPUT

For mic cables, connect the shield to Pin 1 at both ends of the cable.
For line-level signal cables, cut the shield here as illustrated.

**Figure 15-4 (a). Single and dual conductor cables
for use with unbalanced sources**

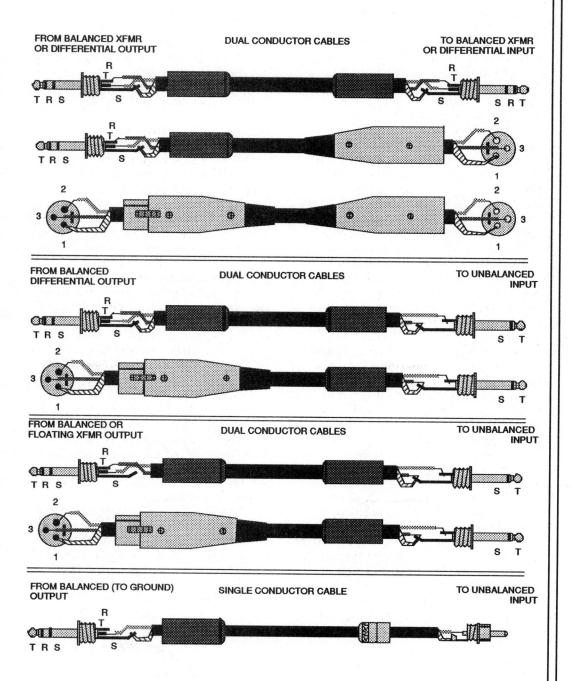

FROM BALANCED XFMR
OR DIFFERENTIAL OUTPUT
DUAL CONDUCTOR CABLES
TO BALANCED XFMR
OR DIFFERENTIAL INPUT

FROM BALANCED
DIFFERENTIAL OUTPUT
DUAL CONDUCTOR CABLES
TO UNBALANCED
INPUT

FROM BALANCED OR
FLOATING XFMR OUTPUT
DUAL CONDUCTOR CABLES
TO UNBALANCED
INPUT

FROM BALANCED (TO GROUND)
OUTPUT
SINGLE CONDUCTOR CABLE
TO UNBALANCED
INPUT

**Figure 15-4 (b). Single and dual conductor cables
for use with transformer or differentially balanced sources**

NOTE: *There are significant differences in the way various balanced outputs are designed. When a balanced output is driving an unbalanced input, it is best to use a dual-conductor shielded cable, connecting the shield at both ends, and allowing the low side of the cable to join the shield at the unbalanced input end of the cable. This provides most of the hum protection of a fully balanced line. In some cases, notably with a balanced to ground output, it is best to use a single conductor shielded cable, as illustrated above. In other cases, such as in equipment racks where jacks are grounded through the rack frame, it may prove necessary to cut the shield at the output end of the cable. Unfortunately, there is no one right way to make a cable for all installations.*

One important aspect of cable construction is the ability of the cable to withstand pulling strain. Cables such as telephone cable are made to be suspended and have high-strength steel-strand wire included in the jacket – not for electrical conduction, but strictly for handling the pulling strain so the softer copper wire is not pulled apart. The cables used for microphones and electric instruments must be reasonably flexible, and light in weight, so steel strands are seldom used. Instead, there is typically some sort of non-conducting cord that is flexible and does not interfere with the impedance of the cable. In larger diameter mic cables, the cord may be made of jute or polyester fiber. Some smaller diameter cable use more exotic fibers such as Dupont Kevlar® which have very high strength for a relatively small diameter. Sometimes the inner conductors or the shield will be fashioned of an alloy that is stronger than pure copper, but such cable will generally be stiffer and less able to withstand repeated bending.

Cables made for installation within a chassis, or that are not intended to be pulled or stressed much, may not have any built-in strain relief. Such cables will not be reliable for live, onstage performances.

It is important that the strain relief in the cable itself be carried through to the connectors at either end of the cable. If the strain relief cords are not secured by a clamp of some sort, then the wire conductors at the connector will have to sustain most of the pulling forces, and premature breakage will occur at the connector. Be sure to use whatever means are available on the connector to securely clamp the cable in the connector.

When clamping a cable, remember that sharp bends also promote premature breakage of conductors. It is best to provide some sort of additional support at the connector that will prevent the cable from bending around too sharp a radius if the cable is pulled sideways. Most XLR type connectors include a tapered rubber extension as part of their clamping mechanism. The taper provides less and less support as the cable exits the connector, which promotes a smooth, maximum radius bend if the cable is pulled sideways. You can create a similar effect with other types of connectors, or where cables exit junction boxes, by using several pieces of heat-shrinkable insulating tubing. Make each piece slightly shorter than the next, and shrink them around the cable so that the ends of all pieces are flush inside the connector (where all are gripped by the cable clamp), and the varying length ends form a tapered support outside the connector.

The Chinese handcuff type of strain relief used on some junction boxes is less desirable than tapered rubber or insulation methods. While it does prevent the cable from being pulled out of the box, it still allows a sharp bend to occur at the end of the handcuff.

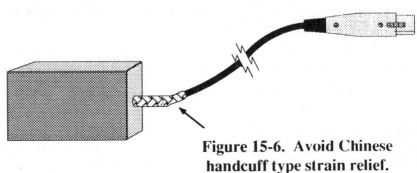

Figure 15-6. Avoid Chinese handcuff type strain relief.

Figure 15-5. Using heat-shrink tubing for strain relief

15.2.5 Unshielded Cables and Speaker Cables

Shielding not only adds capacitance to a cable, it also adds considerable bulk, weight and cost. While one should never consider using unshielded cable for microphones or instruments in a sound system, there are applications, notably long telephone lines, where no shielding is used. Instead, balanced circuits are used with a twisted pair of wires that avoid electromagnetic interference. So long as there is no strong source of electrostatic interference nearby, and so long as the signal level in the wires is high, noise will not be excessive. This same approach applies to speaker cables, although here the signal level is so high that little if any twisting is required. Electromagnetic noise would have to be very high in level to be audible above the relatively higher power being fed to the speaker in this low impedance circuit.

The tens to hundreds of watts that must be handled by speaker cables bring a completely different set of considerations compared to mic or line level audio cables where levels are measured in microwatts or milliwatts. Obviously, wire gauges must be larger to accommodate the higher currents involved. Capacitance remains a problem, though less so because of the lower impedance in the circuit. However, cable inductance can be a serious problem. You will recall that the magnetic field generated by a signal is proportional to the current. The higher currents in speaker wires generate larger fields, with consequently greater sensitivity to low frequency losses due to cable inductance. Because twisting of conductors raises the inductance, speaker cables should not be tightly twisted, and preferably not twisted at all.

It turns out that the requirements for speaker cable are not very different than those for AC power cable and ordinary zip cord (AC power cord) is frequently used for speaker hookup. Also popular for speaker cable is the heavy duty AC cable used for industrial 240 V power extension cords, which has larger gauge wire and flexible, rubberized insulation.

The actual loss of signal due to wire resistance depends on the impedance of the load. Approximate losses in speaker cable for a 100 foot amplifier-to-speaker distance are shown in Table 15-1.

Wire Ga.	Speaker Impedance		
(AWG)	4 ohm	8 ohm	16 ohm
#10	0.44 dB	0.22 dB	0.11 dB
#12	0.69 dB	0.35 dB	0.18 dB
#14	1.07 dB	0.55 dB	0.28 dB
#16	1.65 dB	0.86 dB	0.44 dB
#18	2.49 dB	1.33 dB	0.69 dB

Table 15-1. Signal loss in a 100 foot speaker cable

As you can see, the use of standard 18 gauge zip cord with a 4 ohm speaker results in 2½ dB of loss. A loss of 3 dB would mean half the amplifier's power is being dissipated by the wire, not the speaker, so this is no small loss. Clearly, the larger gauge wire is beneficial in this case. You can also see that a higher impedance results in less loss (and in less power delivered to the speaker, too). This is one of the reasons why large, distributed speaker systems operate at nominal 70 volt amp output levels, and use transformers at each speaker. The impedance seen by the amplifier is kept high so smaller diameter cable can be used to cover large distances (many hundreds of feet) without large losses in the cable.

Incidentally, 300 ohm twin-lead antenna wire may be used (in an emergency) for speaker connections, but it generally has wire of insufficient gauge, and is not durable or flexible enough for portable systems.

NOTE: *Even a relatively slight impedance (or resistance) in the speaker cable significantly lowers the effective damping factor seen at the speaker. While the power loss caused by the cable may or may not be important to you, you may find that the degradation in sound quality caused by the lower damping factor is reason enough to use short, heavy gauge speaker cables.*

15.2.6 Multicore Audio Cables (Snakes)

When you have an 8, 12, 16, or even 24 input mixing console located remotely from the stage, a large number of microphone cables must be run over a relatively long distance. If individual cables are used, the resulting cable bundle can be large, unwieldy, and perhaps impractical for certain venues. Besides, if the stage layout changes, then you may need to use a variety of different length extension cables, which decreases the reliability and further clutters the system. Instead, many sound companies use special *snakes*. These are multi channel audio distribution systems. They utilize multi core cable that consist of from 8 to 24 (or more) shielded pairs. Each shielded pair consists of two twisted center conductors surrounded by a shield, but generally without an insulating jacket. Instead, an overall jacket (and sometimes an overall shield) surrounds the bundle of shielded pairs. The multicore cable sometimes terminates at the console end in pigtails, with each shielded pair separately insulated, strain relieved, and brought to an XLR connector. The other end may terminate in a stage box, which is a junction box that has chassis mounted XLR connectors. Individual mic cables are then used between the stage box and various mics and instruments. Sometimes a similar junction box is used, in lieu of pigtails, at the console end of the snake.

Snakes can save a lot of time in setting up a system, and are certainly neater than a large, loose bundle of separate mic cables. They do have drawbacks. For one thing, it is best to avoid bidirectional snakes in which some line level feeds are sent from the console to the stage. This is sometimes done to drive on-stage power amps with the output of the console, but it can result in feedback. Feedback can occur due to capacitive or inductive coupling from the line level console output in one shielded pair into adjacent shielded pairs that are carrying relatively lower level mic or instrument signals to the console. The lower level signals, including the crosstalk, are amplified in the console, and out they go, completing the feedback loop. If the coupling is largely capacitive, the feedback will occur at a high frequency,

which may even be inaudible. The resulting oscillation can quickly destroy high frequency drivers, and even if the drivers are protected the oscillation can still use up amplifier power, reducing headroom and increasing distortion in the audible spectrum. To avoid this problem, run separate mic cables (or a separate line level snake) from the console back to the stage. Don't share a stage-to-console snake, with primarily low level signals, with a feed from the console to the stage.

In fact, wherever low level and high level lines, or either of these lines and speaker cables, are run parallel for long distances, crosstalk may be great and the potential for oscillation exists. To minimize crosstalk, physically separate low level (microphone) cables from high level (line) cables by the greatest feasible distance. Keep speaker cables away from both low and high level signal cables. At any point they meet, run low level cables perpendicular to high level or speaker cables. If low level (mic) and high level line or speaker cables must be run parallel and in close proximity to one another, they should be bundled separately.

Another thing to examine carefully with snakes is the quality of the construction. Good strain relief should be provided at the point where the multicore cable enters the junction box, and at the point where any pigtails are split out of the multicore cable. The snake itself should have a tough outer jacket that resists being cut if equipment is rolled or dragged over it. If possible, the snake should have at least one or two spare twisted pairs so that, should one develop a broken wire, the entire snake will not have to be scrapped. Some snakes are made with large, locking, multi-pin connectors that enable the snake to be (a) fitted with different junction boxes, (b) fitted with pigtails, and/or (c) extended by connection to another section of multicore cable. This design allows more flexibility for system setups, but is obviously more expensive to implement. Such connectors should have a sturdy shell, a secure lock to prevent accidental disconnection, and gold plated pins to minimize contact resistance. Finally, the same criteria as to wire gauge, capacitance, and shielding density that apply to individual mic cables apply to snakes; check their electrical specifications.

Some cables have multiple conductors, with shielding, but are not optimized for high quality audio transmission. These cables may be built to carry a combination of several of the following signals: intercom, TV cameras, power, computerized controls, and so forth. Be sure the cable you select is specifically made for balanced, mic- or line level audio signals.

Treat snakes with care. Do not bend them too sharply, as this can ultimately cause hidden damage (broken wires).

Coil them carefully for storage and transport, and uncoil them carefully to prevent excess twisting. Some snakes come with, or have optionally available, cable reels. These further expedite setup, and have the advantage of making it easier to store and transport the relatively heavy, bulky snakes. Cable reels should have some sort of locking mechanism to prevent unwanted unspooling, and should have at least a partial friction lock to prevent inertia from throwing extra cable when you're pulling the snakes off the reels.

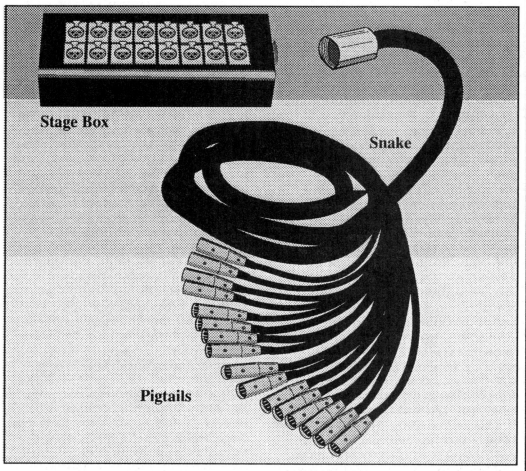

Figure 15-7. Typical multicore snake with stage box and pigtails

15.3.1 General

Ideally, a connector should be easy to use, difficult to accidentally disconnect, and should introduce no resistance and allow no interference to enter the sound system. Depending on the situation, some connectors come closer to this ideal than others. If a system never had to be reconfigured or moved then soldered, crimped or wire-wrapped connections would be best. Such connections have minimal resistance, do not tend to develop resistance over time, and are not likely to be accidentally disconnected. In fact, they often are used in studio wiring, where consoles are interfaced to mic and line cables that are permanently fixed in the facility. In portable systems, we are bound to use other means of interconnection.

Any time a plug and jack are inserted in the audio path, there will be some additional resistance to signal flow. Even if the contact resistance is minimal when the system is assembled, that resistance increases with aging, as dirt enters, or as corrosion forms. When connectors are regularly mated and demated, they tend to wipe themselves clean and resistance does not build up excessively. This is why connectors are best avoided in fixed systems, where the regular cleaning action of assembly and disassembly is not present. Where connectors are used in fixed (or semi-permanent) systems, it is best to specify gold plated pins since these have low initial resistance and they are inert so they don't corrode and cause long term resistance build-up.

This section of the manual discusses some of the pros and cons of typical audio connectors used for microphone and line level signals. Speaker connections are discussed in Section 18.4. In this section, we use the term plug (the male connector) to cover the mating jack (the female connector) as well, unless there is a specific need to differentiate between the two. By convention, XLR connectors are never called plug or jack; they are called XLRs, or XLR-type connectors or simply connectors. (We use XLR even if the connector is an A3, etc.)

Those connectors that are used exclusively for unbalanced circuits need have only two contacts. Examples include two-circuit phone plugs (tip/sleeve), and phono plugs (also known as pin plugs or RCA plugs). Three-circuit phone plugs (tip/ring/sleeve) and XLR connectors are essential for balanced connections, but they may be used for unbalanced connections as well.

Why use one type of connector or another? Often the choice is made for us by the equipment manufacturer, who may install a specific connector. Sometimes there may be more than one option, and the choice is up to the installer. It helps to know the pros and cons of each connector type in making this choice.

15.3.2 Phone Plugs

Phone plugs are so called because they were originally used (and still are in some cases) for patching lines together on telephone switchboards. Since telephone systems relied upon twisted pairs, the original phone plug was a three-circuit plug with a tip, ring and sleeve, as illustrated in Figure 15–8 (next page). Phone plugs are easily wired to the cable, relatively inexpensive (although all-brass "mil-spec" models are costly), and the mating jacks can be set up to automatically switch various circuits when a plug is inserted. Some precautions are in order.

In a balanced audio line, the tip is usually connected to the hot or high side of the audio line, the ring to the low side, and the sleeve to the shield ground. If such a plug is inserted into an unbalanced (tip/sleeve) phone jack, the line will be unbalanced, but the signal polarity will remain correct. Within a mixing console (particularly in large recording or broadcast consoles), the T/R/S phone jacks in the patch bay may be wired for unbalanced operation, with the tip being the audio common, the ring audio high and the sleeve chassis ground. This arrangement avoids pops from static discharge or different ground potentials as a plug is inserted in a jack since the tip (common) makes contact before the

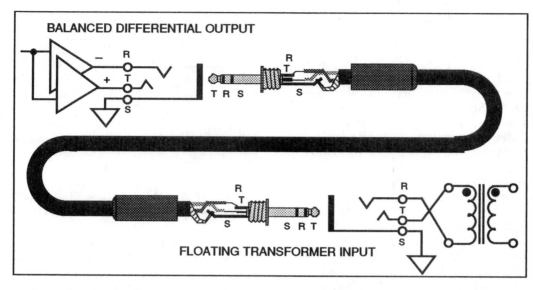

BALANCED DIFFERENTIAL OUTPUT

FLOATING TRANSFORMER INPUT

Figure 15-8. Tip/ring/sleeve phone plugs and jacks in a balanced circuit

signal-carrying ring. If a cable is connected to a patch bay wired this way, and the other end is connected to an unbalanced tip/sleeve jack, then the signal will be shorted out.

The previous paragraph raises one issue about phone plugs; they can cause pops if inserted while a system is in operation. Another potential problem with phone plugs is that the shell (or handle) may crack, particularly if it is plastic. Metal-shell plugs are preferable not only because they won't crack, but also because they afford shielding of the connection. Military style phone plugs are made with brass bodies that include a sturdy integral cable clamp. While these plugs may have a plastic jacket on the handle, they are nonetheless very strong. The brass parts on such plugs are also thicker than the typical stamped metal parts on less costly phone plugs. This enables them to be tapped for small screws, which then enables the cable to be fitted with crimp-on lugs instead of solder contacts. The crimped lugs not only are faster to install than solder, they do not tend to stiffen the wire strands as does solder, so the wire is better able to withstand flexing without breakage. The brass also has lower contact resistance (if regularly wiped clean by usage) than typical nickel or alloy plated plugs. This is a long way of saying that there are benefits to a brass, telephone style plug, even if it does cost three to five times more. The

major disadvantage of this style plug is that it is difficult to provide strain relief where the cable exits the handle.

Phone plugs are the norm for electric guitars. In order to prevent the hum and crackle that is often heard when the cable is unplugged from the guitar, some cables are available with a switch in the phone plug itself. The switch normally shorts the tip to the sleeve when the plug is not inserted in a jack. This grounds out the input to the guitar amp and prevents noise. When the plug is inserted in the guitar (or other instrument), the switch is opened by a small shaft protruding from the shoulder of the plug. Since the cable is not unshorted until it is connected to the guitar, noise is avoided. Such connectors are a good idea, but obviously the added complexity provides another opportunity for something to fail and cause noise or kill the signal. This type of switching phone plug is only for use in guitar cables and should never be used on a speaker cable since it can short circuit the output of the power amplifier.

Other concerns about phone plugs include the lack of a locking mechanism (which means they can be accidentally disconnected), and vulnerability to breakage if knocked sideways. Most phone plug/jack combinations exhibit high contact resistance, which can become a source of power loss and noise in a speaker circuit. There are high current (low loss) phone plugs and jacks that offer significant improvement in this area.

The three-circuit T/R/S phone plug has also been called a stereo phone plug because this is the type of connector used on most stereo headphones. In this case, the circuit is unbalanced and the tip is used for the left channel, the ring the right channel, and the sleeve is the audio common. In other instances, such as the effects send/receive loop of certain mixing consoles and guitar amplifiers, this type of plug accommodates an unbalanced input and output to save space (the tip may be wired to the output, the ring to the input, and the sleeve to the audio common). See Figure 15-10, next page. The disadvantages of such a combined input/output circuit include: (a) the necessity for non-standard cables that enable the two circuits to be split at the far end to connect to the input and output of the remote device, (b) the possibility that the jack may be misused and can either damage or be damaged by external equipment, and (c) possible crosstalk that results in oscillation, though this is not likely in a unity gain circuit, as would generally be present in a loop connection.

The standard tip/ring/sleeve plug or tip/sleeve plug has a shaft diameter of ¼-inch (6.25 mm). There are smaller diameter shafts on similar looking plugs that are sometimes found in special applications. Another similarly constructed class of plugs is known as *tini plugs* and were developed so that patch bays could be miniaturized. These plugs have a shaft diameter of 0.175" (4.45mm) and smaller handles, too. Make sure you purchase the correct plugs or jacks for the job.

Miniature and sub-miniature phone plugs bear some resemblance to standard phone plugs, but you would never accidentally mistake a standard for one of these. The miniature variety is most often found on small, lightweight headphones used for portable cassette and radio units, for inexpensive microphones used with consumer cassette recorders, and occasionally for the connections on 120 volt to 6, 9 or 12 volt power adaptors.

With any phone plug of any size or configuration, make sure that the fingers to which you connect the cable are securely fixed to the plug. Make sure that the tip (ring) and sleeve are concentrically centered, and that the

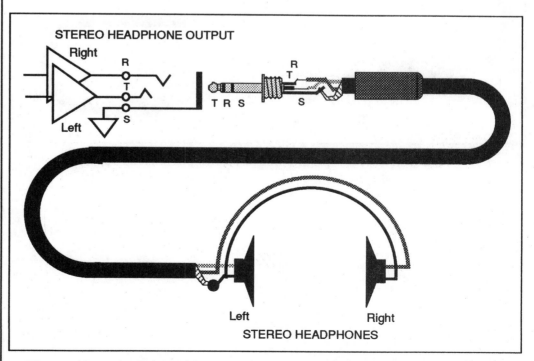

Figure 15-9. A tip/ring/sleeve phone plug wired for stereo headphones

insulators separating them are not cracked, loose or damaged. Make sure there is some means of strain relief for the cable. Avoid handling the plug shaft, and if you do, wipe off finger oils, which promote corrosion. If the connection with a standard phone plug becomes noisy, clean the plug with a brass brush, rubber pencil eraser, or #600 grit emory paper. Clean the jack using a .25 to .30 caliber, brass bristle gun cleaning brush.

The correct methods for wiring T/S and T/R/S phone plugs are illustrated in Figures 15-11 and 15-12 on the following pages.

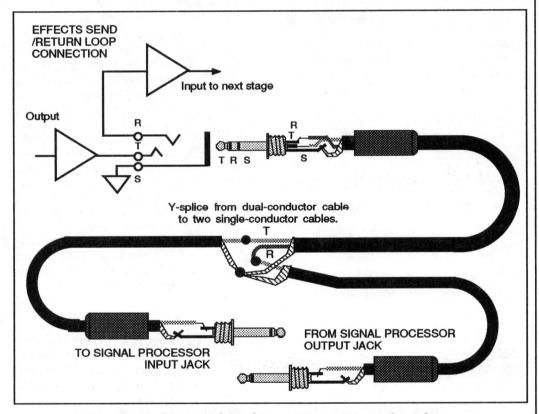

Figure 15-10. A tip/ring/sleeve phone plug wired for a single-cable effects send/return loop

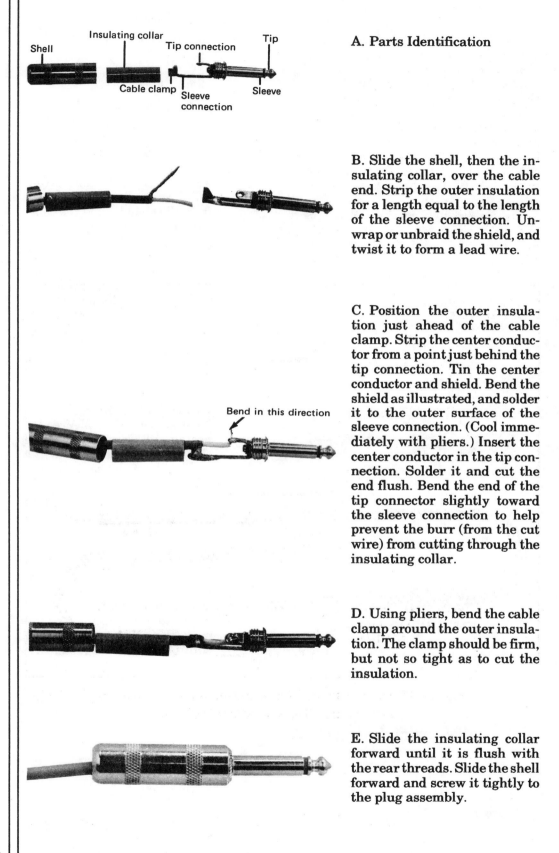

A. Parts Identification

B. Slide the shell, then the insulating collar, over the cable end. Strip the outer insulation for a length equal to the length of the sleeve connection. Unwrap or unbraid the shield, and twist it to form a lead wire.

C. Position the outer insulation just ahead of the cable clamp. Strip the center conductor from a point just behind the tip connection. Tin the center conductor and shield. Bend the shield as illustrated, and solder it to the outer surface of the sleeve connection. (Cool immediately with pliers.) Insert the center conductor in the tip connection. Solder it and cut the end flush. Bend the end of the tip connector slightly toward the sleeve connection to help prevent the burr (from the cut wire) from cutting through the insulating collar.

D. Using pliers, bend the cable clamp around the outer insulation. The clamp should be firm, but not so tight as to cut the insulation.

E. Slide the insulating collar forward until it is flush with the rear threads. Slide the shell forward and screw it tightly to the plug assembly.

Figure 15-11. Wiring a tip/sleeve standard phone plug

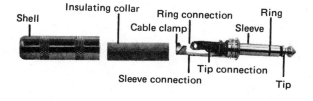

Shell — Insulating collar — Ring connection — Ring — Cable clamp — Sleeve — Sleeve connection — Tip connection — Tip

A. Parts Identification

B. Slide the shell and insulating collar over the cable end. Strip the outer insulation for a length equal to the length of the sleeve connection. Remove any tracer cords and strain relief cords. Form a lead wire from the shield. Hold the cable with the outer insulation just ahead of the cable clamp, and strip the red (or white) conductor just behind the tip connection. Then strip the black conductor just behind the ring connection. Tin all leads, and cut the center conductors so approximately $\frac{1}{8}$" of bare wire remains.

C. Solder the shield to the outer surface of the sleeve connection, allowing enough free shield to bend around to the other side of the cable clamp. Cool the connection immediately with pliers.

Bend slightly in this direction

D. Insert the center conductor leads in their respective connection points, and solder them in place. Trim the leads flush. Bend the end of the tip connection slightly toward the ring connection to help prevent the burr (from the cut wire) from cutting through the insulating collar

E. Using pliers, bend the cable clamp around the outer insulation. The clamp should be firm, but not so tight as to cut the insulation.

F. Slide the insulating collar forward, until it is flush with the rear of the threads. Slide the shell forward and screw it tightly onto the plug.

Figure 15-12. Wiring a tip/ring/sleeve standard phone plug

YAMAHA
Sound Reinforcement
Handbook

15.3.3 Phono (Pin) Connectors

The Radio Corporation of America (RCA) originally developed the pin connector for internal chassis connections in radios and televisions. It became popular for use in the cables that connected phonograph cartridges to preamplifiers because it was inexpensive and easily fitted to the rather small diameter shielded cables used for the cartridge leads (then they were mono cartridges so single conductor shielded cables were adequate). Over the years, the connector became the standard for use in most line level consumer sound equipment. This familiar connector has a protruding pin in the center of a shell. For these reasons, the connector is known variously as an *RCA plug*, a *phono plug* or a *pin plug*. (A variety of this connector is also used for some radio frequency cables, including video in/out connections on many modern video cassette recorders.) This type of plug is used in some professional sound equipment because it is (a) inexpensive, and (b) it allows a lot of connectors to be placed in a relatively small area.

Phono plugs come in two general varieties: a simple one-piece model to which the cable shield must be soldered circumferentially, and a two-piece model with a separate outer shell that allows the shield to be tacked to one finger. It is difficult to uniformly solder a shield all the way around the one-piece plug without overheating the cable and melting the insulation on the center conductor. For this reason, the one-piece plug is best reserved for automated, factory wired cables. The two-piece plugs are relatively small in diameter, and don't allow much room inside. You can't use a very large diameter cable with them, and you may have difficulty sliding the shell over the cable jacket or clamping the jacket with the minimal prongs provided for that purpose.

Because they are tricky to mate with cables, and difficult to clamp, and because there is a high demand for phono cables in the consumer market, such cables are available prewired with molded-in-plastic connectors. If you select such a cable, it may be a good idea to intentionally destroy one and see how well it is made. Look for tightly braided rather than spiral wrapped shielding. Look for an adequate diameter inner conductor with as many strands as feasible. Cut the molded connector apart carefully to determine whether the shield is tacked at one or two points, or whether it covers most of the connector shell to provide good shielding continuity and maximum strength. One drawback of such cables, even if well made, is that the wire itself may have very high capacitance due to its relatively small diameter. Some insulators have better dielectric qualities than others, so similar looking cables may have very different capacitance. A good cable is not cheap, but an expensive one may not always be good.

One of the problems with phono connectors is the tendency to develop high resistance where the plug and jack mate. Particularly in a consumer sound system that may be installed once and not disturbed for years, corrosion at the contact surface can ultimately degrade performance of the entire sound system. To avoid this problem, you can select gold plated connectors, or you can select phono plugs with slightly dished shell fingers and a good, springy contacts that will burnish the contacts to clean them when the connector is twisted in place. Be sure to twist it periodically to achieve the cleaning action.

(Refer to Figure 15-13 on next page.)

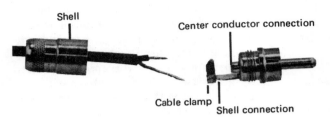

Shell

Center conductor connection

Cable clamp

Shell connection

A. Parts Identification and Cable Preparation: Strip approximately ½" of outer insulation from the cable, and form a lead from the shield. Strip approximately ⁵/₁₆" of insulation from the center conductor. Tin both leads.

B. Solder the shield to the outer surface of the shell connection, allowing enough free shield to wrap the cable around to the center of the connector. Cool the connection immediately with pliers.

C. Insert the center conductor in the hollow pin, and fill that end with solder. Cool the connection immediately with pliers. Clean any solder splashes, and inspect for burned insulation. Pinch the clamp around the insulating jacket with pliers — firmly, but not so tight as to cut the insulation.

D. Slide the shell forward and screw it tightly to the threaded plug.

A Switchcraft Nº 3502 connector is illustrated. Many large diameter cables are more easily wired to simple RCA type pin plugs without a shell (such as a Switchcraft Nº 3501M, or equivalent). The braid can then be soldered directly to the shell of the plug.

Figure 15-13. Wiring a phono plug

15.3.4 XLR Connectors

The 3-pin XLR connector was originally introduced by Cannon (now ITT-Cannon), and that company still owns the rights to the term XLR. There are many models of XLR, but the most common in professional audio is the XLR-3, a connector with three pins for connection of the shield and a twisted pair, plus a separate outer shell that may or may not be tied to the shield connection. (Actually, the XLR-3 is available in male and female, chassis or in-line models, which are all differentiated by additional dash numbers after the XLR-3 designation.) Other manufacturers offer equivalent connectors, which are usually called XLR-type, XLB, or XL-type. For example, Switchcraft makes the A3 connector, and there are similar versions by Neutrik. Two-pin, four-pin, five-pin… even seven-pin XLR type connectors are available, but are seldom found in professional sound systems. (Occasionally 4-pin or 5-pin types are used for specialized intercom, headphone distribution or or bi-amped loudspeaker connections.) All these connectors share attributes that have made the design the de facto standard of the industry.

For one thing, XLR type connectors lock together. They won't pull out if the cable is yanked, yet they are easily released by pressing a tab on the connector. For another thing, the connection is made first by pin 1 (which is always the shield ground) so that when a cable is plugged in, electrostatic charges or ground potential differences are neutralized before the actual audio connection occurs. This prevents distracting and potentially damaging pops that can happen with phone plugs or phono plugs, where the audio connection is generally completed before the shield is grounded. Other advantages of the XLR type connector are its ability to accommodate large diameter mic cables, and to provide good strain relief. Finally, XLR type connectors have large contact areas that afford low contact resistance. The only negatives are the relatively high cost of such connectors, and the care required to properly attach them to the cable.

Figures 15-14 and 15-15 on the following pages show how to connect a male 3-pin XLR connector to a heavy duty microphone cable with braided shield (Belden 8412), and a female 3-pin XLR to a lighter duty cable with foil shield (Belden 8451). Obviously either type connector can be used with either type of cable. The two cables were shown here only to illustrate the ability of the XLR to work with a variety of cables. We would actually suggest adding some heat shrink tubing to the thinner cables to further enhance and extend the strain relief provided by the connector itself.

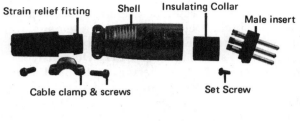

Strain relief fitting — Shell — Insulating Collar — Male insert

Cable clamp & screws — Set Screw

A. Parts Identification (as the connector is usually packaged).

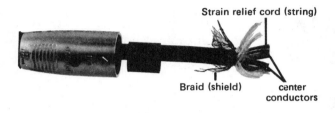

Tracer cord

Braid (shield)

B. Insert the strain relief in the rear of the shell. Then slip the shell onto the cable end, followed by the insulating collar. Strip the outer insulation ½". (Belden № 8412 cable illustrated here.)

Strain relief cord (string)

Braid (shield) — center conductors

C. Cut the tracer cord, unbraid the shield, and cut the cotton strain relief cords.

D. Strip approximately ¼" of insulation from the center conductors. Tin and trim them to approximately ⅛" of exposed wire. Then twist the shield, positioning it in the correct orientation to mate with the insert. After tinning the shield, cut it to the same length as the center conductors.

White wire — Pin 2

Black wire — Pin 3
Shield — Pin 1

E. Solder the center conductors to their respective pins, using just enough solder to fill the ends of the pins. The predominant world standards favor connection of the black lead to pin 3 and the white (or red) lead to pin 2. Solder the shield to pin 1. Clean any solder splashes, and inspect for burned insulation.

F. Slide the insulating collar forward, up to the flange of the male insert. The outer cable insulation must be flush with, or covered by, the end of the insert. (If any of the center conductors is visible, the cable clamp may not be able to firmly grip the cable.) Then slide the collar back onto the shell.

(Continued on next page)

YAMAHA
SOUND REINFORCEMENT
Handbook

Figure 15-14. Wiring a male XLR-3 type connector

(Figure 15-14 continued from prior page)

Keying channel

G. Slide the shell forward, orienting its internal keying channel with the raised lip (key) on the insert. Secure the insert in the shell with the set screw (unscrew it to cause it to rise into the shell and lock the insert). Place the cable clamp over the rear of the shell, with careful attention to the clamp's orientation. A raised lip inside the clamp should be aligned immediately over a lip in the shell for thinner cable (i.e., Belden № 8451). The clamp should be turned around for heavier cable (i.e., Belden № 8412) to provide adequate clearance. Insert the clamp screws, and tighten them fully.

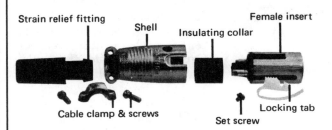

Strain relief fitting   Shell   Insulating collar   Female insert

Cable clamp & screws   Set screw   Locking tab

A. Parts Identification (as the connector is usually packaged).

B. Insert the strain relief in the rear of the shell. Then slip the shell onto the cable end, followed by the insulating collar. Strip the outer cable insulation back approximately $^9/_{16}$". (№ 8451 cable illustrated here.)

C. Pull off the foil wrap. Strip approximately $^5/_{16}$" of insulation from each center conductor, leaving approximately $^1/_4$" of insulation between the bare wire and the outer insulation. Tin the center conductors, and trim them so that about $^1/_8$" of bare wire remains. Then tin the shield conductor, orienting it with the center conductors so they are aligned with the proper pins of the insert. Cut the end of the shield so that it extends $^1/_{16}$" beyond the center conductors.

(Continued on next page)

Figure 15-15. Wiring a female XLR-3 type connector

(Figure 15-15 continued from prior page)

D. Solder the center conductors to their respective pins, using just enough solder to fill the ends of the pins. The predominant world standards favor connection of the black lead to pin 3 and the white (or red) lead to pin 2. Solder the shield to pin 1. Clean any solder splashes, and inspect for burned insulation. Insert the locking tab in the female insert, as illustrated, with the small nib facing the front of the connector.

E. Slide the insulating collar forward, up to the rear edge of the female insert. The outer insulation of the cable must be flush with, or covered by, the end of the insert. (If any of the center conductors are visible, the cable clamp may not be able to grip the cable firmly, and the connector leads will soon fatigue.) Then slide the collar back into the shell.

F. Slide the shell forward, orienting the notch in the shell with the locking tab in the insert. Secure the insert in the shell with the set screw. Place the cable clamp over the rear of the shell, with careful attention to the clamp's orientation. A raised lip inside the clamp should be aligned immediately over a lip in the shell for thinner cable (such as Belden № 8451). For heavier cable (i.e., Belden № 8412), the clamp should be turned around to offset the lips, and thus provide more clearance for the cable. Insert the clamp screws and tighten them fully.

SECTION 16.
SOUND SYSTEM TEST EQUIPMENT

Section 16 describes the most common types of test equipment used in setting up and operating sound systems.

A full course in measurement and instrumentation is clearly far beyond the scope of this handbook. The examples given in this section represent only a small sample of the possible uses for audio test equipment, and are intended to provide an introduction to the basic principles of sound system measurement.

16.1 The Volt-Ohm Meter

Volt-ohm meters (VOMs) are among the most useful tools in the sound technician's tool kit. VOMs can perform a wide variety of tests, and are used in servicing all types of electronic equipment.

As the name implies, a VOM is actually two instruments: a voltmeter (which measures voltage), and an ohmmeter (which measures resistance). Both sections will incorporate switch-selectable ranges.

The voltmeter section of a VOM usually is capable of both DC and AC voltage measurement. For audio purposes, the AC voltage section of the VOM should remain accurate throughout the full audio band (20 Hz to 20 kHz); some VOMs are not accurate above 1 kHz, so be sure to check the meter's specifications.

There is also a difference between average and rms reading voltmeters. For the purpose of measuring pure sine waves, an average reading VOM is sufficient. Accurate measurement of the value of an audio signal, with complex waveforms, requires a true rms detector circuit. Such circuits tend to be expensive, so many VOMs cut corners and use a less complex averaging circuit. Depending on the frequency and waveform, the rms reading obtained with such meters on an audio signal can be inaccurate. For gross audio signal level measurements it may not make a difference to you, but for precise measurements you'll want to use a meter with a true rms detector.

The most common type of display used in VOMs is the meter movement, consisting of a galvanometer-driven needle superimposed over a scale from which readings are taken. In digital VOMs (also called DVMs – an abbreviation for digital voltmeters – not doctors of veterinary medicine), multiple-digit liquid crystal displays are most often used (older types of digital meters may have seven segment LED displays, which draw more power).

VOMs require two wires, called probes, for connection to the electrical points that are to be measured. VOM probes are normally color coded. The red probe is the + or positive connection, and the black is the − or negative. In some measurements, the polarity of connection is crucial to the measurement; in others, it does not matter.

Figure 16-1 shows the use of a VOM to measure continuity in a cable. This measurement uses the resistance-measuring (ohmmeter) circuit of the VOM. Note that polarity of the probe connections does not matter. If more than a few ohms resistance are measured here, the cable conductors may be too small for the length of cable, there may be a frayed conductor (with broken strands), or a bad solder joint at one of the connectors. On the other hand, continuity and resistance measurements rely upon a battery in the VOM to provide a test voltage. As the battery ages, the meter must be recalibrated. Make sure you first zero the meter by touching the meter probes directly to one another and adjusting the calibration knob on the meter (nearly all VOMs have one) until 0 ohms resistance is indicated. If a zero reading cannot be obtained, replace the battery in the VOM.

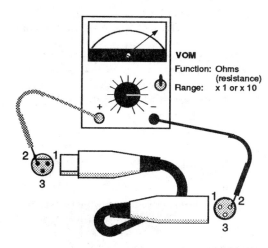

Figure 16-1. Continuity measurement with a VOM

Figure 16-2 shows the use of a VOM to measure a battery. This measurement uses the DC voltage-measuring circuit of the VOM. Polarity of the probe connection is important in this case.

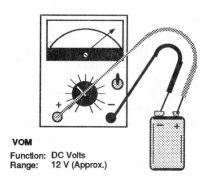

VOM
Function: DC Volts
Range: 12 V (Approx.)

Figure 16-2. DC voltage measurement with a VOM

Figure 16-3 shows the use of a VOM to check the line voltage. This test uses the AC voltage-measuring circuit of the VOM. Polarity of the probe connection is not important, but it is very important to (1) be sure that the range switch of the VOM is set correctly (to AC and a sufficiently high voltage range, and (2) be extremely careful with the handling of the probes, to avoid electrical shock and to avoid short circuiting the outlet by touching the probes together.

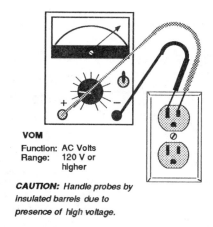

VOM
Function: AC Volts
Range: 120 V or higher

CAUTION: Handle probes by insulated barrels due to presence of high voltage.

Figure 16-3. AC voltage measurement with a VOM

16.2 The Sine Wave Oscillator

A sine wave oscillator is a signal-generator that produces a sine wave output. Both the frequency and the output level are usually adjustable.

For sound system measurements, it is best if the oscillator covers the full audio range from 20 Hz to 20 kHz. Actually, it's better to go beyond this range so that filter cutoff points or amplifier bandwidths can be accurately established. Some sine wave oscillators have output level controls that are calibrated in dBu (or dBm), and this feature can be very useful in audio work (although it is not essential). The distortion figure of the oscillator must be as low as possible.

Sine wave oscillators are used for a wide variety of sound system measurements that require a known signal source. Since the sine wave is the purest wave found in nature and has no harmonics, it is particularly useful for detecting distortion – which will show up as an obvious change in tone quality. The change in tone is caused by added harmonics, which are products of the distortion. Some examples of uses of the sine wave oscillator are given below.

Figure 16-4 shows use of the sine wave oscillator to test a driver. By sweeping the frequency of the oscillator and listening carefully, you can find mechanical defects (such as a loose suspension), most of which will cause a distinct buzzing sound. To test for coil rubbing in a midrange cone type driver, set the frequency of the oscillator to between 5 Hz and 10 Hz. Coil rubbing should show up as a scraping sound. An easier and just as effective technique is to gently press the cone in from the front, and push it out from behind (symmetrically) and to feel for any scraping (and listen for it, too).

In Figure 16-5 (next page), we replace the driver with a loudspeaker system. By sweeping the oscillator in this setup, you can detect not only driver defects, but also cabinet resonances, loose hardware, and other mechanical sources of distortion – all of which will tend to show up at low frequencies. You must be careful not to be confused by resonances in the room (loose ceiling tiles or wallboard, fluorescent light fixtures, and so on). If the test can be done outdoors such spurious sympathetic vibrations can be eliminated. On the other hand, it is sometimes beneficial to run the test in the actual listening environment so that the loose tiles, etc. can be found and dealt with.

Figure 16-6 illustrates use of the sine wave oscillator and an rms-reading voltmeter (or VOM) to check the operating level of a mixer or other component employing VU meters. The normal frequency to use for this test is 1 kHz.

The system levels are first set so that the meter reads 0 VU. This is best done by starting with a known output level from the oscillator (generally

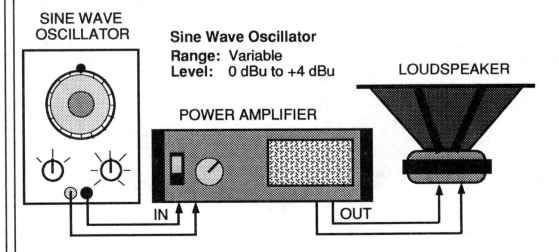

SINE WAVE OSCILLATOR

Sine Wave Oscillator
Range: Variable
Level: 0 dBu to +4 dBu

POWER AMPLIFIER

LOUDSPEAKER

IN   OUT

Figure 16-4. Driver testing with a sine wave oscillator and a power amplifier

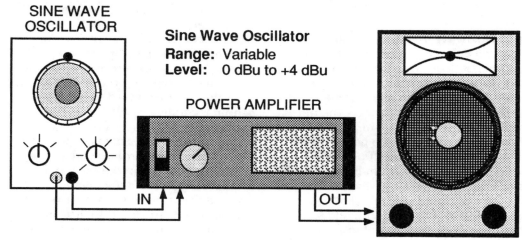

Sine Wave Oscillator
Range: Variable
Level: 0 dBu to +4 dBu

POWER AMPLIFIER

SINE WAVE OSCILLATOR

IN

OUT

Figure 16-5. Loudspeaker system testing with a sine wave oscillator and a power amplifier

0.775 volt rms for 0 dBu rated inputs, or 0.316 volt rms for −10 dBV rated inputs), and then adjusting the level control of the equipment under test.

When the sound equipment's output meter reads 0 VU, the reading on the voltmeter is the nominal operating level. If a dBu scale is not provided on the VOM, the equivalent value in dBu is readily calculated (see Section 8.6, "Operating Levels").

CAUTION: If the equipment has a transformer output, it probably should be terminated by a resistor equal to its rated load impedance (600 ohms, for example), and the speakers, if any, must be disconnected. Consult the equipment manual. With a 600 ohm termination, the dBu scale on the voltmeter will represent the output power in dBm.

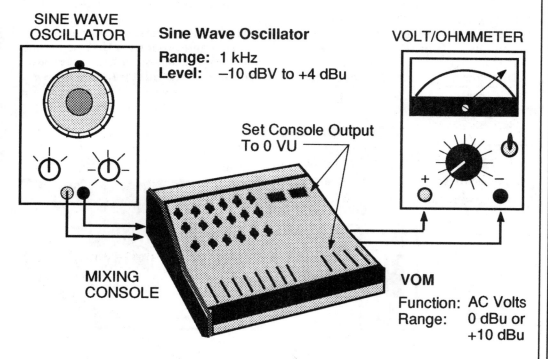

SINE WAVE OSCILLATOR

Sine Wave Oscillator
Range: 1 kHz
Level: −10 dBV to +4 dBu

VOLT/OHMMETER

Set Console Output To 0 VU

MIXING CONSOLE

VOM
Function: AC Volts
Range: 0 dBu or +10 dBu

Figure 16-6. Measuring nominal operating levels with a sine wave oscillator and a VOM

A related test is shown in Figure 16–7. Here we use the sine wave oscillator and rms-reading voltmeter to test the maximum available gain of a signal processor. First, we set the oscillator output to a predetermined level (say, 0.775 volt rms to test a line input). With all level controls on the equipment set at 10 (or fully clockwise), we measure the output level of the equipment. The ratio of the output level to the input level, expressed in dB, is the gain of the device.

NOTE: *The test signal level should not be high enough to overdrive the input of the equipment. If, for example, a microphone input is used, then a mic-level signal should be used for the test; using a line level input here would not yield valid results.*

Sine Wave Oscillator	VOM
Range: AC Volts **Level:** As required	**Function:** 1 kHz **Range:** −10 dBV to +4 dBu *(Note: Connect + terminal to singal + or Hot side of audio line, and − terminal to signal − or audio common or ground.*

SINE WAVE
OSCILLATOR

VOLT/OHMMETER

SIGNAL PROCESSOR

Figure 16-7. Measuring signal processor gain with a sine wave oscillator and a VOM

The oscilloscope displays a visual representation of an electrical signal. The signal is traced on the face of a phosphor coated screen (a CRT or cathode ray tube) by an electron beam, appearing as a line of light on the screen.

The oscilloscope displays a signal as a function of time by sweeping the beam horizontally from left to right across the screen. When the beam reaches the right edge of the screen, it jumps back to the left edge and begins its transit across the screen again. The speed of the sweep determines the time interval that is represented by the width of the screen. The faster the sweep, the shorter the interval.

As in the case of the VOM, the oscilloscope is connected to the circuit points under test using a probe. An oscilloscope probe normally provides connections for both ground (or the reference point) and the signal to be displayed. Figure 16-7 shows a typical oscilloscope and its probe. Sometimes special probes are used for extended range measurements (i.e., greater sensitivity or very high frequencies).

The signal to be displayed is connected so that its instantaneous voltage deflects the beam in the vertical axis around a center line. Points above the line represent a positive signal voltage, and those below the line represent a negative voltage (referred to ground). For example, Figure 16-9 (next page) shows a typical oscilloscope trace of the output of a sine wave generator.

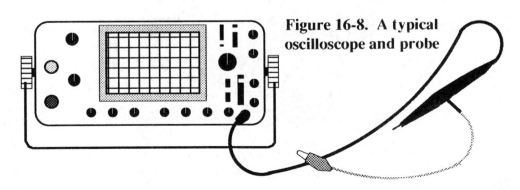

Figure 16-8. A typical oscilloscope and probe

:

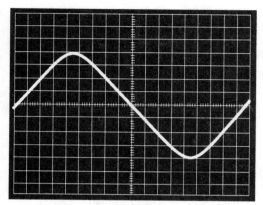

Figure 16-9. Oscilloscope display of a sine wave

An oscilloscope can function as a form of voltmeter if its vertical sensitivity is calibrated. For example, look at the display of Figure 16-9. Note that the total vertical deflection of the sine wave is eight divisions of the graticule grid (four above and four below the center line). If the vertical sensitivity of the oscilloscope is set at 0.25 volts per division, then the sine wave amplitude is 2 volts peak-to-peak. To obtain the RMS value, divide by two times the square root of two; the result is 0.707 volts rms.

If we have an rms-reading voltmeter we can obtain this reading directly, without calculation. Measuring signal levels is a relatively trivial use of the oscilloscope. An oscilloscope tells us much more about a signal than a VOM, and is normally used together with the VOM and other test equipment to get a full picture of the behavior of a circuit.

For example, Figure 16-10 illustrates use of an oscilloscope, a sine wave oscillator, and an rms-reading voltmeter to check the maximum output level of a signal processor.

With the processor level controls (if any) set to maximum, the oscillator output level is adjusted until the sine wave on the oscilloscope appears to just be clipped. Backing off the oscillator level to just below clipping, we read the maximum signal level in rms volts on the voltmeter.

NOTE: The VOM and oscilloscope will normally have very high input impedances. This test should be done with a load termination across the signal processor that is equivalent to a practical real world load if the processor is normally terminated. Otherwise the measured clipping point may be higher than it would be under actual operating conditions.

If the signal processor in Figure 16-10 is a power amplifier, we can use this test to determine its maximum power capability into 8 ohms by loading the output with a high power, non-inductive 8 ohm resistor and repeating the test. The power output is the reading of the voltmeter squared, divided by the resistance value. If we read 45 volts RMS, for example:

$$
\begin{aligned}
P &= 45^2 \div 8 \\
&= 2025 \div 8 \\
&\approx 250 \text{ watts}
\end{aligned}
$$

We can use the oscilloscope wherever we wish to be sure of the presence of a signal and the integrity of that signal. (It becomes clear, for example, what portion of the measured signal is program, and what portion is residual hum and noise.)

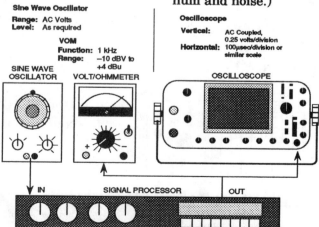

Figure 16-10. Measurement of maximum output level

16.4 The Phase Tester

Phase testers are used to determine the polarity of a circuit. Phase testers work by emitting an electrical pulse of known polarity (usually positive-going) which is connected to pass through the circuit under test. The output of the circuit is connected back to the measurement input of the phase tester, which compares that signal against the pulse that the phase tester is emitting.

Often phase testers give readings using two lights labeled + and − or similar nomenclature. If the pulse coming into the measurement input is in phase with the emitted pulse, the + light will flash; if it is out of phase, the − light flashes.

Figure 16-11 illustrates use of a phase tester to check the throughput polarity of a signal processor.

Phase testers are also sometimes used to check the wiring of loudspeakers to make sure they are in phase with one another. In this case, a microphone is used to capture the loudspeaker output, as shown in Figure 16–12.

Some cautions are in order regarding the use of phase testers. They are relatively sensitive devices, and will give spurious readings under a variety of circumstances. It is important when using a phase tester that you be aware of the following quirks, in order to guard against incorrect readings:

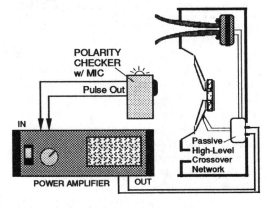

Figure 16-12. Checking the polarity of a loudspeaker

1) Some phase testers are highly level-sensitive: if the input level at the measurement input does not fall within a specific range, the readings may be unstable or inconsistent.

2) Devices exhibiting a nonlinear phase characteristic, limited frequency response, or a substantial amount of pure delay will confuse phase testers, resulting in inconsistent readings.

3) In testing groups of speakers, each speaker must be tested independently, with the others turned off. If one speaker in a group of four is out of phase, and is tested while the others are also reproducing the test pulse, the acoustic signal from the other speakers will swamp that of the out of phase unit, making it appear to be in phase. This effect is most noticeable at low frequencies, where you may not need a phase checker anyway because your ears usually hear the problem.

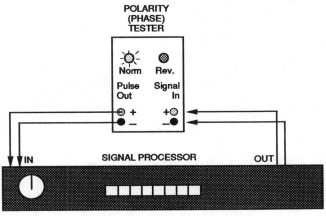

Figure 16-11. Checking the polarity of a signal processor

16.5 The Sound Pressure Level Meter

The SPL meter is a fairly simple instrument consisting of a calibrated microphone, amplifying circuitry, and a meter movement. SPL meters employ both switchable ranges and selectable weighting curves. As its name implies, the SPL meter is used for measuring sound pressure levels in dB.

Four standard weighting curves are used in SPL meters, as shown in Figure 16-13. The function of these curves is to shape the sensitivity of the meter at different frequencies.

The most reliable readings are normally obtained by holding the SPL meter at right angles to the sound source, as far away from the body as possible. Outdoors, the microphone should be pointed upwards. If the microphone is detachable, it may be placed on a stand and aimed directly at the signal source or, outdoors, aimed upwards. These methods are used to minimize the effect of reflections from boundary surfaces and from the body of the observer.

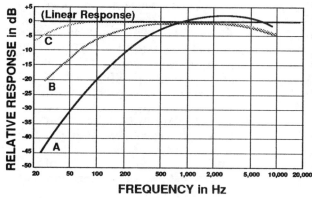

Figure 16-13. Frequency response curves corresponding to sound pressure level meter weighting characteristics

Of the four weighting curves, the two that are most useful in sound reinforcement are the linear (or flat) curve, and the A weighting curve. Inexpensive SPL meters may not give a linear curve, substituting instead the C weighting curve.

Note that the A weighting curve rolls off drastically in the low frequencies. This curve is used to give an approximation of the actual response of the human ear, as determined by Fletcher and Munson. SPL measured using A weighting is given in dB(A) (or dBA). Likewise, linear weighted measurements are given in dB(lin).

Most SPL meters offer both fast and slow response, switch-selected. Slow response is achieved by damping the meter movement to give an indication of the average sound pressure level. Fast response is used to obtain an indication of the peak SPL. More expensive SPL meters may also provide a peak hold function, whereby the meter will hold and continuously display the maximum peak reading that it obtains during the measurement. Peak hold mode makes the reading and recording of peak SPL much easier.

It is important to use an appropriate weighting curve. Often the A curve is used, for example, when measuring the road noise in an automobile, that rolls off a lot of the low-frequency rumble and vibration, making some cars that are noisy at low frequencies appear to be quieter. The A curve is not appropriate for measuring sound levels in the 100 dB SPL range at a concert. The Fletcher-Munson and similar equal loudness curves indicate the ear is more linear at high sound levels, so the C or linear scales would be more appropriate here, though many people incorrectly use the A scale for high level sound measurement. A weighting is more appropriate for low level sounds, where the curve approximates the insensitivity of the human ear to low frequencies at low levels.

16.6 THE REAL-TIME ANALYZER

The real-time analyzer (or RTA) may be the most elaborate and sophisticated piece of equipment in the sound man's tool kit. It is used to obtain an instantaneous display of the frequency response of a sound system or signal processor.

The RTA is basically a form of spectrum analyzer, optimized for audio use. It consists of a specified signal source, a calibrated microphone and preamplifier, signal amplifying and filtering circuitry, and a display. The most common type of display used in RTAs is an array of LEDs, although small, built-in CRT (oscilloscope-like) displays or a video output to a monitor are also found. The signal source normally used is a pink noise generator, although most RTAs will also respond to program material.

A simplified block diagram of an RTA is shown in Figure 16-14. The pink noise source is used to excite the system under test at all audio frequen-

cies, with equal amplitude per octave. The output of the system is filtered in bands, usually one-third octave wide, and the signal amplitude in each band is determined electronically. The display is arranged to indicate the amount of energy in each band, as detected at the output of each filter.

When used to evaluate a sound system, with a calibrated test microphone, the RTA is treated in much the same way as the SPL meter, and the same microphone-handling procedures apply to it. It may be used to measure the frequency response of sound systems at any point in a room or, outdoors, to determine the dispersion characteristics of a system. The RTA typically has a line-level input as well, and may be used to measure the characteristics of an individual signal processor or an entire chain through the preamp, mixer, signal processor and power amp (with appropriate padding after the power amp output).

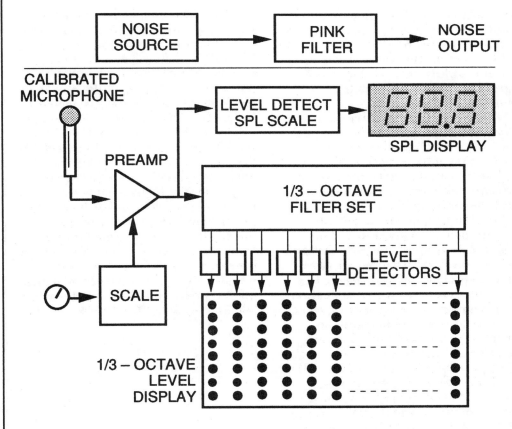

Figure 16-14. Simplified block diagram of a real time analyzer, as used for sound system tests

16.7 The Loudness Monitor

The classical VU meter, devised some 50 years ago, is a quasi-average reading device that almost completely fails to respond to brief peaks. It was never intended to provide acoustical comparisons between processed and unprocessed program material. About ten years after it was developed, a standard emerged for the Peak Program Meter (PPM). It displays and holds only the peak level of the waveforms, giving no indication of the average level. In an attempt to provide both peak and average (VU) information to the engineer, some meters have been made that include a peak-responding LED that turns on when the peak level reaches or exceeds a certain threshold, usually from 3 dB to 10 dB below the maximum output level capability of the circuit. The difficulty here is that one never really knows how much headroom exists until the peak LED turns on, and, at that point, the average level may be too high. It is all but impossible to evaluate the results of compression using such meters.

In response to the need for a meter which shows both rms (average) and peak level, Dorrough Electronics of Woodland Hills, California developed a special loudness monitor. This device vaguely resembles a VU meter, except the scale is comprised of numerous LED segments. Special driver circuitry activates a continuous bar of the LEDs to show the rms level, and another single LED to show the peak level. Peak sensitivity is even faster than a standard PPM. This meter thus provides a continuous readout of peak and average levels, and one can visually see the difference (the distance on the scale) between the two, which constitutes a direct readout of the crest factor of the program. You may begin to see more such meters as engineers realize the value of accurate monitoring of both the average and peak levels.

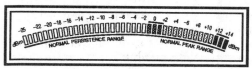

Figure 16-15. The Dorrough loudness monitor

16.8 Summary

We have presented here the basic attributes and uses of standard test equipment for sound reinforcement use. To employ such test equipment effectively and obtain reliable results requires far more knowledge than we can convey here. It is important that those wishing to make sound system measurements study carefully the manuals provided with the equipment they wish to use.

No individual piece of test equipment yields accurate results under all circumstances. Often the source and load impedances used for measurements have a significant impact on levels, noise and distortion measurements. For example, measuring the clipping level of an unterminated graphic equalizer by connecting it to the 100 kohm input of an oscilloscope may yield an apparent error of as much as 6 dB or more compared to the results if a 600 ohm or 1200 ohm terminating resistor (assuming such a termination were specified for the device) were shunted across the EQ's output. The frequency or frequencies at which measurements are made can have a major impact on the measured result. Using a simple VOM that is accurate for 120 volt RMS, 60 Hz power mains voltage measurements may yield wildly inaccurate results when measuring 10 kHz audio signals at 1 volt levels. Even the temperature can be a significant factor, particularly when equipment is used in extremely hot or cold environments. One must know the tolerances of the test equipment. Specifying the total harmonic distortion at 0.001% is meaningless when the distortion analyzer has a noise floor that limits meaningful readings to 0.005% THD. And when measuring noise, the bandwidth of the test equipment is significant. Usually some sort of filter or corrective equation must be applied or else one will end up with a measurement that includes thermal noise well beyond the meaningful audio spectrum. These are but a few of the factors to be considered when testing sound equipment.

Section 17 presents guidelines for selecting, connecting, and troubleshooting the electronic components of sound reinforcement and reproduction systems. Corresponding information covering loudspeaker components is found in Section 18.

The electronics might be termed the nerve center of a sound system. Here, audio signals are routed, processed, and mixed to produce sonic events that are reproduced by the loudspeakers. The controls and indicators of the electronic components are the sound engineer's primary tools. A high-quality electronic system — properly connected and operated — is crucial to superior sound.

The task of specifying and connecting audio equipment involves many interrelated concerns, all of which can decisively affect the system's performance. The key to success in this endeavor is a thorough working knowledge of basic audio electronics, coupled with respect for the practical needs of system operators.

17.1. BASIC SOUND SYSTEM TYPES

Most sound systems fall into one of two basic functional classes: sound reinforcement and sound reproduction. While some applications involve both functions, we will deal with each separately for the sake of clarity — just keep in mind that every application is unique. Combining basic principles in creative ways to solve individual problems is the essence of professional sound.

17.1.1. Sound Reproduction Systems

In sound reproduction, the function of the sound system is to reproduce recorded input signals in accordance with a particular standard of performance. Examples of such applications are night club sound, corporate multimedia shows and location playback in film or video production.

Since the program material will have been recorded and mixed in a studio, any manipulation of the signal is usually confined to level control, basic equalization, and perhaps mixing of multiple sources. These operations may be handled by a small console which need not be functionally complex. The unit should be of high quality since signal distortion and noise are far more objectionable than in live sound — particularly if the audience is familiar with the recorded material (i.e, if a recording doesn't sound as good on the dance floor as it does on their home audio systems, they'll be disappointed.)

Audio performance also must be considered when selecting the playback source equipment, of course, but it is not the only factor. Transport controls should be well suited to the needs and preferences of the system operator, particularly if quick changeovers and/ or tricky musical synchronizations are required. In portable applications such as location playback, ruggedness and reliability are paramount considerations. Finally, corporate multimedia applications often require the ability to synchronize sound playback with image projection (in large multimedia shows, the control and synchronization system may be much more complex than the audio signal handling path).

In sound reproduction, signal processors generally serve not so much to create sonic events as to satisfy the playback standards of the application, be they technical or subjective. For example, master system equalizers are normally employed to tune the loudspeakers for optimum performance in the immediate environment. In some cases, a specified frequency response characteristic may also be imposed on the system. An example of such a house curve is the SMPTE standard for film sound reproduction. Noise gates or other methods of noise reduction may be used to enhance the apparent quality of recordings. On the subjective side, dance club systems sometimes include electronic boom boxes or other types of low frequency enhancement devices.

As the term implies, sound reinforcement is the amplification of a live sound source in order to reach a large audience. Reinforcement applications vary in complexity, from relatively simple paging or conferencing to large-scale music performance.

In paging and announcing, the overriding concern is intelligibility. Voice reinforcement systems are thus electronically very simple, consisting of one or more microphones, preamplification (with mixing, if required) and power amplification. Signal processing is generally confined to loudspeaker equalization, compression and/or gating, all of which can significantly enhance intelligibility. On occasion, filters may be used to curtail low-frequency response in order to compensate for the proximity effect associated with closely placed cardioid mics.

Music reinforcement is another matter entirely. As the technology of concert sound has continually advanced, so have the demands of artists and audiences. The goal of concert sound today is not merely to equal, but to surpass, the impact of studio recordings. As a result, contemporary large-scale concert sound systems attain a complexity unequalled in any other area of professional audio, and the mix engineer is a crucial participant in the creation of the musical event.

A typical music reinforcement system is actually two separate but interdependent electronic systems: the main sound reinforcement system, which delivers sound to the audience, and the stage monitor system, which serves the needs of the onstage performers. In smaller scale applications such as live music clubs, the two may be combined under the control of the house mix engineer. In large concert reinforcement systems they are handled by highly complex individual systems — each controlled by a separate team of engineers — and signals from on-stage microphones and instruments are split to feed both systems.

The main sound reinforcement electronics receive each signal from the stage individually, adding effects as necessary and providing a master mix to feed the house speaker system. The mix is most often mono. On occasion, the sound reinforcement system may be operated in stereo or, more rarely, in three channels (left, right and center). While the output feed is apparently simple, the signal processing at the console may be prodigious, involving numerous submaster busses with outboard effects inserted at several points in the chain. Main sound reinforcement consoles are therefore usually equal in complexity to multi-track recording consoles, and the range of outboard signal processing equipment can exceed that of many studios.

The stage monitor electronics handle the same signals quite differently. Here, the goal is to satisfy the varying requirements of each individual musician, so monitor consoles are designed to provide a large number of separate mixes. While the output feed in this case is far more complicated, the signal processing in each output branch is relatively simple. Individual microphone-loudspeaker combinations must be equalized independently to suppress feedback and maximize acoustic gain. Narrow-band graphic or parametric equalizers serve this function. Limiters or compressors may also be employed to help the monitors compete in the high sound pressure environment of the stage and hold down the level of any feedback that occurs. Beyond this little else is needed, since excess effects only serve to muddy the onstage sound.

17.2. Developing A Logical System Architecture

Every sound system – no matter how simple it may appear – must be the subject of careful planning. The first step in the process is to analyze the intended application for the system, covering both technical and budgetary concerns. From this information, we can determine the functions that will be required, and develop a practical list of equipment.

A successful sound system is more than just a collection of equipment. The individual devices must be connected to function as component parts of a single whole: a system with a logical structure that is optimized to do a job. One could easily argue that an understanding of the importance of logical architecture – the sequence in which devices must be connected and the structure in which they operate – is fundamental to the practice of professional sound.

17.2.1. Functional Grouping

In Section 1.3 , we developed a simplified conceptual model of a sound system (described in Figure 1-6, and repeated below). In that model the system is reduced to three blocks: input, signal processing, and output. When we apply that model to analyzing a practical system, each of these blocks signifies a functional group of components.

The Input Group comprises input transducers and associated interface components such as transformers, pads, external preamplifiers or other in-line signal processors that contribute to a particular input signal.

The Signal Processing and Routing Group is the heart of the electronics system. It encompasses all line-level components that perform centralized control and processing of audio signals in the system.

The Output Group comprises output transducers (usually the loudspeaker system), power amplification and all associated alignment circuitry.

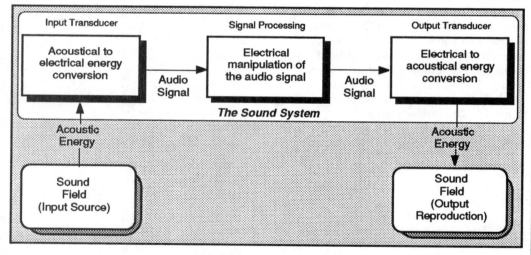

(Figure 1-5 repeated) Conceptual model of a sound system

17.2.2. System Examples

To clarify how these functional classifications are applied to analyzing and planning a system, let's examine some typical sound systems.

Figure 17-1 shows a simple stereo sound reproduction system. The input group consists of: (1) a turntable with moving-coil cartridge, transformer for the cartridge and RIAA preamplification stage; (2) a stereo cassette machine; and (3) a Compact disc player.

The signal processing and routing group consists of a compact mixing console that selects, processes and/or mixes line-level signals from the three input sources.

The output group comprises a stereo graphic equalizer for loudspeaker equalization, a stereo power amplifier, and a pair of full range loudspeakers.

A medium-scale sound reinforcement system, such as might be found in a live music club, is shown on the next page in Figure 17-2.

The input group consists of vocal microphones, drum microphones, and direct inputs from a number of musical instruments. Notice that onstage signal processors which are dedicated to particular instruments are included in the input group, rather than being classified with signal processing and routing.

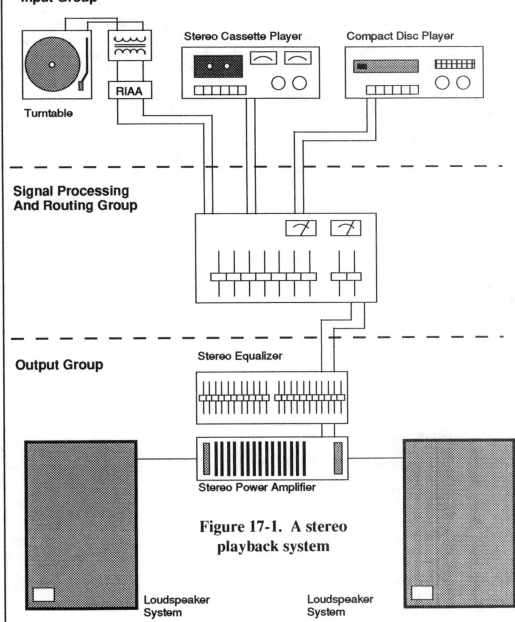

Figure 17-1. A stereo playback system

The house console is central to the signal processing and routing group. A number of outboard signal processors are available for insertion at various points in the signal path, and are to be used for creative enhancement of musical signals from the stage. Since the hypothetical club environment in our example is acoustically dead (particularly with a full house), a master reverberator is provided.

The onstage monitor feed is taken from the house console, so two separate output groups are shown. The main house group, a mono feed, includes master system equalizers, active crossovers, power amplifiers and the house loudspeaker system. The onstage monitor group is a multiple output feed taken from either the house console monitor matrix outputs or from pre-fader auxilliary sends. (For clarity, only a single monitor feed signal path is shown; normally, four to six such feeds would be used in a system of this size.) Pre-fader sends are preferred in order to keep the monitor mix fully independent of the house mix. Each individual branch includes an equalizer for feedback suppression, a limiter, a power amplifier and loudspeaker.

Figure 17-3 (a–c) on pages 320 through 322) shows a full-scale concert sound reinforcement system. A generic listing of typical signal processors and their typical uses in concert reinforcement is shown in Figure 17-3 (d) on page 1-11.

The input group in Figure 17-3 (a) includes a multiple-circuit splitter box that provides separate isolated signal feeds for the house and monitor systems. Notice the audio cassette machine and compact disc player, both local to the house console, which provide recorded music playback at the beginning and end of the show (and a source of sound for preliminary system setup, as well).

The house signal processing and routing group in Figure 17-3 (b) is an expanded version of that shown in the preceding figure.

The order of connections in the output group shown in Figure 17-3 (c) bears detailed study. The house sound reinforcement is assumed to comprise three arrays— Left, Center, and Right— each with associated downfill loudspeakers to cover seating areas that lie outside of the coverage pattern of the array. The Center array is designated as the master system.

A monophonic feed from the house console is routed to an equalization stage which provides correction for the entire main sound reinforcement system. The output of this stage is split. One branch feeds the active crossover package and power amplifiers of the Center array and subwoofers. The other branch feeds separate individual equalizers for the Center downfill and the Left and Right array branches. Each individual array branch incorporates separate equalizer stages that are similarly connected.

This nested connection scheme reflects the logical acoustical hierarchy of the individual loudspeaker components. During setup, the arrays will be tested and equalized in the order implied by this architecture, as follows:

1) The Center main array is tested and equalized alone;

2) The Center downfill loudspeakers are added and equalized to fit into the main array response;

3) The Left and Right main arrays are tested and trimmed using their respective equalizers;

4) The Left and Right downfill systems are added and equalized to fit into the response of their respective main arrays.

A typical companion stage monitor system is analyzed separately in Figure 17-4 on page 323.

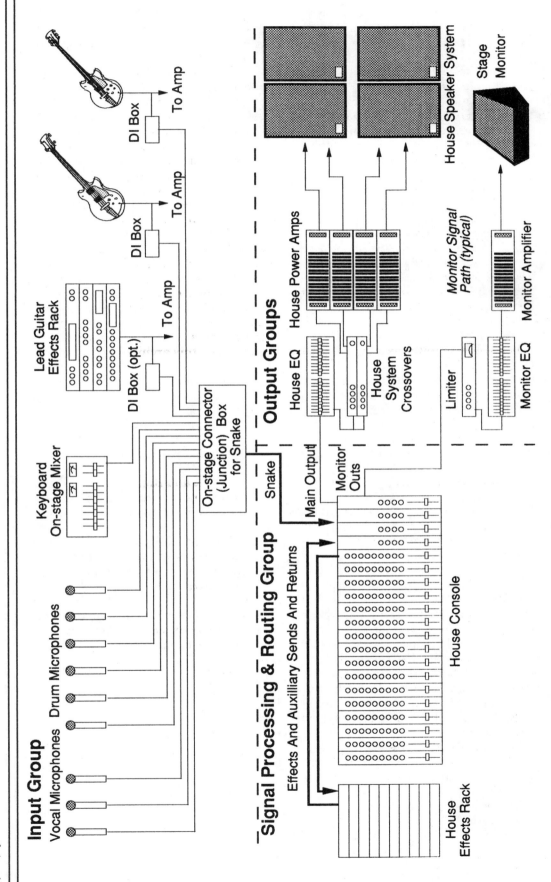

Figure 17-2. A club sound reinforcement system

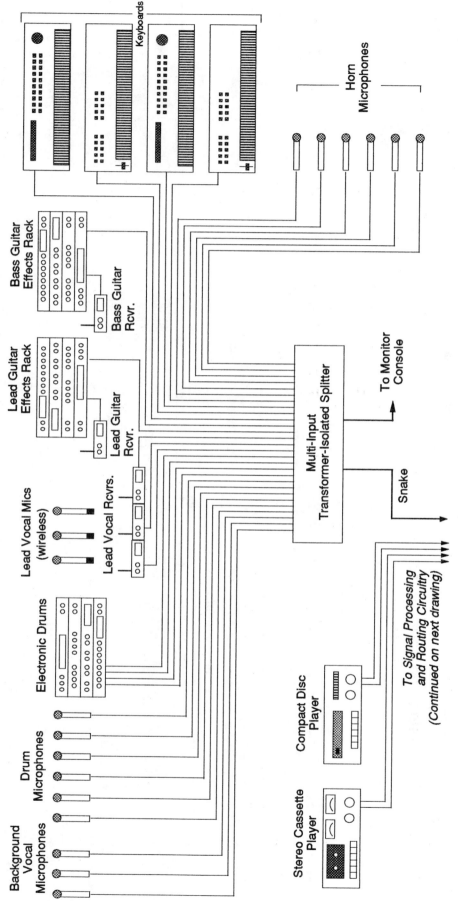

**Figure 17-3. A typical concert sound reinforcement system:
A. Input sources (illustration continued on next page)**

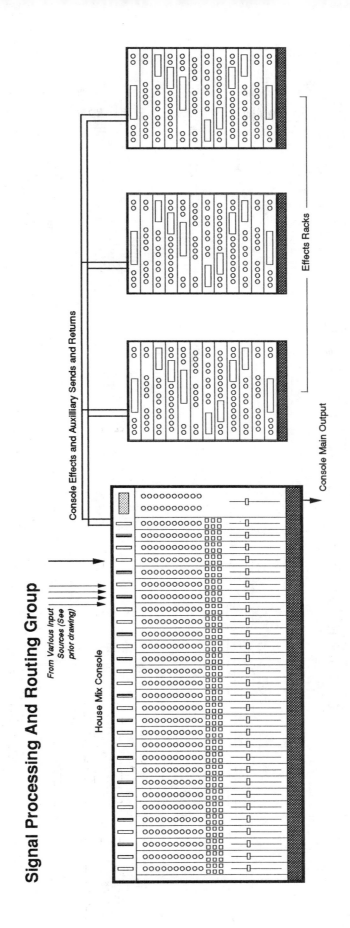

Figure 17-3. A typical concert sound reinforcement system:
B. Signal processing (illustration continued from prior page)

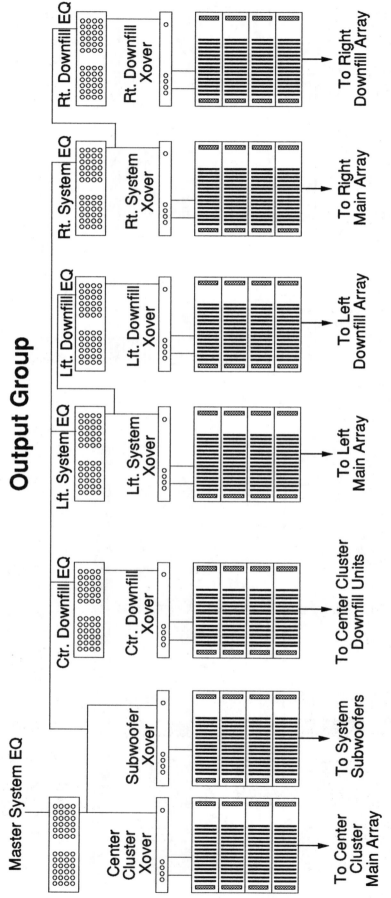

**Figure 17-3. A typical concert sound reinforcement system:
C. Output group (illustration continued from prior page)**

Instrument	Signal Processing
Snare top microphone	Noise gate - Equalizer - Limiter
Snare bottom microphone	Noise gate - Equalizer - Limiter
Hi-hat microphone	*
Rack tom left microphone	Noise gate
Rack tom right microphone	Noise gate
Floor tom microphone	Noise gate
Left overhead	Compression
Right overhead	Compression
Electronic drum snare DI	*
Electronic drum kick DI	Equalizer
Electronic drums left mix out	Equalizer
Electronic drums right mix out	Equalizer
Electric guitar left microphone	Noise gate
Electric guitar right microphone	Noise gate
Bass synth DI	Equalizer - Limiter
Synthesizer DIs	Limiter
Lead vocal microphone	Equalizer - Limiter
	Exciter
Background vocal microphones	Limiter

* No external processing

Figure 17-3. A typical concert sound reinforcement system:
D. Common applications for signal processors

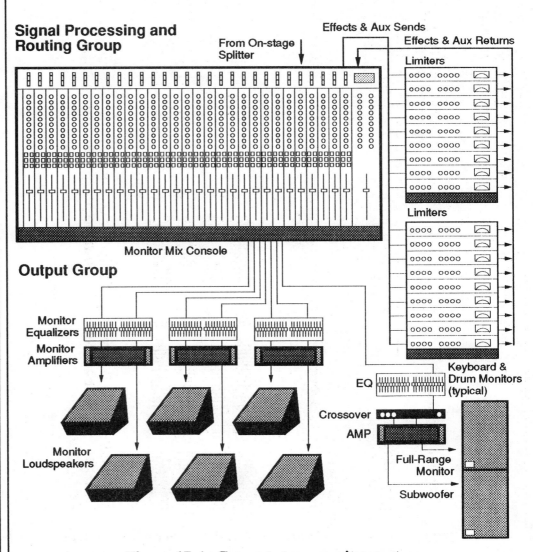

Figure 17-4. Concert stage monitor system

Figure 17-4 (prior page) depicts a typical, separate onstage monitor system that might accompany the main sound reinforcement system of Figure 17-3. This system shares the input group shown in Figure 17-3 (a).

The signal processing and routing group here centers on a console specifically constructed for stage monitor mixing. Note the large number of separate output feeds. Outboard processing is confined to limiters, which provide a degree of compression for vocals and hold down the level of any feedback that might occur.

The output group branches are also quite simple, comprising equalizers for feedback suppression, power amplifiers, and monitor loudspeakers.

17.3. BASIC CONNECTIONS

Despite the fact that audio signal connection practices are reasonably (though not totally) standardized, improper interfacing among components remains one of the most common sources of problems in professional sound. Half of the solution for interfacing problems is to select components that are compatible electrically. The other half is to connect them properly and consistently.

17.3.1. Signal Levels and Impedance

Section 8.7 provides a detailed description of nominal operating levels as they apply to audio equipment. As related there, the standard line level for professional audio equipment is +4 dBu. Simply adhering to this standard when selecting equipment helps to avoid many common interfacing problems. On the other hand, the quality and utility of some contemporary -10 dBV equipment makes strict adherence to the +4 dBu standard less attractive than it once was, especially since -10 dBV equipment (sometimes called semi-pro) is usually less expensive than comparable +4 dBu (pro) gear.

There are solutions to this dilemma. Recognizing the market's desire to have the option to use -10dBV equipment at some places in the signal chain (playback equipment and outboard signal processors are two notable examples), some audio manufacturers supply both +4 dBu and -10 dBV connection points on their equipment. (This is most often true of console manufacturers.) Alternatively, a few companies now offer active interface boxes that convert between the two standards. Use of such interfaces is highly recommended, since they offer a simple, quick and cost effective fix for level (and impedance) matching problems.

Many audio professionals understand the concept of impedance less well than they do signal level, and impedance mismatch is often blamed for problems that have nothing to do with impedance. The confusion stems in part from practices originated in the days of tube equipment, when trans-former interfacing was much more common — if not mandatory — than it is today. (See Section 8.6 for a discussion of input and output impedances.)

Practically speaking, problems at line level are rarely attributable to impedance differences these days. Since modern audio equipment almost invariably features reasonably high input impedances (10k ohms or greater) and low output source impedances (usually 100 ohms or less), line level connections now involve very little power transfer — generally, in the milliwatt-to-microwatt range. Moreover, active transformerless output stages — now the most common type — are not very susceptible to varying load impedance (within practical limits, of course).

This does not mean that impedance can be disregarded. In the majority of sound systems, impedance-related problems are most likely to appear in the input and output groups of components. At both ends, transducers are used and questions of power transfer come into play.

For example, input transducers (microphones, guitar pickups, phonograph cartridges and so on) generally are not capable of sourcing much power at all, and thus require relatively high load impedances. Since their electrical characteristics may also feature significant reactive components (coils or condensers), not only their output level but also their frequency response will be affected by the load they see.

While early microphones (especially ribbon types) incorporated transformers that required specific termination, modern microphones generally present a source impedance of about 150 ohms, and are perfectly happy when connected to a load of 3k ohms or greater. On the other hand, electric guitar pickups are highly load sensitive and significantly reactive, requiring a preamplifier input impedance in the neighborhood of 500k to 1M (1,000,000) ohms. Typical moving magnet phonograph cartridges generally like a load impedance of about 47k ohms; moving-coil cartridges require a much higher input impedance (and their output level is much lower, necessitating a matching step-up transformer or preamp).

It is in the output group that actual impedance calculations are most commonly necessary. The net load impedance presented by a loudspeaker system affects both the size of wire needed for connections to the amplifier output and the amount of power drawn from the amplifier (see Section 12.5 and Section 18.4). Moreover, the design of passive crossovers, though it is not a routine function in day-to-day audio work, must take into account the impedances of the individual drivers.

Finally, wherever transformers are used to solve interfacing problems – and they may be used in the input group, the output group or both – the source and load impedances that they see must be considered. For proper operation, most audio transformers require specific termination (see Section 17.5, following).

Unbalanced connections (sometimes called single-ended) employ two conductors, one at ground potential and the other carrying signal. Unbalanced connections may be transformer-coupled, but the norm is direct coupling. Equipment operating at –10 dBV invariably uses unbalanced connections.

Balanced connections employ two conductors, each of which carries the same signal potential but with the polarity of one reversed with respect to the other. Balanced connections may or may not be referred to ground; if not, they are termed floating connections. A balanced connection referred to ground requires three conductors, the third being at ground potential. (A floating connection may have a third, ground conductor but it is used as a shield and not connected in a way that references the circuit to ground.)

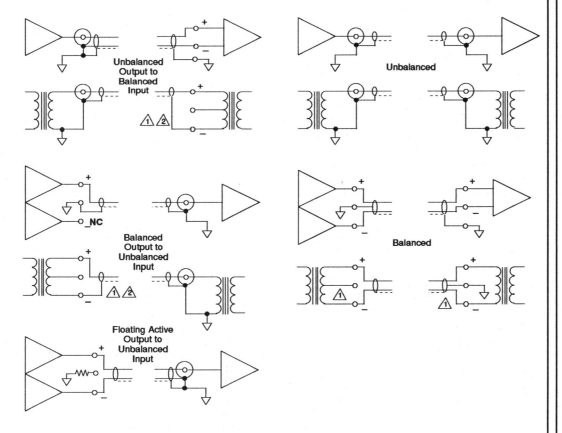

Notes:
1. Do not ground center taps (except in some rare instances).
2. Ground only at the unbalanced end of the cable.

Figure 17-5. Unbalanced and balanced connections

Balanced inputs and outputs are sometimes implemented using a transformer, which may or may not have a center tap. If it does the center tap should usually not be grounded. More often than not, modern professional equipment uses direct coupling. Direct coupled balanced inputs are sometimes called differential inputs. One of the short comings of differential circuits is that they may not be floating, so transformers sometimes must be inserted to break ground loops.

Balanced connections are preferred over unbalanced because they are far less susceptible to pickup of interference. Professional +4 dBu equipment usually (but not always) features balanced inputs and outputs.

Figure 17-5 illustrates the basic recommended practices for handling standard unbalanced and balanced connections in various combinations. Note in particular the method for unbalanced connection of electronically balanced (active) outputs versus transformer-coupled balanced outputs.

The nature of the active output determines the type of cabling that may be used when that balanced output is connected to an unbalanced input. Usually a dual-conductor shielded cable should be employed, allowing the cable to remain more or less balanced right up to the input of the unbalanced device. This actually helps cancel noise because the shield drains noise to the earth ground and is not relied upon to carry the signal. The shield's finite resistance means that grounding the shield and the low side of the cable at the input to the unbalanced device is not the functional equivalent of doing so at the output of the balanced device.

NOTE: The term push-pull has been used to describe a balanced output, but is more correctly reserved for describing the output of power amplifiers, not line-level driver circuits.

Ground is the electrical reference against which potentials (voltages) are expressed. In a practical audio system, a number of different independent references exist in various local subsystems. These may or may not be at the same electrical potential. If handled properly, they certainly need not be at the same potential.

For purposes of clarity in discussing audio connection practices, we will distinguish among three specific ground references:

- **Signal Ground** — the reference point against which signal potentials in a specific piece of equipment or group of components are expressed.

- **Earth Ground** — the local electrical potential of the earth. In practice, earth is the potential of the central, rounded terminal in a U.S. standard three-prong 120-volt outlet. Earth is sometimes obtained from a metal cold water pipe (though this practice has been criticized recently as unreliable due to increasing use of non-conductive ABS plastic pipe sections), or from a chemical earthing rod sunk into the moistened ground.

- **Chassis Ground** — the chassis connection point of a specific component. In equipment fitted with a three prong AC plug, the chassis is normally connected to earth, with provision to connect signal ground to earth as well. Equipment having a two prong AC plug will normally have the chassis connected to signal ground.

As we will see, connections among these various reference points are an all-important factor in assembling a successful audio system.

Grounding has been an area of black magic for many sound technicians and engineers, and certainly for most casual users of sound systems. Everyone knows that grounding has something to do with safety, and something to do with hum and noise suppression, but few people know how to set up a proper AC power distribution system, and how to connect audio equipment grounds so that noise is minimized. This subsection of the manual won't make anyone an expert, but it does point out a few of the principles and precautions with which everyone should be familiar. Whether you read this material or not, before you start cutting shields and lifting grounds, read the warning on the following page.

WARNING: In any audio system installation, governmental and insurance underwriters' electrical codes must be observed. These codes are based on safety, and may vary in different localities; in all cases, local codes take precedence over any suggestions contained in this handbook. Yamaha shall not be liable for incidental or consequential damages, including injury to any persons or property, resulting from improper, unsafe or illegal installation of any related equipment. (IN PLAIN WORDS... IF YOU LIFT A GROUND, THE RESULTING POTENTIAL FOR ELECTRICAL SHOCK IS YOUR OWN RESPONSIBILITY!)

Never trust any potentially hazardous system, such as an AC power system of any type, just because someone else tells you that it's okay. People can get killed by faulty or improperly wired sound equipment, so be sure you check things out yourself.

17.4.1. Why Is Proper Grounding Important?

In practical operating environments, any signal conductor is susceptible to induced currents from several types of sources such as radio frequency (RF) emissions, AC power lines, switching devices, motors and the like. This is why audio signal cables are invariably shielded. The function of the shield is to intercept undesirable emissions. A major goal of grounding technique is to keep unwanted signal currents that are induced in the shield away from the signal conductor(s), and drain them to ground as directly as possible.

Beyond minimizing noise and hum, an equally important consideration in grounding is safety. The connection between a chassis and earth is commonly referred to as a safety ground — and with good reason. Consider the possibility that a chassis might become connected to the hot leg of the AC mains (120 volts RMS AC) due to faulty wiring, an inadvertent short or moisture condensation. Suddenly, that innocuous looking box could be transformed into what engineers gruesomely call a widow maker. Someone who is touching a grounded guitar, mic stand, or other equipment will complete the circuit when touching the now electrically charged chassis, and receive the full brunt of whatever power is available. If the chassis is connected to earth, it will simply blow a fuse or circuit breaker.

Dangerous potential differences can also occur without such shorts. Two individual localized ground points, if they are not directly connected, cannot be assumed to be at the same potential — far from it, in fact. Virtually anyone who has played in a band has, at one time or another, experienced a shock when touching both the guitar and the microphone. The guitar may be grounded onstage while the mic is grounded at the console on the other side of the room but the two grounds are at very different potentials. By completing the circuit between them, the performer gets zapped. Good grounding practice seeks to control such potential differences for the comfort and longevity of all concerned.

17.4.2. Ground Loops

AC line-frequency hum is, without question, the single most common problem in sound systems, and the most common cause of hum is ground loops.

A ground loop occurs when there is more than one ground connection path between two pieces of equipment. The duplicate ground paths form the equivalent of a loop antenna which very efficiently picks up interference currents, which are transformed by lead resistance into voltage fluctuations. As a consequence, the reference in the system is no longer a stable potential, so signals ride on the interference.

Ground loops often are difficult to isolate, even for experienced audio engineers. Sometimes, in poorly designed sound equipment (which sometimes includes expensive sound equipment), ground loops occur inside the chassis even though the equipment has balanced inputs and outputs. In this instance, little can be done to get rid of the hum short of having a skilled audio engineer redesign the ground wiring inside. It's better to avoid this kind of equipment. It is also best to avoid unbalanced equipment in professional sound systems (unless the equipment is all going to be very close together, connected to the same leg of the AC service, and not subject to high hum fields).

If all connections are balanced and the equipment is properly designed and constructed, such ground loops will not induce noise. Unfortunately, much of the so-called professional sound equipment sold today is not properly grounded internally, so system-created ground loops can create very real problems.

Figure 17-6 shows a typical ground loop situation. Two interconnected pieces of equipment are plugged into grounded AC outlets at separate locations, and signal ground is connected to earth in each of them. The earth ground path and duplicate signal ground path form a loop which can pick up interference. Normally, this kind of ground loop should not cause any noise in the audio circuits if (a) the circuits are truly balanced or floating, and (b) the audio common is maintained separately from the chassis ground within the equipment. If one of these conditions is not met, then instead of going directly to earth ground and disappearing, these circulating ground loop noise currents (which act like signals) travel along paths that are not intended to carry signals. The currents, in turn, modulate the potential of the signal-carrying wiring (they are superimposed on the audio), producing hum and noise voltages that cannot easily be separated from program signals by the affected equipment. The noise is thus amplified along with the program material.

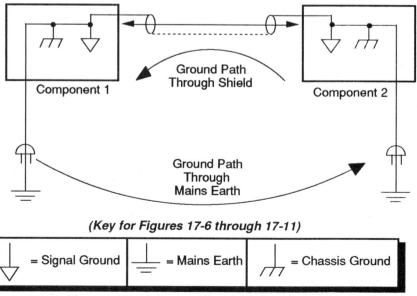

(Key for Figures 17-6 through 17-11)

$\underline{\bigtriangledown}$ = Signal Ground	$\perp$ = Mains Earth	$\perp\!\!\!/\!\!\!/\!\!\!/$ = Chassis Ground

Figure 17-6. Formation of ground loops

17.4.3. Basic Grounding Techniques

We will discuss four basic approaches to handling grounds within audio systems: single point, multiple point, floating, and telescoping shield. Each has specific advantages in different types of systems.

Figure 17-7 illustrates the single-point grounding principle. Chassis ground in each individual component is connected to earth; signal ground is carried between components and connected to earth at one central point. This configuration is very effective in eliminating line frequency hum and switching noise, but is most easily implemented in systems (or subsystems) that remain relatively fixed. Single point grounding is very often used in recording studio installations. It is also effective in the wiring of individual equipment racks. It is almost impossible to implement in complex, portable sound reinforcement systems.

Multiple point grounding is shown in Figure 17-8. This situation is common in systems that use unbalanced equipment having the chassis connected to signal ground. It has the advantage of being very simple in practice, but it is not very reliable – particularly if the connection configuration of the system is changed frequently. Multiple point grounding systems which include unbalanced equipment are inherently rife with ground loops. Hum and noise problems can appear and disappear unpredictably as pieces of equipment are inserted or removed. When they appear, problems are very difficult to isolate and fix. Multiple point ground systems that employ balanced circuits with properly designed equipment may present no special noise problems.

Figure 17-9 shows the floating ground principle. Note that signal ground is completely isolated from earth. This scheme is useful when the earth ground system carries significant noise, but it relies on the equipment input stages to reject interference induced in cable shields.

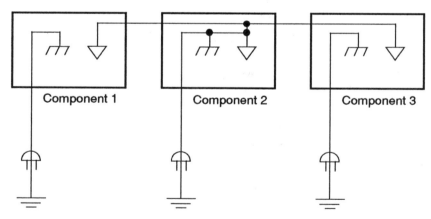

Figure 17-7. Single-point grounding

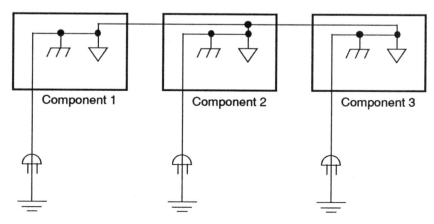

Figure 17-8. Multiple-point grounding

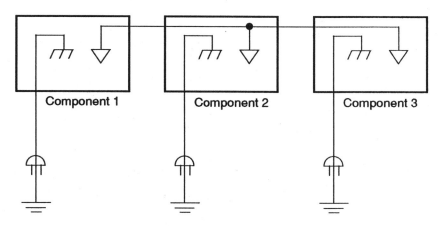

Figure 17-9. Floating connections

The principle of telescoping shields is illustrated in Figure 17-10. This scheme is very effective in eliminating ground loops. If shields are connected only to earth, unwanted signals that are induced in them can never enter the signal path. Balanced lines and transformers are required to implement this approach, since ground is not carried between components. One drawback is that cables may not all be the same – some having shields carried through at both ends, and others not, depending on the equipment – so it becomes more complicated to sort out the cabling upon setup and breakdown of a portable system.

Figure 17-11 (next page) illustrates a typical audio system in which various grounding techniques are combined. The basic rules that guide the choice of grounding schemes may be summarized as:

1) Identify separate subsystems (or equipment environments) that may be contained within an electrostatic shield which drains to earth.

2) Connect signal ground within each separate subsystem to earth at one point only.

3) Provide maximum isolation in connections between subsystems by using transformer coupled floating balanced connections.

Equipment does not have to be grounded to prevent noise from entering the system. The main reason we ground a sound system is for safety; proper grounding can prevent lethal shocks. The next reason for grounding a system that includes AC powered equipment is that, under some conditions, proper grounding may reduce external noise pickup. While proper grounding doesn't always reduce external noise pickup, improper grounding can increase external noise pickup.

The AC power cord ground (the green wire and the third pin on the AC plug) connects the chassis of electronic equipment to a wire in the wall power service that leads through building

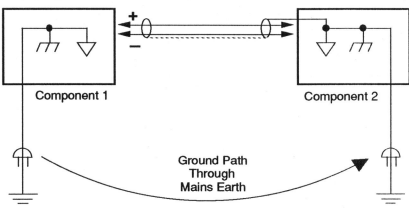

Figure 17-10. Telescoping shields

wiring to an earth ground. The earth ground is required by electrical codes everywhere, and can contribute to ground loops.

If there is only one path to ground, there can be no ground loop. However, one must look carefully. For example, suppose there is just one audio cable joining a console to a power amplifier... can there be a ground loop? Yes! A ground connection through the AC cables and the chassis of the two units makes the second connection. This, along with the audio cable shield, constitutes a continuous ground loop in which noise currents can flow. One way to break this ground loop is to lift the AC ground on one piece of equipment, typically the power amplifier, with a two-wire to three-wire AC adaptor. Leaving the loose green wire on the adaptor unconnected breaks the ground loop, but also removes the AC safety ground. The system now relies upon the audio cable to provide the ground, a practice that can be hazardous. In fact, this type of ground loop

will not automatically cause noise, as stated previously, unless the equipment is unbalanced or improperly grounded internally.

In certain situations you can lift (disconnect) the shield at one end (usually at the output) of an audio cable and thus eliminate the most likely path that carries ground loop currents. In a balanced line, the shield does not carry audio signals, but only serves to protect against static and RFI, so you can disconnect the shield at one end without affecting the audio signal on the two inner conductors of the cable, and with little or no effect on the shielding. Unfortunately, this is not a very practical solution to the ground loop problem for portable sound systems because it requires special cables with shields disconnected on one end. Fortunately, some professional audio equipment is equipped with ground lift switches on the balanced inputs. Ground lifting can be used when multiple unbalanced audio cable join two pieces of equipment; in this

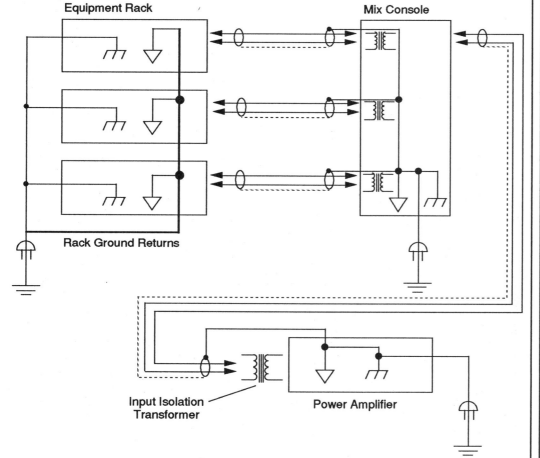

Figure 17-11. Combining grounding techniques in a practical system

case, all but one of the shields can be lifted, thus maintaining the low side of the audio connection without unnecessary duplication, which avoids the ground loops and induced noise. If you want to avoid the ground lifting, try tightly bundling the cables.

Here are some suggestions to minimize the safety conflict while avoiding noise caused by ground loops:

1) Don't lift the safety ground on any piece of equipment unless it significantly reduces the noise level.

2) NEVER defeat the AC safety ground on your console or any other piece of equipment connected directly to your microphones. Microphones take priority in grounding safety because they are handled by performers (who may touch other grounded items, including a wet stage).

3) Where practical, plug all affected equipment into the same AC service "leg." This includes the console, signal processors, and electric instruments such as guitar amps, keyboards, etc. This not only reduces the noise potential if a ground loop occurs, it also reduces the danger of electric shock. Lighting, air conditioning, motors and so on should be connected to a completely different phase (or leg) of the main power distribution system.

WARNING: Microphone cases typically are connected to the shield of the cable, and the shield is tied to the console chassis via pin 1 of the XLR connector. If there is any electrical potential on any external equipment, such as a guitar amp chassis, then a performer who holds the mic and touches the other equipment may be subject to a lethal electrical shock! This is why you should avoid ground lift adaptors on AC power connections if there is any other way to eliminate a ground loop.

17.5. Using Audio Signal Transformers

Due in part to extensive use of inexpensive, poorly designed units, signal transformers have gotten an undeserved bad reputation in some audio circles. True, a poor transformer will seriously degrade sonic quality — just as a cheaply made console or tape machine or microphone will. And it is certainly not necessary for every interconnection in an audio system to be transformer coupled. On the other hand, transformers do offer significant (and, in some cases, absolutely essential) advantages in many applications. The best contemporary audio transformers provide extremely linear performance when they are used properly.

1.5.1. Properties And Functions of Signal Transformers

Figure 17-12 (a) shows a simple transformer. Two independent coils of wire share a common metal core within a shield. By inductive coupling, alternating current signals injected at the primary winding are transferred to the secondary winding. There is no internal DC path from primary to secondary.

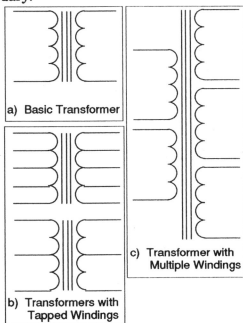

a) Basic Transformer

b) Transformers with Tapped Windings

c) Transformer with Multiple Windings

Figure 17-12. Basic transformer types

The ratio of the number of turns in the primary and secondary windings determines the electrical characteristics of the transformer, as follows:

secondary voltage = primary voltage • T_r

secondary current = primary current ÷ T_r

secondary impedance ÷ primary impedance = T_r^2

Where T_r = # of secondary turns ÷ # of primary turns.

Transformers often have taps (Figure 17-12 (b)) to form various effective turns ratios. A tap at the electrical center of a winding is called a center tap. Multiple windings may also be provided, as shown in Figure 17-12 (c).

Transformers are protected from unwanted induced interference in a number of ways. Normally, both magnetic (iron) and electrostatic (copper) shields are provided. In practice, the electrostatic shield and the core usually are earthed to drain interference currents.

Audio signal transformers can be connected in unbalanced or balanced configurations, as shown in Figure 17–13.

Many audio transformers require resistive termination at the primary, secondary, or both (Figure 17-14) for proper operation. The termination requirements for a particular unit must be determined from the manufacturer's documentation.

The principal benefits of transformer coupling in audio systems are:

- Isolation from high common-mode voltages in signal conductors;

- Ability to achieve complete separation between ground return paths in interconnected components;

- By impedance transformation, ability to avoid undesirable loading (or to provide optimum loading);

- By voltage transformation, ability to step signal levels up or down without substantially affecting the inherent signal-to-noise ratio.

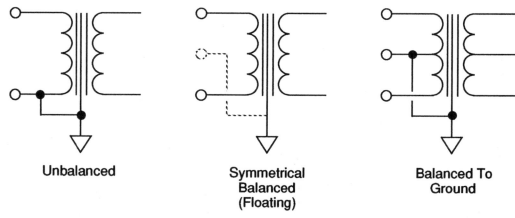

Unbalanced

Symmetrical Balanced (Floating)

Balanced To Ground

Figure 17-13. Unbalanced and balanced connection of transformers

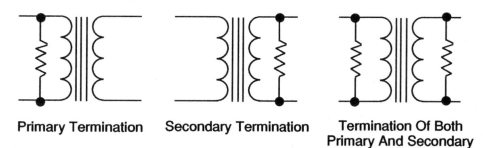

Primary Termination   Secondary Termination   Termination Of Both Primary And Secondary

Figure 17-14. Termination of transformers

17.5.2. Some Practical Applications

Suppose that we wish to connect an electric guitar or electric bass directly to the microphone input of a console. The console input impedance is, say, 3k ohms — which is fine for low to medium impedance microphones. It represents far too great a load for the guitar pickup circuitry, which requires a load impedance of at least 500k ohms. Moreover, the instrument output is unbalanced, and may be very susceptible to noise. The solution is to use a so-called DI (direct injection or simply a direct) box, designed to derive a signal from an instrument directly at its output — before the instrument amplifier.

Figure 17-15 gives a schematic for a simple passive DI box. The specially-designed transformer presents a high input impedance to the unbalanced instrument, and provides a balanced, low impedance source to the console input. Notice the ground lifting switch, which breaks the connection between the console signal ground and the instrument ground. This switch might be left open (as shown), in order to avoid ground loops, when the guitar is also connected to an amplifier or preamplifier.

Some low end mixing consoles employ high impedance unbalanced microphone inputs that are very susceptible to induced RF interference *(Continued on next page.)*

high distortion, tantalum capacitors are not recommended for C1.

2. C2 is an optional high quality (polypropylene or polycarbonate) film capacitor used together with C1 to improve the sonic quality of the input capacitor.

3. C3 is a high quality (polystyrene or polypropylene) film capacitor. Adjust the value for the desired high-frequency rolloff (filter works only with pad in circuit).

4. Pad circuitry must always be used when the source is line or speaker level (synthesizer, guitar amp output, etc.).

5. 1% metal film resistors such as Roederstein (resista) MK-2 are recommended for their low noise and audio quality, although the nearest 5%, ¼ watt carbon film (values shown in parentheses) will work with reduced accuracy.

6. Optional 2.5 kΩ linear taper potentiometer allows continuously variable attenuation between –10 dB and –20 dB. Conductive plastic is recommended, but carbon will work OK.

7. Pin 2 of the microphone-level output connector is "Hi," Pin 3 is "Lo," in order to comply with I.E.C. standards. This is compatible with Neumann, AKG, Beyer, Shure, Sennheiser, Crown, EV, and Shoeps microphones, all of which are Pin 2 "Hot."

8. 3 kΩ resistor across transformer secondary should be installed when the direct box is used with inputs having greater than 2 kΩ actual termination impedance (for example, a standard Yamaha PM2800M input). It is OK to leave the resistor in circuit with 1 kΩ inputs (i.e., a Yamaha PM2800M input with an optional

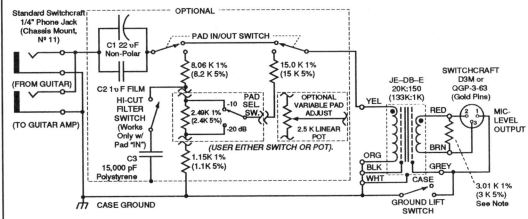

Figure 17-15. A musical instrument DI box

Notes Regarding Figure 17-15:

1. C1 is a high quality, non-polar aluminum electrolytic, such as Roederstein type EKU. Voltage rating should be 25 V or higher. If non-polar cap is not available, use two 47µF, 25V polarized electrolytics in series, as shown on the Jensen Transformers JE-DB-E Data Sheet. Because of their

isolation transformer installed), although better results will be obtained if the resistor is omitted in this case.

9. Parts kit DB-E-PK-1 containing all resistors and capacitors needed to build above circuit available from Jensen Transformers, N. Hollywood, CA for nominal fee.

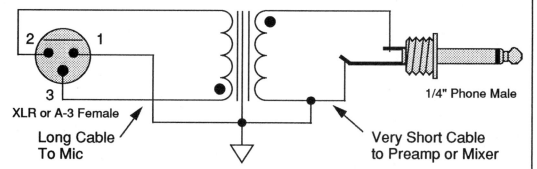

Figure 17-16. Typical Microphone Transformer Connection

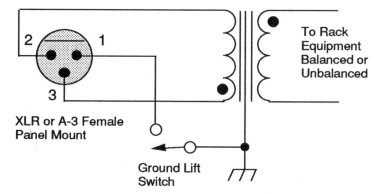

Figure 17-17. Isolated equipment rack input

and hum. The problem is caused both by the impedance mismatch and by the relatively poor noise rejection properties of the unbalanced input circuit. A partial improvement can be obtained by using an external microphone transformer, as shown in Figure 17-16. The transformer's primary winding presents a moderately low impedance

balanced input for the microphone, and the secondary winding presents a higher impedance unbalanced drive to the mixer input. Transformers like this are offered by several manufacturers in a simple in-line package, generally with a female XLR connector at one end and a quarter inch male phone plug at the other.

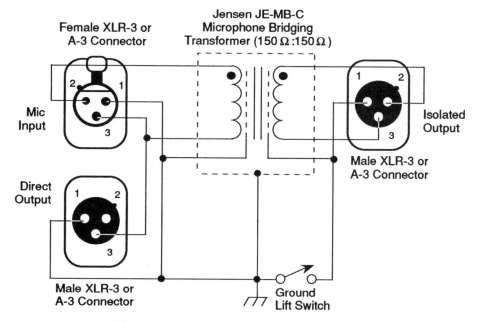

Figure 17-18. Microphone splitter

Figure 17-11 (page 332) shows another very effective use of 1:1 line transformers – isolating local grounds to eliminate ground loops. (Incidentally, just because a 1:1 transformer has the same impedance on the primary and secondary sides, you cannot assume there is no input and output; there can be a significant difference in performance if it is wired backwards. Check the transformer manufacturer's instructions.) Figure 17-17 shows the wiring of a shielded line transformer at an equipment rack input. Note that a balanced (or push-pull) drive is expected.

The isolation properties of transformers are also used to provide separate feeds from on-stage instruments to the house and monitor console systems in large-scale concert systems. Figure 17-18 shows the basic principle of a microphone splitter.

17.6. THE MAIN POWER SOURCE

The preceding discussions clearly demonstrate that from the standpoints of both safety and noise it is important to use securely earthed AC outlets. Figure 17-19 shows the electrical characteristics of a properly wired 120 V AC single phase earthed U.S.A. standard mains duplex outlet. The main power source for your sound system installation should conform to this diagram.

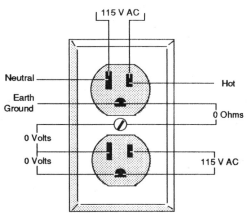

Figure 17-19. Standard duplex outlet

17.6.1 Verify the Correct Mains Voltage

The power supplies of most Yamaha sound equipment sold in the U.S.A. and Canada are designed to operate with 110 to 120 volt, 50 or 60 Hz AC power mains, while General Export models operates on 220 or 240 volt, 50 or 60 Hz AC mains. Other manufacturers typically build equipment to similar standards. If you are traveling with your equipment, be sure to test the power mains, and to use the appropriate power supply. Consult a knowledgeable dealer or the manufacturer for assistance.

Severe over voltage or under voltage in the power mains can damage your equipment. For U.S.A. and Canadian models, the power line must measure more than 105V and less than 130V RMS. The tolerance for General Export models is plus or minus 10%. Some lines are soft, meaning that the voltage drops when the line is loaded due to excessive resistance in the power line, or too high a current load on the circuit. To be certain the voltage is adequate, check it again after turning on the entire sound system, including any power amplifiers turned on if they are connected to the same power mains.

Initially, if the power line voltages do not fall within the allowable range, do not connect the equipment to the mains. Instead, have a qualified electrician inspect and correct the condition. Failure to observe this precaution may damage your equipment and probably void the warranty.

You can test AC outlets with a VOM but you must obviously exercise extreme caution. Alternatively, simple plug-in outlet testers are available from a variety of electronics and hardware stores. An outlet tester is an inexpensive and essential component of the audio practitioner's tool kit. If an outlet appears to be miswired, don't use it. Consult a qualified electrician.

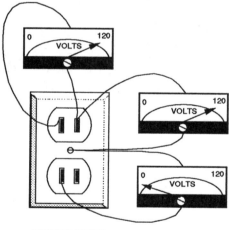

2-WIRE AC OUTLET

Figure 17-20. Testing a two-wire AC outlet

In larger systems it is often difficult to obtain a sufficient number of 20 amp circuits to accommodate the power surges that may occur when the equipment is turned on. Many modern power amplifiers, for example, each require the full capacity of a 20 amp circuit at turn-on, though their operating current requirement is usually much lower. The solution to this problem is to use a stepped turn-on sequence. In fixed installations, the turn-on sequence is sometimes automated with timing and control circuitry.

17.6.2 Ensure There is a Good Earth Ground

Typically, the mixing console must be grounded for safety and proper shielding. A three-wire power cable generally is provided for this purpose. Use a special circuit tester to ensure that the outlet is properly grounded, and that the neutral is not weak or floating. If a grounded, three-wire outlet is not available, or if there is any chance the outlet may not be properly grounded, a separate jumper wire must be connected from the console chassis to an earth ground.

In the past, cold water pipes often were relied upon for an earth ground, although this is no longer the case in many localities. Modern building codes often specify that the water meter be isolated from the water mains by a length of plastic (PVC) pipe; this protects water company personnel working on the water mains from being shocked. It also insulates the cold water pipes from the earth ground. While an electrical wire bypasses the water meter in some locations, this ground path should not be assumed. For similar reasons, avoid hot water pipes. Gas pipes should not be used because if there is a poor electrical connection between two sections of pipe, and if a ground current is being dissipated through the pipe, there exists the potential for a heat or spark-generated fire or explosion. The safest and most reliable approach is to provide your own ground. Drive at least 5 feet (1.5m) of copper jacketed steel grounding rod into moist, salted earth, and use that for a ground, or use one of the specially made chemical-type ground rods available for this purpose.

NOTE: The following discussions of AC outlet wiring are written for U.S.A. and Canadian power systems, although the principles generally apply worldwide. In other areas, however, be sure to check local codes for specific wiring standards.

17.6.3 How to Obtain a Safety Ground When Using a Two-wire Outlet

A two-wire AC outlet does not have a hole for the safety ground prong of a three-wire power cord. A two-wire to three-wire AC adaptor is required if you want to use one of these two-wire outlets with the three-wire AC plug on your sound equipment. These adaptors can maintain a safe ground for the sound system if you connect the loose green wire on the adaptor to a grounded screw on the two-wire outlet. How do you know whether or not the screw is grounded?

1) Connect the adaptor's green wire to the screw on the two-wire outlet.
2) Plug the adaptor into the outlet.
3) Plug in your three-wire AC outlet tester into the adaptor. The AC outlet tester will indicate whether the screw is grounded.

If the screw is not grounded, connect the adaptor's green wire to some other ground point in order to maintain a safe ground for your system. If the outlet tester indicates a good ground but reversed polarity on your two-wire to three-wire adaptor, sometimes you can reverse the adaptor in the outlet by pulling it out, twisting it a half-turn and reconnecting it; this may not be possible if the outlet or adaptor is "polarized" with one prong larger than the other.

17.6.4 Improperly Wired AC Outlets: Lifted Grounds

A lifted ground condition exists if the ground or green wire from the outlet's safety ground is disconnected or missing. In older wiring, the heavy green wire was sometimes omitted from internal wall wiring in favor of letting the flexible metal conduit or rigid conduit (pipe) suffice as the ground path from the electrical service entrance. This method of grounding is generally acceptable, as long as the metal conduit in the wall is intact and all the screws holding the joints together are secure. However, a single loose screw in a conduit joint inside a wall can remove the safety ground from the next outlet box in the line, and from all the subsequent boxes on that same line.

WARNING: NEVER cut the ground pin of a three terminal AC plug. There is no assurance that a component so modified will not one day be used in a manner that would present a serious shock hazard.

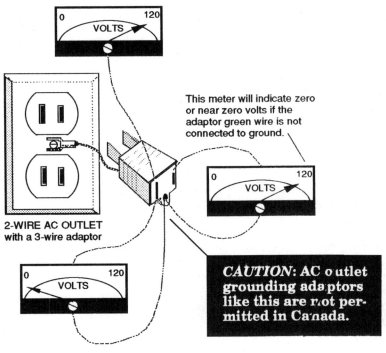

This meter will indicate zero or near zero volts if the adaptor green wire is not connected to ground.

2-WIRE AC OUTLET with a 3-wire adaptor

CAUTION: AC outlet grounding adaptors like this are not permitted in Canada.

Figure 17-21. Testing a 2-wire outlet and a 3-prong to 2-prong adaptor

17.6.5 Improperly Wired AC Outlets: Lifted Neutral

If the neutral becomes lifted at a power outlet, it is possible that items plugged into the outlet will be fed the full 220 to 240 volts available from the power service instead of the desired 110 to 120 volts.

Such outlets may operate, but the voltage can swing from 0 volts to 220 or 240 volts AC (or whatever the maximum voltage at the service entrance), creating a shock hazard and possibly damaging your equipment.

If one piece of sound equipment is plugged into one of the two outlets with a lifted neutral, and a rack of signal processing equipment or power amplifiers is plugged into the other, fuses may blow upon turning on the system, and some of the sound equipment could be destroyed.

Although the white wires (neutral) and the green wires (ground) in the AC wiring are technically at the same potential (voltage), and should measure the same potential using a voltmeter, the ground prong connections at the outlets should be connected to the grounding bar that was driven into the earth as an additional safety precaution in case something should happen to the wires running from the service entrance transformer to the building or within the equipment itself. If a short should occur within the equipment, hopefully the electricity will find its way to ground via the safety ground, instead of via a person's body. When checking AC power lines at the outlet, be sure you have proper testing tools and some familiarity with the danger of shock hazards from AC power.

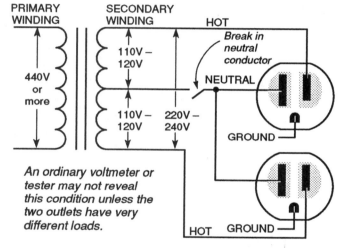

An ordinary voltmeter or tester may not reveal this condition unless the two outlets have very different loads.

Figure 17-22. Schematic of an outlet with a lifted neutral

If you detect any voltage between the larger slot (white wire) in an outlet and the ground terminal (round prong, green wire) when there is no load on that line, you should contact a licensed electrician to check it out and correct the situation.

WARNING: In AC power wiring, black is hot, and white is neutral–the opposite of most audio signal wiring and speaker wiring. It is safer to consider all AC wiring as potentially lethal. It is possible that someone miswired the system, or that a short circuit has developed. Test the voltages yourself, and be safe.

Follow the diagram shown here, being careful not to touch metal with your hands. Do not short the test leads together. If you are not familiar with AC power distribution, don't experiment; have a licensed electrician perform these tests and correct any discrepancies.

17.6.6 AC Safety Tips

1. If you are going to verify the quality of AC wiring, there are two inexpensive items you should carry. One of these is a commercial outlet tester, the other is a neon lamp type AC voltage tester. These items are inexpensive and available at most hardware stores, electrical supply houses, and some lighting stores. It is advisable to also have an RMS (or averaging) voltmeter to measure the exact AC line voltage.
2. The outlet tester should be used on all power outlets. The neon voltage tester should be used to check for voltage differences between microphone and guitar amplifiers, microphones and electric keyboard chassis, and so forth.
3. If you're not sure whether an outlet is good, don't use it. Just in case, carry a long, heavy duty extension cord. A good extension should be made of #12-3 (12 gauge, 3 wires), and no longer than 15 meters (about 50 feet).
4. If there is no suitable power source at a venue, don't plug in your equipment. Any fault in the wiring of the AC outlet is potentially hazardous. Rather than take a chance with damage to equipment and possibly lethal shock, it is best to refuse to use a faulty outlet until it has been repaired by a licensed electrician. Don't take unnecessary risks.

17.6.7 Turn-On Sequencing

In larger systems, it is often difficult to obtain a sufficient number of 20-amp circuits to accommodate the power surges that may occur when the equipment is turned on. Many modern power amplifiers, for example, each require the full capacity of a 20-amp circuit at turn-on, though their operating current requirement is usually much lower. The solution to this problem is to use a stepped turn-on sequence; in fixed installations, the turn-on sequence is sometimes automated with timing and control circuitry.

17.6.8 Power Source Integrity

Finally, make every effort to assure that your source of power is clean and reliable. Synthesizers, computer sequencers and other digital equipment, in particular, normally require a filtered power source with surge protection in order to avoid glitches, system hangups and possible component damage. Power distribution strips with such protection built in are widely available commercially. The ultimate protection is provided by using a power line isolation transformer, such as the "Ultra Isolation" transformers sold by Topaz. Such devices are designed not only to exclude noise and distortion in the AC signal, but also to hold the voltage at the device's output to a nearly constant value regardless of major fluctuations of the line voltage at its input.

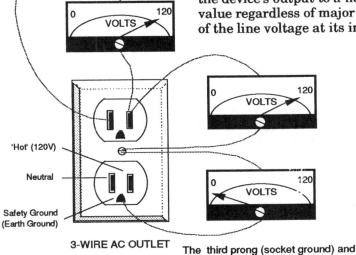

'Hot' (120V)

Neutral

Safety Ground (Earth Ground)

3-WIRE AC OUTLET

The third prong (socket ground) and center screw of the outlet are internally connected and grounded.

Figure 17-23. Testing a three-wire AC outlet

17.7. Configuring Equipment Racks

The great majority of audio equipment manufacturers make provision for their electronic products to be mounted in EIA standard 19 inch wide equipment racks. (The equipment may be only 17 to 18 inches in width, or even less. The rack ears that mount to the rack rails extend to 19 inches.) Panel heights for rack mounting equipment are standardized on multiples of a single unit space of 1.75 inches.

When selecting electronic equipment it is important to bear in mind eventual rack mounting. Not only the height but also the depth of the unit should be considered. Particularly in portable applications, the integrity and strength of the front panel and/or rack mounting ears also must be examined in relation to the chassis weight. Heavy components such as power amplifiers should be supported at the rear as well, rather than relying only on the front rack ears. Even if a piece of equipment seems secure when you screw its front panel to the rack rails, the vibration and shock encountered in the back of a semi-trailer may quickly bend metal or break it right out of the rack.

Before actually mounting the selected components, it is wise to carefully plan out each rack with an eye to signal flow, heat flow, and weight distribution. It might be best to mount together components that function as a group: the equalizer, active crossover and power amplifier for a single loudspeaker or array, for example. On the other hand, some prefer to mount all the equalizers for the system in one rack, all the power amplifiers in another, and so on. If you select the latter approach, you may find that the power amplifier racks are dangerously heavy. Also, if one all the same rack is damaged, you could be out of business, whereas loss of a mixed rack will only partially impair the system. It is far better to put some thought into such matters beforehand than to do all the work and then correct mistakes after they cause major problems.

At its best, configuring equipment racks is a true craft combining a focus on practical utility and careful engineering with a concern for clean appearance. In a well prepared rack, electronic devices are accessible yet protected, and are neatly and consistently mounted with proper hardware. Interior and exterior work lamps, integral power distribution, ground-fault indication and a well stocked spare fuse compartment are among the extra touches that are usually provided. Equipment that may generate strong electromagnetic fields (power amps with large transformers) should be separated from equipment that has high gain (microphone and phono cartridge preamplifiers or cassette decks).

The hallmark of a professional rack is the care that is taken with the internal wiring. Color coding and/or clear and logical cable marking facilitate troubleshooting and reflects an understanding of the electronic signal flow. Related groups of connections are neatly routed and bundled with cable ties. Audio signal cables are kept separate from power cords, and low level signal cables are separated from high level signal cables. Excess cable (including any service loop) is neatly stowed and tied down, and all connections are secured so that they stay in place in shipment.

Finally, touring sound professionals protect their equipment racks in foam-lined flight cases equipped with wheels and handles to facilitate handling. Given the considerable investment in equipment, materials and time that a fully loaded rack represents, such protection is essential. Flight cases in standard sizes are available from a number of manufacturers, and it is generally not necessary or economical to make them yourself.

17.8. Troubleshooting

The ability to efficiently isolate and correct problems in an audio electronic system is one of the greatest assets that a sound professional can possess. Effective troubleshooting requires consistent, logical thought combined with the benefit of experience and a dash of intuition — in precisely that order of importance.

The lessons of experience cannot be adequately conveyed in a text such as this, nor can any number of words bestow an intuitive grasp of electronics. We can describe the logical basis of troubleshooting technique. The principles given here can be expanded to cover a wide variety of problem situations.

17.8.1. Absence of Signal

The tape deck is in play mode, or the performer is speaking into the microphone, but no sound appears at the system output. What to do?

1) Simple as it may seem, check to be sure that every component is turned on, and the fuses are good. Even seasoned pros get caught by this one.

2) Visualize the signal path from input to output, then methodically check the settings of all controls and switches in that path. Are volume controls appropriately set? Is the correct channel selected and properly assigned at the console? Is the channel muted, or is another soloed?

3   Check that the signal path is complete. Are any connections missing?

4) If you make changes, make them one at a time.

If everything looks correct but the problem remains, it is time to begin tracing the signal. In no-signal conditions, tracing proceeds from input to output.

First, check the source itself. If in doubt, replace it with one that you know to be good (a new mic, a test oscillator, a cassette player, etc.). Proceeding along the chain of signal flow, check the source output cable, then the next component in the chain, then its output cable, and so on. Sooner or later, the problem component will reveal itself, and can be replaced or bypassed.

17.8.2. Undesired Signals

Undesired signals include hum, noise, RF, or distortion superimposed upon the desired signal. Any one of a multitude of factors may be at fault. Some are easily identified with experience and intuition, while others may be very difficult to track down.

Assuming that the problem is not due to a familiar faulty cable or component that you've kept alive by jiggling and whacking, the only recourse is to trace the signal. In unwanted-signal conditions, tracing proceeds from output to input. The appropriate starting point for signal tracing depends in part on the character of the unwanted interference. If you are sure that the problem could not possibly be in the loudspeaker cables, start with the power amplifier.

Unplug the cable to the amplifier input. (You may want to plug in a test oscillator or a portable cassette player as an alternate signal source.) If the problem remains, it is certainly in the amplifier. If it goes away, then it is originating farther upstream. Proceed backward through the signal path until you have isolated the component (or cable) that is at fault, then replace or bypass it.

Following are some common unwanted signals and their probable causes:

• **Hum** — Hum is most often caused by ground loops or faulty ground connections. Check the recommendations on grounding given in Section 17.4. Watch out in particular for inadvertent shorts between grounds such as might be caused by setting one chassis atop another or allowing connector shells to touch. (There is nothing wrong with intentionally grounding all chassis together through the rack or with a bus bar, provided your system grounding scheme allows for this.) Never assume that bolting a unit into the rack grounds it; paint, etc. may electrically isolate it from the rack. Try a continuity test of the shield connections in the suspected cable(s).

Hum also can be caused by inductive coupling between adjacent components. Power amplifiers, for example, sometimes radiate a significant hum field that originates from the power transformer. If a sensitive low level component is racked just above such an amplifier, it can pick up and amplify the hum. Inductive coupling can also occur when microphone lines are run too close to power cables. Physically separating the components or cables is the best solution. If you can't separate cables, have them cross one another at right angles rather than near-parallel angles.

• **Buzz** — Generally, this term refers to high frequency harmonics of the power line frequency.

If buzz emanates from the high frequency reproducers of a biamplified loudspeaker system but no corresponding hum is detected from the woofers the high amplifier and the cables connecting to the crossover are suspect. A ground loop may exist, or the cable shield may be ungrounded.

Buzz may also originate from inductive coupling between mic cables and SCR light dimmer circuits. Experiment with alternate positions and orientations of the microphone cables. If the buzz is isolated to a line-level connection, it may be caused by electrostatic coupling. Either insert an appropriate signal transformer with Faraday shielding, or try a different grounding scheme. Some cables, such as Canare 'Star-Quad' 4-conductor balanced cables, are better at rejecting this noise than others.

• **Hiss** — Hiss is most often caused by poor gain staging practices that cause the self-generated noise of components early in the signal path to be amplified to unacceptable levels.

Examine the operating signal level conditions of every component in the chain. Is each working equally hard? The most frequent cause of hiss is excessive gain in the power amplifiers. Is a zero VU signal required from the console to achieve full power? If not, reduce the gain of the power amplifiers. If the masters and channel faders of the console must be at maximum level to get a barely audible signal, reduce the input channel attenuation or turn up the input gain trim and bring the faders down somewhat.

Hiss may also be caused by oscillation or other malfunctions in one or more components in the chain. The offending component can be identified by signal tracing, then checked with an oscilloscope. If the component functions properly when disconnected from the signal path, the input or output connections may be at fault. Check for partial shorts in cables and for excessive output loading. If the equipment features a push-pull output and is driving an unbalanced input, make sure that the low output driver is not shorted to ground at either end of the connecting cable. Unfortunately, some equipment does not have well-designed output driver circuitry, and nothing more than the reactance of a long output cable may be needed to force the output circuit into instability or oscillation.

• **Static and Crackling** — These symptoms are usually due to intermittent signal or shield connections. By signal tracing, the offending cable(s) usually can be isolated and replaced. On occasion, a dirty control may be at fault. Exercising the control can provide a temporary fix, but the part should be cleaned or replaced by a technician as soon as practical.

Static bursts can also be caused by RF interference. Good grounding practice and, possibly, judicious use of transformers will normally solve the problem.

- **Distortion** — Distortion is most often caused by overloading of a stage somewhere in the signal path.

  Examine the gain structure of the system carefully. Are the clip lights on the console or outboard signal processors lit steadily long before the system reaches full power? If so, some gain adjustments are in order. Be sure that you're not trying to drive a −10 dBV input from a +4 dBu output without an intervening pad. Within the console itself, are the input clips lights on before the output VU meters approach zero? If so, this suggests the necessity to reduce the input gain trim or introduce some input attenuation padding, and to then turn up the output level.

  Distortion also may be caused by excessive loading of a device's output. This may be due to an impedance mismatch or a partial short in the cable. Check for both possibilities.

  Finally, distortion may be caused by a failure of an input or output transducer. By testing or substitution, the failed component can be identified and replaced.

SECTION 18.
THE LOUDSPEAKERS

Section 18 presents guidelines for selecting, placing, connecting, testing, and operating loudspeakers in sound reinforcement applications. Section 13 presented details of loudspeaker design and function.

The loudspeaker system is the ultimate link between the performer (or lecturer) and his or her audience. Regardless of the quality of the microphones, mixer, and amplifiers, if the loudspeakers are of poor quality or improperly connected and operated, the result will be inferior sound.

By contrast, a carefully designed and intelligently operated sound system will produce superior results. The key to achieving such results lies in knowing the basic principles of sound reinforcement, and applying those principles with an attitude of care for every detail.

18.1 ANALYZING THE APPLICATION

In specifying a sound system, the first step is to size up the intended application. In doing so, we need to ask a number of specific questions, the answers to which will help to define the requirements that our system must satisfy.

18.1.1 The Program Material

What will the system be used for? Is the application strictly for speech reinforcement, or will music reinforcement be required? If so, what style of music?

The answers to these questions will tell us:

A) what the frequency response requirements will be, and...

B) what the average and maximum sound pressure levels should be.

If the system is for simple speech reinforcement (for a lecture or rally, for example), the low-frequency response of the system need not extend to 20 Hz or even to 50 Hz. In fact, such low end response will tend to emphasize unwanted interference such as wind noise, microphone stand and cable movement, and lectern noise. A good practical low end figure for such a system would be 100 to 150 Hz. At the high end, response to at least 5 kHz is generally regarded as necessary for good speech intelligibility (for reference, a telephone has response from about 300 Hz to 3 kHz).

Speech reinforcement normally requires less power per unit area than music reinforcement. Average levels of between 70 dBA and 80 dBA generally suffice for good speech intelligibility, and one should allow perhaps 10 dB headroom for peaks. In a very loud (or unruly) environment, higher SPLs may be required.

In a reinforcement system for acoustic musical instruments, by contrast, the low end response should extend to between 40 and 50 Hz, and the high end preferably to 16 kHz. Average levels of 80 to 85 dBA may be required, with a minimum of 10 dB headroom, and as much as 20 dB headroom in better quality systems.

A system for rock music playback or reinforcement should have low end response to between 30 and 40 Hz, with most of its power capability concentrated in the low frequencies (below 500 Hz). High frequency response should extend to at least 10 kHz, and preferably to 16 kHz. Average levels up to 100 dBA or so will be expected, again with at least 10 dB of headroom (preferably 15 to 20 dB).

18.1.2 The Environment

Is the system to be used indoors or outdoors? How large is the audience area? What are its dimensions – width, length and, if indoors, ceiling height? If possible, estimate how full the audience area will be.

The answers to these questions will help us to determine:

A) the coverage requirements for the system, and…
B) taken together with the information about the program material, the required SPL capability.

A sound system that is more than adequate for a small club will fall short of satisfying the audience in a large auditorium or concert hall because inadequate power is available to produce the needed SPL, and also because there will be too much reverberation since loudspeaker dispersion is too broad. A sound system that does a good job in the philharmonic concert hall may scarcely be audible in an outdoor amphitheatre due to inadequate sound power capability (it takes power, not just SPL, to fill a large volume of space), and probably inadequate system bandwidth. A system that does a good job in a large concert hall may be unintelligible in a courtroom having relatively lower ceilings because there is likely to be too much reverberation. Such problems are exacerbated by the wide vertical dispersion of a loudspeaker that has been optimized for a taller space and that now throws too much sound at the ceiling, creating the excess reverberation.

Understanding of and control over a sound system's dispersion is an essential ingredient of high quality reinforcement. The reasons for this are twofold.

First, we want the sound quality to be as consistent as possible throughout the audience area. There should be no hot spots, where the sound is significantly louder than in other areas (unless we specifically intend it to be so). The sound should be clear and intelligible everywhere – that is, the system's dispersion should be substantially the same at all frequencies.

Second, we don't want to waste the available energy of the system by directing it where we don't need it. By concentrating the system's energy on the audience area, we increase the effective efficiency of the system.

Only in rare instances will a single loudspeaker cabinet provide all the power and dispersion needed for an application. The trick to constructing multiple-cabinet systems lies in understanding how multiple radiators interact. In practice, every sound system involves compromises dictated by physics, economics and visual aesthetics. Within the limits imposed by such factors there are a few techniques for combining multiple cabinets that yield good directional control.

Each of the techniques presented here assumes multiple full-range cabinets of the same type. This is not necessarily a limiting assumption, since various different types of cabinets can be intermixed in real world systems. It's just easier to conceptualize things if we stick to one type of cabinet for now.

18.2.1 Widening Dispersion

Figure 18-1 shows the general technique for side-by-side placement of full range cabinets to achieve wide horizontal dispersion. Note that the cabinets are placed on an arc, with their -6 dB angles just overlapping.* This allows for a smooth transition between the pattern of each unit and the one next to it, simulating the effect of a single cabinet with a far greater coverage angle. The vertical coverage angle of such a system will be that of an individual cabinet, since this placement configuration does not affect vertical coverage. When multiple loudspeakers are arranged together the arrangement is known as a *cluster*.

Loudspeaker groups such as that shown in Figure 18-1 may be susceptible to a narrowing of their horizontal coverage angle at frequencies where the wavelength is comparable to the total horizontal dimension of the array. The effect is reduced somewhat by splaying the speakers on an arc, and will be most noticeable in smaller groups of speakers. The larger the array, the lower the frequency where the narrowing will occur.

Less commonly, a wide vertical angle may be required. Figure 18-2 (next page) shows one technique for achieving wide vertical dispersion. In this case, the primary consideration is to aim the speakers so that each works independently into its own coverage area and coupling between cabinets is minimized. There will be no appreciable effect on the horizontal coverage, which will be equivalent to that of a single cabinet.

---

*Naturally, the -6 dB point will vary with frequency, so this ideal overlap will exist only in the relatively narrow frequency band around the selected frequency. It is probably best to use a frequency between 2 kHz and 4 kHz, since this is the primary speech intelligibility range, in selecting a -6 dB angle.

Figure 18-1. Splayed loudspeaker arrangement (cluster) for wider dispersion

NOTE: Regarding this configuration – The top cabinet(s) should be tilted upward so that the horns each cover a different area. The bottom cabinet(s) also may be turned upside down for improved low frequency coupling.

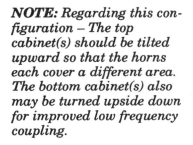

Figure 18-2. Obtaining wider vertical dispersion from multiple cabinets

18.2.2 Narrowing Dispersion

Narrow dispersion is generally desired in situations involving long throws, where the energy of the system needs to be concentrated in one primary direction. This is most often done by narrowing the vertical coverage angle, since reasonably wide horizontal coverage is usually desirable.

A common mistake in sound reinforcement is to deal with long throws by using narrow-dispersion high frequency horns, while allowing wide dispersion of the low frequencies. This results in very unnatural sound quality at long distances from the system. Since the low frequency energy spreads over a greater area than the high frequency energy, the sound from the high horns tends to predominate as one moves farther away from the system. Simultaneously, the very highest frequencies from the horns tend to be differentially absorbed by the air. The result is a characteristic nasal, midrange-heavy quality.

To avoid such effects, the vertical angle of the lows must be narrowed proportionally. One method for doing so is to use horn-loaded low frequency enclosures, which maintain directionality to a higher degree than do infinite baffle or vented, direct radiator enclosures.

Figure 18-3 illustrates a technique that can be used with full range enclosures employing a vented woofer and radial type high frequency horn. The high horns are placed together, since stacking them in this way causes their vertical angle to narrow. At low frequencies, the coverage of the system also narrows somewhat, since the total effective radiating area will be comparable to the wavelength.

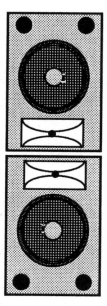

Figure 18-3. Intentionally narrow vertical dispersion

NOTE 1: *The techniques given in this section assume that the loudspeakers in each cluster conform to the following conditions:*
1) All must be of the same design;
2) All must exhibit essentially the same frequency response, dispersion and crossover characteristics;
*3) Driver polarity **must** be consistent throughout.*

NOTE 2: *The configuration shown in Figure 18-3 will work only with loudspeakers employing radial, or modified radial, high frequency horns.*

18.2.3 SPL Estimation

When we add loudspeakers together to form clusters, as shown in the preceding sections, we obviously would like to know how the average and maximum SPL capabilities of the system will be affected. Unfortunately, a number of factors come into play when loudspeakers are clustered, and precise calculations of SPL are difficult to make.

In the near field, the inverse square law will not apply well to the entire cluster, except at low frequencies. In the case of short throws, it is best to work with the figures for the single loudspeaker in the cluster that provides primary coverage for the area in question.

At long distances the inverse square law may be used to estimate SPL resulting from the total acoustical power output of the cluster. We need a means for estimating that output.

As a general rule, for each doubling of the cluster size, the SPL along the composite main axis of the cluster will increase by between 3 dB and the theoretical maximum of 6 dB. The exact level increase depends on the efficiency of addition among the cabinets and the directivity of the cluster, both of which are functions of the specific types of loudspeakers used.

We can start making SPL estimations using the worst case figure of 3 dB, and take any extra SPL that we may realize as a gift — of headroom. From there, as we gain experience with our chosen loudspeaker systems through measurement, the figure can be revised if necessary.

18.3 Placement Considerations

Knowing both the dimensions of the audience area and the directional characteristics of the loudspeaker system, we can plan loudspeaker placements and predict the performance of the system. Our goal is to maximize the system gain, minimize feedback, retain intelligibility, and satisfy the coverage and SPL requirements of the application.

18.3.1 Directionality And Coverage

Figure 18-4 on the following page shows a typical vertical axis polar plot of the high frequency dispersion of a full range loudspeaker. Consider what happens if we place this loudspeaker so as to cover a typical audience area, as shown in that drawing.

We orient the loudspeaker so that its main axis is directed at a point near the rear of the audience area, and take the level at this point to be our reference level, or 0 dB. We designate the distance from the loudspeaker to this point as D. We now wish to determine what the relative level is at various points off-axis, in order to see how even the system's coverage might be.

At point (b), we are 15 degrees off axis. The distance from the loudspeaker is 0.7 D. To determine the relative SPL at this point:

1) Calculate the inverse square level difference relative to our reference point:

$$20 \log (D \div 0.7D) = 3 \text{ dB}$$

2) From the polar plot at 4 kHz, read the loudspeaker's level at 15° off axis, relative to its on-axis level. It is -1 dB.

3) Subtract from the figure obtained in step (1):

$$3 \text{ dB} - 1 \text{ dB} = 2 \text{ dB}$$

The level at (b) is 2 dB higher than at the rear of the audience area.

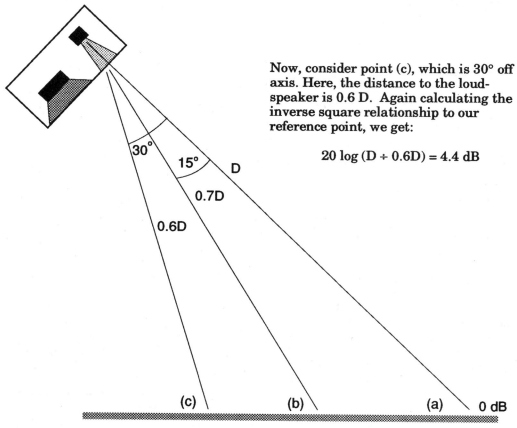

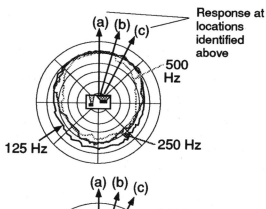

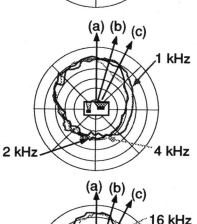

Now, consider point (c), which is 30° off axis. Here, the distance to the loudspeaker is 0.6 D. Again calculating the inverse square relationship to our reference point, we get:

$$20 \log (D \div 0.6D) = 4.4 \text{ dB}$$

30°

15°

D

0.7D

0.6D

(c)   (b)   (a)   0 dB

Aimed Location (a) & Off-Axis Locations (b = 15°, c = 30°)

(a) (b) (c)   Response at locations identified above

500 Hz

125 Hz   250 Hz

Figure 18-4. High frequency coverage of an elevated full-range loudspeaker system: physical locations (above) & corresponding polar response (left)

(a) (b) (c)

1 kHz

2 kHz   4 kHz

Referring to the polar plot, we see that at 30 degrees off axis, the loudspeaker's 4 kHz level is approximately 5 dB down. The level at (c) is thus 0.6 dB lower (4.4 dB - 5 dB) than at the rear of the audience area.

We can conclude that our coverage is very even, since the level varies less than ±2 dB from (c) to the rear of the audience. Calculations will show that, if the loudspeaker were aimed at the middle of the audience area (point b), the uniformity of coverage would actually suffer, with too much sound reaching the front of the audience (point c).

(a) (b) (c)

16 kHz

8 kHz

18.3.2 Feedback Control Review

Reviewing the discussion of sound outdoors, we remember that feedback can be controlled by observing the following guidelines:

A) use the directional characteristics of loudspeakers and microphones to minimize interaction between them,

B) keep the loudspeaker as far from the microphone as is practical, and

C) keep the microphone close to the source.

The effect of each of these practices is to maximize the system gain.

A fourth rule is to obtain the smoothest frequency response from the microphones and loudspeakers. Peaks in response become a trigger for premature feedback, reducing the maximum available gain.

18.3.3 Outdoor Sound Systems

Assuming free-field conditions (absence of any reflecting surfaces), loudspeaker placement outdoors is a fairly simple matter.

First, we determine the required frequency response, average SPL and maximum SPL, and coverage requirements — particularly the length of throws — by analyzing the program material and the environment. Knowing these factors, we choose components on the basis of their frequency response, sensitivity, power handling, and directional characteristics using the knowledge gained in the previous sections of this handbook.

We want to maintain even coverage. That is, we want the sound level to be reasonably even throughout the audience area, within the limits imposed by inverse square losses. This requirement dictates that the speakers be elevated to shoot over the heads of the audience. Using the vertical directivity information supplied in the loudspeaker specifications, together with the inverse square law, we estimate the smoothness of coverage using the procedure of Section 18.3.1 above, and aim the loudspeakers accordingly.

It is common, for practical reasons, to place loudspeakers on either side of the stage area. In this case, the best performance is obtained by aiming each set of speakers at a point in the center of the rear wall, as shown in Figure 18-5 (left). This way, as the sound level gradually drops off in the horizontal axis, the sound from the two systems will combine with and reinforce one another to maintain an even level down the central axis of the audience area.

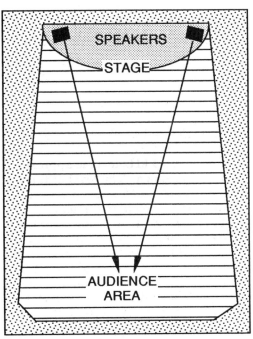

Figure 18-5. Aiming dual speaker clusters on either side of the stage for optimum coverage

18.3.4 Controlling Feedback Indoors

The general principles restated in Section 18.3.2 hold for indoor systems, as well. We assume a reverberant environment indoors, and under this condition the situation becomes a bit more complicated than it is outdoors.

Room modes substantially affect the system's tendency to feed back, and the feedback locks onto the room's resonant frequencies. The system will usually favor a particular frequency*, dependent upon the room geometry and mic placement.

Room modes are essentially independent of the position of the excitation source, so changing the loudspeaker placement won't do any good. Moving the microphone position to a node, if possible, can solve the problem. Tunable equalization filters can also be used to notch out the offending frequency, but this may solve the problem at the expense of fidelity. Of the two, the acoustical solution is preferred. Where EQ must be used, narrow filters are better since a feedback mode tends to be only a few Hz in bandwidth. Use $\frac{1}{3}$, $\frac{1}{6}$ or even $\frac{1}{12}$ octave notch filters. One octave EQ is more suitable for aesthetically adjusting frequency response than for correcting feedback problems, although it can help somewhat. (The problem with very narrow band EQ is that the feedback frequency may shift as the temperature or humidity changes, causing the modes to drift out of the tuned notches in the equalization and thereby creating instability.)

The diffuse reverberant field also affects the system's gain and its potential to feed back. In relatively small, non-reverberant rooms, this may not pose a significant problem. In highly resonant spaces a directional microphone placed close to the source tends to reject most of the room sound. Make sure that the mic has smooth frequency response off axis since lobes in sensitivity can offset any advantage in directivity with regard to feedback prevention.

Both resonant and reverberant effects be minimized by treating the area where the mic is placed (with curtains, for example), or by simply placing the microphone in an area that is isolated to some extent from the general reverberant field (for example, in a stage area treated with absorptive material).

18.3.5 Loudspeaker Placement Indoors

The general guidelines for outdoor loudspeaker placement also apply to indoor systems, but the situation again is complicated by the presence of reflective surfaces.

We want the sound delivered by the system to be as clear as possible, and we wish to have as much control over the sound as we can. These two criteria imply a wish to maximize the system's critical distance – that is, minimize the extent to which we excite the reverberant field, so that the audience hears mostly direct sound and thus enjoys good speech intelligibility. We already know that directional loudspeakers will help. Placement of those loudspeakers is also very important.

By keeping our directional loudspeakers aimed into the audience area, we will assure that the audience is in the direct field of the system, and the reverberant field will be minimized since the audience will absorb most of the sound. The loudspeakers' reduced off axis level also tends to decrease the strength of reflections from the walls and ceiling.

If we aim our loudspeakers near the rear of the audience area we will inevitably end up spilling some sound on the rear wall of the space. This problem is partially solved by aiming the speakers about two-thirds back in the hall, allowing the SPL at the rear to fall off more. A lower level at the rear is not totally unexpected, and usually will be perceived as natural. In fact, many audience members choose rear seats, particularly at rock events, specifically because the sound will not be as loud.

Despite such placement it is best to treat the rear wall of the space with sound absorbent material if at all possible. Simple curtains will usually do a fairly effective job of absorbing the direct sound at mid to high frequencies, but not at low frequencies.

---

* Actually, feedback occurs at a particular wavelength, so the feedback frequency changes with temperature and humidity changes.

18.4 CONNECTIONS

18.4.1 Wire Size

In making connections to reinforcement loudspeakers, we want to minimize losses caused by the resistance of the wire, and thus maximize both the efficiency of the system and the control that the amplifier exerts over the drivers. The longer the wire, the higher its resistance. The thicker the wire, the lower the resistance. The effect of the wire resistance will vary, depending on the impedance of the load.

Table 18-1 can be used as a simple reference when choosing wire gauges for different impedances. Note that lower gauge numbers correspond to thicker wire diameters.

The wire gauges given here are practical minimums. In each case, less than a half dB loss will result from the wire resistance. With low-frequency drivers the damping factor of the amplifier is very important, and the largest practical wire gauge (lower gauge number value) should be used for long runs.

Bear in mind that inductance or capacitance between the two conductors in a speaker cable can have a significant impact on the overall sound. The capacitance or inductance, combined with the resistance of the cable, can create a low or high pass filter, thereby rolling off the frequency response of the signal reaching the loudspeakers. Simply using a cable with thick conductors does not assure good results; coaxial cable and small diameter, thin-insulated multi core cables are not suitable. Heavy insulation not only prevents unwanted short circuits, it also separates the conductors, which reduces capacitive and inductive coupling. Some cables designed for high current AC feeds do make suitable loudspeaker cables (to avoid confusing the power cords with the speaker cables when you're hooking up the system, be sure to use different connectors on the speaker cables).

18.4.2 Connectors

Some very commonly-used connectors on loudspeakers (commercial cabinets) are standard binding posts, pictured in Figure 18-6 (next page). Binding posts accept standard banana plugs, which are sometimes used in studio systems as in Figure 18-6 (a). For reinforcement work the preferred method is to strip the wire, tin it with solder, and insert it through the hole in the binding post, as shown in Figure 18-6 (b), tightening the nut down on the wire. This results in a connection that is less likely to be shaken loose or broken by someone tripping on the wire. Sometimes, particularly if a wire is too large in diameter to fit through the hole in the binding post shaft, a large spade lug is secured to the end of the wire, and the lug is then slipped into the binding post and clamped in place. If the spade lug does not fit around the threaded shaft, one leg of the spade can be inserted into the hole in the shaft, just like the bare wire shown in Fig. 18-6 (b). A poorer alternative is to wrap the wire around the binding post shaft (clockwise), and then tighten down on it with the upper nut of the binding post. Binding posts are color coded, with red for the + connection and black for the − connection.

Another common connector used in sound reinforcement is the ¼-inch phone plug, pictured in Figure 18-7 (next page). This is a two-circuit connector: the tip is used for the + connection, and the sleeve for the − as shown. Phone plugs are common, and do a sufficient job for low level signals (mic and line level), but really are not a good means to connect loudspeakers to amplifiers. The relatively small surface area available for the wipers in the jack to contact the plug create a high resistance contact, one that wastes power and becomes a source of electrical noise. Also, phone plugs do not lock in place and are easily dislodged. Perhaps most significant, phone plugs are prone to short circuits.

Table 18-1. Mimimum recommended wire diameters for loudspeaker connection (lower gauge Nº is even better)

Load Z	Length of Run	
	<100'	>100'
16 ohms	16 ga.	14 ga.
8 ohms	14 ga.	12 ga.
4 ohms	12 ga.	10 ga.

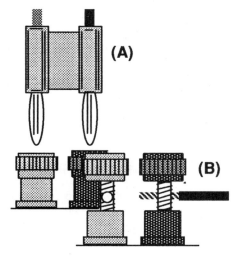

Figure 18-6. 5-Way binding posts accept dual banana plugs (a) or bare wires (b), as well as spade lugs and single banana plugs

The relatively small insulator between the tip and sleeve can crack, and a short will shut down (or damage) the amplifier. These connectors were never really conceived for the high currents involved in large sound reinforcement speaker systems. They are probably OK for quick setup of small, low power sound systems, provided care is exercised to prevent accidental disconnection and regular inspections are made to preclude damaged plugs.

Figure 18-7. Phone plug and phone jack connectors

type cables for loudspeaker connections, we recommend special cables with other types of connectors, and, at the very least, with larger diameter conductors to carry the current).

B) Relatively high voltages may be present at the end of loudspeaker cables. Use of a female on the loudspeaker cable reduces the possibility of shock, since there are no exposed pins carrying the amplifier output.

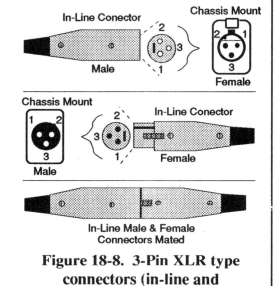

Figure 18-8. 3-Pin XLR type connectors (in-line and panel mounted)

The XLR-type connector, pictured in Figure 18-8, is also often used for loudspeaker connections.

Note that this is a three-circuit connector. When XLR-type connectors are used for loudspeakers, the connector on the loudspeaker is usually a male. The reasons for this are twofold:

A) Since the same connectors are used for microphones and line-level equipment, the use of a male on the cabinet reduces the possibility of an amplifier output being accidentally plugged into a microphone or line-level input in the event a standard mic cable is used. (Instead of mic

Four-circuit XLR-type connectors may also be used for loudspeaker connections, and they offer distinct advantages. First, use of a four-circuit plug eliminates any possibility of accidental connections to microphones or line-level equipment. Second, a four-circuit plug may be used for a single biamplified cabinet, carrying independent connections for both drivers. This eases setup and reduces the possibility of incorrect connections. A suggested pin configuration for a four-circuit XLR-type connector is shown in Figure 18-9 (next page). Similar Cannon 4-pin P type or twist-lock connectors could be used instead of the 4-pin XLR.

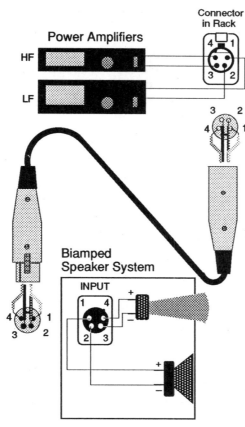

Figure 18-9. A 4-pin XLR Connector utilized for carrying the output from two channels of power amplification to a biamplified loudspeaker system

NOTE: If you use a 4-pin XLR for an additional subwoofer in the biamped system (making it tri amped), connect pin 3 for the subwoofer + terminal and pin 2 for the – terminal; in this way, you cannot accidentally blow up the other biamped section if the cables are crossed. It is also possible to use a 4-pin XLR connector to drive a single, full range loudspeaker system. In this case, two pins would be used for the + and two for the – connection; four-conductor cable would then provide lower resistance and greater redundancy for the connection. If this approach is used be sure that it is never done where biamplified loudspeakers with 4-pin XLRs are present. There's a chance of mixing up the cables and blowing out a high frequency driver in an instant.

18.4.3 Polarity of Connections

NOTE: *Once again, the term polarity is the correct term when discussing the reversal of loudspeaker wires. Phase is often misused here. When one loudspeaker's polarity is reversed (the + and – wires swapped) relative to another, the effect is similar to being 180° out of phase. Phase is frequency dependent, polarity is not. Still, many people continue to use the term out of phase when they really mean reversed in polarity. This misinformed practice may continue, but make sure YOU know the difference.*

The polarity of loudspeaker connections in a reinforcement system is extremely important, and must be strictly observed. There are two main reasons for this.

A) If a single loudspeaker in a reinforcement system cluster (or array) is reversed in polarity, it will cancel part of the in-phase loudspeakers' sound. In a cluster of four loudspeakers, if one is reversed in polarity the cluster output will approximate that of only two loudspeakers, and may be even less.

B) In a cluster of low-frequency loudspeakers, a reversed polarity loudspeaker may actually be destroyed when the system is operated at high levels. When the other loudspeakers in the cluster are moving outward, the out of polarity unit will be moving inward, and vice-versa. The pressure of the in-phase speakers will combine to push the out-of-phase unit to greater excursion. The opposite will occur on the other half-cycle of the wave. In a short period of time, the errant driver can literally be torn to pieces from overexcursion.

For these reasons, it is wise to standardize on color codes and pin configurations for loudspeaker connections, and to strictly observe the standard you have defined. Loudspeaker polarity should always be tested before the system is operated.

18.4.4 General Guidelines

It is best if all connections to the loudspeakers are planned and tested prior to installation. Particularly in the case of portable reinforcement systems, the surest method is to rack amplifiers and active crossovers (if used) together, providing connector panels for loudspeaker cables. This minimizes the chances for misconnection, and speeds both installation and testing. Many professional sound reinforcement companies completely set up a touring sound system in a rehearsal hall, perform a complete sound check, label every connection, and then tear it down for travel to the first show. This not only saves time on the road, it helps identify problems while shop personnel and equipment are handy, and it also provides an opportunity for the performers to participate in evaluating the system, suggest changes, and become familiar with it before the pressure of the tour is a factor.

If the system makes use of parallel connection of loudspeakers to a single amplifier channel, the best place to parallel the loudspeakers is at the amplifier output — particularly if the resulting load impedance is under 8 ohms. While this practice means more loudspeaker cable, it results in better performance from the system— the amplifier will be able to exert better control over each driver, and there will be less chance of interaction between drivers.

The exception to this last rule occurs when two drivers are wired in parallel in a single cabinet. In this case, it is simpler to parallel the drivers in the cabinet, and use a single large-gauge cable for the amplifier connection.

Above all, make certain to observe the polarity of all loudspeaker connections.

18.5 SETTING ELECTRONIC CROSSOVERS

Careful speaker system design assures a flat frequency response and controlled dispersion pattern while avoiding potential response irregularities caused by crossover phase shifts.

18.5.1 Choice of Crossover Frequency and Slope

There is more freedom of choice available to the designer of the biamplified (or triamplified) system than is available to the designer of a non-biamplified system. Many electronic crossover networks enable the user to readily adjust crossover frequencies and slopes for a specific application, with the added advantage of easily fine tuning these parameters after the system is set up. Once a system has been optimized, a special purpose electronic crossover will often be substituted, one with fixed parameters, so that accidental mistuning of the crossover is not possible. Alternately, a protective cover panel may be installed on an adjustable unit. This is important because an act so simple as shifting the crossover frequency can instantly cause the destruction of dozens of compression drivers.

Most manufacturers of quality speaker components provide detailed specifications on power capacity and frequency range. The choice of a crossover frequency can be based on this information; the frequency ranges of all components should overlap somewhat. Below are listed three typical examples, all based on a system having a high frequency compression driver/horn combination having a rated power capacity of 20 watts of pink noise from 2 kHz to 20 kHz, with reasonably good dispersion to at least 12 kHz.

A) Using the above noted compression driver to build a biamplified system, a crossover frequency of 2 kHz is a good starting point. A woofer would then be chosen that yielded usable response to at least 2 kHz, complementing the high frequency driver's response. One concern is the dispersion characteristic of the woofer. It may narrow significantly before reaching 2 kHz, thus providing uneven coverage.

B) In order to obtain more uniform coverage at midrange frequencies, it may be desirable to triamplify a 3-way system. Using the same high frequency driver described above, select a complementary midrange driver and woofer. For example, a woofer specified to have smooth, usable response to 800 Hz could be rolled off at 500 Hz, before its dispersion begins to narrow. Then a midrange driver could be chosen on the basis of smooth response from 500 Hz to at least 2 kHz. If the midrange were capable of response to a higher frequency, say 4 kHz, then the crossover frequency for the high frequency driver could be moved up an octave (to 4 kHz). This would mean the high frequency driver's diaphragm would not have to move through such long excursions, so it could be operated at a higher power level (or would have a longer life at the same power level).

C) An alternative to the triamplified system described in (B) might be the use of the same woofer and tweeter as in example (A), with an addition. We may decide that the high frequency driver does not yield adequate dispersion at the very highest frequencies, and perhaps that its distortion rises when corrective equalization is applied to boost the very highest frequencies (to penetrate longer distances in air). In this case, we might triamplify the system by adding a super tweeter to handle those frequencies from 8 or 12 kHz through 20 kHz. (A quad-amplified system might add the supertweeter to the triamplified system in (B).)

The choice of a crossover slope is related to system response smoothness, and to driver excursion limitations. With some systems, a 12 dB/octave slope rate will produce the best results; with others, best results will be obtained with an 18 dB/octave or 24 dB/octave rate. Slope rates may be mixed within a given loudspeaker system, or even in a given crossover between two drivers. For example, a 12 dB/octave rate might work well between the woofer and midrange, providing a smooth low-to-mid transition, but 18 dB/octave may be necessary to protect the high frequency compression driver from midrange frequencies. Other combinations of slope rates may be called for if one driver has an inherent rolloff, whereas the other does not. For instance, a 15" woofer may exhibit a natural 6 dB/octave rolloff above 500 Hz, whereas the 10" midrange driver has fairly flat response from below 400 Hz up through its primary operating range. In order to realize a complementary 12 dB/octave slope rate at the chosen 500 Hz crossover frequency, the high pass filter for the midrange driver may be set at 12 dB/octave, while the low pass filter for the woofer may have to be set at 6 dB/octave (which combines with the woofer's inherent 6 dB drop in response to yield an effective 12 dB slope rate).

If you are using an electronic crossover in a system that previously had a passive, high level crossover (one that seemed to produce a reasonable overall frequency response and dispersion characteristic), then the transition frequency and slope rates of the electronic crossover may be set to match those of the high level unit. When designing a system from scratch, start with an 18 dB per octave slope rate, and follow the procedures outlined below.

18.5.2 Setting Up the Loudspeaker System

Select high quality professional power amplifiers of appropriate power output capability. The loudspeakers should be chosen to complement each other's frequency response and dispersion characteristics, as well as sensitivity. It is rare to find a high frequency compression drivers with the same sensitivity as a cone woofer of the same power rating, but this is not necessary. The overall sound level that can be delivered to the audience by each section of the loudspeaker system should be similar. This may require some calculation.

For example, suppose the woofer sensitivity is rated at 100 dB SPL, 1 watt, 1 meter, and it can handle up to 100 watts pink noise. This tells us that its maximum on axis SPL at 1 meter is 120 dB (100 watts is 20 dB more power than 1 watt). The high frequency compression driver is rated at 110 dB, 1 watt, 1 meter sensitivity, but can handle only 10 watts maximum power. Is this a mismatch? Not necessarily. 10 watts is 10 dB more than 1 watt, so the high frequency driver can deliver 120 dB SPL maximum— the same as the woofer! Is this a perfect match? Again, not necessarily. The high frequency driver/horn system may have only a third the dispersion angle of the woofer. This means that three of the high frequency drivers are needed to every one of the woofers (a common occurrence in sound systems). The result, in this case, is that we need a 30 watt amplifier for the high frequency driver, and a 100 watt amplifier for the low end, to exactly match the driver's power ratings. To allow for some headroom, we may choose a 200 watt low frequency amp and a 60 or 75 watt HF amp, which are widely available power ratings.

Use of high quality drivers is important because dips or peaks in the middle of a driver's range are not easily corrected. Even so, both the careful physical placement of the low, mid and high frequency drivers and the careful selection of crossover frequencies and slopes are necessary to optimize the system for smooth frequency response throughout its entire range. Once the loudspeakers and electronics are selected, the interconnections should be made with appropri-

ate cable and connectors, as described in Section 18.4.

If the system is assembled entirely from direct radiator type drivers (cone type speakers), try to align their voice coils as closely as possible, as shown in Figure 18-10 (see note on next page).

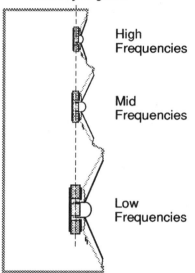

Figure 18-10. Initial positioning of drivers in an all direct-radiator loudspeaker system

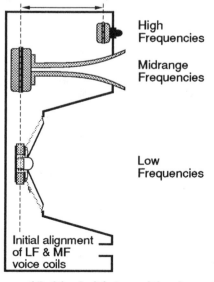

Figure 18-11. Initial positioning of drivers in an all straight horn-loaded loudspeaker system

If the system is entirely constructed of straight horns and drivers (a compression driver and radial/sectoral horn for the mid or high frequencies, and a front loaded horn for the low frequencies), set them up in a configuration similar to that shown in Figure 18-11. This does not apply to systems using one or more folded horns (W bins or re-entrant horns). If you are using a system that is a combination of direct radiator and horn loaded drivers, as in Figure 18-12, or straight and folded horns, their optimum alignment is difficult to ascertain except by trial and error.

NOTE: For time/phase coherence, the ideal initial position of the mid and high frequency compression drivers in any given system should be such that the voice coils (actually, the acoustic centers of the diaphragms) are vertically aligned. Because the midrange driver has a long horn, and the high frequency driver has a very short horn, the midrange horn will cast a large shadow on the high frequency dispersion pattern. It is thus most common to mount the HF driver much closer to the front of the MF horn, and to compensate for the inevitable time difference by using an electronic delay line.

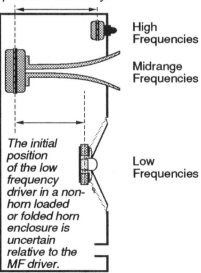

Intentional HF/MF offset to prevent shadowing; time difference is compensated with delay.

High Frequencies

Midrange Frequencies

Low Frequencies

The initial position of the low frequency driver in a non-horn loaded or folded horn enclosure is uncertain relative to the MF driver.

Figure 18-12. Initial driver positions for mixed horn loaded & direct radiator system

18.5.3 Testing and Optimizing the System

The test setup illustrated in Figure 18-13 (next page) requires a source of pink noise, a flat-response (or calibrated) microphone, and a real-time audio spectrum anayzer (RTA), preferably calibrated in one-third octave bands. If you do not have access to this instrumentation, use a male speaking or singing voice as the sound source, and your own ears as the spectrum analyzer.

Since the end goal of system design is to make it sound good (frequency response smoothness is a means towards this goal, not the goal itself), your ears and the human voice make a very acceptable test system.

If you can't test the system in its actual environment, test an indoor sound system in a room with as few reflections (echoes or reverberation) as possible. For an outdoor sound system, do the tests outdoors, away from buildings and out of earshot of any loud traffic or industrial noises. If you have an anechoic chamber it may be helpful for simulating out-of-doors, but will tend to yield misleading results at low frequencies. Such chambers usually cease to be anechoic at low frequencies (it takes a huge chamber to remain anechoic below 150 Hz), so the bass response will seem too heavy, and too much bass cut will be applied. Conversely, outdoor testing is not particularly useful for calibrating loudspeakers if the sound system is intended for indoor use. The lack of boundary-reinforcement will yield too little bass output and will tend to cause too much boost to be applied in this range.

The object of the following instructions is to optimize the loudspeaker system's frequency response and dispersion pattern over a wide frequency range.

When preliminary crossover frequencies and slopes have been selected, and the system is operational, feed the source (pink noise or voice) through the system and monitor it — on the RTA or with your ears.

If the system does not appear to have acceptably flat frequency response (± 6 dB is a reasonable tolerance from 200 Hz to 10 kHz), if its dispersion pattern is not smooth enough, or if it sounds unnatural, first try a different slope rate on all filters.

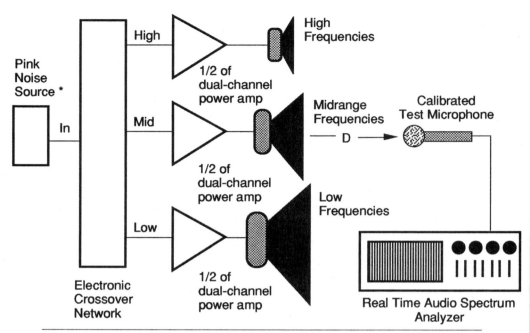

* Alternately, use a microphone, mic preamp or mixer, and a male speaking voice
to replace the pink noise source; use your ears instead of the test mic and RTA.
(Your ears should strongly influence the ultimate setup in any case.)

**Figure 18-13. Test setup for optimizing loudspeaker system
frequency response**

(Response irregularities induced by crossover phase shift cancellations can cause the voice to sound hollow, honky or otherwise unnatural.) If there is no appreciable improvement, switch the slope rate back to the original settings and try reversing the polarity of the feed to the high frequency amplifier (in a biamped system) or the mid frequency amplifier (in a triamped system).

If that doesn't work, go back to the original settings and instead try repositioning the drivers with respect to their voice coil alignment.

Since it is usually easier to move the mid or high frequency drivers, start with them (move the high frequency driver in a biamped system or the mid frequency driver in a triamped system). Move them back and forth until the response is a smooth as possible. This is an especially effective method with systems that combine direct radiators and horn loaded drivers that are mounted in separate enclosures. If all the drivers are in the same cabinet, moving the drivers may be a last resort approach. If possible, determine optimum alignment before completing the cabinet construction.

Finally, if the system still has a noticeable dip in response near a crossover frequency, try overlapping the frequency range of the drivers. At a given transition, use a higher crossover frequency for the lower frequency driver than for the higher frequency driver. Conversely, if there is a peak in the crossover range, try raising the higher frequency driver's crossover frequency or lowering the lower frequency driver's crossover frequency.

At this point, if the system response still is not particularly smooth you may wish to try a new set of crossover frequencies and slopes, select new loudspeakers, or accept the existing system as being adequate for the intended purpose. Only at this point should equalization be considered to smooth out minor response irregularities. Too much equalization causes significant phase shift, decreases headroom, increases noise levels, and actually degrades the sound quality in the process of smoothing the frequency response.

18.5.4 High Frequency Driver Protection Networks

A compression driver or tweeter can be quickly destroyed by transient DC surges, DC shifts in amplifier output due to non-symmetrical waveforms, or turn-on/turn-off thumps from system electronics. While many amplifiers provide DC protection in the form of an output relay, there is no protection from accidentally miswiring the low frequency amplifier of a multi-amped system to the high frequency driver (or misconnecting the electronic crossover network). Such protection can only be provided by carefully checking a system before applying full power, and perhaps by protecting the drivers themselves. For this reason, we discuss this alternate method to protect compression drivers.

One can insert a capacitor in series with the cable to the power amplifier, and possibly a resistor shunt across the driver. This circuit constitutes a half section filter. Even with a multi-amplified system, such protection may be necessary to prevent low frequency energy from damaging the diaphragm or suspension due to overexcursion. The low frequency energy can reach the driver in a multiamped system if it is caused by amplifier clipping (see note below).

NOTE: Clipping a single sine wave generates only harmonics that are higher in frequency than the clipped signal. When two sine waves are clipped simultaneously, they not only produce higher frequency harmonics, they also produce intermodulation products that include lower frequency components. When complex musical signals are clipped it is actually possible for full bandwidth energy to be generated. The extent of this effect depends on the amplifier itself and the degree to which it is over-driven – and some amplifiers exhibit better behavior than others.

When constructing the protection network, select a capacitor that is rated at a minimum of 200 volts. Non-polarized Mylar®, polystyrene, polypropylene, motor start or oil filled types are preferred, but may not be available in high values, so they may have to be paralleled with other types of capacitors. The value should be chosen to

yield a high pass frequency that is an octave below the setting of the electronic crossover's high pass frequency for the driver being protected.

NOTE: When the loudspeaker system includes its own passive, high level crossover network, this protection capacitor is not necessary since one is already provided in the crossover network. Multiamped loudspeaker systems that include low level (passive or active) cross-over networks that are ahead of the power amp benefit from this type of protection for the driver(s). The resistors are used in addition to the capacitor to damp the resulting resonant circuit (caused by the inductance of the driver and the protection capacitor). Such a resonant R-L circuit could actually deliver more voltage to the driver at certain frequencies than is present at the amplifier output!

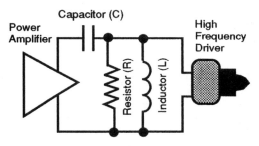

Figure 18-14. High pass filter network for protection of the high frequency driver

This circuit provides a 12 dB/octave roll-off. The inductor constitutes a short circuit for DC components, so in the event of a catastrophic amplifier failure that charges the capacitor, the inductor blocks the low frequency components from reaching the driver. The equation for a constant K network is:

$$X_L = 2 \pi FL \ \dots \text{ or}$$
$$X_C = \frac{1}{2 \pi fC}$$

where X_C is the driver impedance and f is the frequency.

In order to determine the value of the blocking capacitor in microfarads, use the equation below, based on the filter corner (–3dB) frequency equation:

$$C = \frac{500,000}{\pi \text{ x frequency x impedance}}$$

$$= \frac{0.159}{f\,Z}$$

where f is frequency and Z is impedance.

This equation gives you a 6 dB per octave high pass filter whose –3 dB point is at the frequency specified in the equation. *If you want the filter to commence an octave below the crossover frequency, be sure to use that lower frequency in the equation.* These capacitors will end up being quite large and fairly expensive, but in the long run can prove worthwhile by protecting drivers, especially expensive compression drivers.

The resistor R should be about 1.5 times the driver's rated impedance. For example, use a 12 ohm resistor for an 8 ohm driver. The power rating of the resistor should be equal to the driver's power rating. Bear in mind that the resistor, while it damps the resonant circuit, also reduces the effective driver efficiency and places a greater load on the amplifier. For example, an 8 ohm driver in parallel with a 12 ohm shunt resistor constitutes a 4.8 ohm load. Two of these driver/filter circuits in parallel constitute a 2.4 ohm load on the amplifier, not the 4 ohm load that one might casually assume if only the driver impedances are considered. It may be a good idea to use 16 ohm drivers.

In many practical sound reinforcement situations, we find that while the main array satisfies the requirements for 80 to 90 percent of the audience area, there remain some areas where the system response will be degraded. Fill systems are loudspeakers used to fix such problem spots.

Consider the situation shown in Figure 18-15 (next page). Notice that the closest seats (A) are fully 60° off the main axis of the system (C). From the accompanying vertical polar plots for the loudspeaker, we see that while the low-frequency response will still be good 60° off axis, the highest frequencies will have fallen off to between 10 and 15 dB below the on axis level. Despite the fact that these seats are closer to the system, the high frequency energy will be mostly lost.

The solution is to place a second loudspeaker with the main cluster, as shown in Figure 18-16 (next page). Since this loudspeaker is relatively close to the seats that need help, it need not be nearly as powerful as the main cluster. Since the main cluster is omnidirectional at low frequencies, and we wish only to fill in the missing portion of the frequency response, this fill loudspeaker system need only cover the mid and high frequencies. It can thus be relatively smaller and less costly than the main system.

Note that we have placed the fill loudspeaker close to, and in alignment with, the main cluster. This method keeps the arrival times from the fill system coincident with those of the main system. There are two benefits from this approach:

A) phase cancellation between the two systems is minimized, and

B) the effect is of a single sound source placed at the main cluster, and the fill system is not heard as a separate sound source.

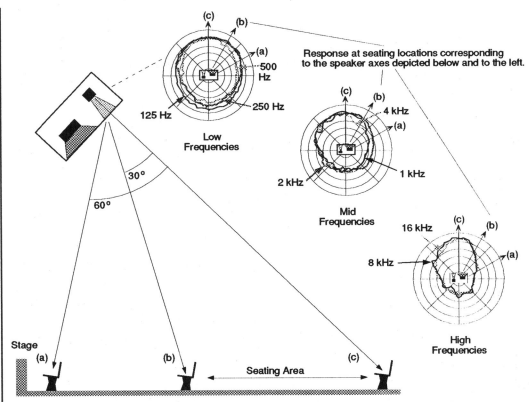

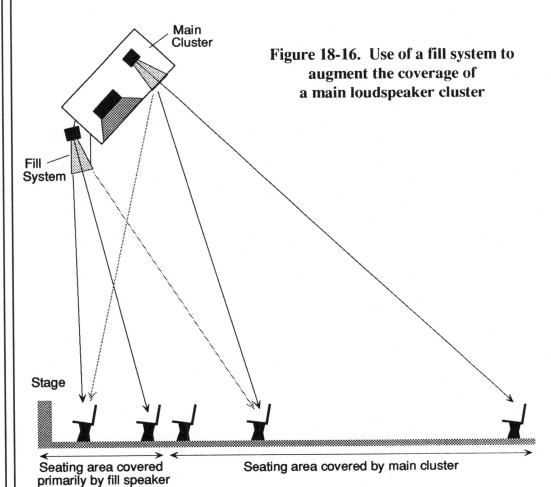

Figure 18-15. Coverage problems of a single loudspeaker cluster (array) for a large audience

Figure 18-16. Use of a fill system to augment the coverage of a main loudspeaker cluster

Another common circumstance calling for use of fill systems is shown in Figure 18-17. Here, an overhanging balcony shadows a large seating area from the main cluster. Figure 18-18 depicts the mechanism by which sound is shadowed (obstructed). Since low frequencies will bend around the overhang and permeate this area, we are again concerned with mids and highs, and our criteria for speaker selection will be the same as in the first example, though perhaps even wider dispersion (or more fill loudpeakers) will be required due to the relatively shorter distance betwen the fill loudspeakers and the seats. As shown, fill systems can be hung inside the balcony overhang.

Note, however, that this area is physically remote from the main cluster, at a distance D. If we simply connect the fill loudspeakers with the main signal feed, the sound will arrive noticeably later than the sound from

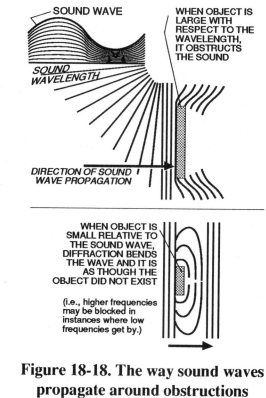

Figure 18-18. The way sound waves propagate around obstructions explains why low frequencies tend to build up under balconies. (More HF than LF fill is needed.)

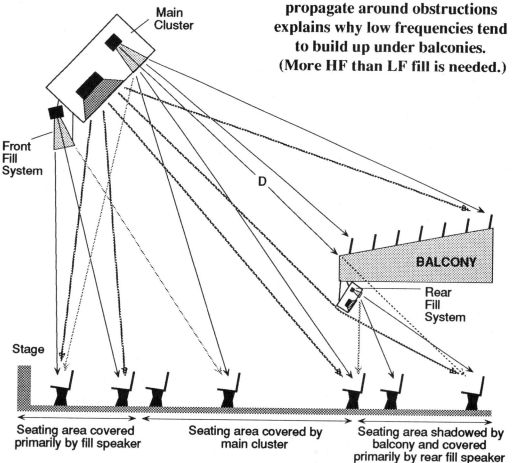

Figure 18-17. Fill loudspeakers used to improve mid and high frequency coverage beneath a balcony

the main cluster. The feed to the fill systems should be electronically delayed so that its sound output coincides with, or actually comes a short while after, the sound arriving from the main cluster. This will not only avoid pre-echo from the stage, it will ensure that the sound is perceived as originating on the stage, which is more natural and less fatiguing for the audience.

Figure 18-19 shows the general connection for inserting a delay for the feed to an under-balcony fill system (or any rear seat fill system).

afternoon rock concert on a hot, humid summer day in Red Rocks, Colorado (one mile high) may require much less delay than an outdoor Inauguration Day rally in Washington DC during a bitterly cold January day. As a rule of thumb you can estimate 88.5 milliseconds delay per 100 feet (at 70° F) distance between main and fill loudspeakers, and you'll be close to the optimum value.

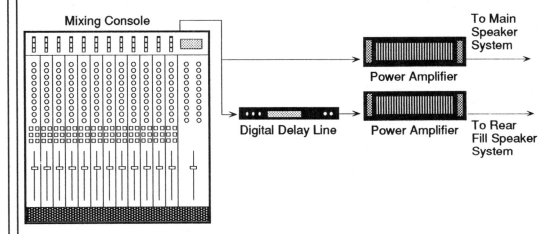

Figure 18-19. Electronics required for delaying the sound to rear fill loudspeakers

The delay must be adjusted to compensate for the propagation delay corresponding to distance D in Figure 18–17. To calculate the required delay time, use the following formula:

$$\text{Delay (milliseconds)} = 1000 \left(\frac{D \text{ (feet)}}{1130} \right)$$

For example, if D is 100 feet, the required delay is approximately 90 msec. One actually wants the sound to be delayed a little bit more than this so that it arrives slightly after the sound from the main cluster. This keeps the perceptual image up front. An additional delay of 10 msec is suitable; much more than this will result in an apparent echo from the fill loudspeakers.

The preceding formula is based on the speed of sound in dry air, at standard temperature, at sea level. If it is warmer, higher, or wetter, the sound travels more rapidly, so slightly less delay may be called for; an outdoor

18.6.1 Balancing Fill Systems

If you have a real-time analyzer, place the measurement microphone in the area covered by the fill system. With the pink noise test source connected to the total system input, first turn the main cluster up to a convenient level and note the frequency response at the measurement position. Then, while the main cluster is still on, bring up the level of the fill system until it just fills in the areas of deficient frequency response, but NOT until the total curve begins to rise in level.

In the case of delay systems, if you see cancellations appear when the fill system is turned on (deep, more or less regularly spaced notches in response), adjust the delay time to see if the notches can be minimized.

If you do not have an RTA, you can balance the fill system adequately by ear. Choose a music selection that you are familiar with — one that covers the full frequency range well. Play it through the main cluster and sit in the area covered by the fill system. Then have someone turn up the level of the fill system just until you begin to hear it as a separate sound source. Now back off on the level slightly until it just recedes into the sound of the main cluster.

18.7 Testing and Equalization

Testing of loudspeaker systems is a relatively simple process if you have the proper tools and follow a logical procedure. In this section we describe the step-by-step principles for testing reinforcement loudspeakers.

18.7.1 Single Loudspeakers

Before a reinforcement system is assembled and installed, it is extremely important that each individual loudspeaker be tested. In doing so, we wish to make certain that:

A) all loudspeakers in the system are working correctly, and

B) polarity is controlled, so that the loudspeakers will work properly together.

The first step in the process is to check the polarity of all visible, low frequency cone drivers in the system. The equipment required is simply a 9–volt transistor radio type battery and a pair of wires. (A 1.5-volt dry cell will suffice, but provides less visible diaphragm excursion.)

Connect the battery – terminal to the – (or black) connection terminal of the loudspeaker. Then, while watching the cone driver (you may need an assistant to do this), briefly connect the + battery terminal to the loudspeaker + terminal. (See Figure 18-20.)

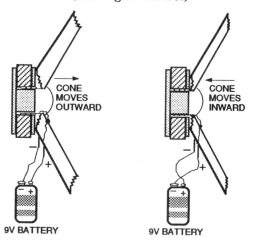

Figure 18-20. Checking loudspeaker polarity with a dry cell

18.7.2 Multiple Loudspeaker Systems

You should hear a distinct pop or thud from the speaker, and the cone should move forward. If the cone moves inward (toward the back of the cabinet), the driver is wired out-of-polarity. If there is no sound, and the cone doesn't move, then there is either a connection problem, or the driver itself may be blown (or the battery is dead!).

Note that if the low frequency elements in the system employ folded horn enclosures, testing the polarity is not as simple since the low frequency driver is not visible. In this case, electronic methods can be used to verify polarity. Most such methods require a fair amount of equipment with known polarity characteristics as well as significant setup time. A simple, relatively reliable solution, however, is to use a phase popper, or polarity popper. This instrument is covered in detail in Section 16, Sound System Test Equipment.

Testing of the polarity of mid and high frequency drivers usually cannot be done visually. Their proper relative polarity depends on the crossover design. These drivers should be considered in phase when the frequency response of the system is smoothest, given that the polarity of the low frequency driver has been verified.

The best test of the polarity of mid and high frequency elements is to check the system frequency response outdoors using a real-time analyzer. If you don't have an RTA, you can test by ear using recorded music, but this is obviously a less accurate method. A detailed description of such tests is given in Section 18.5, Setting Electronic Crossovers.

Once the polarity and frequency response of the loudspeaker are verified, it is a good idea to sweep the cabinet with a sine wave oscillator (if you have one). This test reveals slight coil rubbing, cabinet air leaks, cabinet or hardware resonances and other forms of distortion. All show up as a significant change in the sound of the sine wave to a more buzzing quality. The setup for this test is shown in the adjacent Figure 18-21, and is further described in Section 16.

Last, you may want to listen to recorded music as a final test of the sound of the loudspeaker.

When assembling a system using several loudspeakers, first test each unit individually as described above. Once this has been done, the last step is simply to be sure that all the loudspeakers in the system work together properly.

Place the loudspeaker cabinets side-by-side and turn down the amplifier level to all but one loudspeaker system. Feed music or pink noise, in mono, to the system, and turn up the level to the other loudspeaker(s) one at a time. As each loudspeaker is activated, the sound should increase in level but should not change substantially in quality. If you notice a radical change in quality when another loudspeaker is added, particularly if the bass diminishes, then you should check the polarity of the wiring of that loudspeaker in relationship to the other(s).

If you are using a full range loudspeaker system with a high frequency level control, adjust that control to suit your taste. Once you are sure that your system is operating properly, turn up the amplifier, play some music, and enjoy the sound.

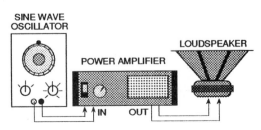

Figure 18-21. Sine wave sweep test of a loudspeaker

18.7.3 Room Equalization

If you have a real-time analyzer, you can test and equalize your sound system to obtain even better sound quality. To equalize the system, the first choice for an equalizer would be a multiple band parametric with good phase characteristics. Alternately, a graphic equalizer may be used. The equalizer should be connected as the last component in the main system before the power amplifiers. As discussed in Section 14, narrower band equalizers, parametric equalizers, (or notch filters) are best in this application. Also, any time correction of multiple drivers (either across a crossover point or in the same band but on dissimilar horns) should be applied before equalizing the system.

NOTE: *Third-octave equalization corresponds well with the critical bandwidth of the ear. The use of narrower band filters or equalizers may not correlate well with audible changes in the sound balance unless guided by sophisticated test equipment.*

First, place the measurement microphone in the near field of the system, approximately 3 to 4 feet away, on axis. This is especially important with an indoor system so that the initial adjustments are made inside the critical distance (before reverberation becomes a factor). With the pink noise source connected to the main system input before the equalizer, turn up the system gain to a convenient measuring level. Use the equalizer to adjust the system for flat frequency response.

Once the system has been made flat in the near field, move the measurement microphone out to a representative listening position at a distance from the system. You will notice two things:

A) the high-frequency response will be rolled off, usually starting at about 10 kHz, and

B) in an indoor system, or an outdoors one with nearby structures, one or more peaks or dips will appear in the low end.

The high frequency rolloff is due to the natural absorption of the highs in the air. If you attempt to boost the highs, you will find that the system sounds unnaturally bright and harsh. This is because the ear is used to hearing a rolloff at a distance, and perceives it as natural. The high-frequency response should not be adjusted on the basis of further measurements. One can adjust high end response to taste, using the ear to judge the results. Be sure to check the sound in the near and far audience areas, however. Some compromise in front-versus-rear highfrequency level may be required, or perhaps the tweeters can be re-aimed.

Low frequency aberrations are generally room related, and may be corrected to some extent. Before doing so, move the microphone around a bit to get a feel for how position dependent the peaks are. Many exist in only a very small area and no attempt should be made to correct them. When you are satisfied that you have identified those peaks that remain present at most locations, use the equalizer to dip them out.

Finally, play recordings with which you are familiar, and adjust the equalization to taste.

Additional information on this topic is contained in Section 14.

SECTION 19.
MIDI

From the very beginnings of audio until the mid-1980's, sound reinforcement engineers dealt exclusively with the audio signal path from performer to listener. While regular technological advances (and greater audience sophistication) spurred increasingly complex sound systems, the essentials remained the same: input transducers, signal processing, and output transducers. An engineer with a good grasp of audio theory could reasonably expect to scope out an unfamiliar system with relative ease.

We can now say with confidence that those days are gone. Today, video projection screens compete for space with the main PA. Lighting controllers resemble desktop computers. Musicians often play to click tracks, in sync with multitrack playback and digitally-sequenced keyboard parts. Snapshot-style console automation, frequently synchronized to music and lighting changes, is increasingly common.

Wherever today's sound engineer turns for employment — the neighborhood music club or house of worship, legitimate theater, industrial productions, all the way to large-scale concert sound — he or she must be able to deal with a world of signals outside of the audio path. The job demands that one speak in new languages and understand foreign signal families.

This chapter provides an introduction to one of the most pervasive and influential of these new languages: MIDI, the Musical Instrument Digital Interface. Developed in the early 1980's by a consortium of music synthesizer manufacturers — Yamaha, Roland, Korg, Kawai and Sequential Circuits — MIDI is a method for communicating music performance data among electronic musical instruments.

19.1 INTERFACE SPECIFICATIONS

Before the advent of MIDI, most synthesizers employed trigger signals and DC voltages to control aspects of sound generation — pitch, volume, when a note began, how long it lasted, how its amplitude and timbre changed over time, and so on. Each manufacturer's synthesizers adhered to somewhat different electrical standards, however. Whereas one might have employed a positive-going 5 volt pulse as a trigger, another would use a contact closure. Similarly, where one synthesizer's control voltage range might have been ±6 volts, another's would be 0 to +12 volts.

If every instrument were to be used only by itself, this relatively chaotic situation might have been perfectly acceptable. Realizing that each synthesizer had some unique merits not found in others, however, musicians inevitably sought to interconnect units made by different manufacturers. The task necessitated custom voltage level and trigger translation circuits, so many musicians found themselves learning to solder. When small computers first became available, some musicians went so far as to learn to program in assembly language and build digital-to-analog converters, in order to explore digital automation.

MIDI was the industry's response to the market demand for compatibility among electronic musical instruments. Taking advantage of the decade's extraordinary advances in digital technology, MIDI-equipped instruments employ integrated-circuit microprocessors to convert performance actions (which key is pressed, how hard it is pressed, which pedals are down, what sound program is used, and so on) into a digitally-coded data stream. The digital data is passed from one instrument to another over a serial interface, requiring only a single cable for each connection. By this method, multiple instruments can share musical data.

19.1.1 Hardware Configuration

Originally conceived as a tool for live music performance, the MIDI interface has proliferated with astounding speed. Today, MIDI ports can be found not only on synthesizers but also on consoles, lighting controllers, effects processors and personal computers. As a tool for inter-device communication and automation, it is one of the most important developments in contemporary audio technology.

The MIDI interface form and data protocol are specified in the *MIDI 1.0 Detailed Specification*, a document promulgated by the MIDI Manufacturers Association* (MMA) and the Japan MIDI Standards Committee (JMSC). These two organizations jointly govern implementation of, and enhancements to, the MIDI standard.

*The MMA shares the offices of the International Midi Association (IMA), though they are not directly affiliated. The IMA is a user-sponsored, non-aligned organization dedicated to dissemination of MIDI information, including the MIDI 1.0 Spec. They can be reached at: 5316 W. 57th St., Los Angeles, CA 90056, phone (213) 649-6434.

The hardware MIDI interface employs DIN 5-pin 180° female panel-mount receptacles throughout. The mating cables are comprised of shielded, twisted conductor pairs with male connectors at both ends, and are limited by the 1.0 Specification to a maximum length of 15 meters (50 feet). Connector pins 4 and 5 carry the digital signal, and the shield is tied to pin 2 (Figure 19-1).

The interface circuit is outlined in the block diagram of Figure 19-2. Data is transmitted serially over the cable as a stream of 0's (current on) and 1's (current off) at a rate of 31.25 Kbaud (31,250 bits per second). Data transmission is controlled by a Universal Asynchronous Receiver/Transmitter (UART) integrated circuit. An opto-isolator (a light emitting diode and phototransistor sealed together in a single housing) at the receiving end provides electrical isolation, to avoid ground loops between the transmitting and receiving circuits. Notice that the

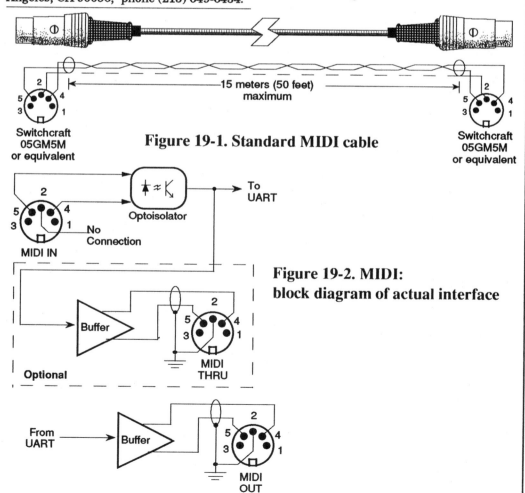

Figure 19-1. Standard MIDI cable

Figure 19-2. MIDI: block diagram of actual interface

ground is lifted in the wiring of the MIDI In connector to form a telescoping shield.

Optionally, the interface specification provides for an additional connector labeled "Thru." This port delivers a direct copy of the MIDI In data for retransmission to other devices, permitting MIDI-equipped instruments to be chained together in series.

The appearance of a typical fully-implemented MIDI port, such as might be found on a music synthesizer, is shown in Figure 19-3. On some keyboard instruments, the Thru jack may be omitted. Similarly, because they normally do not generate MIDI data of their own, effects processors usually will lack a MIDI Out port.

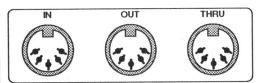

Figure 19-3. Typical instrument MIDI port

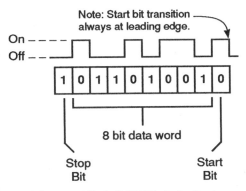

Figure 19-4. MIDI data byte structure

In a typical MIDI data exchange, a transmitting instrument issues at its MIDI Out port a command, or *message*, which specifies an action to be performed ("Play a middle C at mezzoforte dynamics," for example). The receiving instrument then executes the command, unless it is not within its designed capabilities (in which case it ignores it). Each MIDI message is coded as a string of digital data.

MIDI data is organized into 8-bit *bytes* (or *words*) preceded by one *start bit* (always a "0") and followed by one *stop bit* (always a "1"). Figure 19-4 illustrates a typical MIDI data byte, with the binary data shown in the middle of the figure and the corresponding current through the cable appearing just above the data. Each byte carries a different piece of information. The start and stop bits permit the receiving instrument's microprocessor to distinguish the end of one byte from the beginning of the next.

MIDI data bytes are further combined into *messages* consisting of one status byte followed by one or two data bytes (Figure 19-5). *Status bytes* define the kind of command being transmitted (note on, pitch bend, patch change, etc.). *Data bytes* carry specific information relative to the status byte command (key velocity, amount of pitch bend, patch number and so on).

MIDI messages are grouped in two basic classes: *channel messages* and *system messages*.

Note: The channel data can be from 0 through 15, (decimal) whereas the MIDI channel this value represents can be from 1 through 16. Reading from right to left, the binary digits shown here (0001) represent the decimal number one, or MIDI channel 2.

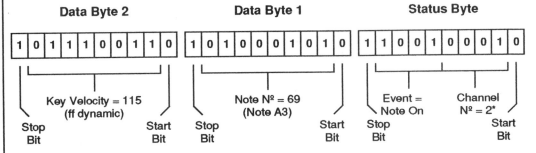

Figure 19-5. MIDI message structure

19.1.3 Channel Messages

To allow for independent control over a number of units in a system, MIDI data may be allocated among a total of 16 *channels*. In the same manner as a television or radio, a MIDI-equipped instrument can be set to receive data on a specific channel (or channels), while ignoring data on other channels (Figure 19-6). The channel on which it receives its main instructions is called the instrument's *basic channel*.

As the name implies, *channel messages* contain information that is intended for a specific receive channel. There are two types of channel messages: *Voice* and *Mode*:

1) **Voice** messages, which comprise the greatest part of the information transmitted over MIDI, are allocated to Voice channels. In most applications, they control synthesizers' sound-generating circuitry, defining when and how notes are played. They can be used for many other purposes, as well: Note On messages, for instance, can be used to trigger percussion sounds on rhythm synthesizers, stage lights, or fader and mute changes on a mixing console.

2) **Mode** messages define the receiving instruments' response(s) to Voice messages — instructing them, for example, to play monophonically or polyphonically (see Section 19.3.2, MIDI Modes). Mode messages must be sent on the *basic channel* of the intended receiver(s).

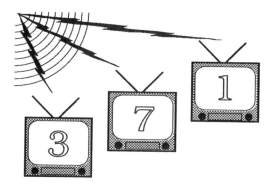

Figure 19-6. Like televisions, MIDI instruments may be tuned to specific receive channels (though you won't see a moving picture).

19.1.4 System Messages

Rather than being coded by channel, *System messages* are directed either to all instruments in the system, or only to those made by a particular manufacturer. There are three types of System messages: *System Common*, *System Real Time* and *System Exclusive*:

1) **System Common** messages are intended for all instruments in a MIDI system, regardless of their assigned channels. Most useful with drum machines and music sequencers, these messages carry such information as the song to be played; where in the song to begin playing; and MIDI Time Code quarter-frame data (see Section 19.6.5).

2) **System Real Time** messages carry timing information to MIDI equipment (such as a drum machine) that utilizes a synchronizing clock. The *Timing Clock message*, for example, provides a clock pulse at the rate of 24 per quarter-note. Other Real Time messages include *Start, Stop* and *Continue* commands for sequenced playback.

3) **System Exclusive** messages take on formats which are unique to specific manufacturers, and are used to send special data (such as patch parameter values, sampler memory or sequencer file data) that are applicable only to a particular instrument. Exclusive messages are directed to individual instruments by a manufacturer's identification number encoded in the Status byte. Each company, in turn, programs its instruments to recognize only its unique ID number, which is issued by the MMA and JMSC to manufacturers upon request.

19.2 Control of Musical Instruments

MIDI originally was developed for live music performance, and this is still a very important application for it. One of MIDI's most basic attributes is that allows multiple synthesizers to be played from a single keyboard. The controlling keyboard is termed the *master*, and the additional instruments that it controls are called *slaves*.

Figure 19-7 shows a typical small MIDI setup for live performance. The MIDI Out jack of a single master keyboard is connected to the MIDI In of the first slave unit, and the MIDI Thru jack of that slave is connected to the MIDI In of a second slave. Performance data originating with the master passes to the first slave, then is echoed to the second via the Thru connection. By controlling channel assignments and the settings of the individual instruments, a variety of doubling and soloing combinations can be achieved with this arrangement.

Notice that the two slaves in the Figure have no keyboards. The advent of MIDI has resulted in a proliferation of such units, variously called *expanders* or *modules*, which contain circuitry that must be controlled externally in order for it to produce a sound. By eliminating the mechanical keyboard and all of the electronics required to make it work, manufacturers have been able to produce very cost-effective MIDI-controlled instruments in small, easily transportable enclosures. Most such units are fitted to mount in a standard 19-inch relay rack, allowing musicians to configure very powerful systems in relatively compact, light-weight packages.

Similarly, several manufacturers offer MIDI master keyboards which incorporate no sound-generating circuitry at all, but are designed solely for the purpose of originating and transmitting MIDI control data. These units usually feature more expensive, specially-weighted keys which approximate the action of a traditional grand piano. Because all of their "intelligence" is devoted to generating control data, they also offer far more thorough and complex MIDI implementations than do ordinary keyboard synthesizers.

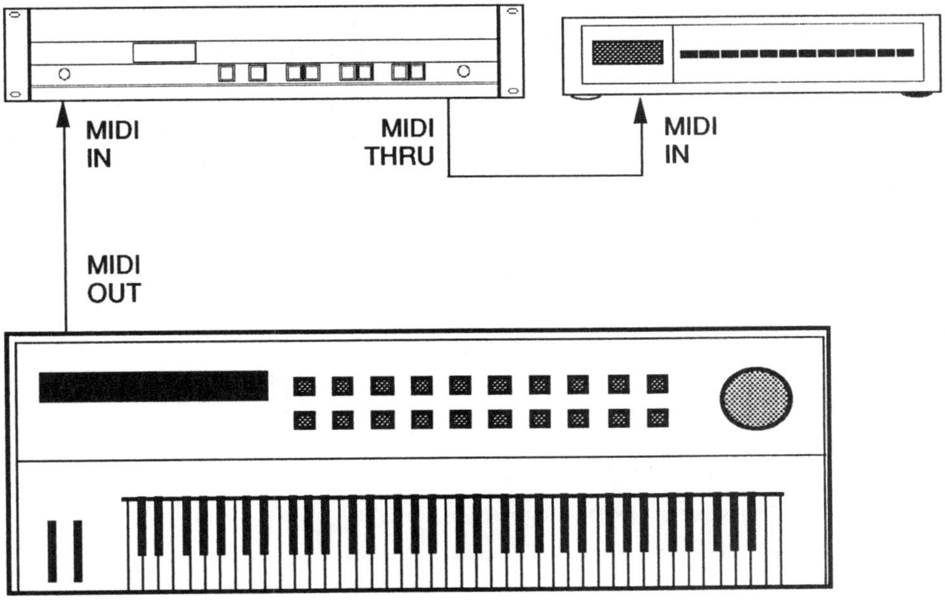

Figure 19-7. Small live performance setup

Figure 19-8 shows another possibility for a live performance setup, this time using three synthesizers, each of which has a keyboard. This setup takes advantage of the distinction between the MIDI Out and MIDI Thru ports to achieve a variety of doublings. If instrument #1 is played, both it and instrument #2 can sound. Instrument #3 cannot sound, though, because its MIDI In is connected to the MIDI Out of #2 (incoming messages are echoed at the Thru port, but not at the MIDI Out). If #2 is played, all three instruments can sound. Playing #3 will cause only it and #1 to sound.

The examples of Figures 19-7 and 19-8 reveal some of the possibilities that can be achieved with basic MIDI setups. These models may easily be expanded — by adding more instruments or some effects processors, for instance — to form larger and more powerful systems.

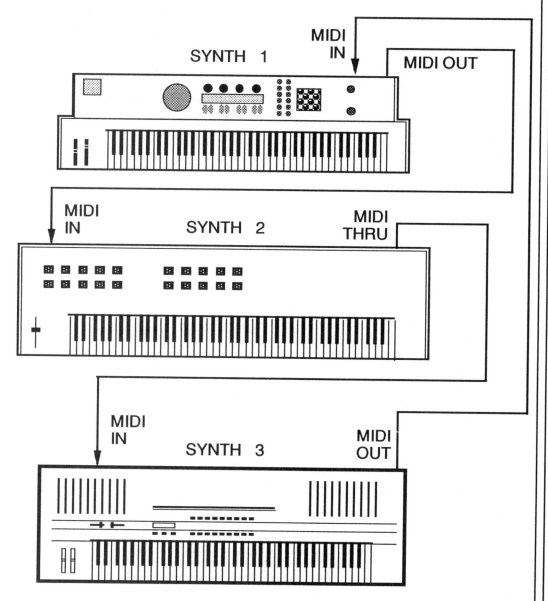

Figure 19-8. Live performance setup using three keyboard synthesizers

19.2.1 MIDI Modes

The MIDI 1.0 Specification defines a set of *Modes* which determine how instruments such as the slaves in Figures 19-6 and 19-7 will respond to incoming MIDI data. MIDI-equipped instruments are designed so that they may be switched among these MIDI Modes, each of which has different advantages in multi-synthesizer systems. In the 1.0 Specification, MIDI Modes are referred to by number.

Mode 1

This mode is also called *Omni On/ Poly*. The term *Omni* refers to the instrument's response to Channel information: with Omni On, the instrument will ignore MIDI Channel assignments and respond to *all* incoming MIDI note data. *Poly* is short for *Polyphonic*, and refers to vertical stacking of notes. In Poly mode, the instrument will play multiple simultaneous notes, up to its designed polyphonic limit. (No presently-available synthesizer is capable of playing an infinite number of simultaneous notes; most units are limited to between six and twenty-four stacked notes.)

Mode 2

Also called *Omni On/Mono*. As above, the instrument will respond to all incoming MIDI data, regardless of channel. *Mono* is short for *Monophonic*, the opposite of polyphonic in musical terminology. In Mono mode, the instrument will play only one note at a time; an instrument set to Mono mode cannot play chords. (Note that, in this usage, the term *monophonic* has nothing to do with whether or not the unit produces a *stereo (stereophonic)* output signal. In other words, MIDI's Mono terminology describes the number of simultaneous notes which can be sounded, not the number of audio output channels or the assignment of a given note or notes to those channels.)

Mode 3

This mode is termed *Omni Off/ Poly*. With Omni Off, the instrument will respond only to MIDI data that is transmitted on its assigned MIDI Channel. In Mode 3 it will, however, play multiple simultaneous notes.

Mode 4

Also termed *Omni Off/Mono*. In this mode, the instrument will respond only to MIDI data transmitted on its assigned Channel, and will play only one note at a time. Some synthesizers can function as multiple *virtual* instruments (playing more than one sound at a time), and are referred to as *multitimbral* synthesizers. Such instruments act like a number of MIDI data receivers, each set to a different MIDI channel (one channel per virtual instrument). Multitimbral synthesizers operate in a non-standard — though increasingly common — MIDI mode called *Multi* mode. Generally, the various receive channels in a Multi mode instrument are all either Mono or Poly, though some synthesizers permit intermixing modes among various receive channels in a multitimbral setting.

Ever since the first electronic synthesizers were introduced, one of the primary design problems faced by instrument development engineers has been the human interface. Music performance generally requires a great deal of expressive control. Most traditional acoustic instruments offer musicians a wealth of possibilities with very simple means: think of all the timbral variations that a violin is capable of, using simply a horsehair bow, gut strings and a fretless fingerboard! To be truly engaging and effective musical tools, electronic synthesizers must offer control mechanisms that provide, at the very least, some proportion of the flexibility afforded by traditional instruments.

Historically, the design approaches that the electronic music industry has applied to this problem have been many and varied, from the proximity-sensing antennae of the early Theremin to the velocity-sensitive, polyphonic-afterpressure keyboards of present-day synthesizers. And while the industry could be seen, at this writing, to have achieved a certain maturity — at least in relation to its status in the 1970's — the human interface is still the subject of much research and development. Nor is this work limited to musical instruments: present-day discussions of future console designs, for example, also revolve partially around the need for new "control surface" models.

Control Number		Controller Function
Dec	**Hex**	
0	00H	Undefined
1	01H	Modulation Wheel (or lever)
2	02H	Breath Controller
3	03H	Undefined
4	04H	Foot Controller
5	05H	Portamento Time
6	06H	Data Entry
7	07H	Main Volume
8	08H	Balance
9	09H	Undefined
10	0AH	Pan
11	0BH	Expression Controller
12-15	0C-0FH	Undefined
16-19	10-13H	General Purpose Controllers 1-4
20-31	14-1FH	Undefined
32-63	20-3FH	LSB for Controller values 0-31
64	40H	Damper Pedal (Sustain)
65	41H	Portamento
66	42H	Sostenuto
67	43H	Soft Pedal
68	44H	Undefined
69	45H	Hold 2
70-79	46-4FH	Undefined
80-83	50-53H	General Purpose Controllers 5-8
84-90	54-5AH	Undefined
91	5BH	External Effects Depth
92	5CH	Tremolo Depth
93	5DH	Chorus Depth
94	5EH	Celeste (Detune) Depth
95	5FH	Phaser Depth
96	60H	Data Increment
97	61H	Data Decrement
98	62H	Non-Registered Parameter Number LSB
99	63H	Non-Registered Parameter Number MSB
100	64H	Registered Parameter Number LSB
101	65H	Registered Parameter Number MSB
102-120	66-78H	Undefined
121-127	79-7FH	Reserved for Channel Mode Messages

Figure 19-9. MIDI 1.0 Specification controller numbers

In order to deal both with the present state of the art and with possible future developments in controller technology, the MIDI 1.0 Specification provides an extensive protocol for assignable controllers. Controller settings are transmitted as *Channel Voice Control Change messages*; two data bytes following the Control Change Status byte identify the controller and its value, respectively.

The controller numbers that have been assigned by the MMA and JMSC (as of document version 4.1 of the 1.0 Specification) appear in the table of Figure 19-9. Some comments apply to this listing:

- Controllers 0 through 31 are of the continuous type; that is, they provide continuously variable settings over a specified range. (This is analogous to a console fader, for example.) Note that controller numbers 32–63 are assigned to the LSB (Least Significant Byte) for numbers 0–31. This allows for much greater resolution in specifying the controller setting, as is appropriate with some continuous functions. (Use of the LSB is optional; if used, it increases data resolution to 14-bit, corresponding to 16,384 increments rather than the usual 128.)
- Controllers 64 through 69 are switch-type; the only data that need be communicated is whether they are ON or OFF. These, and numbers 70–95, are referred to as *single byte* controllers because the Specification does not provide an LSB for them. In theory, numbers 70–90 could be continuous types with 8-bit resolution.
- Data increment and decrement (96 and 97) and Data Entry (6) are MIDI editing controls. They may be implemented in various types of hardware — sliders, alpha wheels and up/down buttons are examples. Their function, regardless, is for remote editing of instrument parameters via MIDI.
- Registered and Non-Registered Parameters are reserved for "sound or performance parameters" (as an example, the three Registered Parameters that are currently defined are Pitch Bend Sensitivity, Fine

Tuning and Coarse Tuning). Registered Parameter assignments are subject to the agreement of MMA and JMSC; Non-Registered Parameters may be freely implemented by manufacturers as they choose. The Specification dictates that Non-Registered Parameter assignments be published in the owner's manual of the instrument.

- *Non-musical* devices such as lighting consoles may use any of these controller numbers as they wish. Don't be surprised to find non-standard implementations in such equipment.

19.2.3 Patch Editor/ Librarian Functions

For reasons of economy, most music synthesizers utilize small data displays (typically, a line or two of LED or LCD characters) that are capable of showing the status of only one or two parameters at a time. They also generally feature a limited number of buttons or knobs, whose functions may change dependent upon the editing action required. As synthesizers have become more sophisticated and complex, therefore, the task of programming them for custom sounds has been hampered by the lack of comprehensive displays and controls. The MIDI *System Exclusive* protocol (Section 19.1.4) was designed in part to address this problem.

The *SysEx* protocol enables manufacturers to develop custom messages exclusively for their own instruments, and to transmit those messages without disturbing the normal flow of MIDI data. In many cases, instrument software engineers have used System Exclusive to provide access to virtually all of the definable parameters of their instruments, including the contents of program or sample memory and the settings of internal control parameters. Given knowledge of the requisite commands and a means to transmit them over MIDI, such an implementation makes possible remote editing of the instrument's internal data (which determine the sounds it can make).

The MMA strongly encourages member companies to publish the details of their SysEx implementations, and stipulates that third-party hardware or software manufacturers may freely make use of the SysEx codes for any existing product without the permission of the original manufacturer. This policy has spawned an after-market industry serving the need for flexible, user-friendly control over instrument patch parameters (patch editing), and for centralized storage of instrument settings (library functions).

Patch editors and librarians are generally implemented in software written for one or more of the desktop computers that are popular for music use. (At this writing, the computers most widely used in music are the Apple Macintosh, Atari 512 and 1040 ST, Commodore Amiga, and IBM PC and its compatibles, including the Yamaha C1.) Editor programs allow the user to *patch* a synthesizer remotely from the computer terminal, making use of the computer's CRT to display all of the patch's parameters at once. Librarian software controls the exchange of patch data between the computer and the instrument, allowing instrument data to be stored on the computer's disk drive(s). The two functions are sometimes combined in a single program.

As a rule, editor/librarian software is custom-written for a specific instrument or family of instruments; commands that make perfect sense to an FM digital synthesizer, for instance, will not relate in any way to the functions of an analog instrument. The exception to this rule involves sampling synthesizers — instruments that play back digitally-recorded waveforms on command, usually transposing them according to the received key number. The 1.0 Specification includes a very comprehensive *Sample Dump Standard* governing exchange of sampler memory data, and this has encouraged the development of more-or-less universal software for samplers. In addition to programs for maintaining sample libraries, utilities have also been developed for computer synthesis of waveform data which may be transferred to samplers over MIDI. (These programs must still address differences in sampling frequency and sample length among the various instruments, but this can be accomplished computationally to some degree.)

19.2.4 MIDI Implementation Charts

To provide end users with a quick reference for ascertaining an instrument's MIDI functions, the 1.0 Specification provides a format for a MIDI Implementation Chart to be included with every instrument's documentation. Figure 19-10 shows a typical MIDI Implementation Chart.

The chart is divided into four columns, the first of which specifies a series of MIDI functions. The second and third columns tell whether each function is transmitted and/or received, and the fourth is reserved for remarks. If an instrument's MIDI implementation is unique in any way, that information will usually be found in the Remarks column, though the middle columns may contain clues, as well.

Implementation charts serve as a guide to compatibility among MIDI instruments. For example, if you have a master keyboard that transmits aftertouch data and you wish to see if a particular slave is capable of responding to that data, check the chart. Similarly, you can also ascertain whether a particular drum machine responds to System Common commands, or whether a sampler's software implements System Exclusive.

Date: 4/2, 1987

Model: DMP7   **MIDI Implementation Chart**   **Version**: 1.0

Function		Transmitted	Recognized	Remarks
Basic Channel	Default	1 − 16	1 − 16	memorized
	Changed	1 − 16	1 − 16	
	Default	x	OMNI off/OMNI on	
Mode	Messages	x	OMNI on/off	
	Altered	★★★★★★★★★★★★★★	x	
Note Number:	True Voice	0 − 127	0 − 127	†1
		★★★★★★★★★★★★★★	x	
Velocity	Note ON	o 9nH, v=0 − 127	o v=0 − 127	
	Note OFF	o 8nH, v=0 − 127	x	
After Touch	Key's	x	x	
	Channels	x	x	
Pitch Bender		x	x	
Control Change	0 − 127	o	o	†1
Program Change		o 0 − 127	o 0 − 127	†2
	True Number	★★★★★★★★★★★★★★	0 − 97	31 − 97: Cartridge
System Exclusive		o	o	Setup Data
System Common	Song Position	x	x	
	Song Select	x	x	
	Tune Request	x	x	
System Real Time	Clock	x	x	
	Commands	x	x	
Aux Messages	Local ON/OFF	x	x	
	All Notes OFF	x	x	
	Active Sensing	x	x	
	Reset	x	x	
Notes		†1: Each parameter can be assigned to any Control Change or Note On number, and these assignment tables can be stored in memory. †2: For program 1 − 128, memory #0 − #97 is selected.		

Mode 1: Omni On, Poly   **Mode 2**: Omni On, Mono   o = Yes

Mode 3: Omni Off, Poly   **Mode 4**: Omni Off, Mono   x = No

Figure 19-10. Typical MIDI implementation chart

Since the MIDI 1.0 Specification combines timing clock information with an extensive protocol for communicating performance actions, the recording and replaying of MIDI data is a natural extension of the interface concept.

MIDI recorders — more commonly termed sequencers — are MIDI's version of tape recorders. Capable of storing and reproducing virtually any event or command that can be transmitted by MIDI, they offer significant advantages in both studio recording and live performance. Playback may be synchronized with either an internal or an external time standard; the playback rate may be altered without affecting musical pitch; and recorded events may even be reassigned to different instruments or sound programs.

The block diagram of Figure 19-11 illustrates the concept of MIDI sequencing. The MIDI Out of a master unit that can generate the requisite MIDI control data is connected to the MIDI In port of a sequencer unit. The sequencer's MIDI Out is then routed back to the master unit, whose MIDI Thru may be connected to other MIDI-equipped slave devices.

In recording mode, performance actions originating at the master are converted to MIDI data and sent to the sequencer, which memorizes them in relation to an internal timing reference. The contents of the sequencer's memory can then be saved to a storage device (normally, a floppy disk or hard disk drive) for later recall.

In playback mode, the sequencer reproduces the recorded MIDI data at its MIDI Out, with events again being timed in relation to its internal clock reference. The sequencer data passes back to the master's MIDI In port and, optionally, is echoed to other devices by its Thru port. The master reproduces the recorded performance actions, as do any slave units chained to it.

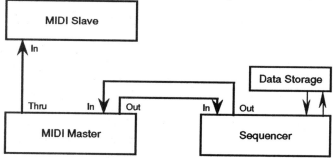

Figure 19-11. MIDI sequencing

Figure 19-12 (next page) shows a simple music recording system implemented according to the model of the previous Figure. Here, the MIDI sequencer unit is a personal computer equipped with a MIDI interface. The master is a keyboard synthesizer, and the slaves are a keyboardless expander module and a drum machine. (Note the similarity to the live performance system of Figure 19-7.) Drum machines usually incorporate sequence memory of their own. With this system, the musician may use that memory for drum patterns, which the drum machine can then play in synch with a MIDI clock pulse derived from the sequencer's internal reference.

For greatest operational flexibility and ease of use, MIDI sequencers are modeled on the multitrack tape recorder. A sequencer may have from one to a hundred or more *tracks* (as with audio tape decks, the number is usually finite). These tracks record MIDI data rather than audio information, and are sometimes called *virtual* tracks because they reside in digital memory rather than on tape.

All of the track functions normally associated with multitrack recording may be performed with a MIDI sequencer. Tracks can be overdubbed in synch with previously-recorded material. Individual tracks can be soloed or muted in playback. Data can be bounced from two or more tracks to another in order to free up track space.

The similarity ends at the concept of channels. In an audio tape recorder, a track *is* a channel. In a MIDI sequencer, data on one or more tracks may be freely assigned to *any* of the sixteen MIDI channels. Moreover, a sequencer track can be made (through track bouncing) to contain events assigned to two or more channels at once, because the MIDI protocol tags each individual event with channel data.

In MIDI sequencers, then, channels and tracks are entirely separate things. A channel is a routing assignment for a particular set of MIDI data; channels are associated with specific receiver instruments, and thus with particular sounds. A track, by contrast, is simply a container for holding recorded MIDI data; the data's channel assignment can be independent of its track assignment.

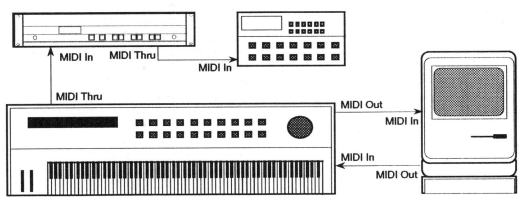

Figure 19-12. A Simple music sequencing system

The multitrack model brings a great deal of flexibility to MIDI sequencing. For example, it is often impractical to store in one pass all of the events (such as fader moves or keystrokes) that you want a particular device to execute. As with conventional multitrack recording, you can overdub two or more successive passes on separate tracks, assigning both to the same MIDI channel to create a composite effect. You may then elect to merge the two tracks, or you can keep them separate for editing purposes.

Some sequencers feature multiple MIDI Out ports, with the ability to route individual tracks to any of the ports. This capability can extend MIDI beyond its sixteen-channel limitation, allowing very complex effects.

For example, Figure 19-13 shows track assignments in a sequencer with two MIDI Out ports and thirty-two tracks. Tracks 1–16 and 17-32 are assigned to MIDI channels 1–16, respectively, so that there are two tracks for each channel. The first sixteen of the tracks have been assigned to port #1, and the other sixteen to port #2. If each MIDI Out port drives a separate MIDI system, this creates the equivalent of thirty-two MIDI channels. Separate devices in each system may *share* the same MIDI channel assignment, yet receive entirely separate track data.

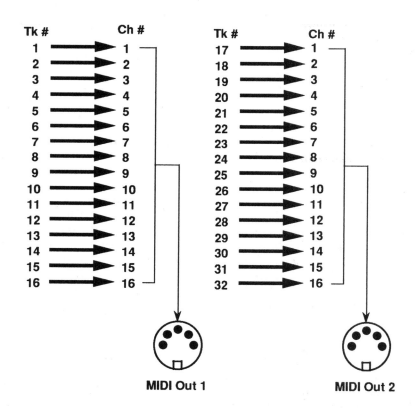

Figure 19-13. Creating a thirty-two channel MIDI system

19.3.3 Hardware vs Computer-Based Sequencers

MIDI sequencers are classified in three different types. Add-on units comprise a hardware interface and software program which, together, turn a personal computer into a MIDI recorder. Stand-alone sequencers are hardware units which perform only sequencing (and, in some cases, patch librarian) functions. Built-in sequencers may be found in a number of MIDI synthesizers.

Of the three, add-on sequencers are probably the most common type. Hardware MIDI interfaces are available for every popular personal computer (a few computers even feature a built-in interface), and are supported by a number of software packages.

Though more expensive than the other two types, add-on sequencers offer numerous advantages. A computer monitor (or CRT — cathode ray tube) can display a lot of information at once, resulting in very fast and efficient operation with less chance of mistakes due to overlooked settings. Mouse-driven computers further enhance efficiency by reducing most operations to a single button-click. Many add-on packages can transcribe recorded MIDI data into music notation (or save disk files that can be accessed by separate notation programs). Moreover, a general-purpose personal computer can be put to other uses such as financial record-keeping, word processing, telecommunications and entertainment. The down side is that, unmodified, many personal computers do not take well to road use.

Stand-alone sequencer units occupy the middle ground in terms of both price and functionality. More cost-effective than personal computers, stand-alone sequencers can be very easy to use, since they feature dedicated controls. Being designed specifically for the task of MIDI sequencing, they generally offer very comprehensive MIDI implementations. Many can sync to a variety of external clock sources without the need for additional clock-translation hardware. The display capabilities of stand-alone units are usually limited, so editing can be a bit more troublesome than with an add-on computer sequencer. Nonetheless, stand-alone sequencers

tend to be much more roadworthy than typical computers. (There are exceptions, such as the roadworthy Yamaha C1 — an MS-DOS compatible laptop computer with a built-in MIDI interface.)

Sequencers built into MIDI-equipped synthesizers offer an obvious price advantage: you get the sequencer, at no additional cost, when you buy the instrument. They don't require separate cases, and are ready to use as soon as the instrument is powered up. Built-in sequencers are the least sophisticated of the three types, though, and usually possess track and note capacity limitations. By and large, their data display is that of the synthesizer and, in most cases, this means that editing is difficult. Still, for performing musicians who don't need a complex sequencing capability, a built-in unit can serve well and be a real bargain.

19.3.4 Typical Sequencer Features

Most sequencers cater primarily to the musician. This is especially evident when reviewing the terminology and graphics associated with these units. Such nuances underscore the sequencer's musical heritage. This should present no real obstacle for those who wish use these sequencers for nonmusical instrument control purposes, as their operation can be quickly learned and they are easily adapted to other functions.

Manufacturers of MIDI sequencers each strive to offer a variety of features that makes their products unique. Still, manufacturers attempt to follow certain basic functions and conventions. Most notably, all sequencers incorporate basic recording controls which emulate those of an audio tape deck. These standard *tape transport* functions (they do not, of course, actually control tape motion) are *play*, *record, pause, stop,* and *punch in.*

Perhaps the most widely used *tape transport* function of the sequencer is *track assignments*. Track assignments control the arming, muting and soloing of MIDI tracks, as well as allocation of each track to a specific MIDI channel.

The remaining sequencer functions are primarily editing tools.

19.3.4.1 Song Editing

The *song editor* is a global editing tool. Sequencers store real time information, not only in terms of actual *elapsed time*, but also in terms of musical *beats* and *bars*. The song editor manipulates these bars. An audio tape recorder logs how much *tape* it uses with a numerical tape counter (which is occasionally calibrated in feet of tape or in hours, minutes and seconds). The sequencer keeps track of how much *data* it stores in terms of musical *beats* and *bars* as well as time (*minutes* and *seconds*). Unlike an audio tape deck, the MIDI sequencer can separate tracks and move them to other tracks at different points. An audio tape recorder can only ping-pong vertical tracks to the same place (i.e., the same time). For example, take a MIDI sequence that has two recorded tracks, each eight bars long. The song editor allows you to either copy those eight bars and insert them, creating a total of sixteen bars of repeated information, or move them to any available track offset to any position in time within the confines of bar delineation. The song editor also adds or deletes measures, copies and pastes measures, and mixes data.

On occasion, a track sheet may become cluttered after only a few moves on one or two tracks that are assigned to the same MIDI port and channel. It is possible to reduce the clutter by combining these channels via the sequencer's *mix data* function.

19.3.4.2 Step Editing

Finer detail can be obtained in another area of the sequencer called the *step editor*. In this area, you can advance or retard MIDI data one beat at a time, or even as little as one clock pulse either direction (a clock pulse is a very small increment, typically 1/96 or 1/128 second). This function is especially useful for sound effects editing.

Some other features in the step editor are: direct point-by-point MIDI recording, such as placing a MIDI note at a specific point in the score, without recording it in real time, by entering the appropriate value; changing the duration of existing notes; altering note on and off commands; and changing the MIDI note number (and hence the pitch) of existing notes. Some sequencers allow block moves of selected (highlighted) areas of the score to be affected in this manner — a powerful means of editing.

19.3.4.3 Common Editing Features

There are also several editing features that relate to both the song and step editor, such as *transposing*. Transposing takes selected MIDI data and moves it up or down by a MIDI note. In musical terms, for example, this would mean taking a piece written in C major and moving it up to C sharp major.

Another important editing feature, *quantizing*, adjusts live performances so notes begin and/or end precisely to synchronize with a specified beat. In musical applications, a performer can play his MIDI keyboard to the sequencer's metronome and later quantize the track to *clean up* his performance. The amount of quantizing, and the precision by which it alters MIDI time values, can generally be controlled in in finite increments so that an aesthetic balance between human performance and technical perfection can be obtained. (A 100% quantized performance tends to sound mechanical and lacks the smooth flow of music performed in real time.) Quantizing can be particularly useful in automating sound reinforcement, where mutes and solos need to occur at a precise point in the music.

The final area is the editing of MIDI *controller data* (values 0–127). MIDI notes and MIDI controllers are recorded concurrently. Controllers such as MIDI control #1 (which represents modulation wheel position) and MIDI controller #7 (which represents MIDI volume) can be altered by editing the MIDI controller data.

19.4 MIDI Data Processors

Just as external signal processors can enhance the quality of an audio production, so there are also MIDI data processors which can optimize and enhance the performance of a MIDI system. These units do not handle audio signals; rather, they process the MIDI data stream.

A growing number of such units continues to appear on the market, and many perform relatively specialized functions. In this Section, we will survey a few of the more common types.

19.4.1 Thru Boxes

As described in Section 19.2, MIDI devices possessing Thru ports can be daisy-chained together so that incoming MIDI data will pass from one to the next. In practice only a limited number of instruments (usually less than five) can be connected in this way because speed limitations of the MIDI interface opto-isolators can accumulate and introduce data errors. Moreover, some instruments do not provide a Thru jack.

MIDI Thru boxes, available from several manufacturers, alleviate these problems. Figure 19-14 illustrates the use of a 1:4 Thru box (a common configuration) in a live performance setup. The master unit's MIDI Out feeds the Thru box MIDI In, and the Thru box's four MIDI Outs each feed a separate slave unit. In theory, two or three slaves could be daisy-chained on each branch.

Engineers accustomed to *multing* audio signals may wonder why the Thru box is necessary. The 1.0 Specification (and the electronic design of the interface) stipulates a +5 volt, 5 mA current loop for the data transmission connection. If you simply split a MIDI Out to two MIDI Ins, the signal level at each input will drop by half, and the input stages may not be able to read the data reliably — or at all. The Thru box provides four separate, buffered MIDI Outs, each with the requisite +5 volt signal level, assuring accurate data transmission.

19.4.2 MIDI Mergers

The inverse relative of the Thru box is the MIDI merger. These devices usually feature two MIDI Ins and one or more MIDI Outs. Data appearing at the MIDI Ins is merged and presented at the MIDI Outs as a single data stream, allowing two masters to control a single MIDI system.

MIDI mergers are necessitated by the synchronization demands of MIDI data transmission. Even if two masters were to share the same clock and phase lock, each would have no way of knowing what the other is doing at any given time. Were both to send a command at precisely the same instant, one would be ignored by the receiving equipment unless some device *merged* the two commands in an ordered, uninterrupted and synchronous manner.

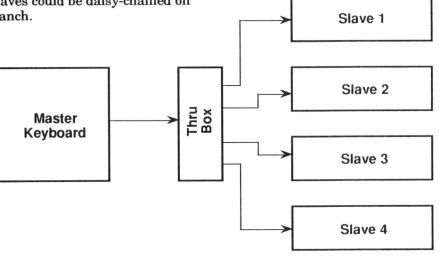

Figure 19-14. Use of a Thru box

Because the task of merging two MIDI data streams requires a fair amount of processing "intelligence," MIDI mergers tend to be much more expensive than Thru boxes.

19.4.3 MIDI Patchers

Despite the considerable flexibility that is built into the MIDI protocol, a single MIDI connection configuration almost never satisfies every contingency.

On the simplest level, for example, one might occasionally wish to make a different synthesizer the master in a live performance system — because its playing characteristics better fit certain styles, or because it possesses some control features that the normal master lacks. The solution in these situations is either to manually re-patch, or to use a MIDI patcher.

MIDI patchers are basically electronic data switchboards that allow programmable routing of MIDI connections in a system. Available in a variety of configurations, these devices normally feature several MIDI Ins and Outs. Different routing configurations may be programmed using front-panel buttons and saved to non-volatile battery-backed memory for later recall. Recall may be triggered by pressing a front-panel switch, an external foot switch, or some other form of control.

19.4.4 Mapping Devices

MIDI mapping devices perform various types of data translation on the MIDI data stream in order to extend the capabilities of the MIDI control system or make up for shortcomings in master units.

One such translation is Program Change mapping. Program Change commands direct the receiver to select a particular *program number* from its memory banks (in synthesizers, *programs* determine the sound characteristics). The Channel Voice Program Change protocol provides for selection of programs by number, in the range of 0–127. Program Change mapping translates a transmitted Program Change number to a different specified value before it reaches the slave unit. This function may be used to select

specific instrument sounds (having different program numbers) on a variety of different *slave* synthesizers with the press of a single Program Change button on the *master* unit.

Another example of a mapping function is keyboard splitting. In some musical situations, it is desirable for one range of keys on the master keyboard to trigger a different key range on the slave. Often, there may be some overlap in the desired ranges. In a multi-instrument MIDI setup, this *splitting* of the keyboard may require that the master transmit different keyboard ranges on different MIDI channels. If the master does not have this capability (most keyboards don't), then a mapping device can provide it.

19.4.5 SysEx Data Storage

SysEx data storage devices exploit the 1.0 Specification *System Exclusive* protocol to store setup information from various devices in a MIDI system at one central facility. Such devices normally comprise one or more disk drives, and the intelligence to learn — and transmit on command — appropriate SysEx commands to a variety of instruments.

Because the unit deals only with storage of SysEx data (and not operations on that data), it handles the data as bulk dumps without regard to content. SysEx storage units allow storing most (if not all) of the instrument settings in a MIDI system on one or two floppy disks. By incorporating the capability to retransmit bulk SysEx data to instruments, these devices permit very fast and reliable setup changes.

19.5 Automation Through MIDI

Over the past decade, technological advances in sound system design have resulted in greatly expanded control over sonic quality, even in acoustically difficult venues. Concurrently, increasingly sophisticated lighting systems and the incorporation of multimedia elements have collaborated in elevating the overall intricacy and dramatic impact of live performances. Most styles of music now make use of relatively elaborate multi-synthesizer setups, necessitating complex mixes with an increased emphasis on outboard processing.

The inevitable result of all of these trends has been escalated demands upon the skills of reinforcement engineers. Rather than simply maintaining a relatively static mix over the course of a show, engineers must effect rapid and accurate changes in levels and mutes, sends, equalization, and outboard effects settings. Even routine scene changes can make a mixer wish he or she had four hands!

Properly implemented, MIDI can help enormously in addressing these challenges by automating common tasks. MIDI also can interface the once-disparate live performance teams of music, sound and lighting: group controls like master fades, lighting moves related to real-time music sequences, and multi-media synchronization in conjunction with SMPTE time code are just a few examples. Even mundane tasks like cueing prompters via sequencing can alleviate performance mishaps and warrant the effort.

In considering MIDI's automation potential, it is important to remember that while the protocol allows for timekeeping functions, MIDI also may be used for so-called "snapshot" automation. In such an implementation, one could store scene change data as a group of presets to be called up on cue from a computer, by pressing footswitches, or from some other encoded controller.

At this writing, MIDI automation is a relatively new development, and is not yet widely used. In the following pages, we will briefly survey some of the possibilities that are presently available.

19.5.1 Instrument Patch Changes

In working with large multi-synthesizer setups, one of the most tedious tasks that keyboard players face is selecting the right sound programs for each song. First of all, one must remember which program each instrument should be playing — and this, alone, introduces a potential for errors since sound programs are always selected by number rather than name.

Assuming that one recalls all the program numbers correctly, there is still the matter of the time it takes to set up each instrument. While some synthesizers allow entering program numbers from a keypad, many others require scrolling through the program list with up/down buttons or a selector wheel. Given that many instruments accommodate a hundred or more programs, this can take a significant amount of time.

The inevitable delays that all of this searching and selection causes between songs can be greatly reduced by using MIDI Channel *Voice Program Change messages* and/or System Exclusive commands. Program Change messages are sent on the receiving instrument's Basic Channel, instructing the instrument to select a specified sound program. System Exclusive messages are directed to a particular instrument by manufacturer ID (rather than channel), and may be used to alter either patch settings or the unit's entire memory contents.

MIDI synthesizers generally transmit Program Change commands when new sounds are selected on them. This capability can be used along with Program Change mapping to cause other (slave) instruments to select complementary programs. Alternatively, other assignable controllers or switches can be used for transmitting Program Change messages to slaves.

In large setups, the most efficient means for effecting program changes is a personal computer running a utility program designed for the purpose; this permits quick, centralized changes of instrument setups. System Exclusive bulk dumps of synthesizer or sampler memory may be handled either by a personal computer or by a disk-based system designed specifically for that purpose.

19.5.2 Signal Processors

Synthesized and sampled sounds cry out for external processing to give them *life* and sonic complexity. Some musical styles rely heavily on multiple effects, with settings changing in different parts of a single song. Visual productions such as industrials or legitimate theater also often call for dramatic effects changes on tight cues.

In response to these practical demands, a number of MIDI-controlled outboard effects units have been produced. While most of these units employ digital delay processing, MIDI-controlled parametric equalization is also coming to the fore. Moreover, present-generation delay processors offer a great deal more than simple echo or reverberation: *non-linear* reverberation programs, phasing, flanging, chorusing, and pitch shifting are all quite common.

MIDI signal processors tend to borrow from the synthesizer model of selectable numbered programs residing in memory, so the most common means of automating effects is to use Program Change commands. In many units, however, this must be done with care since a program change may be accompanied by noise or a momentary muting of the output.

In some cases, basic reverberation parameters such as predelay, reverb time and high-frequency damping may be available for continuous control — usually by the Control Change protocol's General Purpose Controllers. (Similar provisions may be made for center frequency, Q and boost/cut parameters in MIDI-controlled parametric equalizers.) Such an implementation permits one to *play* the processor's settings in real time — or to feed them into a sequencer for later playback. When selected for the duration of a single program, such parameter changes may not cause noise or dropout, depending upon the sophistication of the signal processing unit.

19.5.3 Console Functions

The logical extension of effects and instrument automation is to automate mixing console functions. At this writing, two types of systems are available for this task: add-on units, and built-in MIDI implementations.

Add-on systems are perhaps more common at present. Consisting of a separate enclosure that houses VCAs (voltage-controlled amplifiers) and digital electronics to interpret and execute MIDI commands, these units are usually patched at input strip insertion points. They permit automating only gains and mutes. The manufacturer may provide proprietary software, though third-party sequencers may be used as well.

Built-in MIDI automation is available in some contemporary consoles — though most such units are designed for studio use rather than portable reinforcement. Fader and mute automation is standard. Additionally, it may be possible to automate routing assignments.

In both cases, MIDI *implementations* vary from one unit to another; for example, where one may use Control Change messages for fader data, another may employ Pitch Bend messages. This is fine as long as the system is used only by itself. On the other hand, if two dissimilar systems are expected to interchange data, additional MIDI signal processing (remapping) may be required to translate commands from one unit's protocol to the other's.

Looking to the future, digital signal processing (or digitally-controlled audio) technology will allow automating virtually every feature on a console. The Yamaha DMP-7, for example, is an all-digital 8x2 audio mixing console which features a very extensive MIDI implementation. When operated in conjunction with a sequencer, the DMP-7 permits MIDI automation of not only faders and mutes, but also such parameters as channel equalization, aux and reverb send levels, pan, and effects settings.

At present, such capabilities are targeted primarily at recording studios. But this unit, and other larger devices currently being marketed for studio recording, presage developments to come in the world of reinforcement console design.

In conjunction with SMPTE Time Code (Section 20), MIDI-sequenced parts may be synchronized to a variety of other media such as multitrack audio tape, videotape or film. The Time Code serves as a place marker signal, and a SMPTE-to MIDI Converter handles translation of the time code signal to MIDI clock.

MIDI synchronization takes advantage of provisions in the System Common and System Real Time protocols:

Song Position Pointer — The System Common Song Position Pointer message provides an indication of the number of beats that have elapsed since the beginning of a sequence. It is used to play back a portion of a sequence from a position other than the start of a song. Normally set to 0 at the start of a sequence, SPP increments every sixth clock pulse until playback is stopped; if the sequence is continued, rather than restarted, SPP continues to increment from its previous value.

Sequencers and drum machines which respond to SPP can be made to start at any desired beat in a sequence by sending them an SPP message specifying the beat, then sending a Continue command.

Start, Stop, Continue — These System Real Time messages are used to command "transport" motion of MIDI sequencers and drum machines. *Start* commands the system to start at the beginning of the sequence (SPP = 0). *Stop* halts sequence playback. *Continue* commands the sequence to restart without reverting to the beginning of the sequence.

In MIDI sequence recording, Song Position Pointer allows punch-ins in the middle of a song without reverting to the beginning and running all the way through to the punch point. Used with SMPTE Time Code, it permits the same capability in multitracked overdubs of acoustic instruments or voice.

In MIDI, as in all things electronic, troubles can crop up when you least expect them. MIDI is a microprocessor-based technology — with software consequently playing a major role — and one might therefore expect that a MIDI system would be significantly more complicated to troubleshoot than a standard audio system. Fortunately, most common electronic problems – MIDI or otherwise – yield to the same approach: logical signal tracing and a systematic process of elimination.

There is no substitute for a thorough understanding of the system's layout when tracking down bugs. Nor can we possibly anticipate the myriad problems which *might* occur. We will attempt, in the following paragraphs, to offer suggestions regarding some common MIDI problems.

19.6.1 Lack of Response

Perhaps the most prevalent disorder in MIDI systems is the mute synthesizer; no matter what MIDI commands are sent, the unit refuses to respond.

An obvious immediate cause of the lack of sound might be the audio path so the first places to explore are the audio connections and the mixing console settings. Check, also, to see that the apparently inoperative MIDI unit's volume control is up, and that a sound-generating program is selected.

If you are satisfied that the audio path is OK or if panel indicators on the unit show that it is not receiving MIDI data, then the next step is to check the MIDI connections. MIDI transmission problems can have any of several causes:

1) The MIDI cable may be bad. You can isolate this problem by replacing the cable in question with a known, good cable.
2) The MIDI cable may be misconnected. Remember that master units send commands from the MIDI Out, *not* the MIDI Thru. Conversely, slaves pass data onward via the MIDI Thru, *not* the MIDI Out.
3) The receiver's channel assignment may be incorrect. MIDI data sent on channel 2 will not be received if the

slave is set to channel 3, for example. You can check for this by setting the receiver to Omni On Mode, so that it will respond to data on all channels; if the unit now responds, then check the channel assignments.

4) A unit upstream may not be turned on. MIDI is an active interface, so a unit that is not powered up will *not* echo incoming data at its MIDI Thru port, and hence will break the MIDI signal path. If you must turn off a unit in the middle of the MIDI signal path, you will have to unplug the cable from its MIDI input and instead plug that cable into the input of the next MIDI device.

19.6.2 Stuck Notes

For each note that is to sound, a series of MIDI commands must be sent. The first of these is a Note On command, which is followed by data bytes that give details regarding the pitch and velocity values for the note. When the note is to cease, a separate Note Off command must be sent and received. If the Note Off command is not received, the synthesizer may continue to play indefinitely.

Note Off commands can be interrupted in several ways:

1) The MIDI cable may have become disconnected before the Note Off was received.

2) You may have changed MIDI channels on the master while holding down a note.

3) If sequence playback is involved, an editing operation on the sequencer may have deleted or overwritten the Note Off; or playback may have been stopped in midstream, before the Note Off was sent.

In all cases, the quickest solution is to turn the synthesizer off, wait a few seconds, then turn it on again. This will reset the unit and silence any *hanging* notes.

MIDI *data* feedback — as distinguished from audio feedback — occurs when the MIDI Out data of a sound-producing master finds its way back to the master's MIDI In port. The master transmits data on its basic channel, simultaneously playing the selected notes. The feedback signal appearing at its MIDI In causes it to play the same notes again, but with a slight time delay that is dependent upon the feedback path.

This has two effects. First, it generally results in a distinctive flanging or phasing sound caused by phase cancellation due to the signal delay. Second, because each note is sounded twice, the polyphonic limit of the synthesizer *appears* to be half of what it should be, with the consequence that certain notes will drop out early, or not sound at all.

The solution is, of course, to find and eliminate the feedback path. MIDI feedback occurs most commonly in sequence recording, when the sequencer is set for Thru operation. Referring back to Figure 19-11, observe the MIDI loop between the sequencer and the master. If the sequencer reproduces input data at its MIDI Out, then MIDI feedback will occur. The solution is either to switch off the sequencer's Echo function, or to set the master for Local Off (a mode in which the keyboard will not activate the internal voices).

19.6.4 MIDI Time Delays

MIDI time delays have been the subject of some significant debate. In the early history of MIDI, musicians began to complain that, when they chained several synthesizers using Thru connections, they experienced small but perceptible time delays that threw the *feel* of their tracks out of kilter. For this, they blamed the speed of the interface, and argued that it should have been made parallel, rather than serial. Engineers countered that the speed of the interface made time delays insignificant, and that the musicians were imagining things.

Subsequent investigation has solved the riddle; both were right! The MIDI interface *itself* is, indeed, quite fast if properly implemented; the 1.0 Specification mandates a maximum delay of 2 microseconds. While additional processing delays can occur in individual instruments (though this is due not to MIDI, but to the time required for the instrument's processor to *think things out* before making a sound), they are not likely to be significant. Still, audible problems can occur. How?

The rising edge of the MIDI signal's waveform can be skewed excessively when the signal goes through multiple MIDI In and Thru ports. The waveform is degraded with each such passage so the cumulative degradation can cause errors in data or commands. Such errors may, indeed, be audible.

Once again, the miniscule time delay of 2 or even 10 microseconds is not audible. In fact, delays as large as hundreds of microseconds are not perceptible to a trained ear. The incremental addition of internal processing delay and opto-isolator delay seldom amounts to as much as a millisecond. (A millisecond is 1,000 microseconds.) Delays of less than 5 milliseconds are generally believed to be insignificant. After all, it takes 25 to 30 milliseconds before we hear a discrete echo!

Data errors due to Thru connections are easily solved by adding one or more Thru boxes to the setup (see Section 19.4.1). Internal signal processing delays, however, are harder to handle; if they create a significant problem, the manufacturer of the offending equipment should be responsible for improving the equipment design.

20.1 GENERAL DISCUSSION

Synchronization is the process of causing two or more devices to operate in concert, with an agreement in time and rate of speed. In audio usage, the term customarily denotes an interface between independent, normally free-running machines — two multitracks, for instance, or an audio tape recorder and a video playback deck. Audio synchronization has its origin in post-production for film (and, later, video), but synchronizing equipment is now extremely common in music recording studios, as well.

In the sound reinforcement field, industrial production is the job most likely to involve the engineer with some form of synchronization. Large-scale industrials are quite ambitious affairs, often intermixing prerecorded video, film, slides, multitracked music and effects with live performance. All of these media must operate synchronously, on cue, with no chance for a retake. The importance of understanding how synchronization systems function, therefore, cannot be overestimated — especially since these technologies are making further inroads into the reinforcement world every day.

This chapter surveys some of the synchronization methods that today's sound reinforcement engineers are likely to encounter, with a special emphasis on SMPTE Time Code (SMPTE is the Society of Motion Picture and Television Engineers). The information presented here is not intended to be comprehensive (a full treatment of the subject would require a book in itself), but it should be sufficient to enable a basic understanding of most contemporary systems. The interested reader is encouraged to seek further information in texts that are specific to each technology.

20.1.1 Basic Theory

For two independent machines to be synchronized, there must be a reliable means of determining the movement of each, and adjusting so that the two operate synchronously. This demands that each machine provide a signal — referred to as a sync signal — that reflects its movement. The sync signals from both machines must be compatible; that is, each must reflect its machine's movement in the same way, so that the two can be compared. Sync signals may be either generated directly by the machine transports, or recorded on the media handled by the machines and reproduced when they are in motion.

One machine is taken to be the *master*, and serves as a reference to which the *slave* machine is adjusted. In *closed-loop* synchronization systems (Figure 20-1), a separate synchronizer compares the slave's sync signal to that of the master and generates an error signal which drives the slave's motor, forcing the slave to follow the master. Electronics engineers also refer to this type of control structure as a *servo system* or *feedback control system*.

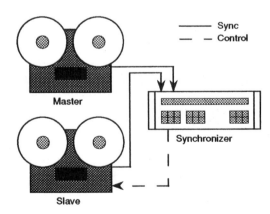

Figure 20-1. Closed-loop synchronization system

Feedback control offers two important advantages:

1) It automatically compensates for variations in the master's movement, be they small (speed variations due to changing load or power conditions), or gross (bumping the master into fast-wind mode).

2) It is self-calibrating. As long as the sync signals are compatible and readable, feedback control will bring the two machines into lock.

Feedback control is the method that is used when two or more normally free-running machines are to be synchronized. A simpler method, *non-feedback* or *open-loop control*, is used when the slave machine is capable of being driven directly from the master. For example, we can run a drum machine from a MIDI sequencer clock source, bypassing the drum machine's internal free-running tempo generator. This is analogous to a physical mechanical linkage between two tape machine transports, causing them to run from a single motor.

We can further categorize existing synchronization techniques in two classes — pulse methods and timepiece methods — according to the information contained in the sync signal.

Pulse synchronization methods rely upon a simple stream of electronic pulses to maintain constant speed among machines. The general term for closed-loop pulse synchronization is *resolving*. (Pulse methods are also used in open-loop systems.) Some of the pulse methods in common use are:

1) **Click Track** — A click track is a metronome signal used by live musicians to stay in tempo with a mechanical, MIDI-sequenced or pre-recorded music or visual program. The click corresponds to the intended beat of the music, so its rate can vary. On occasion, amplitude accents or a dual-tone click may be used to denote the first beat of each measure. Some MIDI sequencers can read and synchronize with click tracks.

2) **Proprietary Clocks** — Before the advent of MIDI, electronic drum machines and synthesizer arpeggiators relied on pulse signals to maintain synchronization. Three different pulse rates predominate, depending upon the manufacturer: 24, 48 and 96 pulses per quarter-note. MIDI adheres to the 24 ppqn standard, but you may still encounter instruments based on the other divisions of the quarter note.

3) **FSK** — FSK (Frequency Shift Keying) is a method for translating a low-frequency pulse (such any of the above proprietary clocks) to a higher frequency for recording to audiotape or transmitting over a medium whose low-frequency response is limited. The clock pulse modulates the frequency of a carrier oscillator, producing a two-tone audio-frequency signal. Units designed for FSK sync read the two-tone signal and convert it back into the corresponding low-frequency pulse.

4) **MIDI Clock** — In its earliest implementations, MIDI constituted a pulse-type sync method at 24 pulses per quarter note. The MIDI standard has since been elaborated into a more sophisticated synchronization system with 48 or 96 pulses per quarter note, but often is still used in its simple pulse sync mode. When synchronizing to tape via a pulse mode, the MIDI clock is con-

verted to an FSK signal or to MIDI time code.

5) **House Sync** — The concept of house sync is exclusive to video. In order to effect clean switching, crossfades or wipes between video signals from different sources, the source signals must normally be synchronized at the video frame level. If they are not, image distortion (usually vertical rolling) will occur at the edit point. House sync employs a single, stable sync signal generator that feeds frame-rate pulses to all sources in a video system. The sources are then locked to that common reference, allowing clean production effects.

6) **Pilot Tone** — Generated by crystal-controlled oscillator circuits in portable sound recorders for film applications, the pilot tone provides a means of resolving camera and recorder speed to keep production audio tracks and images in sync.

7) **Biphase Sync** — Sprocketed film projectors and magnetic film recorders are capable of generating a biphase sync signal, which is used to control motor speed.

Pulse-type synchronization methods share a common drawback: the sync signal in all cases lacks any place-marker function. Pulse sync signals can be resolved so that two systems run at the same rate, but they convey no information beyond speed. To be in sync, the systems must start at the same time, *at the same point in the program* (i.e. a particular measure, or specified frame of film or video).

Timepiece sync methods address this problem by employing a more complex sync signal into which place markers are encoded. These place markers serve to identify individual points in the program material. As a consequence, systems employing time piece synchronization can lock to one another exactly, even though they may not start at precisely the same instant and in precisely the same place in the program.

The balance of this chapter describes the predominant timepiece synchronization method in use today: SMPTE/EBU Time Code.

20.2 SMPTE/EBU Time Code

SMPTE Time Code is a synchronization standard adopted in the United States in the early 1960's for video tape editing. Although still used for that purpose, it has also been embraced by the audio industry as a spinoff of the video sweetening (audio post production) market, and is widely used for audio synchronizing tasks. Sometimes called *electronic sprockets*, SMPTE Time Code allows one or more tape transports (video or audio) to be locked together via a synchronizer, and can also be used for synchronizing MIDI sequencers and console automation systems. EBU is an acronym for the European Broadcast Union, an organization similar to SMPTE that utilizes the same code standard.

The SMPTE Time Code standard is a timekeeping signal protocol, *not* an interface specification. SMPTE Time Code is an audio-frequency signal like other audio signals: it is patched and routed in the same manner (though the path should be the most direct possible). Don't expect to see a Time Code connector on an audio or video tape machine... they exist on only a few such machines. SMPTE Time Code requires the use of an external synchronizer, which will interface with a multi-pin connector on each of the machines that it controls. The time code itself will be recorded on audio tracks, or incorporated within the video signal.

20.2.1 Signal Structure

The SMPTE Time Code signal is a digital pulse stream carrying binary timekeeping information. The data is encoded using Manchester biphase modulation, a technique which defines a binary "0" as a single clock transition, and a "1" as a pair of clock transitions (see Figure 20-2). This affords a number of distinct advantages:

1) The signal is immune to polarity reversals: an out-of-phase connection will not affect the transmission of data.
2) Because the data can be detected using an electronic technique called *zero crossing detection*, the Time Code signal's amplitude can vary somewhat without confusing receiver circuitry.
3) Rate of transmission does not affect recognition of the code, so the receiver can still read the code if the source transport is in fast-wind mode.
4) The data can even be recognized when transmitted backwards, as when the source transport is in reverse wind mode.

Figure 20-2. Manchester biphase modulation encoding

SMPTE data bits are organized into 80- or 90-bit *words* which are synchronized to the image frame rate (see Section 20.2.3), one word per image frame. Data within each word are encoded in BCD (Binary Coded Decimal) format, and express three elements: time code address, user bits, and sync bits. Figure 20-3 illustrates an 80-bit SMPTE Time Code word.

Time code address is an eight digit number, with two digits each for hours, minutes, seconds, and frames. The Time Code Address enables each image frame to be uniquely identified: for example, one hour, two minutes, three seconds, and four frames would appear on the display as 01:02:03:04. Valid time code numbers run from 00:00:00:00 through 23:59:59:29. (Note that the standard is based on a 24-hour clock.)

User bits are eight alphanumeric digits that relay static information, such as the date, reel number, and so on. User bits do not control; they only relay information.

Sync words, among their many functions, indicate the direction of the time code during playback. If you place the tape transport in reverse with the time code playing against the head, it is the sync word that tells the reading device in which direction the code is traveling. For audio purposes, time code address and user bits may be manipulated by the user, while sync words are generally automatic to the system.

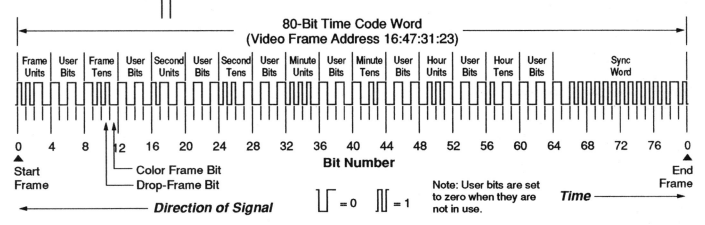

Figure 20-3. SMPTE time code data format (a single frame) —
This example represents 16 hours, 47 minutes, 31 seconds, 23 frames.

20.2.2 Frame Rates and Line References

Four different types of SMPTE Time Code are in wide use at present: 30–Frame, 30 Drop-Frame, 25–Frame and 24–Frame. Each is distinguished by its relationship to a specific film or video frame rate, reflecting once again SMPTE Time Code's heritage in post production. In the United States, black-and-white video runs at 30 fps (frames per second), color video at approximately 29.97 fps, and film at 24 fps. In Europe, both film and video run at 25 fps.

The following paragraphs describe the differences among these standards:

30-Frame — SMPTE time code with a 30-frame division is the original time code, also known as *Non-Drop* (N/D). Its frame rate corresponds to that of black-and-white NTSC video. Non-Drop Frame code is the same as a clock: its Time Code Address data represent real elapsed time.

30 Drop-Frame — When color television was invented, the technology could not adequately transmit color at a 30-frame rate and still remain in phase with black-and-white signals. The color frame rate therefore had to be reduced to approximately 29.97 fps, in order to give the color scan lines adequate time to traverse the screen and still produce a clear image.

This fixed one problem, but created another: time code at that rate ran slower than real time, making an hour of 30-Frame Time Code last 1 hour and 3.6 seconds. A new time code, *Drop-Frame* (D/F), was created to deal with this dilemma, and has remained the U.S. network broadcast standard ever since.

Drop-Frame Time Code alters the frame count by dropping frames Nº 00 and Nº 01, *except on each tenth minute.* This results in a total of 108 frames dropped in a one-hour span, compensating for the 3.6-second per hour difference from 30-Frame Time Code.

Note that, because of this compensation scheme, Drop-Frame Time Code Address data do not accurately represent elapsed time, and are not directly compatible with Non-Drop Time Code Address data.

25-Frame — In Europe, the mains line frequency is 50 Hz. Time code based on that reference is most easily divided into 25 frames per second, which is the frame rate for European video and film (the PAL/SECAM standard, where PAL is Phase Alternation Line, and SECAM is Sequential Couleur á Memoire (sequential colors in memory). The 25-Frame Time Code, also called EBU Time Code, is used in any country where 50 Hz is the line reference. There is no 25 Drop-Frame, because it simply isn't needed: in Europe, both color and black-and-white run at the same frame rate.

24-Frame — Since the film industry uses 24 fps as their standard, 24-Frame Time Code was introduced to correspond with film. This time code is sometimes used by film composers who have all of their music cue sheets marked in frames based on a rate of 24, or for editing film on tape.

There is also a seldom-used standard of 29.97 Non-Drop Time Code, which is what Drop-Frame would be if it did not subtract frames. This is used when a project requires Non-Drop code referenced to the U.S. color video field rate of 59.95 Hz.

Unless doing a video project for the broadcast networks, most people choose Non-Drop code because it always expresses real time. There is certainly no harm in using Drop-Frame for any purpose, however, because most equipment will synchronize to either code. In practical terms, it really doesn't matter which code you use, *as long as the usage is consistent.* Intermixing different frame rates, though, will cause headaches.

20.2.3 Longitudinal, Vertical Interval, and Visible Time Code

Regardless of frame rate, there are two basic versions of SMPTE Time Code that are distinguished by how they are recorded (Figure 20-4).

Londitudinal Time Code — LTC is designed to be recorded on standard audio tape tracks. When recorded to video, LTC is placed on one of the linear audio tracks of the videotape. Its structure is exactly as described above in Section 20.2.1. LTC is the original SMPTE Time Code standard, and older videotapes, if they contain time code at all, will be striped with LTC.

Vertical Interval Time Code — VITC is recorded within the video picture, during the vertical blanking interval. It can be present in a video signal without being visible on screen. VITC is structured similarly to LTC, but includes several housekeeping bits that bring its word length to 90 bits.

LTC is by far the most common in the audio industry, in large part because VITC cannot be recorded on audio tracks. VITC offers distinct advantages for video editing: it can be read from a still frame (whereas LTC cannot) and it provides half-frame (field rate) accuracy for edits. Where video and multitrack audio transports must be synchronized, both VITC and LTC may be used together. In audio-only productions, only LTC is used.

You may receive work videos that have time code printed on the screen; this is called a *window dub* or *burnt time code*. The time code window can be placed anywhere on the screen, in any size, while the tape copy is being made; it cannot be removed from that copy once recorded.

Visible Time Code is simply an image of the time code display, rather than an actual time code signal. A videotape showing a visible code window in the image may have LTC, VITC, both or neither recorded on it.

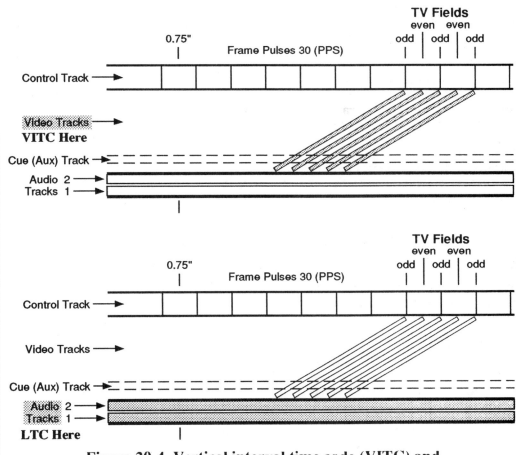

Figure 20-4. Vertical interval time code (VITC) and longitudinal time code (LTC)

The most common method of SMPTE Time Code synchronization is *slave capstan control*, a closed-loop method. A synchronizer monitors the slave and master time code signals, advancing or retarding the slave capstan until the code read from the slave machine matches the master time code. At that point, the system is considered locked.

In reality, there is no such thing as absolute lock. The synchronizer is constantly making minute changes to the slave capstan speed in order to maintain a *phase locked loop* condition between the master and slave code. These minor alterations to the capstan speed may appear as wow or flutter if the system is not properly adjusted.

There are three basic forms of Time Code machine control:

Chase lock is the most common form of synchronization. In chase lock, the synchronizer controls both the slave capstan speed and its transport controls. If the master code is three minutes ahead, for example, the slave transport, when enabled, will be instructed to advance the tape to that area and park. If the master code is already in play, the slave will automatically go to that general area and play. The capstan will then be instructed to speed up or slow down until it reaches lock.

Address lock is a coarse type of synchronization. It locks only the time code addresses of the slave and master machines; the frame count is ignored. Address lock may be used when the time code signal degenerates, leaving the smaller bits (frames and subframes) obscured.

Flywheel is the coarsest of all synchronization modes: it merely considers the master and slave time code carrier frequencies and resolves the two codes as though they were simple pulse sync signals. This causes the slave and the master to run at the same speed.

Flywheel lock may be used when a portion of the recorded time code track is damaged. Just prior to the damaged area, you can switch the lock mode from chase lock to flywheel: the machine will remain locked, and the damaged area (depending on the damage) can be passed over while maintaining lock. *It is inadvisable,* *however, to switch back to chase lock while the tape is running, because it is unlikely that the two codes will be in exactly the same place. This will cause a jump in the sound.*

In practice, the machine transports are normally operated from a synchronizer control panel which displays master and slave time code locations and features a number of buttons for issuing transport commands. The control panel, located at the mix position, communicates with remote synchronizer units which, in turn, communicate with the transports.

From the control panel, edit locations can be specified as SMPTE Time Code Addresses by typing in numbers from a keypad or capturing an address as it is read from a transport in motion. Accurate time offsets between master and slave can be entered and maintained in operation. External events can be triggered at specified time code locations.

The following paragraphs introduce the main concepts involved in effecting these and other SMPTE synchronizer operations.

20.2.4.1 Slave Code Error

Slave code error does not describe a problem with the time code: it is simply the time difference between the master and slave codes. The error can be either positive or negative, depending on whether the slave is ahead of, or behind, the master. The synchronizer displays this number in hours, minutes, seconds, and frames. This error can either be used to determine how far away the slave is from the master, or it can be stored for later calculations.

20.2.4.2 Slave Code Offset

Slave code offset is the slave error added to, or subtracted from, the slave time code. This calculation offsets the slave time code so that it matches the master time code numerically. For example, if the master time code reads 01:00:00:00 and the slave time code reads 04:00:00:00, the offset would be 03:00:00:00. If the master and slave codes were reversed, the offset would be –03:00:00:00. Offsets are extremely useful when matching a pre-striped music track to a new master time code.

20.2.4.3 Flying Offsets

Flying offsets are accomplished using a synchronizer *capture* key, which captures the offset while master and/or slave are in motion. This is useful for defining a specific beat in the music relative to the master time code. For example, if the master is a video deck and you want a particular beat in the music to occur at a specific point in the video, you would park the master at that point, run the music slave (unlocked), and hit the capture key at the desired beat.

20.2.4.4 Slew

Slewing is a way of manually advancing or retarding the slave capstan by increments of frame and subframe. The transports must be locked before slewing can occur. Once you have determined the proper slew value, it can be entered as a permanent offset. If there is already an offset prior to slewing, the slew value will simply be added to or subtracted from the prior offset. This is also referred to as *offset trim*.

20.2.4.5 Advanced Transport Controls

Similar to transport autolocators, some synchronizers autolocate master and slave transports, with one major difference: the location points are related to SMPTE time code. In addition to autolocation, some synchronizers offer such features as *zone limiting* and *auto punch*. Zone limiting sets a predetermined time code number that, when reached by the slave, either stops the transport or takes it out of record. Auto punch brings the slave in and out of record at specified time code locations. These time code numbers can sometimes be stored in event trigger registers.

20.2.4.6 Event Triggers

Event triggers are time code values placed in event trigger registers. Each event produces a physical contact closure somewhere in the synchronizer. The contact closure interface can be used to start and stop tape machines, or to trigger sequences. Event triggers are used for triggering equipment that either cannot, or does not need to, be synchronized.

20.2.5 Time Code and Audio Tape

In order to maintain precise synchronization between machine transports, the time code must be recorded on the tape itself. SMPTE Time Code is an audio-frequency square wave signal, so some cautions apply in handling it. If it bleeds to adjacent tracks, it will be quite annoying, since it lies directly in the midrange and carries substantial harmonics. Conversely, adjacent tracks bleeding onto the time code track can completely disrupt the synchronization process. Finally, audio-frequency magnetic tape recordings are notoriously imperfect at reproducing square wave signals because of bandwidth limitations, so some form of signal conditioning is required if a time code track is to be copied from one tape to another.

20.2.5.1 Printing SMPTE Time Code

The process of printing time code is sometimes referred to as *striping tape*. (This term comes from the motion picture industry, and refers to the stripe of oxide that is placed on the edge of the film after it has been developed; the stripe is used to record audio for the film.) To print time code, you will need a Time Code Generator. Some synchronizers have built-in time code generators, and so do certain tape recorders (i.e., digital multitrack machines, a few analog multitracks, and certain portable 2 or 4 track units intended for field production and news gathering). For those whose synchronizers or tape machines do not have this function, there are many stand-alone generators.

SMPTE time code is generated from a standard frequency. Although generators are very accurate throughout the world, there are significant differences from one to another, so a single point of reference must be obtained. There are four reference methods:

1) **Internal** utilizes the synchronizer's own clock as a reference.
2) **Mains** uses the line frequency from the AC cord as its reference.
3) **Video** utilizes a video signal, generally the master video, which is routed to a video input on the generator. The sync pulse on the video signal is stripped internally and used as reference.

4) **House sync** or *house black* is a stand-alone generator that feeds not only the synchronizer, but generally every other video device in a facility. This is a common practice in the television industry.

LTC must be recorded via the cleanest possible signal chain — preferably, directly from the output of the time code generator to the audio recorder input. This will ensure the most stable time code recording. On audio recorders, time code should be printed at a level which is less than 0 VU but greater than -10 VU. Typically, -7 VU is considered a safe bet for professional machines; on semi-pro machines, the level should be -3 VU. A stand-alone reader can be useful for checking time code stability off of the playback head during striping.

If you are printing time code to a multitrack recorder, it is preferable to use one of the edge tracks, leaving a blank track (or *guard track*) between the code and the next recorded track. Whenever possible, print your time code first, then the audio; this will reduce the likelihood of time code crosstalk into adjacent channels, where the leakage could actually become part of the recorded signal on audio tracks. On large multitrack tape recorders, the edge tracks tend to be unstable; printing the same time code on tracks 23 and 24 will protect you from potential dropouts on track 24. If you are using a multitrack recorder every night during a performance, sooner or later the edge tracks *will get damaged*. A spare time code track then becomes invaluable.

When printing to a video recorder audio track, it is usually recommended that the code be placed on audio channel 2 at a level of +3 VU (as read on the VTR's meter). Some video recorders incorporate audio AGC amplifiers or limiters; these *must* be defeated to ensure a clean, readable code track.

In all cases, be sure to allow a minimum leader of 20 seconds of running time code *before* the program material begins. The leader area provides time for the synchronizer to lock everything up, and can help to avoid the tape running off of the takeup reel when the system attempts to rewind and park at the head. *Never* splice in paper or plastic leader trimmed to the head of the program or between takes: code that begins directly at the head of a take is virtually useless. Takes should always be located by SMPTE number or autolocator address, rather than with leader.

Finally, always use ascending Time Code Address values on a single reel. You may stripe one portion of the reel at one time, and another at a later date: discontinuities in the code are not necessarily a problem, as long as the code is continuous throughout a take. (A code discontinuity within a take requires jam syncing, and an extra track, to fix — see Section 20.2.5.2.) Duplicate Time Code Addresses at different locations on a single reel, though, will confuse both the synchronizer and the engineer.

20.2.5.2 Copying SMPTE Time Code

On occasion, you may need to copy time code from one recorder to another — when making a safety of a multitrack master, for instance. Copying time code always involves some form of signal conditioning. There are three methods of copying LTC: refreshing, jam syncing and reshaping.

Refreshing or *regenerating* time code is performed by copying through a time code generator. The generator locks onto the incoming time code and replicates it, creating a fresh time code signal. Some generators/regenerators can actually fix missing bits in the code.

Jam synchronizing time code is the same as regenerating code, with one exception: if you stop the original time code from playing once jam sync has been started, the jam sync generator will continue to generate code. This is especially useful for code that is too short at the end of a tape, or that has a discontinuity within a take. Some generators can jam sync going backwards, extending the front of the tape, as well. In both refresh and jam sync mode, you can either choose to copy the user bit information or generate new user bits — a different date, for example.

Reshaping is a process that transfers the existing time code through a signal conditioning circuit that re-squares the code waveform. Reshaping is similar to refreshing, but it cannot repair missing bits. In many cases, however, reshaping works adequately for the budget.

20.2.6 SMPTE-To-MIDI Conversion

Used in conjunction with SMPTE Time Code, MIDI provides a powerful extension to the automation capabilities of a synchronized system. (MIDI is detailed in Section 19.)

The device that makes this possible is the SMPTE-to-MIDI Converter, a unit which reads SMPTE Time Code and translates it to MIDI clock with Song Position Pointer data. The converter serves as the interface between the SMPTE-synchronized system and the MIDI-synchronized system. Stand-alone converters which interface with computer sequencers are available from several manufacturers. In addition, some sophisticated synthesizers having built-in sequencers are capable of reading time code and performing the conversion internally.

In the studio, SMPTE-to-MIDI conversion is a tremendous aid in combining pre-sequenced MIDI instrumental parts with multitrack overdubbing of acoustic instruments, vocals and so on. In live sound reinforcement, *virtual tracks* of music and/or or console automation data may be stored in MIDI sequences, then played back in synchronization with multitrack audio, video, or film. This technique is seeing increased use, particularly in industrial production. It provides first-generation sound quality for the sequenced music parts, enhances the polyphonic capability of live ensembles far beyond what the budget might otherwise allow, and affords greater creative leeway for the engineer.

The *Edit Decision List* (EDL), was designed in the 1960's as an editorial standard supporting the video industry. Today, the EDL has evolved into a specific list containing edit events (cues), relative to SMPTE time code, for both video and audio production. An EDL can be generated at any time, although it is customarily created during the video off-line editing process, and is continually updated each time an edit event is performed by the operator. These events can later be fed into a computer either manually or digitally. Digital data for early system was stored on punch tape, and now is stored on floppy or hard disks. The events in computer memory are re-executed automatically in order to create a final on-line master tape.

Note: A pioneer in the field of EDLs is a company known as CMX, and consequently, you may hear old-timers speak of "CMX editing" even if the specific EDL system has not been manufactured by CMX.

20.3.1 The Video Editing Process

While this is a handbook on sound reinforcement, we must mention video here because the EDL – which is now used for audio production — originally came from the video world, where it is still widely used. First, master video tapes are shot (typically on one inch tape). Then these masters must be edited. One inch editing time is expensive, so the masters are transferred (copied) to a more cost effective medium – video cassette or laser disk. The copies, whose SMPTE time code is identical to that on the original tapes, are edited, while the originals (for now) are not touched. The end result of this stage is called the *off-line edit*. The computer then prints out the EDL, a typed listing of all the off-line edits. Then in the on-line editing bay (i.e., the studio containing the more costly one inch video equipment), the EDL that was prepared during the off-line edit is fed into another computer. This computer commands an automatic assembly of the corresponding master

tapes. During this process, last minute on-line EDL updates (such as fades, dissolves, wipes, and special graphics like *paint box*) can be made. The final result of this process is called the *on-line edit*, and this is what airs. It is important to note that video tape is never physically cut; video edits are simply a succession of transfers. The final on-line master is a first generation dub made from segments of other tapes via EDL control.

EDLs are now prepared for audio productions, too, although most often they pertain to audio which is being edited to synchronize with video or film (i.e., for a music video). The list formats are no different for audio or video, just the tape machines and the computer interfaces.

20.3.2 Examples of EDLs

An EDL not only provides a progressive account of all edit events and their sources, but a verbal description of each event, and how it is to be processed. In the following examples, you can see portions of actual edit decision lists. Each horizontal line across the page represents a single edit event. Here is a brief description of the information contained in each line, from left to right.

1. The first vertical column represents the event number. Directly under is the edit description, if any.
2. The second column is the tape identifier (ID).
3. The third column describes whether the edit is video (V), or audio (A). Audio edits generally specify which track is to be edited (A1) or (A2).
4. The fourth column represents how the edit is to be processed. Some of the choices are cuts (C) or dissolves (D). A *dissolve* occurs when the end of one cut (program segment) overlaps the beginning of the next. Even a *fade to black* is in reality a dissolve from picture to black.
5. The fifth column represents the edit in point of the source material.
6. The sixth column represents the edit out point of the source material.

7. The seventh column indicates where the source material is to be inserted into the composite master.

8. The eighth and final column indicates where the end of the source material falls on the composite master. This column also indicates the overall running time.

In Figure 20-5, we see a segment of an EDL which covers a total play time of 7 seconds and 14 frames (i.e., about 7.5 seconds) from master SMPTE time 1 hour, 15 minutes, 50 seconds, zero frames to 1 hour, 16 minutes, 7 seconds, 14 frames. This is obviously a rapid series of very brief cuts with 22 events in less than 8 seconds.

Col. 1: Event Number	Col. 2: Tape ID	Col. 3: Audio or Video edit (A/V) & track	Col. 4: Type of process (C=cut, D=dissolve)	Col. 5: Edit in (begin) point in source reel	Col. 6: Edit out (end) point in source reel	Col. 7: Edit insert begin point in composite master reel	Col. 8: Edit end point in composite master reel
TITLE: 'A' NETWORK "6:00 NEWS — THE ANCHOR WOMAN" PROMO 5-28-89							
FCM: DROP FRAME							
001	BL	V	C	00:00:00:00	00:00:00:00	01:15:50:00	01:15:50:00
001	1	V	D	00:04:26:19	00:04:27:27	01:15:50:00	01:15:51:08
FCM: NON-DROP FRAME							
002	2	V	C	02:06:49:02	02:06:49:18	01:15:51:08	01:15:51:24
FCM: DROP FRAME							
003	1	V	C	00:02:21:26	00:02:22:11	01:15:51:24	01:15:52:09
004	1A	V1	C	01:55:21:06	01:55:22:19	01:15:52:09	01:15:53:22
005	1	V	C	00:04:18:15	00:04:19:00	01:15:53:18	01:15:54:03
006	1	V	C	00:04:57:24	00:04:58:09	01:15:54:03	01:15:54:18
007	1B	V	C	01:27:34:10	01:27:34:28	01:15:54:18	01:15:55:06
008	1	V	C	00:07:04:08	00:07:05:08	01:15:55:06	01:15:56:06
009	1	V	C	00:05:48:16	00:05:49:05	01:15:56:06	01:15:56:25
010	1	V	C	00:05:48:16	00:05:49:05	01:15:56:25	01:15:57:12
011	1	V	C	00:09:04:05	00:09:05:00	01:15:57:12	01:15:58:07
012	1	V	C	00:04:17:16	00:04:18:02	01:15:58:07	01:15:58:23
013	6	V	C	00:01:08:26	00:01:09:24	01:15:58:23	01:15:59:21
014	1	V	C	00:04:22:15	00:04:22:27	01:15:59:20	01:16:00:04
015	1	1	C	00:10:40:23	00:10:41:05	01:15:59:20	01:16:00:04
016	1	V1	C	00:10:47:27	00:10:52:11	01:16:00:04	01:16:00:18
017	1	V1	C	00:04:21:01	00:04:21:11	01:16:01:00	01:16:01:20
FCM: NON-DROP FRAME							
018	6	V	C	00:18:18:06	00:18:19:04	01:16:02:07	01:16:03:05
FCM: DROP FRAME							
019	1	V	C	00:02:17:05	00:02:17:15	01:16:04:18	01:16:04:28
020	6	V	C	00:11:26:13	00:11:28:25	01:16:04:28	01:16:07:10
021	1	V	C	00:06:44:14	00:06:45:09	01:16:06:12	01:16:07:07
022	1	V	C	00:04:20:10	00:04:20:17	01:16:07:07	01:16:07:14

Figure 20-5. An example of an edit decision list (EDL) derived from a segment of a TV news show promo (shading added to clearly indicate columns)

```
TITLE: JOHN JONES RH:BCM 4-6-89 GALLAGHER  CMX FORMAT
GVG SUPER EDIT V4.02    SYSTEM 51EM  SE32785  UNITEL WEST #6
DROP FRAME CODE

0001 149  A2 C  00:00:39:00  00:01:09:02  00:00:10:00  00:00:40:00
MUSIC
0002 BL   V  C  00:00:00:15  00:00:00:15  00:00:10:00  00:00:10:00
0002 002  V  D  02:34:33:06  02:34:35:14  00:00:10:00  00:00:12:08
KISS
0003 002  V  C  00:00:00:15  00:00:00:15  00:00:12:08  00:00:12:08
0003 001  V  D  01:12:36:23  01:12:37:23  00:00:12:08  00:00:13:08
WALKING
0004 001  V  C  01:12:37:23  01:12:37:23  00:00:13:08  00:00:13:08
0004 002  V  D  02:34:25:03  02:34:26:03  00:00:13:08  00:00:14:08
HAND ON BACK
0005 002  V  C  02:34:26:03  02:34:26:03  00:00:14:08  00:00:14:08
0005 004  V  D  04:43:51:06  04:43:52:06  00:00:14:08  00:00:15:08
SHOWS BADGE
0006 004  V  C  04:43:52:06  04:43:52:06  00:00:15:08  00:00:15:08
0006 004B V  D  04:09:17:02  04:09:18:20  00:00:15:08  00:00:16:26
* 2ND KISS B&W SLO-MO @ 50%
```

Figure 20-6. Another segment of an edit decision list (EDL), this one from a dramatic video program, includes examples of notation to describe varous edit points

In the example of Figure 20-6, we see an initial edit event of 30 seconds elapsed time – n musical cut from track 2 of audio tape recorder (ref 149).

The second through sixth events span an elapsed time of six seconds and 26 frames (nearly seven seconds), and constitute a series of brief video dissolves from cuts on video machines 1, 2 and 4.

As you may imagine, the EDL for a relatively short 20 minute show can run many pages in length. This is not as intimidating as it may seem, since the EDL is arranged in a logical chronological sequence, and any given edit point can be searched and located with the editing computer. The printed lists are useful for quickly seeing the overall plan, and for making notes about planned edits.

APPENDIX A.
LOGARITHMS

If you already understand the logarithm (log for short), you can skip this section of the handbook. If you continue reading Section 3.4, we'll assume you're one of those people who avoided, muddled through, or otherwise remained unaware of this corner of mathematical manipulation. Relax, you're not alone. We'll keep this discussion as simple as possible, given the subject matter.

A.1 Raising Numbers to a Power: The Key to Logs

Before we define a logarithm, let's look at a few familiar mathematical relationships that should make sense to everyone.

PROBLEM: What is the square of 3?

$$3^2 = 9$$

PROBLEM: What is the square of 5?

$$5^2 = 25$$

PROBLEM: What is the square of 10?

$$10^2 = 100$$

In all three equations, we have raised a number to the second power (squared it), and have come up with a result. Now, let's label the component numbers in these equations:

The number being raised (3, 5 or 10) can be considered the **base**.

The number to which the base is raised (2 in each case) is the **logarithm**, abbreviated **log**.

$$\overset{\text{Base}}{\searrow} \overset{\text{Log}}{\swarrow} \overset{\text{Antilog}}{\swarrow}$$
$$3^2 = 9$$

The resulting value (9, 25 or 100) is the **antilog**.

A.2 Simple Logs (and Antilogs) to the Base 10

Any number can be used as a base, but in the calculations we use to describe SPL, dBm, and other quantities in most sound systems, the base 10 is standard. When we write "log," we nearly always mean "log base 10," or "$\log_{10}$" unless otherwise noted.

Let's restate the equation in the last problem of Section 3.4.1, using logarithmic terminology.

PROBLEM: What is the **antilog** of 2? We assume base 10, as indicated by the subscript "10" after the "log".

$\text{antilog}_{10} \, 2 = ?$ **(answer is 100)**

What we're really expressing by "$\text{antilog}_{10} \, 2$" is "what is 10 raised to the second power?" The answer, the antilog, is "100."

Now, suppose we know the antilog, and want to solve for the log, the "2" in this case. Let's restate the problem.

PROBLEM: What is the **log** of 100?

$\log_{10} 100 = ?$ **(answer is 2)**

or, restating the same thing, assuming a base 10,

$\log 100 = ?$ **(answer is 2)**

Does this begin to make any sense? If not, here are a few more sample problems (intentionally using whole numbers so you can follow the math in your head).

PROBLEM: What is the log of 1000?

$\log 1000 = ?$ **(answer is 3)**

The log (assumed base 10) of 1000 is 3. This tells us that 1000 is 10 raised to the third power ($10 \cdot 10 \cdot 10 = 1000$).

PROBLEM: What is the log of 10?

log 10 = ? (answer is 1)

The log of 10 is 1, i.e. 10 raised to the first power is 10 (10 • 1 = 10).

A.3 Less Obvious Logs To The Base 10

What about expressing numbers that are not multiples of 10? Logs are just fine here, too, but the actual numbers may extend to many decimal places. For example...

PROBLEM: What is the log of 50?

$$Log_{10}\ 50 = 1.698970$$

This tells us that 10 raised to the 1.698970 power is 50. In other words....

$$10^{1.698970} = 50$$

It's pretty difficult to do this math with a pencil, so how did we know that the log of 50 is 1.698970? In this case, we switched on a scientific calculator, keyed in 50 and pressed the "log" key. The calculator gave us the result. Books are available that have page after page of log tables for almost any number you're likely to need. Either way, you can obtain the log. Let's look at another example.

PROBLEM: What is the log of 2?

$$Log_{10}\ 2 = 0.3010299957$$

The log of 2, then, can be rounded off to 0.301. This means that 10 raised to the 0.301 power is 2.

At this point, we can generalize and provide an equation relating the antilog (the number for which you want to find the log) to the log (the power to which 10 must be raised to equal the antilog).

$$Log_{10}\ A = L$$

where A is the antilog, and L is the log. You can see the relationship of logs to antilogs in the following table.

Antilog	Log (L)
1	0.0000000000
2	0.3010299957
3	0.4771212547
4	0.6020599913
5	0.6989700043
6	0.7781512504
7	0.8450980400
8	0.9030899870
9	0.9542425094
10	1.0000000000
100	2.0000000000
1,000	3.0000000000
10,000	4.0000000000
100,000	5.0000000000
1,000,000	6.0000000000

Table A-1. A few representative logarithms

Log tables, or a scientific calculator, will provide the log for virtually any number. Let's take a number out of thin air: 127.6. The calculator tells us the log of 127.6 is 2.105850674. Raise 10 to the 2.10585... power and you'll get 127.6. What good is all this? There are several advantages:

A) Logs allow us to represent relatively large numbers with relatively smaller numbers (the log of 1 million is 6).
B) Logs relate more closely to the scaling by which the human ear perceives loudness. Because the ear evaluates levels along a logarithmic scale, the decibel (which relies upon logs) is a more meaningful unit.
C) Logs can be more easily manipulated when multiplying and dividing large numbers, as explained in the following text.

A.4 Mathematical Properties of Logs

Logs make it easier to multiply and divide large numbers.

EXAMPLE: How do we multiply two numbers, A and B, using logs? (i.e., what is log (A • B)?)

First, find the log of A. Then find the log of B. Then add the two logs together. Thus,

$$\log (A \cdot B) = \log A + \log B$$

We see that instead of multiplying two numbers, one can take their logs, then add the logs. Adding logs of numbers is the same as multiplying the numbers themselves. Let's verify this relationship using actual numbers.

EXAMPLE: Multiply 100 times 1000 using logs.

$$\log (100 \cdot 1000) = \log 100 + \log 1000$$
$$= 2 + 3$$
$$= 5$$

We see that the log of 100 times 1000 is 5. To check this, we can take the antilog of 5... and the result is 100,000. (10 raised to the fifth power is 100,000!). Check Table 3-5 if you want to verify this.

EXAMPLE: Multiply 7 x 9 using logs.

$$\log (7 \cdot 9) = \log 7 + \log 9$$

Looking at Table 3-5, we find the Log of 7 and the log of 9...

$$\log (7 \cdot 9) = 0.84509804 + 0.9542425094$$

$$\log (7 \cdot 9) = 1.799340549$$

If we raise 10 to the 1.799340549 power, we'll get the same result as multiplying 7 times 9 (that is, 63). To check this, we could look up the log of 63... which turns out to be 1.799340549.

To divide two numbers, we can subtract their logs.

EXAMPLE: How do we divide two numbers, A and B, using logs? (i.e., what is log (A ÷ B)?)

First, find the log of A. Then find the log of B. Then subtract one log from the other. Thus,

$$\log (A \div B) = \log A - \log B$$

We see that instead of multiplying two numbers, one can take their logs, then subtract the logs. Subtracting logs of numbers is the same as dividing the numbers themselves. Let's verify this relationship using actual numbers.

EXAMPLE: Divide 1000 by 100 using logs.

$$\log (1000 \div 100) = \log 1000 - \log 100$$
$$= 3 - 2$$
$$= 1$$

We see that the log of (1000 divided by 100) is 1. To check this, we can take the antilog of 1... and the result is 10. (10 raised to the first power is 10.) This can be verified with Table 3-5.

EXAMPLE: Divide 8 by 4 using logs.

$$\log (8 \div 4) = \log 8 - \log 4$$

Table 3-5 tells us the logs for 8 and 4...

$$\log (8 \div 4) = 0.903089987 - 0.6020599913$$

$$\log (8 \div 4) = 0.3010299957$$

Again, consulting Table 3-5, we find that the antilog of 0.3010299957 is 2. Of course, you already knew that 8 divided by 4 is 2, so this seems like a lot of work for nothing. But when very large numbers are involved, the logs do make things easier.

We won't go into much more detail here. There are negative logs (which is the same as raising a number to its reciprocal power, which is to say, 1 over the number raised to its log). The log of a reciprocal is called a **colog**. You can check a math textbook if you really want to explore this. What's more important for our purposes, however, is to grasp the relationship of logs to decibels.

A.5 One More Look At Logs and Decibels

First, let's restate the formula for the dB as:

$$dB_{power} = 10 \log (A \div B)$$

$$dB_{SPL} \text{ or } dB_{volts} \text{ or } dB_{amps} = 20 \log (A \div B)$$

In each case, A and B are two values, so the dB is expressing the ratio of the powers as a logarithm. Now let's plug in some actual numbers. The "B" in each case can be recognized as a reference value. If we want to express "dBm," then "B" is 1 milliwatt, or 0.001 watts. The "A" in the equation is the power value we wish to restate in dBm.

EXAMPLE: How many dBm is 1 watt?

$$dBm = 10 \log (A \div B)$$

where B = 1 mW

$$dBm = 10 \log (1 \div 0.001)$$
$$= 10 \log (1,000)$$
$$= 10 \cdot 3$$
$$= 30$$

So we see that 10 watts is +30 dBm.

You will recall that the log of one number divided by another can be obtained by subtracting the logs, so here's an alternate way to solve the above equation:

EXAMPLE: How many dBm is 1 watt?

$$dBm = 10 \cdot \log (1 \div 0.001)$$
$$= 10 \cdot (\log 1 - \log 0.001)$$
$$= 10 \cdot (0 - (-3))$$
$$= 10 \cdot (0 + 3)$$
$$= 10 \cdot 3$$
$$= 30$$

You may have gathered that the log of 0.001 is -3, which is $1/10^3$. This second method of solving the equation yields the same result.

Suppose we want to know how many dB greater one power level is than another... just the ratio, not referenced to 1 milliwatt, 1 watt or any other specific value. The same technique applies.

EXAMPLE: How many dB greater is 9 watts than 2 watts?

$$dB_{power} = 10 \log (A \div B)$$
$$= 10 \cdot \log (4.5)$$

We could go on to derive the log of 4.5 and multiply it by 10... but you may not know the log of 4.5. However, in Table 3-5, you do have the logs of 2 and of 9, so lets use the alternate method for solving this problem.

$$= 10 \cdot (\log 9 - \log 2)$$
$$= 10 \cdot (0.9542425094 - 0.3010299957)$$
$$= 10 \cdot 0.6532125138$$
$$= 6.53 \text{ dB}$$

Is this correct? Is 9 watts 6.5 dB more than 2 watts? Well, we know that twice the power is a 3.01 dB increase. From 2 watts to 4 watts is 3.01 dB, and from 4 watts to 8 watts is another 3.01 dB, so 8 watts is 6.02 dB more than 2 watts. Yes, it looks like 9 watts is probably 6.5 dB more than 2 watts.

The above argument shows that a 1 watt increase (from 8 to 9 watts) represents slightly less than $1/2$ dB increase. If we compare 2 watts to 1 watt, that 1 watt increase represents 3 dB (twice the power). The important point here is that dB is a relative scale. The absolute power (or voltage, etc.) involved is not so important to the way we hear as is the relative power. We perceive a 10 dB increase to be twice as loud... regardless of how many watts more power it takes to obtain that 10 dB increase.*

---

* While the absolute power makes no difference, the volume or sound level does, so this statement is not entirely accurate. A 10 dB difference will not sound quite the same at very low volume levels as at high volume levels due to the changing sensitivity of our ears. However, at moderate listening levels, the above relationship is basically true.

Sound Reinforcement Handbook
Index

Colophon

This handbook is a product of "desktop publishing." A few small sections were written many years back, when on a Vydec word processing system, which was "state of the art" in 1974. (It had an 8" 250K floppy disk – not a then-standard cassette tape – and a full page 8-½" x 11" display!) The Vydec data was later transferred to a Corvus Concept system, which also had a full-page *bit mapped* display, and featured an MC68000 CPU, 720K 5-¼" floppy disk, a network with multiple hard disks, and what we considered to be among the most advanced word processing software available in 1982. The bulk of the text for this handbook was written and edited with that Corvus system, and early drafts were printed on various daisywheel and dot matrix printers.

Well, the "state of the art" is constantly in flux. The Corvus system is long gone, replaced in 1986 by an Apple Macintosh system. The copy was ported to the Mac as ASCII (American tandard Code for Information Interchange) text, both via direct cable connection and local modem interconnect. Ralph's copy came via modem, too; early on from his Apple IIe, and later from its replacement – a Macintosh.

Once the ASCII text was in our Mac, we *massaged* it with special software that converted the straight quotes (like "this") to curly quotes (like "this"), removed hard carriage returns except at the end of paragraphs, and did other "clean up" functions. This process was relatively straightforward.

Drawings were prepared with a variety of programs, including *MacPaint, MacDraft, MacDraw, Full Paint, Super Paint,* and *Adobe Illustrator*. Many illustrations were developed by digitizing photos or drawings with an Abaton Scan 300 scanner and *C-Scan* software, then either "editing" them in *Super Paint* or *Desk Paint,* or redrawing them in *Adobe Illustrator*. The connector wiring photos are the only conventionally stripped half-tones in the book, taken from photos we shot years ago for the original PM-1000 manual. These illustrations, and the text, were turned into a near camera-ready proof in the first edition using a page layout program, Aldus' *Pagemaker* 1.2.

After the various consultants and proof readers had an opportunity to mark up that copy, we decided to completely reformat the handbook. Aldus had released *Pagemaker* 2.0a, which offered major improvements in type kerning (letter spacing) and in the way it handled illustrations. We recast all body type, changing from Helvetica to New Century Schoolbook. The first edition's main headings are in Monterey bold, some sub-heads are in Helvetica bold, and the captions are in Times bold.

Hardware and software have continued to evolve rapidly. We began laying out the first edition with a Macintosh Plus (1MB RAM), a 30 MB hard disk, and an Apple Laserwriter. The second edition was created on an accelerated (33 MHz 68030) Mac II with 5 MB RAM, a 19" diagonal monochrome monitor that can display the better part of two pages at full size, and over 240MB of on-line hard disk storage (this handbook alone occupies over 13 megabytes). The second edition also was reformatted and recast, this time in *Pagemaker* 3.01a. Many of the illustrations have been revised, or completely redrawn with updated software for improved quality.

A few pages of this book (table of contents and index) were typeset on a Linotronic L300, which provided about 8 times the resolution of the laser printer, and made these pages of very small type a lot easier to read. Master artwork for the rest of the book was generated by a Qume ScripTEN laser printer.

One of the most satisfying aspects in our production of this book was the ability to get exactly what we wanted, and to make the compromises *we* felt were appropriate whenever something didn't quite work. "Desktop publishing" did more for us than secure total control of the job, it greatly enhanced our creative ability to convey our thoughts with no intermediate interpretations by artists who might not share our insights into the finer points of sound systems and equipment. Ultimately, we did not save time so much as we improved and perfected the end product. If we did our job correctly, you should not be aware of how this book was created.